Just Java 2

SIXTH EDITION

P9-DUT-439

© 2004 Sun Microsystems, Inc.—
Printed in the United States of America.
4150 Network Circle, Santa Clara, California
95054 U.S.A.

Library of Congress Control Number: 2004107483

All rights reserved. This product and related documentation are protected by copyright and distributed under licenses restricting its use, copying, distribution, and decompilation. No part of this product or related documentation may be reproduced in any form by any means without prior written authorization of Sun and its licensors, if any.

RESTRICTED RIGHTS LEGEND: Use, duplication, or disclosure by the United States Government is subject to the restrictions set forth in DFARS 252.227-7013 (c)(1)(ii) and FAR 52.227-19. The products described may be protected by one or more U.S. patents, foreign patents, or pending applications.

TRADEMARKS—HotJava, Java, Java Development Kit, J2EE, JPS, JavaServer Pages, Enterprise JavaBeans, EJB, JDBC, J2SE, Solaris, SPARC, SunOS, and Sunsoft are trademarks of Sun Microsystems, Inc. All other products or services mentioned in this book are the trademarks or service marks of their respective companies or organizations.

Prentice Hall PTR offers excellent discounts on this book when ordered in quantity for bulk purchases or special sales. For more information, please contact U.S. Corporate and Government Sales, 1-800-382-3419, corpsales@pearsontechgroup.com. For sales outside of the U.S., please contact International Sales, international@pearsoned.com.

Acquisitions Editor: *Gregory G. Doench*
Editorial Assistant: *Raquel Kaplan*
Production Supervision: *Julie B. Nahil*
Editor: *Solveig Haugland*
Cover Designer: *Nina Scuderi*
Art Director: *Gail Cocker-Bogusz*
Manufacturing Manager: *Carol Melville*
Marketing Manager: *Chris Guzikowski*
Sun Microsystems Press Publisher: *Myrna Rivera*

ISBN 0-13-148211-4

Text printed on recycled paper
5 6 7 8 9 10 DOC 09 08 07
5th Printing, September 2007

Sun Microsystems Press
A Prentice Hall Title

005.133
J4N
2004

I used to dedicate these books to specific brands of real ale; it was always good for lunch with the chairman when I toured the brewery. Here's something different. I've worked in the computer industry all my life, and in the last few years started teaching programming classes too. You learn a lot when you get immediate feedback about topics that need to be expressed in easier pieces. I would like to dedicate this book to all my students past and present, and all my teachers, young and old.

Mills College Library
Withdrawn

MILLS COLLEGE
LIBRARY

Mills College Library
Withdrawn

Quick Contents

Complete Contents

Preface

The first edition of *Just Java* was one of the earliest books to accompany the original release of Java in 1996. The launch of Java coincided with the explosion of interest in the web and the net which, in turn, drove technology forward at a frantic pace. People talked about "Internet time," which meant three things to me in Silicon Valley: there was immense pressure to rapidly create new hardware and software products; everyone wrote software to display stock prices on their desktops and cell phones; you were forgiven for not showering if you fell asleep at your desk after midnight and woke up there the next morning. Times have changed, but software productivity remains a big reason behind Java's popularity.

Over the last eight years Java has had six major releases, averaging one about every 18 months. With each of these releases, there has been a new edition of *Just Java* to describe and explain the technology. Table 1 shows how the language and libraries have improved.

Table 1   Java changes from JDK 1.0.2 to Java 2 v1.4

Release	Date	Content	See Just Java 6th ed.
JDK 1.0.2	Jan 1996	First general release of the language and libraries	Throughout the book
JDK 1.1	Feb 1997	*Language changes*:	
		Instance initializers	Chapter 5
		Array initializers	Chapter 9
		Nested classes	Chapter 12
		Library changes:	
		Delegation based event-handlers	Chapter 20
		I/O Readers and Writers	Chapter 17
		Object serialization	Chapter 18
JDK 1.2 (rebadged to Java 2)	Dec 1998	*Language changes*:	
		strictfp	Chapter 7
		Weak references	Chapter 10
		Library changes:	
		Java Foundation and Swing	Chapter 21
		Collection classes, JDBC enhancements	Chapter 16, 23-24
		Thread local storage	Chapter 14
Java 2 v1.3	May 2000	Performance and bug fixes, no significant changes	Throughout the book

Table 1   Java changes from JDK 1.0.2 to Java 2 v1.4 *(cont.)*

Release	Date	Content	See Just Java 6th ed.
Java 2 v1.4	Dec 2001	*Language changes*:	
		Assert statement	Chapter 10
		Library changes:	
		Regular expressions	Chapter 19
		New I/O (third attempt)	Chapter 18

This is a remarkable pace of development for a programming system, particularly when Sun keeps such an emphasis on backward compatibility and portability. The Java 1.2 release was a significant one, bundling major functionality improvements like the collection classes and the Swing GUI library. Java 1.3 and 1.4 were comparatively smaller, although 1.4 did bring a new statement ("assert") into the language.

Two and a half years in the making, Sun wanted to make a big splash with its latest release of Java. So Sun switched the name from the confusing old brand of "J2SE version 1.5" to the confusing new brand of "J2SE version 5".

The mysterious "2" slipped in there in 1998, when Sun changed the name at the last minute to emphasize the difference between standard Java and the non-portable version that Microsoft had deviously created. That's all water under the bridge now, and everyone wishes that Sun would use a sensible, simple version number, like "Java 5". But instead, "J2SE version 5" it is. Well, whatever name the marketing geniuses at Sun apply, this release is the biggest and most significant so far. Table 2 on page xxi shows some of the substantial language additions.

There are also the traditional bug-fix, library and performance improvements, including some exciting optimizations for desktop applications.

Table 2   Java 2 v1.5

Release	Date	Content	See Just Java 6th ed.
J2SE 5.0	Jun 2004	*Language changes*:	
		Autoboxing and unboxing	Chapter 3
		Enum types	Chapter 6
		Generic types	Chapter 15, 16
		Variable-arity methods	Chapter 5
		Static import	Chapter 6
		Enhanced for loop	Chapter 4
		Covariant return types	Chapter 11
		Library changes:	
		printf (like C's printf)	Chapter 17
		java.util.scanner (fourth attempt at fixing I/O)	Chapter 17
		java.util.concurrent thread utilities	Chapter 14
		javax.xml XML support bundled	Chapter 27, 28
		Class data sharing	Chapter 2
		Can add Swing components directly to a Container!	Chapter 21

Over the years, I've put a lot of hard work into unlocking the changes in Java, so you don't have to. You're looking at the results of that effort: the sixth edition of *Just Java*.

I'm confident you'll find it easy to read, and packed with the information you need.

I hope that you'll want a copy for yourself.

But if not, I want you to put it back on the shelf, only (as my friend Alan Abel suggested) in a more prominent position.

— P.

Acknowledgments

I'm very grateful to the following people, who are some of the most talented and creative individuals you'll find:

Gilad Bracha

Michael Davidson

Jane Erskine

Marcus Green

Roedy Green

Trey Harris

Karsten Lentzsch

Bob Lynch

Aleksander Malinowski

Simon Roberts

Rick Ross, who provides first-class leadership at http://javalobby.org

Kerry Shetline

Robin Southgate

Lefty Walkowiak

All the cowboys and cowgirls down on the Java Ranch http://javaranch.com

The Limewire team

The unsung heroes and heroines of Sun's Java and Solaris groups

The editorial, marketing, and production teams at Prentice-Hall and Sun Microsystems deserve full appreciation:

Greg Doench, Chris Guzikowski, Julie Nahil, Raquel Kaplan, Nina Scuderi, and Solveig Haugland and her magic editing pixies.

Thanks too, to my wife, family, and friends—hey, if I *wanted* my study to look organized, I'd *keep* it that way, OK?

Part

1

Language

Chapter 1

What Can Java Do for Me?

▼ WHAT JAVA DOES FOR YOU

▼ WHY PORTABILITY MATTERS

▼ LANGUAGE AND LIBRARIES

▼ ONE SIZE DOESN'T FIT ALL

▼ SOME LIGHT RELIEF—A JAVA DESKTOP APPLICATION

Java has become a very popular programming language for the kind of modern software people want to write. Java began as a research project inside Sun Microsystems. The results were posted on the web, and Java took off like a Titan rocket. Sun wisely decided to nurture the market by sharing, and licensed the technology across the computer industry. Today, Java compilers and source code are available for free download from many different organizations. Just about the entire computer industry is backing Java enthusiastically with products and support. In this chapter we'll look at the reasons behind Java's popularity, and summarize the key features of the language.

Java works well for web and server-based applications. It has great features like object-oriented programming, easy database access, and well-designed GUI support. The latest release, Java 2 version 5, has performance tweaks to speed up desktop programs. There are libraries for communicating across networks, and for encryption. It has strong security built in. Most programmers pick up Java quickly. Behind all this, Java is more than just the latest, most popular programming language. It is a way of creating applications that are independent of all hardware and all operating systems.

What Java Does for You: Software Portability

What is meant by "applications that are independent of all hardware and operating systems?" It means you can compile a Java program on any system and run the resulting binary executable file on the same or any other system—on a Macintosh, on Windows 98, NT, 2K, XP, on Solaris, Linux, BSD or any of the varieties of Unix, on IBM's mainframe operating systems, on cell phones, Personal Digital Assistants (PDAs), embedded processors, and even on smart cards (credit cards with a microprocessor and memory), as shown in Figure 1–1.

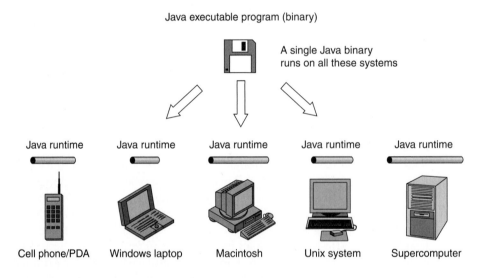

Java executable program (binary)

A single Java binary runs on all these systems

| Java runtime | Java runtime | Java runtime | Java runtime | Java runtime |
| Cell phone/PDA | Windows laptop | Macintosh | Unix system | Supercomputer |

Figure 1–1   Future-proof software: Your Java application runs on every system. No more "requires Windows XP" or "Linux PPC only" , or "compiled for MacOS X version 10.5"; just "built with Java," and you're done.

You will even be able to run on future operating system releases, like Microsoft's Longhorn. Java will be ported to all future operating systems of significance. It's also a fast way for new hardware to get software applications that will run on it.

Java unlocks software from being coupled to any specific OS and hardware platform. This new flexibility has made Java very popular with users, IT departments, and software vendors. All three benefit enormously from software portability.

Why Portability Matters

You might think that software portability does not affect you: your application software runs fine on your PC today and that's all you use. And that's true, right up until the time you want to consider a new or different system.

Say you're in the market to buy a new desktop system, and a friend shows you the video-editing, music, virus resistance, and digital picture capabilities of his Apple Macintosh. You consider switching to a Mac. Switching GUIs is a no-brainer—GUIs all do essentially the same things, and it only takes a day or two to re-train your fingers. The problem is the apps. You are faced with the "choice" of walking away from your investment in your existing PC-only software, or buying yet another Windows PC that has some compatibility with your previous system. You can easily switch hardware from Dell to H-P or IBM, but there's a software barrier to switching from Windows to something with fewer security problems, like Linux or MacOS. You've been locked in.

When your application programs are written in Java, you can upgrade OS and applications independently. You can try Linux and still use your familiar applications. You can move your existing Java programs to any new system, and carry on using them. This is why software portability matters to home users.

For businesses, the problem is worse and far more expensive. Even if your whole organization has standardized on, say, Microsoft Windows XP, there have been numerous releases over just the last decade and a bit: MS-DOS, Win 3.1, Win3.11, Win95A, Win95B, Win98, 98 SE, ME, NT 3.1, NT3.5, NT3.51, NT4, 2K, multiple service packs and required hot-fixes, XP, and Longhorn on the horizon. These platforms have subtle and different incompatibilities among them. Even applications running on a single platform have limited interoperability. Older versions of Microsoft Office cannot read files produced by default from the latest Microsoft Office, even when the files don't use any of the new features.

This is done deliberately, to force upgrades. If even one person in an office upgrades, everyone has to (or risk being cut off from reading new files).

Software portability is all about "future-proofing" your software investment. Rewrite it in Java, and that's the last port you'll ever need to do. Portability is the Holy Grail of the software industry. It has long been sought, but never before attained. Java brings the industry closer to true software portability than any previous system has.

Software portability for office applications

There is today an excellent alternative to costly and incompatible MS Office updates. You can download the free OpenOffice.orgsoftware and use it instead of MS Office.

MS Office Professional Edition 2003 costs $499 in the USA for the basic product—for one computer. OpenOffice.org has the same look and features, and is free for any number of computers. OpenOffice.org can read and save files in MS Office formats. You can even get the source code. Over twenty million users have downloaded it, and you can get your copy at:

`www.openoffice.org`

There are OpenOffice.org versions available for Linux, Windows, MacOS, and Solaris, in many different national languages. OpenOffice.org is not written in Java, so it needs an executable for each platform. OpenOffice.org (like Java) is based on source code made freely available from Sun. There is a programmers guide and SDK at `http://www.openoffice.org/dev_docs/source/sdk/`

Java and jobs

Software portability has a *wonderful* side-effect: skills portability for programmers. Many companies today are out-sourcing programming jobs to countries with low direct labor costs. It's a short-term cost-saving that looks good on paper, until you look at the wider implications.

The beneficiaries of jobs exported from the West are Asian countries with poor performance in the annual global survey of corruption (see `www.transparency.org`). It's a risky long-term bet to move strategic expertise to countries that combine widespread corruption, unproven business privacy and intellectual property laws, with scant free market experience, and no effective environmental or workplace regulation. The bigger picture needs to be thought through when choosing to export jobs and assets from our home economies. As people with a stake in the computer industry, we have a duty to make our views (whatever they are) known to politicians.

Looking at this another way, China (a nation of 1.3 billion) has already standardized on Linux, and India (1 billion people) is reviewing it. Java offers the only viable way to create software targeted at both the West and at emerging markets.

If you're a programmer in the USA or Western Europe affected by jobs moving offshore, Java is a big plus for your career. Employers used to advertise for very specific hardware and OS experience ("must have 2 years of MVS on OS/390") and ignore other resumes. Today, your Java experience gained on any OS is directly transferable to other hardware and jobs.

Java is in demand by employers. An April 2004 review of one of the US's largest job sites reflected these hiring needs. Microsoft's C# was mentioned in about 1400 postings, while C++ was a requirement in about 4000 postings. That's what you would expect. C++ is much more widespread than C#, and runs on many more computers. But Java was a surprise: more than 6800 postings sought Java skills. More employers wanted Java experience than those who wanted C++ and C# combined. This is just an anecdotal datapoint, but it is consistent with other surveys. The *Software Development Times* paper reported in December 2003 that nearly three-quarters of enterprise software development managers are using Java and another 11% plan to start in the next year. Investing some of your time in Java is good for your career.

Java and Microsoft

Java portability poses a real threat to Microsoft's monopoly. Software that can run on any operating system has a larger market than software that is limited to Windows only. Over time ISVs will move their products away from Windows-only to Java—unless Java can somehow be spoiled or broken.

It is unfortunate for you, me, and all computer users that Microsoft uses its monopoly to try to undermine Java. At first, Microsoft introduced deliberate incompatibilities into the Java product it licensed from Sun. Microsoft paid $20 million to Sun to settle the resulting court case. In April 2004, Microsoft paid Sun a further $1.9 billion to settle Sun's litigation over other monopoly abuse.

The current Microsoft plan is to push the C# language, which is Microsoft's barely different copy of Java. But the core C# libraries will be only ever be available on Windows (there's an open source effort to duplicate some C# libraries on Linux, but few believe it will lead anywhere). The C# initiative will last only until Redmond wants to push the Next Incompatible Big Thing. Java is shaped by the computer industry as a whole, and will be around until industry reaches consensus that there is something better to replace Java.

Language and Libraries

Let's spend a minute to review some software terms that are often taken for granted. If you are already familiar with this, just skip ahead until you reach something new. The terminology is spelled out in detail here to give a solid basis for the material that follows in the rest of the book.

What a language is

When people talk about a "programming language", they mean things like:

*   How the language describes data,
*   The statements that work on data, and

- The ways the two can be put together. The set of rules describing how you can put together programs in the language is called a *grammar*. The grammar for a programming language is written in mathematical language, and it defines how expressions are formed, what statements look like, and so on. We'll stay away from mathematics and explain things in English.

Java is a programming language in the same part of the languages family tree as C++, Pascal, or Basic. Java adopts ideas from non-mainstream languages like Smalltalk and Lisp, too. Java is a strongly typed language, meaning that the compiler strictly checks operations and will only allow those that are valid for that type of operand (you can't multiply two character strings, but you may append them). Java is *object-oriented*, meaning that the data declarations are very closely tied to the statements that operate on the data. Object-oriented means more than just tying data to statements, and we expand on that in chapters 2 and 5.

Statements are grouped into what other languages call functions, procedures, or subroutines. In an object-oriented language, we call the functions *methods* as they are the method or way to process some data. Methods can call other methods and can be recursive (call themselves). Program execution begins in a method with the special name `main()`. Statements in Java look similar to statements in many other high-level languages. Here are some examples of Java statements:

```
y = y + 1;
if ( isLeapYear(y) )        // this is a comment
     febDays = 29;
else febDays = 28;
```

Although Java adds some new things, it is equally notable for what is left out. The designer of C++ once wrote, "Within C++, there is a much smaller and cleaner language struggling to get out," (Bjarne Stroustrup, *The Design and Evolution of C++*, Addison-Wesley, 1994: 207). Of the people who agree with that prophetic statement, many think that the name of that smaller and cleaner language is Java.

Java has eight basic or *primitive* datatypes, such as integers, characters, and floating-point numbers. All data is represented as one of these eight built-in elementary types, or as an object or array made up of these types. The size of each type is laid down in the language and is the same on all platforms. Here are some other Java language features that will be covered in later chapters:

- **Threads.** Threads let a single program do more than one thing at once, just as timesharing lets a computer system run more than one program at once.

- **Exceptions.** Exceptions help a programmer deal with error conditions when most convenient, instead of cluttering up the main flow of control with lots of checking and error-handlingcode.

- **Garbage collection.** With garbage collection, the run-time library, not the programmer, manages the use of dynamic storage and reclaims (frees) memory that is no longer in use in a program.

A programming language typically has a specification, which is a weighty document saying what the expressions, statements, and their various groupings actually mean. That is, what changes in memory or control flow will occur when an expression is evaluated or a statement is executed. This is termed the *semantics* of the language. The first half of this book, up to Chapter 15, explains the features and meaning (semantics) of the Java language. Don't worry—the chapters are short and well organized.

Sun has published a Java Language Specification (JLS). It is written mostly for an audience of compiler implementors, and is not intended as a tutorial for programmers (that's what this book is for). But it can be fun to dip into the JLS anyway when you want to play language lawyer or resolve a tricky question, and you can find it online at `http://java.sun.com/docs/books/jls/index.html` .

What a library is

Early in the history of programming, people realized that some routines were needed over and over again in different programs. It makes sense to move frequently reused code into a separate file or *library* that all programs can share. The kind of code that belongs in a library are things like code to open a file, or read in a block of bytes, or get the current timestamp from the operating system.

A library is not an executable program in its own right. It contains executable code that is brought into your program's address space, when your program calls a routine in the library. The work of finding the right library and loading its code into your process memory at run-time is called *dynamic linking* and it's an important feature of Java. "Dynamic" in compiler terminology just means "is done at run-time", and contrasts with "static" meaning "done at compile time".

The entire set of routines in a library (the routine names, what they can return, and the parameter types) is known as the Application Programming Interface, or API. Modern languages check that the calls to a library are consistent with the API of the library implementation. The checking needs to be done twice: at compile time to catch any mismatches as early as possible, and at run-time to confirm that nothing has changed. So the compiler and the run-time environment both need to know where to find the application libraries.

Application Programmer Interface (API)

This is the set of libraries the programmer sees and uses when writing source code. An API consists of the names of the routines in a library, return types, and the number and types of parameters.

For example, the POSIX 1003.1 Operating System standard says that every system complying with the standard will have a function with the following name and argument. It will return nonzero if ch is in the range of the 7-bit ASCII codes:

```
int isascii(int ch);
```

A program that uses only the routines specified in an API is compatible at the source code level with any OS that implements the API. Standard APIs make life easier for software vendors. Java has the same unified API on all computers. This was the part that Microsoft tried to break.

When working on large suites of programs, application programmers will frequently design and implement their own libraries (accumulation of re-usable routines). A retail sales application might have a library for a customer transaction, with all the operations you can do on a transaction: sale, return, void, or cancel. Any time a programmer wants code to process a transaction, he or she calls the appropriate library routine. If a bug is found in transaction code, it only needs to be fixed in one place (the library) and not in all the places where the library routine is called.

What the run-time library is

Just as application suites are supported by libraries, the compiler vendor provides a set of libraries collectively known as the *run-time library*. The run-time library or "the run-time" supports operations needed by programs in the course of execution.

The classic run-time library handles a small number of house-keeping tasks like memory management, maintaining a stack, and dynamic array support. Programmers don't call routines in a classic run-time library; the calls are planted automatically by the compiler when needed. Apart from the implicit calls, there is no significant difference between code in the run-time library and code in an application library. It's implemented the same way and has the same overall goals. Programmers can count on the presence of the run-time library, but because they don't have to tell the compiler where to find it and because they don't call it explicitly, they sometimes aren't really aware of its presence.

Java takes a radically different approach. Java has a very extensive run-time library—greater than any other programming language to date. In addition to the standard house-keeping operations in support of program execution, Java comes bundled with scores of *packages* (the Java term for a library) to carry out tasks useful to many applications. These libraries form part of the Java run-time library by definition, and you can absolutely depend on their standard presence in an implementation. Unlike a classic run-time library, the programmer will explicitly call routines in these Java packages when needed, and hence needs to know about the Java run-times and what they do.

Much of the value of Java is in this set of cross-platform APIs that come with the compiler system. Java has possibly the easiest-to-use networking and windowing (GUI) support of any language. For example, there is a single library function to read a JPEG file and display it as an icon in a GUI. There is another library function to make a standard connection, known as a socket, to any program (not just Java code) on another computer anywhere on the Internet. Java makes network software easy to build.

Some of the standard Java packages are shown in Table 1–1.

Table 1–1   **A few of the many Java libraries (packages) available to all programs**

Package name	Purpose
java.lang	This provides the core support for language features, corresponding to a classic run-time library.
java.io	This package provides basic I/O to the file system
java.net	This library contains the code that lets you implement network applications.
java.util	This library contains data structures (e.g. a tree, a set, a map) and common operations on them. Also other miscellaneous utility classes (date/time support, random numbers, etc.).
java.util.regex	Nested in the java.util package, this library supports text searching using regular expressions patterns.
java.sql	This library provides tools for database access.

You can deduce that there is a hierarchy to package names: nested packages are shown by names separated by a period. E.g. there is a package called java.util full of utilities. One of its members is a package called java.util.regex, which has classes dealing with utilities for regular expressions. The hierarchy helps organize the hundreds of libraries, grouping related ones together. The package names shown in this table are exactly the names used in Java programs.

Once a language has been specified and implemented, it is quite a big deal to make further changes to the language. However, it is trivial to add new libraries because they don't affect any existing programs, they don't need compiler or interpreter changes, and they don't change any tools that process object code. Each new release of Java has added some pretty hefty new packages.

The *Preface* on page xix has a table showing how Java has evolved over a series of successive releases. Up until Java 1.5, there had only been a few new features added to the language. Java 1.5 introduces a major new language feature called "generics" which is explained in Chapter 15. Growth in the language and libraries is a witness to the increasing use of Java in new problem domains and applications.

One Size Doesn't Fit All

It's quite an accomplishment to run the same binary executable on such widely different architectures as MacOS, Windows, Linux and a quarter of a billion cell phones. There's more information about this coming up in Chapter 2, but for now, let's make an over-simplification and say that Java binary executables are interpreted on each platform.

The Java binary format doesn't contain machine code instructions for any one computer. It contains a slightly higher level, more general, set of instructions known as byte code. To run a Java program, you actually run an interpreter. The interpreter reads the binary file containing the byte code and translates it into the machine code for the system where you are executing the program. The full and more complete story is in Chapter 2, remember.

It's also not easy to run software on everything from a smart card to a supercomputer cluster. That encompasses a wide range of hardware capabilities—virtual memory, hard disk, processor speed, file space, GUI abilities, memory size, and so on. Sun has achieved Java support on virtually every computing device[1] by defining different "editions." The smaller editions have a subset of the libraries in the bigger editions.

There are three editions of Java, and the smallest one is further sub-divided. For the sake of clarity, they should just have been called the small, medium and large editions, but the Java marketing folks at Sun gave them these names instead:

Micro Edition (the "small" platform). The Micro Edition is a very low-footprint Java run-time environment, intended for embedding in consumer products like cell phones and other wireless devices, palmtops, or car navigation systems. You will develop your code using J2SE, and then deploy onto the various small devices. The Micro Edition is also known as Java 2 Micro Edition or "J2ME" for short.

The J2ME environment is further subdivided into "profiles." There is a profile (Connected Limited Device Configuration, or CLDC) that defines the libraries available for PDA-type hardware. I have a handheld Sharp Zaurus PDA which

---

1. I have a signet ring that runs Java programs! These rings were given out at the 1998 JavaOne conference. See www.ibutton.com.

runs the Linux operating system just like one of my desktop systems, so PDAs can be pretty capable these days. Another profile (the Mobile Information Device Platform, MIDP) is for wireless devices such as cell phones. Cell phones today are general purpose computers, with a few special peripherals. The smallest profile, which runs in just 128 Kbytes of memory, is intended for smart cards. It's called the Java Card API. The guy at Sun in charge of really dumb names (like J2SE SDK, CLDC and MIDP) must have been on vacation the week the API for Java cards got named "the Java Card API". This profile is allowed to omit support for floating-point arithmetic when the hardware doesn't have it.

The J2ME environment is enjoying enormous success and has shipped in many millions of cell phones already. The year 2002 marked the point at which the number of handheld computing devices sold exceeded the number of PCs sold, so Java's success in this sector has real momentum. The Zelos Group (a company of technology analysts) predicts that Java will run on 450 million handsets by 2007, which is 75% of those shipping that year. As cell phones continue to evolve PDA features, and thus to push PDAs off the market, Java is available for both. Java completely dominates the cell phone programming market and has squeezed all rivals out of this space.

One programmer commented "by learning to program in Java, you free yourself from the limits of programming for just one OS or hardware product. It is an amazing feeling to see my apps running on my Palm Vx and my Motorola i95cl color Javaphone, and to know that they run just as well in any Nokia or Samsung or other java-enabled phone, on a RIM Blackberry, and on Windows CE."

In May 2004, the top cable tv operators and suppliers (CableLabs, Charter, Cox, GoldPocket, Liberate, Motorola, Philips, Sun Microsystems, Time Warner Cable, and Vidiom Systems) jointly announced an initiative to develop a Java digital television API open standard. It is a CDLC profile called OnRamp, intended for legacy, resource-constrained cable television set-top boxes. It will be available to all set-top box vendors and digital tv developers, saving time and money for the entire industry.

Standard Edition (the "medium" platform). Most people will work with this edition, as it is the edition with the libraries for desktop systems. The Standard Edition is also known as Java 2 Platform, Standard Edition or "J2SE" for short. Old-timers also use the abbreviation JDK (Java Development Kit) which was the term in use before Marketing and Legal rebadged it all. Using J2SE, you can write, deploy, and run Java programs for desktops and low-end servers.

This text focuses on J2SE, which is the best edition for those learning Java. Java's compatibility ensures that everything you learn for J2SE also applies to programming the very large and the very small platforms. You can be a cell phone programmer, and a cable tv set-top box programmer, too. NASA's Mars Rover mission, which enjoyed great success in 2004, made extensive use of J2SE to control the vehicle and visually interpret the images sent back to earth.

Sun intends to ship new J2SE releases on a regular 12-18 month cycle, with each update combining improvements in quality and performance as well as a small number of new features. That's the intent, but some releases (like JDK 1.5) have a *lot* of new features and came out on an attenuated timeline (translation: there was so much new stuff, the schedule slipped).

Enterprise Edition (the "large" platform). This development product is intended for those building enterprise-class server-based applications. It contains everything in the standard edition, and additional libraries for enterprise directories, transaction management, and enterprise messaging.

The Enterprise Edition is also known as Java 2 Enterprise Edition or "J2EE" for short. This book describes several of the most popular libraries from the enterprise edition, including Java support for XML, for database access, and for servlets.

Book website/author email
In spite of everyone's efforts, all technical books contain at least one error. If you find an error in this text, please let me know by email.
My email address is at the end of the errata sheet for this book at www.afu.com.

Some Light Relief—A Java Desktop Application

Do you have trouble keeping track of your disk usage? Do you sometimes need to free up space, but have no idea what to start deleting? Have a look at jDiskReport, which is a Java application written by expert programmer Karsten Lentzsch of Kiel in Germany.

jDiskReport is a free cross-platform graphical disk report utility. It lets you understand how much space the files and directories consume on your hard disks.

Figure 1-2 shows jDiskReport but really doesn't do justice to the program.

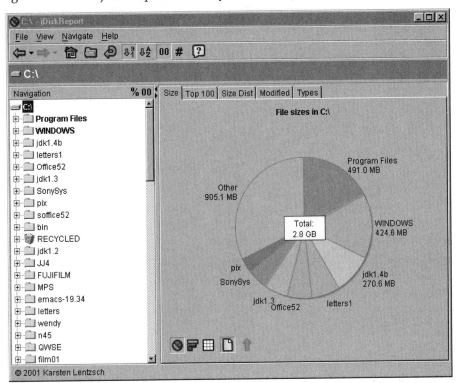

Figure 1–2   The jDiskReport: keeping track of hard disk space.

The jDiskReport software is freely from Karsten's website at `www.jgoodies.com`. Download it and unzip the file. There is a readme.txt and a jar file. Go to the directory containing those files, and start the program with the command line

```
java -jar jdiskreport.jar
```

The application will summarize the disk usage on your system and display it in a large variety of formats: oldest, largest, by type of file, pie chart, bar graph, text, tree display. This software was written once, and it runs on Linux, the Mac, Solaris, an HP Risc system, and so on. It is a very user friendly program, fast, and a good advert for the Java GUI library known as "Swing." Karsten has additional Java software on his website, too. If someone tells you that Java is only good for server software, show them this desktop application. Try it yourself; you'll probably find it very useful.

Chapter 2

Introducing Objects

▼ DOWNLOADING AND COMPILING JAVA

▼ WHAT IS A CLASS?

▼ WHAT IS AN OBJECT?

▼ JAVA DIGITAL CLOCK PROGRAM

▼ SUMMARY

▼ EXERCISES

▼ SOME LIGHT RELIEF—NAPSTER AND LIMEWIRE

Here's where we get to grips with a real Java program. Follow the steps in Appendix A to download a Java compiler. Then you can type in source code and test examples as we go along.

The chapter presents some basics of Object Oriented Programming (OOP). We'll explain exactly what language designers mean by a *type*, and relate that to the *objects* in *OOP*. We'll develop a type called Timestamp, then add a couple of other types to turn it into a complete program. Along the way, we'll clarify the **super-important distinction** between "an object" and "a reference to an object". The chapter ends with the development of a small but complete running Java program that displays a desktop clock.

Downloading and Compiling Java

If you use Solaris or an Apple computer running MacOS X, a Java compiler is already installed on your system. So you folks can skip right ahead to "Running a Java Program". Dell and H-P preload Java libraries on their Windows PCs, but you still need to download a compiler. If you are using Windows, Linux, or Solaris, Sun's website at java.sun.com is the easiest place to get a free Java compiler. There are other places too. IBM has some great Java compiler and tool downloads. If you are using something other than Linux, MacOS, Windows or Solaris, find the Java compiler by searching the manufacturer's website.

Downloading a Java compiler system

Follow the steps in Appendix A to download and install a Java Development Kit (JDK). The current version of the JDK is called "J2SE version 5", i.e. Java 2 Standard Edition version 5 of the Software Development Kit. During beta testing, this release was called version 1.5, and you may still hear old timers call it "JDK 1.5". It was promoted to version 5 in recognition of the large number of core language changes in the release.

Compiling a Java program

A lot of programmers use IDEs to develop their code, and there are many IDEs that support Java, including some free ones such as Sun's NetBeans, Eclipse, or the BlueJ environment. You can get a list by googling for "Java IDE". We'll avoid IDEs here and do everything from the command line, to keep the learning experience focused on Java. Create a separate work directory just for your files, and don't put your directory anywhere under the JDK installation directory.

```
mkdir c:\work
cd c:\work
```

After installing, you can run the Java compiler. Type this at the command shell:

```
javac
```

Assuming you installed the JDK and set the path correctly, you will get back a dozen lines of messages, starting with this line:

```
Usage: javac <options> <source files>
```

Voila, your first Java program (no file at all, which is even easier than "hello world") compiles OK. If you saw something different, like "javac not recognized", troubleshoot your installation and/or the path variable as outlined in appendix A.

Running a Java program

The next step is to run a Java program. Java was originally implemented as an interpreted language. You ran the interpreter program, the interpreter read the bytecode, and interpreted it into the corresponding instructions for that architecture.

And that's still mostly true today for most implementations of Java. Sun refers to the interpreter program as the *Java Virtual Machine* (JVM). The JVM, the run-time library, and the extensive Java libraries together are known as the *Java Runtime Environment* (JRE). The JRE does for Java applications roughly what Microsoft's Common Language Runtime (CLR) does for .net applications. The CLR lets a program be written in any of several Windows languages and only run on Windows. The JRE lets a program (in any language that compiles to Java bytecode) run on every computer system.

That truly means Java runs on just about *every* computer system. Cell phones and digital cameras today contain general-purpose microprocessors, which is the main reason there's a few seconds ofdelay after turning them on—they take time to boot up. I haven't written a Java program for my digital camera yet, but there are plenty for my cell phone.

Interpreter performance boosts
A classic interpreter has a start-up performance issue: instead of the operating system loading your program into memory and executing it, the operating system has to load the interpreter program into memory and execute it, followed by the interpreter program loading the run-time library and your program into memory and executing that. So interpreted programs have twice the start-up overhead of programs that have been compiled to native code. This doesn't matter for server code, but has dampened Java's popularity for desktop applications.

Class data sharing
A huge amount of effort has been devoted to speeding up Java and the JVM interpreter. JDK 1.5 brings in a new and significant optimization called *class data sharing*. This technique maps most of the run-time library into the JVM as a memory image, rather than loading it from a series of class files. Although memory mapped I/O is fast (see Chapter 18 for details), it makes the process look bigger to some Windows tools (wrongly) than if you had loaded the same content through the link-loader.

Footprint reduction
Also in JDK 1.5, as much as possible of the run-time library (several MB) is now shared among JVM instances, rather than loaded into each individually. This will improve performance when you run several Java programs at once. Everyone hopes that class data sharing will give great results, rejuvenating Java on the desktop.

Hotspot
Sun's JVM uses a technique called Just In Time compiling (JIT) to complete compilation at run-time, translating from byte code to native machine code. Sun calls its JIT implementation the "Hotspot"TM compiler. There's a trade-off between the time the JVM spends optimizing the translation, and the time you save because your code now runs faster. The JVM tries to reduce the work by only translating the tight loops or "hot spots" of code, not the whole program. Most benchmarks show that Java code runs as fast as optimized native code, once the program starts.

Continuing the discussion of setting up Java, here's the command that runs a Java program:

```
java classname
```

We are going to use a digital clock program as an example in the rest of the chapter. You can download the clock.java source code file from www.afu.com/jj6 or you can type in the code from the listings later in the chapter. Either way, make sure the files are in your work directory and "cd" to it, so it becomes your current working directory. After successfully compiling, you can run a program with the main code in a class called "clock" by typing:

```
java clock
```

When you compile and run the example program, a window containing a digital clock display appears, and the display keeps updated with the current time. The commands to compile and run are shown in Figure 2–1. The example uses a Mac.

Figure 2–1   Compiling and running clock.java

The javac command will create a file called "clock.class" containing the bytecode. If you create the same files on a windows system (or move the clock.class file from any system over to a windows system), you can execute it with the command "java clock". You will see a window like Figure 2–2 appear, and keep time:

Figure 2–2   Running the same clock program on Windows

Download or type in, then compile and run clock.java now. Don't sweat the details about understanding individual lines of code; we will go over them in the following sections. It's time to say a few words about classes and objects.

What Is a Class?

In a way, Object Oriented Programming (OOP) is a misnomer, as the fundamental things we're dealing with are classes. Perhaps it should have been called "Class-based Programming", but it's too late to change now. So what's a class, and what's an object? There are several different ways of coming at this, and we'll try a couple of them. If you are already familiar with OOP, then just skim through the chapter to pick up the Java specifics. Be sureto visit the "What is an Object?" section, which describes an object-oriented feature handled differently in Java (reference types).

Declaring a variable

To get a good understanding of OOP, you need to understand data types in procedural (non-OOP) languages. The idea of representing real world objects by types and variables in a computer is called *abstraction*. Here's a quick review. You'll be familiar with the idea of declaring a variable. In many languages, a variable declaration will look something like this:

```
int mm = 0;
```

Depending on the exact rules of a language, the keyword for the type might be "int" or "integer" or something similar, and it might come before or after the variable name. In Java, a variable is declared exactly as shown here: type name first, followed by variable name. When you write a declaration like:

```
int mm = 0;
```

you are:

- Allocating some storage, and initializing it to zero,

- Giving it a name, mm,

- Saying that it can only hold values that are compatible with the int type. You cannot put a string of characters into mm.

Simple types

A "type" defines the values that a variable can take, and the operations that can be done on it. When we say "mm has type int" it means that mm can only hold whole numbers, and only in a certain range (usually corresponding to the capabilities of the underlying hardware). It can be used in addition, but not in true/false logical operations. You can't suddenly pull a string of characters out of an int variable. There are ways to convert or *cast* between closely related types. Java is a strongly typed language, so you can only cast between related types.

Data types make software a lot more reliable. The type part of a declaration lays down what kind of values and operations are acceptable for a given variable. The compiler will cross-check every use of a variable against its type declaration, and give error messages for obvious inconsistencies. For example, if you try to divide a string by a floating point number, the compiler will recognize that as an error. The more errors you eliminate during compilation, the fewer you have to debug during execution (or shamefully, after the product has shipped).

Most languages have around ten or so built-in simple or *primitive* types. These are types like character, boolean, int, floating point number, and so on. Primitive types have no visible internal structure, and often correspond to types that are directly supported in hardware. It is easy to overlook the significance of what primitive types add to a programming language, because you get so much behavior implicitly just by mentioning the type name.

Be very clear on the distinction between a type and a primitive variable as shown in Table 2–1.

Table 2–1   Distinction between a type and a primitive variable

Type	Variable
• The name (e.g. int) is shorthand for the allowable values and operations.	• Has a name (e.g. mm) that is used to refer to the storage, to put and get a value there.
• Does not allocate any storage.	• Allocates storage.
• Cannot hold a value.	• The storage can hold one of the acceptable values, and can only be used for the acceptable operations.
• Cannot take part in operations.	
• The type specifies the legal operations (addition, comparison, concatenation, bit shifting, etc.)	• A variable can only take part in operations that are specified by its type.
• The type specifies the legal values (e.g. whole numbers between minus 128 to plus 127).	• A variable can only hold values that are specified by its type.

Composite types

Most programming languages provide a way to group several types, to define a new type. One example would be a "Timestamp" type that is made up of three fields representing hour, minute and seconds. This is called a *composite* type, in contrast to a primitive type. A composite type might be made up of other composite types. An example is a Photo type that may consist of an image type and a Timestamp type (itself a composite type) saying when the picture was taken.

Different programming languages give different names to composite types. Visual Basic calls them User Defined Types. C calls them structs (structures). COBOL calls them records. Fortran calls them derived types. It's just terminology. Java calls composite types *reference types,* and they are popularly known as *classes.*

There are two important things to note about reference types:

- Creating a reference type does not allocate any storage. When you describe a reference type to the compiler, you still have not created anywhere to store a value of that type.

- You'll probably want to define a whole set of allowable operations and legal values to be part of your new type.

Picking up on that second point, the operations for a-type-that-you-define probably won't be as simple as the arithmetic operations on numeric primitive types. For example, say you define a composite type Timestamp. It contains three fields (hh, mm, ss). You'll want a method to update those fields with the current time. You can imagine other operations on Timestamps, too: clear, set to a known time, etc. All the methods should somehow be bundled with the definition of the Timestamp type.

In language terms, data and related functions should be bundled somehow, so you can say, "This is how we represent a Timestamp type, and these are the *only* operations that can be done on Timestamp types." Programming language designers call this *encapsulation*.

Non-OOP languages (like C, Fortran, or classic VB) support encapsulation for built-in types, but not at all for user-defined types. Some languages support "header files" that group variables, definitions of user types, and function declarations, but this is not true encapsulation. Header files do not enforce the integrity of a type: they do not prevent invalid operations (like assigning a float to an int that represents month number), nor do they provide any information hiding. Header files don't provide true encapsulation, so they are not in Java.

Organizing data and methods into larger "chunks"

OOP languages directly support bundling together types and the functions that operate on those types. The feature that allows you to describe and combine a data structure and its methods is (drumroll...) a *class*. A variable whose type is a class is called an *object*. Your programs will typically have a few classes, and many objects belonging to those classes.

Java also supports a feature for grouping related classes together in a library. A library is known as a *package* to a Java compiler, and it's often implemented as a directory of files. Figure 2–3 shows how Java data structures and their methods are put into classes, classes go into source files, and source files are grouped to form packages.

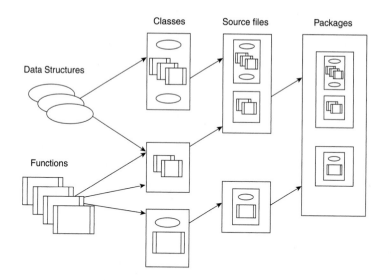

Figure 2–3   Java code is organized into classes, files, and packages

The operations on built-in types tend to be arithmetic operations like +, -, *, and /. The operations on class types are written as statements in methods in the OOP world. Unlike procedural programming where you call functions willy-nilly, in OOP all methods are defined in some class, and you invoke methods on an object of that class. Here's an example using a class from the Java run-time library. Say you have an object of class Calendar, called "now".

```
Calendar now =    /*some initialization, not shown*/
```

Calendar has a method called get() which takes some arguments we will ignore. When we say "you invoke methods on an object", we mean you have to (implicitly or explicitly) provide a Calendar object, and the get() or other method will operate upon that. You don't write:

```
get ( );
```

You have to write

```
now.get ( );
```

That is what it means to invoke a method on an object. Keep going — this will fall into place soon.

A class doesn't just group and organize; it also restricts access to the internal representation of user-defined types. This is done with keywords like "public" and "private" attached to things in the class. Those keywords specify how visible a declaration is.

How do we express "these methods and data declarations together form a class"? It is simplicity itself. You write the methods and declarations in a source file. Then at the head of the things that belong together you write:

```
class classname {
```

and at the end of the methods and data declarations forming the class, you write a matching closing brace:

```
}
```

That's all there is to it! You can precede the keyword `class` with a few keywords that say how widely accessibly this particular class is. At the top of the source file, you can say what package it belongs to, and/or what packages or other classes it will import. Here's a simple Timestamp type. It contains some data declarations, but no methods (yet):

```
class Timestamp {
        int hrs;
        int mins;
        int secs;
}
```

You can put these five lines into a file called Timestamp.java and compile them with the command "javac Timestamp.java". Go ahead and try it now.

We said earlier that Timestamp needs a method to place the current time into the timestamp fields. The class Calendar mentioned previously is in a package called java.util. So the full name of the class is java.util.Calendar, and it does things with dates and times. If we declare an object of Calendar type, we can call some of its methods to extract the current hour, minute and seconds for our Timestamp.

The statements might look like this:

```
        java.util.Calendar now = java.util.Calendar.getInstance();

        hrs  = now.get(java.util.Calendar.HOUR_OF_DAY);
        mins = now.get(java.util.Calendar.MINUTE);
        secs = now.get(java.util.Calendar.SECOND);
```

The first line declares the object "now" of type Calendar, from the package java.util. The dotted notation a.b.c.d is how you refer to classes within packages, and also members within classes. The next three lines are three calls to the `get()` method of Calendar, with three different arguments, each telling it to get a different time-related value. Those words in capitals ("MINUTES" etc) are constant values defined in class Calendar. The argument tells `get()` what date/time values are sought. The return values from these calls are then assigned to the variables hrs, mins, and secs respectively.

We still need to give the method a name, and say that it returns void, i.e. no return value. Here's how:

```
void fillTimes() {
        // the statements from above go here
        java.util.Calendar now;
        now = java.util.Calendar.getInstance();
        hrs = now.get(java.util.Calendar.HOUR_OF_DAY);
        mins = now.get(java.util.Calendar.MINUTE);
        secs = now.get(java.util.Calendar.SECOND);
}
```

Writing "//" makes the rest of the line a comment in Java. We'll sometimes annotate code examples using that. So putting the whole thing together, here's a complete class with data and a method from our clock program. We just defined the Timestamp type in terms of its datafields and methods. All classes are defined by their datafields and methods.

```
class Timestamp {
        int hrs;
        int mins;
        int secs;

        void fillTimes() {
            java.util.Calendar now;
            now = java.util.Calendar.getInstance();
            hrs = now.get(java.util.Calendar.HOUR_OF_DAY);
            mins = now.get(java.util.Calendar.MINUTE);
            secs = now.get(java.util.Calendar.SECOND);
        }
}
```

A data item (as opposed to a method) in a class is a *field*. The methods and fields together are called the *members* of a class (they belong to the class). This class has three fields and one method. You will call its method fillTimes() to update the current hour, minute and second. It provides a convenient interface to extract and format from the more complicated Calendar class in the Java library.

What Is an Object?

The previous section focused on classes and ended with a small but complete user-defined class called Timestamp. We've already let the cat out of the bag that an object is a variable of a class type, not a primitive type. There are several other ways to say that:

- An object is an *instance* of a class

- An object *belongs* to a class

- An object belongs to a *reference type*

However, they all mean the same thing. This section fills in some more of the details on objects: how you declare them and how you create them (two different things), and how you use them.

What "reference type" really means

An object declaration looks exactly the same as a primitive variable declaration. You first write the type name (which is the class name), then follow it by the variable name (which is the object name). So it's just like a declaration of a primitive variable. Here is a declaration of a variable of class type:

```
Timestamp  tick;
```

The following example shows a qualified name that lets you declare an object of a type defined in another package:

```
java.util.Calendar  now;
```

The name Calendar is qualified by the package it is in, java.util.

The Java Language Specification talks about classes being reference types. It means memory references, as in a pointer or address. The variables in the previous examples, *tick* and *now*, look like they can hold an object. Don't be fooled! They *really* only hold something that refers to (is the address of) an object. You have to create the object itself as a separate step!

The big difference between primitive and object

That is a very big difference between primitive variables and objects. When you declare a variable of primitive type, the declaration allocates the memory, and you can start assigning into the variable right away. When you declare a variable of class type, you get somewhere to store the address of an object, but you do not get some storage for the object itself. You have to make the variable point to an existing or newly created object before you can assign to the fields or call the methods of an object.

The "null" reference

When you declare a reference type, it is automatically initialized with the null value, typically represented as zero on the underlying hardware. The null value says "I don't refer to anything" and if you try to get to an object through a null reference, it causes an error condition. You can explicitly assign null or check for it using the literal value "null" as shown in this example:

```
Timestamp t;         // t has the value null at this point

t = new Timestamp(); // this line creates a Timestamp object,
                     // and assigns its address into t.

if (t==null)         // t won't be null here, because it points to the
                     // Timestamp we created in the previous statement
```

We can now use t to access the fields of the object t points to.

```
t.hrs = 12;
```

It's no big deal to create an object. Every class has one or more special methods, known as *constructors*, that create and initialize an object belonging to that class. Someone who wants to create an object will call one of these constructors. A constructor is written with statements like a regular method and has the same name as the class it belongs to. If you didn't explicitly provide any constructors, a simple implicit one is provided on your behalf. Our Timestamp class does not have any explicit constructors, so it gets the implicit one. The next two lines show an object declaration, then a constructor call. The return value from the constructor is a pointer to the freshly created object. Variable cv is assigned that pointer.

```
ClockView cv;
cv = new ClockView();
```

The keyword new is a tipoff that the programmer intends a constructor call, not a regular method. Typically, the two lines are combined into one as below:

```
ClockView cv = new ClockView();
```

Why Java uses reference types

You might ask, why the two-step process of declaring a reference variable, and filling it with a value? That's really two questions: why are constructors used, and why are reference variables used? Chapter 5 explores constructors more thoroughly, and addresses the "why constructors?" question. Reference variables are used for one overriding reason: they greatly simplify automatic memory management at run-time.

Managing memory resources by hand is very error-prone.It is all too easy to introduce leaks, dangling references, and memory corruption. By lifting this burden from the programmer, Java greatly improves software reliability of larger and longer running systems. Reference variables are a central part of Java so we can have automatic memory management, and that's an enabler for more reliable software.

References, pointers, addresses—the same thing

Some people say that Java doesn't have pointers, it has references. They mean that references are a refinement of pointers with restricted semantics.

That is splitting hairs: a reference is another name for a pointer, which is another name for a memory address. If Java doesn't have pointers, it is very suspicious that a common error condition in Java is called a "Null**Pointer**Exception."

Java doesn't have arbitrary arithmetic on pointers (the source of so many bugs in C++), and Java automatically dereferences pointers as needed, making it easy to use.

In particular, when the JLS (Java Language Specification) lays down that all non-primitives are accessed through a reference, it becomes easy for the run-time system to tell if an area of memory is potentially still in use. If nothing points to an object, then it cannot be accessed, so it is not in use. References make it easy to reclaim the storage for an object that's no longer in use, and make it easy to move things about to compact memory. Reference variables bring other simplifications to the compiler and JVM, but automatic memory management is the main reason. As an implementation detail, there might be more than one level of indirection to reach an object, but that is invisible to the programmer. Reference variables also make it easy to build dynamic self-referencing data structures like trees.

```
class Tree {
    int data;
    Tree leftBranch;
    Tree rightBranch;
}
```

There's a cost, of course (there's always a cost). The big cost of reference variables is the "Huh -whuzzat?" factor they cause in people learning the language. The Java design team worked hard to reduce the places where you have to be aware of references. When you access a field in an object, the compiler automatically does the dereference for you, with no special syntax needed. In everyday use, most Java programmers usually say "object" when they mean "reference to an object," and it's perfectly understandable. We'll follow that practice here, and only make a distinction in places where it makes a difference. But it's really important to understand the difference.

"Object" versus "reference-to-object"

You never have an object in Java; you only have a reference-to-an-object. What looks like the declaration of an object variable:

```
Timestamp t;
```

is actually the declaration of a variable that is a *reference to* an object. There is no way in Java to express "a variable that directly contains an object". Variables of a class type always hold the address of some object, not the object itself. This is a big difference from built-in types, and from other OOP languages.

To a programmer, the difference is that a newly declared reference variable contains a null pointer. It does not point to any object. You cannot start accessing a field or calling a method until you make the variable point to some object.

The compiler keeps track of when you are using the variable directly, and when you are using it indirectly to access a member of an object. It generates the right code for you in each case.

Choosing which Object will be operated on

OOP stresses the importance of objects rather than procedural statements. Consider it analogous to the expression "-5", indicating "take the object known as '5' and do the '-' operation on it." In OOP we have "take the object pointed at by t and do the fillTimes() method on it."

As we already mentioned, operations on an object are expressed with method calls rather than operators[1]. To get to any member of an object you say what reference variable you are using, follow that by a "dot," and then say what member you want. This "dot selection" is a common notation in several languages.

Here's an example. Assume we have some class with this declaration and initialization:

```
Timestamp t = new Timestamp();
```

Now we can access the fields of the object t points to.

```
t.hrs = 12;
```

This says "Go to the object that t is pointing to and assign to its hrs field". You invoke a method on an object variable in a similar way. It looks like this

```
t.fillTimes();
```

You specify which object you intend, here it is t, and then which method you want to call. That line of code calls the fillTimes() method on the fields of the object that t points to. If t is not currently pointing at an object a run-time error occurs, so silly mistakes are caught. Reference variables always point at a valid object or contain the value null. They can never hold a pointer to random memory as their contents. (Unless you link some non-Java code with your program; then the non-Java code could forge an invalid pointer.)

In this example, the object t has to belong to a class type that has a fillTimes() method, or else the compiler will flag it as an error. You can't call one of Timestamp's methods on a Calendar object. So if you want to "spiflicate" an object, you'd better make sure that its class contains a "spiflicate" method to do that. You don't call methods on individual fields of an object. You invoke them on the object as a whole.

---

1.   There is ongoing discussion in the Java community about whether Java should be changed to make it possible to use arithmetic operators, not just methods, to express operations on user-defined types. This feature is known as *operator overloading*, and it is not in JDK 1.5, though it may come in future. Operator overloading was left out of Java originally because it is easy to misuse, resulting in confusing and hard-to-maintain code. When used correctly, however, operator overloading can be a cool feature.

Names can be arbitrarily deep. You might have two or three levels of package name, followed by a class nested inside a class, followed by a method call that returns an object that you select a field of. So the naming could look like this:

```
a.b.c.d.e.f().g
```

It's never a problem because you simply read it from left to right, to find out what it means.

Accessing a member from inside a class versus outside a class

Refresh your memory of the Timestamp class, which starts like this:

```
class Timestamp {
        int hrs;
        int mins;
        int secs;

        public fillTimes() {
             /* more code */
            hrs = now.get(java.util.Calendar.HOUR_OF_DAY);
```

Look at the part shown in bold. You can see that the get() method is being invoked on the Calendar object called now. Note also that we can access the field hrs without specifying which object it belongs to! We don't have any reference variable qualifier to the name, like myObj.hrs.

The reason this works just fine is because hrs is a field in the same class as the fillTimes() method. If you do not explicitly provide a reference variable when accessing fields from a method, the compiler makes the reasonable assumption that you are talking about the members belonging to the same object that you invoked the method on.

Under the covers, there is an extra hidden argument, argument_0, passed to all methods at run-time. Argument_0 is a copy of the reference variable that was used to invoke the method at run-time, so it points to the object containing the data for the method to use. Argument_0 would be assigned the value of t here. Argument_0 has a name that shows up in Java: this. You don't declare it; it's provided to you if you want to use it. You can qualify any member name with this:

```
this.hrs = now.get( ...
```

One reason for qualifying a field or method name with this is to emphasize you're talking about a member belonging to this specific object, as opposed to a local declaration inside a method or a member of some other object.

It's time to get back to our digital clock example.

Java Digital Clock Program

Here's the rest of the code that makes up the digital clock. The program is made up of three classes:

- TheTimestamp class that can give you the current hours, minutes, and seconds.

- A class called "ClockView". This holds everything related to the visual appearance of the clock on screen.

- A class called "clock" that has overall control, and is where execution starts.

For a small example like this, we could merge everything into one class, and make it a dozen lines shorter. By keeping the design elements in separate classes, you can form a better idea of how classes should be used in bigger programs and systems.

The main() routine where execution starts

We'll start with the class that has overall control, where execution starts. Every Java application ever written starts in a method called "main" that has this general appearance.

The "method signature"

```
public static void main ( String[] args ) {
     // statements...
}
```

As the diagram indicates, the name and parameters of a method are together known as the *signature*. The signature of a method comes up later in some other class features. Those three qualifiers at the front of the main name "public static void" always appear on the front of the main routine, so just take them as given for now. We've already seen that "void" means "this method does not have a return value". Chapter 6 has an explanation of static if you want to peek ahead.

You write your main method, and put it in whichever of your classes is going to have overall control of the program.

The actual statements in our digital clock main routine are quite brief. Here they are in full (line numbers added on the left for ease of description):

```
1    public static void main(String[] args) {
2
3        ClockView cv = new ClockView();
4        cv.setVisible(true);
5        // loop about every 0.5 seconds
6        try {
7            for (;;) {
8                cv.refreshTimeDisplay();
9                Thread.sleep(500);
10           }
11       } catch (Exception e) {System.out.println("Error:"+e) ; }
12   }
```

Line 3 is the declaration of a variable to hold an instance of ClockView. That's the class that does everything to do with visual appearance, and it is coming up soon. Line 3 also initializes cv with a call to a constructor of ClockView. Now we have an object we can invoke methods on.

Line 4 calls the method setVisible() with an argument of true. We know that ClockView holds everything about the GUI, so it's a safe bet this makes it appear on the screen.

Line 5 is a comment.

Lines 6 and 11 are the start and end of a statement that says "try the code inside me, and if an error occurs take the action on line 11, i.e. print out a message."

Lines 7 and 10 are the start and end of an infinite loop. Whatever is in the scope of the for loop will be repeated over and over until some external act stops it.

Line 8 calls the method refreshTimeDisplay() on object cv. That obviously puts the latest current time onto the screen.

Line 9 causes the program to sleep for 500 milliseconds (half a second). Thread is a class within the Java library. That's all there is to the main routine: call a ClockView routine to update the time on the screen, wait half a second, and do it again. Repeat forever.

The clock class

Putting the whole thing in a class, we end up with this code.

```
public class clock {

    public static void main(String args[]) {
        ClockView cv = new ClockView();
        cv.setVisible(true);
        // loop about every 0.5 seconds
        try {
            for (;;) {
                cv.refreshTimeDisplay();
                Thread.sleep(500);
            }
        } catch (Exception e) {System.out.println("Error:"+e) ; }
    }

}
```

Put the clock into a file called clock.java. You don't have any choice over the file name. A public class has to go into a file of the same name as the class, so it should be called clock.java. If you try to compile clock.java at this point, the compiler will complain that it cannot find any class called ClockView. We have used ClockView but not written it yet. The compiler needs to see the bytecode for all the classes that you use when you compile a file. This is needed so the compiler can check that you are using all the other methods and fields correctly. Let's go on to look at ClockView so we have a complete example.

The ClockView class

The last piece of the program is the class called ClockView. It contains everything related to the visual appearance of the clock on the screen. If you got tired of a digital clock, and wanted an analog clock with a face and hands, you would be able to achieve that by modifying this class only. The Timestamp and clock classes would not need to be changed at all. If you have ever done any maintenance programming, you'll understand what a benefit it is to separate the concerns. You get this benefit partly from Object Oriented Programming, and partly from a well thought-out design.

We'll base our clock display on two existing GUI components from the Java library. We'll use a JFrame as the small window to display the clock, and a JLabel to hold the digits of the time display. Both these classes are in package javax.swing. JFrame is a resizeable window with a menu bar, close icon etc. It's a convenient backdrop. JLabel is a fast cheap way to put read-only text on a GUI. It's ideal for displaying the time digits.

If you type the ClockView code in, you can put it in the same file as either Timestamp or clock, or put it in a file of its own. Sometimes it is convenient to put related classes in the same file. No two public classes can be in the same file, though. Here is the class, and it is followed by some notes at the end of the listing.

```
class ClockView extends javax.swing.JFrame {

    private javax.swing.JLabel tLabel = new javax.swing.JLabel();

    ClockView() {    // constructor
        this.setDefaultCloseOperation(
                javax.swing.WindowConstants.EXIT_ON_CLOSE);
        this.setSize(95,45);
        this.getContentPane().add(tLabel);
        this.refreshTimeDisplay();
    }

    protected String getDigitsAsString(int i) {
        String str = Integer.toString(i);
        if (i<10) str = "0"+str;
        return str;
    }

    public void refreshTimeDisplay() {
        Timestamp t = new Timestamp();
        t.fillTimes();
        String display = getDigitsAsString(t.hrs) + ":"
                     + getDigitsAsString(t.mins)  + ":"
                     + getDigitsAsString(t.secs);
        tLabel.setText("  " + display );
        tLabel.repaint();
    }

}
```

The first line of the class "... extends javax.swing.JFrame" is very important. It says that this class is based on some other class we have. This is an OOP concept called *inheritance* and it is important enough to have Chapter 8 devoted to it. Inheritance is what you get from your parents, and it means that ClockView has all the fields and methods of its parent, the JFrame class. That explains how the clock.main() routine can call a ClockView method called setVisible, even though we don't see setVisible() defined previously. It comes from the parent JFrame.

ClockView has one field, tLabel, and three methods. The first "method" is actually a constructor. When this is invoked, the run-time system allocates the storage for a ClockView object, then executes the statements in the body to initialize the new object. The initialization done in the constructor is a one-timeGUI set-up: the label is added to the frame, the frame is told that the program should exit if someone closes it, and the frame is given a size of 95 pixels wide by 45 pixels high.

The second method getDigitsAsString() takes the integer argument, and returns the equivalent string, zero-padded to be exactly two digits long. The plus sign in this method and the next one is not arithmetic addition. It is a special operator that is defined to take a string as the first operand and anything else as the second operand. It will convert the second operand into a string and append it onto the first string. In compiler terminology, you could say the "+" operator is overloaded for Strings.

The final method in ClockView is refreshTimeDisplay(). It creates a new Timestamp object and calls its fillTimes() method to get the most up-to-date time. Then it assembles those values into a string containing hours, minutes and second separated by colons. Finally, it updates the label with this string, and calls repaint() to make the new text appear on the screen. Again, repaint is a library call that tells the GUI "some part of this component may have changed, please update that part of the screen with the new appearance".

In describing these classes there are several places where we've used a library class. When you start out as a Java programmer, that large API is an unknown for you. But the library classes are as important as learning the language; you need to learn them both. As we go through the book, most chapters will present a class or two from the API, starting with the ones you'll use most. We'll also suggest some tips on how to learn more of the API. A lot of people have already trodden that path, and it has a gentle gradient.

Compiling and running the Digital Clock program

At last you can compile the code and run the complete clock program. You'll run the javac compiler and give the names of the source code files you created. If you put all three classes in one file, the command will be:

```
javac clock.java
```

If you put each class in its own file, the command will be something like:

```
javac clock.java  Timestamp.java  ClockView.java
```

(use the actual filenames you used, and note that class names are case-sensitive, and file names should match exactly). You're sure to make a couple of typing mistakes the first couple of times, and the compiler will give you error messages with the line numbers. Correct all those, and repeat until you get a clean compilation. The compiler will create three new files, one for each class it found. The files will be clock.class, Timestamp.class and ClockView.class. These files will contain byte code.

When you get a clean compilation of all three classes, you can run the program by typing:

```
java clock
```

That will cause the JVM to look for the file clock.class, load it, and run its `main()` method. Here's the result on Windows, shown in Figure 2–4.

Figure 2–4   Compiling and running the clock program

Summary

You have now covered two of the four cornerstones of object-oriented programming: abstraction and encapsulation. This section summarizes what we've seen.

OOP is all about special support for class types and the operations on them. Objects are variables whose type is a class. Classes, objects, and methods belong together in a unbreakable way. The methods in a class can only be invoked on objects that belong to that class. If you don't have an object, you cannot invoke one of the object methods. You cannot write a method in class A that is invoked on an object of some unrelated class B. There is no way to get that past the compiler in Java.

There are no structures or records in Java. The most important way to group related things is to put them in a class. You also put classes together into a package. Packages are usually implemented as directories in the file system, though the JLS doesn't demand that. You can have nest packages within a package. This is called a sub-package.

The rest is just details (although there are a lot of them). We've touched on constructors and hinted about inheritance. This is a short summary, but the concepts are critical to object oriented programming and being an effective Java programmer. It's a good idea to turn the corner of this page down, and come back periodically to ensure the concepts stick.

Exercises

1. Write down an explanation of how a class, object, and method are related.

2. A rectangle can be defined by the length of two adjacent sides. Write a class that holds these two pieces of integer data, and provides useful rectangle-related operations, like calculating the area, updating the side data, and calculating the combined area of two rectangles. You'll write a method with a signature like this:

```
int combinedArea(secondRect sr) // the first rect is "this" of course
```

3. Rewrite the ClockView class (only) so the clock displays the time in Roman numerals. The Roman numerals from 1 to 12 are I, II, III, IV, V, VI, VII, VIII, IX, X, XI, and XII.

4. Rewrite the ClockView class so it uses the 12-hour clock and also displays AM or PM as appropriate.

5. Rewrite the ClockView class so that it includes tenths of seconds, and change the main routine in the clock class to update the display every tenth of a second. This code in Timestamp will obtain the tenths of a second from a Calendar object:

```
int mlsec = now.get(java.util.Calendar.MILLISECOND);
tenths = mlsec / 100;
```

You'll need to declare tenths as a field of Timestamp. You also need to put that number into the display of the clock in ClockView.

Some Light Relief—Napster and LimeWire

Everyone knows the story of Napster by this point. College student Shawn Fanning (baby nickname: "the napster" because of his sleeping habits) threw together some rickety old Windows software to transmit the titles of any music tracks you had on your PC to a central database.

Other users could search that database looking for titles they wanted. When they found a match, the Napster software would set up a peer-to-peer connection and allow direct transfer of the music bits from your PC to the unknown fan elsewhere. Your incentive to share was that you in turn would be able to get files from other people similarly sharing their titles.

That was the concept at least. In practice, the record companies and some bands took exception to freelance distribution. By this time, Fanning had parlayed his idea and some prototype software into a start-up venture backed by premier venture capitalist company Kleiner Perkins Caulfield and Byers. At its peak,

Napster claimed it had 70 million users, and even if they only exaggerated by the industry standard factor (ten-fold), that's still a lot of users.

Napster's demise took a couple of years to wind through the legal system, but the central point never seemed that subtle to me: you cannot legally broker the wholesale transfer of other people's intellectual property. Naturally, the record companies conducted themselves with their usual rapacious shortsightedness. Instead of licensing the Napster software to supply what customers clearly wanted, and charging fees, they tried to sue Napster out of existence. It's a reprise of 1992 when they killed DAT (Digital Audio Tape) by encumbering it with anticopying hardware backed by law. Incredible.

Which brings us to the current situation. Napster is just about completely dead. Apple has taken the largest slice of the online music market by offering the service that everyone wanted all along: reasonably priced legal music downloads through its iTunes Music Store. The music you buy on iTunes can easily be played on iPods, which are a high profit margin product for Apple. Microsoft is poised to leverage its monopoly and belatedly bundle its imitation of Apple's Music Store. And a number of underground, peer-to-peer file-sharing distributed databases have replaced Napster's centralized model, most notably a service called BitTorrent.

When I tried the Napster software in its heyday, all the way back in the last millennium, my first thought was, "Why on earth didn't they write this in Java?" It was a simple network database lookup with peer file transfer capability front-ended by a simple GUI. Tailor-made for Java! Fanning was not familiar with Java, so he churned out his Windows-only software. Though Napster has now passed on to that great big recording studio in the sky, others still carry the conductor's baton.

Bearshare, Gnutella, and LimeWire are currently three popular applications for sharing files (including .mp3 music files) across the net. They use the Gnutella client protocol, which is a search engine and file serving system in one. It is wholly distributed. Anyone can implement it to share their content (any files) with others. The great thing about LimeWire is that it is written in Java. You can download the application from www.limewire.com and see for yourself. The main screen is shown in Figure 2–5.

Since LimeWire is written in Java, the program runs on Windows, Macintosh, Linux, Solaris, IBM mainframes, and other computing platforms. The application has a solid, professional feel to it, and is fully functional. It has more than 3 million users, and is estimated to be present on 1.5% of all PCs.

LimeWire is now being sued by the record industry. Win or lose, the record industry will probably be able to drive LimeWire out of business. LimeWire has responded by going open source, so download a copy of the application while you can, and see how the experts write Java GUIs.

When someone asks me about Java client applications, LimeWire, in Figure 2–5, is one of the programs I like to show them.

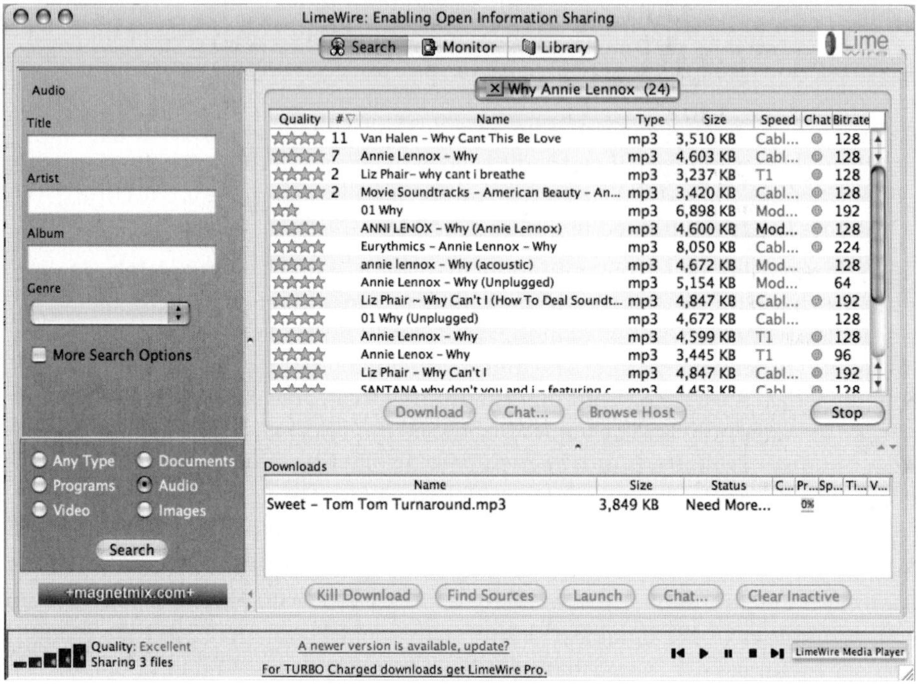

Quality	# ▽	Name	Type	Size	Speed	Chat	Bitrate
★★★★	11	Van Halen – Why Cant This Be Love	mp3	3,510 KB	Cabl...	◉	128
★★★★	7	Annie Lennox – Why	mp3	4,603 KB	Cabl...	◉	128
★★★★	2	Liz Phair– why cant i breathe	mp3	3,237 KB	T1		128
★★★★	2	Movie Soundtracks – American Beauty – An...	mp3	3,420 KB	Cabl...	◉	128
★★		01 Why	mp3	6,898 KB	Mod...	◉	192
★★★★		ANNI LENOX – Why (Annie Lennox)	mp3	4,600 KB	Mod...	◉	128
★★★★		Eurythmics – Annie Lennox – Why	mp3	8,050 KB	Cabl...	◉	224
★★★★		annie lennox – Why (acoustic)	mp3	4,672 KB	Mod...		128
★★★★		Annie Lennox – Why (Unplugged)	mp3	5,154 KB	Mod...		64
★★★★		Liz Phair ~ Why Can't I (How To Deal Soundt...	mp3	4,847 KB	Cabl...	◉	192
★★★★		01 Why (Unplugged)	mp3	4,672 KB	Cabl...		128
★★★★		Annie Lennox – Why	mp3	4,599 KB	T1	◉	128
★★★★		Annie Lenox – Why	mp3	3,445 KB	T1	◉	96
★★★★		Liz Phair – Why Can't I	mp3	4,847 KB	Cabl...	◉	192
★★★★		SANTANA why don't you and i – featuring c...	mp3	4,453 KB	Cabl...		128

Figure 2–5   LimeWire: Napster's successor

Primitive Types, Wrappers, and Boxing

There are eight built-in, non-object types in Java, known as primitive types. Every piece of data in a class is ultimately represented in terms of these primitive types. The eight primitive types are:

- boolean (for true/false values)
- char (for character data, ultimately to be input or printed)
- int, long, byte, short (for arithmetic on whole numbers)
- double, float (for arithmetic on the real numbers)

Primitive types are simpler than class types, and are directly supported in hardware on most computers. That is, most of the operations on primitive types are a single machine instruction, like ADD, whereas the operations on class types are statements in a method.

Older high-level languages don't specify the sizes of primitive data types. On an 8086 an int was naturally 16 bits, but on the first SPARC processors it was 32 bits. Compiler writers for C were allowed to select the best sizes on each architecture for performance. That turned out to be a Very Bad Idea. Types that vary with the platform greatly impede program portability, and programmer time is a lot more expensive than processor time.

Java does away with all the uncertainty by rigorously specifying the sizes of the primitive types and making clear that these sizes are identical on all platforms. We'll examine the properties of each primitive type in turn.

Literal Values

As we mention each of the eight primitive types, we'll show a typical declaration; say what range of values it can hold; and also describe the literal values for the type.

A "literal" is a value provided at compile time. Just write down the value that you mean, and that's the literal. Here's a snippet of code showing several literals:

```
int   i = 2;       // 2 is a literal
double d = 3.14;   // 3.14 is a literal
if ( c == 'j' )    // 'j' is a literal
```

Every literal has a type, just like every variable has a type. The literal written as 2 has type *int*. The literal written as 3.14 belongs to the type *double*. For booleans, the literals are the words false and true.

It is not valid to directly assign a literal of one type to a variable of another. In other words, this code is invalid:

```
int   i = 3.14;  // type mismatch! BAD CODE
```

The literal 3.14 is a double floating-point number literal, and cannot be assigned directly to an int variable. You can do it by forcing an explicit type conversion, known as a *cast*. The details are coming up shortly.

A language that allows assignment and conversion only between closely related types is called a *strongly typed* language. Java is a strongly typed language. Strong typing reduces the power of a language, but reduces some errors even more.

boolean

This is the data type used for true/false conditions. To speed up memory access, implementations don't pack boolean values into the theoretical one-bit minimum space, but put each boolean into a byte.

example declaration:

```
boolean b = false;
```

range of values: false, true

literals: `false    true`

In the code below,

```
boolean found = false;

/* more code */

if (x == 99) found = true;
```

x is compared with value 99. If x matches 99, then the boolean found is set to true.

You cannot assign or cast a boolean value to any other type. However, you can always get the same effect by using an expression, like the following:

```
if (b) i=1; else i=0; // set i according to boolean b value.

// set boolean b according to int i value
if (i==1) b = true; else b = false;
```

Unlike some other languages, the Java boolean type is not based on integers. In particular, the Java programmer cannot increment, decrement, shift, or add boolean values. Inside a JVM, however, there are no instructions specifically for booleans, so integer operations (like assigning zero) *are* used. In the Sun JVM, the byte containing a boolean is promoted to 32 bits when pushed onto the stack during execution. So don't think booleans are a 1-bit type that economizes on storage.

char

This type is a 16-bit unsigned quantity that is used to represent text characters. You'd use this to hold a single character. If you want to store several successive characters, such as a name or an address or phone number, you would use the predefined type String, which keeps track of multiple consecutive characters at once. String is a class in the java.lang package, not a primitive type. We'll get to String a little later.

The type char has been made 16 bits long because that's what you need to support character sets from every locale in the world. The USA can get by with just 7-bit ASCII, and Western Europe is fine with 8-bit ISO 8859-1 characters giving a few accented characters. Many other places such as China, Korea, India, and Japan need and use 16-bit character sets. So Java does too. If you are using a computer in the 8-bit western world, characters are automatically converted to/from 16 bits on the way in and out of Java.

Although char holds a text character, inside the JVM char is just a 16-bit binary number. So all the arithmetic operators are available on type char. But unlike all the other arithmetic types, char is unsigned—it never takes a negative value. You should only use char to hold character data or bit values. If you want a 16-bit quantity for calculations, don't use char, use short. If you ignore this advice, a cast (conversion) of a negative value into char will make the value magically become positive without the bits changing. If you cast that char value back to an int, the int will now have a positive value. That's a surefire way to introduce bugs into your code.

example declaration:

```
char testGrade;
char middleInitial;
```

range of values: a value in the Unicode code set 0 to 65,535

You have to cast a 32- or 64-bit result if you want to put it into a smaller result. This means that assignments to char must always be cast into the result if they involve any arithmetic. An example would be:

```
char c = (char) (c + 13); // the cast is required
```

literals: Char literals are always between single quotes. String literals are always between double quotes, so you can tell apart a one-character String from a char. A char variable can be assigned directly to all of the arithmetic types: byte, short, int, long, float and double. It's not clear why you would want to assign a char literal to a double, but you can. Here are the four ways you can write a char literal:

- A single character in single quotes, e.g.

  ```
  char tShirtSize = 'L';
  ```

- A character escape sequence. The allowable values are:

'\n' (linefeed)	'\r' (carriage return)	'\f' formfeed
'\b' (backspace)	'\t' (tab)	'\\' (backslash)
'\"' (double quote)	'\'' (single quote)	

- An octal escape sequence. You probably will never use these. See the following box.

- A Unicode escape sequence. You probably will never use these. See the following box.

Character escape sequences

An octal escape sequence looks like `'\nnn'` where nnn is one-to-three octal digits in the range 0 to 377. They are meant for programmers who need to express an ASCII control character and are used to doing it in octal. Some examples are `'\0'` or `'\12'` or `'\277'` or `'\377'`. Octal escape sequences are best avoided.

A Unicode escape sequence looks like `'\uxxxx'` where xxxx is exactly four hexadecimal digits. They give the programmer a way to represent any Unicode character even on an outdated ASCII-only or eight-bit-only systems that don't have a way to directly input multibyte characters. Unicode escape sequences can appear anywhere at all, even in the middle of String literals, and the translation immediately takes place to a single Unicode character. Unicode escape sequences are best avoided.

Choosing Unicode for the Java char type was a very sensible design choice. Although a few people complained about the cost and waste of using 16 bits per character, these are the same misers who a few years ago didn't want to shift from two-digit years to four-digit years, and who still hold onto their abacuses while they evaluate the "cutting edge" slide rule technology.

Switching to Unicode

OS vendors missed a big opportunity to move from ASCII to Unicode as the native character set of various operating systems. It could all have been done as part of the transition to 64-bit system software. Since that isn't happening, we'll all have two big "flag-days" in our future: one to make our applications 64-bit compatible, and one to make our applications globally compatible by converting all ASCII text to Unicode.

The extra storage requirements of Unicode are a no-brainer. Rotating magnetic media just keeps getting cheaper and cheaper. Even if my 50GB of data doubled in size—which it won't because I have a lot of non-text files—that is only about another $40 worth of disk.

When the operating system vendors catch up, Java is already there.

Designers of forward-looking systems like Java have a responsibility to include proper support for more than just Western alphabets. Apart from anything else, customers are more likely to buy your software if it supports their native language. Until all systems have adopted Unicode, however, handling it on an ASCII system is clumsy, so avoid sprinkling Unicode literals through your code.

int

The type int is a 32-bit, signed, two's-complement number, as used in virtually every modern CPU. It will be the type that you should choose by default whenever you are going to carry out integer arithmetic.

example declaration:
```
int i;
```
range of values: −2,147,483,648 to 2,147,483,647

literals: Int literals come in any of three varieties:

- A decimal literal, e.g., 10 or −256

- With a leading zero, meaning an octal literal, e.g., 077777

- With a leading 0x, meaning a hexadecimal literal, e.g., 0xA5 or 0Xa5

Uppercase or lowercase has no significance with any of the letters that can appear in integer literals. If you use octal or hexadecimal, and you provide a literal that sets the leftmost bit in the receiving number, then it represents a negative number. (The arithmetic types are stored in a binary format known as "two's-complement"—google for full details).

A numeric literal is a 32-bit quantity, even if its value could fit into a smaller type. But provided its actual value is within range for a smaller type, an int literal can be assigned directly to something with fewer bits, such as byte, short, or char. If you try to assign an int literal that is too large into a smaller type, the compiler will insist that you write an explicit conversion, termed a "cast."

When you cast from a bigger type of integer to a smaller type, the high-order bits are just dropped. Integer variables and literals can be assigned to floating-point variables without casting.

long

The type long is a 64-bit, signed, two's-complement quantity. It should be used when calculations on whole numbers may exceed the range of int. Using longs, the range of values is -2^{63} to $(2^{63}-1)$. Numbers up in this range will be increasingly prevalent in computing, and 2^{64} in particular is a number that really needs a name of its own. In 1993, I coined the term "Bubbabyte" to describe 2^{64} bytes. Just as 2^{10} bytes is a Kilobyte, and 2^{20} is a Megabyte, so 2^{64} bytes is a Bubbabyte. Using a long, you can count up to half a Bubbabyte less one.

example declaration:
```
long nationalDebt;
```
range of values: −9,223,372,036,854,775,808 to 9,223,372,036,854,775,807

A word about casts (type conversion)

All variables have a type in Java, and the type is checked so that you can't assign between two things that are incompatible. You cannot directly assign a floating-point variable to an integer variable.

It is reasonable, however, to convert between closely related types. That is what a cast does. You cast an expression into another type by writing the desired new type name in parentheses before the expression, as follows:

```
float f = 3.142;
int i = (int) f; // a cast
```

Some numeric conversions don't need a cast. You are allowed to directly assign from a smaller-range numeric type into a larger range—a byte to int, or int to long, or long to float—without a cast. Assigning to a more capacious type is called a *widening primitive conversion*, and it does not lose any information about the overall magnitude of the numeric value. When you want to do an assignment that can potentially lose data, such as a float-to-int assignment that would drop any fractional part, you must use a cast. The cast tells the compiler that you, the programmer, understand about the potential data loss, and it is ok.

A cast can be used to convert between two objects of related classes, as well as between two primitives. Casting is "type safe," meaning that the validity of an object type conversion is checked at run-time. It will cause an error if you try to cast an object to a type that is just plain wrong for it.

You never used to be able to cast from an object to a primitive value or vice versa. There was no fundamental theoretical reason for the restriction, and it was loosened up in JDK 1.5. There is a predefined class type corresponding to each of the eight primitive types. You can now cast both ways between values of a primitive type and its corresponding object type. In fact, you don't even have to cast! You can make the assignment directly. There is more about this in *Autoboxing and Unboxing* on page 55.

literals: The general form of long literals is the same as int literals, but with an "L" or "l" on the end to indicate "long." However, never use the lowercase letter "l" to indicate a "long" literal as it is too similar to the digit "1." Always use the uppercase letter "L" instead. The three kinds of long literals are:

- A decimal literal, e.g., 2047L or −10L

- An octal literal, e.g., 0777777L

- A hexadecimal literal, e.g., 0xA5L or OxABadBabbeL

All long literals are 64-bit quantities. A long literal must be cast to assign it to something with fewer bits, such as byte, short, int, or char.

byte

The byte type is an 8-bit, signed, two's-complement quantity. The reasons for using byte are to hold a generic 8-bit value, to match a value in existing data files, or to economize on storage space where you have a large number of such values. Despite popular belief, there is no speed advantage in arithmetic on shorter types like bytes, shorts, or chars—modern CPUs take the same amount of time to load or multiply 8 bits as they take for 32 bits.

example declaration:

```
byte heightOfTide;
```

range of values: −128 to 127

literals: There are no byte literals. You can use, without a cast, int literals provided their values fit in 8 bits. You can use char, long, and floating-point literals if you cast them.

You always have to cast a (non-literal) value of a larger type if you want to put it into a variable of a smaller type. Since arithmetic is always performed at least at 32-bit precision, this means that assignments to a byte variable must always be cast into the result if they involve any arithmetic, like this:

```
byte b1=1, b2=2;
byte b3 = b2 + b1; // NO! NO! NO! compilation error
byte b3 = (byte) (b2 + b1); // correct, uses a cast
```

People often find this surprising. If I have an expression involving only bytes, why should I need to cast it into a byte result? The right way to think about it is that most modern computers do all integral arithmetic at 32-bit or 64-bit precision (there is no "8-bit add" instruction on modern CPUs). Java follows this model of the underlying hardware.

An arithmetic operation on two bytes potentially yields a bigger result than can be stored in one byte. The philosophy for numeric casts is that they are required whenever you assign from a *more* capacious type to a *less* capacious type. This is termed a *narrowing primitive conversion*, and it may lose information about the overall magnitude of a numeric value. It may also lose some digits of precision, and sign information (when converting to char, because chars are always interpreted as positive values).

The cast tells the compiler that you, the programmer understand the information that may be lost, and have programmed accordingly. You might check the data before the conversion to ensure it is within a range where no information will be lost, for example.

short

This type is a 16-bit, signed, two's-complement integer. The main reasons for using short are to match external values already present in a file or to economize on storage space where you have a large number of such values.

range of values: −32,768 to 32,767

literals: There are no short literals. You can use, without a cast, int literals provided their values will fit in 16 bits. You can use char, long, and floating-point literals if you cast them.

As with byte, assignments to short must always be cast into the result if the right-hand side of the assignment involves any arithmetic.

The last two primitive types, double and float, are floating-point arithmetic types. Before we look at the features of double and float, *Limited Accuracy of Floating Point Types* on page 49 describes some problems you may encounter in any language, when using floating-point arithmetic.

Limited Accuracy of Floating Point Types

Before we describe double and float, we need to point out two limitations of floating-point arithmetic. People are still getting Ph.D.s for probing the mathematics underlying floats, but the short story is:

- Floating-point numbers only hold a limited number of significant figures. The float type only holds six to seven significant figures. So you can hold the number 123,456 accurately, and you can hold the number 0.123456 pretty accurately, but it's certain that you cannot hold the number 123,456.123456 in a float variable accurately because that would require 12 significant figures. You can write the number in your program, and you'll actually get a number that is approximately the value you want, but not exactly equal. (You'll get 123456.125, in fact).

- Floating-point numbers may contain tiny inaccuracies that can mount up as you iterate through an expression. Don't expect ten iterations of adding 0.1 to a float variable to cause it to exactly equal 1.0F!

Floating-point numbers have these limitations in every programming language. It is inherent in the type. You are trying to represent an infinite quantity of numbers in a finite type. The only way this can be done is by picking points on the real-number continuum and representing those exactly. Then use those model values to represent approximations to all other real numbers. It's as though we could only store tenths, and so everything from 0.0 to 0.049 becomes 0.0. Everything from 0.05 to 0.149 becomes 0.1, and so on. With floats, we're working with millionths, not tenths. But it is still not perfectly accurate for most numbers. With this background about the limitations, let's review the two floating point types.

double

The type double refers to floating-point numbers stored in 64 bits, as described in the IEEE[1] standard reference 754. The type double will be the default type you use when you want to do some calculations that might involve decimal places (i.e., not integral values).

range of values: These provide numbers that can range between about −1.7E308 to +1.7E308 with about 15 significant figures of accuracy. The exact accuracy depends on the number being represented. Double precision floating-point numbers have the range shown in Figure 4–1.

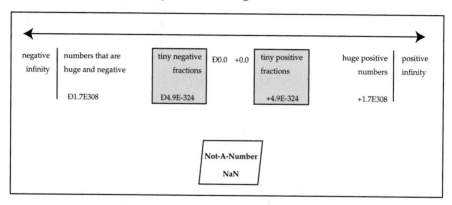

Figure 4–1   Type double should be used when calculations involve decimal places

IEEE 754 arithmetic has come into virtually universal acceptance over the last decade, and it would certainly raise a few eyebrows if a computer manufacturer proposed an incompatible system of floating-point numbers now. IEEE 754 is the standard for floating-point arithmetic, but there are several places where chip designers can choose from different alternatives within the standard, such as rounding modes and extended precision. Java originally insisted on consistency on all hardware by specifying the alternatives that must be used. That is now loosened somewhat with strictfp.

---

1.   IEEE is the Institute of Electrical and Electronic Engineers, a U.S. professional body.

Make mine a double: how large is 1.7E308?

The largest double precision number is a little bit bigger than a 17 followed by 307 zeroes. That's an amazingly huge number.

The volume of the observable universe is about (4pi/3)(15 billion light-years)^3 = 10^{85} cm^3. Protons, the fundamental particle found in the nucleus of an atom, have an average density (averaged over all space, not just on planets) of about 10^{-7} cm^{-3}. Multiplying the universe volume by the proton average density, the number of protons in the observable Universe is about 10^{78}, or "only" 1 followed by 78 zeros, give or take two-fifty.

It's possible to come up with problems where you want accuracy to 14 significant figures, such as figuring the national debt, but it is unusual to need to tabulate numbers that are orders of magnitude greater than the number of protons in the universe.

IEEE 754 has an ingenious way of dealing with the problem of representing, on limited hardware, the unlimited amount of infinite precision real-world numbers. The problem is resolved by reserving a special value that says, "Help! I've fallen off the end of what's representable and I can't get up." You're probably familiar with infinity, but the "Not-a-Number" might be new if you haven't done much numerical programming. Not-a-Number, or NaN, is a value that a floating point can take to indicate that the result of some operation is not mathematically well-defined, like dividing zero by zero.

If you get a NaN as an expression being evaluated, it will contaminate the whole expression, producing an overall result of NaN—*which is exactly what you want!* The worst way to handle a numeric error is to ignore it and pretend it didn't happen.

You may never see a NaN if your algorithms are numerically stable, and you never push the limits of your datasets. Still, it's nice to know that NaN is there, ready to tell you your results are garbage, if they head that way.

literals: It is easiest to show by example the valid formats for double literals:

```
1e1   2.   .3   3.14   6.02e+23d
```

The format is very easy-going; just give the compiler a decimal point or an exponent, and it will recognize that a floating-point literal is intended. A suffix of "D", "d", or no suffix, means a double literal. In practice, most people omit the suffix.

It is also permissible to assign any of the integer literals or character literals to floats or doubles. The assignment doesn't need a cast, as you are going from a less capacious type to a more capacious type.

So a line like this, while perverse, is valid:

```
double newline = '\n';
```

It takes the integer value of the literal (0x0a in this case), floats it to get 10.0d, and assigns that to "newline." Don't ever do this.

float

The type float refers to floating-point numbers stored in 32 bits, as described in the IEEE standard reference 754.

The justification for using single-precision variables used to be that arithmetic operations were twice as fast as on double precision variables. With modern extensively pipelined processors and wide data buses between the cache and CPUs, the speed differences are inconsequential. The reasons for using floats are to minimize storage requirements when you have a very large quantity of them or to retain compatibility with external data files.

Floats are best avoided if possible, because they have such limited accuracy. They are in Java because they are supported in hardware so it costs little, and provides compatibility with existing code and expectations.

range of values: The type float provides numbers that can range between about −3.4E38 to 3.4E38 (i.e., 340,000,000,000,000,000,000,000,000,000,000,000,000) with about six to seven significant figures of accuracy. The exact accuracy depends on the number being represented.

literals: The simplest way to understand what is allowed is to look at examples of valid float literals, as follows:

```
1e1f   2.f   .3f   3.14f   6.02e+23f
```

A suffix of "F" or "f" is always required on a float literal. A common mistake is to leave the suffix off the float literal, as follows:

```
float cabbage = 6.5;
Error: explicit cast needed to convert double to float.
```

The code must be changed to the following:

```
float cabbage = 6.5f;
```

Also, a double literal cannot be assigned to a float variable without a cast, even if it is within the range of the float type. This is because some precision in the decimal places may potentially be lost.

That concludes the description of the eight primitive types, and we now continue with an explanation of how each of these eight primitives also has a class type to represent it.

Object Wrappers for Primitives

Each of the eight primitive types we have just seen has a corresponding class type, predefined in the Java library. For example, there is a class java.lang.Integer that corresponds to primitive type int. These class types accompanying the primitive types are known as *object wrappers* and they serve several purposes:

- The class is a convenient place to store constants like the biggest and smallest values the primitive type can store.

- The class also has methods that can convert both ways between primitive values of each type and printable Strings. Some wrapper classes have additional utility methods.

- Some data structure library classes only operate on objects, not primitive variables. The object wrappers provide a convenient way to convert a primitive into the equivalent object, so it can be processed by these data structure classes. One example of a data structure class that only operates on objects is the class java.util.SortedSet, which keeps a collection of objects in sorted order for you.

Why use object wrappers instead of primitive types directly?

There is one more big reason why we wrap primitive types. There is a "joker" reference type that can hold a pointer to any type of object at all. This is the type java.lang.Object. Code like this is perfectly legal (and common in some kinds of program):

```
Timestamp t = new Timestamp();
java.lang.Object o = t;
```

There is no corresponding primitive type that can hold any kind of primitive variable. Therefore, if you want to have an algorithm that operates on arbitrary or unknown variables, make it work with variables of type java.lang.Object. If the arbitrary values are primitives, wrap them and use java.lang.Object references to manipulate them.

You might wonder what kind of processing you can do to an object, if its true type (and therefore its methods) are concealed from you. You can hold it in a data structure such as a stack, queue, set, etc. You may be able to compare it to others of the same type, and therefore sort the collection. You can do enough things to be useful.

Table 3–1 shows the names of the wrapper classes for primitive types.

Table 3–1   Object wrapper classes for primitive types

Primitive type	Corresponding wrapper class
boolean	java.lang.Boolean
char	java.lang.Character
int	java.lang.Integer
long	java.lang.Long
byte	java.lang.Byte
short	java.lang.Short
double	java.lang.Double
float	java.lang.Float

These wrapper classes are all found in package java.lang. You have to tell the compiler where to find most of the packages you use, but java.lang is an exception to this rule. The classes in package java.lang are regarded as the most fundamental, and the compiler makes them available to every compilation automatically. You don't have to give the full name java.lang.Byte in your code; it's enough to write Byte.

The names follow the Java convention that class names should start with a capital letter, and method, object, and field names should start with a lowercase letter, to help you tell them apart when reading code. The names Integer and Character do not mirror exactly the names of their primitive type counterparts (int and char). There's no good reason for that, just sloppy code review by the original implementors.

Here's an example of how the wrappers for primitive types might be used. This example shows some methods of Integer. Similar methods exist for the other wrapper classes.

```
int i = 15;
Integer myInt = new Integer(i); //wrap an int in a object

// get the printable representation of an Integer:
String s = myInt.toString();

// gets the Integer as a printable hex string
String s = myInt.toHexString(15); // s is now "f"

// reads a string, and gives you back an int
i = myInt.parseInt( "2047" );

// reads a string, and gives you back an Integer object
myInt = myInt.valueOf( "2047" );
```

To see the full capabilities of the wrapper classes, peruse them in the HTML documentation of the Java API.

Autoboxing and Unboxing

Autoboxing is a feature that came into Java with the JDK 1.5 release. It recognizes the very close relationship between primitive variables and objects of their corresponding wrapper type, and provides a little extra help from the compiler. Autoboxing says that you can convert from one to the other without explicitly writing the code. The compiler will provide it for you.

New!

In releases before 1.5, you could get an int value into a java.lang.Integer like this:

```
int i = 27;
Integer myInt = new Integer(i);
```

With autoboxing, you can make the assignment directly, and the compiler looks at the types of the variables, and says "yes, I know how to wrap (or "put a box around") an int to get an Integer object". Then it allows the expression, and generates the code to do it. So you may write this instead:

```
int i = 27;
Integer myInt = i;          //  autobox!
```

Unboxing is the same concept going the other way, from a primitive-wrapper object to a primitive type. Here's an example with a wrapper object for the Double type:

```
Double dObj = 27.0;   // autobox
double d = dObj;      // unbox, gets value 27.0
```

Boxing isn't just for variable creation or initialization. You can use it wherever the context expects a primitive and you have the corresponding wrapper. It gets automatically wrapped for you. Here's an example showing how we can use a Boolean object where a boolean primitive is expected:

```
Boolean isReady = new Boolean(false);

if (isReady)  { /* more code */
```

Here's an example where unboxing is done in an expression:

```
Float fObj1 = 20.0F;  // boxing
Float fObj2 = 10.0F;  // boxing
float result = fObj1 * fObj2;  // unboxing
Float fObj3 = fObj1 * 23.0F;   // boxing and unboxing
```

When you compile programs with new JDK 1.5 features, you'll need to add two options on the command line, like this:

```
javac  -source 1.5  -target 1.5  myfile.java
```

(This was true at the time we went to press, but Sun may make last minute changes to the compiler options. The latest information will be on the website afu.com/jj6.)

Performance Implications of Autoboxing

The autoboxing feature was introduced to Java for programmer convenience, particularly in the Collections classes that provide ready-made data structures for use on Objects. Where the intent is obvious, you no longer have to write it all out explicitly.

Just because you don't write the code explicitly, it doesn't mean the code goes away. The compiler generates actual instructions for the implied type promotions between a primitive and its object wrapper.

Those actual instructions have a performance cost at run-time, even though you don't see them at compile time. Take this autoboxing, for instance:

```
Integer myInt = i; // autobox!
```

The compiler will treat that the same way as if you had written a constructor call:

```
Integer myInt = new Integer(i);
```

When a constructor is invoked, it causes a chain of calls to constructors in successively higher parent classes back until a constructor in java.lang.Object is invoked. The parent class of Integer is java.lang.Number, and the parent of Number is java.lang.Object. So there are three constructor calls, a memory allocation, and an assignment in that innocuous-looking autoboxing.

CPU cycles get cheaper every year, but they're not completely free or infinitely fast. Be aware of the cost of autoboxing, and avoid doing it unnecessarily or in a loop. Autoboxing costs no more and no less than the equivalent explicit statements. But it's easy to inadvertently overlook the cost of statements that aren't written explicitly.

No methods on primitives in Java

The C# language goes one step further than Java in autoboxing—you can invoke methods on primitives! The primitive value will be autoboxed to create an object, then the method will be invoked on that object. You can't do that in Java, but if you could, it would look like this:

```
int i = 15;
String s = i.toString();  // gets autoboxed, but not valid in Java
```

There's no strong reason in favor of allowing or disallowing this. It's a question of how much the language designer wants to blur the distinction between primitives and objects. Some languages, Smalltalk is an example, don't have any primitive types at all—everything is an object.

java.lang.Object

We'll finish this chapter by describing a couple of much-used classes that we have seen informally already: Object and String.

The class java.lang.Object is the ultimate parent of every other class in the system, and it has half-a-dozen methods which therefore can be invoked on any and all objects. (An object is able to invoke the methods in all its parent classes — remember how ClockView objects could call setVisible() because they got it from their parent JFrame). Following are some of the members Object has. You can skim through this now, jumping ahead to the description of type String, and return if you need more information about something specific in Object.

```
public class Object {
    public java.lang.Object();  // constructor

    public java.lang.String toString();

    public boolean equals(java.lang.Object);
    public int hashCode();

    public final Class getClass();

    protected java.lang.Object clone()
                throws CloneNotSupportedException;

    // methods relating to thread programming
    public final void notify();
    public final void wait() throws InterruptedException;
}
```

The "throws *SomeException*" clause is an announcement of the kind of unexpected error return that the method might give you. Object does have a few more methods than shown here. The API documentation has the full description.

Most of the methods in Object provide some useful, though often elementary, functionality. Programmers are supposed to write their own version of any of these methods to replace the basic one if necessary. When an object (any object) calls a method, its own version of that method is preferred over an identically named method in a parent class, as we'll see in Chapter 8. The technical term for this is *overriding*. Object makes sure there is a basic version of the methods; the programmer specializes them if necessary.

String toString(); This is a handy method. You can call it explicitly, and it will return a string that "textually represents" this object. It's actually the name of the class of the object, the "@" sign, and the address of the object. Use it while debugging to see if your objects really are what you thought they were. These lines in file ClockView.java will invoke Object's toString() on a Timestamp object, and print the String.

```
Timestamp t = new Timestamp();
t.fillTimes();
String s = t.toString();
System.out.println(s);
```

When you run the clock program with these lines, the output will have this general form (the actual number, being an address, will vary from system to system):

Timestamp@af9e22

Many programmers supply their own implementation of Object's toString() for some of their more important classes. They may put other debugging information into the string returned. Or they may make the toString() method provide a printable representation for output. Here is a such a method for Timestamp:

```
class Timestamp {
        int hrs;
        int mins;
        int secs;

        public String toString() {
            String result = Integer.toString(secs);
            if (secs<10) result = "0" + result;
            result = Integer.toString(mins) + ":" + result;
            if (mins<10) result = "0" + result;
            result = Integer.toString(hrs) + ":" + result;
            if (hrs<10) result = "0" + result;
            return result;
        }
  //  rest of class omitted
```

With this change, when you re-run the program, each time toString is called the output will look similar to:

```
13:24:42
```

boolean equals(Object obj). If you compare two objects for equality using the "==" comparison, e.g. `if (o1==o2)` the reference variables are compared, not any of the contents of either object. If you think about it, that's exactly what you've written. The `equals()` method in Object is there to give you a "hook" to do a more sophisticated comparison.

As implemented in class Object, the `equals()` method does the same comparison of reference variables. Variables `obj1` and `obj2` compare equal if both point to the same object. You invoke it as here:

```
if (obj1.equals(obj2) ) /* more code */
```

If this is not adequate for one of your classes, supply your own version of equals to look at the fields of each object and do a more detailed comparison. For example, two Strings are usually considered equal if they contain the exact same sequence of characters. So String has an `equals()` method that iterates down one String, comparing all its characters with the characters in the other String.

int hashCode (). A hashcode is a value that can be used to uniquely identify an individual object. The most natural implementation is to use the memory address of an object as its hashcode, since every object has a unique address.

The hashcode of an object is used as a key in one of the standard data structure classes—java.util.Hashtable. Although you might program for a long time without needing this, it turns out to be useful to be able to put any kind of object in a hashtable, should we so desire. Therefore we need to be able to get a hashcode for every single object in the system. So the method was put in the Object class.

When you provide your own version of `equals()` for your own class, you should also provide your own version of `hashCode()` for that class, to make sure that equal Objects get the same hashcode. If you fail to do this, your objects will mysteriously fail to work in some data structures in the Collections classes. Collections have their own chapter later on.

final Class getClass(). All class types have an object that represents them at run-time. This run-time representation is known as *Run Time Type Identification* or RTTI. The method `getClass()` gets that object containing the RTTI information, returning it in an object of type `java.lang.Class`.

Say you have an object pointer, o:

```
Object o;
```

At some point in execution, this can get assigned to point to different objects:

```
o = new Integer(27);
```

or

```
o = new Character('?');
```

Using methods from `java.lang.Class`, you find out the actual more-specific class to which an arbitrary object belongs. You call the `getClass` method to do this:

```
Class whatAmI = o.getClass();
```

Application programmers rarely need to do this. It is intended for people writing compilers, IDEs and system programs.

```
Object clone() throws CloneNotSupportedException
```

Java supports the notion of cloning, meaning to get a complete bit-for-bit copy of an object. Java does a shallow clone, meaning that when an object has data fields that are other objects, it simply copies the reference. The alternative is to recursively clone all referenced classes, too, known as a *deep clone*.

As a programmer, you can choose the exact cloning behavior you want. If a class wants to support deep cloning on its objects, it can provide its own version of `clone()`.

Application programmers do want to clone objects occasionally. Say you have an object representing a new customer who is buying something. You might clone the object representing the new customer so it can be added to the customer database in a separate thread. In the meantime, the original object is processed to complete the sale. That way, both tasks have all the data they need, and neither task has to wait for the other.

java.lang.String

To complete this chapter, here is the standard Java class java.lang.String. That's obviously a class type, contrasting with the primitive types with which we started the chapter. You will use String instances a lot—whenever you want to store some characters in a sequence or do human-readable I/O.

As the name suggests, String objects hold a series of adjacent characters, similar to an array. Strings have methods to extract substrings, to put into lower case, to search a String, to compare two Strings, and so on. Arrays of char have none of these. String is a very convenient class and you'll use it extensively in many programs.

literals: A string literal is zero or more characters enclosed in double quotes, like these two lines:

```
"That'll cost you two-fifty \n"
"" // empty string
```

The empty String is different from the null pointer. The empty String is a pointer to a String object which happens to have zero length. You can invoke all the compare, search, extract methods on an empty String. They do little, but they don't cause errors.

Strings are used so frequently that Java has some special built-in support. Everywhere else in Java, you use a constructor to create an object of a class, such as:

```
String drinkPref = new String( "I like tea" );
```

String literals count as a shortcut for the constructor. So this is equivalent:

```
String drinkPref = "I like tea";
```

Each string literal behaves as if it is a reference to an instance of class String, meaning that you can invoke methods on it, copy a reference to it, and so on. For convenience or performance, the compiler may implement it another way, but it must be indistinguishable to the programmer. Here's a method invoked on a literal:

```
String s = "ABCD".toLowerCase();
```

String s is assigned a pointer to the newly created String "abcd".

Like all literals, string literals cannot be modified after they have been created. Variables of class String have the same quality—once you have created a String, you cannot change a character in the middle to something else. Some people use the term "immutable" to describe this, as in "Strings are immutable."

But don't worry: you can always discard any String and make the same reference variable refer to a different String with different content. You can construct a new String out of pieces from other Strings. So being unable to change a given String after it has been created isn't a handicap in practice, and it makes programs more reliable. Programmers can be certain that a String object won't be changed out from under them, via some other reference to it.

Language Support for String Concatenation

There is another String feature with special built-in compiler support: *concatenation*, or joining of two Strings. Whenever a String is one operand of the "+" operator, the system does not do addition. Instead, the other operand (whatever it is, object or primitive) will be converted to a String, and the result is the two Strings appended together. If the operand is an object, it is converted to a

String by calling its `toString()` method. The `toString()` method of Object is described on page 58; String has its own special version of this.

Concatenation is a piece of "magic" extra operator support for type String. The "+" operator used to be the only operator that could be applied to an object, until unboxing was brought into JDK 1.5. You will use this String "+" feature in many places. Here are a few examples:

- To print out a variable and some text saying what it is:

```
System.out.println( "x has value " + x
                + " and y has value " + y );
```

- To break a long String literal down into smaller strings and continue it across several lines:

```
  "Thomas the Tank Engine and the naughty "
+ "Engine-driver who tied down Thomas's Boiler Safety Valve"
+ "and How They Found Pieces of Thomas in Three Counties."
```

- To convert the value to a String (concatenating an empty String with a value of a primitive type is a Java idiom):

```
int i = 256;
    ...
... "" + i // yields a String containing the value of i.
```

That's much shorter than the alternative of using the conversion method of the String class `String.valueOf( i )`.

The source code for the Java run-time library

Amazingly, Sun provides the source code for the Java API, so you can look at classes, see how things are implemented, and get a deeper understanding. When you install the JDK, it places a file called src.zip in the top level directory that you chose or approved for the installation.

It's a *badly behaved zip file* in that it unzips into multiple top-level directories. So you first want to create a single directory to contain the source files; say, c:\jdk15\src. Then run these commands to make a directory and unpack the source. %JAVAHOME% stands for the directory where you installed Java (refer to Appendix A for the pathname, and use that here):

```
cd c:\jdk15
mkdir src
cd src
move %JAVAHOME%\src.zip   .
jar -xvf src.zip
```

That will unzip the source. Start looking in directory c:\jdk15\src\java\lang to see source files Object.java, String.java, and the source files for the wrapper classes described earlier.

String Comparison

Just a reminder about String comparisons. Compare two Strings like this:

```
if ( s1.equals(s2) )
```

not like this:

```
if (s1 == s2)
```

The first compares string *contents*, the second, string *addresses* (this is another artifact of reference types, remember?). Failing to use equals() to compare two strings is probably the most common single mistake made by Java novices.

Tip: Using intern() on Strings

There is one exception to rule of comparing Strings by calling equals(). The exception has been put in place as a performance optimization. String has a method called intern(). You can call intern() on one of your strings, to put it into a private program-wide pool that the String class maintains. You get back a pointer to that string in the pool. Each string is only in that pool once. If you later call intern() on a string that is already in the pool, you get the shared version back to use. This works because string contents never change after creation.

All String literals and String-valued constant expressions are interned for you automatically. That ensures that you don't have two copies of a string literal with the same contents. You can call intern() on your own strings in addition, if you wish. There is some cost to interning a string, so only do it when the number of string comparisons in your program is a lot more than the number of string creations. The key reason to use intern() is that all strings returned from intern() can be compared for equality by using s == t instead of s.equals(t)! (Exercise: why?) The reference comparison is obviously quicker than invoking the equals method. A second benefit is that since all references to Strings of the same value use only a single object, you may save memory. The answer to the question why (start of paragraph) is that if strings are unique, then every pointer to Foo will point to the same one copy of Foo. There will never be two Foo's at different addresses. So address equality can be used for comparing string equality.

String uses another built-in class called StringBuffer to help it operate. StringBuffer differs from String in that you can change characters in the middle of a StringBuffer after it has been instantiated. StringBuffer doesn't have any support for searching for individual characters or substrings though. StringBuffer is widely used by the compiler to implement support for concatenating two Strings into a longer String. You'll use the class String in every program; you may never use StringBuffer.

JDK 1.5 introduced the class java.lang.StringBuilder. StringBuilder has the same API as StringBuffer, but it has performance optimizations that make it appropriate to use only in single-threaded code. This is an optimization for experts only. All the programs we have seen so far are single-threaded (no two pieces of the code are running in parallel). If you do have multiple threads of control in your programs and you want mutable Strings in those threads, you need to use StringBuffer.

The following code shows the important methods of the String class.

```
public final class String implements CharSequence, Comparable, Serializable {
        // constructors with various arguments
    public String();
    public String(java.lang.String);
    public String(java.lang.StringBuffer);
    public String(byte[]);
    public String(byte[],int);
    public String(byte[],int,int);
    public String(byte[],int,int,int);
    public String(byte[],int,int,java.lang.String)
                                    throws UnsupportedEncodingException;
    public String(byte[],java.lang.String) throws UnsupportedEncodingException;
    public String(char[]);
    public String(char[],int,int);
        // comparisons
    public char charAt(int);
    public int compareTo(java.lang.Object);
    public int compareTo(java.lang.String);
    public int compareToIgnoreCase(java.lang.String);
    public boolean endsWith(java.lang.String);
    public boolean equals(java.lang.Object);
    public boolean equalsIgnoreCase(java.lang.String);
    public boolean regionMatches(int, java.lang.String, int, int);
    public boolean regionMatches(boolean, int, java.lang.String, int, int);
    public boolean startsWith(java.lang.String);
    public boolean startsWith(java.lang.String, int);
        // search, extract and other routines
    public String concat(java.lang.String);
    public static String copyValueOf(char[]);
    public static String copyValueOf(char[], int, int);
    public byte [] getBytes();
    public void getBytes(int, int, byte[], int);
    public byte [] getBytes(java.lang.String)throws UnsupportedEncodingException;
    public void getChars(int, int, char[], int);
    public int hashCode();
    public int indexOf(int);
    public int indexOf(int, int);
    public int indexOf(java.lang.String);
    public int indexOf(java.lang.String, int);
    public native java.lang.String intern();
    public int lastIndexOf(int);
    public int lastIndexOf(int, int);
    public int lastIndexOf(java.lang.String);
```

```
public int lastIndexOf(java.lang.String, int);
public int length(); // gets the length of the string
public String replace(char, char);
//new in JDK 1.4, splits the string according to the pattern
public String[] split (String pattern);
public String[] split (String pattern, int limit);

public String substring(int);
public String substring(int, int);
public char toCharArray()[]; public java.lang.String toLowerCase();
public String toLowerCase(java.util.Locale);
public String toString();
public String toUpperCase();
public String toUpperCase(java.util.Locale);
public String trim(); // chops off leading & trailing spaces
        // conversion to String
public static String valueOf(char);
public static String valueOf(double);
public static String valueOf(float);
public static String valueOf(int);
public static String valueOf(long);
public static String valueOf(java.lang.Object);
public static String valueOf(boolean);
public static String valueOf(char[]);
public static String valueOf(char[], int, int);
}
```

Some Light Relief—Hatless Atlas

Here's a cheery song that was written by top programmer David H. Zobel and circulated on the Internet for more than a while. It's sung to the tune of *Twinkle, Twinkle, Little Star*, but to sing it you have to know how some programmers pronounce the shifted and control characters on a keyboard. The "^" character above the "6" is often pronounced "hat" because it looks like a little hat. Some people give the name "huh" to "?", and "wow" to "!". Both of those are a lot shorter than more conventional names.

The song is called *Hatless Atlas* and it goes like this.

^ < @ < . @ *	Hat less at less point at star,
} " _ # |	backbrace double base pound space bar.
- @ $ & / _ %	Dash at cash and slash base rate,
!(@ | = >	wow open tab at bar is great.
; ' + $? ^?	Semi backquote plus cash huh DEL,
, # " ~ |) ^G	comma pound double tilde bar close BEL.

This song can be enjoyed on more than one level. While the theme is not totally transparent, key elements are revealed. The bare-headed strong man relishes nature ("point at star"), and then enjoys the full hospitality of a tavern ("Wow, open tab at bar is great"). Soon he finds that the question of payment does arise, after all; hence, the veiled reference to the Treasury lending policy ("slash base rate") and the finality overshadowing that closing lament "bar close BEL"!

I like to think that in the years to come wherever programmers gather in the evening, after the pizza is all eaten and a sufficient quantity of beer has been drunk, a piano may start to play softly in the corner. Quietly, one member of the group will sing, and then more and more of the programming staff will join in. Any systems analysts who haven't yet quaffed themselves unconscious might sway unsteadily with the beat. Soon several choruses of *Hatless Atlas* will roll lustily around the corners of the room. Old-timers will talk of the great bugs they have overcome and the days of punching clocks, cards, and DOS machines.

Or maybe we'll all stay home and watch reruns of *Star Trek: Kirk Violates the Prime Directive with Xena, Warrior Princess* instead. Who knows?

Chapter 4

Statements and Comments

Huh? What is it, Lassie? What is it, girl?

You say someone has left the braces off their if statement,

and that it's likely to be a maintenance problem? Good girl, Lassie!

Statements are the way we get things done in a program. Here are the most common statements in Java.

Organizing statements	`{ /*statements*/ }` and *emptyStatement ;*	
Expression statement	*someExpression ;*	
Selection statements	`if`	
	`switch`	
Looping statements	`for`	
	`while`	
Transfer of control	`return`	

There are two statements, "throw" and "catch" relating to a form of error handling known as "exceptions". There is also a statement called the "thread statement" which uses the "synchronized" keyword. When there are several threads contending for a shared resource, the synchronized keyword serializes access to the resource, the same way a turnstile allows a crowd of people to enter a stadium one at a time. The thread statement and the exception statements are covered in their own chapters later. The statements described in this chapter, plus Chapter 10, "Exceptions," Chapter 13, "Doing Several Things at Once: Threads," and Chapter 14, "Advanced Thread Topics," cover all statements in Java.

Statements cannot float loose in programs—they are always inside a block. The Java Language Specification says that a block is itself a statement, which makes sense because it is the way you group a number of related statements. A "block" is a programming language term for a pair of curly braces plus everything inside it. A block contains local variable declarations, class declarations, and statements, collectively known as the *block statements*. Here is an example block.

```
{
    int i = 0;                     // block statement
    class x { /* some code */ }    // block statement
    i = 27;                        // block statement
}
```

A method body is a block.

```
public static void main(String[]args) {
    /* an empty method body block */
}
```

Any statement may be prefixed by a label, as shown here:

```
processMonths:
    for(int m = 1; m <= 12; m++) { ...
```

Java doesn't have a goto statement that could be used to branch to a label. If a label appears, it is either just empty documentation (rare—use a comment instead), or it is used to break out of certain enclosing statements in a clean way.

Even though there is no goto statement, there is a reserved word "goto" in Java. The designers grabbed the keyword to ensure that no one uses it as a variable name. That way, if it later turns out to be convenient to support a goto (perhaps for automatically generated code, or to fix the appalling "switch" statement), it can be introduced without breaking any existing code.

Most of Java's statements are very similar to their counterparts in other languages and will be readily recognizable to any programmer. Accordingly, we can limit our discussion to showing the general form of each statement and noting any special rules or "gotchas" that apply.

Organizing Statements

Wherever you can legally put one statement, you can put a block of several
statements. We've seen blocks many times. Use them to group statements in a
loop or an "if" clause, or to declare a variable that will be used only within the
block. This is called a *local* variable because it is local to the block and the name
cannot be seen outside the block. A block looks like this:

```
for (;;) {
    int timeMsecs = 500;        // local variable
    Thread.sleep(timeMsecs);
}
```

This makes the entire block be the subject of the "for" loop. In this example, the
for statement causes the block to be repeated in an infinite loop. It can be stopped
by an exception error condition or by something external to the loop, like closing
the window containing the program, or stopping the Thread it is running in.

Empty statement

Java has the empty statement, which is simply a semicolon by itself. The empty
statement does nothing, and is used to make things clearer. In the example below,
we are saying "if the condition is true, do nothing; otherwise, invoke the
method."

```
boolean noRecordsLeft = /*some calculation*/
if (noRecordsLeft)

    ; // empty statement

else
    alertTheMedia();
```

The code is written this way to make it clearer. If you rewrite it so the "else" part
becomes the "then" part to avoid an empty statement, the condition becomes a
double negative ("not no records left").

```
if (noRecordsLeft==false) {

    alertTheMedia();
}
```

Double negatives don't unconfuse code, so if the empty statement helps you
never fail to avoid them, then don't not go for it. Wherever you can legally put a
statement, you can put an empty statement. It's usual to comment the empty
statement and put it on a line by itself.

Expression Statements

Certain kinds of expression are counted as statements. You write any expression, put a semicolon after it, and voila, it's an expression statement. In particular, an assignment, method invocation, the creation of a object by calling a constructor (looks like a method call, and the keyword "new" is used so we can tell them apart), and pre-increment, post-increment, and decrement are all expressions that can be statements.

```
a = b;                   // assignment
w.setSize(200,100);      // method invocation
new WarningWindow(f);    // instance creation
++i;                     // pre-increment
```

An expression statement is executed by evaluating the expression.

If the expression is an instance creation, you usually save a reference to it so that you can access fields and invoke methods on that object. For example, you have:

```
foo = new WarningWindow(f); // instance creation
```

not:

```
new WarningWindow(f); // instance, but no ref saved
```

However, there are certain classes we'll see later that you can instantiate for which you don't necessarily need to save a reference. The two main examples are Threads and inner (nested) classes. They are fine doing their work without further input from you. So, while you usually keep a reference to a newly instantiated class, you might occasionally see no reference kept.

Selection Statements

The general form of the "if" statement looks like this:

```
if ( Expression ) Statement  [ else  Statement ]
```

Statement Notes

✔ The Expression must have boolean type. It can be a Boolean object which will be unboxed to a boolean. Requiring a boolean (in contrast to an integer) has the delightful effect of banishing the old "if (a=b)" problem, where the programmer mistakenly taps the "=" key once instead of twice, and does an assignment instead of the intended comparison, (a==b).

✔ If that typo is written in Java, the compiler will give an error message that a boolean is needed in that context—unless a and b are booleans. For this reason, people sometimes write code like if (false==b) because the compiler will output an error message for the typo if (false=b)

✔ The Statement can be any statement, in particular a block statement, { /*more code*/ }, is normal.

The general form of the "switch" statement is impossible to show in any meaningful form in a syntax diagram with less than about two dozen production rules. That tells you something about how badly designed the statement is right there. If you look at Kernighan and Ritchie's C book, *The C Programming Language*, you'll note that even they were not up to the task of showing the syntax in any better way than this:

```
switch (Expression) Statement
```

Ignoring syntax diagrams, the switch statement is what some other languages call a "case" statement. It causes control to be transferred to one of several statements depending on the value of the Expression, which must be of type:

* char, byte, short, or int

* Object versions of these, Character, Byte, Short, Integer, which will be unboxed

* An enumerated type (Chapter 6 has the scoop on enums)

The switch statement has this general appearance:

```
switch (Expression) {
    case constant_1 : Statement; break;
    case constant_5 :
    case constant_3 : Statement; break;
          . . .
    case constant_n : Statement; break;
         default : Statement; break;
    }
```

The expression is evaluated. The flow of control transfers to the case clause whose constant matches the expression, if there is such a case. You can't have two cases with the same value.

The value following the keyword "case" has to be a constant. You can't use a variable as the value. Java compiler-writers have put a lot of effort into generating efficient code for switch statements, using techniques like jump tables. A jump table lets the code branch directly to the right case, without testing whether all the intervening cases match the switch variable.

Statement Notes

✔ If you omit a "break" at the end of a branch, control falls through to execute any remaining branches after that branch is executed, up to the next break! This is almost *never* what you want. Implicit fall-through (in the absence of "break") is a huge bug-prone misfeature!

✔ There can be only one "default" branch, and it doesn't have to be last. The "default" branch can be omitted. If it is present, it is executed when none of the "case" values match the Expression.

✔ A Statement can be labeled with several cases. (This is actually a trivial case of fall-through.) In the example above, the case for constant_5 has no statements, so execution falls through to the case for constant_3.

✔ If none of the cases match, and there is no default case, the statement does nothing.

Switch is very badly designed

Looking through about 100,000 lines of the Java Development system source, there are about 320 switch statements. Based on a random sample of files, implicit fall-through is used in less than 1% of case branches. A statement in which you must take explicit action 99% of the time to avoid something is a disaster. Death to the switch statement!

Microsoft fixed this when they copied Java to make C#. They made "*not* falling through" be the default. If you want fall-through, you have to use C#'s goto statement. Alas, Java is most unlikely to get a similar fix, because it would not be backwards compatible with hundreds of millions of existing programs.

When Java was reviewed inside Sun in 1995, I emailed James Gosling (the main language designer) to suggest improving the switch statement. James sent a polite reply back saying that it was too late. At the time there were probably a dozen Java programmers, and hundreds of Java programs.

JDK 1.4 introduced a compiler option to check for and warn about switch fall-through! Imagine: a language feature so broken that there's now a compiler option to check that you didn't use it. It's too late to change it now because of the vast number of programs that use it. The best you could do would be to introduce a non-bug prone replacement for the switch statement and call it something different.

Use this command line option to check for broken code:

```
javac -Xswitchcheck filename.java
```

Looping Statements

The "for" statement looks like this:

> for (*Initial; Test; Increment*) *Statement*

There are new versions of "for" to use with collection classes, arrays and enumerated types:

> for (*SomeType varOfSomeType* : *SomeCollectionVariable*) *Statement*

> for (*SomeType varOfSomeType* : *ArrayVariableOfSomeType*) *Statement*

> for (*SomeType varOfSomeType* : *EnumSet*) *Statement*

These versions of "for" allow you to cycle easily through all elements in a collection or an array or an enumeration, or subranges of an enumeration. They are covered in Chapter 16, "Collections," Chapter 9, "Arrays," and Chapter 6, "Static, Final, and Enumerated Types."

Statement Notes

✔ Initial, Test, and Increment are all expressions that control the loop. The semicolons are required, but any or all of the expressions are optional. The Test expression must be a boolean or a Boolean. A typical loop will look like this:

```
for( i=0; i<100; i++ ) { /*loop body*/  }
```

An infinite loop will have blank Initial Test and Increments, like this:

```
for (;;)
```

✔ It is possible and handy to declare the loop variable in the "for" statement, like this:

```
for( int i=0; i<100; i++ ) { /*loop body*/  }
```

This is a nice feature created for the convenience of the programmer.

✔ The comma separator "," is allowed in the Initial and Increment sections of loops. This is so you can string together several initializations or increments, like this:

```
for(i=0,j=0; i<100; i++, j=i*2 ) { /*loop body*/ }
```

The "while" statement comes in two varieties. The first looks like this:

```
while ( Expression ) Statement
```

Statement Notes

✔ While the boolean or Boolean-typed expression remains true, the Statement is executed.

✔ This form of loop is for iterations that take place zero or more times. If the Expression is false on the first evaluation, the Statement will not execute.

Example:

```
while ( moreData() ) {
    readData();
    processData();
}
```

The "do while" variety of the while statement looks like this:

```
do Statement while ( Expression ) ;
```

Statement Notes

 The Statement is executed, and then the boolean or Boolean-typed expression is evaluated. If it is true, you loop through the Statement again and test again. If it is false, execution drops through to the following statement.

 This form of loop is for iterations that need to be done at least one time. If the Expression is false on the first evaluation, the Statement will already have executed once.

Example:
```
do {
    getCreditAuthorization();
    processSale();
} while ( tenderType().equals("credit card") );
```

There may be "continue" statements in a for or while loop. These look like:

```
continue;
continue  Identifier;
```

Continue statements occur only in loops. When a continue statement is executed, it causes the flow of control to pass to the next iteration of the loop. It's as though you say, "Well, that's it for iteration N; increment the loop variable (if this is a for loop), do the test, and continue with iteration N+1."

The "continue *Identifier*" form is used when you have nested loops, and you want to break out of an inner one altogether and start with the next iteration of the outer loop.

The flow of control will continue with the test for the next iteration of the outer loop with the matching identifier label. Here's the right way to read it. When you see "continue articleMainLoop;" look backwards in the code for a loop labelled like any one of these three:

```
articleMainLoop: for (int i=0;  /*loop*/  or
articleMainLoop: while (int i=0;  /*loop*/  or
articleMainLoop: do { /*loop*/
```

That is the place that the test and next iteration will continue. The following code shows an example continue statement:

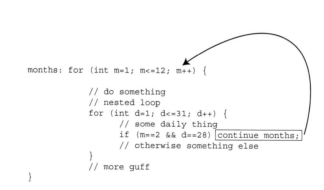

```
months: for (int m=1; m<=12; m++) {

         // do something
         // nested loop
         for (int d=1; d<=31; d++) {
              // some daily thing
              if (m==2 && d==28) continue months;
              // otherwise something else
         }
         // more guff
}
```

There may be "break" statements in a loop or a switch. These look like this:

```
break;
```

Or they look like this:

```
break identifier;
```

Break is a more dramatic version of continue. Break with no identifier causes control to pass to just after the end of the immediately enclosing "for, do, while," or "switch" statement. The loop or switch statement is "broken out of." Break with no identifier can appear only in a statement by virtue of the whole thing being nested in an iteration or switch statement. You will break to the end of the iteration or switch, *not* any "if" statement it's immediately nested in.

```
for (int i=1; i<=12; i++){

   if (LeapYear()) {

        if (i==2)    break;

   }

   getTotalforMonth(i);

}

// break to here. Is that what you want?
```

If an identifier is included, it must be an identifier matching the label on some enclosing statement. The enclosing statement can be *any* kind of statement, not just an iterative or switch statement. In other words, it's OK to break out of any kind of enclosing block as long as you explicitly indicate it with a label.

In practice, it's almost always a loop or switch that you break out of, not an if or block. There is the slightly confusing feature that statements are labeled at their *beginning*, but "break" causes you to jump to their *end*. Here is an example:

```
months: for (int m=1; m<=12; m++) {

                // do something
                // nested loop
                for (int d=1; d<=31; d++) {
                        // some daily thing
                        if (cost > budget) break months;
                }
        }
        cost=0;
```

Transfer of Control Statements

A "return" statement looks like this:

```
return;
```

or

```
return  Expression;
```

Statement Notes

✔ "Return" (with no accompanying expression) is only used in a method that has a return value of void. It gets you out of the method and back to where you were called from. The code below is an example:

```
void resetFields(Customer c) {
    if (c==null) return;
    // otherwise, go on to reset the fields of c
}
```

✔ A "return Expression" is always used in every method that actually does
return a value. It cannot be used in a method whose return value is void.
The code below shows an example:

```
int hourOfDay( ) {
    java.util.Calendar now = java.util.Calendar.getInstance();
    int hrs = now.get(java.util.Calendar.HOUR_OF_DAY);
    return hrs;
}
```

There two other statements that can transfer the flow of control: the "throw"
statement that raises an exception, and the "assert" that does sanity-checking of
important conditions. These are described in chapter 10 *Exceptions*.

Comments

Java has comment conventions similar to those of C++. Two slashes together,
"//" make the rest of the line a comment, as follows:

```
i = 0;  // the "to end-of-line" comment
```

Comments starting with "/*" make all the characters up to and including the first
"*/", be a comment. It might stretch over several lines:

```
/* the "regular multiline" comment
   goes here.
 */
```

Commenting out code

Since comments do not nest in Java, to comment out a big section of code, you
must either put "//" at the start of every line, or use "/*" at the front and immediately
after every embedded closing comment, finishing up with your own closing
comment at the end.
You can also use the following around statements you want to temporarily delete:

```
if ( false ) {
    ...
}
```

Each of these approaches has advantages and disadvantages. Perhaps the best
way to remove unwanted code is to use a source code control system. Delete the
code. If you later need to recover it, fallback to a previous revision that included the
code.

Javadoc comments

There's a third variety of comment starting with "/**". This indicates text that will
be picked up from the source code by javadoc, an automatic HTML

documentation generator. The entire Java API has been documented by putting these "/** ... */" comments in the source code, and running javadoc on it. The resulting run-time library HTML documentation is on the Sun website at java.sun.com. Before we describe the format of javadoc comments, let's describe the javadoc output that forms the API documentation.

Reading the Java API

This is a very, very important section! The Java Application Programmer Interface (API) is a vast collection of libraries. Luckily, it is well documented, and the documentation is easily accessed using a browser starting at
http://java.sun.com/docs/index.html

You can also download the html and install it locally. I prefer to download it because local access is faster than web access, and we're mostly Type A individuals in programming. However you do it, start up your favorite browser and browse the URL for the Java API for the release you installed on your computer. When the page comes up, set a bookmark for it. Your browser should be displaying something like Figure 4–1.

This is the standard format for the Java API documentation. There is a tool called "javadoc" that generates this HTML documentation from ordinary source code files. All the Java library code is heavily annotated with comments, which javadoc processes and displays to you (see Figure 4–1).

There are three frames in the window. Frame 1 has a scrolling list of all package names in the release. Frame 2 has an alphabetical list of all classes. Frame 3 starts off by displaying more detail on each package.

To look at a particular class, you can either click on its name in Frame 2, or if you know the package it is in, you can click on that package in Frame 1. That causes Frame 2 to display all the classes in that package. Try it now, with package java.lang. You might have to scroll the frames a bit. Then click on class "Object" in Frame 2.

That brings up all the information about class java.lang.Object in Frame 3. You will see documentation on all the methods of the class, the constructors, the error conditions it can hit, and often some more general information too.

You should get into the habit of using the javadoc documentation heavily. You should read through the API of every class described here, and every class before you use it in your own programs. You can look at the source of the run-time library, if the javadoc isn't clear enough. Repeat with each new release of the JDK. Yes, it's a lot of reading. Do it as you use each class. That's what it takes to be a highly productive programmer.

Frame 1

Frame 2

Frame 3

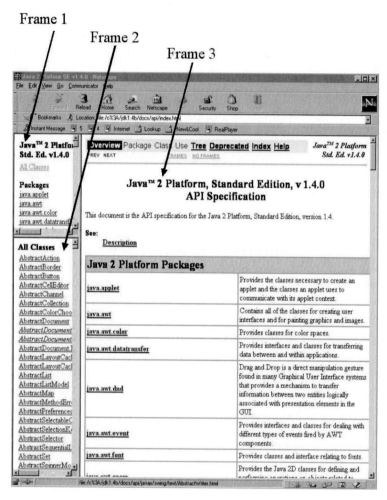

Figure 4–1   The API documentation

You can use javadoc on your own code and generate some HTML documentation for it. Many professional Java software suites are documented using javadoc.

Format of Javadoc comments

Javadoc is an implementation of the *literate programming* system invented by Donald Knuth. The javadoc tool (included with the JDK) parses source code looking for comments that start "/**". If it finds any, it extracts them into a set of HTML pages describing the API. There are a few special tags inside a javadoc comment (they look like "*@tagname*") that tell javadoc the text that follows

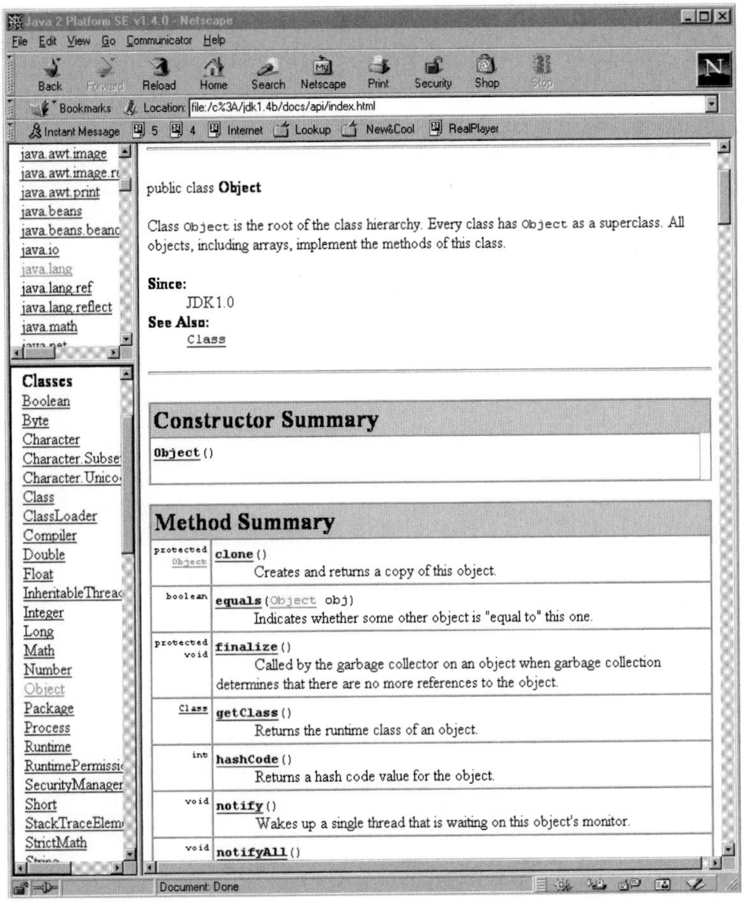

Figure 4–2   Detailed information on classes in the Java API

describes a parameter, or a return value, or the author, etc. Some of the tags and the way you write them is shown in this example:

```
/** the API comment for HTML documentation
    @version anyLinesOfHTML
    @author anyLinesOfHTML
    @see SomeOtherClassOrMethodName
    @param anyLinesOfHTML
    @return anyLinesOfHTML
    @exception anyLinesOfHTML
    @since JDK1.1
 */
```

The javadoc comments for a class come immediately before the class. The javadoc comments describing a method come immediately before the method. You can

see the formatted HTML output for the class java.lang.Object on the previous
pages. Here's some of the corresponding raw source code for that class, showing
the extensive javadoc comments.

```
/**
 * Class <code>Object</code> is the root of the class hierarchy.
 * Every class has <code>Object</code> as a superclass. All objects,
 * including arrays, implement the methods of this class.
 *
 * @author   unascribed
 * @version  1.65, 12/19/03
 * @see      java.lang.Class
 * @since    JDK1.0
 */
    public class Object {
      /**
       * Creates and returns a copy of this object.
       * @return     a clone of this instance.
         *   @exception  CloneNotSupportedException  if the object's class
         *               doesn't support <code>Cloneable</code> interface.
       * @see java.lang.Cloneable
       */
          protected Object clone() throws CloneNotSupportedException {
```

Try javadoc. You can easily annotate your own code with comments javadoc
recognizes. javadoc works on .java files, not .class files, because the .java files
contain the comments. Add some of the javadoc tags to the clock example
program and run javadoc like this:

```
javadoc clock.java
```

or

```
javadoc -source 1.5 clock.java
```

This will create several HTML files and a style sheet, listing the file names as it
generates them. (A style sheet is an update to HTML that lets you customize the
appearance of other tags. You can change colors, fonts, and sizes throughout a
document by using a style sheet that overrides the default appearance).

View the javadoc output using a browser. It shows the chain of class inheritance
and all the public fields in the class, along with your comments.

Whether or not you agree with the idea of using web pages to store program
documentation, it offers some compelling advantages. Documentation
automatically generated from the program source is much more likely to be
available, accurate (what could be more accurate than the documentation and the
source being two views of the same thing?), and complete (the documentation is
written at the same time as the code and by the same person).

Exercises

1. Write the `if` statements that call different methods `do0_9()`, `do10_99()`, and `do100_999()` based on the value of i being in the range 0-9, 10-99, or 100-999. Don't forget to allow for other values of i, including negative values.

2. Write a switch statement that corresponds to the if statement in question 1. Which is more compact? Which is easier to read?

3. Write a method that counts the number of "1" bits in an int value. You can get successive bits from the end of an int by checking to see if the int is an odd number. An int is an even number if a division by two followed by a multiplication by two gives you back the original number (truncation of a fraction gives a smaller result for an odd number). If it is an odd number, the least significant bit is 1, otherwise it is zero. Then divide the int by 2 to get the next bit. Don't do this check-and-divide-by-two more than 31 times. Why shouldn't you do the shift more than 31 times with an int?

4. Write another method that counts the number of "1" bits in a long value. Is there any way to share code between the two? (Hint: a long is two ints wide.) Would you do so in practice? Explain why or why not. Then look up the javadoc API and reimplement it using `java.math.BigInteger.bitCount()`.

Some Light Relief—MiniScribe: The Hard Luck Hard Disk

Most readers will know the term "hard disk," which contrasts with "floppy disk," but how many people know about MiniScribe's pioneering efforts in the fields of *very* hard disks, inventory control, and accounting techniques?

MiniScribe was a successful start-up company based in Longmont, Colorado, that manufactured disk drives. In the late 1980s, Miniscribe ran into problems when IBM unexpectedly cancelled some very big purchasing contracts. The venture capitalists behind MiniScribe, Hambrecht & Quist, brought in turnaround expert Q.T. Wiles to get the company back on track.

Wiles mercilessly drove company executives to meet revenue targets, even as sales fell still further. In desperation, the beleaguered executives turned to outright record falsification. It must have seemed so easy. Over the space of a couple of years they came up with an impressive range of fraudulent techniques for making a failing company have the appearance of prospering.

The Miniscribe executives started off with the easy paper-based deceit, like:

- Counting raw inventory as finished goods (with a higher value).
- Anticipating shipments before they were made to customers.
- Counting imaginary shipments on non-existent ships.

When they were not found out, they graduated to more brazen activities like parading inventory past the accountants twice, so it would be counted twice, and shipping obsolete product to a fake customer called "BW." "BW" stood for "Big Warehouse" and was a MiniScribe storage building. And so it went, with smaller crimes leading to bigger crimes, just the way your kindergarten teacher warned it would.

Miniscribe employed more than 9,000 people worldwide at the height of its fortunes, so this was no fly-by-night, two-guys-in-a-garage undertaking. This was a fly-by-night, 9,000-guys-in-a-Big-Warehouse undertaking. The companies that supplied Miniscribe were doing less and less business with them and were finding it hard to get paid. One analyst surveyed the entire computer industry and found only one large MiniScribe customer. At the same time, MiniScribe was issuing press releases talking about "record sales."

The most breathtaking coup, though, was the brick scam. Desperate to show shipments on the books, executives brought in their assistants, spouses, and even children for a crazy weekend of filling disk shipping boxes with house bricks. They also created a special computer program called "Cook book" (these guys were well aware of what they were doing) that facilitated shipping the bricks to good old "BW" and recognizing the "revenue" from that customer. These bricks were surely the ultimate hard drive.

Of course, it all came unglued in the end. On January 1, 1990, MiniScribe announced massive layoffs and filed for bankruptcy. Chief Financial Officer Owen Taranto, the genius who devised the brick shipment plan, was granted immunity for his testimony. The stock went into a precipitous decline, but not before the aptly named Wiles had unloaded a parcel of it at premium prices. So the people who lost their jobs and the stockholders bore the brunt of all this dishonesty.

There was plenty of blame to go around. After a trial, Cooper & Lybrand, Hambrecht & Quist, and sixteen MiniScribe executives were ordered to pay $568 million in restitution to defrauded stockholders. Wiles was sentenced to three years in the Big House. The remains of MiniScribe were bought out by rival Maxtor. The later Maxtor model 8541s looked just like Miniscribe 8541s, so they were still being made, but any resemblance to a brick was long since gone.

You want to know the thing that really kills me about this case, though? It's just not that unusual an event. I taught a programming class at beautiful Foothill College, in Los Altos Hills, California, recently. As well as filling the students' heads with knowledge about stacks, interrupts, kernels, device drivers, heaps, and such, I took pains to talk about the computer industry as a whole. As part of that, I wanted to give a brief lecture on ethics in the computer industry.

I figured I'd dredge up a few shocking tales about benchmark shenanigans, mention whatever was the most recent abuse of an unregulated monopoly by Microsoft corporate executives, and remind the class to avoid dealing from the bottom of the deck. I started collecting news stories and reports of ethical lapses within the computer industry to provide material for the lecture.

To my horror, I found that lack of integrity at high levels within a company was not as rare as I had supposed. My files swelled up with material and case studies to the point where I stopped collecting it. So if the MiniScribe story tells us anything, it is this: you will likely be confronted with something ethically wrong at some point in your programming career. When that happens, you'll have a choice between going along with it, or refusing to. If you have thought beforehand about what you want to be known for, it will be easier to do the right thing. That's all.

Chapter 5

OOP Part II— Constructors and Visibility

▼ CREATING NEW OBJECTS: CONSTRUCTORS

▼ MORE ABOUT METHODS

▼ VARIABLE-ARITY METHODS

▼ PACKAGES

▼ HOW THE JDK FINDS CLASSES

▼ ACCESS MODIFIERS

▼ EXERCISES

▼ SOME LIGHT RELIEF—IT'S NOT YOUR FATHER'S IBM

All the way back in Chapter 2, we briefly mentioned two concepts that are used a lot with classes: constructors (to create new objects), and access control (to deliberately restrict or increase the visibility of classes and things in classes). This chapter is where we deliver the full details on these two topics. Constructors are usually described as being like methods "with a few differences" and method is the object-oriented name for a function or procedure. So there's a section on methods and parameter passing in here too. We look at the ways you can organize groups of classes into packages, and how you can store packages in jar files. At the end of this chapter, you'll have enough knowledge to read and write basic Java object-oriented programs.

Polymorphism Is a Long Word for a Short Topic

In Chapter 8, we'll cover *inheritance* and *polymorphism*. Don't be put off by the term *polymorphism*. It's just a long word meaning "how child classes provide specialized versions of the methods inherited from the parent". You'll need to read and understand the advanced OOP chapter be an effective Java programmer. The good news is that object-oriented programming is based on a few simple ideas. Here are the key OOP ideas that we have met so far:

Object-oriented programming: key ideas so far

- A class is another name for a datatype.

- An object is a variable belonging to a class datatype.

- The methods and data defined in a class implement the operations of the type. The compiler permits only these operations on objects of this type. You have to provide a specific object when you call a method. The statements are executed on that specific object.

- Every class has a parent class, and has full access to the data and operations of its parent (access to your parent's stuff is called "inheritance").

We also saw that Java object variables are really just pointers to objects, "references" in Java terminology. This is a big difference between Java and most other object-oriented programming languages. Some implications that flow from this design decision are summarized in the next section.

Reminder: Java object variables are really references to objects

- All objects are accessed through references (these are, effectively, pointers).

- Declaring what looks like an object variable actually gets you a variable that can hold a reference to an object.

- When you declare that variable, it contains a null value that does not point to any object. To start using the object, you must first make the variable point to an object. You can make it point to an existing object, or you can create a new object for it to reference.

We have reinforced the point that object variables don't start out pointing to an object. It's time to describe in detail how you create a new object when you want one.

Creating New Objects: Constructors

You call a *constructor* to create a new object. A constructor is a special kind of method that you write as part of a class. It looks like an ordinary method, but a constructor magically allocates memory for a new instance of an object, then executes the statements that you write in the constructor body. Your statements typically initialize the fields of the new object.

Like any method, a constructor needs to be given a name. A constructor also needs to indicate that its return type is "an object of the class that this constructor belongs to". The Java design team chose to roll these two needs together, by adopting the conventions that:

- A constructor has *the same name as the class it belongs to.*

- A constructor is *written without an explicit return type.* In some sense, its name *is* the return type.

The purpose of a constructor is to allocate and initialize a newly created object. Here's the Timestamp class with the obvious constructor:

```
class Timestamp {
        int hrs;
        int mins;
        int secs;

        // a constructor returns a new Timestamp object
        // implicitly allocates memory for the object
        // explicitly initializes the fields of the object
        Timestamp() {
            java.util.Calendar now =
                        java.util.Calendar.getInstance();
            hrs = now.get(java.util.Calendar.HOUR_OF_DAY);
            mins = now.get(java.util.Calendar.MINUTE);
            secs = now.get(java.util.Calendar.SECOND);
        }
}
```

Notice there is no explicit statement to allocate memory; the run-time library knows that this is a constructor, not an ordinary method, and does the allocation behind-the-scenes for you. Also, there is no "return TimestampObjectRef" statement, even though the constructor does return a Timestamp object reference at the place where it was called. These are just language quirks to get used to.

Here is what a call to a constructor looks like:

```
t = new Timestamp(); // t now points to an obj
```

The keyword "new" is always used when you call a constructor, it tips you off that it's not a method call. It's very common to declare a variable and initialize it by a constructor call in one shot:

```
Timestamp t = new Timestamp();
```

An expression with the "new" keyword is the *only* way to get a new object created (sole exception: cloning, described in Chapter 11). Even if it looks like you got an object some other way (like a string literal, or the `java.lang.Class.newInstance()` method) a constructor was called for you behind the scenes.

A call to a constructor creates a new instance of a class, so the process is also known as *instantiation* or doing an instantiation.

The default no-arg constructor

All classes always have at least one constructor. If you write a class without any explicit constructors (this is allowed), the *default no-arg constructor* is assumed for you. The default no-arg (meaning "no arguments") constructor for a class takes no arguments and does nothing except create an object.

Here's the Timestamp class, with no explicit constructors:

```
class Timestamp {
        int hrs;
        int mins;
        int secs;
}
```

The default no-arg constructor is provided by the compiler, and it's exactly equivalent to writing this:

```
class Timestamp {
        int hrs;
        int mins;
        int secs;

        Timestamp() { } // explicit no-arg constructor

}
```

When not to allow a no-arg constructor

Some classes shouldn't have a no-arg constructor. An example would be a class that represents Employee records. Assume that every employee must have a unique ID number, and you intend this will be passed as an argument to the constructor. If that class also had a no-arg constructor, that's a potential way to create an object without the ID getting set. So Java says when you provide any constructor at all, you do not get the default no-arg constructor. That ensures that a careless programmer can't call it, and create a half-baked employee object with no ID.

When you want it all

There are other cases where you need some explicit constructors, and you also want a no-arg constructor. If you also want a no-arg constructor, you just write one explicitly, as in the Timestamp code above. You can put some statements in the no-arg constructor body if you wish.

Constructors can call sibling constructors

Most classes have at least one explicit constructor. You can define several different constructors and tell them apart by their parameter types. Sometimes you may want one constructor to call another. It's quite common to have a series of constructors that accept several different types of arguments, and each call a single constructor with the arguments in a standardized form to do the rest of the processing in one place. You use the keyword this() to call a different constructor in the same class. We have seen this in a method means "the object I was invoked on." Here it is re-used to mean "one of my other constructors; pick the one with the matching signature."

Here's an example of one constructor calling another. These are two constructors that could be added to Timestamp, allowing a programmer to pass in the hour, minute, and second that he wants the Timestamp to represent. The second Timestamp constructor allows the programmer to just set the hour, and zero should be set in the other fields. The second constructor will call the first.

```
Timestamp(int h, int m, int s) {
    hrs = h;
    mins = m;
    secs = s;
}

Timestamp(int h) {
    this(h, 0, 0); // calls the other constr.
}
```

When one constructor explicitly invokes another, that invocation must be the very first statement in the constructor. This is because you can't call a constructor on something that has already had its memory allocated, and the memory has already been allocated by the time the system starts executing your statements in a constructor.

A constructor cannot be invoked explicitly by the programmer other than in object creation, although this might otherwise be quite a useful operation to, say, reset an object to a known initial state.

A second glimpse at inheritance

To fully understand constructors, we need to say a few more words about inheritance. All the constructor calls we have seen so far have been like this:

```
Timestamp t = new Timestamp();
```

But you may also see a constructor called with a different name (and therefore a different type) from the reference variable type:

```
Fruit lime = new Citrus();
```

Here we are getting a Citrus-type object back from the constructor, but we are assigning it to a variable of type Fruit. You can only do this with compatible types.

One class can be based on another class. That class is compatible with the class it is based on. The technique of basing one class on another is called "inheritance." Inheritance is what you get from your parent, and a child class has all the fields and methods that are in the parent.

It's a neat thing: A class can be related to another class in a parent/child relationship. You are saying "this class *extends* that class over there, with these additional members or changes." A variable of a parent type can also hold a value that points to a child object. When you see a line of code as above, you can conclude that since Fruit can hold a Citrus object pointer, Fruit must be the parent of Citrus (or grandparent or somewhere above it). So there must be a definition similar to this somewhere:

```
class Fruit {  /* */  }

class Citrus extends Fruit { /*  */ }
```

In those lines of code, there is obviously a class called Fruit and a class called Citrus that extends Fruit. That means Citrus has all the methods and fields that Fruit does, plus its own special operations that apply only to citrus fruit. Citrus is a child class of Fruit. It is also termed a subclass or subtype. Subclass objects can always be assigned to parent objects, but not the other way round. All Citrus are Fruit. But not all Fruit are Citrus (it might be AppleVariety or FruitGrownOnVine).

Even if you don't explicitly give it one, all classes that you write have a parent class. If you do not specify a parent, your class extends the fundamental system class known as *Object*. A class is a type, and a child class is just a subtype. All objects in the system are subtypes of `java.lang.Object`, and have all the members of that root class.

What happens during instantiation

When an object is instantiated, this is the order in which things happen:

1. The memory for the object is allocated.

2. That memory is cleared, causing data fields to be filled in with the default values zero, 0.0, null, and so on. Thus, all objects start with a known state.

3. The constructor is called and might explicitly call another constructor in the same class.

4. A constructor in the object's parent class is *always* called, either explicitly with super(someArguments), or implicitly. This is recursive, meaning that the parent then calls a constructor in its parent and so on all the way back to the constructor in the java.lang.Object class.

5. Any data fields with explicit initializers have those initial assignments executed.

6. Any *Instance Initializers* are executed. Most of your classes won't use instance initializers, but see the following box for information about them.

7. The rest of the statements in the object's constructor are executed.

What's an "Instance Initializer"?

An instance initializer is a delicious hack! They were introduced with JDK 1.1 so that anonymous classes can be initialized. An instance initializer is simply a block of code in a class outside the body of any method. Because it doesn't have a name, you can't write a constructor for an anonymous class. We haven't covered anonymous classes yet, but here's an example instance initializer with a regular, non-anonymous class.

```
class Timestamp {
    int hrs;
    int mins;
    int secs;

    {
        System.out.println("I am an instance initializer!");
        hrs = 0;   mins = 0; secs = 0;
    }

    Timestamp() {
        System.out.println("I am a constructor!");
    }

}
```

Any instance initializer blocks are executed in the order in which they appear in the source code, every time a new object is constructed. Where you have a choice, use constructors in preference to instance initializers, otherwise you will confuse other programmers and make them think you don't know what you're doing.

People sometimes doubt that a constructor calls a constructor in the parent class, even if you didn't explicitly code it that way. Take a look at this example. There are three classes (Grandparent, Parent, and Child) in a superclass, class, subclass relationship. The phrase "class Child extends Parent" makes class Child a child of class Parent. You can use any names; I used Child and Parent to make the hierarchy obvious.

```java
class Grandparent {
    Grandparent() {
        // parent constructor (java.lang.Object) is always called here
        // or you may call it explicitly with super();
        System.out.println("Grandparent");
    }
}

class Parent extends Grandparent {
    Parent() {
        // parent constructor is always called here
        // or you may call it explicitly with super();
        System.out.println("Parent");
    }
}

public class Child extends Parent {

    public static void main(String[] args) {
        Child c = new Child();// invokes the chain of parent constrs.
        System.out.println("Child");
    }
}
```

The class called "Child" has a default no-arg constructor. However, when you instantiate a child object, you will see that the parent and grandparent (and so on) constructors are called, even though there is no explicit statement doing that. The right way to think about it is that constructors do object-specific initialization. So you definitely want the parent constructor called because it knows best how to initialize the fields that you got from the parent. You should compile and run the program, and check that you see this output:

```
Grandparent
Parent
Child
```

Grandparent is printed first because its constructor is called before the first statement in the Parent constructor is executed. Constructing a new object can take several method calls and be expensive in terms of processor time and system resources.

No destructors

Java has automatic storage management, including automatic reclamation of objects no longer in use. The run-time system does not need to be told when an object has reached the end of its lifetime.

Accordingly, there are no "destructor" methods to reclaim an object. Just delete, overwrite, or null out the last reference to an object, and it becomes available for destruction so the memory can be reused.

More About Methods

Methods are the OOP name for functions. A method is always declared inside a class; methods can't exist outside a class. A method has this general form:

This part is known as the "method signature"

```
optAccess  optModifiers  returnType  (methodName ( optParamList )  )
```

```
optThrowsClause
```

```
        {   optStatements  }
```

The parts marked *"opt"* in the previous example are optional, and we will deal with these in due course. An example method may look like this:

```
void setValue(int i) {
     something = i;
}
```

The main routine, where execution starts, is another example:

The "method signature"

```
public static void(main ( String[] args )){

     /* statements */
}
```

Arguments and parameters

What's the difference between an argument and a parameter? Here's a bit of terminology which is frequently ignored. A *parameter* is any variable declared within the method signature. The list of parameters is enclosed in parentheses. Each parameter consists of a type name followed by a variable name. In the code fragments shown previously, i is an int parameter to setValue(), and args is a String array parameter to main(). Parameters are sometimes called "formal parameters".

Arguments only appear in calls to a method. An argument is the actual value used in a particular call to a function. If we invoke setValue twice like this:

```
setValue(17);
setValue(x);
```

Then 17, and x are arguments passed in these calls, respectively. Arguments are sometimes called "actual parameters".

The String array parameter in main is usually given the name arg or args, even though it's a parameter, not an argument. (This tradition comes from C, which has the same misnomer.) Args holds the command line arguments passed to the program when you started it up. If you run your Java program by typing

```
java myClass 12 file.txt Birmingham
```

then the String array that the run-time library passes to the main method of myClass will have three elements with the String values "12", "file.txt" and "Birmingham" respectively.

Reference variables and passing parameters to methods

The difference between variables of primitive types and objects (reference types) has implications for parameter-passing. Variables of primitive types are passed by value; objects are passed by reference.

"*Passing by value*" means that the argument's value is copied and is passed to the method. Inside the method you can modify the copy at will, and the modifications don't affect the original argument.

"*Passing by reference*" means that a reference to (i.e., the address of) the argument is passed to the method. Using the reference, the method is actually directly accessing the argument, not a copy of it. Any changes the method makes to the parameter are made to the actual object used as the argument. After you return from the method, that object will retain any new values set in the method.

What's really going on here is that a *copy* of the value that references an object argument is passed to the method. This is why some Java books say (misleadingly) "everything is passed by value"—the copy of the *object reference* is passed by *value,* yes, but that effectively passes the *object itself* by *reference.*

The one difference is that with "references passed by value" (as in Java), there is nothing you can do to an argument to change where the original parameter points. With true "pass by reference," assigning to the argument will make the original parameter change too. In Java, a method can change the contents of an object parameter, but not which object it is.

Overloaded method names

You invoke a method by its name. You can have several methods with the same name in a class. The same-named methods are said to *overload* the name.

```
void someMethod(int i) {
      // some statements
}

void someMethod(double d, char c) { // overloaded
      // some statements
}
```

Those two methods in the previous example are overloaded. As long as they have different arguments, the compiler will be able to tell which one you intend to call. The ten-dollar way of saying this is, "The method signature is used to disambiguate overloaded method calls."

Methods with the same name should do the same thing. Don't have a method called validate() that validates a customer record, and another one in the same class called validate(int i) that calculates the square root of its argument.

Unlike primitive variables inside an object (data fields), primitive variables declared inside a method have an undefined initial value. For those familiar with compiler internals, it's too big a performance hit to keep clearing stack frames, so it's not done. Primitive local variables get an initial value of whatever old junk was left on the stack. Your compiler may try to warn you about places where you have possibly left a local variable without an initial value. But you cannot rely on this, so it's important to initialize local variables before use.

Variable-Arity Methods

Arity is a computer science term meaning the number of arguments a method or operator takes. It was originally a joking term, taken from "polarity" meaning the number of poles something has, so by extension "arity" must mean "number of". Well, just like your mother told you if you pulled a face it would stick like that, the term *arity* stuck.

In some languages, methods may have *variable-arity* which means their last or only argument is actually a list of arguments. Congratulations; with JDK 1.5, Java is now one of the languages with variable-arity! This is another hack that was put in Java because some engineers really liked C's printf() function, and wanted Java to have the same convenience.

Luckily, variable-arity (also called var-args by some) has been implemented in a very straightforward way in Java. Here's the code you write to tell the compiler "this is a variable-arity method" in Java:

```
public PrintWriter format(String format, Object... args)
```

This declaration actually comes from the API class java.io.PrintWriter. The three dots tell the compiler *"args is a sequence of Objects"*, so this is a variable-arity method. Inside the body of format(), the args parameter is regarded as type "array of Object", i.e. it is exactly as though the method were declared:

```
public PrintWriter format(String format, Object[] args)
```

Where you see a difference is in *calls* to variable-arity methods. If the last parameter is declared with those three dots known as an ellipsis, then you can call the method with a variable number of objects as that last parameter. They will be automatically assembled into an array for you.

So you can make a call like this:

```
myPW.format( myFormatStr, t1, t2 );
```

Primitive variables will even get autoboxed for you.

```
myPW.format( myFormatStr, 1, 2, 3, 4 );
```

It doesn't buy all that much. It saves you having to create the array by hand:

```
Integer[] i = { 1, 2, 3, 4 };    // int literals get autoboxed
myPW.format( myFormatStr, i );
```

Where variable-arity shines is in formatting text. That first argument is a string that can contain ordinary text, and special *format specifiers*. The ordinary text is carried through literally, and the format specifiers are applied to modify the appearance of the remaining parameters before adding them to the text. The sort of thing you can do is round numbers, specify how many digits should appear, and how many characters wide they should be in all.

The format specifiers are very powerful, very involved, and really make up a special-purpose (rather ugly) programming language of their own. And they work on more than just numbers. There are format specifiers for everything you might want to print: dates, times, text messages, and so on. We'll look at format specifiers in Chapter 17. But you may now write

```
System.out.printf("%s is %d years old \n", name, age );
```

and get a result like

```
Ruprecht is 17 years old
```

You can call the same method with a different number of arguments:

```
System.out.printf("My favorite %d primes are %d,%d,%d\n", 3, i, j, 2 );
```

to get the result:

```
My favorite 3 primes are 17,11,2
```

There's potential for some confusion with variable-arity methods. When you look at the call, the number of arguments no longer matches the number of parameters. You should try to restrict your use of variable-arity to the purpose intended when it was brought into Java: text string formatting and printing.

Packages

There are several keywords that control the visibility of a class or the members of a class. *Access Modifiers* on page 103 summarizes these modifiers (private, no keyword, protected, and public). Some of these access modifiers apply to packages, so we'll start with the "how and why" of Java packages.

What a package is

When you're just writing a few programs for your personal use, you can put the classes in any old directory and use any old names. When you have a team of twenty programmers working on five different software products that interact, you need a better way to organize your files than "putting them in any old directory."

Java uses the term *package* to mean a collection of related classes that form a library, and which are kept together in the same directory. Strictly speaking, packages and classes do not *have* to be directories and files. The Java Language Specification is written to allow implementations to store code in a database or any other kind of repository, and some IDEs do just that. However, "package equals directory" and "class equals file" is the simplest implementation, and the best way to understand the topic.

Package naming rules

A package name needs to match the directory name where the source and class files are stored. So a package called "java.lang" must have its class files in a directory where the last part of the pathname is java\lang (on Windows) or java/lang (on Unix, Linux, the Mac, etc). Java uses the computer's filesystem to organize and locate packages.

The requirement means that if you know the name of a class, you also know where to find it (as long as you know where to begin looking). Classes that are part of the same package will be in the same directory. It simplifies things for the compiler-writer, and gives the programmer less to remember.

Packaging classes

How do you tell the compiler that a class D is part of some package, like a.b.c ? It's simplicity itself—just put the source in file a/b/c/D.java and write the first few lines in the file like this:

```
package a.b.c;
class D   {
          /* more code */
}
```

Class D will go in file D.java and the byte code output by the compiler will go in D.class. Package names are hierarchical, and the packages can be nested arbitrarily deep. The prize in the Java API currently goes to

```
package javax.swing.text.html.parser;   // 5 levels of pkg!
```

That package contains half-a-dozen classes relating to parsing HTML within Text components that belong to the Swing GUI package in the Javax API. Classes in this package are in directory $JAVAHOME/javax/swing/text/html/parser.

A class's package name is used as a prefix to create the full name of the class. If a class was identified only by classname and nothing else, we'd need some scheme to distinguish between duplicate names. If I wrote a class called `ReadData` that was in a library installed on a customer's system, and you wrote a class called `ReadData` that was in another library installed on the same customer's system, the JVM wouldn't know which of the two classes to load when it hit a reference to `ReadData`.

All the compiler tools recognize classes that are qualified by package name. In the case of class a.b.c.D, if you are in the parent directory of "a", you can compile with:

```
javac a/b/c/D.java
```

and if D has a public main method, you can run it with:

```
java a.b.c.D
```

When your source code doesn't explicitly mention a package, the class is compiled into an unnamed package in the current directory. This is fine for toy programs and examples, but professional software always uses packages.

Creating unique package names

The JLS tells you how to form package names that are distinct from everyone else's. Within a given organization, start with its Internet domain name, and reverse it, so the most general part appears first. In IBM's workstation division, the package names would start with com.ibm.wkstn. How, and how far, they subdivide it further is totally up to them. They'll probably want to add, at a minimum,"product within division."

Since domain names are unique across the entire Internet, you can also easily create package names that have this quality. It allows different vendors to provide class libraries with no danger of namespace collisions. There are thus three purposes to packages:

- To organize namespaces in your program so your classes don't collide with each other

- To organize namespaces for all organizations, so all program names don't collide with each other

- To control visibility of classes

Picking up on these points, the next section, *How the JDK Finds Classes,* explains how the JDK uses packages to locate the classes to load. *Access Modifiers* on page 103 describes the keywords that make classes more visible or less.

How the JDK Finds Classes

Unlike many other language or compiler systems, Java doesn't link all your code into one big, freestanding program. Instead, it leaves everything in separate classfiles. Packages, and hence directory paths, impose some order on that. The JDK always knows where to find the Java run-time library classes, but the run-time class loader still needs to know where to find your classes.

The first point to note is that you can zip all your class files into a *jar file*, so you don't really need umpteen levels of directory on the customer's system. A jar file (Java Archive) works exactly like a zip file and can be used to store a whole directory tree in a single file. You can put other files that the application needs, such as image files, sound files, and translations for Strings, in the jar, too. Then you have to put the jar file (or the complete directory tree) where Java can find it, or tell Java the possible places to look for it. You can even set a jar file up so it will execute when its icon is double-clicked.

How to create a jar file

You can create your own jar files by using standard WinZIP, other software, or the jar utility that comes with the JDK. The jar program has a command line that looks like this in general form:

```
jar [ options ] [manifest] destination input-file [input-files]
```

The options that jar takes are similar to those of tar—the Unix tape archive utility—but the formats are different, and tar files are not used in Java. To create a compressed archive of all the class files and .jpg files for package a.b.c, you would use the commands

```
cd parent-of-a
jar cvf myJarFile.jar a/b/c/*.class a/b/c/*.jpg
```

Don't forget that once you put some code in a jar, it's not enough to recompile when you change something. You must also rebuild the jar file with the new .class; otherwise, you'll continue to get the old version of the program. Don't encrypt the jar file. Since JDK 1.2 there has been an option to update (replace a file in) an existing jar file. The example below shows how to replace the file Foo.class in archive myJarFile.jar.

```
jar u myJarFile.jar Foo.class
```

The directory pathnames stored inside the jar must match the package names exactly, with no extra or missing qualification. The pathnames are case sensitive within a jar file, and must exactly match the case of package, file, and class.

Applications can be stored in jars, too

You can store a complete application in a jar file and run it without unpacking the contents. The command will execute the application contained in the jar file.

```
MyApp.jar
```

or

```
java -jar  MyApp.jar
```

For this to work, there needs to be a manifest file in the jar file, to say which class has the `main()` routine where you want execution to start. You provide this information with the Main-Class header, which has the general form:

```
Main-Class: a.b.c.MyMainClassName
```

Put that line of text into a file called "Manifest.mf." That will be our manifest file (manifest in the sense of "ship's manifest" that lists all the cargo packed in the hold). When you create the jar file, ensure that the information gets put into the manifest of the jar by using the command

```
jar cmf Manifest.mf write.jar write.class
```

Making jar files double-clickable

You can even make a jar file double-clickable, so that the application it contains will run automatically. This is a function of the file-to-program associations of the operating system, and you can find the procedures described at these URLs:

MacOS X: `http://developer.apple.com/java/javatutorial/doubleclick.html`

Windows: `http://mindprod.com/jgloss/jar.html`

If any of these move about, do a web search for "jar file double-clickable" combined with the OS or window environment name. There really ought to be a tool within the JDK to create double-clickable jar files automatically, by supplying another option to jar.

Putting the jar file where Java will find it

Java looks in the directory $JAVAHOME/jre/lib/ext for jar files. You can install your programs just by placing the jar file containing them in this directory. They will be found automatically without further action on the user's part. Now, this directory is reserved for use by the Java system, and it is intended for optional system libraries that weren't bundled with the JDK. However, it is super-convenient to put jar files there while you are learning about Java. Just don't do it for any deployed applications.

Java also looks in the directory $JAVAHOME/jre/classes for a directory hierarchy containing class files that corresponds to your package hierarchy. You may have to create the classes subdirectory the first time. If your program doesn't use packages, you can just dump the .class files directly in this directory. That gets messy for more than a few files, though.

Telling Java where to look for the jar file or package roots

The JDK will look at the CLASSPATH environment variable to know where to look for top level packages/directories. CLASSPATH tells the class loader all the possible places (roots) to begin looking for Java packages to import in a compilation or to load at run-time. Other Java compiler systems may use other arrangements, and their documentation will give the details.

You set CLASSPATH to be a list of all the directories where the JDK should start looking for your top level package/directory names. For class a/b/c/D.java, we would set CLASSPATH to contain the parent directory of "a", and any other parent directories that contain the start of a package/directory path. Environment variables are shell and operating system specific, and the appendix that explains how to install the JDK also explains how shell variables are set, and how directory names are separated in the list.

Access Modifiers

It's important to know the information in this section, but you can skim through it on the first reading. It explains how we can use keywords to make things more widely or narrowly visible.

There are three or four keywords that are applied to class members. These keywords are collectively called the *access modifiers*. By default, a member is only visible to classes in its own package. Certain keywords make them visible inside the class (only), or inside the inheritance hierarchy, or to classes in other packages.

Access modifiers for a class

Class declarations can be nested inside other classes. It's a design choice you'd make when the nested class is a helper or utility for the top level class. E.g. the top level class java.lang.Character contains a nested class called java.lang.Character.UnicodeBlock.

```
package java.lang;
public class Character {    /* a top level class */
      /* lots of code */
      public class UnicodeBlock { /*a nested class*/  }
}
```

That nested class organizes and gives names to several chunks of Unicode characters. You've got your Basic Latin block, your Extended Latin block, your Greek block, your Cyrillic block, and so on all the way to the Chinese and Japanese character blocks. The UnicodeBlock class was put inside Character because it provides some services intimately tied to Character. However it is public so anyone can use it (e.g. to test if a certain character is in the range of Greek characters).

Most of the classes you write will be top level (not nested) classes. Top level classes are always visible to other classes in the same package. They are only visible in other packages when you prefix the class definition with the access modifier "public". The term "visible" means you can see and access the resource (call a method, read a field, whatever it is). Here are the two cases of visibility of a top level class:

- *If you don't use any access modifier*

  ```
  package a.b.c;
  class D {  /*some code */ }
  ```

  Class D will be visible only to classes in the same package a.b.c, (typically this means the same directory) and nowhere else.

- *If you use the* public *access modifier*

  ```
  package a.b.c;
  public class D {  /*some code */ }
  ```

  Class a.b.c.D will be visible to all packages everywhere.

Good programming practice says that you should give resources the least possible visibility compatible with them being able to carry out their work. Certainly the only public resources should be those that you intend to be part of the API of your system.

Access modifiers for a method, field, or nested class

The constructors and members of a class have finer granularity of visibility than top-level classes. That lets you fine-tune the visibility of resources beyond just the on/off that classes provide. But if a class isn't visible, then none of its members

will be either, regardless of their access modifiers. Here's a reminder of how
constructors and members look in a class.

```
package a.b.c;
public class D {
      D() { /*some code*/ }              // constructor

              // the class members
      int i;                             // data field
      int getValue() { return i; }       // method
      class mynested { /*more code*/ } // nested class
}
```

Just like top-level classes, a member might have no access modifier or the
keyword public. There are two additional modifiers for members, protected and
private, giving four cases of visibility.

- *No access modifier*

  ```
  /*no modifier*/ int getValue() { return i; }
  ```

  The member will be visible only to classes in the same package a.b.c, and
  nowhere else. This is often called "package access" because that starts
  with a "P" like the other choices. The JLS calls it "default access".

- *The* public *access modifier*

  ```
  public int getValue() { return i; }
  ```

  The member will be visible to classes in all packages everywhere.

- *The* private *access modifier*

  ```
  private int getValue() { return i; }
  ```

  The member will be visible only inside the top level class, and nowhere
  outside.

- *The* protected *access modifier*

  ```
  protected int getValue() { return i; }
  ```

  The member will be visible to classes in this package, and subclasses
  everywhere. But watch out! This does not work the way you might think.
  See the discussion of "clone" in Chapter 11.

Here is an OOP code idiom that uses access modifiers to allow read-only access to
a field:

Rationale for the "protected" access modifier

Visibility for top-level classes is simple. If you make them public, they are visible everywhere. Otherwise they are only visible to other classes in the same package.

You can't have the same simple access rules with members, though. Classes can be joined in a parent/child relationship, and the child usually needs to see all the fields of the parent.

Unless we make a special provision, any class that could be extended would need to have all its members made visible everywhere. But encapsulation demands that visibility be as restricted as possible. If we had to open up visibility everywhere to accommodate inheritance, it would conflict with encapsulation.

How it got resolved: two new access modifiers

- "protected", for potential parent classes to open up visibility of their members to their child classes, but not to others.

- "private", for classes to prevent access anywhere outside the body of this class, even by subclasses.

```
public class Employee {
    private long salary;      // field is NOT visible to other classes

    public long getSalary() { // method is visible to other classes
         return salary;
    }
    /* more code*/
}


class SomeOtherClassEntirely {

    public void main() {
        Employee e = new Employee(); /*more code*/

        long pay = e.getSalary();// gets the salary field of e
```

In the preceding example, the salary field is private and cannot be accessed outside the Employee class. However, the Employee class can define an *accessor* method that is not private and that reads the value and returns it. Accessor functions frequently occur in pairs, with the name getSomething() to read it, and setSomething(x newValue) to set it. The setSomething() method is called a *mutator* method, and is often given protected visibility. Do this when you want any class to be able to get a field, but only child classes to be able to set the field.

That finishes the discussion of visibility. On to the Light Relief!

But first the Exercises!

Exercises

1. Distinguish between class and object, member and field, primitive type and class type.

2. Write a sample program that demonstrates the compiler will not let you access a private member from another class, but that you can write a public accessor function to set the value of a private field. (Compile the first part, compile and run the second part.)

3. Write a class with a static block, some constructors, and instance initializers that print out the order in which these are executed.

4. Describe why a setSomething() method is often given protected visibility.

Some Light Relief—It's Not Your Father's IBM

Probably the biggest single supporter of Java is IBM. The largest computer company on the planet demonstrates its support with products, with research, with free downloadable code, and with open participation in the user community. IBM's Java initiative mirrors its Linux initiative. The company supports these two technologies for the same reasons: software compatibility across product lines, freedom from proprietary operating systems that IBM doesn't own, and recognition that these technologies have become a major force in IT.

IBM announced in 2000 that it would invest $1 billion in Linux, and did exactly that. In 2004, IBM announced a plan to migrate all its internal desktop PCs to Linux! This isn't "the standard is whatever we sell" IBM of a generation ago. The company is showing a new face that is lively, cooperative, and engaging. For example, to show how the Linux operating system is viable across all platforms— from large enterprise servers to the smallest embedded devices—IBM demonstrated a wristwatch-sized Linux device at a San Jose conference in August 2000 (see Figure 5–1). The wristwatch had wireless capability, and could be used to read email. It ran Linux 2.2 and the X window system!

Figure 5–1   The IBM Linux wristwatch

Now, granted a wristwatch running Linux is not the big deal today that it was in 2000, but it's a measure of IBM's commitment to Linux. On the Java side, IBM has released a large amount of useful software through its Alphaworks early release research program. One Java package that you can download from Alphaworks is the Robocode software.

Robocode is an intriguing "learn Java while having fun with a game" system. Recreational software is one of the last things I would have expected to come out of IBM! The game part is shown in the screenshot in Figure 5–2. There is a troop of robot battle tanks that roll all over the window, chasing and shooting one another. The Java part is that each tank is programmed in Java. There is a library of tank actions to change speed or direction and fire the gun. Other tanks are detected and reported asynchronously. It's wonderfully easy to get started with this software. You can have tanks clanking around blasting each other within minutes of the download, and read the documentation later!

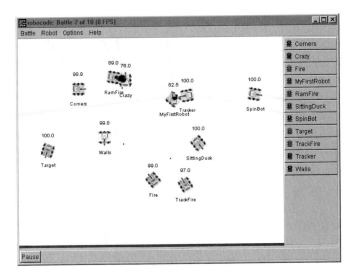

Figure 5–2   Java's Robocode

There is a simple editing and compiling environment built in so you can very quickly start programming and deploying your own robot tanks (see Figure 5–3).

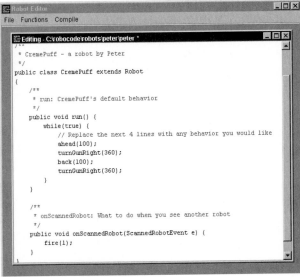

Figure 5–3   Robocode software

It is very similar to the old "Turtle Graphics" educational software, but instead of guiding a toothless old turtle that can draw a line, you control a radar-guided tank that chases down and explodes other tanks. That's *much* more educational.

You can download IBM's Java Robocode software from `robocode.alphaworks.ibm.com/home/home.html`.

Robocode is all the work of one talented guy: IBM researcher Mat Nelson. The Alphaworks site has a community bulletin board, regular software updates, and robot competitions. What are you waiting for, General Patton? Roll those tanks!

Chapter 6

Static, Final, and Enumerated Types

▼ What Field Modifier static Means

▼ What Field Modifier final Means

▼ Why Enumerate a Type?

▼ Statements Updated for Enumerations

▼ More Complicated Enumerated Types

▼ Some Light Relief—The Haunted Zen Garden of Apple

New! **E**numerated types were brought into Java with the JDK 1.5 release. They are not a new idea in programming, and lots of other languages already have them. The word "enumerate" means "to specify individually". An enumerated type is one where we specify individually (as words) all the legal values for that type.

For a type that represents t-shirt sizes, the values might be *small, medium, large, extraLarge*. For a bread flavors type, some values could be *wholewheat, ninegrain, rye, french, sourdough*. A DaysOfTheWeek enumerated type will have legal values of *Monday, Tuesday, Wednesday, Thursday, Friday, Saturday, Sunday*.

The values have to be identifiers. In the USA, ladies' dress sizes are 2, 4, 6, 8, 10, 12, 14, 16. As a Java enumeration, that would have to be represented in words as two, four, or any other characters that form an identifier, such as size2, size4 etc.

When you declare a variable that belongs to an enumerated type, it can only hold one value at a time, and it can't hold values from some other type. A t-shirt size enum variable can't hold "large" and "small" simultaneously, just as an int can't

111

hold two values simultaneously. You can't assign "Monday" to a t-shirt size variable. Though enumerated types aren't essential, they make some kinds of code more readable.

---

enum is a new keyword

Although JDK 1.5 introduced extensive language changes, "enum" is the only new keyword brought into the language. If any of your existing programs use the word "enum" as an identifier, you will have to change them before you can use JDK.5 features.

The identifier enum might well be in programs that use the older class java.util.Enumeration. That class has nothing to do with the enum type, but is a way of iterating through all the objects in a data structure class. Many people (including me) declared variables such as

```
java.util.Enumeration  enum;
```

The java.util.Enumeration class has been obsoleted by a class called Iterator, also in the java.util package, so if you're updating some code to change a variable called "enum", you might want to modify it to use an iterator too. We cover iterators in Chapter 16.

Before JDK 1.5, a common way to represent enumerations was with integer constants, like this:

```
class Bread {
    static final int wholewheat = 0;
    static final int ninegrain = 1;
    static final int rye = 2;
    static final int french = 3;
}
```

then later

```
    int todaysLoaf = rye;
```

In the new enum scheme, enumerations are references to one of a fixed set of objects that represent the various possible values. Each object representing one of the choices knows where it fits in the order, its name, and optionally other information as well. Because enum types are implemented as classes, you can add your own methods to them!

The main purpose of this chapter is to describe enumerated types in detail. To do that, we first need to explain what the *field modifiers* "static" and "final" mean. Here's the story in brief:

• The keyword `final` makes the declaration a constant.

- The keyword `static` makes the declaration belong to the class as a whole. A static field is shared by all instances of the class, instead of each instance having its own version of the field. A static method does not have a "this" object. A static method can operate on someone else's objects, but not via an implicit or explicit *this*.

  The method where execution starts, `main()`, is a static method. The purpose of `main()` is to be an entry point to your code, not to track the state of one individual object. Static "per-class" declarations are different from all the "per-object" data you have seen to date.

The values in enumerated types are always implicitly static and final. The next two sections, *What Field Modifier static Means* and *What Field Modifier final Means*, have a longer explanation of the practical effect of these field modifiers. After that, we'll get into enumerated types themselves.

What Field Modifier `static` Means

We have seen how a class defines the fields and methods that are in an object, and how each object has its own storage for these members. That is usually what you want.

Sometimes, however, there are fields of which you want only one copy, no matter how many instances of the class exist. A good example is a field that represents a total. The objects contain the individual amounts, and you want a single field that represents the total over all the existing objects of that class. There is an obvious place to put this kind of "one-per-class" field too—in a single object that represents the class. Static fields are sometimes called "class variables" because of this.

You could put a total field in every object, but when the total changes you would need to update every object. By making total a *static* field, any object that wants to reference total knows it isn't instance data. Instead it goes to the class and accesses the single copy there. There aren't multiple copies of a static field, so you can't get multiple inconsistent totals.

Static is a really poor name

Of all the many poorly chosen names in Java, "static" is the worst. The keyword is carried over from the C language, where it was applied to storage which can be allocated statically (at compile time). Whenever you see "static" in Java, think "once-only" or "one-per-class."

What you can make static

You can apply the modifier static to four things in Java:

- **Data.** This is a field that belongs to the class, not a field that is stored in each individual object.

- **Methods.** These are methods that belong to the class, not individual objects.

- **Blocks.** These are blocks within a class that are executed only once, usually for some initialization. They are like instance initializers, but execute once per class, not once per object.

- **Classes.** These are classes that are nested in another class. Static classes were introduced with JDK 1.1.

We'll describe static data and static methods in this chapter. Static blocks and static classes are dealt with later on.

Static data

Static data belongs to the class, not an individual object of the class. There is exactly one instance of static data, regardless of how many objects of the class there are. To make a field "per-class," apply the keyword "static," as shown here.

```
class Employee {
    int     id;                  // per-object field
    int     salary;              // per-object field

    static int total; // per-class field (one only)

        . . .
}
```

Every Employee object will have the employee_id and salary fields. There will be one field called totalPayroll stored elsewhere in an object representing the Employee class.

Because static data is *declared* in the class right next to the instance data, it's all too easy to overlook that static data is *not kept* in each object with its instance data. Make sure you understand this crucial point before reading on. Figure 6–1 represents the previous code in the form of a diagram.

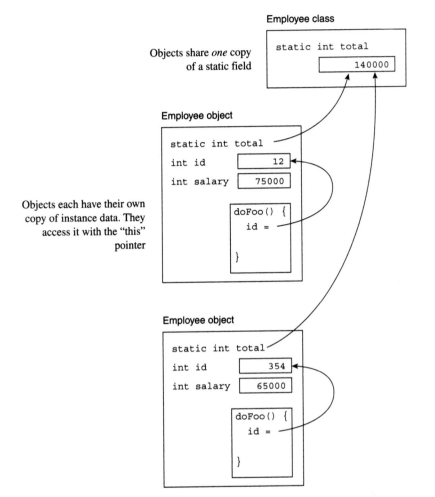

Figure 6–1   There is one copy of a Static field, shared by each object

In methods inside the class, static data is accessed by giving its name just like instance data.

```
salary = 90000;
total = this.total + this.salary;
```

It's legal but highly misleading to qualify the name of a static field with "this." The "this" variable points to an instance, but static data doesn't live in an instance. The compiler knows where the static data really is, and generates code to access the field in the class object.

Outside the class, static data can be accessed by prefixing it with the name of the class *or* the name of an object reference. It is considered poor form to use the object reference method. It confuses the reader into mistaking your static member for an instance member.

```
Employee newhire = new Employee();

// static reference through the class (preferred)
Employee.total += 100000;
```

Static methods

Just as there can be static data that belongs to the class as a whole, there can also be static methods, also called *class methods*. A class method does some class-wide operations and is not applied to an individual object. Again, these are indicated by using the static modifier before the method name.

The main() method where execution starts is static.

```
public static void main(String[] args) {
```

If main weren't static, if it were an instance method, some magic would be needed to create an instance before calling it, as is done for applets and servlets.

Any method that doesn't use instance data is a candidate to be a static method. The conversion routines in the wrappers for the primitive types are static methods. If you look at the source code for java.lang.Integer, you'll see a routine like this

```
public static int parseInt(String s)
                                throws NumberFormatException {
    // statements go here.
}
```

The method is a utility that reads the String passed to it as an argument, and tries to turn it into an int return value. It doesn't do anything with data from a specific Integer object (there isn't even an Integer object involved in the call). So parseInt() is properly declared as static. It wouldn't be actively harmful to make it an instance method, but you would then need to whisk up an otherwise unnecessary Integer object on which to invoke it. Here's an example of calling the static method parseInt:

```
int i = Integer.parseInt("-2048");
```

The Java Language Specification says "A class method is always invoked without reference to a particular object" (section 8.4.3.2). So some compilers generate an error if you invoke a static method through an instance variable. Other compilers take the view "it's OK to reach static data through an instance reference (and the JLS has an example of this), so it should be OK for static methods too". Stick to invoking static methods using the class name, to avoid compiler problems and to show other programmers that this a class method.

A common pitfall with static methods

A common pitfall is to reference *per-object* members from a *static* method. This "does not compute". A static method isn't invoked on an object and doesn't have the implicit "this" pointer to individual object data, so the compiler won't know which object you want. You'll get an error message saying "Can't make static reference to non-static variable."

Java novices often make this mistake when they write their first class with several methods. They know the `main()` method has to be static, but they try to invoke the instance methods from inside `main`. The simplest workaround is to declare an instance of the class in question inside `main()`, and invoke the methods on that.

```
class Timestamp {
    void someMethod() { // ...

    public static void main(String[] args) {
        someMethod(); // NO! does not work

        Timestamp ts = new Timestamp();
        ts.someMethod(); // Yes! does work
```

Another workaround is to add the `static` modifier to everything you reference. Only use this kludge for small test programs.

What Field Modifier `final` Means

This section looks at `final`, which makes something constant. Why was the word "const" or "constant" not chosen? Because "final" can also be applied to methods, as well as data, and the term "final" makes better sense for both.

A class or a class member (that is, a data field or a method) can be declared final, meaning that once it is given a value it won't change. We will look at what it means for a class or a method not to change in Chapter 8. A couple of final data declarations are:

```
final static int myChecksum = calculateIt();
final Timestamp noon = new Timestamp(12, 00, 00);
final int universalAnswer = 42;
```

When a reference variable is declared final, it means that you cannot change that variable to point at some other object. You can, however, access the variable and change its fields through that final reference variable. The reference is final, not the referenced object.

JDK 1.1 introduced the ability to mark method arguments and variables local to a method as final, such as:

```
void someMethod(final MyClass c, final int a[]) {
    c.field = 7;        // allowed
    a[0] = 7;           // allowed
    c = new MyClass();  // final means this line is NOT allowed
    a = new int[13];    // final means this line is NOT allowed
}
```

Programmers rarely use this, because it clutters up the signature and makes the parameter names harder to read. That's a pity. Marking a declaration as final is a clue to the compiler that certain optimizations can be made. In the case of final primitive data, the compiler can often substitute the value in each place the name is used, in an optimization known as *constant propagation*. As my friend, talented compiler-writer and builder of battle robots Brian Scearce pointed out, that in turn may lead to other optimizations becoming possible.

The "blank final variable"

JDK 1.1 also introduced something called a *blank final variable,* which is simply a final variable (of any kind) that doesn't have an initializer. A blank final variable must be assigned an initial value, and that can be assigned only once. If you give a value to a blank final in a constructor, every constructor must give it a value. This is because you don't know which constructor will be called, and it must end up with an initialization.

```
class Employee {

    final String name;// blank final variable - has no initializer

    Employee (String s) {  // constructor
        name = s;          // the blank final is initialized
    }

    // more stuff
}
```

Use a blank final when you have a value that is too complicated to calculate in a declaration, or that might cause an exception condition (more on that later), or where the final value depends on an argument to a constructor.

That completes the description of static and final. The next section, *Why Enumerate a Type?*, explains a new feature in Java, the enumerated type, which is built up from final static values.

Why Enumerate a Type?

Here's the older approach of simulating enumerations:

```
class Bread {
    static final int wholewheat = 0;
    static final int ninegrain = 1;
    static final int rye = 2;
    static final int french = 3;
}
```

You would then declare an int variable and let it hold values from the Bread class, e.g.

```
int todaysLoaf = Bread.rye;
```

Drawbacks of using ints to enumerate

Using final ints to represent values in an enumeration has at least three drawbacks.

- All the compiler tools (debugger, linker, run-time, etc.) still regard the variables as ints. They are ints. If you ask for the value of todaysLoaf, it will be 2, not "rye". The programmer has to do the mapping back and forth mentally.

- The variables aren't typesafe. There's nothing to stop todaysLoaf getting assigned a value of 99 that doesn't correspond to any Bread value. What happens next depends on how well the rest of your code is written, but the best case is that some routine notices pretty quickly and throws an exception. The worst case is that your computer-controlled bakery tries to bake "type 99" bread causing an expensive sticky mess.

- Use of integer constants makes code "brittle" (easily subject to breakage). The constants get compiled into every class that use them. If you update the class where the constants are defined, you must go and find all the users of that class, and recompile them against the new definitions. If you miss one, the code will run but be subject to subtle bugs.

How enums solve these issues

Enumerated types were introduced with JDK 1.5 to address these limitations. Variables of enumerated types

- Are displayed to the programmer or user as Strings, not numbers
- Can only hold values defined in the type
- Do not require clients to be recompiled when the enumeration changes

Enumerated types are written using a similar syntax to class declarations, and you should think of them as being a specialized sort of class. An enumerated type definition can go in a file of its own, or in a file with other classes. A public enumeration must be in a file of its own with the name matching the enumeration name.

You might create an enumerated type to represent some bread flavors. It would be defined like this:

```
enum Bread { wholewheat, ninegrain, rye, french }
```

That lets you declare variables of type Bread in the usual way:

```
Bread todaysLoaf;
```

You can assign an enum value to a variable of Bread type like this:

```
todaysLoaf = Bread.rye;
```

All the language tools know about the symbolic names. If you print out a Bread variable, you get the string value, not whatever numeric constant underlies it internally.

```
System.out.println("bread choice is: " + todaysLoaf);
```

This results in output of:

```
bread choice is: rye
```

How enums are implemented

Under the covers, enum constants are static final objects declared (by the compiler) in their enum class. An enum class can have constructors, methods, and data. Enum variables are merely pointers to one of the static final enum constant objects.

You'll understand enums better if you know that the compiler treats them approximately the same way as if it had seen this source code:

```
class Bread extends Enum {
    // constructor
    public Bread(String name, int position) { super(name, position); }

    public static final Bread wholewheat = new Bread("wholewheat",0);
    public static final Bread ninegrain = new Bread("ninegrain", 1);
    public static final Bread rye = new Bread("rye", 2);
    public static final Bread french = new Bread("french", 3);

    // more stuff here
}
```

This is an approximation because the parent class, java.lang.Enum, uses a generic parameter, and we cover generics later. Bringing generics into the definition of Enum was an unnecessary complication aimed at improving the type-safety of enums. The work could and should have been moved into the compiler. The previous code should give you a good idea of how enums are represented.

Namespaces in Java and in enumerations

Namespace isn't a term that occurs in the Java Language Specification. Instead, it's a compiler term meaning "place where a group of names are organized as a whole." Some older languages only have one global namespace that holds the names of all methods and variables. Along with each name, the compiler stores information about what type it is, and other details.

Java has many namespaces. All the members in a class form a namespace. All the variables in a method form a namespace. A package forms a namespace. Even a local block inside a method forms a namespace.

A compiler will look for an identifier in the namespace that most closely encloses it. If not found, it will look in successively wider namespaces until it finds the first occurrence of the correct identifier. You won't confuse Java if you give the same name to a method, to a data field, and to a label. It puts them in different namespaces. When the compiler is looking for a method name, it doesn't bother looking in the field namespace.

Each enumeration has its own namespace, so it is perfectly valid for enumeration values to overlap with other enums or other variables, like this:

```
enum Fruit { peach, orange, grapefruit, durian }
enum WarmColor { peach, red, orange }
```

Some more Java terminology: the enumeration values apple, red, peach, plum and orange are known as *enum constants*. The enumeration types Fruit and WarmColor are *enum types*.

Enum constants make software more reliable

Here's an amazing thing: the constants that represent the enumeration values are not compiled into other classes that use the enumeration. Instead, each enum constant (like Bread.rye previously) is left as a symbolic reference that will be linked in at run-time, just like a field or method reference.

If you compile a class that uses Bread.rye, and then later add some other bread flavors at the beginning of the enumeration (pumpernickel and oatmeal), Bread.rye will now have a different numeric value. But you do not need to recompile any classes that use the enumeration. Even better, if you remove an enum constant that is actually being used by some other class (and you forget to recompile the class where it's used), the run-time library will issue an informative error message as soon as you use the now-removed name. This is a significant boost to making Java software more reliable.

Statements Updated for Enumerations

Two statements have been changed to make them work better with enumerations: the switch statement, and the for statement.

Using a for statement with enums

Language designers want to make it easy to express the concept *"Iterate through all the values in this enumeration type"*. There was much discussion about how to modify the "for" loop statement. It was done in a clever way—by adding support for iterating through all the values in any array.

Here is the new "get all elements of an array" syntax added to the "for" statement.

```
// for each Dog object in the dogsArray[] print out the dog's name
for (Dog dog : dogsArray ){
    dog.printName();
}
```

This style of "for" statement has become known as the "foreach" statement (which is really goofy, because there is no each or foreach keyword). The colon is read as "in", so the whole thing is read as "for each dog in dogsArray". The loop variable dog iterates through all the elements in the array starting at zero.

Zermelo-Fränkel set theory and you

Keywords don't have to be reserved words. So keywords don't have to be prohibited for use as identifiers. A compiler can look at the tokens around a keyword and decide whether it is being used as a keyword or an identifier. This is called *context-sensitive parsing*.

I would have preferred an actual keyword "in" rather than punctuation, but the colon has been used this way in Zermelo-Fränkel set theory by generations of mathematicans. It's just syntactic sugar. And if we've always done something this way, hey, don't not go for it.

Using the new foreach feature, we can now write a very brief program that echoes the arguments from the command line. The command line arguments (starting after the main class name) are passed to main() in the String array parameter. We print it out like this:

```
public class echo {
    public static void main( String[] args) {
        for (String i : args )
            System. out. println("arg = " + i);
    }
}
```

Compiling and running the program with a few arguments gives this:

```
javac -source 1.5 -target 1.5 echo. java

java echo test data here
arg = test
arg = data
arg = here
```

Note: The final decision on whether to have a "-source 1.5" compiler option and what it should look like had not been made when this book went to press. See the website www.afu.com/jj6 for the latest information. You can set it up in a batch file so you don't have to keep typing it.

The same for loop syntax can be used for enums if you can somehow get the enum constants into an array. And that's exactly how it was done. Every enum type that you define automatically brings into existence a class method called values().

The values() method for enums

The values() method is created on your behalf in every enum you define. It has a return value of an array, with successive elements containing the enum values. That can be used in for loops as the example shows:

```
for (Bread b : Bread.values() ) {

    // b iterates through all the Bread enum constants
    System.out.println("bread type = " + b);

}
```

In addition to the enum constants that you write, the enum type can contain other fields. The values() method is one of them. Bread.values() is a call to a class method belonging to the Bread enum. The method is invoked on the enum class type Bread, not on an instance, so we can conclude it must be a class method.

You can even iterate through a subrange of an enum type. The class java.util.EnumSet has a method called range() that takes various arguments, and returns a value suitable for use in the expanded for statement.

You would use it like this:

```
public class Example {
    enum Month {Jan, Feb, Mar, Apr, May, Jun, Jul, Aug, Sep, Oct, Nov, Dec }
    public static void main(String[] args) {

        for (Month m : java.util.EnumSet.range(Month.Jun, Month.Aug) )
                System.out.println("summer includes: " + m );
    }
}
```

When compiled and run, that prints:

```
summer includes: Jun
summer includes: Jul
summer includes: Aug
```

The method range() belonging to class EnumSet returns, not an array (as you might guess), but an object of type EnumSet. The "for" statement has been modified to accept an array *or* an EnumSet in this kind of loop (it can accept a Collection class too).

Modifying the "for" loopto allow a special type here was done as a concession to performance improvement. An EnumSet is a collection class that can hold multiple enum constants from any one enum type. They don't have to be a consecutive range of enum constants. If there are 64 or fewer enum constants in the set, it will store the set as a long word of bits, and not as an array of references. This makes it very fast to tell if an enum constant is in or out of the set, and very fast to iterate through a range of enum constants.

Using a switch statement with enums

You can now use an enum type in a "switch" statement (Java's name for the case statement used in other languages). Formerly, the switch expression had to be an int type. Here's an example that uses an enum in a switch statement.

```
Bread myLoaf = Bread.rye;
int price = 0;

switch (myLoaf) {
    case wholewheat: price = 190;
                     break;

    case     french: price = 200;
                     break;

    case ninegrain: price = 250;
                    break;

            case rye: price = 275;
                      break;
}

System.out.println( myLoaf + " costs " + price);
```

The "break" statement causes the flow of control to transfer to the end of the switch. Without that, program execution drops through into the next case clause. Running the program gives the output:

```
rye costs 275
```

The enum value in the case switch label must be an unqualified name. That is, you must write "rye" and not "Bread. rye". That (unfortunately) contrasts with an assignment to an enum variable. In an assignment:

```
myLoaf = Bread.rye;
```

you must use the qualified name Bread.rye, unless you import the type name.

Dropping the need to qualify names—import

We mentioned above that you must use the qualified name, such as Bread.rye, *unless you import the type name.* This section explains how to do that, using a wordy example from the digital clock in Chapter 2. That program had a statement saying:

```
this.setDefaultCloseOperation(javax.swing.WindowConstants.EXIT_ON_CLOSE);
```

The statement is setting how the window should behave when the user clicks on the close icon on the title bar. There's a choice of four alternatives, ranging from "ignore it" to "terminate the program". The alternatives are represented by integer constants in class WindowConstants, which is part of package javax.swing. Here is the source code from the Java run-time library, defining those constants:

```
public static final int DO_NOTHING_ON_CLOSE = 0;
public static final int HIDE_ON_CLOSE = 1;
public static final int DISPOSE_ON_CLOSE = 2;
public static final int EXIT_ON_CLOSE = 3;
```

Those could be better expressed as an enum type, but this code was written long before Java supported enum types. It would be nice if the programmer using those constants didn't have to mention the lengthy names of the package and subpackage they come from.

That's exactly what the "import" statement gives you. The import statement has been part of Java from the beginning. It lets a programmer write this:

```
import java.swingx.*;    // import all classes in package java.swingx
```

or

```
import java.swingx.WindowConstants;  // import this class
```

The "import" statements (if any) appear at the top of the source file, right after the optional line that says what package this file belongs to. The imports apply to all the rest of the file. The import statement brings into your namespace one or more classes from a package. The import with the asterisk is meant to be like a wildcard in a file name. It means "import all classes from the package". So "import javax.swing.*;" means you can drop the "javax.swing" qualifier from class names from the javax.swing package.

The second version, importing a single class, means that you do not have to qualify that one class with its package name at each point you mention it.

Import is purely a compile time convenience feature. It does not make a class visible that was not visible before. It does not make any change to the amount of code that is linked into your executable. It just lets you refer to a class without qualifying it with the full name of the package it is in.

Either of these imports would allow us to cut down our "close window" statement to:

```
this.setDefaultCloseOperation( WindowConstants.EXIT_ON_CLOSE );
```

Using "import static"

We are still required to mention the class name, and this is where the new feature of *static import* comes in. JDK 1.5 adds the ability to import the static members from a class, or the enum values from an enum type. It is analogous to the ordinary import statement, and it looks like this:

```
import static qualified_class_name.*;
```

or

```
import static qualified_enum_name.*;
```

So you can now write

```
import static javax.swing.WindowConstants.*;
   /* more code */
  this.setDefaultCloseOperation(EXIT_ON_CLOSE);
```

The *this* can be implicit, so what started out as

```
this.setDefaultCloseOperation(javax.swing.WindowConstants.EXIT_ON_CLOSE);
```

can now be written as

```
import static javax.swing.WindowConstants.*;
   //  lots more code here
setDefaultCloseOperation(EXIT_ON_CLOSE);
```

Similarly, using enums and static import we can write:

```
import static mypackage.Bread.* ;
     // more code here

     Bread myLoaf = rye;
```

You can import just one enum value or static member, by appending its name instead of using the "*" to get all of them. Don't forget that to compile anything with the new JDK 1.5 features, you need to use these options on the command line:

```
javac -source 1.5 -target 1.5 sourcefiles.java
```

You can use import static on the System class to shorten the name of the utility that does console I/O. Before import static, I used to create an alias like this:

```
java.io.PrintStream o = System.out;
o.println("hello Bob");
```

Now you can "import static" instead.

```
import static java.lang.System.out; /* more code omitted */
out.println("hello Bob");
```

The compiler is quite capable of figuring out whether you are importing a static member or a classname within a package, so the "import static" keywords could have been left as just the old "import" keyword. It was considered better to remind the programmer that only static members can be imported, not instance members.

What if you import static WarmColors and Fruits? You can do this (they will need to be in a named package, not the default anonymous package used in the examples). But any place where you use one of the named constants whose name is duplicated, you will have to provide the full qualified name:

```
Fruit f = Fruit.peach;
Fruit f2 =      apple;  // unique name, so no qualifier needed.
```

At this point we've covered everything relating to enums that you'll see 99% of the time. There is some more material, but you can safely skip the rest of the chapter, and return when you have some specific enum construct to decode.

More Complicated Enumerated Types

Since enums are effectively classes, you can do pretty much everything with them that you can do with a class. In particular, you can provide one or more constructors for an enum type! That may seem a little weird to you (it does to me), because you never call an enum constructor anywhere in your code, or use the "new" operator to instantiate an enum. The definition of an enum brings the class enum constants into existence. You always work with static fields of an enum, not instances.

You might want to write a constructor when you have enumerations with a close relationship to numeric values. An example is an enumeration of hens' egg sizes, shown in Table 6–1. In the U.S., these are the names and weights associated with eggs:

Table 6–1   U.S. names and weights associated with eggs

Name	weight per dozen
Jumbo	30 oz
Extra large	27 oz
Large	24 oz

Adding constructors to your enums

We're going to create an enum class called egg, with enum constants of jumbo, etc. You can tie arbitrary data to each enum constant by writing a constructor for the enum class. In other circumstances, a constructor has the same name as the class, so you'd expect it to be called egg here. And indeed it is, but that's not the full story. You declare an enum constant (jumbo, etc) and that *name declaration* is regarded as a *call* to your constructor. You may pass data values as arguments to the call. Arguments are passed in the usual way, by enclosing the comma-separated list in parentheses.

Putting it together, the enum now looks like this:

```
enum egg {
            // the enum constants, which "call" the constructor
            jumbo(30.0),
            extraLarge(27.0),
            large(24.0);

            egg(double w) {weight=w;} // constructor

            private double weight;

}
```

The beta JDK 1.5 compiler requires the enum constants to come before the constructor. There's no good reason for that and I filed it as a bug, but no word yet on whether Sun sees it the same way. As well as constructors, you can add practically any methods or data fields in an enum class. The "private" keyword makes a member inaccessible from outside the class. So you probably want to add this method to the enum to be able to retrieve the weight of an enum variable:

```
double getWeight() { return this.weight; }
```

Here's a small main program that uses the enum, and prints out the weight for jumbo eggs.

```
public class bigegg {
    public static void main( String[] args) {
        egg e = egg.jumbo;
        double wt = e. getWeight();
        System.out.println( e + " eggs weigh "+ wt +" oz. per doz.");
    }
}
```

Running the code gives this output:

```
jumbo eggs weigh 30.0oz. per doz.
```

The language specification guarantees that all enum constants are unique. There may be two different reference variables pointing to Bread.rye, but there are never two different Bread.rye enum constants. That ensures programmers can compare enums using e == Bread.rye as well as e.equals(Bread. rye).

You need to avoid declaring any members in your enums with names that duplicate those in java.lang.Enum. The box below has a list of most of the methods. The compiler will tell you if you make this mistake.

Predefined members that belong to every enum
The compiler automatically creates several other members in addition to values() in every enum class. These additional members help the enum do its work. The compiler will warn you if you re-use one of these names. Furthermore, each enum type is regarded as a child of class java.lang.Enum, and therefore inherits those methods from there too. Some of the methods in java.lang.Enum are:

```
public int compareTo( Enum e );
// returns negative, 0, positive for this earlier, equal, or later
// in declaration order than e

public int ordinal();
// returns the position of the enum constant in the
// declaration, first enum constant is at position 0

public static EnumType valueOf( java.lang.Class ec, String s );
// turns a String into its corresponding enum constant
// the ec argument is the class object of the enum type we are using

public boolean equals( Object o );
// returns true when this equals the enum specified by Object o.
```

Instance methods and enum variables
We mentioned back at the start of the chapter that enum types are implemented as classes, so you can add your own methods to them. Here's an example showing how you can do that:

```
enum Month {
    Jan, Feb, Mar, Apr, May, Jun, Jul, Aug, Sep, Oct, Nov, Dec;

    int days() {
        if ((this==Sep)|(this==Apr)|(this==Jun)|(this==Nov)) return 30;
        if (this==Feb)
            throw new UnsupportedOperationException("need leap year status");
        return 31;
    }
}
```

We added the method days() to enum Month. It returns a count of the number of days in the month, except for Feb when it will throw an exception. That's a lame response, but better than allowing the day count to be wrong. What this says is that the days() method should not be part of the enum Month (in real world code), because it does not have enough information to do its job.

You can declare an enum variable like this:

```
Month easterMonth;
```

You can use it like this:

```
// Easter is always between March 22 and April 25
easterMonth = calcMonthOfEaster(); // this method not shown!
if (easterMonth == Month.Mar )   /* do something*/ ;

if (easterMonth.days() != 31)    /* do something else */ ;
```

Constant-specific class bodies

There's only one more aspect of enums to cover, and it's something that you will encounter rarely in practice: a feature known as constant-specific class bodies. We've seen previously how enums are implemented in terms of classes, and how they can have their own constructors, methods and data, as well as the enum constants.

Going a step beyond this, each enum constant in an enum type can be given its own class body. You write it as the enum constant name followed by a block like this

```
{ body_of_a_class }
```

and anything that can appear in a class can go in that body.

This kind of class body attached to an enum constant is called a constant-specific class body, and it is regarded as an anonymous (cannot be referred to by a name) class that extends the enum type. When a child class extends a parent, it may provide its own version of a method with the same signature in the parent. This process of replacing a method is known as *overriding*. In particular, an instance method in a constant-specific class body will override an instance method of the same signature that belongs to the enum type. Phew!

Here's an example, building on the basic egg enum:

```
enum egg {

    large { /* this is a constant-specific class body*/ },
    extraLarge { /* so is this, and they are empty*/ },
    jumbo { /* yep, same here*/ };

    public double recipeEquivalent() { return 1.0; }
}
```

The example shows three enum constants, each with an empty constant-specific class body. The enum type also has an instance method called `recipeEquivalent()`.

As you may know, when a recipe calls for eggs, it always means large eggs[1]. We are going to override the enum type method `recipeEquivalent()` and provide a constant specific method that gives the "scaling factor" for jumbo and extra large eggs. To make your recipes come out right, you need to use fractions of eggs when using the bigger eggs. The method `recipeEquivalent()` provides the scaling factor for each egg size.

Referring back to table 6-1, by weight,

  1 large egg == (1extra-large egg * 24/ 27) == (1 jumbo egg * 24/ 30).

That can be expressed in the code like this:

```
enum egg {
    large,
    extraLarge { public double recipeEquivalent(){ return 24.0/ 27.0; }},
    jumbo { public double recipeEquivalent(){ return 24.0/ 30.0; }};

    public double recipeEquivalent() { return 1.0; }
}
```

There are other ways to get the same effect of scaling different egg sizes. This example is meant to show how you might use a constant-specific class body. Here's a main program to test the feature:

```
public class eggtest {
    public static void main( String[] args) {
        System.out.println(" when the recipe calls for 1 egg, use:");
        for (egg e : egg.values() ) {
            System.out.printf("%f %s eggs %n", e.recipeEquivalent(), e );
        }
    }
}
```

1.   If you didn't know this, I don't want to eat sponge cake at your house.

The result of compiling and running that code is:

```
when the recipe calls for 1 egg, use:
1.00 large eggs
0.88 extraLarge eggs
0.80 jumbo eggs
```

Note the use of the new `printf()` method. Chapter 17 has the full details. Remember to add an option on the command line to compile these new features:

```
javac -source 1.5 egg.java eggtest.java
```

Finally, if your enums start to sprout constructors, methods, constant specific bodies and instance data, maybe your enum type should just be a class in the first place.

Some Light Relief—The Haunted Zen Garden of Apple

I've always made a point of exploring new and unfamiliar places, particularly when I'm trying a new shortcut and forgot to bring the map with me. My colleague Lefty is just the opposite. Lefty (who I taught to count on his fingers in binary—you can count up to 1023 that way) likes to stick to paths so well beaten they are practically pulverized.

Lefty and I were on the Apple Computer campus in Cupertino, California. If you know the area, we were in the Bandley 3 building, and late for a meeting in nearby De Anza 7. You can almost see these two buildings from each other, so I was practically sure that if we jogged through the parking lots as the crow flies, we'd get to De Anza 7 in the shortest amount of time.

"I hope you're not trying one of your shortcuts," accused Lefty as he sprinted behind me, vaulting over fences and bushes. "Don't be ridiculous!" I retorted. We would have arrived almost on time too, if my shortcut hadn't taken us through a small and mysterious grove of trees at the side of the De Anza 7 parking lot. Lefty ran into the grove, then straight into a large waist-high stone.

Figure 6–2   The Haunted Zen Garden of Apple (De Anza 7 in background)

The big southpaw went down with a curse that would curl the hair of a software architect. While he threshed on the ground, mouthing incoherent criticism of me and shortcuts, I examined the stone with interest. It appeared to be a tombstone covered in Japanese writing.

I tried to redirect his attention to the mysterious stone "Check this out Lefty," I noted, "It's just like that slab on Jupiter in 2001!". His reply cannot be printed in a text that family members may read. Looking around more widely, I was very surprised to see that the grove was an abandoned Zen garden. My first thought was to wonder if the tombstone meant the Zen garden was haunted, cursed, or at least full of bugs.

A mystery like this needs a solution. Even if it doesn't, it's going to get one. The first theory was that the haunted Zen garden had been created by an Apple executive who'd fallen prey to the "Japan does everything better" management fad of the month. But nobody at Apple wanted to confess to knowing anything about *that*.

To cut a long story short, the true story became clear when I got the stone inscription translated. It reads:

"This place has been cultivated by Ernest and Lillian Wanaka as part of the Cupertino Nursery since 1947. The Wanakas have dreamed of creating an elegant Japanese Garden at this tranquil land that can be viewed from their residence. At last they decided to start working on the dream. The completed garden was opened in 1954 as a place of contemplation for Cupertino citizens."

The rest of the story soon emerged. The property all around was formerly owned by the Japanese Wanaka family of Cupertino, who lived on it and tended it as a nursery. When Apple bought the land from them, a clause in the contract stipulated that the Zen garden had to be left in place in perpetuity. (Lefty gasped at this bit, and pointed out that Apple could park another 15 cars in the space the garden occupied. Lefty is a very practical person.) The abandoned Zen garden is more than 50 years old, and predates the Macintosh, Apple, and Silicon Valley itself.

The abandoned Zen garden remains there today, at the corner of De Anza 7. That building was at one time the hub of executive power at Apple. As some used to joke, De Anza 7 was "where the rubber meets the air". The stone that tripped Lefty wasn't a tombstone on unhallowed ground; it was a dedication in a garden. If that land is haunted, it is only by the spirits of past Apple executives like Sculley, Spindler, Yocom, Graziano, Sullivan, Stead, and Eisenstat.

"Why doesn't Apple pay a gardening service to keep up the garden?" Lefty asked.

I thought about how you can't pay someone to maintain a Zen garden for you. That would be karma-lama-ding-dong. The point of a Zen garden is that you maintain it yourself and rake the sand around the rocks according to your meditations of the day. Today all the Zen is in the Apple products, not in the parking lots.

"There are no shortcuts to Zen, Lefty" I loftily replied.

Chapter 7

Names, Operators, and Accuracy

- ▼ KEYWORDS
- ▼ PUNCTUATION TERMINOLOGY
- ▼ NAMES
- ▼ IDENTIFIERS
- ▼ EXPRESSIONS
- ▼ ARRAYS
- ▼ OPERATORS
- ▼ ASSOCIATIVITY
- ▼ HOW ACCURATE ARE CALCULATIONS?
- ▼ WIDENING AND NARROWING CONVERSIONS
- ▼ WHAT HAPPENS ON OVERFLOW?
- ▼ SOME LIGHT RELIEF—FURBY'S BRAIN TRANSPLANT

This chapter covers more of the language basics. The information here follows a progression: first, the basics of names and identifiers, then how names are connected in expressions by operators, followed by the rules to evaluate expressions.

The last part of the chapter describes practical limits on accuracy, casting and conversions. If you are new to floating point arithmetic, some of this may come as a bit of a shock. The chapter finishes up by presenting the standard class java.lang.Math.

135

Keywords

Keywords are reserved words, which means they cannot be used as identifiers. Java now has 50 keywords ("enum" became a keyword in JDK 1.5). These are the keywords.

abstract	continue	for	new	switch
assert	default	goto	package	synchronized
boolean	do	if	private	this
break	double	implements	protected	throw
byte	else	import	public	throws
case	enum	instanceof	return	transient
catch	extends	int	short	try
char	final	interface	static	void
class	finally	long	strictfp	volatile
const	float	native	super	while

The keywords `const` and `goto` are reserved words, even though they are not used anywhere in Java. This allows future expansion, or (unlikely but claimed) better diagnostic messages if a programmer uses them in a way they might be used in C++.

The words "true" and "false" look like keywords, but technically they are boolean literals. Similarly,"null" looks like it should be in the keyword list, but it is technically the null literal for reference types. The classification of these three words as literals, not keywords, doesn't have any subtle side effects, and it keeps the type system a bit cleaner.

Punctuation Terminology

You might find it useful to refer back to this table in the chapters ahead.

These characters are called parentheses: ( ). They go around expressions and parameter lists.

These characters are called square brackets: [ ]. They go around array indexes.

These characters are called braces or curly braces: { }. They indicate the start and end of a new block of code, or an array literal.

These characters are called angle brackets: < >. They go around generic parameters.

The ellipsis token ... came into Java in JDK 1.5. It indicates the last argument to a method is a sequence of objects.

Names

What is the difference between an *identifier* and a *name?* An identifier is just a sequence of letters and digits that don't match a keyword or the literals "true," "false," or "null." A name, on the other hand, can be prefixed with any number of further identifiers to pin-point the namespace from which it comes. An identifier is thus the simplest form of name. The general case of name looks like the following:

```
package1.Package2.PackageN.Class1.NestedClass2.NestedClassM.memberN
```

Since packages can be nested in packages, and classes nested in classes, there can be an arbitrary number of identifiers separated by periods, as in:

```
java.lang.System.out.println( "goober" );
```

That name refers to the java.lang package. There are several packages in the java hierarchy, and java.lang is the one that contains basic language support. One of the classes in the java.lang package is System. The class System contains a field that is an object of the PrintStream class, called out. PrintStream supports several methods, including one called `println()` that takes a `String` as an argument. It's a way to get text sent to the standard output of a program.

By looking at a lengthy name in isolation, you can't tell where the package identifiers stop and the class and member identifiers start. You have to do the same kind of evaluation that the compiler does. Since the namespaces are hierarchical, if you have two identifiers that are the same, you can say which you mean by providing another level of name. This is called *qualifying the name.* For example, if you define your own class called BitSet, and you also want to reference the class of the same name that is in the java.util package, you can distinguish them like this:

```
            BitSet myBS = new BitSet();
    java.util.BitSet theirBS = new java.util.BitSet();
```

java.util qualifies the class name BitSet.

Identifiers

Identifiers are the names provided by the programmer, and can be any length in Java. They must start with a letter, underscore, or dollar sign, and in subsequent positions can also contain digits.

A letter that can be used for a Java identifier doesn't just mean uppercase and lowercase A–Z. It means any of the tens of thousands of Unicode letters from any of the major languages in the world including Bengali letters, Cyrillic letters, or

Bopomofo symbols. Every Unicode character above hex 00C0 is legal in an identifier. Legal Java identifiers shows some example valid Java identifiers.

Table 7–1   Legal Java identifiers

calories	Häagen_Dazs	déconnage
_99	Puñetas	fottío
i	$_	p

The more accented characters you use in your variable names, the harder it is for others to edit them and maintain the code. So you should stick to the simple ASCII characters.

When a field or method can be forward-referenced

A forward reference is the use of a name before that name has been defined, as in the following:

```
class Fruit {
    void setWeight() { grams = 22; } // grams not yet declared

    int grams;
}
```

The example shown compiles with no problem. You can declare fields in any order, with one exception. The rule of thumb is that the compiler needs to see a field before it is used in the initialization of another field:

```
int i = grams;
```

The declaration of grams would have to appear before the int i declaration. The actual rule is somewhat more complicated, involving cases of nested classes (JLS section 8.3.2.3), but if you follow the rule of thumb you'll avoid the complexities. It is intended to avoid circular initializations.

When a class can be forward-referenced

A class can always be forward-referenced. The declaration of a class generally doesn't need to appear before the use of that class, as long as the compiler finds it at some point during compilation.

This is another benefit of "object variables are really pointers". The compiler already knows how much memory to allocate for the object reference (one pointer's worth), and it knows how to reach members through the reference. It doesn't know how much space to allocate for the object itself, nor what the offsets of the members are, and it doesn't need to know this, because everything is accessed indirectly.

Expressions

There's a lengthy chapter in the Java Language Specification on expressions, covering many cases that would be interesting only to language lawyers. What it boils down to is that an expression is any of the alternatives shown in Table 7–2.

Table 7–2   Expressions in Java

Expression	Example of expression
A literal	245
this object reference	this
A field access	now.hh
A method call	now.fillTimes()
An object creation	new Timestamp(12, 0, 0)
An array creation	new int[27]
An array access	myArray[i][j]
Any expression connected by operators	now.mins / 60
Any expression in parens	(now.millisecs * 1000)

You *evaluate* an expression, to get a result that will be:

- A variable (as in evaluating this gives you an object you can store into), or

- A value, or

- Nothing (a void expression). You get nothing as the result when you call a method with a return value of void.

An expression can appear on either side of an assignment. If it is on the left-hand side of an assignment, the result designates where the evaluated right-hand side should be stored. Here's an example:

```
myArray[i][j] = now.hh + 12;
```

The expression on the lefthand side of the assignment is evaluated, meaning that we take the name myArray, calculate index i, go to that element, take the array reference there, calculate index j, go to that element, and that place is where we will store the result that we will get from evaluating the expression on the righthand side.

The type of an expression is either known at compile time or checked at run-time to be compatible with whatever you are doing with the expression. There is no escape from strong typing in Java.

Here's an example of an expression whose type is not known until run-time. We know o is an object, but we don't know what type it actually holds.

```
Object o;
if (Math.random() > 0.5)
     o = new int[7];
else o = new String("surprise!");
```

Arrays

This is just a confirmation that Java has arrays. When you see a pair of square brackets like this [ ], it always means you're dealing with an array. The full description of arrays has its own chapter, Chapter 9.

An example array is the set commandline arguments, which is passed to the main() routine as an array of Strings.

```
void main(String[] args) { /* code */ }
```

The individual elements in an array can be any type: primitive or reference type. The array as a whole is an object in Java. That means array types are reference types, and an array variable is really a reference to an array object.

Operators

An *operator* is a punctuation mark that says to do something to two (or three) *operands*. An example is the expression "a * b". The "*" is the multiplication operator, and "a" and "b" are the operands. Most of the operators in Java will be readily familiar to any programmer.

One unusual aspect is that the order of operand evaluation in Java is well-defined. For many older languages, the order of evaluation was been deliberately left unspecified to allow the compiler-writer more freedom. In other words, in C and C++, the following operands can be evaluated and added together in any order:

```
i + myArray[i] + functionCall();
```

The function may be called before, during (on adventurous multiprocessing hardware), or after the array reference is evaluated, and the additions may be executed in any order. If the functionCall() adjusts the value of i, the overall result depends on the order of evaluation. The trade-off is that some programs give different results depending on the order of evaluation. A professional programmer would consider such programs to be badly written, but they exist nonetheless.

The order of evaluation was left unspecified in earlier languages so that compiler-writers could reorder operations to optimize register use. Java makes the trade-off in a different place. It recognizes that getting consistent results on all computer systems is a much more important goal than getting varying results a trifle faster on one system. In practice, the opportunities for speeding up expression evaluation through reordering operands seem to be quite limited in many programs. As processor speed and cost improve, it is appropriate that modern languages optimize for programmer sanity instead of performance.

Java specifies not just left-to-right operand evaluation, but the order of everything else, too, such as:

- The left operand is evaluated before the right operand of a binary operator. This is true even for the assignment operator, which must evaluate the left operand (where the result will be stored) fully before starting any part of evaluating the right operand (what the result is).

- An array access has this general form:

  `ArrayInstance[index1] [indexN]`

  The `ArrayInstance` expression before the square brackets is fully evaluated before any part of the indexes in square brackets are evaluated. This can make a difference if any of these expressions involves calling a method that has side effects, such as changing the value of an index expression that has not yet been evaluated. The indexes are evaluated one by one from left to right.

- A method call for an object has this general form:

  `objectInstance.methodName(arguments);`

  The `objectInstance` is fully evaluated before the `methodName` and `arguments`. This can make a difference if the objectInstance is the return value from a method that has side effects, such as changing the value of one of the arguments. Any arguments are evaluated one by one from left to right.

The Java Language Specification 2nd Edition (James Gosling, Bill Joy, and Guy L. Steele, Addison-Wesley, 2000) uses the phrase, "Java guarantees that the operands to operators *appear to be* evaluated from left-to-right." This is an escape clause that allows clever compiler-writers to do brilliant optimizations, as long as the appearance of left-to-right evaluation is maintained.

For example, if some subexpressions is repeated in the same basic block, like this subexpression "x+10" on both the left and right hand side of the assignment,

```
a[ x*10 + y ] = x*10;
```

a clever compiler-writer might be able to arrange for the reuse of the first time it was calculated, instead of going through all the steps to calculate it again. In general, because of complications involving infinity and not-a-number (NaN) results, floating-point operands cannot be trivially reordered.

Note that the usual operator precedence still applies. In an expression like the following, the multiplication is always done before the addition.

```
b + c * d
```

The Java order of evaluation says that for all binary (two argument) operators, the left operand is always fully evaluated before the right operand. Therefore, the operand "b" in the previous example must be evaluated before the multiplication is done (because the multiplied result is the right operand to the addition).

Left-to-right evaluation means in practice that all operands in an expression (if they are evaluated at all) are evaluated in the left-to-right order in which they are written down on a page. Sometimes an evaluated result must be stored while a higher precedence operation is performed. Although *The Java Language Specification* only talks about the apparent order of evaluation of operands to individual operators, this is a necessary consequence of the rules.

Java operators

The Java operators and their precedence are shown in Table 7–3. The arithmetic operators are undoubtedly familiar to the reader. We'll outline the other operators in the next section.

Table 7–3   **Java operators and their precedence**

Symbol	Note	Precedence (highest number= highest precedence)	COFFEEPOT Property (see *Associativity*)
++ --	pre-increment, decrement	16	right
++ --	post-increment, decrement	15	left
~	flip the bits of an integer	14	right
!	logical not (reverse a boolean)	14	right
- +	arithmetic negation, plus	14	right
(typename)	type conversion (cast)	13	right
* / %	multiplicative operators	12	left
- +	additive operators	11	left
<< >> >>>	left and right bitwise shift	10	left
instanceof < <= > >=	relational operators	9	left
== !=	equality operators	8	left
&	bitwise and	7	left
^	bitwise exclusive or	6	left

Table 7–3   Java operators and their precedence *(cont.)*

Symbol	Note	Precedence (highest number= highest precedence)	COFFEEPOT Property (see *Associativity*)
|	bitwise inclusive or	5	left
&&	conditional and	4	left
||	conditional or	3	left
? :	conditional operator	2	right
= *= /= %=	assignment operators	1	right
+= -=			
<<= >>= >>>=			
&= ^= |=			

Char is considered to be an arithmetic type that only ever holds positive values. It is a 16-bit integer whose bit patterns run from 0 to 0xFFFF, which is 65535 in base ten.

The ++ and -- operators

The pre- and post-increment and decrement operators are shorthand for the common operation of adding or subtracting one from an arithmetic type. You write the operator next to the operand, and the variable is adjusted by one. These are all equivalent ways of increasing the value of i by one:

```
i = i+1;  // expression assignment
i += 1;   // assignment operator
++i;      // pre-increment
i++;      // post-increment
```

The pre- and post-increment operators can appear in the middle of an expression, whereas the two assignments cannot. Pre- and post- differ if you bury the operator in the middle of a larger expression, like this:

```
int result = myArray[++i]; // pre-increment
```

The pre-increment here will increment i *before* using it as the index. The post-increment version will use the current value of i, and after it has been used, add one to it. It makes a very compact notation. Pre- and post-decrement operators (--i) work in a similar way.

The % and / operators

The division operator "/" is regular division on integer types and floating point types. Integer division just cuts off any decimal part, so -9/2 is -4.5 which is cut to -4. This is also (less meaningfully) termed "rounding towards zero."

The remainder operator "%" means "what is left over after dividing by the right operand a whole number of times." Thus, -7%2 is -1. This is because -7 divided by 2 is -3, with -1 left over.

Some people call "%" the modulus operator, so "-7 % 2" can be read as "-7 modulo 2". If you have trouble remembering what modulo does, it may help to recall that all integer arithmetic in Java is modular, meaning that the answer is modulo the range. If working with 32 bits, the answer is that part of the mathematically correct answer that fits in a 32-bit range. If working with 64 bits, the answer is that part of the answer that fits in 64 bits. If doing "-8 modulo 3", the answer is that remainder part of the division answer that fits in 3, i.e., -2.

The equality shown below is true for division and remainder on integer types:

```
(x / y) * y + x%y == x
```

If you need to work out what sign some remainder will have, just plug the values into that formula.

The << >> and >>> operators

In Java the ">>" operator does an arithmetic or signed shift right, meaning that the sign bit is propagated. In C, it has always been implementation-defined whether this was a logical shift (fill with 0 bits) or an arithmetic shift (fill with copies of the sign bit). This occasionally caused grief, as programmers discovered the implementation dependency when debugging or porting a system. Here's how you use the operator in Java:

```
int eighth = x >> 3; // shift right 3 times same as div by 8
```

One Java operator not in other languages is ">>>" which means "shift right and zero fill" or "unsigned shift" (do not propagate the sign bit). The ">>>" operator is not very useful in practice. It works as expected on numbers of canonical size, ints, and longs.

It is broken, however, for short and byte, because negative operands of these types are promoted to int with sign propagation before the shift takes place, leaving bits 7-or-15 to 31 as ones. The zero fill thus starts at bit 31, and doesn't show up in the original byte or short. So >>> is completely useless for non-canonical types, and best avoided.

If you want to do unsigned shift on a short or a byte, mask the bits you want and use >>.

```
byte b = -1;
b = (byte)((b & 0xff) >> 4);
```

That way programs won't mysteriously stop working when someone changes a type from int to short.

The instanceof *Operator*

The other new operator is instanceof. We've seen in several places how a class can be set up as a subclass of another class. The instanceof operator is used with superclasses to tell if you have a particular subclass object. For example, we may see the following:

```
class vehicle { /* some code */ }
class car extends vehicle { /* some code */ }
class convertible extends car { /* some code */ }

vehicle v; /* some code */ }
convertible c;
if (v instanceof convertible)
    c = (convertible) v;
```

The instanceof operator returns true or false depending on whether the object is actually of the class you mention. The operation is often followed by a statement that casts the object from the base type to the subclass. Before attempting the cast, instanceof lets us check that it is valid. There is more about this in the next chapter.

The & | and ^ operators

The "&" operator takes two boolean operands, or two integer operands. It always evaluates both operands. For booleans, it ANDs the operands, producing a boolean result. For integer types, it bitwise ANDs the operands, producing a result that is the promoted type of the operands (type long if you are working with longs, otherwise int).

To illustrate the & operator and the >> shift operator, you can get the two nibbles out of a byte with this code.

```
byte byteMe = someValue;
byte loNibble = (byte) (byteMe & 0x0F);
```

The low nibble (least significant 4 bits) are extracted by ANDing the byte with a literal that has the lowest four bits set. The high nibble (most significant 4 bits) are extracted by shifting the byte right four bits (to move the bits to the low end), and doing the AND again.

```
byte hiNibble = (byte) ((byteMe >> 4) & 0x0F);
```

If that looks like a lot of casting to (byte), the section called *Widening and Narrowing Conversions* on page 152 explains why it is needed.

" | " is the corresponding bitwise OR operation.

"^" is the corresponding bitwise XOR operation. In case you're wondering XOR is used in some graphics operations, and it's included mainly because it's cheap to do so.

The && and || Operators

The "&&" is a conditional AND that takes only boolean operands. It avoids evaluating its second operand if possible. Consider the expression a && b. If a evaluates to false, the overall AND result must be false and the b operand is not evaluated. This is sometimes called *short-circuited evaluation.* "||" is the corresponding short-circuited OR operation. There is no short-circuited XOR operation.

You often use a short-circuited operation to check if a variable points to an object before invoking an instance method on it.

```
if ((myString != null) && (myString.equals("credit sale")) { /*code*/
```

In the example above, if the variable myString is null, then the second half of the expression is skipped. Here's a mnemonic you might find helpful: the longer operators "&&" or "||" try to shorten themselves by not evaluating the second operator if they can.

The ? : operator

The "? :" operator is unusual in that it is a ternary or three-operand operator. It is best understood by comparing it to an equivalent if statement:

```
if (someCondition)     truePart          else     falsePart
    someCondition ?     trueExpression      :      falseExpression
```

The conditional operator can appear in the middle of an expression, whereas an if statement cannot. The value of the expression is either the true expression or the false expression. Only one of the two expressions is evaluated. If you do use this operator, don't nest one inside another, as it quickly becomes impossible to follow. This example of ? is from the Java run-time library:

```
int maxValue = (a >= b) ? a : b;
```

The parentheses are not required, but they make the code more legible.

The assignment operators

Assignment operators are another notational shortcut. They are a combination of an assignment and an operation where the same variable is the left operand *and* the place to store the result. I like to think of it as "factoring out" in some sense, the common operand. For example, these two lines are equivalent:

```
i = i + 4;    // i gets increased by 4.

i += 4;       // factored out the common "i".
```

There are assignment operator versions of all the arithmetic, shifting, and bit-twiddling operators where the same variable is the left operand and the place to store the result. Here's another example:

```
ypoints[i] *= deltaY;
```

The assignment operator "i += something" is short for "i = i + something" with one subtle difference. When you use the assignment operator, the "i" part of it is only evaluated once. In the long hand form, "i" appears in the statement twice, and is evaluated twice. Say the expression wasn't "i" but was an array reference like this:

```
points[j++] += deltaY; // assignment operator version
```

Writing that longhand gives:

```
points[j++] = points[j++] + deltaY; // long hand version
```

A different element is referenced in the second `points[j++]` expression in the long hand version because `j` was bumped up by the post increment in the first `points[j++]` expression!

Assignment operators are carried over from C into Java, where they were originally intended to help the compiler-writer generate efficient code by leaving off a repetition of one operand. That way it was trivial to identify and reuse quantities that were already in a register. Assignment operators are most useful when the operand is a long complicated name. It saves you from having to repeat it (possibly making a typo) and it saves the maintenance programmer from having to inspect it carefully to make certain it is the same operand.

The comma operator is gone

Finally, note that Java cut back on the use of the obscure comma operator. Even if you're quite an experienced C programmer, you might never have seen the comma operator, as it was rarely used. The only place it occurs in Java is in "for" loops. The comma allows you to put several expressions (separated by commas) into each clause of a "for" loop.

```
for (i=0, j=0; i<10; i++, j++)
```

It's not actually counted as an operator in Java, so it doesn't appear in Java operators and their precedence. It's treated as an aspect of the `for` statement.

Associativity

Associativity is one of those subjects that is poorly explained in most programming texts. In fact, a good way to judge a programming text for any language is to look for its explanation of associativity. Silence is not golden.

There are three factors that determine the ultimate value of an expression in any algorithmic language, and they work in this order: precedence, associativity, and order of evaluation.

Precedence says that some operations bind more tightly than others. Precedence tells us that the multiplication in a + b * c will be done before the addition, i.e., we have a + (b * c) rather than (a + b) * c. Precedence tells us how to bind operands in an expression that contains different operators.

Associativity is the tie breaker for deciding the binding when we have several operators of equal precedence strung together. If we have 3 * 5 % 3, should we evaluate it as (3 * 5) % 3 or as 3 * (5 % 3) ?

The first is 15 % 3, which is 0. The second is 3 * 2, which is 6! Multiplication and the "%" remainder operation have the same precedence, so precedence does not give the answer. But both operators *, % are left-associative, meaning when you have a bunch of them strung together you start associating operators with operands from the left. Push the result back as a new operand, and continue until the expression is evaluated. In this case, (3 * 5) % 3 is the correct grouping.

There is no extra charge for parentheses. Use parentheses generously in expressions, so that future programmers (and the compiler) can avoid imposing its own view about how you wanted the operands grouped.

Associativity is a terrible name for the process of deciding which operands belong with which operators of equal precedence. A more meaningful description would be, *"Code Order For Finding/Evaluating Equal Precedence Operator Textstrings."* This is the "COFFEEPOT property" mentioned in Table 7–3.

Note that associativity deals solely with deciding which operands go with which of a sequence of adjacent operators of equal precedence. It doesn't say anything about the order in which those operands are evaluated.

Order of evaluation, if it is specified in a language, tells us the sequence for each operator in which the operands are evaluated. In a strict left-to-right language like Java, the order of evaluation tells us that in (i=2) * i++, the left operand to the multiplication will be evaluated before the right operand, then the multiplication will be done, yielding a result of 4, with i set to 3. Why isn't the auto-increment done before the multiplication? It has a higher precedence after all. The reason is because it is a *post* increment, and so by definition the operation is not done until the operand has been used.

In C and C++, this expression is undefined because it modifies the same value more than once within an expression. It is legal in Java because the order of evaluation is well defined.

How Accurate Are Calculations?

The accuracy when evaluating a result is referred to as the *precision* of an expression. The precision may be expressed either as number of bits (64 bits), or as the data type of the result (double precision, meaning 64-bit floating-point format).

The precision of an expression

In Java, the precision of evaluating an operator depends on the types of its operands. Java looks at the types of the operands around an operator and picks the biggest of what it sees: double, float, and long, in that order of preference. Both operands are then promoted to this type, and that is the type of the result. If there are no doubles, floats, or longs in the expression, both operands are promoted to int, and that is the type of the result. This continues from left to right through the entire expression.

A Java compiler follows this algorithm to compile each operation:

- If either operand is a double, do the operation in double precision.
- Otherwise, if either operand is a float, do the operation in single precision.
- Otherwise, if either operand is a long, do the operation at long precision.
- Otherwise, do the operation at 32-bit int precision.

In summary, Java expressions end up with the type of the biggest, floatiest type (double, float, long) in the expression. They are otherwise 32-bit integers.

Limited significant figures in floating-point numbers

The precision tells you how many bits you get in your answer. But if your calculation involves floating point, you also have to be wary about the limited accuracy of the answer. Accuracy is not just the range of values of a type, but also (for real types) the number of significant figures that can be stored. The type float can store some numbers exactly, but in general you can only count on about six to seven digits of significant figures. When a long (which can hold at least 18 places of integer values) is implicitly or explicitly converted to a float, some precision may be lost there too. Here's an example showing loss of precision when floating a long and casting back.

```
public class inexact2 {
    public static void main(String s[]) {
        long  orig = 9000000000000000000L;
        float floatMe = orig;       // assign the long into a float
        long now = (long) floatMe; // put the float back into a long

        System.out.println("orig: " + orig + "\n" +
                           " now: " + now);
    }
}
```

The output is as follows:

```
orig: 9000000000000000000
 now: 9000000202358128640
```

As you can see, after being assigned to and retrieved back from the float variable, the long has lost all accuracy after six or seven significant digits. The truth is that if a float has the value shown, 9000000202358128640, it could stand for any real value in the interval between the nearest representable floating-point number on each side. This is true for *every* float and double value. That's what floating point means.

The limitations of floating-point arithmetic apply to all programming languages. But people notice them a lot more in Java because Java doesn't round floating point numbers to six decimal places when it prints them. The C and C++ languages do round by default, hiding the floating point limitations from the unwary.

JDK 1.5 introduced a notation to pass methods a varying number of arguments. This was specifically intended to bring the much-loved (by some) C function printf() into Java. Printf outputs formatted numbers, and can be used to round numbers on printing. Chapter 17 has some examples of formatting numbers using printf.

Inaccuracies of floating-point numbers

Because floating-point numbers are (in general) approximations of the precise number, you must be wary about the accuracy of calculations. If this comes as a surprise to you, try this test program immediately, and thank your good fortune at having the chance to learn about it before you stumble over it as a difficult debugging problem.

```
public class inexact {
    public static void main(String s[]) {
        float total = 0.0F;
        for (int i=0; i<10; i++)
            total = total + 0.1F;

        if (total!=1.0F) System.out.println("total is "+total);
    }
}
```

You will see this results in the following output:

```
total is 1.0000001
```

0.1 cannot be represented exactly by summing several powers of two, which is the internal representation of floating point numbers. Summing ten "approximation to 0.1" does not exactly amount to one. This is a limitation of floating-point numbers in all programming languages, and not unique to Java. You can even reproduce it on many pocket calculators that uses floating point, unless the manufacturer has taken steps to round results and hide it.

This is why you should never use a floating-point variable as a loop counter. A longer explanation of this thorny topic is in "What Every Computer Scientist Should Know about Floating Point" by David Goldberg, in the March 1991 issue of *Computing Surveys* (volume 23, number 1). You can find that paper with a web search at the site docs.sun.com.

Floating-point extension

A new keyword was added to JDK 1.2: strictfp. The keyword is applied in front of a method or class when you need strictly identical floating point arithmetic on all your different platforms, and this is more important than faster, slightly more accurate results on some platforms. There are more details at java.sun.com/docs/books/jls/strictfp-changes.pdf.

Here's the wording for telling a method not to use extended precision:

```
strictfp void doCalc (float x, float y) {
    // some calculations not to be done in extended precision
}
```

By default, the JVM will feel free to use extended accuracy if the platform supports it, allowing slightly different and faster arithmetic results on PowerPC and x86 systems. The default (omitting the keyword) is the right choice unless you have a special reason for needing less accurate but more uniform answers.

Widening and Narrowing Conversions

This section provides more details on when a cast is needed, and also introduces the terminology of type conversions. This is explained in terms of an assignment between one variable and another, and exactly the same rules apply in the transfer of values from actual parameters to formal parameters.

When you assign an expression to a variable, a *conversion* must be done. Conversions among the primitive types are either identity, widening, or narrowing conversions.

- **Identity conversions** are an assignment between two identical types, like an int to int assignment. The conversion is trivial: just copy the bits unchanged.

- **Widening conversions** occur when you assign from a less capacious type (such as a short) to a more capacious one (such as a long). You may lose some digits of precision when you convert either way between an integer type and a floating point type. An example of this appeared in the previous section with a long-to-float assignment. Widening conversions preserve the approximate magnitude of the result, even if it cannot be represented exactly in the new type.

- **Narrowing conversions** are the remaining conversions. These are assignments from one type to a different type with a smaller range. They may lose the magnitude information. Magnitude means the largeness of a number, as in the phrase "order of magnitude." So a conversion from a long to a byte will lose information about the millions and billions, but will preserve the least significant digits.

Widening conversions are inserted automatically by the compiler. Narrowing conversions always require an explicit cast.

Expressions are evaluated in one of the canonical types (int, long, float or double). That means if your expression is assigned to a non-canonical type (byte, short, or char), an identity or a narrowing conversion will be required. If a narrowing conversion is required, you must write a cast. The cast tells the compiler, "OK, I am aware that the most significant digits are being lost here. Just go ahead and do it." Now it should be clear why we have to use a cast in:

```
byte loNibble = (byte) (byteMe & 0x0F);
```

Each operand in the expression "byteMe & 0x0F" is promoted to int, then the "and" operation is done yielding a 32-bit int result. The variable receiving the expression is an 8-bit byte, so a narrowing conversion is required. Hence, the cast "(byte)" is applied to the entire right-hand side result to mollify the compiler.

Casts and assignment operators

As a reminder, assignment operators are expressions like:

```
b += 7;
```

If b is a byte and you had written that as the equivalent

```
b = b + 7; // NO! NO! NO!
```

you will find that the first statement compiles fine, but the second produces an error message about loss of precision. You have to use an explicit cast in the second statement, like this:

```
 b = (byte) (b + 7);
```

Why is a cast required in one case, but not in an apparently equivalent one? For an answer, we have to travel to *The Java Language Specification*, which is online at `java.sun.com/docs/books/jls/second_edition/html` and pull on our language lawyer caps.

Section 15.26.2 "Compound Assignment Operators" says:

> A compound assignment expression of the form
> E1 op= E2
> is equivalent to
> E1 = (T)((E1) op (E2))
> where T is the type of E1, except that E1 is evaluated only once. Note that the implied cast to type T may be either an identity conversion (§5.1.1) or a narrowing primitive conversion (§5.1.3).

That last sentence is the key one. It says that you get the cast for free ("implied cast … to a narrowing primitive conversion"). This was done for pragmatic reasons: the assignment operators would be totally lame if they didn't work on non-canonical types. And a cast is needed when they do. Ergo, it is provided automagically.

Not all questions are answered so easily in the JLS, but it is always worth checking. I have it bookmarked in my browser.

What Happens on Overflow?

 When a result is too big for the type intended to hold it because of a cast, an implicit type conversion, or the evaluation of an expression, something has to give! What happens depends on whether the result type is integer or floating point.

Integer overflow

When an integer-valued expression is too big for its type, only the low end (least significant) bits get stored. Because of the way two's-complement numbers are stored, adding one to the highest positive integer value gives a result of the highest negative integer value. Watch out for this (it's true for all languages that use standard arithmetic, not just Java).

There is only one case in which integer calculation ceases and overflow is reported to the programmer: division by zero (using / or %) will throw an exception. To "throw an exception" is covered in Chapter 10. It means the flow of control is changed to go to an error-handler that you provide.

There is a class called Integer that is part of the standard Java libraries. It contains some useful constants relating to the primitive type int.

```
public static final int   MIN_VALUE = 0x80000000; // class Integer
public static final int   MAX_VALUE = 0x7fffffff; // class Integer
```

There are similar values in the related class Long. Notice how these constants (final) are also static. If something is constant, you surely don't need a copy of it in every object. You can use just one copy for the whole class, so make it static.

One possible use for these constants would be to evaluate an expression at long precision, and then compare the result to these int endpoints. If it is between them, then you know the result can be cast into an int without losing bits, unless it overflowed long, of course.

Floating-point overflow

When a floating-point expression (double or float) overflows, the result becomes infinity. When it underflows (reaches a value that is too small to represent), the result goes to zero. When you do something undefined like divide zero by zero, you get a NaN. Under no circumstances is an exception ever raised from a floating-point expression.

The class Float, which is part of the standard Java libraries, contains some useful constants relating to the primitive type float.

```
public static final float POSITIVE_INFINITY;
public static final float NEGATIVE_INFINITY;
public static final float NaN;
public static final float MAX_VALUE = 3.40282346638528860e+38f;
public static final float MIN_VALUE = 1.40129846432481707e-45f;
```

One pitfall is that it doesn't help to compare a value to NaN, for NaN compares false to everything (including itself)! Instead, test the NaNiness of a value like this:

```
if (Float.isNaN( myfloat ) )  // It's a NaN
```

There are similar values in the class Double.

Overflow summary
- Integer arithmetic:
  Division by zero (using / or %) will throw an exception.
  Out of range values drop the high order bits from the result.
- Floating point arithmetic:
  Never throws an exception.
  Out of range values are indicated by a NaN result.

Arithmetic that cannot overflow

There is a class called java.math.BigInteger that supports arithmetic on unbounded integers, and a class called java.math.BigDecimal that does the same thing for real numbers. They simulate arbitrary precision arithmetic in software. Because the operations are implemented by software, not hardware, they are not as fast as arithmetic on the primitive types, but they offer arbitrary precision operands and results.

Some Light Relief—Furby's Brain Transplant

The smash hit toy of Christmas 1998 was Furby. Furby was designed by Californian toy inventor Dave Hampton. Part of Dave's motivation to develop Furby was a reaction against the previous "virtual pet," the Japanese Tamagotchi. Tamagotchis are bland, inert lumps of plastic. Dave knew he could do better, and he created a fur-covered toy that sings, farts, and wobbles—sometimes all at once. No kid could resist that. In 1998, Furby sold over two million units, and they were actually being rushed by air from mainland China factories to satisfy U.S. market demand! Toys have a limited life. Furby was red hot in 1998, warm in 1999, and by 2000 you could buy one for $9.99 in Target.

Furby is an animated doll about 7 inches high. It looks like a Gremlin from the 1984 movie of that name, and toy distributor Hasbro had to settle an infringement claim from Warner Brothers. Inside, Furby is packed with a rich assortment of devices. It has a microphone, a loud-speaker, infrared transmitter/receiver, light detector, speech generation chip, CPU, EEPROM, and RAM. It has a motor and various cams to animate ears, eyes, body, etc. Obviously, it was imperative to take one of these apart and reprogram it for more useful tasks.

Unfortunately, at some point in the past, Furby architect Dave Hampton had been rudely surprised by "potty-mouth Barney," and he was determined that no one would pull the same stunt with Furby. There was another reason to make it difficult to reverse-engineer Furby: to prevent other toy companies from copying the technology. The world of children's toys is (apparently) a cutthroat, rapacious, dog-eat-dog world, where intellectual property is Napstered on a daily basis, and only the strong survive. The main defense against reverse-engineering Furby was a brittle epoxy shell that completely encased Furby's CPU, ROM, RAM, audio data, and the I/O interfaces such as driver transistors and an analog-digital convertor.

The epoxy made it impossible to clamp a logic analyzer onto the CPU, read the bus traffic, and dump out the control program. It is impossible to chip or grind off the epoxy without destroying the components underneath. Certain U.S. government labs are equipped with the right acids and neutralizers to break into equipment like this. But I don't know anyone at the CIA or NSA, and this didn't seem like the right project to introduce myself. Furby's software and sound data is not accessible for reading, writing, disassembly, replacement, or even examination. There are no exposed data/address buses, interrupt lines, or I/O lines other than those that directly drive the peripherals. Conclusion: Reprogramming Furby would require junking the existing CPU and fitting another CPU and memory—effectively, a Furby brain transplant.

So I issued the "Hack Furby" challenge from my website at afu.com (where I also keep the Java Programmers FAQ). The Hack Furby challenge offered a cash prize for the first person to reverse-engineer Furby or retrofit it with a different CPU. It was similar to challenges issued in the early days of aviation. Almost all the early aviation milestones—Bleriot's flight across the channel, Alcock and Brown across the Atlantic, Lindbergh's solo Atlantic crossing—were in response to a cash challenge, and I felt sure that computer engineers were no less motivated. This was no easy task and almost a year passed by before a winner claimed the prize.

The challenge was finally met by Jeff Gibbons, a talented Canadian computer consultant working for Motorola. Jeff chose the Intel 8051 processor to drive Furby because of the vast amount of free support tools and low cost hardware available. The 8051 is an 8-bit CPU that's been around for about 20 years, and that fully meets the time-honored Intel processor tradition of "ignore all design suggestions from the software guys." Jeff architected and built replacement circuit boards that fit into the existing space in Furby, after you junk the epoxy-protected boards. The new circuit boards carry the 8051, EEPROM, 1Mbyte RAM, an RS232 port, a power regulator, an amplifier, a digital-analog converter, and tons of support hardware. This was an incredible achievement on Jeff's part. He essentially designed and built a complete general-purpose computer system in four months of evenings and weekends.

After Jeff produced the working hardware, I wrote the first draft of the *Furby Programmer's Reference Manual*. For a while, Jeff was selling Furby upgrade kits, too. For well under $100 you could convert your Furby into a TV remote controller, a speaking clock, a pocket calculator, a chess machine or anything else that will run on a 20MHz processor and a little over 1Mbyte of RAM. Furby can be programmed in assembler or in C, and you download the program through a tether cable to the serial port on a PC. Clearly, the next step is to get a JVM running on Furby, and bring up Java 2 Micro Edition on Furby. Put a telnet connection on the serial port, and we're really cooking.

For legal and policy reasons, I can't show you a picture of a modified Furby in this book. (*How about that!*) You've no idea how easily those toy moguls take offense.

But if you hustle over to www.afu.com/furby you can feast your eyes on all the "stripped and re-chipped" Furby pictures that anyone could want.

This whole project was done under GPL, the Gnu Public License, which means we openly published all the schematics, results, software, etc. The goal is to enable volunteers to carry the project forward. If you know a lot about embedded systems and are trying think of what to do with all your plentiful spare time, perhaps Java-powered Furby could be in your future.

The last word should come from Furby himself. I did the FCC compliance testing on the Furby prototype "borrowing" some time in one of the hardware labs at Sun Microsystems.

FCC testing measures the amount of electronic interference that a product generates. It has to be lower than certain limits to comply with FCC rules. In the photo here, Furby is on the lower TV screen, on a table on a large turntable,

Figure 7–1   Hardware labs where work on Furby was done

executing all his motions and new vocabulary. The upper TV screen shows the very sensitive "bow tie" antenna six meters away, which sweeps for electromagnetic radiation as Furby revolves. The oscilloscope on the right graphs the radio frequencies that Furby radiates in every direction.

There was a lot of unwanted radio wave leakage, known as noise, coming out of hacked Furby. Upgraded Furby failed FCC parts A and B, so Jeff could not sell pre-assembled programmable Furbies, alas. The chief engineer of Sun's FCC lab came in unexpectedly, listened to Furby chirping and jabbering away, and sized up what I was doing in his lab. Then he glanced at the measurements and grunted, "Noisy little critter, ain't he?"

Chapter 8

More OOP—
Extending Classes

▼ INHERITANCE

▼ POLYMORPHISM

▼ THE CLASS WHOSE NAME IS Class

▼ EXERCISES

▼ SOME LIGHT RELIEF—THE NERD DETECTION SYSTEM

We now come to the main part of object-oriented programming, covering inheritance and polymorphism. Despite the unusual names, they describe some clean concepts. You need a solid understanding of inheritance and polymorphism to program in an object-oriented language and to use some of the Java library routines.

As we have seen several times, inheritance means basing a new class on a class that is already defined. The new class will extend the existing class in some way. Just as inheritance in real life is "what you get from a parent," inheritance in OOP is "what you get from a parent class." Every class has one immediate parent class. This is either a parent that you name explicitly or the parent that you get implicitly. The implicit parent you get if you don't name one explicitly is java.lang.Object.

```
class A { /*code*/ }
```

is equivalent to:

```
class A extends java.lang.Object { /*code*/ }
```

The class java.lang.Object is the ultimate parent class of all classes. The phrase "class A extends B" is how you indicate that A is a child of class B. A child class is also known as a *subclass* or *subtype*. A subclass can access all the non-private members of its superclass/supertype just as though they were declared directly in the subclass.

159

Table 8–1 provides some terminology.

Table 8–1   **Object-oriented programming terminology**

Term	Definition
class	A data type.
extend	To make a new class that inherits the contents of an existing class.
superclass or supertype	A parent or "base" class. Superclass wrongly suggests that the parent class has more than the subclass. It means "super" in the sense of "above." The superclass is above its children in the inheritance tree.
subclass or subtype	A child class that inherits, or extends, a superclass. It is called a subclass because it only represents a subpart of the universe of things that make up the superclass. It usually has more fields to represent its specialization, however.

Inheritance

In this section we are going to look at a real-world example of type inheritance, and turn that into code fragments to give you a solid understanding of the big picture. Then we'll look at a more substantial example of inheritance in OOP, and present that in terms of a complete program you can type in and run.

Real-world example of inheritance

To see what inheritance means in practice, consider a real-world example of the Linnaean taxonomy of the animal kingdom, as shown in Figure 8–1.

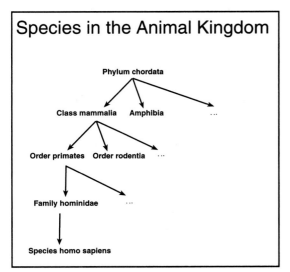

Figure 8–1   **A real-world example of an inheritance hierarchy**

Animals are classified by whether they have a spinal cord or not. Developing the example with code, we have:

```
class Animal {    }
class Chordata extends Animal { final boolean spine=true; }
```

All mammals have a spinal cord. They inherit it as a characteristic because they are a subclass of the chordata phylum (fancy words for "the group with spines"). Mammals, like humans, also have specialized characteristics: they feed their young milk, they have hair, they have two generations of teeth, and so on.

```
class Mammal extends Chordata { final int teeth_gens = 2; }
```

Primates inherit all the characteristics of mammals, including the quality of having a spinal cord, which mammals inherited from their parent type. The primate subclass is specialized with forward facing eyes, a large braincase, and so on to increasingly specialized subtypes.

```
class Primate extends Mammal { final String braincaseSize = "large"; }
```

An important part of OOP is figuring out and advantageously using the inheritance hierarchies of the class data types. Inheritance is one of the concepts people mean when they say object-oriented programming requires a special way of thinking. Get ready to spring forward with that "conceptual leap."

A Java example of inheritance

There is a GUI library class in Java called Window that implements the simplest kind of window. The class Window doesn't even have borders or a titlebar, so you can't move it or close it using a mouse. If you look at the src/java/awt/Window.java source file, you'll see code similar to the following (slightly simplified for clarity):

```
package java.awt;
import several-packages;
public class Window {
    // about 900 lines of code of methods and fields

    public Window(Frame owner) { /*a constructor*/ }
}
```

Read the code carefully on this and the following pages, as we're going to stick with this example for much of the chapter.

A Window object can be moved or written on by your code and can hold other GUI objects. Here's a program to instantiate a Window object and display it on the screen:

```
import java.awt.*;
public class example {
    public static void main(String args[]) {
        Frame f = new Frame();// Window must belong to a Frame
        Window w = new Window(f);
        w.setSize(200,100);
        w.setVisible(true);
        w.setLocation(50,50);
    }
}
```

The constructor for Window requires a more fully featured GUI object with a title bar, namely a Frame, so we create one here just to give it to the constructor. We don't do anything else with the Frame. We don't even bother making it visible. If you compile and run the code, you will get the window shown in Figure 8–2.

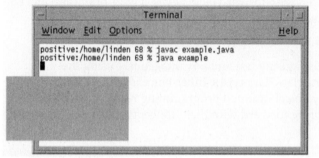

Figure 8–2   Window and Frame

For the sake of this inheritance example, let's assume that your program needs a slightly different kind of window: a WarningWindow. The only change from Window is that you want WarningWindows to be colored red to highlight their importance. Everything else should work exactly like Window and should have all the same methods and fields.

There are at least three alternative ways to implement WarningWindow:

- Change the Window class and add a constructor for a special Window that is colored red. This is a bad approach because application programmers should never, ever change the standard run-time library, even if you do have the source for it.

- Copy all the code in Window.java into file WarningWindow.java, making the change you need. This is a bad approach because it is impossible to keep duplicated code in synchronization. Whenever the code for class Window changes in future releases, class WarningWindow will be out of sync and may well stop working.

- Make WarningWindow a *subclass* of Window, so it *inherits* all the functionality from Window. *Add* a small amount of code for the different behavior you want.

The preferred OOP approach is the third one: make WarningWindow *extend* the class Window so that WarningWindow inherits all the data and methods of Window.

```
class WarningWindow extends java.awt.Window {
    // put any additional or changed members in here
}
```

This is exactly how the OOP process is supposed to work: Find a class that does most of what you want, and then subclass it to provide the exact functionality. There's nothing special about the libraries that come with Java. You are supposed to subclass system classes and your own classes as needed.

There are two points to watch here. First (unlike real life), the child class chooses its parent class. The parent has some say in the matter in that it can control its visibility with access modifiers, and it can make itself final to say "no class is permitted to extend me." Second, you have to know what a class does and how it is implemented in order to extend it successfully. Despite the goals of encapsulation, you cannot treat a superclass like a black box and completely ignore its inner workings. This is because a subclass is essentially a statement that says, "I belong inside the same black box as the superclass."

I happen to know that the Window class, like many graphical classes, has a method called setBackground() that can be used to change the color of its background.[1] All we have to do is make sure that every WarningWindow calls that method when it is being instantiated. A good way to ensure that is to put the call in a constructor. The code should go in a file called WarningWindow.java, as follows:

```
class WarningWindow extends java.awt.Window {

    WarningWindow(java.awt.Frame anyFrame) { //a constructor
        super(anyFrame);
        setBackground(java.awt.Color.red);
    }
}
```

The class java.awt.Window does not have a default no-arg constructor. So we need to explicitly call one of the constructors in Window when our subclass is instantiated. We write a WarningWindow constructor that takes a Frame parameter, call the constructor of its superclass (that's the `super(anyFrame)` statement), and then call `setBackground()` to set the window color to red.

Why call `super(anyFrame)`?

As we saw in Chapter 5, a chain of superclass constructors is always invoked when you create a subclass object. If you don't explicitly call a superclass constructor, then the no-arg constructor of the superclass is called for you.

In this situation the superclass must *have* a no-arg constructor (either an implicit one because it doesn't have any explicit constructors, or an explicit no-arg constructor). If you break this rule, the compiler won't be able to find a constructor to call, and you will get a compilation error along the lines of "*no constructor found in superclass.*"

Window is our superclass. To forestall the compiler error message, we check the API to see what constructors it has, and explicitly write a call to the most suitable one.

Here's an example program that instantiates a regular window and a WarningWindow. We can call the three `setSomething()` methods, even though we didn't declare them in WarningWindow. We inherited them from Window. All the non-private members of the chain of superclasses (stretching back to Object) are available in the subclass just as if they were declared directly in the subclass.

1. Actually, `setBackground()` and many of the other "Window" routines really come from a *parent* of Window; in this case, the class called Component.

```
import java.awt.*;
public class example { // example use of 2 kinds of Window

    public static void main(String args[]) {
        Frame f = new Frame();

        Window w = new Window(f); // standard Window
        w.setSize(200,100);
        w.setVisible(true);
        w.setLocation(300,300);

        // The new red-hued WarningWindow we created
        WarningWindow ww = new WarningWindow(f);
        ww.setSize(200,100); // setSize is in a superclass
        ww.setVisible(true);
        ww.setLocation(370,370);
    }
}
```

Put example.java in the same directory with WarningWindow.java and compile them. Try running the program and you will see the result shown in Figure 8–3. Since the red window won't show up red in a printed book, you're going to have to try it to prove that I'm not kidding you.

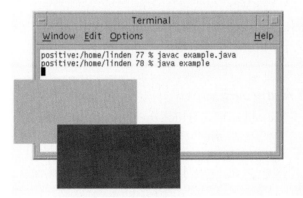

Figure 8–3   Program results: A regular window and a WarningWindow

Choosing the right parent saves a lot of work

That's your first example of inheritance. We have reused the functionality of 900 lines of code in a new six-line class that is in a separate file and only contains the differences and specializations from its superclass. How is this any different from a library? What we have here is a powerful way to take an existing library and *modify* some of its behavior without modifying the library itself.

You might ask how this is any different from instantiating an ordinary Window and always remembering to color it red. The answer is that inheritance lets the compiler and run-time do the hard work of keeping track of what an object is, and whether it has the library behavior or the modified behavior. Inheritance lets you *superimpose* some new behavior on an existing class, creating a new class without copying everything. I use this all the time when debugging or prototyping some code. "What if I did it this way?" I ask myself, and I write a subclass that extends the original class and contains my experimental changes. If the idea is bad, I just throw away the new class, and I haven't changed one line of source code in the underlying class.

"Is a" versus "Has a"

Don't confuse inheritance with nesting (having a member that refers to another object).

Declaring an object as a data field inside a class just sets up a reference variable to the object with no special privileges or relationship. In contrast, inheritance says the subclass is a variation of the superclass that extends its semantics in some way.

The way to distinguish between these two cases is to ask yourself the "is a" versus "has a" question. Let's assume you have a "car" class and an "engine" class, and you want to decide whether to use inheritance or nesting to associate the two. Would you say "a car has an engine" or "a car is an engine?" If the answer is "has a," use nesting. If the answer is "is a," use inheritance. Similarly, if we have a "mammal" class and a "dog" class, we know that a "dog is a mammal." We would use inheritance to add the canine specializations to the mammal class resulting in the dog class.

The rule of thumb is that inheritance is for specialization of a type or changing its behavior. Container classes are for data structure reuse.

The super *keyword is not really very super*

The most common use of super is the call super() which invokes a constructor in the superclass, as in the WarningWindow class above.

The keyword can also be used to access fields of any superclass (not just the immediate superclass) that are hidden or *shadowed* by an identically named field in the subclass. Similarly the super keyword can be used to invoke overridden methods in the superclass. Neither of these techniques is very common.

There is no way to "chain" several supers together, however, and reach back higher into the parent class hierarchy. Do not think that because super.x means "the x of a superclass" therefore "super.super.x" means "the x of grandparent." This is a very common mistake. There is no super.super.x. Super doesn't work that way at all. The right way to think of super is as *a reference to the current object, but typed as an instance of its superclass*. This is weird and goes against the OOP philosophy that you chose methods and fields based on the actual type of an object, not the type of any reference to it. Super is a "safety hatch" so you can get hold of parent members if absolutely necessary.

Java does not use multiple inheritance

You may have heard about "multiple inheritance." That means having more than one immediate parent class. The resulting subclass thus has characteristics from all its immediate parent types.

Multiple inheritance is much less common than single inheritance. Where it has appeared in languages (like C++), it has been the subject of considerable debate on whether it should be in the language at all. Multiple inheritance poses additional problems in both implementation and use. Say there is a class A with some data members, and classes B and C inherit from A. Now have a class D that multiply-inherits from B and C. Does D have one copy of A's data members, or two identical copies? When you access a method in D, do you get B's or C's version of it? All this can be worked out, if you don't mind having a language reference manual the size of the Gutenberg Bible.

Some people say that no convincing examples have been produced where there was no alternative design avoiding multiple inheritance. Java bypasses any difficulties by not permitting multiple inheritance. The *interface* feature described in Chapter 11 fills in the gap left by multiple inheritance.

Inheritance usually provides increasing specialization as you go from a general superclass class (e.g., vehicle) to a more specific subclass (e.g., passenger car, fire truck, or delivery van). It can equally well restrict or extend the available operations, though.

Summary of key idea: inheritance

The purpose of inheritance in an OOP language is twofold:

1. To model a data hierarchy in the application area that you are programming.
2. To provide code reuse while allowing customizations.

Inheritance means being able to declare a type that builds on the fields (data and methods) of a previously declared type. The child inherits all the operations and data of the parent, plus you get the chance to declare new versions of the parent methods. A child class refines, specializes, replaces, or adds to the parent class.

What happens when data field names collide?

It's bad style to give a data field in a subclass the same name as a field in a superclass. If you do this, the subclass field hides the superclass field. The visible subclass field is said to *shadow* (put in the shade) the superclass field. The superclass field is still available by using the `super` keyword. It is also available if you assign the subclass to the superclass type. Be careful here.

```
class Fruit {        // example of variable name hiding
    boolean zestySkin= false;
}

public class Citrus extends Fruit {
    boolean zestySkin= true;    // same name hides the Fruit one

    public static void main (String args[]) {
        Citrus c = new Citrus();
        Fruit f = c; // f and c now refer to the same object
        System.out.println( " f.zesty = " + f.zestySkin );
        System.out.println( " c.zesty = " + c.zestySkin );
        System.out.println( " Parent cast sees child field = "
                                + ((Fruit) c).zestySkin );
    }
}
```

When you run the above code, you get this output:

```
f.zesty = false                    •
c.zesty = true
Parent cast sees child field = false // surprise!
```

Be sure to note that *a cast of something to its superclass makes it see the superclass variables where there is name hiding*. The reason Java allows name duplication is to permit new fields to be added later to superclasses without breaking existing subclasses that might already use that name. The subclasses will continue to use their own copies of those fields, except when you tell them to behave like superclass objects. Methods are intended for overloading, but not fields. Don't hide field names as a general practice.

A data field may have the same name as a method in its own class or superclass without either hiding the other.

```
class Example {
    public int total = 22;   // overloading field and method is dumb,
    public int total () {    // but it works OK
```

Name duplication should be rare, because the Java Language Specification says that method names should be based on verbs, while field names should be based on nouns (JLS, sect. 6.8).

In the case of a method with the same name in both a superclass and the subclass, the run-time system figures out exactly what class this object really is and calls the method that is a member of that particular class. This is dealt with in *Polymorphism* on page 171.

It turns out that all objects carry around a little bit of extra information about their type and the characteristics of that type. The run-time system needs to keep track of the type of an object reference to check casts to invoke the right version of overloaded methods. The information is known as Run Time Type Information

(RTTI), and it is kept in an object of its own. You get to the RTTI object through the getClass() method that is in class Object and thus inherited by every class. The type of an RTTI object is a reference type whose name is Class. That class called Class is featured in *The Class Whose Name Is Class* on page 179.

Objects keep their identity, regardless of reference type!

One of the great things about inheritance is that it lets you treat a specialized object as a more general one. In other words, my WarningWindow, by virtue of being a subclass of Window, counts as a Window and can be used anywhere in code where a Window is used. If you have a method that expects a Window as an argument, you can pass it a WarningWindow, and it will work fine.

If you have a Window variable, you can assign a WarningWindow into it, like this:

```
WarningWindow ww = new WarningWindow( new Frame() );
Window w = ww; // the Window obj now refers to a WarningWindow
```

Here's the really magical thing: that Window object will continue to behave as a WarningWindow! It will display with a red background whenever someone invokes a Window operation on it that causes it to be updated on the screen. Even though we access the object using a Window pointer, the object knows it is a Warning Window and still behaves as one.

This is the *key point* of OOP. When you have a variable of SomeClass, it might actually be referring to a much more specialized subclass. If a method takes some particular superclass type as a parameter, you can actually call it with any of its subclasses and it will do the right thing. Add some lines of code to the example class a few pages back to try this. You can even assign a WarningWindow object to an Object, then later cast it back to a Window or WarningWindow, and it won't have lost its type information.

Casting

Let's look a little more closely into compatibility between subclass and superclass. We'll use the following code for examples:

```
public class Mammal {  }
public class Dog extends Mammal {   }
public class Cat extends Mammal {   }

Dog fido = new Dog();
Cat kitty = new Cat();
Mammal m = fido;
```

Notice the assignment of m (a Mammal variable) = fido (a Dog object). You can always make a more general object hold a more specialized one, but the reverse is not true without an explicit type conversion. All dogs are mammals, but not all mammals are dogs. Cats, horses, pigs, and people are also mammals. You can assign m=fido, but not (directly) fido=m, because m could be referring to a Cat object.

Just as you can cast (convert) an integer into a double, you can cast a superclass into one of its more specialized subclasses. To cast any type, write the typename in parentheses immediately before the object being cast. In this case:

```
fido = (Dog) m;     // The cast allows the compilation to work
                    // and the conversion is checked at run-time
```

Type hierarchies are often drawn as tree diagrams with Object (the ultimate superclass) at the top, and all subclasses beneath their superclass as Figure 8–4 exemplifies. In a drawing of this kind, you can only cast "downward" from a superclass to some subclass (or subclass of a subclass, and so on). You can never cast "sideways" to force an object to become something it is not.

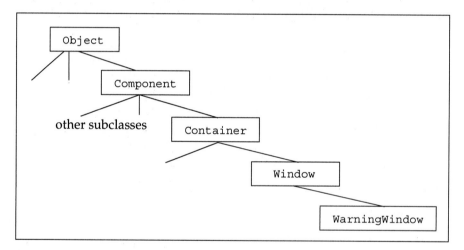

Figure 8–4   An inheritance hierarchy may be many levels deep

The general rules for casting classes are:

- You can always assign parent = child; a cast is not needed because a specific child class also belongs to its general parent class. You can assign several levels up the hierarchy; that is, the parent may be a more remote ancestor. Chordata c = new Dog() is valid.

- You can cast `child = (child) parent`, and it will be checked at run-time. If the parent is referring to the correct child type, the assignment will occur. If the parent is actually pointing to some unrelated subclass, an exception ClassCastException will be raised. Exceptions are a recoverable interruption to the normal flow of control. They are described later.

- You cannot assign or cast at all between arbitrary unrelated classes, as in `fido=kitty;`

Because every class is a subclass of the built-in system class Object, every object can be assigned to something of type Object, and later cast back to the type that it really is. In this way, the type Object can be used as a general reference to anything.

Some Java utility classes store and manipulate Object. You can use them for any object, later casting to get back the same type that you put in. You can be certain that, if a cast succeeds, you really have an object of the type you cast to. This is another illustration that there is no evading strong typing in Java.

Summary: superclass/subclass compatibility

They must really love this topic on the Java Certification exam, because they ask it in several different questions. Make sure you have it down before taking that test. Here are possible assignments and a note about their compatibility:

```
superclass = subclass // always valid
subclass = (subclass) superclass //valid at compile time, checked at run-time
subclass = superclass // not valid as written, requires a cast to compile
someClass = someUnrelatedClass // won't even compile
someClass = (someClass) someUnrelatedClass // won't even compile
```

Polymorphism

Polymorphism is a complicated name for a straightfoward concept. It is Greek for "many shapes," and it means *allowing the same code to be used with different types*. In Java, it is implemented by allowing several different methods to have the same name, making it look like one method to the API user. "Name reuse" would be a better term. There are two types of polymorphism in Java: the really easy kind (overloading) and the interesting kind (overriding).

Overloading

The really easy kind of polymorphism is called *overloading* in Java and other languages, and it means that in any class you can use the same name for several different (but hopefully related) methods. The methods must have different

Here are two overloaded methods:

```
public static int parseInt(String s) throws NumberFormatException
public static int parseInt(String s, int radix)
                                    throws NumberFormatException
```

These methods come from the class `java.lang.Integer` class wrapper for the primitive type `int`. The first method tries to interpret the String as an int, and return the corresponding binary int value. The second method does the same thing, but uses an arbitrary base that you specify. You could parse a hexadecimal String by supplying 16 as the radix argument.

The return type and the exceptions that a method can throw are not looked at when resolving same-named functions in Java.

The I/O facilities of a language are one typical place where overloading is used. You don't want to have an I/O class that requires a different method name depending on whether you are trying to print a short, an int, a long, and so on. You just want to be able to say "print(thing)."

Overriding

The second, more complicated kind of polymorphism, true polymorphism, is resolved dynamically at run-time. It occurs when a subclass class has a method with the same signature (number, type, and order of parameters) as a method in the superclass. When this happens, the method in the derived class overrides the method in the superclass. Methods cannot be overridden to be more private only to be more public.

An example should make this clear. Let's go back to our base class Window, and our subclass WarningWindow. I happen to know that one of the operations you can do with a Window is `setSize()` on it. That's even in our example program. We will give WarningWindow its own version of `setSize()` to reflect the fact that WarningWindows are more important and should be bigger than regular Windows. We add a `setSize()` method to our subclass:

```
class WarningWindow extends java.awt.Window {

    WarningWindow(java.awt.Frame apple) { // constructor
        super(apple);
        setBackground(java.awt.Color.red);
    }

    public void setSize(int x, int y) { // overriding method
        int bigx = (int) (x*1.5);
        int bigy = (int) (y*1.5);
        super.setSize(bigx, bigy);
    }
}
```

The method setSize() in WarningWindow replaces or overrides the superclass's version of setSize() when the method is invoked on a WarningWindow object. C++ programmers will note that you do not need to specifically point out to the compiler (with the C++ "virtual" keyword) that overriding will take place. Here's some example code:

```
public static void main(String args[]) {
        Frame f = new Frame();
        Window w = new Window(f);
          w.setSize(200,100);
          w.setVisible(true);
          w.setLocation(300,300);

        Window w2 = new WarningWindow(f); // the only change
          w2.setSize(200,100);
          w2.setVisible(true);
          w2.setLocation(370,370);
}
```

The code creates two Window variables, w and w2. The first variable, w, is assigned a Window and various properties are set. The second Window variable, w2, is assigned a WarningWindow. The same properties are set (it's put in a slightly different location, so it doesn't obscure the first Window).

When you try running this, you will note that when we apply the setSize() method to a Window, we get the base class version, meaning it comes out the regular size. When we apply the setSize method to a WarningWindow, we get the WarningWindow specialized version which it displays 50% bigger in each direction as shown in Figure 8–5. Wow!

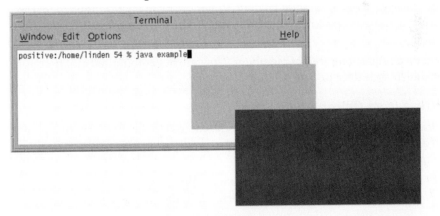

Figure 8–5   A Window variable invokes setSize() but ends up bigger! It is actually pointing to a variable of subclass WarningWindow which overrides Window.setSize() with its own version.

When we invoke the method on something that started out as a general Window, but may have been assigned a WarningWindow at run-time, the correct method is chosen at run-time based on what the object actually is. And *that* is polymorphism. It is a powerful tool for letting a class implement an operation in a way that is unique to itself.

It would clearly be bad design to override a method in a way that fundamentally changes what it does. You wouldn't *really* want to make setSize() use different values from its arguments. It makes a great demonstration for teaching purposes, though, because the difference is so visible.

The difference between overloading and overriding

Overloading, the shallow kind of polymorphism, is resolved by the compiler at compile time. Overloading allows several methods to have the same one name, and the compiler will choose the one you mean by matching on argument types.
Overriding, the deep kind of polymorphism, is resolved at run-time. It occurs when one class extends another, and the subclass has a method with the same signature (exact match of number and argument types) as a method in the superclass.
Question: Which of them gets invoked?
Answer: If it's an object of the subclass, the subclass one; if it's an object of the superclass, the superclass one. The reason this is "fancy" is that sometimes you cannot tell until run-time, so the compiler must plant code to work out which method is appropriate for whatever this object turns out to be, then call that at run-time. This is called a "virtual call".

The technical term for "choosing the correct method for whatever object this is at run-time" is *late binding* or *delayed binding*. Polymorphism is the language feature that allows two methods to have the same name, such that late binding may be applied.

Constructor declarations are not members. They are never inherited and therefore are not subject to hiding or overriding.

Inheriting from Object

So the meaning of inheritance is that a class has access to the members of a parent class. If a class has its own version of a method in a parent class, its own version will be called.

This has implications for program maintenance. When you see a class accessing some member, if you cannot find the declaration in the class itself, look in the parent class, and then in the parent of the parent class, all the way back to the ultimate base class Object, if necessary.

Inheritance is the reason why you can call toString() on any object. If you look back at the listing of Object at the end of Chapter 3, you'll see it has a number of methods that are inherited by every class. The method toString() is one of these. If you provide your own version of toString() for one of your classes, that will be used instead of the Object toString(), *even if you are accessing your object through an Object pointer.* To see this in action, add some code to Timestamp to print its values like "12:15:03", e.g.

```
class Timestamp {
    int hrs;
    int mins;
    int secs;

    public String toString() {
        String result = "" + hrs;
        String pad = ":";
        if (mins<10) pad = ":0";
        result += pad + mins;
        if (secs<10) pad = ":0";
        else pad = ":";
        result += pad + secs;
        return result;
    }
    /* constructor and more code omitted */
}
```

Then put two lines like this in a method that will be executed.

```
Object o = new Timestamp();
System.out.println("Object o is " + o );
```

You will see output like this, confirming that polymorphism and late binding are taking place:

```
Object o is 19:03:17
```

Defining toString for your classes can also be used to provide debugging output.

Forcing overriding off: final

We have already seen final applied to data to make it constant. There are two further adjustments to fine-tune inheritance of methods: abstract and final. You will be able to use these when you get more practiced in defining type hierarchies.

Let's consider the class java.lang.Math that provides various trig and math operations.

One feature of the class is that all trig operations are done in radians, not degrees. Would it be possible to *extend* java.lang.Math and *override* just the trig functions so that they worked with degrees instead? You could leave all the other rounding and comparing Math functions alone, and you would have specialized the subclass for your needs.

Your code might look like this:

```
public class DegreeMath extends java.lang.Math { // won't work
    public double sin(double d) {
        double rads = super.toRadians(d);
        double result = super.sin(rads);
        return super.toDegrees(result);
    }
}
```

That is a great idea in theory, but it cannot be done this way for the Math class in practice for two reasons. One, the Math class is labeled as final, so cannot be extended. Two, all the Math methods are static.

```
public final class Math { /*more code*/
    public static native double sin(double a);
```

Static methods do not participate in overriding. Overriding is used when an object might be one type or might be a more specialized subtype. Class methods don't belong to an object and never have this possible ambiguity. It's another reason why you should always invoke class methods using the name of the class, not an instance of it: to remind yourself that the method will not be overridden.

When the keyword final appears at the start of a class declaration, it means "no one can extend this class." Similarly, an individual method can be made final, preventing it from being overridden. It is final in the sense that it is a leaf of an inheritance tree. Typically, you might wish to prevent further inheritance to avoid further specialization or for security reasons: you don't want to permit this type to be further adjusted. A "final" method is also a hint to the compiler to inline the code. Inlining the code means optimizing out the overhead of a method call by taking the statements in the body of the method and duplicating them inline instead of making the call. This is a classic space versus time trade-off.

The class java.lang.Math is labeled as final for performance reasons. Even if a method is not inlined, the method call can be made much more quickly if the compiler can compile the call directly, rather than have the run-time system figure out during execution what the actual class is, and hence which is the right overriding method. The performance cost is the reason overriding is off by default in C++.

The class java.lang.String is labeled as `final` for reasons of security and performance. String objects are read-only. The class does not provide any public methods to change characters in the middle of an existing String. If you could override String, you could write a subclass that was not read-only, and that also could be used in all the places that String is used. Specifically, you could change the String pathname to a file after it had been checked for access permission, but before the open operation had been done.

Private methods are all implicitly final—because no one outside the class can see them, no one can override them.

Forcing overriding on: *abstract*

Just as `final` tells the compiler "This thing is complete and must not be changed or extended or overridden," there is a keyword to *require* overriding to take place. The keyword `abstract` tells the compiler "This thing is incomplete and must be extended to be used." You can think of `final` and `abstract` as opposites of each other, as they cannot occur together for a method or class. The keyword `final` or `abstract` can be applied to an individual method or an entire class.

When the keyword `abstract` appears at the start of a class declaration, it means that zero or more of its methods are abstract. An abstract method has no body; its purpose is to *force* some subclass to override it and provide a concrete implementation. Labeling a method `abstract` requires you to label the class abstract.

You make a class `abstract` when three conditions are fulfilled:

* There will be several subclasses.

* You want to handle all the different subclasses as an instance of the superclass.

* The superclass alone does not make sense as an object.

That set of conditions indicating an abstract class probably made no sense at all, so I'll show what it means in terms of an example. We will use java.awt.Component as an example of an abstract class. Think back to the GUI class Window. We showed a few pages back how Window is a subclass of Component (not directly, but two levels down).

It turns out that Component is the window toolkit superclass for many Java library objects that you can display on the screen. In particular, many screen widgets (Unix terminology) or controls (Microsoft terminology) are Components. Scrollbars, panels, dialogs, tabbed panes, cursors, labels, textfields, and so on are all subclasses of Component. Thus, Component meets the first condition of abstract classes: it has more than one subclass.

There are many operations that we can do on a control without precisely knowing or caring which control it is. One common operation is to add it to a container for display. A container is a GUI backdrop or pinboard whose purpose is to arrange and display the group of components it is given. We don't want to have umpteen individual methods—one for adding each individual type of control to a panel—we just want to be able to say the following:

```
myContainer.add(Component c);
```

We have the second condition: for convenience, you want to handle all the different subclasses as an instance of the superclass. The most frequently seen case is where the superclass is a parameter to a method, as it is here.

Finally, all the subclasses of Component are real, concrete objects. You can actually display them on the screen. Component itself is not a concrete object. You cannot sensibly display a Component object on the screen (even if you could instantiate it, what would be drawn?). Only the subclasses have the actual semantics of shape, behavior, and look. An instance of Component itself doesn't really make sense. You need an instance of a concrete subclass of Component. In this way, the third condition has been met: an instance of the superclass does not make sense as an object. Hence, java.awt.Component is an abstract class.

Although making a class abstract forces a programmer to extend it and fill in some more details in the subclass before it can be instantiated, it allows the class to stand in for any of the concrete subclasses. Saying a class is abstract imposes the requirements "you must implement the abstract method(s) in a subclass" and "you cannot instantiate an object of the abstract class, it is still incomplete in some way."

Here's the general form that Component has in source code:

```
public abstract class Component {
        public void setBackground(java.awt.Color){ /*more code*/ }
        public void setVisible(boolean) { /* more code*/ }
        public void setLocation(int, int){ /*more code*/ }
          // 3800 lines of code omitted
        public abstract void DrawMeOnScreen();
}
```

Some methods in Component are concrete. These are the methods that set various flags and keep track of options, like the current position of the Component on the screen and whether it has been made visible or not. Some methods of Component are abstract, like anything to do with drawing its appearance on the screen. The subclasses of Component will implement the DrawMeOnScreen() and other abstract methods in a way that makes sense for them. Button will implement it so that it draws a rounded rectangle with a label. Scrollbar will implement it so it draws an "elevator bar" and associated arrow icons.

```
// some concrete subclasses of Component
public class Button extends Component {
     public void DrawMeOnScreen(){ /*more code*/ }
}

public class Scrollbar extends Component {
     public void DrawMeOnScreen(){ /*more code*/ }
}
```

The last piece of the picture is some other class entirely that wants to operate on any of the Component subclasses. It treats them all as a Component, and when it needs the component to be drawn, it can call its DrawMeOnScreen() method, and be assured that one exists.

```
public class Container {
     public void remove(Component comp) { /*code*/ }
     public Component add(Component comp){ comp.DrawMeOnScreen(); }
}
```

I have fudged a bit on the name and use of DrawMeOnScreen() to make the example simpler. That's what the method does, but it is called something less intuitive—paintComponent(), if you must know. We'll meet it in a later chapter.

We could get by without abstract. Polymorphism would still take place, and overriding methods called. Abstract provides a way for library writers to force programmers to implement certain methods. The use of extends is at least twenty times more common than the use of abstract to fine-tune class hierarchies in the Java run-time library.

The Class Whose Name Is Class

Here's where the terminology admittedly can get a little confusing. We saw a few pages back that every object has some Run Time Type Information associated with it. The RTTI for any object is stored in an object whose class is called "Class." Class could certainly use a better, less self-referential name, like ClassInformation or just RTTI.

A big use of Class is to help with loading new classes during program execution. A lot of other languages load an entire program before they start execution. Java encourages dynamic loading. Classes only need to be loaded on demand when they are first referenced.

When you compile a class called, say, Fruit, the compiler creates the bytecode file Fruit.class. When the first reference to a Fruit type or object is encountered at runtime, the JVM asks the java.lang.ClassLoader class to find and load that class file. Typically, the ClassLoader transforms the fully qualified name into a file name and looks for that in certain places locally (and for applets, it looks across the net back to the server). It will look in the directories on the class path; it will look in the lib\ext directory in the run-time library; it will look at any jar files you have named, and so on. If the class file is not found, an error is reported. Otherwise the JVM loads the bytecode instructions into memory and automatically creates a Class object to represent the class.

Class provides the information for checking casts at run-time, and it also lets a program introspect all the members of a class—the data fields and the methods. These are systems programming activities, unlikely to occur in your programs, but providing Class makes it easy to program them without stepping outside the Java system. You can safely skim over the rest of this section and return when you have a specific need to look at RTTI.

To access the run-time type information for a class, you need an object of type Class. You can get one in three ways. Here's some code showing the alternatives:

```
Object o = new Timestamp();

Class which = o.getClass(); // getClass is a method in Object
```

or

```
Class which = Class.forName("Timestamp"); // forName is a static method
```

or

```
Class which = Timestamp.class; // class literal
```

The second alternative will throw a ClassNotFoundException if no class of that name can be found, so if you are experimenting with this code, you'll need to put that statement in a try/catch clause described in the Exceptions chapter.

The last alternative is called a *class literal*. You can jam the characters .class onto the end of any type at all, even a primitive type like int, and it gets you the Class RTTI associated with the type. You'll choose which of the alternatives to use depending on whether you have an object, the classname in a String, or the class.

Once you have the class object you can invoke its methods. The strict left-to-right evaluation of Java allows method calls to be chained together in one statement. You can do this with any methods where the result of one method is the reference used in the next:

```
String name = myobject.getClass().getName();
```

Method getName() returns a String containing the name of the class, e.g. "java.awt.Window" or "Timestamp".

Extra type information in JDK 1.5

JDK 1.5 introduced the big new feature of generics. Generics are a fancy way of providing extra type information to library classes, and they have a whole chapter to themselves. The main users of generics in Java are the collection classes in package java.util. However, class java.lang.Class has been updated to use generics too.

We'll defer the full explanation to the generics chapter, and just mention here the key points:

- When you instantiate a Class object, you are now able to tell the compiler what type you are doing it for (if you wish to do this).

- The way you provide that information is to mention the typename in angle brackets, like this:

```
Class <Timestamp> ct = Timestamp.class;
```

It is read as "Class of Timestamp"

- With this extra information, the compiler knows enough to give you back the correct type from newInstance() and an explicit cast is no longer needed:

```
Timestamp t = ct.newInstance();
```

You don't have to use this new feature. If you want to use it, you need to use the compiler "-source 1.5" option.

The class whose name is Class looks like this in **JDK** 1.4. The **JDK** 1.5 version has been retrofitted to give it a generic parameter. Instantiations now specify the type for which they are a Class object. Chapter 15 has the full story.

```
public final class java.lang.Class  {
    public java.io.InputStream getResourceAsStream(java.lang.String);
    public java.net.URL getResource(java.lang.String);

    public native String getName();
    public static native java.lang.Class forName(java.lang.String);
    public native java.lang.Object newInstance();

    static native Class getPrimitiveClass(java.lang.String);

    public native boolean isInstance(java.lang.Object);
    public native boolean isAssignableFrom(java.lang.Class);
    public native boolean isInterface();
    public native boolean isArray();
    public native boolean isPrimitive();

// security related
    public native ClassLoader getClassLoader();
    public native Object getSigners()[];
    native void setSigners(java.lang.Object[]);

// introspection on the class, its ancestors, members and constructors
    public native Class getSuperclass();
    public native Class getInterfaces()[];
    public native Class getComponentType();
    public native int getModifiers();
    public Class getDeclaringClass();
    public Class getDeclaredClasses()[];
    public Class getClasses()[];
    public reflect.Constructor getConstructors()[];
    public reflect.Constructor getConstructor(java.lang.Class[]);
    public reflect.Constructor getDeclaredConstructors()[];
    public reflect.Constructor getDeclaredConstructor(java.lang.Class[]);

    public reflect.Field getFields()[];
    public reflect.Field getField(java.lang.String);
    public reflect.Field getDeclaredFields()[];
    public reflect.Field getDeclaredField(java.lang.String);

    public reflect.Method getMethods()[];
    public reflect.Method getMethod(java.lang.String, java.lang.Class[]);
    public reflect.Method getDeclaredMethods()[];
    public reflect.Method getDeclaredMethod(
                         java.lang.String, java.lang.Class[]);

    public java.lang.String toString();
}
```

A description of some methods of Class follow. We've already covered the
method that returns the name of the Class.

```
public native String getName();
```

This next example is a surprising method—it allows you to create an object of the
class for which this is the RTTI. Coupled with the forName() method, this lets you

create an object of any class whose name you have in a String. Highly dynamic! The no-arg constructor of the appropriate class is called, so it better have one.

```
public native Object newInstance()
          throws InstantiationException, IllegalAccessException
```

In the following example, if you have an instance of a class, and you cast it to the class that you know it is, you can call its methods:

```
String s = "java.awt.Window";
Object f = Class.forName(s).newInstance();

java.awt.Component c = (java.awt.Window) f;
c.setVisible(true);
```

Exercises

1. What are the four attributes that distinguish object-oriented programming? What are some advantages and disadvantages of OOP?

2. Give three examples of primitive types and three examples of predefined Java classes (i.e., object types).

3. What is the default constructor, and when is it called? What is a no-arg constructor?

4. Describe overriding, and write some code to show an example.

5. Consider the following three related classes:

```
class Mammal {}
class Dog extends Mammal { }
class Cat extends Mammal { }
```

There are these variables of each class:

```
Mammal m;
Dog d = new Dog( );
Cat c = new Cat( );
```

Which of these statements will cause an error at compile time, and why? Which of these statements may cause an error at run-time, and why?

```
m = d;         // 1.
d = m;         // 2.
d = (Dog) m;   // 3.
d = c;         // 4.
d = (Dog) c;   // 5.
```

6. Create a class that provides all the same methods as java.lang.Math, but which operate on degrees, not radians. Do this by creating a wrapper for each method in Math, in your class. Recall that a wrapper is a thin layer around a type or a method call to make some convenient adaptation, then call the underlying version.

Some Light Relief—The Nerd Detection System

Most people are familiar with the little security decals that electronic and other high-value stores use to deter shoplifters. The sticker contains a metallic strip. Unless deactivated by a store cashier, the sticker sets off an alarm when carried past a detector at the store doors.

These security stickers are actually a form of antenna. The sticker detector sends out a weak RF signal between two posts through which shoppers will pass. It looks for a return signal at a specific frequency, which indicates that one of the stickers has entered the field between the posts.

All this theory was obvious to a couple of California Institute of Technology students Dwight Berg and Tom Capellari, who decided to test the system in practice. Naturally, they selected a freshman to (unknowingly) participate in the trials. At preregistration, after the unlucky frosh's picture was taken but before it was laminated onto his I.D. card, Dwight and Tom fixed a couple of active security decals from local stores onto the back of the photo.

The stunt card was then laminated together, hiding the gimmick, and the two conspirators awaited further developments. A couple of months later they caught up with their victim as he was entering one of the stores. He was carrying his wallet above his head. In response to a comment that this was an unusual posture, the frosh replied that something in his wallet, probably his bank card, seemed to set off store alarms. He had been conditioned to carry his wallet above his head after several weeks of setting off the alarms while entering and leaving many of the local stores.

The frosh seemed unimpressed with Dwight and Tom's suggestion that perhaps the local merchants had installed some new type of nerd detection system. Apparently though the comment got the frosh thinking, because on the next occasion when he met Dwight he put him in a headlock until he confessed to his misdeed. **Moral:** Never annoy a computer programmer.

Chapter 9

Arrays

▼ UNDERSTANDING AND CREATING ARRAYS

▼ ARRAYS OF ARRAYS

▼ HAVE ARRAY BRACKETS, WILL TRAVEL

▼ THE MATH PACKAGE

▼ SOME LIGHT RELIEF—THINK BIG (AND SMALL)

In this chapter, we introduce arrays and describe how to use them. Arrays in Java have pretty much the same features as arrays in many languages—the ability to store multiple variables all of one type, and access them by an index value.

Understanding and Creating Arrays

There are some neat features that flow from Java's rule that arrays are objects. That's a good place to start reviewing arrays.

Arrays are objects

When Java says arrays are objects, it means array types are reference types, and your array variable is really a reference to an array. What looks like the declaration of an array:

```
int day[];
```

is actually a variable that will point to an array-of-ints *when you create that array*. Notice that the array size is not mentioned in the declaration. When we finally fill in the pointer, it can point to any size of int array, and in the course of execution you can assign it different values to point to different arrays. You can't suddenly make an int array point to a char array, of course.

185

Here are some ways in which arrays *are* like objects:

- They *are* objects because the language specification says so ("*An object is a class instance or an array*", section 4.3.1).

- Array types are reference types, just like object types.

- Arrays are allocated with the "new" operator, similar to constructors.

- Arrays are always allocated in the heap part of memory, never in the stack part of memory. Objects follow the same rule.

- The parent class of all arrays is Object, and you can call any of the methods of Object, such as toString(), on an array.

On the other hand, here are some ways arrays *are not* like objects:

- You can't extend an array type to create a new child array type.

- Arrays have a different syntax from other object classes.

- You can't define your own methods for arrays.

Regard arrays as funny kinds of objects that share some key characteristics with regular objects. Operations that are common to all objects can be done on arrays. Operations that require an Object as an operand can be passed an array.

When you write an array as the parameter to a method, you write it like this:

```
void main(String[] args) { ...
```

The array size is not part of the signature, so you can send across different-sized arrays as arguments in different calls. String[] matches any size array-of-Strings.

Index checking

Array indexes are all checked at run-time. If a subscript attempts to access an element outside the bounds of its array, it causes an exception and the program will cease execution rather than overwrite some other part of memory. Exceptions are described in Chapter 11.

The length of an array (the number of elements in it) is a data field in the array class. You can get the size of an array by referencing the following:

```
myArray.length      // yes
```

People always want to treat that as a method call, and write the following:

```
myArray.length()    // NO! NO! NO!
```

To remember this, remind yourself that arrays only have the method calls defined in java.lang.Object, and length() isn't one of them. So length must be a field for arrays. java.lang.String, on the other hand, is a regular class in all respects, is not an array of chars, and does have a length() method.

The length of an entire array versus a string in an array

Think back to the main() method and its String argument array. You may wonder how to get the length of the array (the total number of Strings) versus the length of a given String in the array. Here is some code that demonstrates the two scenarios:

```
public static void main(String args[]) {
    int i=0;
    System.out.println( "number of String args:" + args.length );
    System.out.println( "length of i'th String:" +args[i].length() );
}
```

Creating an array

When you declare an array, as in the following example, that declaration says "carrot can hold a reference to any size array of int."

```
int carrot [];
```

You have to make the reference point to an array before you can use it, just as with class types. You might make it point to an existing array, or you might create the array with a new expression, just as with objects.

```
carrot = new int[100];
```

An array is explicitly created by an array creation expression. Once an array has been created, it cannot change in size. You can make the reference variable point to a bigger array into which you copy the same contents.Class.

Array size

You can never specify the size of an array in a declaration like this:

```
int sprout [256];                    // NO! NO! NO!
```

The array's size is set when you assign something to it, either in an initializer or a regular assignment statement.

```
int carrot [] = new int[256];
```

Once an array object has been created with a given size, it cannot change for that array, although you can replace it by assigning a different-sized array object to it.

When you create an object, the fields that are primitive types are created and initialized to zero. The fields that are reference types are initialized to null (don't point to anything yet).

It is exactly the same with arrays. If the array element type is a primitive type, space for the values is allocated when the array is new'd[1]. The primitives are all set to zero, and you'll want to initialize them with whatever the appropriate value is before use.

```
carrot = new int [256];// creates 256 ints
carrot[7] = 32;          // ok, accesses 1 element.
```

If the array elements are a reference type, space for the references-to-objects is allocated, they are initialized to null, *and you must fill them in before use!*

```
Timestamp appts [] = new Timestamp[256]; // creates 256 null references
appts[7].hh = 10; // NO! NO! NO! (appts[7] is still null)
```

You need to make each individual reference element point to an object before you can access the object. You need to do something like this:

```
Timestamp appts [] = new Timestamp[256];
for (int i=0; i<appts.length; i++) {
    appts[i] = new Timestamp();
}

appts[7].hh = 10; // now OK!
```

Failing to create the objects in an array of reference types is the most common novice mistake with arrays, and it causes a NullPointerException error.

Array compatibility

Although you cannot declare an array type that extends another array type (the way you can with a class), there is a notion of type compatibility between arrays that have objects as their elements. If you have two arrays, one of a Parent class and one of a Child class, you can assign the array-containing-Child to the array-containing-Parent, and generally use it wherever an array-containing-Parent is expected.

Java has some standard classes like this:

```
class Number extends Object { /* more code */ }
class Integer extends Number { /*more code */ }
```

---

1.   *New'd* is shorthand that some programmers use in place of *instantiated.*

We can declare:

```
Number [] na;
Integer [] ia = new Integer[12];
void example(Numbers[] x) {/*more code */}
```

These statements are legal:

```
example(ia);  // sends an Integer[] which is compatible with Number[]
na = ia;      // assignment compatible
```

Initializing an array

You can initialize an array in its declaration with an *array initializer* like this:

```
byte b[] = { 0, 1, 1, 2, 3 };
String wkdays[] = { "Mon", "Tue", "Wed", "Thu", "Fri", };
```

A superfluous trailing comma is allowed in an initialization list—an unnecessary carryover from C. The permissible extra trailing comma is claimed to be of use when a list of initial values is being generated automatically.

A new array object is implicitly created when an array initializer expression is evaluated. You can't use an array initializer anywhere outside a declaration, like in an assignment statement. So this is not valid:

```
wkdays = { "Mon", "Tues" }; // NO! NO! NO!
```

But it is really useful to be able to allocate and initialize an array in a statement, so *array creation expressions* were brought to the rescue. It provides the explicit extra information about the type of the thing in braces. This is valid:

```
wkdays = new String[] { "Mon", "Tues", "Wed", "Thur", "Fri"};
```

That `new type[] {value1, value2 }` is an array creation expression, and it was introduced in JDK 1.1. You *can* use an array creation expression in a declaration or anywhere a reference to an array is expected. Here is one in a declaration.

```
Fruit orchard[] = new Fruit [] {new Fruit(),
                                new Fruit(4,3),
                                null };
```

Duplicating arrays

There is a method called `arraycopy()` in class `java.lang.System` that will copy part or all of an array, like this:

```
String midweek[] = new String[3];
System.arraycopy ( /*source*/      wkdays,
                   /*src offset*/  1,
                   /*dest*/        midweek,
                   /*dest offset*/ 0,
                   /*len*/         3 );
```

You can clone an array, like this:

```
int p[] = new int[10];
int p2[] = (int[]) p.clone(); // makes a copy of p
```

Cloning creates a new array, whereas arraycopy just copies elements into an existing array. As with the clone of anything, you get back an Object which must be cast to the correct type. That's what (int[]) is doing.

Arrays of Arrays

We'll discuss how the terminology of arrays is not universally consistent among all programming languages. Java uses the terminology consistently, though. Then we'll show how to declare arrays of arrays in Java.

Array terminology

The language specification says there are no *multidimensional* arrays in Java, meaning the language doesn't use the convention of Pascal or Ada to put several indexes into one set of subscript brackets. Ada allows multidimensional arrays like this:

```
year : array(1..12, 1..31) of real;
```
Ada code for multidimensional array.

```
year(i,j) = 924.4;
```

Ada also allows arrays of arrays, like this:

```
type month is array(1..31) of real;
```
Ada code for array of arrays.
```
year : array(1..12) of month;
year(i)(j) = 924.4;
```

Perhaps Ada and Pascal are a bit obscure these days, but I wanted to show you the different terminology and different design choices these languages have made, compared with Java. In some cases the terminology in one language is in conflict with the terminology in another language. Make sure everyone has a consistent view of the terminology before you start designing your software.

What "multidimensional" means in different languages

The Java language only has arrays of arrays, and it only calls these arrays of arrays.

- The Visual Basic language only has multidimensional arrays, and only calls them multidimensional arrays.
- The ANSI C standard says C has what other languages call arrays of arrays, but it also calls these multidimensional.
- The Ada standard explicitly says arrays of arrays and multidimensional arrays are different. The language has both.
- The Pascal standard says arrays of arrays and multidimensional arrays are the same thing.

When using an array of arrays, you can treat each individual component array as a free-standing array, and use it in any way you can use a free-standing array (assign to it, clear it, copy it, etc.). The different component arrays can be different sizes. When using a multidimensional array (in a language that supports it) there are no nested component arrays. You just have a table of M by N (or M by N by P, etc.) elements.

Declaring arrays of arrays

Java arrays of arrays are declared like this:

```
Fruit plums [] [] ;
```

Array "plums" is composed of an array of elements each of which is an array whose elements are Fruit objects. You can allocate and assign to any arrays individually.

```
plums = new Fruit [23] [9]; // an array[23] of array[9]
plums [i] = new Fruit [17]; // an array[17]
plums [i][j] = new Fruit(); // an individual Fruit
```

Because object declarations do not create objects (I am nagging about this repeatedly—it's an important point for bug free programs), you will need to fill out or *instantiate* the elements in an array before using it. If you have an array of arrays, like the one in the following example, you will need to instantiate both the top-level array and at least one bottom-level array before you can start storing ints:

```
int cabbage[][];
```

The bottom-level arrays do not have to all be a single uniform size. Here are several alternative and equivalent ways you could create and fill a triangular array of arrays:

- Use several array creation expressions, like this:

```
int myTable[][] = new int[][] {
                      new int[] {0},
                      new int[] {0,1},
                      new int[] {0,1,2},
                      new int[] {0,1,2,3},
                  };
```

- Lump all the initializers together in a big array initializer, like this:

```
int myTable[][] = new int[][] {
                  {0},
                  {0,1},
                  {0,1,2},
                  {0,1,2,3}, };
```

- Initialize individual arrays with array creation expressions, like this:

```
int myTable[][] = new int[4][];
// then in statements
myTable[0] = new int[] {0};
myTable[1] = new int[] {0, 1};
myTable[2] = new int[] {0, 1, 2};
myTable[3] = new int[] {0, 1, 2, 3};
```

- Use a loop, as outlined in the next section.

Looping over arrays

JDK 1.5 introduced a new form of the "for" loop, intended for iterating over an entire array. You provide three names: the element type, a name for the loop variable that will hold successive elements, and the array that you want to get elements from. Looping over a single array looks like this:

```
public static void main(String[] args) {
for(String s : args) {
    System.out.println(s);
}
```

Iterating through an array of arrays is similar. Say we have this array:

```
int myTable[][] = new int[][] {
                      new int[] {0},
                      new int[] {0,1},
                      new int[] {0,1,2},
                      new int[] {0,1,2,3},
                  };
```

We can loop over it with the following code. The outer loop has an element type of "array of int", and the inner loop has an element type of int.

```
for (int[] mt : myTable) {
    for (int i : mt) {
        System.out.print( i + " ");
    }
    System.out.println();
}
```

Put it in a main() method in a class, and compile the code with:

```
javac -source 1.5 arr.java
```

Run the code to get this output:

```
java arr
0
0 1
0 1 2
0 1 2 3
```

More about arrays of arrays

If you don't instantiate all the dimensions at one time, you must instantiate the most significant dimensions first. For example:

```
int cabbage[][] = new int[5][];    // ok
int cabbage[][] = new int[5][3];   // ok
```

but:

```
int cabbage[][] = new int[][3];    // NO! NO! NO! (bad allocation order)
```

Arrays with the same element type, and the same number of dimensions (in the C sense, Java doesn't have multidimensional arrays) can be assigned to each other. The arrays do not need to have the same number of elements because (as you would expect) the assignment just copies one reference variable into another. For example:

```
int eggs[] = {1,2,3,4,5};
int ham[] = new int[2] {77, 96};
ham = eggs;
ham[3] = 0;     // OK, because ham now has 5 elements.
```

This doesn't make a new copy of eggs; it makes ham and eggs reference the same array object.

Watch the size of those arrays of arrays. The following declaration allocates an array of 4 * 250 * 1000 * 1000 bytes = 1GB.

```
int bubba[][][] = new int[250][1000][1000];
```

Do you have that much memory on your system? In 1998, that was an hilarious joke. In the great post-bubble memory glut of 2001, 1GB was about $120 worth of synchronous 133MHz DRAM. By Spring 2004, 1 GB of DRAM cost about $150, but it was on two chips not four, and ran at 333 MHz not 133MHz. This is the power of Moore's Law. (And I have always admired the way Gordon Moore had exactly the right last name to give to his observation. Moore's law does indeed give you "More and more").

Have Array Brackets, Will Travel

There is a quirk of syntax in that the array declaration bracket pairs can "float" to be next to the element type, to be next to the data name, or to be in a mixture of the two. The following are all valid array declarations:

```
int a [] ;
int [] b = { 5, 2, 3 } ;

char c [][] = new char[12][31];
char[] d [] = { {1,1,1,1}, {2,2,2,2} }; // creates d[2][4]
char[][] e;

byte f [][][] = new byte [3][3][7];
byte [][] g[] = new byte [3][3][7];

short [] h, i[], j, k[][];
```

If array brackets appear next to the type, they are part of the type, and apply to *every* variable in that declaration. In the code above, "j" is an array of short, and "i" is an array of arrays of short. If the array brackets are next to the variable name, they apply only to that variable name.

Allowing (encouraging, actually) array brackets next to the type name is done so declarations of functions returning arrays can be read more easily. Here is an example of how returning an array value from a function would look following C rules. (You can't return an array in C, but this is how C syntax would express it if you could.)

```
int funarray()[] { ... }                    Pseudo-C code
```

Here are the alternatives for expressing it in Java (and it is permissible in Java), first following the C paradigm:

```
int ginger ()[]  { return new int[20]; }    Java code
```

A much better way is to express it as shown in Figure 9–1.

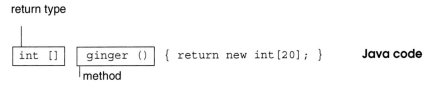

Figure 9–1   Better array declaration

Figure 9–1 allows the programmer to see all the tokens that compose the return type grouped together.

Chapter 10 has an explanation of what the stack and heap do for you. In some languages the stack lets you get into trouble by re-using memory that is already in use somewhere else in your program. Arrays are never allocated on the stack in Java, so you cannot get into trouble this way (see Chapter 10 for the full story). The takeaway here is that Java closes a loophole that's a big source of bugs in C/C++.

Indexing arrays and 64-bit Java

Arrays are indexed by int values. Values of types byte, short, and char are promoted to int when they are used as an index, just as they are in other expression contexts. Arrays may not be indexed by long values. That means arrays are implicitly limited to no more than the highest 32-bit int value, namely, 2,147,483,647. That's OK for the next year or so—but the lack of 64-bit addressing will eventually make itself felt in Java arrays, and the rule will need to be relaxed.

So what is meant by a 64-bit version of Java, available for the Solaris 64-bit operating system? It means that the JVM on that platform does not incur the emulation penalty of a 32-bit application on 64-bit hardware.

Instead, the JVM has been compiled as a 64-bit program, and supports 64-bit addresses on 64-bit Sparc-v9 platforms when using the Java HotSpot Server VM. With a 64-bit address space, heap memory above 4 GB is available. But you can't use it for a single massive array, because ints don't count that high. Until this language rule is relaxed, an array can hold no more than 2.1 billion elements.

The Math Package

Let's introduce another of the standard classes. This one is called java.lang.Math and it has a couple of dozen useful mathematical functions and constants, including trig routines (watch out—these expect an argument in radians, not degrees), pseudorandom numbers, square root, rounding, and the constants pi and e.

There are two methods in Math to convert between degrees and radians:

```
public static double toDegrees (double); // new in JDK 1.2
public static double toRadians (double); // new in JDK 1.2
```

You'll need these when you call the trig functions if your measurements are in degrees.

You can review the source of the Math package at $JAVAHOME/src/java/lang/Math.java and in the browser looking at the Java API.

How to invoke a Math.method

All the routines in the Math package are static, so you can invoke them using the name of the class, like this:

```
double probability = java.lang.Math.random(); // value 0.0..1.0
```

All the classes in java.lang are automatically imported, so you can write this as:

```
double probability = Math.random(); // value 0.0..1.0
```

Most people will write an import static line near the top of their code (right after the package statement):

```
import static java.lang.Math.*;
```

That allows you to shorten the method call to:

```
double cabbage = random();
```

Don't forget to compile with the "-source 1.5" option to javac if you use import static.

The Math.log() function returns a natural (base e) logarithm. Convert natural logarithms to base 10 logarithms with code like this:

```
double nat_log = ...

double base10log = nat_log / Math.log(10.0);
```

The list of members in the java.lang.Math class is:

```
public final class Math {
    public static final double E = 2.7182818284590452354;
    public static final double PI = 3.14159265358979323846;
    public static native double IEEEremainder(double, double);
    public static double abs(double);
    public static float abs(float);
    public static int abs(int);
    public static long abs(long);

// trig functions
    public static double toDegrees(double);
    public static double toRadians(double);
    public static native double sin(double);
    public static native double cos(double);
    public static native double tan(double);
    public static native double asin(double);
    public static native double acos(double);
    public static native double atan(double);
    public static native double atan2(double, double);
    public static native double exp(double);
    public static native double pow(double, double);
    public static native double log(double);
    public static native double sqrt(double);

// rounding and comparing
    public static native double ceil(double);
    public static native double floor(double);
    public static double max(double, double);
    public static float max(float, float);
    public static int max(int, int);
    public static long max(long, long);
    public static double min(double, double);
    public static float min(float, float);
    public static int min(int, int);
    public static long min(long, long);
    public static long round(double);
    public static int round(float);

// returns a random number between 0.0 and 1.0
    public static synchronized double random();

// rounds the argument to an integer, stored as a double
    public static native double rint(double);
}
```

To "strictfp" or not to "strictfp", is that the question?

The strictfp modifier has a performance cost. CPU's that can do 80-bit double length arithmetic have to take extra steps to get rid of the additional accuracy to mimic processors with standard 64-bit double arithmetic. People doing serious number crunching usually want programs to run as fast as possible, but sometimes consistency of results on all platforms is important too.

The best policy in this situation is to give users a choice. Provide one class that guarantees the fastest best results that a processor is capable of, and provide a second class that will give identical results on all processors.

This is exactly the approach that Java has chosen, support two math libraries with an otherwise identical API: java.lang.Math and java.lang.StrictMath. From the names, you can probably guess that StrictMath uses the strictfp modifier and produces identical results on all platforms. Indeed, that is what javadoc claims for java.lang.StrictMath.

Unhappily, if you look at the source code in the run-time library for these two classes, you'll see that the StrictMath class *does not* use the strictfp keyword, and java.lang.Math *does*. When there is a conflict between the documentation and the source code, I generally believe the source code. I filed bug 5050978 against JDK 1.5 beta, but no word back from Sun yet.

You can review and file bugs against Java at
`http://bugs.sun.com/bugdatabase/index.jsp`
It's very rare to find a bug in the JDK, and such bugs often result in compiler crashes. If you have a run-time problem in your program, it is almost guaranteed to be a bug you caused.

Originally, all the Math methods were "strictfp", meaning that the JVM could not use an extended exponent range to represent intermediate results on x86 hardware. That was changed in JDK 1.3, which introduced the package java.lang.StrictMath. StrictMath and Math have the same API. Use StrictMath when absolute portability of numeric results is an issue for you.

Some Light Relief—Think Big (and Small)

One early Java technology was applets—a Java program that runs in a browser. Someone who sets up a website can serve up executable Java programs referenced from HTML pages. When a user browses such a page, the Java code is downloaded to his or her system, along with the HTML text and images. A JVM inside the browser (safely and securely) executes the applet on the user's system.

You write an applet by extending the class javax.swing.JApplet, supplying your own child versions of some of the methods in the base class. At one time applets were very popular on the Internet, and they are still widely used for some applications on company intranets. They are also widely used at some educational sites.

Applets were wounded in the "browser wars" of the late 1990s. Microsoft crushed all competition in web browsers by bundling the Internet Explorer application, and paying off large ISPs to use Explorer. Eventually Netscape went out of business, and then people had to download complicated browser plug-ins to use applets. Many decided it was more trouble than it was worth. Pulling this kind of stunt is illegal when you're a monopoly. Microsoft settled out of court by paying $750 million to Netscape's owner AOL. But Netscape was still out of business, and there was still no competition in the browser market, and there was still no native support for applets.

People write applets to do all kinds of things, usually focused on a graphical and/or dynamic presentation of data from the server. There's one particularly good applet which you can easily find on the web. Known as the "Powers of 10" demo, it was written by Matthew J. Parry-Hill, Christopher A. Burdett, and Michael Davidson of the National High Magnetic Field Laboratory at Florida State University. The applet is based on the book *Cosmic View: The Universe in 40 Jumps* written by brilliant Dutch engineer and educator, Kees Boeke. Figure 9–2 shows a screen shot of the Powers of 10 applet.

The Powers of 10 applet presents a series of images, starting with the galaxy at 10 million light years from earth. Each image brings you, the observer, 10 times closer to earth. After about 15 such zoom-ins, there is a recognizable planet earth in the picture. Further zooms bring you to the Western hemisphere, the state of Florida, to a tree by the National High Magnetic Field Laboratory. You then zoom into a leaf, a leaf cell, DNA, and sub-atomic protoplasmic primordial globules.

Powers of 10 is an interactive Java-based tutorial on comparative sizes, fun as well as educational. Michael used a couple of interesting techniques to speed up performance. Only a couple of the images are downloaded before the applet starts. The rest are brought from the server as the applet is running, so the user does not have to wait. The "zoom in" effect on an image is done by re-drawing the images at different sizes rather than inefficiently using a succession of different-sized images. The applet is at
`http://micro.magnet.fsu.edu/primer/java/scienceopticsu/powersof10/index.html`
and it has been run by more than 14 million people in the last six years. Check it out; it's shown in Figure 9–2.

Figure 9–2   Powers of 10 interactive Java-based tutorial at
http://micro.magnet.fsu.edu/primer/java/scienceopticsu/powersof10/index.html

Exceptions

When people say "it's the exception that proves the rule" they mean prove in the sense of "test", as in *proving grounds*. They also mean exception in the sense of "infringement". In other words, you're really hearing "it's the infringements that test whether the rule is any good or not", but never mind that. In Java, the word "exception" relates to an unwanted error condition, and how we recover from it.

In this chapter, we'll cover the purpose of exceptions, what kinds of things cause them, and how to handle them when they happen. We'll start with a look at two data structures used by the run-time system, because some knowledge of these will give you much better insight into exceptions. We'll end the chapter with a description of the assert statement added to Java in JDK 1.4.

Exceptions and asserts are two ways of dealing with unexpected and unwanted error situations. Exceptions give you a chance to recover from the error and continue program execution. Assert statements provide a way to stop a program dead when it notices some serious inconsistency (like a checksum being incorrect). You can configure at run-time whether you want this "stop on error" behavior or not.

Run-time Internals: The Heap

We made the point in Chapter 2 that the purpose of reference variables is to allow automatic memory management. Many languages allow storage to be allocated dynamically (at run-time). This is good, because it allows a program to adapt to the size of the data it is trying to process, rather than being compiled with a fixed upper limit.

Memory is allocated implicitly by creating an object

In low-level languages like C, the programmer asks for a block of memory with a call to one of the malloc routines. In more structured languages like Java, you get memory by instantiating an object. That object can be an array of arbitrary size, limited only by the maximum value that an int index can hold, or by process size or by the virtual storage on the system.

Memory is a scarce resource, and you should free it up (return it to the system) when it is no longer needed. This can be done by the programmer explicitly managing memory resources, or by the system keeping track of what is in use and freeing up memory that is no longer in use. When the system has responsibility for freeing unused memory the process is known as *garbage collection*, although garbage recycling would be a more accurate term.

Since its first incarnation as the Oak language, Java has included garbage collection. Automatic garbage collection takes the burden of a challenging and error-prone task away from the programmer, leading to better memory utilization and higher reliability software.

A heap of memory

The *heap* is the run-time data structure used to support dynamic memory management. It is a large storage area that can allocate memory when the run-time library requests it, and can accept previously allocated memory back for deallocation and returning to the pool. Why is it called a heap? In English, a heap is a quantity of things lying in any old order on top of one another. That's what a heap is in a run-time library. It starts as a large segment of memory given to the process when it starts. As the process runs, it allocates memory, gives it back, allocates some more, and pretty soon you have a heap. The heap itself keeps track of what is in use and what is free. In C, you manage the heap manually. In Java, it is done for you.

Your programs start with a default total heap size, and you can change that maximum using a compiler flag like " -Xmx64m" for the JDK ("64m" means 64 MB). There are several other compiler flags to give guidance to the heap manager. You would only use them if you are tuning an application to make it fit on hardware that may be slightly too small. Search at java.sun.com for the document "Garbage Collector Ergonomics" if you want more information on these flags.

Memory leaks—rare in Java

Java designer James Gosling once asked a software engineer at an investment bank why they became a Java early adopter. The engineer replied that they had a large C++ system that had a memory leak (a common C++ bug that Java virtually eliminates). They were unable to do anything about this bug.

They adopted the workaround of rebooting the production system every day. The reboot would set everything back to a good initial state. The C++ program would start again, gradually leaking memory (holding onto it when it should be returned, causing the process to grow bigger and slower) until the next day's reboot.

As the bank's business increased and moved to more timezones, they got to the point where they didn't have a window of opportunity in which to reboot the server. So they rewrote the application in Java, and one day when the server was down for maintenance they decided to swap in the Java version. And, as the engineer reported, "It just stayed up, and it just stayed up, and it just stayed up."

There are automated tools for instrumenting and tracking C++ leaks. Sometimes these show leaks in vendor libraries, which are outside your control. SmartHeap from MicroQuill detects memory leaks in MFC, which Microsoft won't fix. Therefore, if you build a server using MFC, you risk falling into this situation.

Memory leaks are *much* less common in Java. You can use jvmstat to provide statistics about the heap and garbage collection. This will let you drill down on a performance issue. Search for "jvmstat" at `http://developers.sun.com`

Storage lifetime

Whenever something is allocated on the heap, its lifetime is independent of the scope in which it was allocated. In other words, it may have been allocated *inside* a method which has now returned. But if there is still a reference to it *outside* the method, it is still live.

```
int[] saveIt;

void foo() {
    int i;
    int[] a = new int[1000000];
    saveIt = a;
}

/*more code*/
  foo();
  saveIt[1000] = 23; // is it valid? array was allocated in foo
                     // and foo is no longer live
```

In the code above, an int array is allocated in a method and a reference to that array is stashed away for later use (the "saveIt=a" statement). Later, after the method has returned, the saved reference is used to access the array.

This is perfectly valid for languages like Java that use heap-based storage. It is a potent source of bugs for languages like C that allocate local variables on the stack. That part of the stack is freely overwritten after the flow of control returns from a method call. If the run-time allocated an array there, the array can be freely overwritten with other values.

Garbage Collection

Many programming languages support heap-based memory allocation. All objects in Java are allocated on the heap; no objects are ever allocated on the stack (an additional special-purpose storage data structure). Different pieces of storage can be allocated from and returned to the heap in no particular order, leading to problems of fragmentation—you have enough total storage free to satisfy a large allocation request, but it is not in the usable form of one contiguous chunk.

Solving the fragmentation problem

Heap fragmentation is resolved by the run-time system periodically reorganizing the heap, and possibly relocating some live (in-use) objects. All this will be transparent to the application, apart from the time it takes. Most algorithms require the application to stop while the heap is being reorganized.

Languages with dynamic data structures (structures that can grow and shrink in size at run-time) must have some way of telling the underlying run-time when they need more memory. C does this with the `malloc()` library call. Java does this with the "new" operator.

Conversely, you also need some way to indicate memory that is no longer in use (e.g., threads that have terminated, objects that are no longer referenced by anything, variables that have gone out of scope, etc.) and hand it back to the run-time system for reuse. C and C++ require explicit deallocation of memory; C does this with the `free()` library call, C++ uses `delete()`. The programmer has to say what memory (objects) to give back to the run-time system, and when. In practice, this has turned out to be an error-prone task. It's all too easy to create a "memory leak" by not freeing memory before overwriting the last pointer to it. It can then neither be referenced nor freed, and is lost to further use for as long as the program runs. The process address space grows bigger and bigger, and the process gets slower and slower as it is swapped out to make room for other tasks. Java takes a different approach to reclaiming memory.

To avoid the problems of explicit memory management, Java takes the burden off the shoulders of the programmer and puts it on the run-time storage manager. One subsystem of the storage manager is the "garbage collector." The automatic reclaiming of memory that is no longer in use is known as "garbage collection" in computer science. Java has a thread that runs in the background whose task is to do garbage collection. It looks at memory, and when it finds objects that are no longer referenced, it reclaims them by telling the heap that memory is available to be reallocated.

The costs and benefits of garbage collection

Taking away the task of memory management from the programmer gives him or her one less thing to worry about, and makes the resulting software much more reliable in use. It may take a little longer to run compared with a language like C++ with explicit memory management, because the garbage collector has to go out and look for reclaimable memory rather than simply being told where to find it. On the other hand, it's much quicker to debug your programs and get them running in the first place. Most people would agree that in the presence of ever-improving hardware performance, a small performance overhead is an acceptable price to pay for more reliable software.

What is the cost of making garbage collection an implicit operation of the run-time system rather than a responsibility of the programmer? It means that at unpredictable times, a potentially large amount of behind-the-scenes processing will suddenly start up when some low-water mark is hit and more memory is called for. This has been a problem with past systems, but Java addresses it somewhat with threads. In a multithreaded system, some of the garbage collector might run in parallel with user code and have a less intrusive effect on the system.

We should mention at this point that there is almost no direct interaction between the programmer and garbage collection. It is one of the run-time services that you can take for granted, like keeping track of return addresses, or identifying the correct handler for an exception. The discussion here is to provide a little more insight into what takes place behind the scenes.

If you want to tell the system that you are done with a data structure and it can be reclaimed, all you do is remove all your references to it, as in:

```
myBigDataStructure = null;
```

If there are other references to the data structure, it won't be garbage-collected. But as soon as nothing points to it, it is a candidate for sweeping away.

Finalizers

A "finalizer" is a Java term related to but not the same as a C++ destructor. When there are no further references to an object, its storage can be reclaimed by the garbage collector.

A finalizer is a method from class Object that any class may override. If a class has a finalizer method, it will be called on dead instances of that class before the memory occupied by that object is reused.

Garbage collection algorithms

A number of alternative garbage collection algorithms have been proposed and tried over the years. Three popular ones are "reference counting," "mark and sweep," and "stop and copy."

- **Reference counting** keeps a counter for each chunk of memory allocated. The counter records how many pointers directly point at the chunk or something inside it. The counter needs to be kept up to date as assignments are made. If the reference count ever drops to zero, nothing can ever access the memory and so it can immediately be returned to the pool of free storage. The big advantage of reference counting is that it imposes a steady constant overhead, rather than needing periodic bursts of the CPU. Reference counting has to be a bit more complex so it isn't fooled by circular references. If A points to B, and B points to A, but nothing else points to A and B they will not be freed even though they could be. It's also a little resource-intensive in multithreaded environments because reference counts must be locked for mutual exclusion before reference counts are updated.

- **Mark and sweep** is the garbage collection algorithm used by the current JDK. The marker starts at the root pointers. Root pointers are things like references to all threads, stacks and static (global) variables. You can imagine marking with a red pen every object that can be accessed from the roots. Then the marker recursively marks all the objects that are directly or indirectly referenced from the objects reachable from the roots. The algorithm continues until no more red marks can be placed. The entire virtual process may need to be swapped in and looked at, which is expensive in disk traffic and time. A smart garbage collector knows it doesn't have to bring in objects that can't contain references, like large graphics images and the like. Then the "sweep" phase starts, and everything without a red mark is swept back onto the free list for reuse. Memory compaction also takes place at this point. Memory compaction means jiggling down into one place all the memory that is in use, so that all the free store comes together and can be merged into one large pool. Compaction helps when you have a number of large objects to allocate.

- **Stop and copy** is a third garbage collection algorithm. As the name suggests, it halts all other threads and goes into a garbage collection phase. The heap is split into two parts: the currently active part and the new part. Each of these is known as a "semi-space." Non-garbage is identified by tracing active pointers, just as in mark and sweep. It copies all the non-garbage stuff over into the new semi-space and makes that the currently active semi-space. The old currently active semi-space is just discarded completely. The advantage of "stop and copy" is that it avoids heap fragmentation, so periodic memory compaction is not needed. Stop and copy is a fast garbage collection algorithm, but it requires twice the memory area. It also can't be used in real-time systems, as it makes your computer appear to just freeze from time to time.

The Java Language Specification says this on the topic:

> The purpose of finalizers is to provide a chance to free up resources (such as file descriptors or operating system graphics contexts) that are owned by objects but cannot be accessed directly and cannot be freed automatically by the automatic storage management. Simply reclaiming an object's memory by garbage collection would not guarantee that these resources would be reclaimed.

You don't need this in your code 99% of the time. The run-time library does control several resources like this, such as *graphics contexts*. They usually come with a method called dispose(), which you call to tell the run-time to give the resource back to the OS.

Interpose a finalizer by providing a body for the method finalize() in your class to override the Object version. It will look like this:

```
class Fruit {

        protected void finalize() throws Throwable {
                // do finalization
        }
```

It must have the signature shown (also be protected and return void). If present, a class's finalizer is called by the garbage collector at some point after the object is first recognized as garbage and before the memory is reclaimed, such that the object is garbage at the time of the call. A finalizer can also be called explicitly. There is no guarantee that an object will be garbage collected, and hence there is no guarantee that an object's finalizer will be called. A program may terminate normally without garbage collection taking place. So you could not rely on a finalizer method being called, and you cannot use it to carry out some essential final housekeeping (release a lock, write usage statistics, or whatever).

Finally (uh...), don't confuse "final" (a constant) or "finally" (a block that is always executed after a "try{}") with "finalize"—the three concepts are unrelated.

Weak references

JDK 1.2 brought in the notion of *weak references*. Weak references allow a program to have a reference to an object that does not prevent the object from being considered for reclamation by the garbage collector. This is an advanced technique that won't appear in your programs much, if at all.

Weak references are useful for building caches that can be flushed if memory gets low. They also permit scheduling post-mortem cleanup actions in a more flexible way than the finalization mechanism. Finally, weak references allow a program to be notified when the collector has determined that an object has become eligible for reclamation.

Let us move on to look at the other great run-time data structure, the stack.

Run-time Internals: The Stack

The *stack* is a run-time data structure that provides the storage space needed for method calls and returns. All modern block-structured languages use stacks, and many processors have some hardware support for them. Unfortunately in recent years, the terminology has got a little looser; marketing people started using *stack* to mean any layered system service, such as the TCP/IP library, or an application server and container. In this chapter, stack means the LIFO (Last In First Out) data structure that provides space for local variables, and implements the method-calling conventions.

When you call a method, some housekeeping data, known as an *activation record* or *stack frame*, is pushed onto the stack. The activation record contains the return address, the arguments passed to the function, the space for local variables, intermediate calculations, and so on, for that invocation of that method in that thread of control. When you return from a function, the activation record is popped from the stack. The next function call will push another record into the same space.

Figure 10–1 shows how each method call results in a new activation record being pushed onto (added to) the stack. Stacks are only ever meant to be used for data, never for storing code.

Stack cracking—impossible in Java

If you have any pointers back into the old activation record on the stack, memory can be corrupted, as the pointer references an area that the next function call will reuse for a different purpose. A cracker can do this deliberately, overwrite the return address on the stack, and have the program "return" to other code that he places on the stack.

This is the source of a large number of high-profile bugs and failings in C/C++ code. The Internet Worm of 1988 used a related flaw to subvert a large part of the Internet. Ten years later, the Hotmail bug of 1998 was due to the same flaw! In 2008, I fully expect the latest Windows virus to exploit this C/C++ design flaw, just as so many do today. In other words, the lifetime of stack-based storage is tied to the scope in which it was allocated; although many languages let you get this wrong, Java doesn't!

Intel is currently considering hardware modifications so that a CPU can recognize when it is executing from addresses in a stack, and cease execution! Only a hardware company would consider using a silicon sledgehammer to crack a software nut.

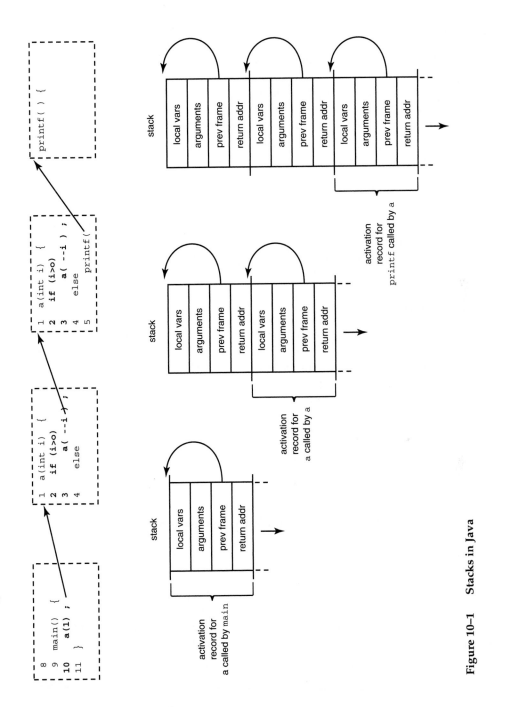

Figure 10–1   Stacks in Java

Although we have talked about "the stack", there will actually be one stack allocated for each thread of control within your program. If a thread in your Java code (or any Java libraries you are using) calls out to a C library, another stack will be allocated to hold the C activation records. You don't have to do anything special to get your stacks. As part of instantiating a new thread, the run-time allocates a new stack for it to use. The heap is usually put at the opposite end of the address space to the stacks, and they grow towards the holes between them.

The JDK compiler option -Xoss determines the size of the Java stacks. The default value depends on the hardware you are using, and the JDK version. You can set the value to 64Kb with compiler option: -Xoss64k. If a thread runs out of stack space or collides with the bottom of another stack, you will get the exception java.lang.StackOverflowError. (Sun uses the standard trick of mapping a page at the end of each stack with no permission, so if a thread bumps into it, the OS memory protection catches it at once). This is a good point to pick up with the description of exceptions, starting in the next section.

Exceptions

We'll cover the purpose and use of exceptions following this order. The one sentence summary is *"Exceptions are like software interrupts—they are generated by error conditions like division by zero, and they divert the flow of control to a place where you have said you will handle this kind of error."*

First, we'll look at the basics of:

- Why exceptions are in the language.

- What causes an exception (implicitly and explicitly).

Once an exception has occurred, you'll want to know how to take steps to deal with it:

- How to handle ("catch") an exception within the method where it was thrown.

- Handling groups of related exceptions.

You'll also need to know what happens if you do not provide code to handle each type of exception. You can skip this on a first reading if you just want the exception basics. These sections have information saying how methods tell the compiler about exceptions they might generate but do not handle:

- How the exception propagates if not handled in the method where it was thrown.

- How and why methods declare the exceptions that can propagate out of them.

- Fancy exception stuff.

The purpose of exceptions

Exceptions are for changing the flow of control when some important or unexpected event, usually an error, has occurred. They divert processing to a part of the program that can try to cope with the error, or at least die gracefully.

There are many possible errors that can happen in non-trivial programs: these range from "unable to open a file" to "array subscript out of range" to "no memory left to allocate" to "division by zero." It would obscure the code greatly to check for all possibilities at all places where they may happen. Exceptions provide a clean way for you to write general or specific error handlers, and have the run-time system watch for these errors and transfer control when necessary. Your error handler code thus does not clutter up the mainstream processing.

Java exceptions are adapted from C++, which itself borrowed them from the functional language ML, developed by Bell Labs, Princeton, and recently Yale. Java exception terminology is shown in Table 10–1.

Table 10–1   Exception terminology of Java

Note	Java	Some other languages
An error condition that happens at run-time	Exception	Exception
Causing an exception to occur	Throwing	Raising
Capturing an exception that has just occurred and executing statements to resolve it in some way	Catching	Handling
The block that does this	Catch clause	Handler
The sequence of method calls that brought control to the point where the exception happened	Stack trace	Call chain

What happens when an exception is thrown

An exception is set in motion by the program doing some illegal or invalid action, such as trying to reference through a null pointer. An exception can also be caused explicitly by the "throw" statement. Two things happen:

- An exception object is instantiated to record the details of what went wrong

- The run-time system then diverts the normal flow of control, to search back up the call chain for a place where you have put a statement saying you can handle this kind of exception object.

That place can be in the same method, in the method that called the one where the exception occurred, or in the one that called that method, and so on. You might want to refresh your memory on how the stack keeps track of method invocations, by looking at Figure 10–1.

Because control propagates back up the call chain, we say that the exception object is *thrown*. It's not really "thrown" anywhere; the exception object is really held ready to one side, while the run-time system looks further and further up the call chain for a catch clause that covers this kind of exception.

If the run-time system gets to the top where your program execution started, and no handler for the exception has yet been found, then program execution will cease with an explanatory message.

How to cause an exception (implicitly and explicitly)

As stated previously, exceptions occur when:

- The program does something illegal (common case), or
- The program explicitly generates an exception by executing the throw statement (less common case)

The throw statement has this general form:

```
throw ExceptionObject;
```

The *ExceptionObject* is an object of a class that extends the class java.lang.Exception.

Example of causing an exception

Here is a simple program that results in an "int division by zero" exception:

```
class example10 {
    public static void main(String[] a) {
        int i=1, j=0, k;

        k = i/j;    // line 5 causes division-by-zero exception
    }
}
```

Compiling and running this program gives this result:

```
> javac example10.java
> java example10
    java.lang.ArithmeticException: / by zero
        at example10.main(example10.java:5)
```

The message "/ by zero" is the unknown compiler writer's goofy shorthand for "division by zero". There are a certain number of predefined exceptions, like ArithmeticException, known as the run-time exceptions. Actually, since *all* exceptions are run-time events, a better name would be the "irrecoverable" exceptions. The Javaheads mean "run-time" in the sense of "thrown by the run-time library code, not your code."

Run-time exceptions contrast with the user-defined exceptions which are generally held to be less severe, and in some instances can be recovered from. If a filename cannot be opened, prompt the user to enter a new name. If a data structure is found to be full, overwrite some element that is no longer needed.

You don't have to (but can) make provisions for catching run-time exceptions. You *do* have to make provision for user-defined exception types. The user-defined exceptions are called *checked exceptions* because the compiler checks your code for consistency across: where they are thrown, the methods that say they can throw them, and where they are caught (handled).

The class hierarchy for exceptions looks like Figure 10–2.

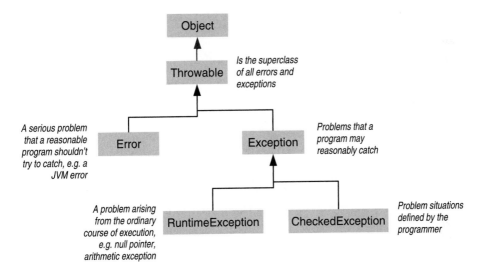

Figure 10–2   Class hierarchy for exceptions

User-defined exceptions

Here is an example of how to create your own exception class by extending class java.lang.Exception:

```
class OutofGas extends Exception {}

class Airplane {
      /* more code */
      if (fuel < 0.1) throw   new OutofGas();
}
```

Any method that throws a user-defined exception must also either catch it or declare it as part of the method interface. What, you may ask, is the point of throwing an exception if you are going to catch it in the same method? The answer is that exceptions don't *reduce* the amount of work you have to do to handle errors. Their advantage is they let you collect it all in well localized places in your program so you don't obscure the main flow of control with zillions of checks of return values.

Figure 10–3   **Exception notice an error, but don't necessarily allow recovery**

How to handle ("catch") an exception within the method where it was thrown

Here is the general form of how to catch an exception:

```
try  {  /* exception-raising statements here */ }
```

There must be at least one of
the two choices below. Both are OK.

```
catch (arg)  { /*code*/}
```
◄———— There can be zero or many of these.

```
finally    { /*code*/}
```
◄———— There can be zero or one of these.

The try statement says, "Try these statements and see if you get an exception." The try statement must be followed by one (or both) of these two clauses:

- The catch clause
- The finally clause

You can have multiple `catch` clauses, and you can have `catch` clauses with a `finally` clause.

Each `catch` says, "I will handle any exception that matches my argument." Matching an argument means that the thrown exception could legally be assigned to the argument exception (assignment compatible—it's the same class or a subclass of the argument exception). There can be several successive catches, each looking for a different exception. Here's an example `try` statement that catches just one type of exception.

```
try {
    i = method_A(len, 0);
    j = method_B( );
} catch (CharConversionException cce) {
    n = assignDefaults();
}
```

It's generally regarded as bad style to attempt to catch *all* exceptions with one clause, like this:

```
catch (Exception e) { /* more code */
```

That is too general to be of use and you might catch more than you expected. You should catch specific checked exceptions and let run-time exceptions propagate up to give you a reasonable error message when they hit the top. However, you'll see it in books and sample programs, where people are trying to avoid "code explosion" of unnecessary detail.

The `finally` block, if present, is a "last chance to clean up" block. It is *always* executed—even if something in one of the other blocks did a "return!" The `finally` block is executed whether an exception occurred or not and whether it was caught or not. It is executed after the `catch` block, if present, and, regardless of the path taken, through the `try` block and the `catch` block.

The `finally` block can be useful in the complete absence of any exceptions. It is a piece of code that is executed irrespective of what happens in the `try` block. There may be numerous paths through a large and complicated `try` block. The `finally` block can contain the housekeeping tasks that must always be done (counts updated, locks released, and so on) when finishing this piece of code.

Cleaning up with `finally`

Most resources in a program are simply memory, but there are a few resources known to the operating system outside the program. Graphics contexts are one example. They are used to keep track of something on the screen and carry around a lot of information about font, resolution, size, color, and pixel data. There are usually a limited number of graphics contexts available at any one time.

Sockets, file descriptors, database connections, and window handles are other common examples. These usually have a `dispose()` method to hand the resource back to the operating system. If you just null out the last pointer to the resource, the Java side of it will eventually be garbage-collected, but that doesn't do anything about recycling the native resource.

By putting a call to `dispose()` in the `finally` clause, we can be certain that the scarce resource will always be given back to the operating system, regardless of any exceptions raised or avoided.

After the whole *try ... catch ... finally* series of blocks is executed, if one of those blocks doesn't divert it, execution continues after the last `catch` or `finally` (whichever is present). The kinds of things that could make execution divert to elsewhere are the regular things: a `continue`, `break`, `return`, or the raising of a different exception. If a `finally` clause also has a transfer of control statement, then that is the one that is obeyed.

Handling groups of related exceptions

We mentioned before that "matching an argument" means that the thrown exception can be assigned legally to the argument exception. This permits a refinement. It allows a handler to catch any of several related exception objects with common parentage. Look at this example:

```
class Grumpy extends Exception {}
class TooHot   extends Grumpy {}
class TooTired extends Grumpy {}
class TooCross extends Grumpy {}
class TooCold  extends Grumpy {}
    /* more code */

    try {
      if ( temp > 40 ) throw (new TooHot() );
      if ( sleep < 8 ) throw (new TooTired() );
    }
    catch (Grumpy g) {
        if (g instanceof TooHot)
           {System.out.println("caught too hot!"); return;}
        if (g instanceof TooTired)
           {System.out.println("caught too tired!"); return;}
    }
    finally {System.out.println("in the finally clause.");}
  }
```

The catch clauses are checked in the order in which they appear in the program. If there is a match, then the block is executed. The instanceof operator can be used to learn the exact identity of the exception.

How the exception propagates if not handled in the method where it was thrown

If none of the catch clauses match the exception that has been thrown, then the finally clause is executed (if there is one). At this point (no handler for this exception), what happens is the same as if the exception was raised and there wasn't a try statement. The flow of control abruptly leaves this method, and a premature return is done to the method that called this one. If that call was in the scope of a try statement, then we look for a matching exception again, and so on.

Figure 10–4 shows what happens when an exception is not dealt within the routine where it occurs. The run-time system looks for a "try . . . catch" block further up the call chain, enclosing the method call that brought us here. If the exception propagates all the way to the top of the call stack without finding a matching exception handler, then execution ceases with a message. You can think of this as Java setting up a default catch block for you around the program entry point that just prints an error message and quits.

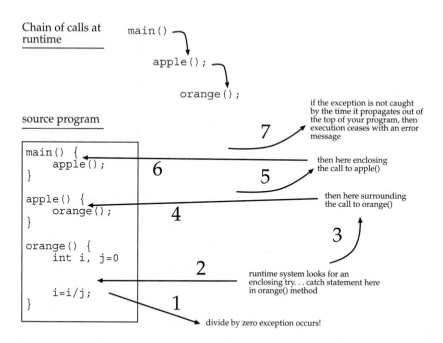

Figure 10–4   The result of an exception not handled within the occurring routine

There is no overhead to putting some statements in a `try` statement. The only overhead comes when an exception occurs.

How and why methods declare the exceptions that can propagate out of them

Earlier we mentioned that a method must either catch the exception that it throws or declare it along with its signature,[1] meaning it must announce the exception to the outside world. This is so that anyone who writes a call to that method is alerted to the fact that an exception might come back instead of a normal return. It also allows the compiler to check that you are using exceptions consistently and have covered all the cases.

When a programmer sees that a method can raise an exception, he or she makes the choice between handling the exception or allowing it to propagate further up the call stack. A method declares the exceptions that might be thrown out of it by listing them in a throws clause like this:

```
public static int parseInt(String s, int radix)
                        throws NumberFormatException {
      /* body of method */
}
```

1.   The exceptions a method throws are not part of the signature, though.

If the routine can throw more than one exception, list them all, separating the names with commas. The names must be exception or error names (that is, any type that is assignable to the predefined type Throwable). Note that just as a method declaration specifies the return *type*, it specifies the exception *type* that can be thrown, rather than an exception object.

The rules for how much and what must match, when one method that throws an exception overrides another, work in the obvious way. Namely, if you never do this, you will never obviously be bothered by it. Well, OK, another way to think about it is to consider the exception as an extra parameter that must be assignment-compatible with the exception in the class being overridden.

Fancy exception stuff

When you create a new exception by subclassing an existing exception class, you have the chance to associate a message string with it. The message string can be retrieved by a method. Usually, the message string will be some kind of more detailed indication about what's gone wrong.

```
class OutofGas extends Exception {
    OutofGas(String s) {super(s);}  // constructor
}

    /* more code */
    // in use, it may look like this
    try {
        if (fuel<1) throw  new OutofGas("less than 1 litre fuel");
    }
    catch ( OutofGas o) {
        System.out.println( o.getMessage() );
    }
```

At run-time, if there is less than one unit of fuel where it is tested, the OutOfGas exception will be thrown, and the handler will cause this message to appear:

```
less than 1 litre fuel
```

You might log the message, or write it to a diagnostics file instead of displaying it. Another method that is inherited from the superclass Throwable is printStackTrace().

How to find out which method threw the exception

Developers sometimes need code that gets the name of the method the code is currently in. Often this is needed for logging or diagnostic purposes. The old way of finding the current location in a program involved generating an exception, printing the stack trace to an in-memory buffer, and then parsing the trace to find out the exact information.

Since JDK 1.4, there is a much better and briefer way: use the StackTraceElement class. The code looks like this:

```
Throwable t = new Throwable();
StackTraceElement elements[] = t.getStackTrace();
String method = elements[0].getMethodName();
```

If you're interested in this, also review the java.util.logging package, which has similar helpful features.

Invoking this method on an exception will cause the call chain at the point where the exception was thrown (not where it is being handled) to be printed out. For example:

```
// catching an exception in a calling method

class test5p {
    static int myArray[] = {0,1,2,3,4};

    public static void main(String[] a) {
        try {
            bob();
        } catch (Exception e) {
            System.out.println("caught exception in main()");
            e.printStackTrace;
        }
    }

    static void bob() {

        try {
            myArray[-1] = 4; //obvious out of bounds exception
        }
        catch (NullPointerException e) {
            System.out.println("caught a different exception");
        }

    }
}
```

We have a handler for null pointer, but that has nothing to do with the exception that occurred. So the exception propagated back to the top and execution ended. At run-time it will produce output like this:

```
caught exception in main()
java.lang.ArrayIndexOutOfBoundsException: -1
    at test.bob(test5p.java:19)
    at test.main(test5p.java:9)
```

Summary of exceptions

- Their purpose is to allow safer programming by providing a distinct path to deal with errors.

- Many methods in the API throw exceptions, so you can't avoid using them. Do define your own error conditions. But don't over-use them and make them do the work that an if statement should do. Exceptions are a useful tool for organized handling of true error conditions.

- The main use of exceptions is getting a decent error message explaining what failed, where, and why. It's a bit much to always expect recovery. Graceful degradation is often the most you can obtain.

We will next review the assert statement.

The Assert Statement

Introduced with Java 1.4, the assert statement helps to debug code and also troubleshoot applications after they have been deployed. You write an assert statement stating some very important condition that you believe will always be true at this point in your program. If the condition *is not* true, the assertion throws an Error (a Throwable thing that is not intended to be caught). You can do that already in Java. The part that is new is that assertion statements let you choose at run-time whether the assertion checking is on or off.

Two key steps in using assert

There are two key pieces to using asserts.

- First, you sprinkle assert statements at a few critical places in your program. For example, after calculating a checksum, you could assert that the calculated value equals the stored checksum. You only use assert statements for fatal errors—something has gone so wrong that the only thing to do is stop before more data disappears or whatever.

- The second half of assert statements is that you control whether the assert statements are in effect, or not, at run-time. There is a command line option to the JVM that enables or disables whether the assertions are executed, and this can be applied to individual packages and even classes.

The usual scenario is that you keep the assert statements on during debugging and testing. After testing, when you are confident that the application works correctly, you no longer need to do all that checking. So you disable the assert statements, but leave them compiled in the source code. If the application later hits a problem, you can enable asserts and rerun the failure case to see if any assertions are untrue. This can be done in the field or over telephone support.

An assert statement looks like either of these alternatives:

```
assert booleanExpression;

assert booleanExpression : Expression2;
```

If the boolean is not true, a java.lang.AssertionError is thrown. The second form of the statement allows you to write an expression that will be passed to the constructor of the AssertionError. The expression is supposed to resolve to a message about what went wrong. You should just pass a String. An expression of other types (such as int) is allowed to accommodate those crazies who want to number their error messages or label them with a character instead of using self-identifying strings.

Complete example of assert

Here's a complete example of the use, compilation, and run of a program with assert.

```
public class asst {
    public static void main(String[] args) {

        int a = Integer.parseInt(args[0]);
        System.out.println("a = "+a);

        assert a>=0 : "argument too negative";

        // if a OK, go on with program
    }
}
```

That assert statement is equivalent to this line of code:

```
if (a<0) throw new java.lang.AssertionError("argument too negative");
```

except that you have the additional ability to configure whether such statements should be executed or not.

When using assert statements, Sun's JDK 1.4 compiler needs the `-source 1.4` command line option. That option is not needed when using Sun's Java 5 compiler. This is to avoid code breakage with people who have created their own version of assertions in the past and used the identifier "assert". Compile as follows:

```
javac -source 1.4 asst.java
```

Even after you have compiled them in, by default assertions are *disabled* at run-time. Here is a regular program execution where no error occurs, even though we provided a command line argument that triggers the problem.

```
java asst -3
```

To turn on the assertion checking for a particular run, use the "-ea" (enable assertions) option to java:

```
java -ea asst -3
Exception in thread "main" java.lang.AssertionError: argument too
negative at asst.main(asst.java:7)
```

There is also a syntax for enabling just one package tree or a class, but you might as well do everything. A separate switch is provided to enable asserts in the system classes (i.e., to set the assertion status for java.* packages to true).

```
java   -esa   MyProgram
```

If you ever get a run-time error in the JVM, such as a core dump, try running with the "-esa" option and including the output in your bug report to Sun. You can search and file bug reports on the JDK at the Java Developer Connection site `developer.java.sun.com`.

Points to watch with assert

There are a couple of caveats with assertion statements. First, you must test your code both ways, with assertions enabled and disabled.

Second, you must avoid side effects in the assertion expression. Otherwise, program behavior would be different depending on whether you run with assertions on or off. A "side effect" is a change to the value of some variable, as part of evaluating the expression, e.g.,

```
boolean noMoreData = true;

boolean checkingMethod() {
    noMoreData = false;
    return noMoreData;
}
assert checkingMethod();
```

Just Java 2

Finally, assertions are supposed to be unrecoverable errors, so do not try to repair the problem and continue. That is what exceptions are for. Assert statements provide the ability to check for significant errors and to make the checking configurable at run-time.

Further Reading

There is more information on the assert statement, including a couple of clever idioms, at the Sun site `java.sun.com/j2se/1.5/docs/guide/lang/assert.html`. One of the idioms is code to prevent a program from running at all if assertions are turned off.

Some Light Relief—Making an Exception for You

In June 2003, NASA launched two robot geologist missions to Mars. After a space voyage of six months, the Spirit Rover was the first to arrive safely and start its exploration, looking for signs of water and other geological features. For two and a half weeks on the surface, Spirit sent a series of stunning pictures. Suddenly and inexplicably, it dropped contact with mission control.

The team back at California's Jet Propulsion Lab who designed and built the rovers were mystified and despondent. The Spirit mission manager, Jennifer Trosper, talked to her husband on the phone. "I asked him first how his day was. He said it was okay. And then he asked me how my day was going," recalled Trosper. "Well... I think I'm personally responsible for the loss of a $400 million national asset," she confessed. I hate those kind of "rainy Monday" days, don't you?

The Rover is a reprogrammable embedded system that is directed by remote control instructions over wireless from Earth. If Spirit didn't make contact, it wouldn't get instructions for more tasks, or even to diagnose the failure. Things perked up a little the next day when JPL sent a command, and Spirit acknowledged it before once again falling silent.

The Spirit rover is built from off-the-shelf hardware and software. Wind River's VxWorks real-time embedded OS runs on top of a radiation-hardened RAD6000 CPU chip from Lockheed-Martin. This chip is based on the same Power-PC CPU that IBM uses in its RS/6000 Unix workstations. It's a 32-bit RISC processor clocked at 33MHz with 120MB main memory, which is plenty for the tasks it has to do. Mars is a hostile environment for anything mechanical, so the rover has a 256 MB flash memory filesystem instead of disk.

The flash filesystem stores data files (such as photo files), and also executable programs. It's designed so that when the system boots up, some filesystem data is copied from flash into a main memory cache. Obviously the amount of RAM reserved for the cache places an overall limit on the size and number of files the RAM disk can hold. JPL was aware of this limit, and had calculated that regular operations would stay well within it.

Everything about the software was designed to be maintained over radio links from planet Earth. Indeed, the mission team had uploaded a completely new software revision a week after the June 2003 launch, as the Spirit rover raced towards Mars. You never want to delete the old software until you've had a chance to check that the new software works in all circumstances, so the flash memory now held two sets of executables.

The software upload fixed the bugs that had been identified, and mission control made a note that they'd have to delete the old files after the new ones had been shown to work on the ground. Six months later, Spirit landed on Mars, and started collecting data. Each set of data, each image, each instrument reading was stored in a new file in the flash file system. On Martian day 15 of the mission, the ground team uploaded in two parts a utility that would clean out the obsolete files and free up a lot of room in the flash filesystem.

Unhappily, the second half of the upload failed, and was rescheduled for the next communications window between Earth and Mars, four days later. In the meantime, Spirit continued taking pictures and measurements, and storing the results in the rapidly filling filesystem. Before the file delete utility could be uploaded, the portion of RAM dedicated to the flash filesystem filled up completely.

No new files could be written. The very next task that tried to write a file got a "memory allocation failure" exception instead (this part of the Rover is written in C++, but it was an exception of the same type discussed in this chapter). The exception handler put the task on hold, waiting for space. That in turn eventually led to a system reboot. And when the system rebooted, it tried to mount the flash filesystem and build the RAM cache. Again, it ran out of RAM space while making the attempt. That led to a reboot, and the cycle now repeated over and over again. Spirit was unable to complete a reboot and spent most of the time resetting itself instead of listening to signals from Earth.

As the team on earth searched for possible causes of failure, someone recalled the incomplete upload of the delete utility. Analyzing this further, the team recalled that they had used the VxWorks option that causes a task to be suspended on a memory allocation failure. The team uploaded a new program that instructed Spirit to reboot without mounting the flash memory filesystem. They transmitted it repeatedly until they hit the narrow window when Spirit was able to listen during its reboot attempts. Spirit acknowledged the transmission just as it was supposed to. The message had gotten through!

They then wrote code to go through the flash memory image, and delete the obsolete files there, without using the RAM cache. Finally, they ran an fsck (filesystem check) utility. To everyone's great relief, Spirit started functioning again! But, just in case, the software team is updating the exception-handler to recover from a memory allocation failure more gracefully! So there you have it—whether you are in the computer room down the hall, or 1.52 Astronomical Units away on the surface of another planet, exception handlers really matter.

Interfaces

Interfaces are an important concept in Java. In this chapter, we'll explain what interfaces do, and how you use them. Here's a summary of what interfaces do, so you can see where we're headed.

In a few words, an interface is similar to a class that only abstract methods. You can't instantiate an abstract class; its purpose is to force any subclasses to implement its methods. That allows other classes to rely on those methods being present in the subclasses.

An interface does the same job as a class, but without the requirement that there is a parent/child relationship. Interfaces are reference types, like classes and arrays. Interface types are used as parameters, and an actual class with that behavior will be used as an argument. A class associates itself with an interface by saying it *implements* an interface, thereby promising that it provides all the methods that the interface specifies.

Let's start by describing the problem that interfaces solve.

What Problem Does an Interface Solve?

We've seen in previous chapters how classes can be related in a hierarchy, with the common behavior higher up the tree. An example is given in Figure 11–1.

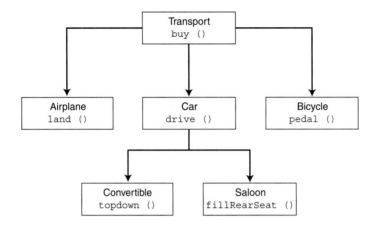

Figure 11–1 **Where should the `refuel()` method go?**

Figure 11–1 shows some classes relating to means of transport. Each box is a class, labeled with the class name, and with an example method that belongs in that class. The parent class is called "Transport" and has a method called `buy()`. Whatever kind of vehicle you have, you have to buy it before it becomes yours. Putting the method in the parent class means that all subclasses inherit it.

Transport has three child classes. The class called "Car" has a method called `drive()`, and this is inherited by its two subclasses, Convertible and Saloon. Whatever kind of car it is, the way you move it is to `drive()`. It belongs in Car, not Transport, because you ride a bicycle or fly an airplane, not drive them.

Now let's imagine we want to keep refuelling information in this class hierarchy. We want to add a method called `refuel()` that fills the fuel tank of each vehicle. The class that keeps track of our supply depot will call the refuel method on vehicle objects. Where is the right place to add `refuel()` in the tree of classes?

We cannot add a `refuel()` method in the transport class, because Bicycle would inherit it, and bicycles are not refuelled. We can add the method individually to Airplane and Car and any other unrelated Classes, like Generator, which represent something you can refuel.

That's good, but it causes problems for our supply depot class. The supply depot class will call an object's `refuel()` method. What should be the type of the things we pass to it for refuelling? We cannot pass a Transport, because not all transport objects have a refuel() method, and some non-Transport things (like Generator or Pump) need refuelling.

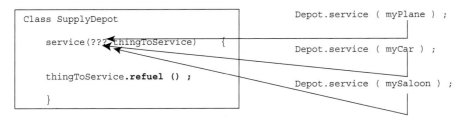

Figure 11–2 **What type should thingToService be to represent everything that has a refuel() method?**

We could overload service() with one version for each type that has a refuel method.

```
public class SupplyDepot {
    public void service(Airplane a)  { /* more code */ }
    public void service(Car c)       { /* more code */ }
    public void service(Generator g) { /* more code */ }
    public void service(Pump p)      { /* more code */ }
        // more methods, omitted
}
```

But that's not very convenient. If we come along with some new thing that is capable of being refuelled, like a JetSki, we now have to modify the SupplyDepot class to add a service (JetSki j) method. Well designed systems don't cause changes to ripple across classes this way.

We are looking for a way to say "I represent any type that has a refuel() method" (see Figure 11–2). Then we just make the argument to service() be that type. Some OOP languages allow classes to have more than one parent, a feature known as "multiple inheritance." Multiple inheritance would solve this problem by having a class called CapableOfBeingRefuelled with a single method called refuel(). Everything that can be refuelled will be where it is now in the class hierarchy, but it will also have CapableOfBeingRefuelled as a second parent.

When a language has multiple inheritance, it often proves to be a controversial feature because it seems to need a great many confusing and unintuitive language rules. Java does not have a multiple inheritance feature, but it has something that fills a similar role in a simpler way. Step forward, interfaces!

Interfaces are in the Java language to allow a class to say it has some particular behavior. An interface type acts as a placeholder for real classes in any place where that behavior is expected.

We already saw something similar with inheritance, but you can inherit only from *one* class. A class can implement *any number* of interfaces. Interfaces say, "*I offer these methods, and you can later use any object from a class that implements me in any place you are using me.*" Interfaces provide the functionality of multiple inheritance, without the difficulties.

Remember some of the sample Java classes, like java.lang.String and java.lang.Integer we have presented, saying "here is the API" and showing a list of the method names (but not the code inside the methods)? The "I" in API even stands for "Interface" (Application Programmer Interface).

This is what a Java interface is: A class-like item that has a list of method names, not the method bodies. For this reason, some people say that "Java has multiple inheritance of interface, but not multiple inheritance of implementation." An interface is a skeleton of a class showing the methods the class will have when someone implements it. An interface looks like the following:

```
public interface CapableOfBeingRefuelled {
    public int refuel();
}
```

An interface looks a bit like a class (actually, with no bodies, it's more like an abstract class), is counted as a reference type, and can generally be used in most of the same places as a class. It doesn't have any behavior, though—it's just a description of promised behavior. Here's how the members behave, regardless of whether you supply these modifiers:

- The members of an interface—the fields and methods—are public, even if you don't label them so.

- Any data fields in an interface are final, even if you don't label them so.

- The methods in an interface are abstract, even if you don't label them so.

Any class that has a refuel method should say that it implements the CapableOfBeingRefuelled interface, as follows:

```
public class Airplane implements CapableOfBeingRefuelled {
    public int refuel() {
        purgeTanks();
        leftTank = this.capacity;
        rightTank = this.capacity;
    }
        // more methods, omitted
}
```

Now here comes the clever part. The SupplyDepot's service method will take an argument that is type CapableOfBeingRefuelled! Class Airplane, Generator,

JetSki, Car and so on all have that type by virtue of implementing that interface. Therefore, they can all be passed to the service method. SupplyDepot will look like the following.

```
public class SupplyDepot {
    public void service(CapableOfBeingRefuelled thingToService) {
        thingToService.refuel();
    }
        // more methods, omitted
}
```

(To make this completely functional we'd need to provide parameters that tell the supply depot the capacity of the item to refuel, and decrement that amount of fuel from the depot).

When we come along with something additional that needs to be refuelled, like a snowmobile, no change is needed in the SupplyDepot class. The snowmobile is declared as follows, and it is therefore already compatible with the argument to SupplyDepot's service() method:

```
public class Snowmobile implements CapableOfBeingRefuelled {
    public int refuel() {
                . . .
    }

    ... // more methods, omitted
}
```

The fundamental reason for interfaces is to allow classes to say, in a way the compiler can check on it, "*I have the behavior X, and you can use one of my objects wherever you have something that needs to do X*".

In summary:

- Use the interface type as a parameter for a method M. *Inside that method M, you can call any of the methods promised by the interface parameter.* When you actually call the method M, you will have to provide an object that implements the interface and thus has all the methods promised by the interface.

- Interfaces let you compile your code now. But you need to provide an object with actual code for the thing to work at run-time.

- The interface specifies the exact signatures of the methods that must be provided by the implementing classes.

A class can extend only one superclass, but it can implement any number of interfaces. Two interfaces can make the same demand for a method of a given name in a class without. For example, interface A specifies a refuel() method, interface B specifies a refuel() method, and class C implements both interfaces.

This is one of the situations that causes teeth grinding among the multiple inheritance fans. In C++ that class is going to inherit two different refuel methods with the same signature. It doesn't cause any problem in Java. In Java, class C implements one `refuel()` method and it satisfies both interfaces.

Interface java.lang.Comparable

Interfaces are used frequently in the Java run-time library. Here is the source of interface Comparable in the java.lang package up to JDK 1.4. (We'll show the JDK 1.5 code, which is different, soon).

```
public interface Comparable {
    public int compareTo(Object o);
}
```

All classes that implement Comparable have to provide a `compareTo()` method. It allows two objects of the same class to be put in order with respect to one another, that is, they can be compared.

If you read the API documentation, you will see that implementations of `compareTo()` must return a negative, zero, or positive int, depending on whether "this" is smaller, equal to, or greater than the object parameter. There isn't any way for the compiler to enforce this level of meaning, and if you make `compareTo()` do anything different for one of your classes, this code will be broken anywhere you use that class in place of a Comparable.

Here's a complete example that implements the Comparable interface. To keep it simple, the example is a class that "wraps" an int as an object.

```
class MyInt implements Comparable {
    private int mi;
    public MyInt(int i) { mi = i; }        // constructor
    public int getMyInt() { return mi; } // getter

    public int compareTo(Object other) {
        MyInt miOther = (MyInt) other;    //cast Obj param back to MyInt
        return (this.mi - miOther.mi);
    }

}
```

You can declare `MyInts` and compare them like this:

```
MyInt m4 = new MyInt(4);
MyInt m5 = new MyInt(5);

int result = m4.compareTo(m5);   // negative, zero or positive
```

That's the way Comparable looked before JDK 1.5. In JDK 1.5, classes and interfaces are allowed to take generic parameters, and Comparable was changed for that.

Generic types in JDK 1.5: A preview

JDK 1.5 introduced the generic feature, allowing you to use types as parameters, just as you can use variables as parameters. The java.lang.Comparable interface was upgraded. You have the choice of compiling for the new syntax or the old syntax. The old syntax is shown in this chapter and the new syntax is explained in the chapter on generics. To give you an appetizer, here's what the new feature looks like:

- Comparable now takes a *generic type parameter*, which looks like a name in angle brackets. It is read as "Comparable of T". The name is used inside the interface to specify that the argument to compareTo must be of this yet-to-be-specified type:

```
public interface Comparable <T> {
    public int compareTo(T t);
}
```

- Any class that implements Comparable must provide an actual type argument, to be used in place of the generic type parameter. This gives the type of the thing to which you are comparing. You usually compare two objects of the same type, so it will usually be a repetition of the class name (here MyInt):

```
class MyInt implements Comparable <MyInt> { int mi; /* code */
```

- The compareTo() method now uses an argument of the type you are comparing to, not of type Object, so no casting is necessary. The main benefit is that the compiler will not let you compare a MyInt with an object of some other class.

```
    public int compareTo(MyInt other) {
        return (this.mi - other.mi);  // NEW - no cast from Obj
    }
```

- If you add these four lines to MyInt, you have a complete compilable example:

```
    private int mi;     // stores the int value
    public MyInt(int i) { mi = i; }        // constructor
    public int getMyInt() { return mi; }   // getter
}
```

- If you add a main method with these lines, you can run the example. These lines are the same whether you use the old style or you use the new generic feature.

```
    MyInt m4 = new MyInt(4);
    MyInt m5 = new MyInt(5);

    int result = m4.compareTo(m5);
    if (result<0) System.out.println("m4 < m5");
```

There is no change in the *use* of Comparable classes. The only changes for generics in this example are in the *definition of Comparable* and the *definition of classes that implement the Comparable interface.*

Interfaces Versus Abstract Classes

While you use an interface to specify the form that something *must* have, it does not actually provide the implementation for it. In this sense, an interface is a like an abstract class. The abstract class must be extended in exactly the manner that its abstract methods specify.

An interface differs from an abstract class in the following ways:

- An abstract class is an incomplete class that requires further specialization in child classes. The subclasses are closely related to the parent. An interface doesn't have any overtones of specialization that are present with inheritance. It merely says, "We need something that does 'foo' and here are the ways that users should be able to call it."

- A class can implement several interfaces at once, whereas a class can extend only one parent class.

- Interfaces can be used to support callbacks (inheritance doesn't help with this). This is a significant coding idiom. It essentially provides a pointer to a function, but in a type-safe way. *Using Interface Callbacks for GUI Event Handlers* on page 239 explains callbacks.

Here's the bottom line: You'll probably use interfaces more often than abstract classes. Use an abstract class when you want to initiate a hierarchy of more specialized classes and provide a partial implementation with fine control over what is private, public, protected, etc. Use an interface when you need multiple inheritance of design to say, "This class has behavior (methods) A, B, and C."

An interface can be extended, but only by another interface. It is legal for a class to implement an interface but only have some of the methods promised in the interface. You must then make it an abstract class that must be further extended (inherited) before it can be instantiated.

Granting Permission Through an Interface—Cloneable

When we looked at the Object class in Chapter 3, we saw that it has this method:

```
protected native Object clone() throws CloneNotSupportedException;
```

Java supports the notion of *cloning*, meaning to get a complete bit-for-bit duplicate of an object. Cloning, perhaps surprisingly, does not invoke any constructor.

Not every class should support the ability to clone. If I have a class that represents a set of objects that are unique in the real world, such as the ships in a company fleet, the operation of cloning doesn't make sense. You buy new ships, but you can't get exact duplicates in *every* detail (including, say, registration number) of an existing ship. However, methods (including the clone() method) in the class java.lang.Object are inherited by all classes.

So Java places a further requirement on classes that want to be cloneable: They must implement the cloneable interface to indicate that cloning is valid for them. The cloneable interface is this:

```
public interface Cloneable { } // completely empty
```

The empty interface as a marker is not the most common use of interfaces, but you do see it in the system libraries. To have a class that can be cloned, you must state that the class implements the Cloneable interface.

```
public class ICanBeCopied implements Cloneable { ...
```

Why wasn't the method clone() of Object made part of the Cloneable interface? That seems like the obvious place to put it, instead of in Object. The reason is that we have two conflicting aims.

- We want to provide a default implementation of clone so that any cloneable class can automatically inherit it. A method body cannot be put in an interface, so Object is the only possible place for it.

- We also want individual classes to take an extra step to permit cloning on their object, so an interface is needed. The class Object has a clone() method, but does *not* implement the Cloneable interface, otherwise all its descendants (which is every object in existence) would too.

The end result is that we require, at minimum, an extra step of having cloneable classes implement the Cloneable interface. We provide a default implementation by putting the method clone, with a body, into the root superclass Object. That implementation does a shallow clone. If you want a deep clone, implement it in your own class. If you write your own clone(), the first statement should be a call to super.clone().

If you call `clone()` on an object that does not implement the Cloneable interface, you get a CloneNotSupportedException.

Shallow versus deep clone

There is some subtlety to a class that has data fields that are references to other classes. Do you simply copy the reference and share the referenced object (a *shallow clone*), or do you recursively clone all referenced objects as well (a *deep clone*)?

While `Object.clone()` does a shallow clone, supplying the method in class `Object` and making it overridable allows you to choose the behavior you want. You can disallow any kind of clone. You can override clone as public rather than the default protected (outside this package, only subclasses can clone). You can implement a deep clone, if you want.

Cloning an object is not that common. People sometimes clone a shared object, such as a customer record, when they need to keep track of its state for later read-only processing, but they don't want to tie up access to the real object for everyone. The specifics of your class determine if you need to implement a shallow clone or a deep clone. A shallow clone is cheaper, so if that's all you need, great. An alternative to cloning is to instantiate a new object, and individually copy all the fields from the object you want duplicated. That way you don't need to catch exceptions, or worry about the scope of protected.

Note that `clone()` returns an `Object`. The object returned by `clone()` is usually cast immediately to the correct type, as in this example:

```
Vector v = new Vector();
Vector v2;

v2 = (Vector) v.clone();
```

Since Arrays are considered to implement the Cloneable interface, they can be copied by `System.arrayCopy` or by `clone()`.

You cannot clone any enum object—java.lang.Enum disallows it with a final clone() method that throws an exception. Recall that enum constants are final values. Since they are guaranteed not to change, everyone can share one copy of them, and no duplicates are needed.

A common pitfall with clone

There is a commonly encountered pitfall with cloning. When you try to clone an object in the most obvious way, you get a compilation error:

```
class B implements Cloneable {
    int i = 22;
}

public class C {
    public static void main(String [] args) {
        B b = new B();
        B duplicate = (B) b.clone();
    }
}

ERROR: clone has protected access in java.lang.Object
```

It's true, too. The relevant signature in java.lang.Object is:

```
protected native Object clone() throws CloneNotSupportedException;
```

What Protected *Really* Means

The "protected" access modifier says the member is visible to any classes in the same package, and to subclasses everywhere. The same package part is clear enough: your code is never in the same package as java.lang.Object.clone(). The "subclasses everywhere" part is more accurately expressed as *a protected member can be accessed from within a class* **through references that are of at least the same type of the class.** Consider this example, which uses a protected field called "teeth", which is simpler to follow than the clone() method:

```
package animals;
class Mammal {protected int teeth;  }

package pets;
class Cat extends Mammal { }

class Dog extends Mammal {
    Cat housemate = new Cat();
    int cats_teeth = housemate.teeth; // NO!! field is protected.
}

class Dalmatian extends Dog { }
```

Cat and Dog both inherit the protected field teeth from Mammal. Since Mammal is in a different package, the subclass rule applies. That stipulates that code in the Dog class can access the protected teeth field only through a reference that is Dog or a subtype of Dog, like Dalmatian.

Code in the Dog class cannot access the protected field using a reference to Cat. Cat can access the protected field using a reference to Cat. If you have a reference to Mammal, and if you can successfully cast it to Dog, you can use that Dog value inside Dog to access the field. You can't use the Mammal reference inside Dog to access the field.

This rule is aimed at making sure that protected instance members are accessed only by the part of the class hierarchy they belong to, and not by siblings. It's a funny rule because unlike public, private, or package access, a line of code that accesses a protected member can be valid in one class and not valid in the next class you write in the same package. Even when both classes are subtypes of the class with the protected member! The rule doesn't apply to static protected variables and methods. Those are accessible from any child class, since there is no "object" through which to access them.

The member in question is Object.clone in package java.lang. Clearly, my class C is not in package java.lang, and is not a subclass of class B. Therefore class C cannot access B's clone(). This means that a method can clone its own objects inside its own class and nobody in other packages can, which is not terrifically useful.

The fix? Just override Object's-version-of-clone in the class that implements Cloneable and make the method public! You can give the same or more generous access when you override a method.

Furthermore, Java now has "covariant return types". That means when you override a method, you don't have to return the exact same type that the parent method does. You may now return an *subtype* of the

What the JLS says about protected

The Java Language Specification (JLS) says in section 6.6.2:

> Let *C* be the class in which a `protected` member m is declared. Access is
> permitted only within the body of a subclass *S* of *C*. In addition, if *id* denotes
> an instance field or instance method, then if the access is by a qualified name
> *Q.id*, where *Q* is an *ExpressionName*, then the access is permitted if and only
> if the type of the expression *Q* is *S* or a subclass of *S*.

People learning about this subtlety often wonder if they have wandered into a C++
book by mistake. Don't worry! There are hardly any other pitfalls like that in Java.
Well, at least compared with some other languages. For historians and language
theologians, this meaning of protected was a change made to Java between JDK
1.0 Beta 1 and Beta 2 in December 1995.

Using Interface Callbacks for GUI Event Handlers

So far we've discussed examples of the Comparable and Cloneable interfaces.
These interfaces solve compile time issues of forcing a class to have certain
behavior. There is an additional way that an interface can be used, to obtain more
dynamic behavior. It forms the basis of GUI programming in Java. We have
already seen most of this; the only piece that's new is the way that the object-
which-implements-an-interface tells the servicing class about itself.

In our earlier example, we called a service method and passed an instance of our
handler object as an argument:

```
Depot.service( myPlane );
```

Inside the body of service, the method `myPlane.refuel()` was immediately called
back, and that really did the servicing. The piece that is new for GUI callbacks is
this. We don't pass our handler object to the service routine *each time* a service is
needed. Instead, we pass the handler object in a *one-time* registration with the
service. The service saves the pointer to our handler. From then on, whenever an
event happens, the service looks at its list of saved references. It will call back to
every handler object that has registered with it. You will write the handler object
so that it does whatever needs to happen when that part of the GUI is tweaked. If
it is a handler for a button marked "quit", the handler will quit the program. If it
is a handler for a file open dialog, it will open the file.

This one time registration of the callback target is not such a big change. But it
allows the run-time library to take the initiative on deciding when a call back to

an event handler must occur, rather than the handler deciding that. Let's look at this in terms of code.

1.   The run-time library defines an interface that promises a method called *itHappened()* like this:

```
interface ActionListener {
    public void itHappened();
}
```

The run-time library makes calls to the method promised by the interface. Your code implements the interface.

2.   In your application code, provide a class that implements the interface:

```
class MyCode implements ActionListener {
    public void itHappened() {
        System.out.println("All your base are belong to us");
    }
    // other code
}
```

This is your event handler.

3.   In your application code, make a one-time call to the run-time library to register your interest in button push, mouse click, or other events, and tell it your event handler code.

```
MyCode myobj = new MyCode()
runtime.registerActionListener( myobj );   // it saves a copy of myobj
```

4.   In the run-time library, the registration routine saves a reference to any objects that register with (i.e., call) it :

```
private ActionListener[] registeredObjects; /* init code omitted */

registerActionListener( ActionListener myobj ) {
    // it saves a copy of myobj
    registeredObjects[i] = myobj;
}
```

5.   This is the step all previous steps have been leading up to. Whenever the run-time library notices a GUI event has occurred, it will call back any *itHappened()* methods that have registered for this event:

```
for (ActionListener a : registeredObjects)
        a.itHappened();
```

There may be a list of ActionListeners that have registered with the run-time to be informed when that event happens. Often there is just one.

This is how event handling works in the GUI. The whole point is that step 5 runs in a separate thread to your code, and so can call back to your ActionListener at any time. This is therefore known as a *callback*. That's the end of interfaces. It's time to look at another class from the run-time library.

The Class Double

The following is the declaration of class java.lang.Double. This class implements the Comparable interface, which has been updated to be a generic interface. Apart from the appetizer in this chapter, we defer further explanation of generics until Chapter 15.

```
public final class java.lang.Double extends java.lang.Number
                              implements java.lang.Comparable {
    // constructors
    public java.lang.Double(double);
    public java.lang.Double(java.lang.String)
                    throws java.lang.NumberFormatException;
    public static final double POSITIVE_INFINITY = 1.0 / 0.0;
    public static final double NEGATIVE_INFINITY = -1.0 / 0.0;
    public static final double NaN = 0.0d / 0.0;
    public static final double MAX_VALUE = 1.79769313486231570e+308;
    public static final double MIN_VALUE = longBitsToDouble(1L);
    public static final java.lang.Class TYPE=
                         Class.getPrimitiveClass("double");

    public byte byteValue();
    public short shortValue();
    public int intValue();
    public long longValue();
    public float floatValue();
    public double doubleValue();

    public int compareTo(java.lang.Double);
    public int compareTo(java.lang.Object);
    public boolean isInfinite();
    public static boolean isInfinite(double);
    public boolean isNaN();
    public static boolean isNaN(double);
    public boolean equals(java.lang.Object);
    public int hashCode();
    public static native long doubleToLongBits(double);
    public static native double longBitsToDouble(long);

    public static double parseDouble(java.lang.String) throws
                         java.lang.NumberFormatException;
    public java.lang.String toString();
    public static java.lang.String toString(double);
    public static java.lang.Double valueOf(java.lang.String) throws
                         java.lang.NumberFormatException;
}
```

Exercises

1. Describe, without excessive handwaving, two common uses for interfaces.

2. Given the SupplyDepot, Transport, and CapableOfBeingRefuelled classes/interfaces described earlier in this chapter, add a main routine to Airplane. Then add fields, parameters, and code to SupplyDepot and elsewhere so that a CapableOfBeingRefuelled can tell the service routine how much fuel it takes. Make sure that amount of fuel is decremented at the Depot, and incremented in the object that implements CapableOfBeingRefuelled.

3. Look at the Cloneable interface in javadoc. Take any class that you have written and make it cloneable by making it implement the Cloneable interface.

4. Override `Object.clone()` to do a shallow copy for your class, and also keep count of the number of objects of your class that have been created. Don't forget to count those created via a constructor, too.

5. Write some code to clone an object of your class. Change your version of `clone()` to do a deep copy for your class. Run the clone program again, and make it print out enough information that you can tell the difference between a shallow clone and a deep clone.

Some Light Relief—The Java-Powered Toaster

First prize for the "most entertaining Java application of 2001" goes to Robin Southgate. For his final year project as an Industrial Design student at Brunel University in England, Robin designed and built a bread toaster. Not just any toaster though. Robin's toaster is powered by a Java program that dials a weather service, retrieves the forecast, and singes the outlook onto the toast. Examples of the toast are shown in Figure 11–3.

Robin's design integrates a standard domestic toaster with the Tiny InterNet Interface (TINI) microcontroller from Dallas Semiconductor. The TINI is a $20 microcontroller chip set that supports an incredible software development platform. TINI contains a Java virtual machine, a web server, and a TCP/IP network stack running on top of a real time operating system, all in less than half a Mbyte of flash RAM. You program the chip and control the I/O to its peripherals completely in Java. The peripherals can include ethernet, a parallel port, a wireless network interface, as well as the usual RS232 serial port and I2C bus.

Toast on a sunny day   Toast on a rainy day

Figure 11–3   Java-powered toaster

Robin modified the toaster so that it works automatically. When a piece of toast is put in, the microcontroller wakes up and dials out through a modem on the serial port to remotely access the weather information. The Java code then condenses the forecast into a choice between "sunny," "overcast," "rain," or "snow," and chooses the appropriate baffle to move in front of the toast heater element. The baffle is made of polytetrafluorethylene (more commonly known as "teflon" or PTFE) which is both food-safe and heat resistant at toaster temperatures. The baffle has a hole in the shape of the weather icon, exposing that area of the toast to more radiant heat than adjacent masked areas. The toast pops up in about 30 seconds with the weather icon burned onto it.

When he started on the project, Robin appealed to the TINI engineering mailing list for advice. About half the engineers made a lot of fat-headed suggestions, like using cocoa powder for toner to print on the bread. Another proposed using a CO2 laser to reduce cooking time into the 1-2 second range. They just didn't seem to be taking the project seriously. Other engineers could see the value of Java-powered toast, and gave Robin guidance on how he could refine his design.

The project involved sensing toaster operation, communicating with a remote site, decoding the data returned, moving the baffles, and controlling the toaster element. The prototype shown in Figure 11–4 needed special attention to switch the high current for the heating element safely. TINI is an excellent choice for this kind of embedded design. It has a built-in serial port that can trivially drive an external modem. There are readily available modules to monitor current, temperature, baffle position, and to switch loads. A key element with all projects is to build and debug the new design in stages rather than trying the whole thing at once. And of course, all the programming was done in Java.

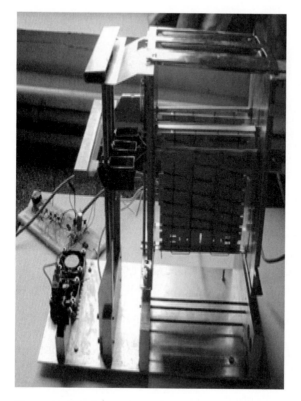

Figure 11–4   Java-powered toaster

See `www.dalsemi.com` for more information on the amazingly capable Java products from Dallas Semiconductor. As one engineer on the mailing list concluded, "when it comes to domestic appliances for toast-related processing, Java has the biggest appetite."

If, like me, you have often wondered what a Java program to control a weather-forecasting toaster looks like, here is the answer. It is just the regular "put bit patterns into ports" that comprises most embedded programming, but expressed in Java quite neatly.

```
//  The toaster main control program

import java.util.*;
import java.io.*;
import com.dalsemi.onewire.*;
import com.dalsemi.onewire.adapter.*;
import com.dalsemi.onewire.container.*;
import com.dalsemi.onewire.container.OneWireContainer.*;
import com.dalsemi.onewire.utils.*;
import com.dalsemi.onewire.utils.Address;

public class WeatherSwitch {

    public static void main(String args[]) {
        // details omitted...
        // contact server, get forecast
        // translate it into a command for the Switch.
    }

    public static void Switch2405(byte[] ID) {
        // "ID" is a byte array of size 8 with the address
        // of a part we have already found.
        // "access" is a DSPortAdapter
        DSPortAdapter access = new TINIExternalAdapter();
        int i=0;
        OneWireContainer05 ds2405 =
                    (OneWireContainer05) access.getDeviceContainer(ID);
        ds2405.setupContainer(access,ID);
        byte state[] = {}; // declare variable first, we'll assign it below

        try // catch exception {
          state = ds2405.readDevice();
        } catch (Exception e) {};

        // I know that the 2405 only has one channel (one switch)
        // and it doesn't support 'Smart On'
        boolean latch_state = ds2405.getLatchState(0,state);
        System.out.println("Current state of switch: "+latch_state);
        System.out.println("Current output level:" +
                                            ds2405.getLevel(0,state));

        if (!latch_state) {
            System.out.println("Toggling switch");
            ds2405.setLatchState(0,!latch_state,false,state);
            try {
                ds2405.writeDevice(state);
                state = ds2405.readDevice();
                latch_state = ds2405.getLatchState(0,state);
            } catch (Exception e) {};

            System.out.println("Current state of switch: "+latch_state);
            System.out.println("Current output level:"
                                            +ds2405.getLevel(0,state));
```

Chapter 12

Nested Classes

▼ INTRODUCTION TO NESTED CLASSES

▼ NESTED STATIC CLASSES

▼ INNER MEMBER CLASSES

▼ INNER LOCAL CLASSES

▼ INNER ANONYMOUS CLASSES

▼ HOW INNER CLASSES ARE COMPILED

▼ THE CLASS CHARACTER

▼ EXERCISES

▼ SOME LIGHT RELIEF—THE DOMESTIC OBFUSCATED JAVA
   CODE NON-COMPETITION

This chapter covers all aspects of nested classes. In compiler terminology, *nesting* means "putting something inside another thing". Everyone who has read this far will be comfortable with nesting *methods* and *data fields* inside classes. In this chapter we explain the different ways a class can be nested inside another class, and what it all means.

Introduction to Nested Classes

Nested classes are another in the (ever-lengthening) list of "Java features that were introduced to make one specific thing quicker to write". There's a trade-off though. While nested classes make event-handlers simpler to write, they also add complexity to the compiler and to the features that programmers must learn.

Nested classes will make more sense when we have covered event-handlers for the GUI (Chapter 20), so you could skim the rest of this chapter until then. For now, just note that there are ways you can nest classes inside each other like Russian dolls, and postpone an in-depth reading until you need it.

The name "nested class" suggests you just write a class declaration inside a class, and you're done! Actually, there are four different kinds of nested classes specialized for different purposes, and given different names.

All classes are either:

- *Top-level* or *nested*
- Nested classes are:
  - *Static classes* or *inner classes*
  - Inner classes are:
    - *Member classes* or *local classes* or *anonymous classes*

Figure 12–1 represents the hierarchy and terminology of nested classes in a diagram.

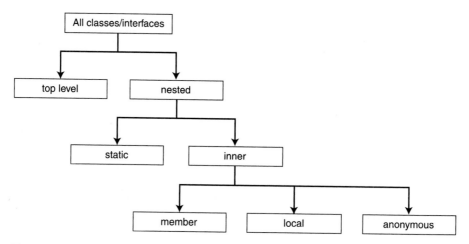

Figure 12–1   The hierarchy of nested classes

A nested class is any class whose declaration occurs within the body of another class or interface. Up to now, we have been dealing exclusively with top-level classes. A top-level class is any class that is not nested.

You can declare nested classes as final, private, protected, or public, just like other members. Access protection protects against classes outside the enclosing class. It never affects the enclosing class or other classes inside it. They have full visibility into each other. A nested class declared as final ensures that the nested class cannot be extended.

Nested Static Classes

Nested static classes are the simplest of the nested classes to write, understand, and use. Table 12–1 shows how to create a nested static class. You simply write the declaration of your class in the usual way, give it the modifier static, and put it inside a top-level class.

Table 12–1   **Creating a nested static class**

Java term	Description	Example code
Nested static class	```class Top { static class MyNested { } }```	A nested class that is declared "static." This acts like a top-level class.

Qualities of a nested static class

You recall that static means "there is only one of these". A static thing is not tied to an individual instance object. If you think about it, there is only one of any top-level class (though it might have a large number of instances). A static nested class acts exactly like a top-level class. The only differences are:

- The full name of the nested static class includes the name of the class in which it is nested, e.g. Top.MyNested. Instance declarations of the nested class outside Top would look like:

  ```
  Top.MyNested myObj = new Top.MyNested();
  ```

- The nested static class has access to all the static methods and static data of the class it is nested in, even the private members.

If it helps, think of the "static" as having more to do with labelling the field of the top-level class, than with the nested class that is that field. Since the nested class is static, it does not have a "this" pointer to an instance of the enclosing class. Therefore, a nested static class has no direct access to the instance data in objects of its enclosing class. It can declare instances of itself or its outer class and access instance data that way.

This code shows how a static nested class can access instance data of the class it is nested within:

```
public class Top {

    int i; // instance data within Top

    static class MyNested {
        Top t = new Top();
        {
            t.i = 3;  // accessing Top instance data
        }
    }

}
```

Where to use a nested static class

Imagine you are implementing a complicated class. Halfway through, you realize that you need a "helper" type with some utility methods. This helper type is self-contained enough that it can be a separate class from the complicated class. It can be used by other classes, not just the complicated class. But it is tied to the complicated class. Without the complicated class, there would be no reason for the helper class to exist.

Before nested classes, there wasn't a good solution to this, and you'd end up solving it by making the helper class a top-level class, and perhaps make some members of the complicated class more public than they should be. Today, you'd just make the helper class nested static, and put it inside the complicated class.

Example of a nested static class

There's an example of a nested static class in the run-time in `java.lang.Character`. Simplifying it to omit irrelevant detail, it looks like the following:

```
public class Character {
  /* more code */

      public static class UnicodeBlock  {
          /* various methods, omitted */
      }
```

The nested static class Character.UnicodeBlock stores the names of groups of characters (blocks) in the Unicode codeset. Often, there's a canonical name, like "Greek and Coptic" plus several aliases, all of which get stored. There are several dozen block names, corresponding to runs of adjacent characters: Cyrillic, Armenian, Hebrew, Arabic, and so on.

The class gives a way to associate names with Unicode code pages. You can see how that is tightly bound to class `Character`, but also useful outside it. Finally, it's all static final data; you don't need a unique but identical copy of all the code page names for every `Character` object. That would duplicate a large amount of unchanging data for every single char wrapper you have! The combination of requirements makes UnicodeBlock a perfect candidate for a static class nested inside java.lang.Character.

Inner Member Classes

Java supports an instance class being declared within another class, just as an instance method or instance data field is declared within a class. It is called an inner class, and the class is associated with each instance of the class in which it is nested.

The three varieties of inner class are *member class*, *local class*, and *anonymous class*, each one being a refinement of the one before it. We will look at the special features of each of these kinds of classes and how to use them in the pages ahead. Information on member class is shown in Table 12–2.

Table 12–2   Member class

Java term	Description	Example code

Member class	This is an inner class.
	
	It is a nested class that *is not* declared "static." It is an instance member of a class.
		`class Top {`
		`    class MyMember {`
		`        /* code */`
		`    }`
		`}`

The comment saying /* code */ is a reminder that in practice the classes will have bodies with methods and fields.

A member class is like a nested static class *without* the keyword static. That says, "The class appears in every instance".

Qualities of an inner member class

Just as any instance member in a class can see all the other members, the scope of an inner class is the entire parent in which it is directly nested.

That is, the inner class can reference any members in its parent. The parent must declare an instance of an inner class before it can invoke the inner class methods, assign to data fields (including private ones), and so on.

The following code shows an example of use.

```
class top {
    int i=33;

    class myNestedMember {// member inner class
        int k = i;          // note 1 below
        int foo() { return this.k;}  // note 2 below
    }

    void doCalculations () {
        myNestedMember mn1 = new myNestedMember(); //instantiate member
        myNestedMember mn2 = new myNestedMember(); // get another one too
        mn1.k = 564 * mn2.foo();
    }

}
```

The right way to think of an inner class object is that, because it is associated with
an instance of its enclosing class, it has two "this" pointers: One to its own
instance data and one to the instance data of its enclosing object. Look at the line
marked note 1. The reference to i is a reference to instance data of its enclosing
object. Similarly on the line marked note 2, the this.k is a reference to the instance
data within the nested class.

Unlike nested static classes, inner classes are not directly part of a package and are
not visible outside the class in which they are nested.

Where to use an inner member class

One of the criticisms that people sometimes (rightly) make of OOP is that
everything has to be a class. In particular, even if you just want a single function
for some utilitarian purpose, you still have to create a class and instantiate an
object of that class and invoke a method on that instance. The code for that class
might have to be pages and pages away from the place in the source file where
you use it. It's a bit heavyweight if your utility function is just a few lines of code.
Inner classes are intended to improve the situation.

One of the main uses of inner classes is for GUI event handlers, and we'll see
plenty of real examples of them in Chapter 20. They allow you to put the event
handling class and method right next to the place where you declare the GUI
objects.

Example inner member class from the Java run-time library

The class java.awt.ScrollPane has a member class, as follows:

```
public class ScrollPane extends Container implements Accessible {
    class PeerFixer implements AdjustmentListener, java.io.Serializable {
        // methods, omitted
    }
    /* more code */
}
```

The run-time library uses the class `PeerFixer` which is a member class of ScrollPane to keep a scrolling window in the native GUI aligned with scrolling window object in Java when the user makes adjustments. (The AWT GUI toolkit attempted to use native window system objects with a thin Java layer on top that represents their state to/from Java. This was a clever idea, and achieved a quick'n'dirty implementation of portable windowing. But it proved to be a long-term maintenance nightmare of corner-case bugs where the semantic differences among Windows, Mac, and Unix window systems leaked through).

Inner Local Classes

Inner local classes are perhaps the simplest of the nested classes to write, understand, and use. The following table shows how to create an inner local class. You simply write the declaration of your class in the usual way, and put it inside (local to) a block. The block almost always instantiates an object of the inner class.

Information on the local class is shown in Table 12–3.

Table 12–3   Local class

Java term	Description	Example code
Local class	This is an inner class. It is local to a block, typically within a method.	```void myMethod() {` ` class MyLocal {` ` /*code*/` ` void something() { }` ` }` ` MyLocal m = new` `MyLocal();` ` foo(m);` `}```

Qualities of an inner local class

A local class is an inner class. It is a class that is declared within a block of code, so it is *not* a member of the enclosing class. Typically, a local class is declared within a method.

A local class is not visible outside the block that contains it, but the block can create an object of the inner local class and give away a reference to it. Then the object lives on, and its methods can be invoked by whoever holds the reference.

Where to use an inner local class

Figure 12–2 shows a local class. This inner class is the event handler for a button. The overwhelming use of local classes is to create an object that can be called back as an event handler. The value that local classes add is that you can write the handler close to the code that creates the button (or whatever) that generates the events.

You can find this code example at `www.afu.com/jj6`, and you can try compiling and running it.

Example inner local class

You could easily convert this local class to a member class by moving it outside the method.

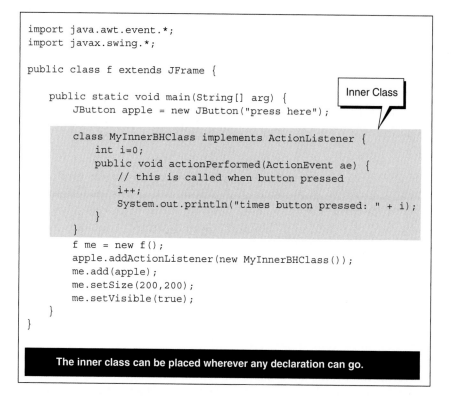

Figure 12–2   A local inner class

The distinction between member classes and local classes is a fine one. The most important limitation is that inner local classes can access only `final` variables or `final` parameters. The reason for this apparently strange restriction is given later in the chapter. It has to do with the way inner local classes are implemented.

To explain Figure 12–2 a little, an applet is a Java program that runs inside a browser. It is invoked by some HTML which I have put in the source code as a comment. If you browse this source file, the applet will start running.

Applets begin execution in a method called init(). You extend java.applet.Applet or javax.swing.JApplet and provide your own overriding init method. The init() method in this example contains an inner class that has a method which is called when the button is pressed. The method is the *event handler* for the button.

Inner Anonymous Classes

It's possible to go one step further from a local inner class to something called an *anonymous class*. An anonymous class is a refinement of inner classes, allowing you to write the *definition* of the class, followed by the *instance allocation*.

The anonymous class is explained in Table 12–4.

Table 12–4   Anonymous class

Java term	Description	Example code

Anonymous class	This is an inner class. It is a variation on a local class.
	
	The class is declared and instantiated within a single expression.
		`void foo () {`
		
		`    JFrame jf = new JFrame();`
		`    jf.addEventHandler(`
		`        new EventAdapter() {`
		`            myOverridingMethod(){`
		`            /* some code */`
		`            } // end method`
		`        } // end anon class`
		`    );`
		`}`

Qualities of an inner anonymous class

Instead of just nesting the class like any other declaration, you go to the

```
new SomeClass ()
```

part of the statement where an object is instantiated, and immediately follow it with a block containing the class body, such as the following:

```
{
    public void actionPerformed(ActionEvent e) {
        System.out.println(e.paramString() + " pressed");
    }
}
```

We have already seen something like this before. Think back to the *constant-specific class bodies* of enums. Those could hold a method that overrides a method in the base enum. The same kind of thing is going on here. The full example is shown in Figure 12–3.

Where to use an inner anonymous class

This is quite specialized. The block that you provide is held to be an anonymous (no-name) class that *extends* the class or interface name. The whole purpose is that you provide overriding versions of one or more of the methods in the base class. If SomeClass is an interface, you have to provide all the methods, of course.

It's an even more concise way of writing an event handler than a local class. With a local class you have to provide all method bodies. With an anonymous class, you cram it into the instantiation and only provide method bodies for the methods you want to change.

You never *have* to use any kind of an inner class. You can always get the same effect with top-level classes. Inner classes are intended as conveniences to make certain common coding constructs quick to write.

Example inner anonymous class

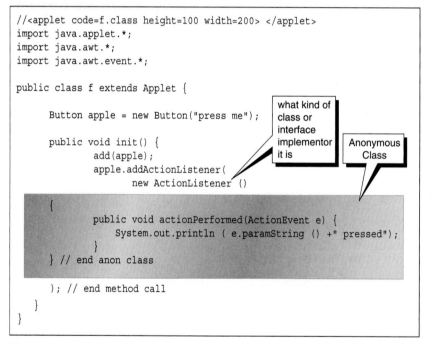

Figure 12–3   An anonymous class.

Try compiling and running this example. Your f2.java file generates class files called f2.class and f2$1.class. The second of these represents the anonymous ActionListener inner class.

Be sure you are clear on what is going on here, even if the code doesn't make total sense until we reach Chapter 20. This is saying that there is an Interface (or class—we can't tell from looking at the code here) called ActionListener. We are declaring an object of an anonymous class type that either implements the interface or extends the class. If it extends the class, then any methods we define override the corresponding methods of the base class.

You should only use inner classes and anonymous classes where the event handler is just a few lines long. If the event handler is more than a screenful of text, it should be in a named top-level class. We have to admit; however, that the notational convenience for smaller cases is considerable. Just don't get carried away with it.

How Inner Classes Are Compiled

You might be interested to learn that inner classes are completely defined in terms of a source transformation into corresponding freestanding classes, and that is how the Sun compiler compiles them. In other words, first it extracts them and pretends they are top-level classes with funny names. Then it fixes up the extra *this* pointers that are needed, and compiles them. The following is an inner class called `pip`:

```
public class orange {
     int i=0;
     void foo() {   }

     class pip {
          int seeds=2;
          void bar() { }
     }
}
```

Here's how the compiler transforms an inner class into JDK 1.0 compatible code. If you understand this process, a lot of the mystery of inner classes will disappear. First, extract the inner class, make it a top-level class, and prefix the containing-class-and-a-dollar-sign to its name.

```
class orange$pip {
     int seeds=2;
     void bar() { }
}

public class orange {
     int i=0;
     void foo() {   }
}
```

Then, give the inner class a private field this$0 that keeps a reference to the object in which it appears. Also, ensure all the constructors are passed an extra argument (the pointer to the containing instance) so they can initialize the this$0 field. Note: The name this$0 is reserved for internal use, so you can't completely replicate this process manually, but this is what the compiler is doing.

```
class orange$pip { // the transformed inner class
    private orange this$0;   // the saved copy of orange.this

    orange$pip(orange o) {  // constructor
        this$0 = o; // initialize the ref to enclosing obj
    }
    int seeds=2;
    void bar() { }
}
```

The manufactured field this$0 allows the inner class to access any fields of its containing class, even private fields that could not otherwise be accessed. If you try compiling this example, you will note that the compiler produces class files with names like orange$pip.class.

That embedded dollar sign in the name of nested classes is part of the definition. Having a consistent explicit policy for naming inner classes allows everyone's tools (debugger, linker, and so on) to work the same way. It's just a bit confusing that $ signs are also used by the Unix shell in shell variables.

Why you can access only final variables

One restriction on local and anonymous inner classes is that they can't access variables of the method in which they are embedded. The reason becomes clear if you think it through.

The source transformation shown previously lets an inner class reach back to its outer class, but the scoping rules don't give it any way to see the local variables of a method in that class. In addition, the life of the object might well outlast the life of the method in which it was created. If you gave the object a pointer to method local data in the stack, you'd be breaking the integrity of the language. Therefore, the compiler prevents this. If you break this "do not access non-final local variables" rule, as in the following code, the compiler displays an error message along the lines of the one shown:

```
public void init() {
    int i = 20; // local variable i
    s.addAdjustmentListener(
        new AdjustmentListener() {
            public void adjustmentValueChanged( AdjustmentEvent ae) {
                    something.setSize( i, ae.getValue() );
ERROR Attempt to use a non-final variable i. From enclosing blocks,
only final local variables are available.
```

The simplest fix is to make the variable final, if possible. You can use a constant (final) variable because the compiler passes a *copy* of it to the inner class constructor as an extra argument. Since it is final, the value of which it is a copy won't later change to something else.

Some people feel that inner classes take more away from the simplicity and purity of model than they provide. Don't make the problem worse by using them for large classes.

We now finish the chapter by featuring the class Character.

The Class Character

The following is the declaration of class java.lang.Character. The important point here is to notice all the routines for classifying a character as an identifier, a digit, etc:

```
public final class java.lang.Character
        implements java.io.Serializable, java.lang.Comparable {
    public java.lang.Character(char); // constructor



    public static final int MIN_RADIX = 2;
    public static final int MAX_RADIX = 36;
```

```
    public static final char MIN_VALUE = '\u0000';
    public static final char MAX_VALUE = '\uffff';
    public static final java.lang.Class TYPE = Class.getPrimitiveClass("char");
    public static final byte UNASSIGNED;//about 20 other Unicode types
    public static final byte UPPERCASE_LETTER;
    public static int getType(char); // returns the Unicode type

    public char charValue();
    public int compareTo(java.lang.Character);
    public int compareTo(java.lang.Object);
    public static int digit(char, int);
    public boolean equals(java.lang.Object);
    public static char forDigit(int, int);
    public static int getNumericValue(char);
    public int hashCode();

    public static boolean isDefined(char);
    public static boolean isDigit(char);
    public static boolean isISOControl(char);
    public static boolean isIdentifierIgnorable(char);
    public static boolean isJavaIdentifierPart(char);
    public static boolean isJavaIdentifierStart(char);
    public static boolean isJavaLetter(char); // deprecated
    public static boolean isJavaLetterOrDigit(char); // deprecated
    public static boolean isLetter(char);
    public static boolean isLetterOrDigit(char);
    public static boolean isLowerCase(char);
    public static boolean isSpace(char);
    public static boolean isSpaceChar(char);
    public static boolean isTitleCase(char);
    public static boolean isUnicodeIdentifierPart(char);
    public static boolean isUnicodeIdentifierStart(char);
    public static boolean isUpperCase(char);
    public static boolean isWhitespace(char);
    public static char toLowerCase(char);
    public java.lang.String toString();
    public static char toTitleCase(char);
    public static char toUpperCase(char);

    // class Character is continued on the next page ...
    // class Character continued ...
    // Character contains two top-level nested classes

    public static class java.lang.Character.Subset {
// represents a particular subset of the Unicode characters
        protected java.lang.Character.Subset(java.lang.String);
        public final boolean equals(java.lang.Object);
        public final int hashCode();
        public final java.lang.String toString();
    } // end of Subset
```

```
        public static final class java.lang.Character.UnicodeBlock
                              extends java.lang.Character.Subset {
// Names for Unicode Blocks. Any given character is contained by
// at most one Unicode block.
        public static final UnicodeBlock BASIC_LATIN;
        public static final UnicodeBlock LATIN_1_SUPPLEMENT;
        public static final UnicodeBlock LATIN_EXTENDED_A;
        public static final UnicodeBlock LATIN_EXTENDED_B;
        public static final UnicodeBlock IPA_EXTENSIONS;
        public static final UnicodeBlock SPACING_MODIFIER_LETTERS;
        public static final UnicodeBlock COMBINING_DIACRITICAL_MARKS;
        public static final UnicodeBlock GREEK;
        public static final UnicodeBlock CYRILLIC;
        public static final UnicodeBlock ARMENIAN;
        public static final UnicodeBlock HEBREW;
        public static final UnicodeBlock ARABIC;
        public static final UnicodeBlock DEVANAGARI;
            ... there are about 65 of these in all ...
        public static final UnicodeBlock COMBINING_MARKS_FOR_SYMBOLS;
        public static final UnicodeBlock LETTERLIKE_SYMBOLS;
        public static final UnicodeBlock NUMBER_FORMS;
        public static UnicodeBlock of(char);
    } // end of UnicodeBlock class
} // end of Character class
```

Java coding style

This seems like a good point in the text to tell you about the recommended coding style for Java. These recommendations are actually in section 6.8, "Naming Conventions," in the Java Language Specification (JLS).

- Package names are guaranteed unique by using the Internet domain name in reverse order, as in com.afu.applications.arby. The com (or edu, gov, etc.) part used to be in uppercase, but now lowercase is the recommendation.

- Class and interface names should be descriptive nouns with the first letter of each word capitalized, as in PolarCoords. Interfaces are often (not always) called *something*-able, e.g., Runnable or Sortable. There is a caution here: java.util.Observable is not an interface, though java.util.Observer is. These two classes are not well designed.

- Object and field names are nouns or noun phrases with the first letter lowercase and the first letter of subsequent words capitalized, as in currentLimit.

- Method names are verbs or verb phrases with the first letter lowercase and the first letter of subsequent words capitalized, as in calculateCurrentLimit.

- Constant (final) names are in caps, as in UPPER_LIMIT.

If you keep to these simple conventions, you'll be giving useful stylistic hints to those who must maintain your code. Maybe they will do the same for you. There aren't any recommendations in the JLS on brace style, but all the Java run-time code I've ever seen uses this style:

```
compoundStatement {                     void someMethod() {
    statement;                              statement;
    statement;                              statement;
}                                       }
```

It's a slight variant of "K&R style" (it comes from Kernighan and Ritchie who developed C), known as "The Original One True Brace Style" (TOOTBS).[1] With this style, the else part of an if-else statement and the while part of a do-while statement appear on the same line as the close brace. With most other styles, the braces are always alone on a line. When maintaining someone else's code, *always* use the style used in that code.

The One True Brace Style has methods formatted like the following:

```
void someMethod()
{
        statement;
        statement;
}
```

The *Original* One True Brace Style, and Java, has them like this:

```
void someMethod() {
        statement;
        statement;
}
```

The Java way is more consistent, but makes it a little harder to find functions and review their signatures. You'll be enchanted to hear that there are many further styles and variations that different programmers champion. Stick with TOOTBS.

Exercises

1. Describe the three different kinds of inner class. Find an example of one kind of inner class in the Java run-time library source code. Describe it.

2. What is a static nested class? Give an example of where you might use one.

---

1. I'm not making another one of my acronym wisecracks here—this is all true.

3. Find an example of a local inner class in the Java run-time library, and explain why it is used there.

Some Light Relief—The Domestic Obfuscated Java Code Non-Competition

Readers of my book *Expert C Programming* will be aware of the International Obfuscated C Code Competition (IOCCC). It's an annual contest run over Usenet since 1984 to find the most horrible and unreadable C programs of the year. Not horrible in that it is badly written, but in the much subtler concept of being horrible to figure out what it does and how it works.

The IOCCC accepts entries in the winter, which are judged over the spring, and the winners are announced at the summer Usenix conference. It is a great honor to be one of the dozen or so category winners at the IOCCC, as many very good programmers turn their talents to the dark side of the force for this event. If you know C pretty well, you might be interested in figuring out what this IOCCC past winner does:

```
main() {printf(&unix["\021%six\012\0"],(unix)["have"]+"fun"-0x60);}
```

Hint: It *doesn't* print "have fun."

Here, in the spirit of the IOCCC, are two Java programs that I wrote for April Fool's Day a few years back. You should be pretty good at reading Java code at this point, so I won't spoil your fun.

This program looks like one big comment, so it should compile without problems. When you run it, it greets you! But how?

```
/*    Just Java
      Peter van der Linden
      April 1, 1996.
\u0070\u0075\u0062\u006c\u0069\u0063\u0020
 \u0050\u0076\u0064\u004c\u0020\u0031\u0020\u0041\u0070\u0072\u0039\u0036
  \u002a\u002f\u0020\u0063\u006c\u0061\u0073\u0073\u0020\u0068\u0020\u007b
   \u0020\u0020\u0070\u0075\u0062\u006c\u0069\u0063\u0020\u0020\u0020\u0020
    \u0073\u0074\u0061\u0074\u0069\u0063\u0020\u0020\u0076\u006f\u0069\u0064
     \u006d\u0061\u0069\u006e\u0028\u0020\u0053\u0074\u0072\u0069\u006e\u0067
      \u005b\u005d\u0061\u0029\u0020\u007b\u0053\u0079\u0073\u0074\u0065\u006d
       \u002e\u006f\u0075\u0074\u002e\u0070\u0072\u0069\u006e\u0074\u006c\u006e
        \u0028\u0022\u0048\u0069\u0021\u0022\u0029\u003b\u007d\u007d\u002f\u002a

  */
```

```
% javac h.java

% java h

Hi!
```

The second program is my attempt to greatly improve program portability. This one source file can be compiled by an ANSI C compiler and executed. The same code can also be compiled and executed by a Java compiler and by a C++ compiler! Was that a great day, or what? True source portability! Every program should do as well. This program is on the website www.afu.com/jj6.

```
/*  Peter van der Linden,    "Just Java"
    April 1, 1996
    Real portability: a Java program, C program and C++ program.

    Compile and run this Java program with:  javac b.java     java b
    Compile and run this C program with:     cc    b.c        a.out
    Compile and run this C++ program with:   CC    b.c        a.out
    \u002a\u002f\u002f*/

#define String char*
#define t struct
#include <stdio.h>
t{t{int(*print)(const char*,...);}out;}
System={{printf}};/*\u002a\u002f

public class b {
                           public static void
/* The main routine                          */       main (
/* The number of arguments \u002a\u002f\u002f*/          int     argc,
/* The array of argument strings             */         String argv[]  )
                      {
                            System.out.print("Hi!\n");
                      }

/*\u002a\u002f}/**/
```

How does this trilingual program work?

Please don't suggest an International Obfuscated Java Code Competition! It works for C because there are so many opportunities to abuse the preprocessor, the expression semantics, the library calls, and so on. Java doesn't offer half as many opportunities to unscrew the unscrutable, so let's keep things that way, OK?

Part

2
Key Libraries

Chapter 13

Doing Several Things at Once: Threads

▼ WHAT ARE THREADS?

▼ TWO WAYS TO OBTAIN A NEW THREAD

▼ THE LIFECYCLE OF A THREAD

▼ THREAD GROUPS

▼ FOUR KINDS OF THREADS PROGRAMMING

▼ SOME LIGHT RELIEF—THE MOTION SENSOR SOLUTION

Multithreading is not a new concept in software, but it is new to come into the limelight. People have been kicking around experimental implementations for 20 years or more, but it is only in the last few years that desktop hardware (especially desktop multiprocessors) became powerful enough to make multithreading popular.

There is a POSIX[1] document 1003.4a (ratified June 1995) that describes a threads API standard. The threads described by the POSIX model and the threads available in Java do not completely coincide. The Java designers didn't use POSIX threads because the POSIX model was still under development when they implemented Java. Java threads are simpler, take care of their own memory management, and do not have the full generality (or overhead) of POSIX threads.

What Are Threads?

A computer system can give the impression of doing several things simultaneously, like print from one window, compile in another, while downloading music in a third. The OS runs each process for a few milliseconds,

---

1. POSIX is an operating system standard heavily weighted to a common subset of Unix.

then saves the process state, switches to the next process, and so on. Threads simply extend that concept from *switching between several different programs* to *switching between several different functions executing simultaneously within a single program*, as shown in Figure 13–1.

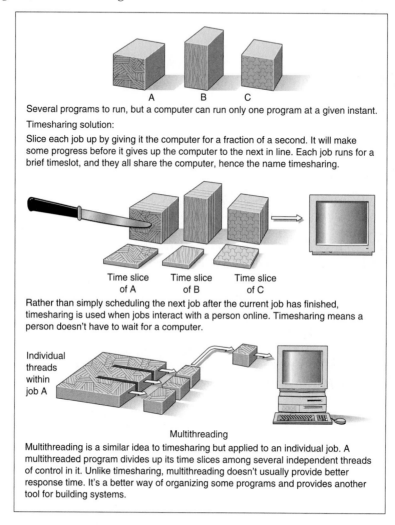

Figure 13–1   **An explanation of processor time sharing and multithreading**

A thread isn't restricted just to one method. Any thread in a multithreaded program can call any series of methods that could be called in a single-threaded program. You often have one thread that waits for input from a GUI and another thread that processes the input when it arrives.

When the operating system switches from running one process to running another for its time slice, there is a somewhat costly overhead of saving all program state (virtual memory contents and map, file descriptors, interrupt settings, etc.). When the JVM switches from running one of your threads to running another of your threads, the cost is much lower. The context switch takes place within the same address space, so the JVM just saves a few registers, changes the stack pointer and the program counter, and the next thread is ready to go. Threads can actually achieve the counterintuitive result of making a program run faster, even on uniprocessor hardware. This occurs when there are calculation steps that no longer have to wait for earlier output to complete, but can run while the I/O is taking place.

Threads (an abbreviation of "threads of control," meaning control flow) are the way we get several things to happen at once in a program. Why is this a good idea? In an unthreaded program (what you have been using so far in Java, and what you have always used in Fortran, Pascal, C, Basic, C++, COBOL, and so on), only one thing happens at a time. Threads allow a program to do more than one thing at a time. There are three reasons why you would do this:

- You can write interactive programs that never "go dead" on the user. You might have one thread controlling and responding to a GUI, while another thread carries out the tasks or computations requested, while a third thread does file I/O, all for the same program. When one part of the program is blocked waiting on some resource, the other threads can still run.

- Some programs are easier to write if you split them into threads. The classic example is the server part of a client/server. When each request comes in from a client, it is convenient if the server can spawn a new thread to process that one request. The alternative is to have one larger server program algorithmically try to keep track of the state of each individual request.

- Some programs are amenable to parallel processing. Writing them as threads allows the code to express this. Examples include some sorting and merging algorithms, some matrix operations, searching for aliens (à la http://seti.org), and many recursive algorithms.

Two Ways to Obtain a New Thread

There are two ways to obtain a new thread of control in Java. Either extend the Thread class, or write a class to implement the java.lang.Runnable interface and use it in the Thread constructor. The first way can be used only if your class doesn't already extend some other class (because Java disallows multiple parents).

1. Extend class java.lang.Thread and override `run()`:

```
class Plum extends Thread {
    public void run() { /* more code */ }
}

Plum P = new Plum();
P.start();
```

or

2. Implement the Runnable interface (the class Thread itself is an implementation of Runnable), and use that class in the Thread constructor:

```
class Mango implements Runnable {
    public void run() { /* more code */ }
}


Mango m = new Mango();

Thread t1 = new Thread( m );
t1.start();
```

Figure 13–2 shows how a subclass of Thread is created by extending Thread.

Creating a thread looks confusing, because you have to start the thread running by calling a method that you did not write, namely `start()` in Figure 13–2. You extended or constructed Thread, so you will have `Thread.start()` by inheritance and all will be well.

Then, continuing to refer to Figure 13–2, declaring an object of class Plum gives you a new thread of control whose execution starts in the method `run()`. That isn't an OOP mechanism, it's just a name convention you have to know. Declaring two Plums (or more likely one Plum and one object of some other thread subclass) gives you two independently executing threads of control, and declaring and filling an array of Plums gives you an entire array.length of threads of control.

New threads do not start executing on creation. For some applications, programmers want to create threads (which incurs some system resource cost) in

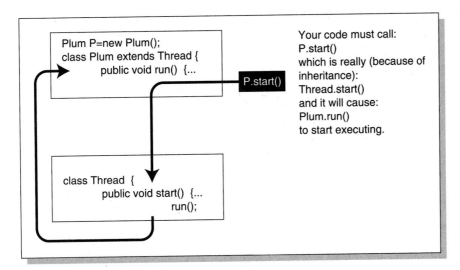

Figure 13–2   Subclass of Thread created by extending Thread

advance, then explicitly start them when needed (cheap), so this has been made the way it works. Create a thread like the following:

```
Mango m = new Mango();
```

You start it running by calling the start() method, like the following:

```
m.start();
```

Or you can create and start it in one step, like the following:

```
new Mango().start();
```

Execution then begins in the run() method, from where you can call other methods in this and other classes as usual. Remember: run() is the place where it starts, and start() gets it running. Another way to think of this is that run() is the equivalent of main() for a thread. You do not call it directly, but it is called on your behalf. If you ever see a call to run, like either of the following lines,

```
run()
something.run()
```

it means someone who didn't understand what they were doing wrote the code.

A few words on Runnable

The following is the alternative way to create your own threads. The Runnable interface looks like this:

```
public interface Runnable {
    public void run();
}
```

All it does is promise that an implementing class will have a no-arg method called run(). To turn a Runnable object into a Thread, you pass it as an argument to a Thread constructor, like this:

```
class Mango implements Runnable {
    public void run() { ... }
}
  /* more code */

Thread t1 = new Thread(new Mango());
```

Now you have a thread t1 that you can invoke all the Thread methods on, such as:

```
t1.start();
t1.stop();
```

You have to call start() to get t1 executing (just as if you had extended Thread). It's common to instantiate and start in one statement like the following:

```
new Thread (new Mango()).start();
```

However, you cannot have statements *within the Runnable interface implementation* of run() that invoke the Thread methods, like sleep() or getName() or setPriority().

This is because there is no Thread in our Runnable instance. So our Runnable doesn't know, and cannot directly invoke, any Thread-y things. This perhaps makes an implementation of Runnable slightly less convenient than a subclass of Thread. The code example coming up shows what *won't* work.

There is a simple workaround shown after the code example.

```
// Show the two ways to obtain a new thread
//    1.  extend class java.lang.Thread and override run()
//    2.  implement the Runnable interface,

class example {
   public static void main(String[] a) {

     // alternative 1
      ExtnOfThread t1 = new ExtnOfThread();
      t1.start();

     // alternative 2
      Thread t2 = new Thread (new ImplOfRunnable());
      t2.start();
   }
}

class ExtnOfThread extends Thread {
   public void run() {
        System.out.println("Extension of Thread running");
// next line compiles and runs just fine
        try {sleep(1000);}
        catch (InterruptedException ie) {return;}
   }
}

class ImplOfRunnable implements Runnable {
   public void run() {
        System.out.println("Implementation of Runnable running");

// next line will not compile - thread method sleep() not known
//         try {sleep(1000);}
//         catch (InterruptedException ie) {return;}
   }
}
```

The class Thread has many other methods shown later in the chapter. You can call these Thread methods only if you have a Thread object on which to invoke them. You don't get that automatically in a class that implements Runnable.

To get a Thread object, you call the static method Thread.currentThread(). Its return value is simply the currently running thread. Once you have that, you can easily apply any thread methods to it, as shown in the next example.

```
class ImplOfRunnable implements Runnable {
   public void run() {
        System.out.println("Implementation of Runnable running");
        Thread t = Thread.currentThread();
        try { t.sleep(1000); }
        catch  (InterruptedException ie) { return; }
   }
}
```

A call to currentThread() can appear in any Java code, including your main
program. Once you have that thread object, you can invoke the thread methods
on it.

The official word from the Java team is that you should use the Runnable interface
if the run() method is the only one you are planning to override. The thinking is
that, to maintain the purity of the model, classes should not be subclassed unless
the programmer intends to modify or enhance the fundamental behavior of the
class.

As with exceptions, you can provide a string argument when you create a thread
subclass. If you want to do this, you must provide a constructor to take that string
and pass it back to the constructor of the base class. The string becomes the name
of the object of the Thread subclass and can later be used to identify it.

```
class Grape extends Thread {
        Grape(String s){ super(s); } // constructor

        public void run() { /* code */ }
}
    /* more code */
    static public void main(String s[]) {
        new Grape("merlot").start();
        new Grape("pinot").start();
        new Grape("cabernet").start();
```

You cannot pass any parameters into the "run()" method because its signature
would differ from the version it is overriding in Thread. A thread can, however,
get the string with which it was started, by invoking the "getName()" method.
This string could encode arguments or be an index into a static array of
arguments as needed.

You have already seen enough to write an elementary Java program that uses
threads. So do it. Write two classes that extend Thread. In one, the run() method
should print "I like tea" in a loop, while the other prints "I like coffee". Create a
third class with a main() routine that instantiates and starts the other two threads.
Compile and run your program.

The Lifecycle of a Thread

We have already covered how a thread is created, and how the start() method
inherited from Thread causes execution to start in its run() method. An individual
thread dies when execution falls off the end of run() or otherwise leaves the run
method (through an exception or return statement).

If an exception is thrown from the run method, the runtime system prints a
message saying so, the thread terminates, but the exception does not propagate
back into the code that created or started the thread. What this means is that once

you start up a separate thread, it doesn't come back to interfere with the code that spawned it.

Priorities

Threads have priorities that you can set and change. A higher priority thread executes ahead of a lower priority thread if they are both ready to run.

Java threads are preemptible, meaning that a running thread will be pushed off the processor by a higher priority thread before it is ready to give it up of its own accord. Java threads might or might not also be time-sliced, meaning that a running thread might share the processor with threads of equal priority.

A slice of time

Not guaranteeing time-slicing might seem a somewhat surprising design decision as it violates the "Principle of Least Astonishment"—it leads to program behavior that programmers find surprising (namely threads can suffer from CPU starvation). There is some precedent in that time-slicing can also be missing in a POSIX-conforming thread implementation. POSIX specifies a number of different scheduling algorithms, one of which (round robin) does do time-slicing. Another scheduling possibility allows a local implementation. In the Solaris case of POSIX threads, only the local implementation is used, and this does not do any time-slicing.

Many people thought that the failure to require time-slicing in the Java scheduler was a mistake that will be fixed in a future release. But it hasn't happened for so many years, that now it probably won't ever.

Since a programmer cannot assume that time-slicing will take place, the careful programmer assures portability by writing threaded code that does not depend on time-slicing. The code must cope with the fact that once a thread starts running, all other threads with the same priority might become blocked. One way to cope with this would be to adjust thread priorities on the fly. That is *not* recommended because the code will cost you a fortune in software maintenance.

A better way is to yield control to other threads frequently. CPU-intensive threads should call the yield() method at regular intervals to ensure they don't hog the processor. This won't be needed if time-slicing is made a standard part of Java. Yield allows the scheduler to choose another runnable thread for execution.

Java thread priorities run from 1 (lowest) to 10 (highest). Threads start off with the same priority as their parent thread (the thread that created them), and you can adjust the priority as follows:

```
t1.setPriority ( t1.getPriority() +1 );
```

On operating systems that have priorities, most users cannot adjust their processes to a higher priority (because they can gain an unfair advantage over other users of the system).[2] There is no such inhibition for threads, because they all operate within one process. The user is competing only with himself or herself for resources.

Thread Groups

A Thread group is (big surprise!) a group of Threads. A Thread group can contain a set of Threads as well as a set of other Thread groups. It's a way of bundling several related threads together and doing certain housekeeping things to all of them, like starting them all with a single method invocation.

There are methods to create a Thread group and add a Thread to it. You can get a reference to your Thread group for later use:

```
private ThreadGroup mygroup;
mygroup=Thread.currentThread().getThreadGroup();
```

Thread groups exist because it turned out to be a useful concept in the runtime library. There seemed no reason not to just pass it through to application programmers, as well. The designers of the new `java.util.concurrency` package suggest that thread groups were never much use, and might be deprecated in future. So avoid them.

How many threads? Sometimes programmers ask, "How many threads should I have in my program?" Ron Winacott of Sun Canada has done a lot of thread programming, and he compares this question to asking, "How many people can I take in my transport?"

The problem is that so much is left unspecified. What kind of transport is it? Is it a motorbike or a jumbo jet? Are the people children, or 250-pound pro wrestlers like Ric Flair? How many are needed to help get to where you want to go (e.g., driver, radio operator, navigator, tail gunner, nanny, observer)? In other words, what kind of program is it, what's the workload, and on what hardware are you running it?

The bottom line is: Each thread has a default stack size of 400K in the JDK current release. It will also use about 0.5K to hold its internal state, but the stack size is the limiting factor. A 32-bit UNIX process (UNIX is the most capable of all the systems to which Java has been ported) effectively has a 2 GB user address space[3], so in theory, you could have around 5,000 threads. In practice, you would be limited by CPU availability, swap space, and disk bandwidth before you got up there. In one experiment, I was able to create almost 2,000 threads before my

---

2. Hence, the infamous message from the system operator, "I've upped my priority, now up yours."
3. The kernel has the other 2 GB of the 4 GB that can be addressed using 32 bits.

desktop system ground to a halt. That was just to create them; I'm not making any claims about them doing any useful work.

Now, back to the real question. Overall, there is no unique correct answer. How many is "reasonable"? There is only one person who can accurately answer this question and that is the programmer writing the threaded application. The runtime library used to have a comment mentioning 26 threads as being the maximum concurrency that one might reasonably expect. That precision lends spurious plausibility, but it's just a rule of thumb.

The best estimate is "the number of threads needed to perform the task". If this number is too high for the address space or the CPU power, then you must redesign the tasks (and the number of threads) to use what is available. Use threads to achieve concurrency or to gain overlapping I/O. Do not try to create a new thread for every single method, class, or object in your program.

Inner class thread

One Java expert on the team pointed out that you can write an anonymous inner class to create and start a background thread close to the place where it's relevant:

```
(new Thread() {
    public void run() {
        // 2 or 3 lines to do in the background
    }
} ).start();
```

That's true, but for goodness sake, don't make your programs impossible to maintain by putting more than two or three lines in an inner class.

You might be wondering, "What if you start a thread and don't save the reference to it (like the previous code)? Will it be immediately garbage collected?" The answer is no. *You* might not have a reference to the thread, but the *run-time system* still does, and the thread will not be reclaimed until it returns from its run method. This is also the reason your GUI programs don't terminate when the flow of control reaches the end of your main() method: there are still some window system threads running.

Four Kinds of Threads Programming

Coordination between different threads is known as *synchronization*. Programs that use threads can be divided into the following four levels of difficulty, depending on the kind of synchronization needed between the different threads.

1. Unrelated threads
2. Related but unsynchronized threads
3. Mutually exclusive threads
4. Communicating mutually exclusive threads

We will deal with the first two here and the second two in the next chapter. Figure 13–3 is the key for all illustrations dealing with this topic.

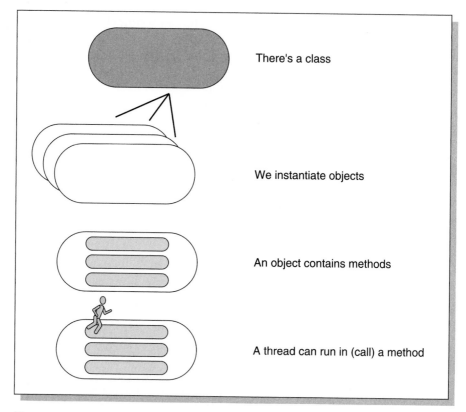

There's a class

We instantiate objects

An object contains methods

A thread can run in (call) a method

Figure 13–3   Key to threads diagrams

Unrelated threads

The simplest threads program involves threads of control that do different things and don't interact with each other.

A good example of unrelated threads is the answer to the programming challenge set a few pages back.

The code is as follows:

```
public class drinks {
    public static void main(String[] a) {
        Coffee t1 = new Coffee();
        t1.start();
        new Tea().start();  // an anonymous thread
    }
}

class Coffee extends Thread {
    public void run() {
        while(true) {
            System.out.println("I like coffee");
            yield();  // did you forget this?
        }
    }
}

class Tea extends Thread {
    public void run() {
        while(true) {
            System.out.println("I like tea");
            yield();
        }
    }
}
```

When you run this program, you will see output similar to the following:

I like coffee
I like tea
I like coffee
I like tea
I like coffee
I like tea

It is repeated over and over again until you press control-C or otherwise interrupt program execution. This type of threads programming is easy to get working, and it corresponds to Figure 13–4.

Related but unsynchronized threads

This level of complexity uses threaded code to partition a problem, solving it by having multiple threads work on different pieces of the same data structure. The threads don't interact with each other. Here, threads of control do work that is sent to them, but they don't work on shared data, so they don't need to access it in a synchronized way.

An example of this would be spawning a new thread for each socket connection that comes in. A thread that just does "work to order" like that is a good example of a demon thread—its only purpose is to serve a higher master. See Figure 13–5 for a graphical representation of how this kind of thread interacts with objects.

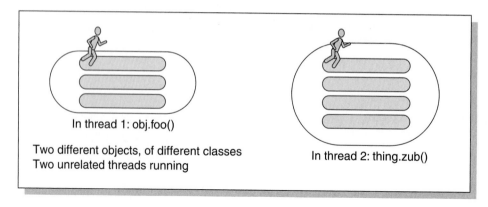

In thread 1: obj.foo()

Two different objects, of different classes
Two unrelated threads running

In thread 2: thing.zub()

Figure 13–4   Unrelated threads

Demon threads

A thread can also be marked as a demon or daemon (the spelling varies) thread. Demon threads are those that exist only to carry out work on behalf of others. The following marks a thread as a demon:

```
myThread.setDemon(true);
```

If a Java program finds that only demon threads are running, it has nothing further to do and terminates. A thread that maintains a queue for a printer is an example of a system demon thread.

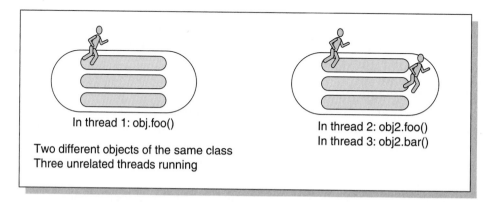

In thread 1: obj.foo()

Two different objects of the same class
Three unrelated threads running

In thread 2: obj2.foo()
In thread 3: obj2.bar()

Figure 13–5   Related but unsynchronized threads.

A less common but still interesting example of related but unsynchronized threads involves partitioning a data set and instantiating multiple copies of the same thread to work on different pieces of the same problem. Be careful not to duplicate work, or even worse, to let two different threads operate on the same data at once.

The following is an example program that tests whether a given number is a prime number. That involves a lot of calculations that don't affect each other so it's a good candidate for parcelling the work out among a number of threads. Tell each thread the range of numbers it is to test-divide into the possible prime. Then let them all loose in parallel.

The driver code is:

```
// demonstrates the use of threads to test a number for primality

public class testPrime {

    public static void main(String s[]) {
        long possPrime = Long.parseLong(s[0]);
        int centuries = (int)(possPrime/100) +1;

        for(int i=0;i<centuries;i++) {
            new testRange(i*100, possPrime).start();
        }

    }
}
```

This main program gets its argument, which is the value to test for primarily, and then calculates how many 100s there are in the number. A new thread is created to test for factors in every range of 100. So if the number is 2048, there are twenty 100s. Twenty one threads are created. The first checks whether any of the numbers 2 to 99 divide into 2048. The second checks the range 100 to 199. The third checks 200 to 299, and so on, with the 21st thread checking the numbers 2000 to 2100.

The line "`new testRange(i*100, possPrime).start();`" instantiates an object of class testRange, using the constructor that takes two arguments. That object belongs to a subclass of Thread, so the `.start()` jammed on the end starts it running. This is the Java idiom of invoking a method on the object returned by a constructor or method invocation. The listing of class testRange is as follows:

```
class testRange extends Thread {

    static long possPrime;
    long from, to;

    // constructor
    //    record the number we are to test, and
    //    the range of factors we are to try.
    testRange(int argFrom, long argpossPrime) {
        possPrime=argpossPrime;
        if (argFrom==0) from=2; else from=argFrom;
        to=argFrom+99;
    }

    public void run() {
        for (long i=from; i<=to && i<possPrime; i++) {
            if (possPrime % i == 0) {  // i divides possPrime exactly
                System.out.println(
                        "factor "+i+" found by thread "+getName());
                break;   // get out of for loop
            }
            yield();
        }
    }

}
```

The constructor saves a copy of two things: The number we are to test for primarily, and the start of the range of potential factors for this thread instance to test. The end of the range is the start plus 99.

All the run() method does is count through this range, trying each divisor. If one divides the number exactly, then print it out and stop this thread. We have the answer that the number is not prime. There are many possible improvements to the algorithm (for instance, we need only test for factors up to the square root of the possible prime). These improvements have been omitted so as not to clutter up the code example.

A sample run of this program might look like the following:

```
% java testPrime 2048
 factor 2 found by thread Thread-4
 factor 512 found by thread Thread-9
 factor 1024 found by thread Thread-14
 factor 128 found by thread Thread-5
 factor 256 found by thread Thread-6
```

So, 2048 is not a prime number and five of the 21 threads found factors. The default name for the first thread you create is Thread-4 (not Thread-1) because there are already several threads running in your program, including the garbage collector and your main program.

Deprecated thread methods and interrupting I/O

When a method or class in the Java API is replaced, the old one is said to be "deprecated." It is left in the library so that old programs don't fail, but you should use the newer version.

Three methods in the thread class have been deprecated:

```
Thread.suspend();
Thread.resume();
Thread.stop();
```

Suspend and resume were always just a bad idea. They were methods in the run-time code that someone thought would be helpful to make available as part of the API. Applications shouldn't be doing thread scheduling.

Most uses of stop should be replaced by code that just modifies some variable to tell the target thread it should stop running. The target thread should poll this synchronized variable regularly, and return from its run method when some other thread sets it.

If you wanted to stop a thread because it is hung in I/O, send it an exception instead, by calling `probablyBlockedThread.interrupt();` If it is blocked in I/O that will send it an exception. There is more information about all of these in the Java HTML documentation.

The following code shows the non-private members of the class `java.lang.Thread`. You can look at the full source at `src\java\lang\Thread.java`.

```
public class java.lang.Thread implements java.lang.Runnable {
    java.lang.InheritableThreadLocal$Entry values;
    public static final int MIN_PRIORITY;
    public static final int NORM_PRIORITY;
    public static final int MAX_PRIORITY;
// constructors
    public java.lang.Thread();
    public java.lang.Thread(java.lang.Runnable);
    public java.lang.Thread(java.lang.Runnable,java.lang.String);
    public java.lang.Thread(java.lang.String);
    public java.lang.Thread(ThreadGroup,java.lang.Runnable);
    public Thread(ThreadGroup, Runnable, String);
    public java.lang.Thread(ThreadGroup,String);

    public static int activeCount();
    public final void checkAccess();
    public static native java.lang.Thread currentThread();
    public void destroy();
    public static void dumpStack();
    public static int enumerate(java.lang.Thread[]);
    public java.lang.ClassLoader getContextClassLoader();
    public final java.lang.String getName();
    public final int getPriority();
    public final java.lang.ThreadGroup getThreadGroup();
    public void interrupt();
    public static boolean interrupted();
    public final native boolean isAlive();
    public final boolean isDaemon();
    public boolean isInterrupted();
    public final void join() throws java.lang.InterruptedException;
    public final synchronized void join(long) throws
                                    InterruptedException;
  public final synchronized void join(long, int) throws
                            InterruptedException;
    public void run();
    public void setContextClassLoader(java.lang.ClassLoader);
    public final void setDaemon(boolean);
    public final void setName(java.lang.String);
    public final void setPriority(int);
    public static native void sleep(long) throws
                                    java.lang.InterruptedException;
public static void sleep(long, int) throws java.lang.InterruptedException;
    public java.lang.String toString();
    public static native void yield();
    public native synchronized void start();

// deprecated methods: do not use.
    public native int countStackFrames();              // deprecated
    public final void stop();                          // deprecated
    public final synchronized void stop(java.lang.Throwable); //deprecated
    public final void suspend();                       // deprecated
    public final void resume();                        // deprecated
}
```

Some Light Relief—The Motion Sensor Solution

A while back I moved into a new office building at Sun Microsystems. This was good in that it gave me an excuse to discard all the flotsam and jetsam I had not yet unpacked from the previous such move. You should move your office every three years for that reason alone. Not me, you. But my move was bad in that there were a few things about the new office that didn't suit me.

Number one on the list was the motion sensor connected to the lights. All modern U.S. office buildings have power-saving features in the lighting, heating, and ventilation. These building services are usually installed in a false floor at the top of a building, but that's another storey[4]. Improving the energy efficiency of buildings is part of the U.S. government's Energy Star program. Energy Star is the reason that the photocopier is always off when you go to use it. There are Energy Star power management guidelines that apply to desktop computers, too. At that time, I was responsible for Sun's desktop power management software in the Solaris kernel, so I know how essential it is to allow users to retain control over power-saving features. Apparently, our building designers did not appreciate this.

The light in my new office was wired up to a motion sensor, and it would automatically switch itself off if you didn't move around enough. This was something of a nuisance as there are long periods in the day when the only thing moving in my office are my fingertips flying over the keyboard. Periodically, my office would be plunged into darkness, a sharp transition which spoils my concentration. And concentration is very important to programmers.

After that unpleasant business with the glitter booby trap[5] I installed in the VP's office, it would have been futile to ask the facilities guys to replace the motion sensor with a regular switch. So I considered other alternatives. A gerbil on an exercise wheel? They're high maintenance, noisy, smelly, and they keep erratic hours. One of my colleagues suggested installing folks from the marketing department in my office and having them flap their arms intermittently, thus getting some productive use out of them. I did consider it, but they have many of the same disadvantages as the gerbil, and are not so easy to train.

The final answer was one of those kitschy dippy bird things. I position it next to the sensor and dip the beak in the glass of water in the morning. It continues to rock backwards and forwards for a good long time, and everyone is happy. I plan to camouflage the dippy bird with a water lily in a dish, which motivates the housekeeping staff to keep the water level topped up. That makes it zero

4.   Another *storey*! Geddit?
5.   Booby-trapped ceiling tile, hinged like a trapdoor and piled with confetti on top. The trap is triggered by a thread attached to the back of a desk drawer. It pulls out the safety latch when the drawer is opened. Treat your boss to one today.

maintenance from my perspective and the closest we'll get to perpetual motion, and furthermore the lights no longer go out on me.

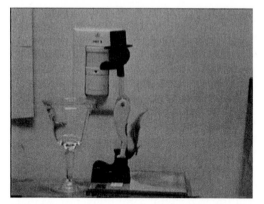

Figure 13–6   Perceptual motion: The dippy bird

How do dippy birds work?

Dippy birds work on the same general principle as the steam engine, but with less splendor.

The bird is essentially two balanced globes connected by a small tube, with the lower globe full of a very volatile (easy to evaporate) liquid. You start it going by tipping the upper globe forward into a glass of water, and releasing it back upright. Water evaporation from the surface of the upper globe soon cools it, cooling the air inside too, thus dropping its pressure. The lowered air pressure in the upper globe sucks some of the fluid up the tube from the lower globe. That change in delicate weight distribution causes the bird to tip forward, and dunk its beak in the water. Now that the bird is tipped forward, the bottom of the tube comes out of the volatile liquid. A bubble of normal pressure air will travel up the tube, thus releasing the column of fluid to the bottom of the bird. That weight change in turn makes the bird bob upright again. Why does the liquid have to be volatile? So it doesn't inhibit the tiny cooling effect of water evaporation from a surface.

As the water droplets left on its beak start to evaporate, the pressure in the higher globe drops again, and the cycle repeats until the water source is used up.

You can get a dippy bird of your own (see Figure 13-6) from Edmunds Scientific at www.edsci.com. Don't forget about the glitter trap, either. Email me your results!

Chapter **14**

Advanced
Thread Topics

In this chapter we will cover the advanced thread topics. Specifically, we will explain how threads synchronize with each other when they have data that they must pass to each other. That is, they cannot solve the problem merely by staying out of each other's way and ignoring each other.

In Chapter 13, we reviewed the easy parts of thread programming as items 1 and 2 in a list there. This chapter covers items 3 and 4 from the same list. These are the hard parts of thread programming. We are about to plunge into level 3: when threads need to exclude each other from running during certain times.

Mutually Exclusive Threads

Here's where threads start to interact with each other, and that makes life a little more complicated. In particular, we have threads that need to work on the same pieces of the same data structure.

These threads must take steps to stay out of each other's way so they don't each simultaneously modify the same piece of data, leaving an uncertain result. Staying out of each other's way is known as *mutual exclusion*. You'll understand better why mutual exclusion is necessary if we motivate the discussion with some code. You should download or type the example in and run it.

This code simulates a steam boiler. It defines some values (the current reading of, and the safe limit for, a pressure gauge), and then instantiates ten copies of a thread called "pressure," storing them in an array. The pressure class models an input valve that wants to inject more pressure into the boiler. Each pressure object looks to see if we are within safe boiler limits, and if so, increases the pressure. The main routine concludes by waiting for each thread to finish (this is the join() statement) and then prints the current value of the pressure gauge. Here is the main routine:

```
public class p {
    static int pressureGauge=0;
    static final int safetyLimit = 20;

    public static void main(String[]args) {
        pressure []p1 = new pressure[10];
        for (int i=0; i<10; i++)   {
            p1[i] = new pressure();
            p1[i].start();
        }
        // the 10 threads are now running in parallel
        try{
            for (int i=0;i<10;i++)
                        p1[i].join();   // wait for thread to end
        } catch(Exception e){ }

        System.out.println(
            "gauge reads "+pressureGauge+", safe limit is 20");
    }

}
```

Now let's look at the pressure thread. This code simply checks whether the current pressure reading is within safety limits, and if it is, it waits briefly, then increases the pressure.

The following is the thread:

```
class pressure extends Thread {

    void RaisePressure() {
        if (p.pressureGauge < p.safetyLimit-15) {
            // wait briefly to simulate some calculations
            try{sleep(100);} catch (Exception e){}
            p.pressureGauge += 15;
        } else
            ; // pressure too high -- don't do anything.
    }

    public void run() {
        RaisePressure();
    }
}
```

If you haven't seen this before, it should look pretty safe. After all, before we increase the pressure reading we always check that our addition won't push it over the safety limit. Stop reading at this point, type in the two dozen lines of code, and run them. The following is what you might see:

```
% java p
gauge reads 150, safe limit is 20
```

Although we always checked the gauge before increasing the pressure, it is over the safety limit by a huge margin! Better evacuate the area! So what is happening here?

The problem is a race condition

This is a classic example of what is called a *data race* or a *race condition*. A race condition occurs when two or more threads update the same value simultaneously. What you want to happen is:

1.   Thread 1 reads pressure gauge
2.   Thread 1 updates pressure gauge
3.   Thread 2 reads pressure gauge
4.   Thread 2 updates pressure gauge

But it might happen that thread 2 starts to read before thread 1 has updated, so the accesses take place in this order:

1.   Thread 1 reads pressure gauge
2.   Thread 2 reads pressure gauge
3.   Thread 1 updates pressure gauge
4.   Thread 2 updates pressure gauge

In this case, thread 2 reads an erroneous value for the gauge (too low), effectively missing the fact that thread 1 is in the middle of updating the value based on what it read. For this example we helped the data race to happen by introducing a tenth-of-a-second delay between reading and updating. But whenever you have different threads updating the same data, a data race can occur even in statements that follow each other consecutively. It can even occur in the middle of expression evaluation! At Sun, inside the OS kernel group, for years every time we prototyped a faster speed processor or a new multi-processor, we uncovered (and fixed) new data race problems in Solaris.

Data race bug caused power blackout

Remember the great North American power blackout of August 14 2003? As many as 50 million people lost electrical power in a region stretching from Michigan through Canada to New York City. It took three days to restore service to some customers.

There were several factors that contributed to the blackout, but the official report highlights the failure of the alarm monitoring software written in C++ by GE Energy. The software failure wrongly led operators to believe that all was well, and precluded them from rebalancing the power load before the blackout cascaded out of control.

Because the consequences of the software failure were so severe, the bug was analyzed exhaustively. The root cause was finally identified by artificially introducing delays in the code (just like in our example program previously). There were two threads that wrote to a common data structure, and through a coding error, they could both update it at the same time. It was a classic race condition, and eventually the program "lost the race", leaving the structure in an inconsistent state. That in turn caused the alarm event handler to spin in an infinite loop, instead of raising the alarm. The biggest power failure in the history of the United States and Canada was caused by a data race bug in some threaded C++ code. Java is equally vulnerable to this kind of bug.

In this example, we have highlighted what is happening and rigged the code to exaggerate the effect, but in general data races are among the hardest problems to debug. They typically do not reproduce consistently and they leave no visible clues as to how data got into an inconsistent state.

Synchronization solutions

The following are some common operations that are used to ensure data integrity in the face of concurrency. These have evolved over the years, as understanding of the problems has increased. The operations are not specific to Java; they are used for synchronization on all kinds of systems.

- **Test-and-set instructions**. All general purpose processors now have this kind of instruction, and it is used to build higher-level synchronization constructs. Test-and-set does not block; that has to be built on top of it.

- **P-and-v semaphores.** Introduced by Prof Dijkstra in the 1960's, the semaphore was the main synchronization primitive for a long time. Semaphores count down and up: P is short for the Dutch words *proberen te verlangen*, to try to decrement. V stands for *verhogen*, to increment. It's easy to build semaphores from test-and-set instructions. Semaphores are low-level, and can be hard for programmers to read and debug. They can be used to implement higher-level primitives.

- **Read/write locks**, also known as "mutexes" (although some people use the term mutex to mean a semaphore). A lock provides a simple "turnstile": only one thread at a time can be going through (executing in) a block protected by a lock. It's easy to build a lock from semaphores.

- **Monitors**. A monitor is a higher level construct built out of a lock plus a variable that keeps track of some related condition, like "number of unconsumed bytes in the buffer". It's easy to build monitors from read/write locks. A monitor defines several methods as part of its protocol. Two of those predefined methods are wait() and notify().

There are a surprising number of special-purpose variations on these basic themes, and there is no universal agreement on the terminology. The first item in the previous list is a hardware instruction, and Java has all three of the other synchronization primitives listed.

To avoid data races, follow this simple rule: Whenever two threads access the same data, they must use mutual exclusion. You can optimize slightly, by allowing multiple readers at one instant. A reader and a writer must never be accessing the same data at the same time. Two writers must never be running at the same time. As the name suggests, mutual exclusion is a protocol for making sure that if one thread is touching some particular data, another is not. The threads mutually exclude each other in time.

In Java, thread mutual exclusion is built on objects. Every object in the system has its own semaphore (strictly speaking, this will only be allocated if it is used), so any object in the system can be used as the "turnstile" or "thread serializer" for threads. You use the synchronized keyword and explicitly or implicitly provide an object, any object, to synchronize on. The run-time system will take over and apply the code to ensure that, at most, one thread has locked that specific object at any given instant, as shown in Figure 14–1.

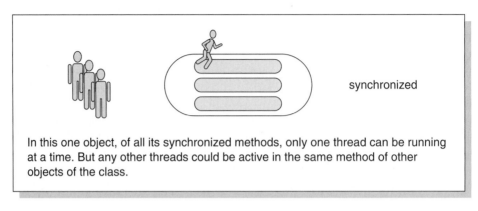

In this one object, of all its synchronized methods, only one thread can be running at a time. But any other threads could be active in the same method of other objects of the class.

Figure 14–1   Mutually exclusive threads

Synchronized blocks

You can apply the synchronized keyword to class methods, to instance methods, or to a block of code. In each case, the mutex (mutual exclusion) lock of some named object is acquired, then the code is executed, then the lock is released. If the lock is already held by another thread, then the thread that wants to acquire the lock is suspended until the lock is released.

The Java programmer never deals with the low-level and error-prone details of creating, acquiring, and releasing locks, but only specifies the region of code and the object that must be exclusively held in that region. You want to make your regions of synchronized code as small as possible, because mutual exclusion really chokes performance. The following are examples of each of these alternatives of synchronizing over a class, a method, or a block, with comments on how the exclusion works.

Mutual exclusion over an entire class. This is achieved by applying the keyword synchronized to a class method (a method with the keyword static). Making a class method synchronized tells the compiler, "Add this method to the set of class methods that must run with mutual exclusion," as shown in Figure 14–2. Only one static synchronized method for a particular class can be running at any given time, regardless of how many objects there are. The threads are implicitly synchronized using the class object.

In the preceding pressure example, we can make RaisePressure a static synchronized method by changing its declaration to this:

```
static synchronized void RaisePressure() {
```

Since there is only one of these methods for the entire class, no matter how many thread objects are created, we have effectively serialized the code that accesses

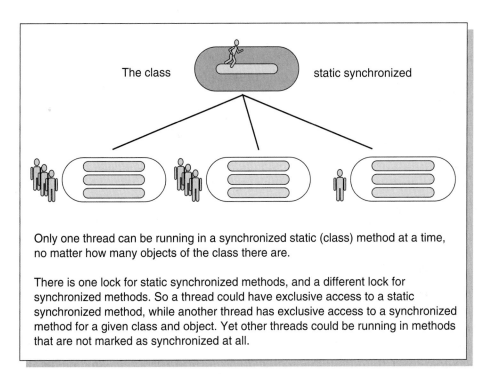

The class   static synchronized

Only one thread can be running in a synchronized static (class) method at a time, no matter how many objects of the class there are.

There is one lock for static synchronized methods, and a different lock for synchronized methods. So a thread could have exclusive access to a static synchronized method, while another thread has exclusive access to a synchronized method for a given class and object. Yet other threads could be running in methods that are not marked as synchronized at all.

Figure 14–2   Mutual exclusion over the static methods of a class

and updates the pressure gauge. Recompiling with this change and rerunning the code will give this result (and you should try it):

```
% java p
gauge reads 15, safe limit is 20
```

Mutual exclusion over a block of statements. This is achieved by attaching the keyword "synchronized" before a block of code. You also have to explicitly mention in parentheses the object whose lock must be acquired before the region can be entered. Reverting to our original pressure example, we could make the following change inside the method RaisePressure to achieve the necessary mutual exclusion:

```
void RaisePressure() {
    synchronized(O) {
      if (p.pressureGauge < p.safetyLimit-15) {
           try{sleep(100);} catch (Exception e){} // delay
           p.pressureGauge += 15;
      }  else ; // pressure too high -- don't add to it.
    }
}
```

We will also need to provide the object O that we are using for synchronization. This declaration will do fine:

```
static Object O = new Object();
```

We could use an existing object, but we do not have a convenient one at hand in this example. The fields pressureGauge and safetyLimit are ints, not Objects, otherwise either of those would be a suitable choice. It is always preferable to use the object that is being updated as the synchronization lock wherever possible. Recompiling with the change and rerunning the code will give the desired exclusion:

```
% java p
 gauge reads 15, safe limit is 20
```

Mutual exclusion over a method. This is achieved by applying the keyword "synchronized" to an ordinary (non-static) method. Note that in this case the object whose lock will provide the mutual exclusion is implicit. It is the this object on which the method is invoked.

```
synchronized void foo() { ...  }
```

This is equivalent to:

```
void foo() {
  synchronized (this) {
     ...
  }
}
```

Note that making the obvious change to our pressure example does not give the desired result!

```
// this example shows what will NOT work
synchronized void RaisePressure() {
     if (p.pressureGauge < p.safetyLimit-15) {
          try{sleep(100);} catch (Exception e){} // delay
          p.pressureGauge += 15;
     } else ; // pressure too high -- don't add to it.
}
```

The reason is clear: The "this" object is one of the ten different threads that are created. Each thread will successfully grab its own lock, and there will be no exclusion between the different threads at all. Synchronization excludes threads working on the *same object*; it doesn't synchronize the *same method* on different objects.

Be sure you are clear on this critical point: Synchronized methods are useful when you have several threads that might invoke methods simultaneously *on the same one object*. It ensures that, at most, one of all the methods designated as synchronized will be invoked *on that one object* at any given instant.

In this case we have the reverse. We have one thread for each of several different objects calling the same method simultaneously. Some system redesign is called for here.

Note that synchronized methods all exclude each other, but they do not exclude a non-synchronized method, nor a (synchronized or non-synchronized) static (class) method from running.

Communicating Mutually Exclusive Threads

Warning: Specialized threads topics ahead
Here's where things become downright complicated until you get familiar with the protocol. This is an advanced section, and you don't need to understand it unless you are tackling sophisticated concurrent programming. You can safely jump over this material to the end of the chapter, returning to study it in depth when you see the words wait/notify in a program.

The hardest kind of programming with threads is when the threads need to pass data back and forth. Imagine that we are in the same situation as the previous section. We have threads that process the same data, so we need to run synchronized. In our new case, however, imagine that it's not enough just to say, "Don't run while I am running." We need the threads to be able to say, "OK, I have some data ready for you," and to suspend themselves if there isn't data ready. There is a convenient parallel programming idiom known as *wait/notify* that does exactly this. Figure 14–3 shows this in four stages.

Wait/notify is a tricky language-independent protocol that has been developed by ingenious minds. Wait/notify wasn't invented by Java, and it's not Java-specific. If you've ever taken a college-level course in operating system concurrency, you have probably seen it. Otherwise, you just need to appreciate it as the accepted solution to this problem. Wait/notify is used when synchronized methods in the same class need to communicate with each other. The most common occurrence of this is a producer/consumer situation—one thread is producing data irregularly and another thread is consuming (processing) it.

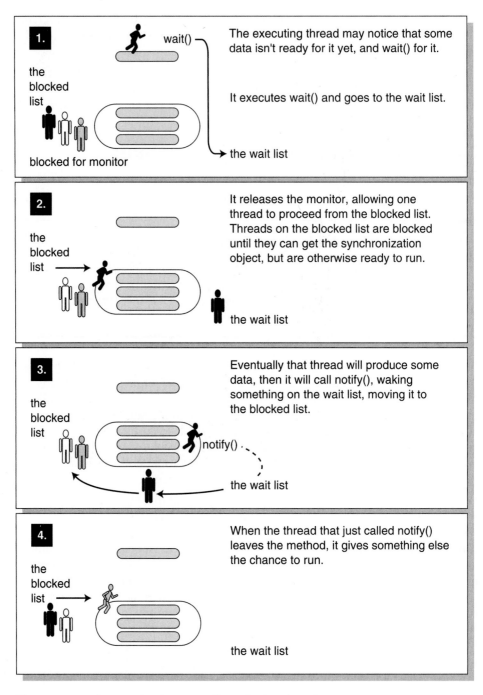

1. wait()

the blocked list

blocked for monitor

the wait list

The executing thread may notice that some data isn't ready for it yet, and wait() for it.

It executes wait() and goes to the wait list.

2.

the blocked list

the wait list

It releases the monitor, allowing one thread to proceed from the blocked list. Threads on the blocked list are blocked until they can get the synchronization object, but are otherwise ready to run.

3.

the blocked list

notify()

the wait list

Eventually that thread will produce some data, then it will call notify(), waking something on the wait list, moving it to the blocked list.

4.

the blocked list

the wait list

When the thread that just called notify() leaves the method, it gives something else the chance to run.

Figure 14–3   Communicating mutually exclusive threads

`wait()`/`notify()` come from Multics

"Wait/notify" is one of two interprocess synchronization mechanisms pioneered by Multics. Multics (Multiplexed Information and Computing Service) was a mainframe timesharing operating system begun in 1965 and used until 2000, thirty five years! Multics began as a research project and was an important influence on operating system development for thirty years. It was large and took longer to implement than anyone expected, but it's a treasure house of solved engineering problems. Multics was the inspiration for the name Unix, and hence indirectly Linux.

A process goes to "wait for" a certain "event", such as "page has arrived from disk". The process is suspended until some other process "notifies" of that event, whereupon one or more processes waiting on it are resumed. Part of the protocol is the possibility of false notifications, so no data is sent with the notification, and the waiter must test for data upon resumption.

Methods in the threads are called only from within synchronized code, which means they are called only when a mutex lock is held. However, simple synchronization is not enough. The consumer might grab the lock and then find that there is nothing in the buffer to consume. The producer might grab the lock and find that there isn't yet room in the buffer to put something. You could make either of these spin in a busy loop continually grabbing the lock, testing whether they can move some data and releasing the lock if not. But busy loops are never used in production code. They burn CPU cycles without any productive result.[1]

The correct approach lies in the two method calls `wait()` and `notify()`. This protocol allows a thread to pause or wait while another thread takes over the lock.

- The `wait()` method says, "Oops, even though I have the lock I can't go any further until you have some data for me, so I will release the lock and suspend myself here. One of you notifiers carry on! I'll wake up when the lock becomes free, and try to grab it."

- The `notify()` method says, "Hey, I just produced some data, so I will release the lock and suspend myself here. One of you waiters wake up, take the lock back, then carry on!"

The pseudo-code for the way the producer works is:

```
// producer thread
grab mutex lock
produce_data()
notify() // this includes releasing the lock.
```

1. Well, OK, one of my colleagues pointed out a research paper that showed a brief busy loop followed by a wait/notify was superior to either used alone. Let's leave research papers out of this for now.

The pseudo-code for the consumer is:

```
// consumer thread
grab mutex lock, i.e. enter synchronized code
while( no_data )
      wait()          // releases lock and stalls here till notified
                      // then it tries to re-acquire the lock
                      // if it does not get the lock, it stays waiting
                      // otherwise it proceeds to check the while again
                      // if there now is data, it falls through
consume_the_data()
leave synchronized code
```

The consumer waits in a loop, testing whether there is yet data, because a
different consumer might have grabbed the data, in which case it needs to wait
again. As we have already seen, entering and leaving synchronized code is
trivially achieved by applying the keyword "synchronized" to a method, so the
templates become like this:

```
// producer thread
produce_data()
notify()
```

```
// consumer thread
while( no_data )
     wait()
consume_the_data()
```

Usually, the producer is storing the produced data into some kind of bounded
buffer, which means the producer can fill it up and will need to wait() until there
is room. The consumer needs to notify() the producer when something is
removed from the buffer.

The pseudo-code is:

```
// producer thread—produces one datum
while( buffer_full )
     wait()
produce_data()
notify()
```

```
// consumer thread—consumes one datum
while( no_data )
     wait()
consume_the_data()
notify()
```

The reason we walked through this step-by-step is that it makes the following
program easier to understand. If you didn't follow the previous pseudo-code, go
back over the previous section again. This code directly implements the pseudo-

code, and demonstrates the use of wait/notify in communicating mutually exclusive threads.

There are three classes that follow. The first is a class that contains a main driver program. It simply instantiates a producer thread and a consumer thread and lets them go at it.

```
public class showWaitNotify {
  public static void main(String args[]) {
    Producer p = new Producer();

    Consumer c = new Consumer(p);
    p.start();
    c.start();
  }
}
```

The second class is the Producer class. It implements the previous pseudo-code and demonstrates the use of wait/notify. It has two key methods: one that produces data (actually, it just reads an incrementing ID value) and stores it into an array. The other method, called consume(), will try to return successive values from this array. The value of this setup is that you can call produce() and consume() from separate threads: They won't overrun the array; they won't get something before it has been produced; they won't step on each other; and neither ever gets in a busy wait.

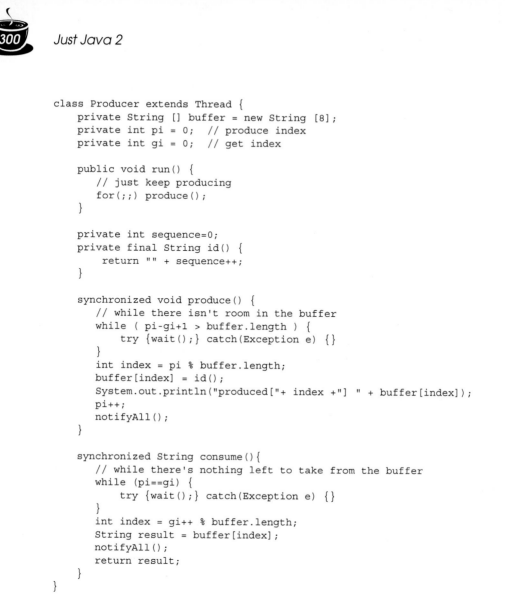
```
class Producer extends Thread {
    private String [] buffer = new String [8];
    private int pi = 0;   // produce index
    private int gi = 0;   // get index

    public void run() {
        // just keep producing
        for(;;) produce();
    }

    private int sequence=0;
    private final String id() {
        return "" + sequence++;
    }

    synchronized void produce() {
        // while there isn't room in the buffer
        while ( pi-gi+1 > buffer.length ) {
            try {wait();} catch(Exception e) {}
        }
        int index = pi % buffer.length;
        buffer[index] = id();
        System.out.println("produced["+ index +"] " + buffer[index]);
        pi++;
        notifyAll();
    }

    synchronized String consume() {
        // while there's nothing left to take from the buffer
        while (pi==gi) {
            try {wait();} catch(Exception e) {}
        }
        int index = gi++ % buffer.length;
        String result = buffer[index];
        notifyAll();
        return result;
    }
}
```

The produce() method puts a datum in the buffer, and consume() can be called from within a Consumer class to pull something out for the consumer.

Expressions like "pi % buffer.length" are a programming idiom to index an array as a circular buffer. It is a cheap way to let the pi and gi be used as subscripts, be incremented without limit, and also make sure that pi never gets more than one buffer's worth ahead of gi. We want the pi and gi values to count up serially 1 2 3 4 5 6 7 8 9 10 11 12, so we can make sure pi never gets more than 8 ahead of gi. We need the subscripts to count 1 2 3 4 5 6 7 0 1 2 3 "modulo the buffer size". Plug in some actual values to see how this works.

Finally, the third class is another thread that will be the consumer in this example. It starts off with a common Java idiom: Another class is passed into the constructor, and all the constructor does is save a copy of this object for later use. This is the way that the consumer can call the consume() method of the producer.

```java
class Consumer extends Thread {
    Producer whoIamTalkingTo;
    // java idiom for a constructor
    Consumer(Producer who) { whoIamTalkingTo = who; }

    public void run() {
        java.util.Random r = new java.util.Random();
        for(;;) {
            String result = whoIamTalkingTo.consume();
            System.out.println("consumed: "+result);
            // next line is just to make it run a bit slower.
            int randomtime = Math.abs(r.nextInt() % 250);
            try{sleep(randomtime);} catch(Exception e){}
        }
    }
}
```

The technique of passing an object into a constructor that saves the reference to it, for later communicating something back, is a common idiom known as a "callback." We already saw this in the Interfaces chapter. Make sure you understand the previous example, to see how this is written and used.

The run method of this consumer simply repeats over and over again a get method, printing what it got, followed by a sleep for a random period. The sleep is just to give the producer some work to do in adapting to an asynchronous consumer.

When you compile these three classes together and try running them, you will see output similar to the following (not necessarily identical, because of asynchronicity):

```
% java plum
produced[0] 0
produced[1] 1
produced[2] 2
consumed: 0
produced[3] 3
produced[4] 4
produced[5] 5
produced[6] 6
produced[7] 7
produced[0] 8
consumed: 1
produced[1] 9
produced[2] 10
consumed: 2
produced[3] 11
consumed: 3
produced[4] 12
consumed: 4
produced[5] 13
consumed: 5
produced[6] 14
```

And so on.

Notice that the producer filled much of the buffer before the consumer ran at all. Then each time the slow consumer removed something from the buffer, the producer reused that now empty slot. And always the consumer got exactly what was stored there with no data race corruption. If this explanation of wait/notify seems complicated, your impression is correct. Programming threaded code is hard in the general case and these methods supply a specialized feature that makes one aspect of it a little easier.

The good news is that, for simple producer/consumer code, you don't have to bother with any of this! Two classes, PipedInputStream and PipedOutputStream, in the I/O library can be used in your code to support simple asynchronous communication between threads. We will look at this later.

The wait and notify methods are in the basic class Object, so they are shared by all objects in the system. There are several variants:

```
public final native void notify();
public final native void notifyAll();

public final void wait() throws InterruptedException;
public final void wait(long time, int nanos) throws InterruptedException;
public final native void wait(long timeout) throws InterruptedException;
```

The difference between notify() and notifyAll() is that notifyAll() wakes up all threads that are in the wait list of this object. That might be appropriate if they are all readers or they are all waiting for the same answer, or can all carry on once the data has been written. In the example, there is only one other thread, so notify() or notifyAll() will have the same effect. There are three forms of wait, including two that allow a wait to time out after the specified period of milliseconds or milliseconds and nanoseconds(!) have elapsed. Why have a separate wait list or wait set for each object, instead of just blocking waiting for the lock? Because the whole point of wait/notifying is to take the objects out of contention for systems resources until they are truly able to run! A notify notifies an arbitrary thread in the wait list. You can't rely on FIFO order.

An older thread bug in the collections library

Thread programs are notoriously difficult to get right. Up to and including JDK 1.3, there was a thread bug in the library class java.util.Vector. The code involved two versions of the lastIndexOf() method, one of which invokes the other. The code is:

```
public int lastIndexOf(Object elem) {
    return lastIndexOf(elem, elementCount-1);
}
public synchronized int lastIndexOf(Object elem, int index) {
    if (elem == null) {
    for (int i = index; i >= 0; i--)
    if (elementData[i]==null)
    return i;
    // ...
}
```

Vectors offer the feature of being properly synchronized in the presence of threads. Now, imagine if one thread calls the first method and evaluates the argument involving elementCount. What happens if another thread comes along at the same time (because that first method is not synchronized) and changes the size of the Vector? Then the elementCount given to the second method when it is called from the first method could refer to a value that is not even in the Vector any more. This code was fixed in JDK 1.4.

Interrupting a thread

Now we have all that theory behind us, let's explain the minor point of why statements like this have an exception handler:

```
try {sleep(randomtime);} catch(Exception e){}
try {wait();} catch(Exception e) {}
```

It's quite easy. One thread can interrupt another sleeping thread by calling its `interrupt()` method. This will make the interrupted thread wake up and take the exception branch. The thread must be able to tell the difference between waking up because it has been "notified" and waking up because it has been "interrupted". So the second case is detected by raising the exception InterruptedException in the thread. Statements like `sleep()`, `join()`, and `wait()` that are potentially prone to being interrupted in the middle need to catch this exception, or declare that their method can throw it.

The `interrupt()` method of Thread sets the interrupt state (a boolean flag) of a thread to "true." A thread can query and clear its own interrupt state using the `Thread.interrupted()` method. (You call it twice to clear it!) You can query the interrupted state of any thread using `isInterrupted()`. The method `interrupt()` does not wake a thread that is waiting to acquire a synchronization lock.

Two further points: In this text, I generally use the parent type Exception, instead of the correct subtype, InterruptedException. This is to minimize the size of the lines in the example. Always catch the narrowest type of exception you can or you might catch more than you bargained for. And do something sensible with it, like print an error message. Finally, note that the `interrupt()` method was not implemented in the first major release of the JDK.

Synchronized code isn't a perfect solution, because a system can still get into deadlock. Deadlock or *deadly embrace* is the situation where there is a circular dependency among several threads between resources held and resources required. In its simplest form, Thread "A" holds lock "X" and needs lock "Y," while Thread "B" holds lock "Y" and is waiting for lock "X" to become free. Result: That part of the system grinds to a halt. This can happen all too easily when one synchronized method calls another. The "volatile" keyword can also be applied to data. This informs the compiler that several threads might be accessing this simultaneously. The data therefore needs to be completely refreshed from memory (rather than a value that was read into a register three cycles ago) and completely stored back on each access.

Volatile is apparently intended for accessing objects like real-time clocks that sit on the memory bus. It is convenient to glue them on there, because they can be read and written with the usual "load" and "store" memory access instructions, instead of requiring a dedicated I/O port. They can return the current time via a single cycle read, but the value will change unpredictably due to actions outside the program. Volatile doesn't seem intended for general use on arbitrary objects in applications. The keyword isn't used anywhere in the current version of the run-time library.

Generalized thread programming is a discipline in its own right and one that is growing in importance with the use of multiprocessor systems and server systems.

Piped I/O for Threads

A pipe is an easy way to move data between two threads. One thread writes into the pipe, and the other reads from it. This forms a producer/consumer buffer, ready-programmed for you! There are two stream classes that we always use together in a matched consumer/producer pair:

- PipedInputStream – Gets bytes from a pipe (think "hosepipe"; it's just a data structure that squirts bytes at you).

- PipedOutputStream – Puts bytes into a pipe (think "drainpipe"; it's just a data structure that drinks down bytes that you pour into it).

An object of one of these classes is connected to an object of the other class, providing a safe way (without data race conditions) for one thread to send a stream of data to another thread.

As an example of the use of piped streams, the following program reimplements the Producer/Consumer problem, but uses piped streams instead of wait/notify. If you compare, you'll see that this is considerably simpler. There is no visible shared buffer—the pipe stream between the two threads encapsulates it.

The next example shows one thread sending primitive types to another. You can also send Strings using the classes PipedWriter and PipedReader. These four Piped classes are part of the java.io package.

Pipe pitfall

Most operating systems support a pipe feature to communicate between threads or processes. All of these have one common pitfall! The pipe between the threads is implemented by a buffer in shared memory, and this buffer has a limited capacity. If your input and output happens at different rates, the availability of data will become a bottleneck. The faster thread blocks until the slower thread has either added something to the empty buffer (the output thread is slower), or made some room in an otherwise full buffer by reading something from the buffer (the input thread is slower).

If your system design relies on the two threads taking turns, your program can deadlock and not run satisfactorily. This pipe problem is common to all languages. You can extend these two streams to give the buffer a different size, but that might merely postpone but not solve the pipe problem.

Their use should be clear from the examples here, and it is fully explained in the two chapters on I/O.

```
import java.io.*;
public class expipes {

  public static void main(String args[]) {
      Producer p = new Producer();

      Consumer c = new Consumer(p);
      c.start();
      p.start();
  }
}


///// This class writes into the pipe until it is full, at which
///// point it is blocked until the consumer takes something out.

class Producer extends Thread {
    protected PipedOutputStream po = new PipedOutputStream();
    private DataOutputStream dos = new DataOutputStream(po);

    public void run() {
       // just keep producing numbers
       for(;;) produce();
    }

    private int sequence=0;
    private final int id() {
        return sequence++;
    }

    void produce() {
       long t = id();
       System.out.println("produced " + t);
       try {dos.writeLong( t );}
       catch (IOException ie) { System.out.println(ie); }
    }

}
```

```
///// This class consumes everything sent over the pipe.
///// The pipe does the synchronization. When the pipe is full,
///// this thread's read from the pipe is blocked.
class Consumer extends Thread {
    private PipedInputStream pip;
    private DataInputStream d;

    // java constructor idiom, save argument.
    Consumer(Producer who) {
        try {
            pip = new PipedInputStream(who.po);
            d = new DataInputStream( pip );
        } catch (IOException ie) {
            System.out.println(ie);
        }
    }

    long get(){
        long i=0;
        try {   i= d.readLong();   // read from pipe.
        } catch (IOException ie) {System.out.println(ie);}
        return i;
    }

    public void run() {
        java.util.Random r = new java.util.Random();
        for(;;) {
            long result = get();
            System.out.println("consumed: "+result);
            // next lines are just to make things asynchronous
            int randomtime = r.nextInt() % 1250;
            try{sleep(randomtime);} catch(Exception e){}
        }
    }
}
```

The output of this program is a list of serially increasing numbers. The numbers
are passed in a buffer in a thread-safe way from the producer thread to the
consumer thread. The piped streams allow for real simplification in interthread
communication.

Thread Local Storage

Thread local storage is a term for data that is accessible to anything that can access the thread, but that can hold a value that is unique in each thread. A common use for thread local storage is to give a different identifier to each of several newly constructed threads (as in, "if I am thread 5,...") or tells them what they need to work on. ThreadLocal objects are typically private static variables used to associate some state with a thread (e.g., a user ID, session ID, or transaction ID).

Thread local storage was introduced with JDK 1.2 and allows each thread to have its own *independently initialized* copy of a variable. It's easy enough to give threads their own variables. The bit that's tricky is in getting them initialized with a value that's different for each thread in a thread-safe way. It's tough for the thread to do it because each copy of the same thread is (naturally) executing exactly the same code.

The following describes how you give your threads an int ID. You will create a subclass of ThreadLocal. You extend the ThreadLocal class and add members as needed. The unfamiliar thing in <anglebrackets> is a generic parameter:

```
class MyThreadLocal extends ThreadLocal <Integer>{
    private static int id = 0;

    // this method overrides a method in ThreadLocal
    protected synchronized Integer initialValue() {
        return id++;   // autoboxing at work for you.
    }

    // this method overrides a method in ThreadLocal
    public Integer get() {
        return super.get();
    }

}
```

We'll explain the use of generics in full in the next chapter. For now, it's a way of telling a class "this is the specific type I want you to work on in this subclass". It's a way of getting better type checking than if you just use Object everywhere. Here the <Integer> says we providing an Integer to each thread. We can provide any object as thread local storage, including a container class (i.e. large amounts of data).

If you look at the API for java.lang.ThreadLocal, you'll see that it has an initialValue() method that we are overriding. Here, the underlying int is incremented each time the initialValue() method is called (so everyone gets a different initial value).

ThreadLocal also has get() and set() methods. An overriding version of get() is used, just to show explicitly that it is calling the ThreadLocal.get().

The following is our thread that uses local storage. It holds a static instance of the previous class:

```
class ThreadWithTLS extends Thread {
    private static MyThreadLocal tls = new MyThreadLocal();
    public void run() {
        System.out.println("My thread local value is " + tls.get());
    }
}
```

To show it in operation, we need a program that starts up a few of these threads, so you can see them get() different TLS values:

```
public class tls {

    public static void main(String args[]) {
        for(int i=0; i<5; i++)
            new ThreadWithTLS().start();
    }
}
```

When you try running the program you'll see each different thread has its own value for the integer that MyThreadLocal maintains.

```
% javac -source  1.5 tls.java
% java tls
My thread local value is 0
My thread local value is 1
My thread local value is 2
My thread local value is 3
My thread local value is 4
```

What's happening behind the scenes is that the class ThreadLocal is maintaining a table of threads versus values. Any thread can get its local value from the table and any thread can set a new value for itself into the table. The access is through tls.get() and tls.set(). The ThreadLocal class translates that into table lookup, indexed by thread ID. How does it know thread IDs? It's just the value returned by Thread.currentThread!

Wait—I hear you ask, "How does the initial value get set, since we didn't write a call to it?" It doesn't! At least, it doesn't until you call ThreadLocal's get() for the first time. When you do, it calls initialValue() as its first action to put a value in the table for you to get. That happens in each Thread.

Thread local storage is another thread idiom, and you won't use it in many (perhaps any) of your Java threaded programs. But when you want it, it is there. It's designed and implemented in a particularly clever way that makes it easy for the programmer to use, but also makes the maximum use of Java features to do all the work. The Thread API didn't change at all for the addition of thread local storage. It gets "two thumbs up" from this reviewer.

Thread local storage uses weak references (mentioned in chapter 10). The thread local storage has a table that connects threads with corresponding local storage data items. Each thread has a regular reference to the thread id that it uses for a key, and to the local storage entry. The table is a data structure that ties these together, allowing quick retrieval of an entry corresponding to a key. The thread has regular references, but the table just has weak references to all its keys/entries. A key and entry stay around as long as the strong references from the thread do. But when the thread ends, and is garbage collected, there are only now weak references to that key/entry in the table. Voila, key and entry are suddenly and automatically also candidates for garbage collection.

Package java.util.concurrent

New!

JDK 1.5 introduced several new packages and a couple of dozen new classes to beef up support for threads and thread-based systems. These are centered around package java.util.concurrent. In one sentence, the goal is "to do for threads what java.util.Collection did for data structures". Namely, provide a central, consistent, "bullet-proof" way of expressing best practices, so that programmers no longer need to create them by hand for each new problem.

You can view the concurrent package as a set of design patterns implemented for Java threads (if design patterns are new to you, we mention the basics in the next section). This new package will see the most use in large and sophisticated server systems, and is beyond the scope of this book.

The following is a summary of java.util.concurrency to provide a road map when you are ready to look into it further. The new package contains some utility classes for threads, and some new frameworks.

- There are a small number of new frameworks built around the interface java.util.collections.Executor. It is now easy to use thread pools (which recycle existing threads instead of creating a new thread for each new request). There is support for delayed and periodic task execution. You can have threads that return results, not just fall off the end of the run() method. You can start a long-running thread, query it for completion, and cancel it.

- There are some new Collection data classes that you can use when many threads share access to a common data structure. There is a new Queue class called java.util.concurrent.ConcurrentLinkedQueue, which is suitable for holding the collection for producer-consumer, messaging, parallel tasking, and other threads. There are some other concurrent collections that are thread safe but not bottle-necked by a single lock (a single lock undermines scalability). These containers support multiple readers as well as a tunable number of concurrent writes.

- Improvements in time-related code. There are proper definitions for periods of nanoseconds, microseconds, milliseconds, and seconds. They can easily be converted into one another. There are timeouts for "wait at least this long before giving up".

- Synchronization primitives. There are new classes for common synchronization idioms, including a class that represents a counting semaphore.

- Five new exceptions (e.g. TimeoutException, CancellationException).

The package java.util.concurrent also does some major work on atomicity. That's a performance optimization to support thread safe programs on single variables, without using locks. It's going to take time for all this to sink in, and find its way into the mainstream. It's a very good thing to have sophisticated thread use put on a more formal foundation. The hard work was done by an industry group led by Professor Doug Lea.

An Aside on Design Patterns

There's an area of increasing importance in OOP technology, known as *design patterns*. A design pattern is a set of steps for doing something, like a recipe is a set of steps for cooking something.

There is a key book on the topic called *Design Patterns—Elements of Reusable Object-Oriented Software* by Erich Gamma, Richard Helm, Ralph Johnson, and John Vlissides (Addison Wesley, 1994: ISBN 0-201-63361-2). The book would be a lot more valuable if it were easier to read and gave examples that ordinary programmers could relate to. In spite of its dry, excessively academic style, it's an important text.

As the authors explain, design patterns describe simple, repeatable solutions to specific problems in object-oriented software design. They capture solutions that have been refined over time; hence, they aren't typically the first code that comes to mind unless you know about them. They are code idioms writ large. They are not unusual or amazing, or tied to any one language. Giving names to the common idioms and describing them, helps reuse. Some common idioms/design patterns are shown in Table 14–1.

Table 14–1   Design patterns overview

Design pattern	Purpose and use
Abstract Factory	Supplies an interface to create any of several related objects without specifying their concrete classes. The Factory figures out the precise class that is needed and constructs one of those for you.
Adapter	Converts the interface of a class into another interface that the client can use directly. Adapter lets classes work together that couldn't otherwise. Think "hose to sprinkler interface adapter."
Observer	Defines a many-to-one dependency between objects, so that when the observed object changes state, all the Observers are notified and can act accordingly. Think "monitoring the progress of something coming in over the network."
Singleton	Ensure that only one object is instantiated from some class, and provide a global point of access to it.
Command	Encapsulate a request as an object, rather than a method call. That lets you parameterize servers to handle different requests, and support requests that can be undone.

The recommended book describes a couple of dozen design patterns, and repays further study.

Further Reading

There are several great websites giving additional information on the SCJP tests described in the Light Relief section. Marcus Green has one at www.jchq.net/, and Bill Brogden's is at www.lanw.com/java/javacert/. These sites have examples of the kinds of questions you'll face, FAQs, advice, and suggestions on books that prepare you for the tests.

Exercises

1. Give three examples of when threads might be used to an advantage in a program. Describe a circumstance when it would not be advantageous to use threads.

2. What are the two ways of creating a new thread in Java?

3. Take your favorite sorting algorithm and make it multithreaded. *Hint*: A recursive partitioning algorithm like quicksort is the best candidate for this. Quicksort simply divides the array to be sorted into two pieces, then moves

numbers about until all the numbers in one piece are smaller (or at least no larger) than all the numbers in the other piece. Repeat the algorithm on each of the pieces. When the pieces consist of just one element, the array is sorted.

4. What resources are consumed by each individual thread?

5. Refer back to the text giving the information about the synchronization bug in the thread library. What code change would you recommend to fix that bug and why? Look at the source code for Vector in the current run-time library. Did they follow your recommendation?

6. Rewrite the code example in the previous chapter that shows how to test a range of prime numbers for primes. Give the argument range to the threads by using thread local storage.

Some Light Relief—Are You Certifiable? I Am.

These Light Relief sections are pieces of "infotainment" about Java and the computer industry. This one is heavy on the info, and light on the 'tainment.

Sun Microsystems, the company that originated Java, started offering a Java test and pass certificate to programmers back in 1996. People take these tests for different reasons. Some companies send their employees on Java training courses and buy them this test at the end so they will have a qualification they can take away with them. Other people (like me) took the test at the invitation of the folks at Sun running the program to help them calibrate the results. Some people just like an extra qualification to put on their resume.

The Java Technology Certifications

Java 2 Platform, Standard Edition:
- Sun Certified Java Programmer
- Sun Certified Java Developer

Java 2 Platform, Enterprise Edition:
- Sun Certified Web Component Developer
- Sun Certified Enterprise Architect
- Sun Certified Business Component Developer

Java 2 Platform, Micro Edition:
- Sun Certified Mobile Application Developer

It is not (yet) common to see a job advert that mentions Java certification as a prerequisite for the position, but I think it's safe to assume that if you were a hiring manager trying to choose between two otherwise equal candidates, one of whom had demonstrated commitment and interest by obtaining a Java technology certification, you'd probably choose that applicant first. It's a rough, tough world out there in software development, and any steps you can take to boost your own career are worth considering.

Sun Certified Java Programmer

After you have learned Java from this book, the way to become a "Sun Certified Java Programmer"(SCJP) is straightforward, but it takes an investment of time. The steps are:

1. **Learn the SCJP curriculum.**

   What are they testing for? The test objectives can be found online at
   `suned.sun.com/US/images/certification_progj2se_07_01.pdf`
   (just search for "certification" at `java.sun.com` if Sun has moved it). Testing covers only four packages: `java.lang`, `java.io`, `java.util`, and `java.awt` (GUI). So you're wasting your time boning up on other packages, until the test is updated. There are plenty of questions on things you use only infrequently, like `wait()` and `notify()` in threads.

2. **Learn the SCJP test rubric.**

   The exam lasts two hours and has 59 questions with no optional parts. You should attempt every question, and spend no more than two minutes on each. There are three kinds of question:

   Multiple-choice questions with *a single* correct answer.

   Multiple-choice questions with *multiple* correct answers.

3. **Practice on the sample tests.**

   Sample tests and sample questions can be found at the websites listed in *Further Reading* and at this URL:
   `suned.sun.com/US/certification/java/index.html`
   Some of these resources are free, and some of them are for sale.

4. **Take the SCJP test.**

   You sign up with Sun Education Services for $150 (in the U.S.). The tests are locally administered in centers run by a company called Prometric, who also run the Novell and Microsoft certifications. You have to make an appointment for the test with Prometric, then on the due day go along to their local branch. The test is computer-administered and marked, so you get your result immediately after completing it. Sun sends you official confirmation a week or two later in the form of a nice letter that includes a Java lapel pin (if you passed).

You might think you can skip some of the preparatory steps, but that would be a big mistake. You should maintain a healthy respect for the SCJP examination. It is not easy to pass, and many inadequately prepared candidates fail on their first try.

Some of the questions on the test have the form *if you were to run this really stupid piece of code that no one would ever write in practice, what would the output be?* People don't like those kind of questions, but you may encounter that code when you are helping maintain someone else's code.

Other questions are downright tricky, and focus on a difference between Java and other OOP languages. But they are not phrased that way! You just have to know how Java does something, and a familiarity with C++ could hurt you.

A sticking point for me was the multiple choice questions that expected multiple answers. Such a question may say something like this:

What can cause a thread to stop executing?

1) The program exits via a call to System.exit(0);

2) Another thread is given a higher priority.

3) A call to the thread's stop method.

4) A call to the halt method of the Thread class.

You may read this list and choose an answer like "1." The correct answer is "1," "2," and "3." If you miss one of these, you still got two-thirds right, but your score is zero. If you get too many questions like this, you risk failing even though you know quite a bit of the material.

The bottom line on all this is that Java certification can't hurt, and as long as you know what you're getting into you'll succeed. Plus, you get the cool lapel pin (Figure 11-4).

MADE IN U.S.A.

Figure 14–4   A pin to prove it

Explanation
<Generics>

New!

The biggest, most far-reaching new feature to come into Java with the JDK 1.5 release is "type genericity"—the ability to pass *types* as arguments, just the way we can pass *values* as arguments. In this chapter we'll take a close look at generic types, see what software problem they solve, and describe how they were retrofitted into the language and run-time system (not an easy thing).

Explanation <Generics>
Generics introduced some new syntax to Java – writing a typename in angle brackets, like this:

```
LinkedList <Character>
```

That is read as *LinkedList* **of** *Character*. So this chapter title is read as *Explanation of Generics*. It's a nudge toward getting familiar with the new syntax ;-)

We'll start with a reminder on terminology—if we don't keep the terminology straight here, we're lost! We'll finish with a look at some advanced features of generics, features really intended for library designers, but also useful for everyone else to know how to read. There's a small corner of generics (specifically, generic *methods* rather than *classes*) that we'll defer to the next chapter.

Generics are based on an idea that seems simple—code can be parameterized with types as well as variables. However, the topic quickly moves into compiler theory and challenging intellectual rigor. We'll surely see entire books on Java generics in due course, just like there are entire books on C pointers. To help things along, this chapter sometimes introduces new concepts that depend on previous concepts and previous examples. To get a clear picture you'll need to read the sections in sequence.

Terminology Refresher: Parameters Versus Arguments

Everyone is familiar with the concept of methods having parameters. When you write the method, you write the parameters in a comma-separated list. Here's the declaration of the power() function in Java.lang.Math:

```
static double pow(double a, double b) { /*more*/ }
```

The method returns the value of a raised to the power b. The variables a and b are *parameters* to the method. Here's the point: The method will calculate that value for any a and b. Parameters let us write that method once, use it on any pairs of numbers, and refer to the different numbers coming into the method by unchanging names in the method body.

Arguments are the converse. At the place where we invoke the method, we write the method name and supply the specific variables or values that we want the method to work on, in this particular case:

```
import static java.lang.Math.*;

double result = pow(10.0, PI );
```

The literal 10.0 and the constant Math.PI (the closest approximation to PI that a double can hold) are the *arguments* for this call. Other calls may have different arguments.

```
result = pow(x, y);
```

The compiler plants code to do a parameter = argument assignment for each parameter on every call. This takes place right before the call, in a method prolog that you don't see.

In a single sentence, the concept of generics is *"We want to have a parameter that represents a **type**, not a value. We'll instantiate objects-of-the-generic-class using different types (Integer, Timestamp, Double, Thread) as the type argument. Each object will be specialized to do work on that specific actual type argument."* OK, three sentences. We indicate that something is a type parameter by enclosing it in angle brackets, e.g. `<String>`. The type parameters come right after the name of the class being parameterized. e.g. `class List <String>`. That is read as *List specialized for String*, abbreviated to "List of String".

Why the ugly <Type> syntax?

The first question that comes to mind is why did the Java language designers use the ugly < >? Why not just pass the plain old typename as a parameter nested in parentheses?

It was done to help you, silly! By making type parameters look different from variable parameters, it is always possible to tell them apart at a glance.

Maybe using parentheses would have been a good idea for generic classes. But it is also possible to give generic parameters to a method. Having a method take two different types of parameters that look the same, but mean different things, could be tricky. What if only one set of parameters were present? In programming languages, different things should look different, and have different names.

Let's motivate the feature by looking at the problem.

The Problem that Generic Code Addresses

Generics, also known as templates or parametric polymorphism, seem to be a popular feature in modern programming languages. Ada has them, so does C++, and so does Microsoft's copy of Java, C#. The overall design for Java generics was published in 1998, long before C# was launched. C# is again following Java's lead and adopting generics, although with a different design. The popularity might lead you to think that generics solve a big and important problem.

If you look at some of the written material justifying generics in Java, however, a different picture emerges. Some texts suggest that a purpose of generics is to reduce the amount of casting needed, particularly when using the Java data structure classes known as the *collection classes*. From JDK 1.2 (where collections were introduced) up to and including JDK 1.4, collections held Objects. Variables of any class type could be put into any collection, because all class types are compatible with the type used in a collection, Object. When you retrieved something from a collection, you had to figure out what type it really was, then cast it back to that.

The Java Collection classes

JDK 1.2 introduced some really robust data structure container classes. There are about 20 classes and a dozen interfaces kept in the package java.util.

These classes are termed *the collection classes*, and they do some amazing things. They maintain standard data structures, such as lists, sets, and maps (pairing of a key and value) and several subtypes of these. You can create a data structure that holds your own objects merely by instantiating one of these types.

The collection classes were updated to work with generic types in the JDK 1.5 release. Generics can work with all software libraries, not just the collection classes, but the collection classes are the main beneficiaries within the Java API. The chapter on collection classes comes right after this chapter and gives practical examples of generic use.

Usually, your collections just hold one kind of type, e.g. a given collection of yours holds String objects. A different collection holds Timestamps. A typical collection does *not* hold a mixed bag of String, Integer, Date, Thread, JFrame, and Timestamp objects. So figuring out what's in the collection isn't a problem. And casting something back to the right class isn't a big deal either:

```
String result = (String) myDict.get(i);   // without generics
```

Using generics, the collection gives you back the right type, i.e. String, not Object. You can thus omit the cast, and that statement becomes:

```
String result = myDict.get(i);                   // with generics
```

Yippee! The casts aren't written in the source, but they don't vanish altogether. They are still there in the generated code. It's like autoboxing; the compiler will insert the required code for you. So what's the reason behind this apparent paradox: lots of people want generics, but all generics seem to do is save you writing a few casts?

The answer is that analyzing generics in terms of saving casts misses the big picture. The *real* purpose of generics is to improve type safety by moving the detection of errors earlier in the development cycle. The value of Java generics is quite a bit less than a cure for software bit-rot, but more than just a confusing new syntax to avoid a few casts.

The purpose of generics

The generic feature in Java lets you tell the compiler about the type that you expect to load into a collection class. You find out sooner (at compile-time, rather than run-time) about any errors you have made involving the types of objects you put into or take out of collections. Further, with generics, you catch all the errors. In the bad old days, you only caught the errors you particularly exercised. Obscure bugs could hide for years before surfacing.

A lagniappe (small extra benefit) is that you no longer need to write certain casts.

Imagine that you have a collection class that does something with objects of some other type: It keeps a pool of them, stores them in a stack, or holds them in sorted order, for example. One instance of your class can do this magical processing on type A, another instance on type B, a third on C, and so on. Previously, you were not able to make this distinction. You had to code "all instances of that collection class process the type Object" and then keep clear in your head which of your instances dealt with type A objects, which with B, which with type C, etc.

Generics let you explicitly tell the compiler which specific type each instance of your class processes. The compiler will look at the generic information where you say "I intend this object to process only type A objects", and it will make sure that you don't slip a few B's in.

What used to happen was that you thought you had a collection of say, Strings. But some buggy code occasionally put an Integer in there too. Everything was held as an Object so the compiler couldn't catch it. When you retrieved the Integer at run-time and tried to cast it back to a String, it would throw a class cast exception. This error could be rare enough that it wouldn't happen until after a long time after the application was deployed.

With generics the compiler has enough information to notice when you try to slip an Integer into a collection of Strings. Errors are reported at compile time, when it is *much* cheaper to fix problems. Remember you probably need an option on the command line to compile code with these new features:

```
javac -source 1.5  myGenerics.java
```

Let's look at the three steps involved in conveying the extra information to the compiler.

What Generic Code Looks Like

There are three parts to generics:

1. Declare the class which will have generic type parameters

2. Declare/instantiate an object of that class, passing the actual type arguments to it.

3. Invoke methods on the object of the instantiated generic class.

Using the instantiated generic class is no different to using a non-generic class, so we won't spend a lot of time looking at that. The class declaration has to come before any instantiations, so let's look at declarations first.

A use of generics outside the Collection classes

The class java.lang.Class has been updated to take a generic parameter. Recall that the run-time system creates a separate Class object for each class in your program, when it loads the class. Class allows programs to get information about the classes it's using. Here's how Class was used *before* generics:

```
Class t = Timestamp.class;    // old style variable declaration
Timestamp ts = (Timestamp) t.newInstance();// old style, cast needed
```

Now when you declare a Class object, you may tell the compiler what type it will hold.

```
Class <Timestamp> t = Timestamp.class;  // declare with generic param
Timestamp ts = t.newInstance();       // with generics, no cast needed
```

The purpose of this change is to tell the compiler to which type you are going to dedicate the Class variable t. If you don't use generics, the variable t can hold a class literal for any type, such as String.class or Long.class. You would do this if that's what your code needs.

When you use the generic parameter, variable t can hold a Class object *only for type Timestamp*. You would do this if that's what you intend for your code. It's all about using the compiler to catch mistakes before run-time, by using strong typing.

Declaring a class with generic type parameters

One of the collection classes in the Java API is a class that maintains a linked list data structure; it is class java.util.LinkedList. When you have some objects that you want to keep in a linked list, you create an instance of the LinkedList class. You can then call methods like add(), getFirst() on the instance to put your objects in a list, and retrieve them.

Up until JDK 1.4 LinkedList looked like this (simplified to omit extraneous detail):

```
public class LinkedList {
    boolean add(Object o)  { /*more*/ }
    Object  getFirst()     { /*more*/ }
}
```

In JDK 1.5, LinkedList, along with many other classes in the API, was updated to accept a generic type parameter, and it now looks something like this:

New!

```
public class LinkedList <Element> {
    boolean add(Element o)    { /*more*/ }
    Element getFirst()        { /*more*/ }
}
```

The key piece is the <Element> after the classname. The notation is similar to that used in Backus-Naur Form beloved of compiler-writers everywhere, though the chief designer told me this was not his inspiration. In BNF, a word in angle brackets <word> stands for something that will be explained, described, or filled out later, which is exactly the role of a generic parameter. The angle brackets say, "Here are generic type parameters", and the identifiers are the names of the parameters. C++ uses angle brackets for type parameters, and the similarity to C++ was considered a plus (yikes!) But if the team could have found some unused punctuation that didn't need the shift key, they would have done so.

Once you have declared the name, you can use it nearly anywhere in the body of the generic where a type name is expected. It's as simple as that. You can provide any identifiers, "Element" is only an example. Sun recommends you use names that are one character long for type parameters, such as 'E' instead of "Element".

In the sample code above, the argument to the add() method has been updated. It now takes an object of type Element (whatever that eventually turns out to be). And the getFirst() method now returns an Element, not an Object.

A couple of questions come to mind. How does this work if you want your linked list to contain arbitrary objects of different types, say, it's a list holding all the different objects in your program? If they have a common parent type, then you could parameterize the list with that type. Ultimately, you would need to set the list up to accept Objects. The more general the type that the list works on, the less and less the generic feature buys you.

The Table example

We're going to switch to an example over the next few pages. It is class Table that takes two generic parameters, Key and Value. A Table stores Key/Value pairs. The key can be any type suitable for a key, such as an Integer or a String. No key is duplicated in the table. The Value can be any type.

You put a key/value pair of objects into a Table object. You can later retrieve the value by calling the get method, giving the key as an argument. It will return the associated value from the table, or the value null if that key hasn't been put into the table.

When you want to use more than one generic type parameter, just use a comma-separated list in the angle brackets. The generic class is:

```
public class Table <Key, Value> {
    Value put(Key k, Value v) {/*code omitted*/ }
    Value get(Key k)          {/*code omitted*/ }
}
```

This class can be instantiated with <String, Integer> to use as a name, number phone book.

You could instantiate it with <Integer, Integer> for a part number, stock-on-hand table.

You could instantiate it with <Timestamp, String> for a day's worth of appointment times and their descriptions.

Here is the code to create the three data structures mention in the previous box:

```
Table<String, Integer> phonebook  = new Table<String, Integer> ();

Table<Integer, Integer> partsTable = new Table<Integer,Integer>();

Table<Timestamp, String> appts = new Table<Timestamp,String>();
```

Generic parameters are intended for classes that do all their work on one specific type at a time, and where this work can be applied to many different types. There are several classic examples of this:

- **Container classes**, which implement a data structure holding objects of type X.

- **Input/output**, where you want to output a value in a formatted way, such as a byte, a short, an integer, and so on. Java I/O uses a completely different model (Gulp! Actually it has several different models as successive designers have tried to plug past gaps. JDK 1.4 had "new I/O" so the JDK 1.5 improvements are "even newer new I/O"). Java I/O *wasn't* changed to use generics.

- **Sorting and Searching classes**. These utilities are part of the collection classes, and so have been genericized.

- **Cloning**. The `clone()` method in Object did not need to be updated to use generics. Instead, when we override it, we can use the covariant return type feature to make it return an object of precisely the correct type (see page 238).

That's the basics of declaring a generic type; next we'll walk through showing how to pass type arguments to a generic.

Instantiating an object and passing arguments to the generic type

After you have set up your parameterized class, you need a way to create an instance of it and at the same time pass the actual type arguments. As usual, you create instances with constructors. You pass the type arguments in angle brackets, right before the parentheses for the constructor arguments. So you've got both sets of arguments appearing: type arguments in angle brackets, and constructor variable arguments in parentheses. Here's an example:

```
LinkedList<String> familyAddresses = new LinkedList<String> ( );
```

As always, you can use a super class on the left, and instantiate a more specific subtype:

```
Collection <String> familyAddresses = new LinkedList<String> ( );
```

Doing that keeps your options open for changing the underlying container (to say, ArrayList) without affecting pages and pages of code.

You use the same general form when you have more than one generic parameter. We can instantiate a Table to work with String keys, and integer values that are phone numbers:

```
Table<String,Integer> phonebook = new Table<String,Integer> ( );
```

To summarize what's going on here:

- The left-hand side says "phonebook" is an object of type Table parameterized with *String, Integer* to match parameters names *Key,Value* respectively. Refer back to the code in the box headed "The Table Example".

- The right-hand side calls a constructor of the Table<String, Integer> class.

- The Table-object-referenced-by-phonebook has been specialized so that it can only store values that are Integer objects. The integers are accessed by keys that are Strings.

- When you see "*Type <OtherType>*" you usually read it as "this is a *Type* of *OtherType*'s", so here, "this is a Table of String/Integer pairs". Since String is the key, we know it will be the phone subscriber's name. (This example works in small cases, but falls apart in real world scenarios of multiple phone lines and multiple people with the same name).

Invoking methods on objects of the instantiated generic type

If we also want to create a Table that can hold Strings that are accessed by Timestamps keys, we can use the same generic Table, and give it different parameters like this:

```
Table<Timestamp,String> appts = new Table<Timestamp,String> ( );
```

The appts object holds a schedule of appointments throughout a day, keyed by timestamp, each with a String saying what the appointment is at that time. You then use the newly created appts instance in the normal way, without regard to how its class started off as a generic class. You might add a few appointments by invoking Table's put() method like this:

```
appts.put(new Timestamp(7,30,00), "Feed dogs");
appts.put(new Timestamp(9,30,00), "Dentist");
appts.put(new Timestamp(12,00,00), "Lunch with Bob");
```

The appts Table is happy to hold <Timestamp, String> values.

The phonebook Table holds <String, Integer> pairs. If you forget what you're doing, and try to put a Timestamp, String pair into the phonebook Table:

```
phonebook.put(new Timestamp(9,30,00), "Dentist");
```

you'll get a compiler error message like this: *"Error: put(String,Integer) in Table<String, Integer> cannot be applied to (Timestamp, String)"*. Before generics, when Tables just held Objects, this level of type checking was not possible. With generics, Tables still deal with Objects at run-time, but the extra information at compile time allows stronger type checking. If you use generic parameters for all your collections, and all your program compiles without errors or warnings, and you don't use native code, then your program is guaranteed not to fail at run-time with a class cast exception on a collection.

Generic Interfaces

Interfaces, as well as classes, can be parameterized with generic types. As you'd expect, it looks exactly the same as when a class is parameterized. We'll walk through a complete "before and after" example here, because we'll use it in the next section as part of a more complicated generic parameter declaration.

This example uses the standard java.lang.Comparable interface type that defines a compareTo() method used for comparing two objects. The method returns an int which is negative, zero, or positive to indicate this is smaller, equal, or bigger than the argument.

java.lang.Comparable without generics

The Comparable interface looks like this in JDK 1.4:

```
public interface Comparable {
    int compareTo(Object obj)
}
```

A class that implements the interface would be declared like this in JDK 1.4:

```
public class Timestamp2 implements java.lang.Comparable {
    int hrs;
    int mins;
    int secs;

    public int compareTo(Object t) {
        Timestamp2 t2 = (Timestamp2) t;
        return (this.hrs - t2.hrs);
    }
}
```

The subtraction in the compareTo method is a cheap, fast way of getting the necessary negative, zero, or positive result. As long as the subtraction never overflows, it will give an accurate answer. To keep things simple, we'll define two timestamps as equal if their hour component matches.

When a class implements the Comparable interface, you can compare two of its objects like this:

```
int result = myTimestamp.compareTo(yourTimestamp);
```

Adding generics to java.lang.Comparable

In JDK 1.5, the Comparable interface now looks something like this:

```
public interface Comparable<T> {
    int compareTo(T thing)
}
```

That's the same notation for a type parameter that we saw earlier with classes. A class can implement the interface like this:

```
public class Timestamp implements java.lang.Comparable<Timestamp>{
    int hrs;
    int mins;
    int secs;

    public int compareTo(Timestamp t) {
        return (this.hrs - t.hrs);
    }
}
```

We thus provide the arguments to the generic parameters in the definition of the implementing class, rather than in the object instantiation. The compiler knows that class Timestamp is implementing the Comparable interface on Timestamps, not Objects. So method compareTo can take a Timestamp parameter, not an Object, and explicit casting is not needed inside the method. The compiler still needs to insert it in the generated code.

Method calls look the same as if you didn't use generics:

```
int result = myTimestamp.compareTo(yourTimestamp);
```

The most common case is comparing two objects of the same class. If a class wants to allow its objects to be compared to objects of some other class, you can also express that using the generic parameter. One example might be allowing Timestamps to be compared to Strings. They are equal if the String contains the text representation of the Timestamp, e.g. "noon" and 12:00:00. Here's how you would write that:

```
public class Timestamp implements java.lang.Comparable<String>{
        int hrs;
        int mins;
        int secs;

    public int compareTo(String s) { /*more code here*/ }
```

Restrictions on a generic type

As designed for Java, genericity is a compile time feature. Practically nothing about the actual type parameters persists through to run-time. There is just one class file for a generic class, no matter how many times the generic class is instantiated. At run-time, an instance of a generic class has no information about what type argument was actually given to some instance as its type parameter at compile time. (There's some structural information in the class file, available through reflection). It may actually *be* a String, but the generic class holds it as an Object. That's why the compiler still needs to insert casts.

This run-time amnesia has been termed *type erasure*. There are three limitations on the use of generic parameters, some of which follow from type erasure:

1.   You cannot use a type parameter to create a new instance:

```
        public class Table <Key, Value> {
           Value v = new Value();  //  illegal!
        }
```

Creating an instance out of a type parameter makes little sense. The actual type parameter might be an interface or a class with private constructors.

2.   You should not use a type parameter in a cast. The compiler cannot check the validity of the cast. You're opening up the possibility generics try to avoid—a run-time class cast exception:

```
Key k2 = (Key) someObj;   //  causes compiler warning!
```

If you do write this code, the compiler will issue a warning, and suggest that you recompile using the "-Xlint" option to get a list of the specific lines it is warning you about. That option should have been made the default for every Java compilation.

3.   All reference types have the methods defined in the ultimate parent class, Object. So it is legal to call methods of Object, like toString() on any generic parameter:

```
public class Table <Key, Value> {
    boolean add(Key k, Value v) {
        String s = v.toString();   //  legal
    }
}
```

There's no fundamental theoretical requirement for type erasure. It was one design among several possibilities, chosen because it did not require any changes to the JVM. C# made a different design choice, keeps the information around, and does the parameter substitution at run-time including compiling each instantiation of a new type on-the-fly! It has a slightly richer choice of operations because of this, along with a more complicated compiler/run-time and larger run-time performance penalty (while the code is compiled).

C++ does something else again. The designer of C#, Anders Hejlsberg, summarized the different approaches as "C# generics are really just like classes, except they have a type parameter. C++ templates are really just like macros, except they look like classes". C++ does the instantiation of a new type at compile or link time, but it doesn't check that a generic type actually has the methods you invoke on it. So those operations can fail with a cryptic message at run-time. That won't happen in Java.

You may need to call more methods on a type parameter, than just those in Object. You can arrange this in the usual way - tell the compiler that the actual type argument has to implement some interface or extend some class. The way to do that is explained in the next section.

Bounds—Requiring a Type Parameter to Implement an Interface or Extend a Parent Class

You'll get more use out of generic types if there's a way to call additional methods on them, more than just the handful of methods implemented in java.lang.Object. You can call a specific method, such as compareTo(), on a generic type within the body of a generic class, if you can be sure that the type has such a method. There are two ways to ensure that some class has a given method:

- Make the class a child of some parent that has the method, or
- Make the class implement an interface that has the method.

In general terms, we want a way to tell a generic that one of the parameter types *must implement some interface* or *extend some parent*. We express this with a Java generics feature called *bounds*. Bounds are limitations or restrictions put on type parameters.

Bounds say "The type that you use as an argument to the generic *must* extend this class" or "... *must* implement this interface". The purpose of bounds is to inform the compiler of methods that are guaranteed to be present in the type argument. Then we can call them, and it is guaranteed not to fail at run-time with a "method not found" exception.

An ordinary generic parameter is written as:

```
class SomeGenericClass <X>
```

We want a way to add this kind of condition to X:

```
<X has-to-extend-or-implement Comparable>
```

Then we can call Comparable's methods on X, like this:

```
class SomeGenericClass <X has-to-extend-or-implement Comparable> {
    void check(X x1, X x2) {
        int result = x1.compareTo(x2);

        /* more code, omitted*/
```

Bounds are *restrictions* in the sense that not every type will meet the requirements. But they are really *permissions* in the sense that they grant extra capabilities inside the body of the generic class. They guarantee that objects of the type parameter will have certain methods and therefore you can invoke those methods. I mentioned above that at run-time, an instance of a generic class has no information about the type argument and holds it as an Object. That was a simplification to avoid confusing you too soon. If a generic type parameter has a non-trivial bound, that information is carried through to run-time.

The pseudo-keyword used above "has-to-extend-or-implement" is a bit longer than necessary. The important thing here is guaranteeing the availability of certain methods on X, and the Java compiler doesn't care whether it is done by implementing an interface or by extending a class. So the actual form uses the keyword "extends". (In the beta compiler, you can't substitute the obvious word "implements" if you are talking about an interface. "Extends" does double duty here for a class and for an interface. Everyone hopes that changes in the final version).

```
class SomeGenericClass <X extends SomeInterfaceOrClass> {
```

You could set up a generic class that will only accept subtypes of Thread as a parameter:

```
class SomeGenericClass <X extends Thread> {
```

Inside that generic class, you may now invoke Thread methods on X objects:

```
void makeItGo(X myThr) {
    myThr.start();
```

That's easy to understand and read. Don't worry, it gets more complicated: What if you need the generic parameter X to extend some other class or interface *that is itself generic*? What then, eh? What if you need X to extend, not Thread, but Comparable? Comparable takes a generic parameter saying what type something can be compared to. So what we have above, won't quite work for Comparable as written. Keep on reading for the full details!

Generic parameter bounds that mention a generic type

Here's where the syntax starts to get hard to read. If the interface or class that you mention as a bound, is itself generic, then you must give its full signature, *including its generic type parameters*. For instance:

```
class SomeGenericClass <X extends Comparable<X> > {
```

So here it says "X is a type parameter to this class, and X has a bound. X must extend/implement Comparable. And not just any old Comparable, but Comparable of X". The net effect is that only types which implement Comparable on themselves will be allowed as type arguments to the generic class. That would ensure you could call x.compareTo(x2) within the generic body.

Some more syntactic sugar with your generics?

There's a phrase among compiler writers, coined by Prof. Peter Landin and popularized by Prof. Alan Perlis, that something is "syntactic sugar".

It describes syntax (keywords, etc.,) added to a language just to make it more palatable to programmers. The phrase is used dismissively ("Curse you Perkins, and your syntactic sugar too!") which I think is a mistake. What's wrong with making something simpler for programmers to understand and use?

Case in point, here's the "before" and "after" of one method in class java.util.Collections:

Before generics:

```
public static void sort(List list)
```

With generics:

```
public static <T extends Comparable<? super T>> void sort(List<T>list)
```

But don't let the unfamiliar notation throw you off. We'll decode this in the next chapter, on Collections. To be honest, I can't think of a way to improve the notation, short of turning it all into keywords, which itself has drawbacks. It gets familiar quickly if you stick with it and keep reading. But in the meantime, I'd like a big old spoonful of that syntactic sugar.

Going back to the Table example, here's how you require that all types, X, used as a Key type parameter must implement the Comparable<X> interface:

```
class Table <Key extends Comparable<Key>, Value> {

        boolean add(Key k, Value v) { /*more code*/ }
```

That allows us to call compareTo() on Key values within the generic, so we can tell the ordering of keys and perhaps keep them sorted for efficient access.

Using a concrete example from earlier in the chapter, here's how you would instantiate a Table object with Integer keys, and String values. If you check the declaration of Integer in the Java API, you will see that it does implement Comparable<Integer>. Therefore Integer can be used for the Key parameter in this declaration.

```
Table<Integer,String> digitStrings = new Table<Integer,String>();
```

You might set up a table like this so that you can translate easily between int digits and their text equivalent. Some code to do this might be:

```
String old;
old = digitStrings.put(0,"zero");
old = digitStrings.put(1,"one");
old = digitStrings.put(2,"two");
```

Notice that we provided an int value as the first argument to the put() method where the declaration called for a Key, and which we instantiated with an Integer.

We don't have to write:

```
old = digitStrings.put(new Integer(0),"zero");
```

because autoboxing does that conversion from int to Integer for us automatically.

If you want to try compiling this example, use the name java.util.Hashtable instead of Table. Not everyone is familiar with Hashtables yet, but everyone knows what a table of <key, value> pairs is. A hashtable lets you put or retrieve a value using a key, instead of a position in a list like some of the other collection classes. When you put() something in a Hashtable, the method returns the old value that was in the table under that key, if there was one. That way you can tell if you replaced something already there, or genuinely added something fresh into the table.

Several generic parameter bounds

You might find that some of your generic types need to implement several interfaces. That is expressed in a generic parameter by using the "&" ampersand character:

```
class Table <Key extends Comparable<Key> & java.io.Serializable, Value> {
```

You can include up to one bound for a specific parent class (such as Thread, or Employee) in there too. The limit is one in Java, because you have exactly one immediate parent class (no multiple inheritance).

Table 15–1 summarizes in one place these new terms, and examples of what they look like. We have not yet covered the last two items in the table, but they are included here for completeness. The last two items, wildcards and generic methods are not intended for use in generic classes directly. These features are mainly in Java to support *your* methods in non-generic classes which use a generic type from the library. You will use wildcards and/or generic methods when you write an application method that needs to accept a generic type as an argument. As such, we will cover these two features in the next chapter, which describes generic collections, and how to use them. That's the end of generics for now.

Table 15–1   Summary of terminology

Concept	Example
Generic class	`class LinkedList <E>  { }`
Generic interface	`interface Comparable <T> {` `                    void myMethod(T t) {  }  }`

Parameterized type	`class LinkedList <E>  { }`
	`// LinkedList is a parameterized type`
	`//  the generic parameter is E`

Type parameter	`<E>`
Type argument	`String` // (the thing that replaces the type parameter)
Instantiation	`LinkedList<String> sll = new LinkedList<String>()`
Bounds	`<E extends SomeClass & SomeInterface<E> >`
Wildcard	`LinkedList<?>`

Generic method	`public static <T> void copy(`
	`                    List<? super T> dest,`
	`                    List<? extends T> src   )`

Some Light Relief—On Computable Numbers with an Application to the Entscheidungsproblem

Generics in Java got me thinking about methods and subroutines in general. Computer science is a young enough field that it might be possible to pinpoint where subroutines were first used, and maybe even who came up with the idea. Like the answer to "What was the first computer?" the origin of subroutines is more a question about definitions than about history. Depending on how you define it, the first computer was:

- The ENIAC (Electronic Numerator, Integrator, Analyzer and Calculator/Computer [accounts differ]). Built by John Mauchley and J. Presper Eckert at the Moore School in the University of Pennsylvania, it was dedicated in February 1946. As originally built, it was not a stored program computer. ENIAC led to a follow-on project, EDVAC (Electronic Discrete Variable Automatic Calculator/Computer), and eventually a spin-off company that built Univac and morphed into the company of the same name (today known as Unisys).

- The SSEC (Selective Sequence Electronic Calculator) in January 1948, built by Wallace Eckert of IBM (no relation to John Eckert). Programs were read from paper tape or plugboards, but the system had the ability to cache in memory, and in theory operate like a stored program computer some of the time.

- The Manchester Mark 1 in June 1948, built by Fred Williams, Tom Kilburn and a team at Manchester University, England. This is the first machine that everyone recognizes as a computer, because it is the first system that stored its programs in the same memory used for data. The Manchester Mark 1 is unrelated to the Harvard Mark 1 built by IBM in 1943. The Harvard Mark 1 was a big calculator built out of relays, and driven by programs on paper tape (like a player piano).

- The EDSAC (Electronic Delay Storage Automatic Computer) in May 1949 by Maurice Wilkes's team at Cambridge University in England. This was the first operational, full-scale stored-program computer. It was closely based on the EDVAC design.

There are other candidates for the title "first computer", too. I would characterize the evolution as, before World War II—paper designs, during World War II—electronic calculators, and right after World War II—the first true computers. The Manchester Mark I is the one I am putting my money on as the very first true computer. They rebuilt the Mark I to commemorate its golden anniversary in 1998, and there's a plaque on the wall of the building where it was originally constructed. Last time I was in Manchester, England I took a photo of it.

One of the first programmers on the Manchester Mark I was legendary computer pioneer Alan Turing. Even before he joined the Mark I team in 1948, he sent them a routine to do long division. When I get time, I want to write a simulator in Java for the Mark 1— imagine the thrill of coding that retraces the footsteps of a great pioneer! Turing wrote the first ever Programmer's Handbook, some of which you can find online at http://www.computer50.org/kgill/mark1/progman.html.

Alan Turing had worked on systems that encapsulated all three phases of early computer evolution: paper designs, electronic calculators, and true computers. His 1937 paper, which I generically re-used for the title of this light relief (ho ho), *On computable numbers, with an application to the Entscheidungsproblem* appeared in summer 1936 in the Proceedings of the London Mathematical Society Vol. 42, pp. 230--265. It was very influential and ground-breaking work[1]. Original copies of

---

1. Some say that John Von Neumann got the idea from Turing's paper of having one memory that would store data *and* instructions, and a "Von Neumann machine" should therefore be called "Turing's Other Machine". Turing completed his PhD under von Neumann's supervision, so the big Hungarian was certainly familiar with Turing's work. Ideas likely flowed both ways, and they were both intellectual giants who deserve enormous credit as computer pioneers.

this paper sell for $35,000, so if you find one in your home magazine rack, get down to eBay.

The *Entscheidungsproblem* ("decision problem") is the challenge to find a general algorithm that can evaluate whether arbitrary statements in symbolic logic are valid or not. The statements are written in mathematical terms. Turing's contribution was to come up with a standard computing model that set aside implementation details and allowed the focus to be on underlying logic. His model came to be known as the Turing machine, and Turing proved in his paper that the Entscheidungsproblem was equivalent to trying to decide in advance if an arbitrary program for the Turing machine would halt or not. And he knew the answer to that problem!

It causes major pants-wetting excitement among mathematicians when they prove one deep problem is equivalent to another. Turing's breakthrough is a fundamental finding of theoretical computer science. He showed that it is undecidable to determine in advance whether an arbitrary computer program will halt or loop endlessly. This is formally known as the Halting Problem. When I read Turing's 1936 paper, I was looking for any mention of subroutines. To my joy, I found that he clearly understood and used parameterized subroutines.

Figure 15–1   **In this laboratory in Manchester, England, on June 21, 1948, the world's first computer was powered up**

Since the word subroutine hadn't been invented yet, Turing called them *m-configuration functions*. This is a paper design, not something that pushes electrons. Still, it's pretty cool that Turing used the concept at the dawn of computing. Turing had great success cracking Nazi Enigma codes during the war years, with a special purpose electrical calculator called the Bombe.

In February 1946, Turing wrote a design proposal for a project known as the Automatic Computing Engine, in which he unequivocally spelled out subroutines and their implementation. Because the terms "call" and "return" were not yet in use, Turing coined the terms "bury" and "unbury" for these actions. He also proposed a stack of return addresses, and now referred to subroutines as "subsidiary operations".

Turing wrote:

"We also wish to be able to arrange for the splitting up of operations into subsidiary operations. This should be done in such a way that once we have written down how an operation is done we can use it as a subsidiary to any other operation. ... When we wish to start on a subsidiary operation we need only make a note of where we left off the major operation and then apply the first instruction of the subsidiary. When the subsidiary is over we look up the note and continue with the major operation. Each subsidiary operation can end with instructions for this recovery of the note." A.M. Turing, *"Proposals for the development in the Mathematics Division of an Automatic Computing Engine (ACE)."* Report E882, Executive Committee, NPL February 1946. Reprinted in April 1972 as NPL Report Com. Sci 57.

So Turing invented the modern concept of the subroutine, but it was still only a paper proposal. The ACE project was delayed by resource constraints (Britain was still on rationing for eight years after World War II ended), bureaucracy, and Turing's limitations as a salesman. Eventually Turing gave up his ACE project and accepted an offer to move to Manchester and work on the prototype Mark I. Around this time, Turing hypothesized the "Turing Test" for artificial intelligence: if a human observer, conversing over a teletype with a computer, could not distinguish whether a person or a computer was at the other end, such a computer would have A.I. Unfortunately, this conjecture was a busted flush for Turing. The Turing test has been shown many times to be inadequate: people are just too ready to see patterns where there are none, and to confuse superficial appearance with reality.

Meanwhile, progress was forging ahead in Britain. The earliest subroutines that ran on real hardware were developed by David Wheeler for the EDSAC in Cambridge, working with M. V. Wilkes and Stanley Gill. The call/return became known as a "Wheeler Jump" and was set up as follows. Before you make the call, an instruction loads its own address into the accumulator. A second instruction will set up the return branch. It adds a predetermined constant to the accumulator to transform the address bit pattern into a branch to the first instruction's address plus some number of words (the length of instructions two to four) needed to cause a proper return branch. Note that you're working with a word that includes the op-code as well as the address portion, so you want to be careful about overflow. Then a third instruction stores the new "return" branch from the accumulator to an address at the end of the subroutine. Finally, you branch to the beginning of the subroutine!

David Wheeler was the chief programmer for the EDSAC project and went on to a career of great renown. He was the one who pointed out that *all problems in Computer Science can be solved by another level of indirection*. Wheeler also invented the concept of a bootstrap – a ROM program that is run every time the machine is turned on. The first bootstrap was put in the read only memory of the EDSAC system in August 1949. It was a very advanced bootstrap/loader which loaded the programs to be executed, and also allowed the programs to be relocated to different parts of memory.

Bottom line: We *do* know who invented the subroutine, which 55 years later led to generics in Java. Alan Turing invented the concept, and Dave Wheeler was the first to see it implemented on a real system. So the next time you write foo(), you know who to thank.

3

Server-side Java

Collections

We come now to a most important part of Java: the java.util and related packages that provide off-the-shelf data structures for your programs.

Computer science has a couple of dozen standard data structures (such as the linked list, the binary tree, the stack, etc). Java provides many of these standard data structures directly as library classes, and makes it easy for you to implement additional ones in a consistent way. These data structures hold collections of objects, called *elements*, and the library is known as the Java Collection Framework.

The Java Collection Framework has been updated to use generics starting in JDK 1.5, and you need to read Chapter 15 to understand this chapter. Collections are expected to be *homogeneous*: an instance of a collection class should only hold elements of one type. The code change is that you use generics to tell the compiler what that type is. The compiler will then detect attempts to add an object of the wrong type into a collection.

341

Collection API

We mentioned there are a couple of dozen basic data structures in computer science. Java provides the most important of these (including all three mentioned earlier) in a set of library classes. There is a common interface, java.util.Collection, giving the method signatures for insertion, deletion, and other common operations. Whatever java.util data structures you use, you can access them in a uniform way.

There are three main data structure classes that implement java.util.Collection:

- **List**. Lists can contain duplicate elements. Lists are kept in the order that elements are added. A list might contain an element for each tire sold in a tire store on one day. In this example, if someone buys four "Road Hugger" tires, four identical elements will get added to the list.

- **Set**. Sets cannot contain duplicate elements. Sets have their own idea of order, which is not the order that elements are added. A Set might contain "all customer objects who have not bought from us in the last six months".

- **Queue**. Queues were added in JDK 1.5. They are intended for holding elements prior to processing. Queues came into Java to help Threads. They typically deliver elements in a FIFO (first in, first out) order, but don't have to. You might use a queue to hold service requests while waiting for a server thread to become free.

On top of these three basic structures, there are many additional flavors or variations:

- Lists that are kept in an array (allowing fast random access)

- Lists in which each element points to adjacent elements rather than being stored next to them (enabling lists of arbitrary size)

- Sets specialized for fast access to enum objects

- Sets that support "copy on write" operations for sharing mostly read-only data between threads,

- Blocking queues of various types that wait for space before completing an add().

There are also a few simple data structures from JDK 1.1, updated to implement Collection: Vector and Stack.

There is a fourth basic data structure in java.util. It doesn't implement the Collection interface because it's about *pairs* of related objects.

- **Map**. Lists and Sets just hold individual objects. Maps are for pairs of objects, where one is the key (such as "person name"), and the other is a value associated with that key (e.g. phone number). Maps have lots of variations too, depending on the underlying data structure: HashMap, TreeMap, WeakHashMap, HashTable and others. A *map* is a mathematical term for how one group of things (the keys) is related to another group of things (the values).

You choose List, Set, Queue, or Map depending on the characteristics of your data. Then you drill down onto a specific concrete class that gives the performance or other quality you need. You don't typically extend the Collection classes. You declare an object of one of the classes. Then you add your objects into your Collection object. Later, you iterate through the collection and process those objects, perhaps updating or sorting or removing some of them. There are umpteen other secondary operations too, like getting the count of the number of objects, and adding or removing a complete other collection from this one.

Most texts launch into an involved and highly detailed description of the individual data structures at this point. You can quickly get overwhelmed with low level information on weakly referenced hash maps, or abstract sequential lists. Instead, let's take a look at characteristics of collections, and some examples.

The Collection interface

The class java.util.Collection is just an interface that defines a dozen or so methods for adding to, removing from, and querying a data structure. Now all the individual java.util data structures (and others that *you* write) can implement this interface, and everyone adds and retrieves data with the same method signatures. Collection has a single generic parameter, E, so you can specify what Element type it is a collection of. It looks like this (simplified for ease of reading):

```
public interface java.util.Collection <E> {
    // basic operations
    public int       size();
    public boolean isEmpty();
    public boolean contains(E element);
    public boolean add(E element);
    public boolean remove(E element);
    public Iterator<E> iterator();

    // bulk operations on an entire collection
    public boolean addAll(Collection c);
    public boolean removeAll(Collection c);
    public boolean retainAll(Collection c);
    public boolean containsAll(Collection c);
    public void    clear();

    // put the collection into an array
    public Object[] toArray();
    public <T> T[] toArray(T[] a);

    // a reminder that you may need to override these
    public boolean equals(Object o);
    public int       hashCode();

}
```

Again, generic parameter E says what type you're going to keep in this instance. Here's how you would declare a collection that will hold Double objects (refer to the previous chapter if you are wondering about <Double>):

```
Collection <Double> myReadings;
```

Of course, that only gives you a place to hold a reference to the collection object. Say we decide to hold our readings in a PriorityQueue. The whole thing will look like this:

```
Collection<Double> myReadings = new PriorityQueue<Double>();
```

Declare Collection objects with Collection type

In the previous code, we declared the collection object c, to have type *Collection of Double*. We could equalled have given it the specific subtype that we instantiated it with:

```
PriorityQueue<Double> myReadings = new PriorityQueue<Double>();
```

The preferred style is to declare the variable as having type Collection:

```
Collection<Double> myReadings = new PriorityQueue<Double>();
```

It gives you more flexibility, by making it easy to later change to a different kind of collection class, such as:

```
Collection<Double> myReadings = new Stack<Double>();
```

When myReadings is typed as Collection, the compiler will ensure that you do not inadvertently call any methods that are specific to PriorityQueue or Stack.

Let's take a closer look at the methods that the Collection interface promises. All of the basic methods should be self-explanatory, with the possible exception of iterator(), which we will get to shortly.

add() and remove() will add or remove the argument element and return true if that operation changed the Collection. In other words, if you try to remove something that is not in the collection, no exception is thrown, but the method call returns false. If the argument object actually was part of the collection, that element is removed from it and the method returns true. If you try to add something that is already in the collection, the result depends on what kind of collection it is. Some collections allow duplicate elements, and will add it again quite happily. Other collections do not allow duplicates. They will notice that they are already holding the element, and will return false to indicate that the operation did not change the collection.

There is no get() method to obtain an individual object back from a collection! The older way uses an iterator, which will give you *all* the objects one-by-one. You can stop iterating when you reach one you particularly like, if you wish. In JDK 1.5 use the for statement. There is a get() method on some of the classes that implement Collection.

The retainAll() method does set intersection. It goes through this Collection and compares it with the Collection passed as the argument. It keeps all the elements that are in both collections and removes the others from this Collection.

The addAll() method adds all the elements of the argument collection to this collection. The removeAll() method removes all elements from this collection that are also contained in the argument collection. After this call returns, this collection will hold no elements in common with the argument collection.

All concrete Collection classes have a constructor that takes a Collection as an argument. The collection must be of the same type or a subtype of E. There is no way for the Collection interface to specify the existence of these constructors. It's just a generally accepted protocol. This constructor allows you to get a view of an existing Collection in one of the other Collection data structures. No cloning takes place.

Collections only ever hold references to objects, so sorting, or adding, or other operations are quick—just rearrange a few pointers. But if you change an object through some other pointer, the collection gets changed too. That might or might not be what you intend.

There is a helper class, Collections, that consists exclusively of static functions to do useful things to a Collection argument (get the maximum element, reverse a collection, sort it, do a binary search, etc.). We come back to that later with an example. Next we'll take a look at the way you add elements to any collection, and how you can use an iterator to visit all the elements.

Adding to a Collection

One of the concrete classes that implements Collection is java.util.HashSet. This class implements Set interface, so we know it cannot have duplicates. It is implemented using a hash table, and it acts like a Set, hence HashSet. Here is the code that shows how you would populate a HashSet Collection object and invoke some common methods on it:

```java
Collection<Double> c = new HashSet<Double>();

for(int i = 1; i <= 5; i++)
    c.add( (double)i );  // add element to collection

if ( ! c.isEmpty() )
    System.out.println("c has " + c.size() + " elements");


for(Double d : c )      // iterate through a collection!
    System.out.println("c has " + d );
}
```

If you put those statements in a main routine and add an "import java.util.*" at the top of the class, you'll be able to compile and run the program with this result:

```
% javac -source 1.5 foo.java
% java foo
c has 5 elements
c has 3.0
c has 4.0
c has 5.0
c has 1.0
c has 2.0
```

HashSet is one of the collections that uses an order that suits itself, hence the elements come out in a seemingly funny order. To see why, you have to understand how hash tables work, and in particular what is going on with the methods equals() and hashcode() that are defined in java.lang.Object, and hence present in every Object. We'll defer this discussion to a little later in the chapter.

Foreach statement—iterating through a Collection

There are two things to note here. First, Sets don't generally give you back the elements in the order in which you add them. Second, iterating through a collection is now quick and simple to write. Just mention the element type, a loop variable, and the collection you are taking it from:

```
for(Double d : c )      // iterating through a collection!
```

Let's take a more detailed look at iterators, the older way of traversing a collection

public interface Iterator <E>

Iterator is an interface that allows you to visit all the elements in a collection without having to know the details of how or where they're stored. The collection class knows all those details, and it implements the Iterator interface. The Iterator interface looks like this:

```
public interface java.util.Iterator<E> {
    public boolean hasNext();
    public E next();
    public void remove();
}
```

The interface java.util.Iterator replaces an earlier attempt to do the same thing, java.util.Enumerator (mnemonic: each improvement makes the name shorter: Enumerator, Iterator, foreach). Use foreach when you can. Use Iterators instead of Enumerators because:

- Iterators provide a safe way to remove an element that you have just arrived at, whereas Enumerator does not have this feature.

- The names are shorter in Iterator (next() versus nextElement()).

- Iterators have been updated to take a generic parameter, so that the next() method returns something of the correct type, not type Object.

The Collection interface promises that each implementing class will have a method that returns an Iterator:

```
public Iterator<E> iterator ()
```

Calling a collection's iterator() method returns you back an object that fulfills the Iterator (with a capital "I") interface. The obvious implementation for iterator() is to return an inner class that implements Iterator, and is local to the method, possibly anonymous[1]. For an array, iteration is simply going from a[0] to a[n-1], but for a binary tree a little more effort is needed. The Iterator interface allows that effort to be encapsulated, kept in the Collection, and hidden from user classes.

The method hasNext() allows you to test whether there is a next element in the collection. The methods hasNext() and next() are robust. You can call them in any order, and they are not tied to each other at all. The method hasNext() can be called multiple times without moving to the next element, and it will return the correct answer.

The method next() returns the first then subsequent elements of the iteration. If there is no next element, it will throw the exception NoSuchElementException. When you visit an element with next(), you can then call remove() on it to delete it from the collection. This is much simpler than having every individual Java programmer trying to implement remove() for a linked list or whatever the structure is, for themselves.

---

1.   If that sentence seemed like mumbo-jumbo, please review Chapter 12 and tackle the collections questions in the exercises at the end of this chapter.

Fail fast Iterators and ConcurrentModificationException

It is defined to be a bug if a collection is modified during the course of iterating through it, perhaps by another thread. That is really just a special case of a race condition. You are only allowed to modify a collection during the course of iterating by using the `remove()` method of the Iterator, or the `add()`, `remove()`, or `set()` methods of ListIterator.

All the iterators that are part of the Java run-time library try to detect illegal concurrent modifications, and throw a ConcurrentModificationException. In other words, if you have a program that adds elements to a List in one thread, while another thread is trying to iterate through the same list, the list iterator will use its best efforts to detect this and throw a ConcurrentModificationException. This is so the Iterator fails quickly and cleanly, rather than risking arbitrary, non-deterministic behavior at an undetermined time in the future. The behavior is called *fail-fast*. It's not guaranteed to throw an exception, it's a best effort approach to help you uncover bugs in your code.

Assume we are using the Collection created in the previous example. We can work our way through each element with an explicit Iterator like this:

```
Collection<Double> c = new HashSet<Double>();

//  code to fill the collection, omitted.

for (Iterator i = c.iterator(); i.hasNext(); )
    System.out.println("c has " + i.next() );
```

The new syntax of the for statement is a lot easier and quicker to write:

```
for(Double d : c )
    System.out.println("c has " + d );
```

Iterators will drop out of use, as the 1.5 release grows in popularity. You'll only see Iterators in old code, and in loops where you need to remove elements from the collection.

Let's go on to look at another class that implements Collection: LinkedList.

List, LinkedList, and ArrayList

One of the concrete classes that implements Collection is java.util.LinkedList. This class is just a plain old "Data Structures 101" forward-and-backward-linked list. You provide separate objects that you want stored, and the library class does the work of setting up and copying references to make a list. You start by instantiating an empty LinkedList, then anything you add is put on the list as a new element.

The class LinkedList implements List which implements Collection. The exact parent-child relationship of interfaces is shown in Figure 16–1.

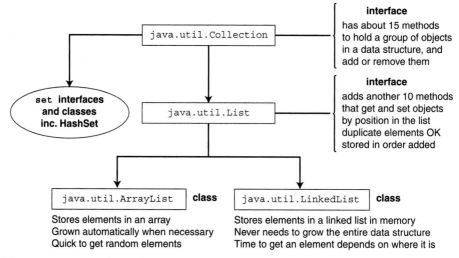

Figure 16–1   Interface relationship

The interface java.util.List adds about another ten methods to the elementary data access methods specified in java.util.Collection. Slightly simplified, the methods are:

```
public interface java.util.List<E> extends java.util.Collection <E> {
    public boolean addAll(int index, Collection);
    public Object get(int index);
    public Object set(int index, E element);
    public void add(int index, E element);
    public Object remove(int index);
    public int indexOf(Object o);
    public int lastIndexOf(Object o);

    public java.util.ListIterator<E> listIterator();
    public java.util.ListIterator<E> listIterator(int index);
    public java.util.List<E> subList(int from, int to);
}
```

Most of these List methods let the programmer access elements by their integer index (position in the list), and search for elements in the list. Unlike sets, lists allow duplicate elements. Say you owned a store, and wanted to record each item as it is sold so that you know what you need to re-order. A list would be a good choice for this kind of collection. As you complete each sale, say for a 21-inch

Sony color TV model ABC-1, a new element representing that product is added to the list. If you sell ten of them during the day, there will be 10 "TV model ABC-1" records on the list.

A HashSet would not be a good choice for this collection, because after you have added the first ABC-1 record to the collection, it's already in the set and you cannot add it again.

The subList() method returns a new list that points to the elements in the first list between the *from* argument, inclusive but not including the *to* argument. Lists start at element zero, just like arrays.

Note the two listIterator() methods. A ListIterator is a subinterface of Iterator. The first listIterator() obtains a ListIterator starting at the first element in the collection. The second one gets a ListIterator starting at the position specified by the int argument. Listiterator promises these methods:

```
public interface java.util.ListIterator<E> extends java.util.Iterator<E> {
    public boolean hasNext();
    public E next();
    public boolean hasPrevious();
    public E previous();

    public int nextIndex();
    public int previousIndex();

    public void remove();
    public void set(E e);
    public void add(E e);
}
```

A ListIterator allows you to iterate backwards over a list of objects as well as forwards. If you want to start at the end of the list, create a ListIterator passing an argument of list.size(). Then a call to list.previous() will return the last element, and you can keep going back through previous objects.

Unlike an Iterator, a ListIterator doesn't have a current element. The position of the ListIterator always lies in between two elements: the one that would be returned by a call to coll.previous(), and the one that would be returned by a call to coll.next().

The remove() and set() methods operate on the element returned by the most recent next() or previous(). The set() method replaces that element by the argument element. The remove() method removes that element from the list.

Here is the code for iterating backwards through a list:

```
LinkedList <String> cs = new LinkedList<String>();
// code to add elements
cs.add( "hello" );
cs.add( "there" );
cs.add( "everybody" );

ListIterator<String> li = cs.listIterator( cs.size() );
while( li.hasPrevious() ) {
    String s = li.previous();
    System.out.println(s);
}
```

```
% javac -source 1.5 example.java
% java example
everybody
there
hello
```

ArrayList implements List

We now come to another class that implements List. ArrayList is a concrete class that implements the List interface using an array as the underlying type. The ArrayList class should be thought of as an array that grows as needed to store the number of elements you want to put there.

When you want to put your data in a List, ArrayList is always an alternative to LinkedList. The reason for choosing one over the other is a performance versus function trade off.

- An ArrayList offers immediate access to all its elements (they are stored in an array, remember). You can only reach a LinkedList element by starting at one end or the other of the list, and traversing all the intervening elements.

- A LinkedList lets you add a new element very quickly. The time to add an element to an ArrayList is normally quick, too. But when the array is full, adding another element causes a new bigger array to be allocated and the old one copied over into it. LinkedList does not have that drawback.

The ArrayList class has the following public methods (slightly simplified to omit bounds on generic parameters), in addition to those promised by the List interface:

```
public class java.util.ArrayList<E> implements
            java.util.List, java.util.RandomAccess,
                java.lang.Cloneable, java.io.Serializable {
    public ArrayList();        // constructors
    public ArrayList(int size);
    public ArrayList(Collection c);

    public void trimToSize();
    public void ensureCapacity(int size);

    public Object clone();
}
```

You don't access ArrayList elements with the array brackets "[]," instead, you use the List methods to get and set the elements at particular indices.

To cut down on incremental reallocation, you can tell the constructor how many elements the array should allow for initially. The default allocation is ten elements, or 10% more than the size of a Collection you pass to the constructor, in the JDK.

Set, HashSet, and SortedSet

One of the concrete classes that implements Collection is java.util.HashSet. We briefly visited HashSet at the beginning of this section on Collections, and now it is time to expand on it a little. This class is just a plain old "Data Structures 101" hash table.

You provide each object that will be stored as data in the hash table, and the library class does the work of maintaining the table and putting the elements in the right places. You start by instantiating an empty HashSet, then anything you add is placed in the table. If an object is already in the table, it won't be added again.

The class HashSet implements Set which implements Collection. The exact parent-child relationship of interfaces is shown in Figure 16–2.

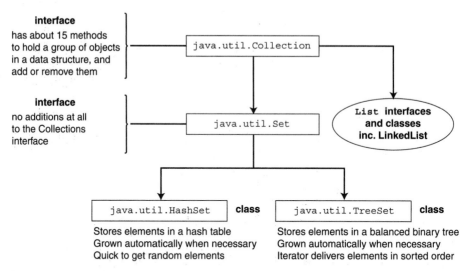

Figure 16–2   HashSet relationship

The interface java.util.Set does not add any methods at all to the elementary data access methods specified in java.util.Collection. It is written as a separate interface to help document and represent the design of the Collections Framework. It shows the symmetry between classes that are Sets, and classes that are Lists. As a reminder, the Collection interface, and thus the Set interface, looks like this.

```
public interface java.util.Set<E> extends Collection<E> {
    // basic operations
    public int size();
    public boolean isEmpty();
    public boolean contains(Object element);
    public boolean add(E element);
    public boolean remove(Object element);
    public Iterator iterator();

    // bulk operations on an entire collection
    public boolean addAll(Collection c);
    public boolean removeAll(Collection c);
    public boolean retainAll(Collection c);
    public boolean containsAll(Collection c);
    public void clear();

    // put the collection into an array
    public Object[] toArray();
    public T[] toArray(T a[]);

    // a reminder that you may need to override these
    public boolean equals(Object o);
    public int hashCode();
}
```

A Set is *a collection that has no duplicate elements*. The interface represents the mathematical concept of a set, as applied in set theory. It is easy to calculate the intersection of two collections, or take the set difference between this set and another. An example of a set is the set of all colors that a system can display on its monitor. Here is how we would calculate the intersection of two collections:

```java
import java.util.*;
import java.awt.Color;
import static java.awt.Color.*;

public class d2 {

    public static void main(String[] args)  {

        // populate first collection
        Collection <Color> hs1 = new HashSet<Color>();
        hs1.add( red );
        hs1.add( green );
        hs1.add( blue );
        hs1.add( magenta );

        // populate second collection
        Collection<Color> hs2 = new HashSet<Color>();
        hs2.add( red );
        hs2.add( green );
        hs2.add( yellow );

        // intersect is the things that are in hs1 AND in hs2
        Collection <Color> intersect = hs1;
        boolean ok = intersect.retainAll(hs2);

        System.out.println("intersect:   " + intersect);

    }
}
```

Running this code results in this output:

```
intersect:   [java.awt.Color[r=0,g=255,b=0],
              java.awt.Color[r=255,g=0,b=0]]
```

Java has a type Color in the GUI library. Colors are stored as bytes containing the level of RGB (red/green/blue) shading for a monitor. If you inspect the output, you'll confirm that indeed the intersection of the two collections is green, red. We should note that these methods (addAll(), retainAll(), and removeAll()) are promised by the Collection interface, so you can use them on any Collection data structure including linked lists, not just on sets! The Collection framework is very powerful, and will save you many hours of programming once you master it.

You would use a HashSet when you have a collection that is not going to have duplicates and you want fast retrieval.

TreeSet

The fourth and final concrete Collection class that we'll mention is the TreeSet class. This class is a set (i.e., collection of arbitrary elements), and it has the additional feature that the elements are kept in a way that makes it easy to fetch them in ascending order of elements.

TreeSet automatically sorts an element into its correct place in the collection whenever you add it! The sort order will either be the natural order for the class, as expressed by Comparable, or the order defined by a Comparator that you pass to the constructor. When you get an Iterator for a TreeSet, it is guaranteed to deliver the elements in this order.

A TreeSet collection is implemented by ("has a") a TreeMap behind the scenes. TreeMap in turn uses a red/black tree as its data structure. If you haven't met red/black trees yet, they are a variety of binary tree that is always kept balanced.

TreeSet works just like HashSet, but it takes a little extra work to keep everything in sorted order. Therefore, you will choose TreeSet when the ordering of the elements is important to you, and HashSet otherwise. There's no sense in incurring a performance penalty if you don't need to.

TreeSet has a few additional methods of its own, relating to the fact that it keeps elements in order. The extra features it offers, over and above Collection, are:

```
public class TreeSet<E>   extends AbstractSet<E>
          implements SortedSet<E>, Cloneable, java.io.Serializable {
    public TreeSet(); // constructors
    public TreeSet(Comparator);
    public TreeSet(Collection);
    public TreeSet(SortedSet<E> s);

    public SortedSet subSet(E from, E to);
    public SortedSet headSet(E lessThan);
    public SortedSet tailSet(E gte);

    public Comparator comparator();
    public E first();
    public E last();
    public Object clone();
}
```

The methods `first()` and `last()` obviously return you the lowest and highest element currently in the collection. The method `headSet()` returns a view of this Collection, containing only elements that are strictly less than the argument object. The method `tailSet()` returns a view of elements that are greater than or equal to the argument object. The method `subSet()` returns a view into the collection that holds only objects starting at the from object inclusive, and going up to but not including the to object.

The four constructors of TreeSet shown will instantiate, respectively, an empty TreeSet, an empty tree set that will use this comparator, a TreeSet containing the elements in this collection, and a TreeSet containing the elements in this SortedSet. SortedSet is an interface that is only implemented by one class in the JDK: TreeSet. It is there so you can use it if you extend the framework with your own classes and designs.

The Collections Helper Class

As we mentioned above, there is a "helper" class that contains about 50 static methods and nested classes that operate on or return a Collection. Here's the API for that class **Collections**, simplified to omit generic parameters.

We'll first show the class, then look at generic parameters in more detail.

```
public class Collections extends Object {
    public static final Set EMPTY_SET;
    public static final List EMPTY_LIST;
    public static final Map EMPTY_MAP;

    public static void sort(List);
    public static void sort(List, Comparator);
    public static int binarySearch(List, Object);
    public static int iteratorBinarySearch(List, Object);
    public static int binarySearch(List, Object, Comparator);
    public static int iteratorBinarySearch(List, Object, Comparator);
    public static void reverse(List);
    public static void shuffle(List);
    public static void shuffle(List, Random);
    public static void swap(List, int, int);
    public static void fill(List, Object);
    public static void copy(List, List);
    public static void rotate(List, int);
    public static boolean replaceAll(List, Object, Object);
    public static int indexOfSubList(List, List);
    public static int lastIndexOfSubList(List, List);
    public static List nCopies(int, Object);
    public static List list(Enumeration);

    public static Object min(Collection);
    public static Object min(Collection, Comparator);
    public static Object max(Collection);
    public static Object max(Collection, Comparator);
    public static Collection synchronizedCollection(Collection);

    public static Set synchronizedSet(Set);
    public static SortedSet synchronizedSortedSet(SortedSet);
    public static List synchronizedList(List);
    public static Map synchronizedMap(Map);
    public static SortedMap synchronizedSortedMap(SortedMap);

    public static Set singleton(Object);
    public static List singletonList(Object);
    public static Map singletonMap(Object, Object);
    public static Comparator reverseOrder();
    public static Enumeration enumeration(Collection);
}
```

About half of the methods provide further List operations, including sorting and searching. These operations are not needed for Sets because there is a subtype of Set that is defined to be held in sorted order. The API documentation has the full description of each of these methods.

One useful thing is to sort a List into order. The helper class java.util.Collections contains a static method that sorts a List. Here's an example List of String.

```
LinkedList <String> cs = new LinkedList<String>();
// code to add elements
cs.add( "data" );
cs.add( "element" );
cs.add( "boolean" );
cs.add( "computer" );
cs.add( "algorithm" );
```

Here's the one-liner (excellent!) to sort that list:

```
Collections.sort( cs );
System.out.println("lexicographic order: " + cs );
```

Here's how to compile and run the code:

```
% javac -source 1.5 example.java
% java example
lexicographic order: [algorithm, boolean, computer, data, element]
```

Comparable and Comparator

You might wonder how the Collections class is able to sort a List: how does it know how elements are compared with each other? The answer is that you tell it. You tell Collections or anyone who is interested how objects-of-your-class-in-a-collection are ordered by implementing one of two available interfaces:

- java.lang.Comparable – Implement this interface when there is a single obvious natural ordering for the objects.

```
public interface java.lang.Comparable<T> {
    public int compareTo( T rhs);
}
```

We described this generic interface in the previous chapter. String implements Comparable, with a natural ordering of alphabetic. They call it "lexicographic order," rather than "alphabetic order," because lots of string values are digits, punctuation, or other non-alphabetic characters.

- java.util.Comparator – Implement this generic interface when there are several equally good orderings for the objects. Create one Comparator for each ordering you want to offer.

```
public interface java.util.Comparator <T> {
    public int compare(T lhs, T rhs);
    public boolean equals(Object comp);
}
```

The compare() method returns a negative, zero, or positive int, for <, equal, > exactly like Comparable's compareTo().

The `equals()` method is a tricky one. It is used to check two Comparators (*not* the objects they are comparing) to see if they are the same. If the Comparators are the same, and your List is already in the order of one of them, you don't need to sort it again. Usually you leave this method out and let your Comparator inherit the `equals()` method from Object.

Any class implementing one of these interfaces must be very careful to keep the normal mathematical properties expected of comparisons. If a equals b, and b equals c, then it is expected that a equals c. Further, a should equal a, and the method should be consistent with its own or any parent object's `equal()` method. The API documentation has a lengthy discussion of this topic.

A common optimization is wrong!

A common technique for comparing one quantity with another, returning the result as a negative/zero/positive quantity, is to use subtraction:

```
public int compareTo(int lhs, int rhs) {
    return (lhs-rhs);
}
```

So, if you were comparing 7 and -3, the answer is 7 - -3, or +10, which is positive, indicating that 7 is indeed bigger than -3. You get a three-way comparison in one line of code. This technique is widely used and is independent of programming language. It works as long as the operation fits in 32 bits, but disastrously returns the wrong answer when the subtraction overflows.

Recall from Chapter 7 that ints never give an overflow exception, except for division by zero. The result just rolls over like an odometer. If you subtract two numbers that cause such a rollover, you may get the wrong answer. You can only compare using subtraction when you are certain the values cannot overflow, or when the operands are unsigned as with type char.

Why `compare` and `compareTo` have different arguments

You may wonder why Comparator.compare takes two Object arguments, where Comparable.compareTo takes a "this" and one Object argument. The reason is that Comparable is used for natural order. By definition there is only one natural order for each class. Therefore, its comparison method might as well be put in the class directly.

Comparator is used to give any order you like, so there may be several Comparators for a given class. At most, one of these could go into the class (further ones would be disallowed because you cannot have multiple methods with the same signature in the same class).

It is, therefore, convenient to implement Comparator with a separate class, perhaps statically nested in, rather than a method of, the class you are comparing. Once it is not a method of the class you are comparing, the "this" no longer refers to objects you are comparing, and you have to explicitly pass those objects as two arguments. The comparison methods have different names to emphasize the difference between the interfaces.

The class java.lang.String has a Comparator, as well as implementing Comparable. The Comparator is implemented as a static nested class that is private inside the String class, and which does a comparison ignoring letter case.

```
private static class CaseInsensitiveComparator
                implements Comparator, java.io.Serializable {
       public int compare(Object o1, Object o2) {
         // 20 lines of code, omitted
       }
}
```

Then, also inside String, the Comparator is instantiated and made publicly available as part of String's API:

```
public static final Comparator CASE_INSENSITIVE_ORDER
                              = new CaseInsensitiveComparator();
```

The point of that is that String exports one case insensitive comparator, and you cannot declare your own copies, or extend String's one.

It's time to present the final piece of generics, and we'll use the class java.util.Collections as our example in the next section.

Wildcard Parameters and Generic Methods

The final piece of generics relates to the interaction between *generic type parameters* and *methods*. Most of the generic features we have seen so far are intended for API and library programmers. The main thing regular programmers need to remember is that:

```
public class HashSet <E> { /*more code*/
```

means that (to use this class) you will declare and instantiate a HashSet to work with a specific type:

```
HashSet<Timestamp> ht = new HashSet<Timestamp>();
```

The generic features presented in this section are different. These features are intended for use by regular programmers. You'll need these features in your own code, when you use somebody else's generic class.

There are two main generic-related features we are going to cover. Both of them concern methods and generics. The two features are:

- **Expressing various bounds on a generic** that is used as a method parameter. Here's an example method signature with a generic parameter:

  ```
  static void shuffle(List<Double> list)
  ```

  We need a way to get rid of that too-detailed <Double> and express "this method can work with a List of <AnyType> or <AnySubclassOf T> or <AnySuperclassOf T>".

- **Parameterizing a method**, (rather than a class or interface) with a generic parameter. From our experience with generic classes, we would expect to write a generic method something like this:

  ```
  static <genericParam> void sort(List<genericParam> list)
  ```

We'll cover these new features in this order in the next two major sections.

Wildcarding a Generic Parameter

Say we want to write a method that will shuffle the elements in a Collection. We can shuffle a list regardless of what type the elements are. We don't want to have to write one shuffle method that works on List<Integer> and another for List<String> and another for List<Byte>. We need to give shuffle() a parameter that is a *"List of anything"* and have it move elements around. The usual way to express "List of anything" is "List of Object", which in the new world of generics is written "List <Object>"

363

However, there's a big problem with passing around a nice, type-safe, homogeneous "List <String>" and letting someone untrustworthy, like our shuffle() method, get their hands on it as a "List <Object>" A parameter that points to a "List <Object>" can easily be used to add *any* Objects to the list: Strings, Integers, Timestamps, or anything else. The whole generics initiative is about limiting collections to only hold one type of object, and endowing the compiler with the information to check this. Unhappily List<Object> would blow our type-safe homogeneous collection model out of the water.

There's a piece of new syntax introduced here to express "parameterized type, but I don't care what it was parameterized with, they all match". It's called a *wildcard*, and it's written like this:

```
LinkedList <?>
```

You pronounce it "LinkedList of unknown", and it's intended to make you think of regular expression symbols where a "?" matches any single character. LinkedList<?> is the superclass of every LinkedList<T>. Collection<?> is "any class that implements Collection". Wildcards can be used with any parameterized type. This is the actual declaration of the shuffle() method in class java.util.Collections

```
static void shuffle(List<?> mylist, Random rnd)
```

Shuffle will thus take an argument that is a List of any type, just as we need.

With <?> come a couple of rules to preserve type safety:

• The compiler will treat parameterized types as incompatible with each other. I.e. List<A> and List<B> are incompatible and can't be assigned to each other, even when the types A and B are parent and child. The compiler must prevent an assignment like this:

```
LinkedList <Number> parent;
LinkedList <Integer> child;    // Integer is a subclass of Number
parent = child;  // compiler must reject this as "inconvertible"
```

• The elements of an array can be an unbounded wildcard type, such as List<?>,

```
List<?>[] arrayOfLists;  // OK
```

but no other kind of generic type is acceptable in an array.

```
List<Integer>[] arrayOfLists; // NOT ALLOWED!!
```

To expand on that last point, a declaration "List<?>[] arrayOfLists;" says *"arrayOfLists is an array; each element of the array holds a list of unknown type"*. You can therefore do list operations on an array element, but if you pull an individual element out, you can only do object operations on it. Furthermore, the list is

MILLS COLLEGE
LIBRARY

incompatible with any other kind of list you might have, even a parent or child of the actual type.

Here is how you would declare and initialize an array containing an unbounded wildcard type:

```
List<?>[] arrayOfLists = new List<?>[128];
```

Here is something (a List of anything) that you could put in the array:

```
LinkedList<Double> ld = new LinkedList<Double>();
ld.add( 2.71 );
```

Here is how you could put it into the arrayOfLists:

```
arrayOfLists[0] = ld;
```

You could use the array as an actual parameter:

```
example(arrayOfLists);
```

Here is the corresponding method body that uses the array as a formal parameter:

```
static public void example(List<?>[] arrayOfLists) {
    List<?> list = arrayOfLists[0];
    int size = list.size();
}
```

Inside the method you can invoke methods of List, such as size(), on elements of the array parameter.

Bounds on wildcards

There are two refinements of a wildcard on a generic parameter: forcing a wildcard generic parameter to be a *subtype* of something, and forcing it to be a *supertype* of something. Remember bounds—the feature that allowed you to force a generic type parameter to extend some other class? Here's a reminder:

```
class Example <T extends java.lang.Number>
```

That says *"When you instantiate this class, the actual type parameter must be Number or a subclass of Number, and therefore I can call methods of Number on objects of type T inside class Example"*.

It's possible to add bounds to a wildcard, to require that the parameter of the parameterized type implement some interface or extend some class. That way you can rely on those methods being available, and you can call them from inside your method.

The abstract class Number is the superclass of classes BigDecimal, BigInteger, Byte, Double, Float, Integer, Long, and Short. Say you wanted to process linked lists of Numbers, and keep it all type-safe. Here is the syntax:

```
LinkedList<? extends Number>
```

You could use it as the argument to a method that prints the first element of any list of numbers:

```
static void printFirst(LinkedList<? extends Number> n) {
    Number e = n.getFirst();
    System.out.println(e);
}
```

You could set up some lists of Numbers and call your printFirst() method as follows:

```
LinkedList<Double> ld = new LinkedList<Double>();
ld.add( 2.71 );
printFirst( ld );

LinkedList<Integer> li = new LinkedList<Integer>();
li.add( 21 );
printFirst( li );
```

The key point here is that we have a way to express a formal parameter to a method such that it can accept many different varieties of a generic type as the actual parameter. The terminology is that "Number is the *upper bound*" of the wildcard. Use an upper bound on a wildcard when you want to process elements from several collections of related types, in a type-safe way. Inside printFirst you can invoke any of the methods of LinkedList on the argument, n. You can invoke any of the methods of Number on elements that you get from the list. You are not allowed to use the wildcarded variable, n, to write into the linked list.

Lower bounds on wildcards

You can also specify a *lower bound* on a generic that's a parameter to one of your methods:

```
LinkedList<? super Integer>
```

That denotes a type that is required to be the class Integer or a superclass (parent class). The superclasses of Integer are Number and then Object. It's the opposite of requiring a type to be a child class, and so this is called a *lower bound*.

The most common use of a lower bound is in conjunction with assignments. An instance of a superclass can always hold an instance of one of its child classes. If a programmer tells the compiler *this thing has to be Integer or a supertype of Integer*, pretty soon you'll probably see it get assigned an object of *this other thing that has to be Integer or a subtype of Integer*.

Generic Methods

So far we have seen the wildcard feature used to give the methods you write some minimal knowledge about parameters that are generic types. You may be surprised (appalled, dismayed, horrified, or even delighted) to learn that individual methods can also be generic. In other words, there is a way to parameterize your methods with one or more type parameters.

As with classes, the type parameters are spelled out in angle brackets before the variable parameters. The type parameter comes immediately before the return type for the method, and after any access modifier. Here is the printFirst() method from the previous section rewritten to be a generic method:

```
public <T> void printFirst(LinkedList <T> e) { }
```

The generic parameter, T, comes before the method name to make the job of parsing easier for the compiler. It also separates the generic parameters away from the method signature. Once you have given names to the type parameters, like T here, you can use them in the argument list or the method body. Here we are using T to say that printFirst() takes an argument which is a LinkedList of T, whose name is e.

It may be that the return type uses the parameter type in some way, in which case you'll have two sets of angle brackets together, as in this example from the Java API:

```
static <T> Set<T> emptySet()
```

static	<T>	Set<T>	emptySet()
Modifiers	Generic parameter	Return type	Method signature

The method emptySet() has one type parameter, T, and it returns a value "set of T".

Let's emphasize that this feature is intended for your methods that have parameters that are collection types. If you don't write code to pass around and process collection types, you probably won't need to use generic methods.

There's a difference between generic methods and generic classes. You never pass actual type arguments to a generic method, but you have to do this with a generic class. In the case of a generic method, the compiler looks at the types used in the method call, and figures out what actual type the generic type must be. The rule of thumb is that it chooses the most specific type argument that will make the call type-correct. So it would prefer Integer to Number, and it would prefer Number to Object.

Since we can implement some methods using either feature, wildcards or generics, you may wonder how to choose between them. Here are the guidelines.

1. Choose wildcards when you want to convey the message "this method works on all the subtypes". E.g. "this method works on a LinkedList of anything". This is preferred over saying "this is a LinkedList of Object".

2. Sun advises that wildcards are "clearer and more concise" than generic methods, so wildcards are preferred when you have a choice.

3. Use a generic method when you need to express a subtle connection or dependency between the argument types and/or the return type of a method. For example we mentioned above the generic method emptySet():

```
static <T> Set<T> emptySet()
```

Here the generic parameter is type <T> . The return type, which is Set<T>, depends on that type. We cannot express the return type except in terms of T. So this is a proper use of a generic method.

If there is no such dependency, do not use a generic method.

Combining a generic method with a wildcard

Just when you thought it couldn't get any better, here comes the news that it's possible to *combine* a generic method with a wildcard. Here's the JDK 1.4 declaration of the static method Collections.copy().

```
static void copy(List dest, List src)
```

The copy() method copies all of the elements from the source list into the destination list. In JDK 1.5, the method changed to:

```
public static <T> void copy(List<? super T> dest, List<? extends T> src)
```

Breaking it down piece by piece,

- copy() is a method with one generic parameter, T
- copy() has two ordinary parameters, dest and src
- dest can be a List of any type T or superclass of T
- src can be a List of any type T or subclass of T

The thrust of that should jump off the page at you. It's saying when we assign "dest = src" the destination has to be a type that can hold the source. In other words, assignments like "ParentType = ChildType" are OK, but not the other way round.

Decoding the generics

Here's the promised decoding of:

```
public static <T extends Comparable<? super T>>void sort(List<T> list)
```

Reading from the inside out is the best way of decoding this. As you can see there's a method called "sort" that takes a generic parameter that's a "List of T".
The angle brackets tip us off that this is a generic parameter. The method has to describe its generic parameter, and the description appears right before the void return value. T is a type that must implement the Comparable interface. Specifically, the Comparable interface must have been implemented for type T, or any of T's parent classes. Phew!

That wraps up the last part of generic types, and how you will see them used in the class java.util.Collections. The rest of the chapter is dedicated to reviewing the Map interface and related types that store pairs of values.

Summary of Collection

- JDK 1.2 introduced support for Collections, also known as "container classes." There are two basic interfaces that extend Collection in different directions, Set and List.

- A List is a collection that has an order associated with its elements. That order is the order in which the elements were added to the collection. There does not need to be any logical relationship between elements.

- The List interface is implemented by two concrete classes, LinkedList and ArrayList. LinkedList is a doubly linked list. The time to access elements depends on where they are in the list, but there is no overhead to growing or shrinking the collection. ArrayList is a list stored as an array. It provides quick access to any element, but it is expensive to grow or shrink the array.

- A Set is a collection that never has any duplicate objects. Unlike a mathematical set, the objects may come in some order, but it is not the order in which you add them to the collection.

- The Set interface is implemented by two concrete classes, HashSet and TreeSet. HashSet is a set backed by hash table. It is quick to add and retrieve elements, but the elements are in no particular order. TreeSet is a set backed by a red/black tree. The elements are kept in sorted order, so it costs more to insert them.

- JDK 1.5 introduced support for generic classes, interfaces, and methods. The collection classes are the main user of these.

We saw the helper class for collections, and there is a similar one for arrays. These support some very useful sorting and extraction utilities for collections and arrays. It's possible to flatten any collection into an array, although you'll probably never need to.

All of these features together make up the Collections Framework, and there is one additional piece to it, which we will review in the next section. So far, all these data structures have dealt with individual objects. There is another interface backed by concrete classes that you can use to process pairs of key/values together. This is the Map interface.

Map, HashMap, and TreeMap

Map is a data structure interface that connects keys and values. Each key has at most one associated value. Some examples of key/value pairs would be driver's license number and "Object representing a licensed driver", username and password, ISBN and book title. The first of each of these pairs is a key for uniquely retrieving the second. The most obvious way of storing a Map is as a two-column table, and you can get fancier from there.

The Map interface provides three views onto its collection of keys/values. You can see the map as a collection of keys, or as a collection of values, or as a collection of key/value pairs. Once you have these collections back, you can invoke the standard Collection method to get an iterator and visit all the elements.

The order of a map is defined as the order in which the iterators on a map's collection views return their elements. Some Map implementations, like the TreeMap class, make specific guarantees as to their order; others, like the HashMap, do not.

The Map interface looks like this:

```
public interface java.util.Map <K, V> {
    public java.util.Set<K> keySet();          // get keys
    public java.util.Collection<V> values();   // get values
    public java.util.Set<Map.Entry<K,V>> entrySet();// get mappings

    public boolean containsKey(Object);
    public boolean containsValue(Object);

    public V get(Object key);
    public V put(K key, V value);
    public void putAll(Map<? extends K,? extends V> t);

    public V remove(Object key);
    public boolean isEmpty();
    public int size();
    public void clear();
    public boolean equals(Object);
    public int hashCode();

    public static interface java.util.Map.Entry<K, V> {
        public K getKey();
        public V getValue();
        public V setValue(V v);
        public boolean equals(Object o);
        public int hashCode();
    }
}
```

The keys, values, and mappings are returned as collections so that you can easily compare entire maps to one another, and answer questions like "does this map have all the keys that are in that map?" or "does this map have any values in common with that map?" You answer these kind of questions by using the set difference, intersection, and union operations that we have already seen for collections.

If you have a class that implements map, you can iterate over all its mappings like this:

```
Set<Map.Entry<String,String>> s = myMap.entrySet();
for (Map.Entry<String,String> me : s) {
```

The set returned by entrySet() is a collection of objects that belong to the static nested interface java.util.Map.Entry. You can then get an iterator for that Set, and each object that it returns will belong to type (class that implements Map.Entry). You can invoke any of the methods promised in the nested interface on that returned object. You can get each key in turn, or get/set each value in turn.

```
        // nested inside the for loop, above
        String k = me.getKey();
        String v = me.getValue();
}
```

To review, the objects ok and ov represent a single entry in the Map. The object ok is the key for value ov. We got the entry set from the Map, we get the key and value from the entry set.

Maps and their concrete subclasses are part of the Collections Framework, but they are not in themselves collections. You can get pieces from them that are collections, but Map is not a subinterface of Collection.

In the next section, we'll look at a couple of concrete classes that implement Map. Before we do that, we'll briefly outline how hash tables work, and what it means for you in practice.

What Is a hash table?

A hash table is a data structure that stores keys/values like an ordinary table, but offers fast retrieval. A symbol table in a compiler is often maintained as a hash table. When a name is first read in from the source program, it is *hashed,* or converted to a table index—say, 379—by an algorithm designed to spread the hash keys around the table. It is then entered in the table at location 379 along with its value (the unhashed name, type, scope, etc.).

Then, when you get the same name again, it is hashed, and the same result, 379, is used as a subscript for immediate access to all its details in the hash table. It is marvelous that a hash table is a library data structure in Java!

If two or more elements hash to the same index value, the extra ones are stored in a linked list, hanging off that table entry.

Why is a hash table better than just maintaining a sorted list or vector? Because hashing is fast, and sorting is slow.

Now the purpose of the method hashCode() in class java.lang.Object should be clear. It ensures that every single object in the system has a hashcode, and thus can be put in a hash table without further work on your part. The hashcode is a 32-bit int, and the hash table algorithm will typically reduce it modulo the size of the table, and take the remainder as an index value.

The hashcode returned by Object.hashCode() looks like the address of the object in virtual memory, which is a good way of ensuring that unique objects have unique hashcodes. That's fine for many classes, but not so fine for others. There are some classes where objects can be unique (i.e., at different memory addresses) but still be equal.

String is an example of a class with that property. I may have a String object that holds the value "mudflap". For all purposes, the content of the string should be used to determine equality to some other String, not the unique memory address. I want any other string with those characters to compare equal. Therefore, the `Object.hashCode()` isn't very useful for String, and the String class should override it.

String does override `Object.hashCode()`, and it replaces the method with one where the hashcode is calculated based on the characters in the string. The algorithm takes each character in the String and multiplies it by 31 to the power i, where i is the character offset within the String. It sums all these values to get the hash for a given string. (Another way of looking at this is that, loosely, it converts the String to a base 31 int.)

String also overrides `java.lang.Object.equals()` and replaces it with an equality test that looks at content, not address. There is a rather large pitfall here that you must be careful to avoid. You must always make sure that you override `equals()` and `hashCode()` in pairs, and you must make sure they are implemented in mutually compatible ways. If two objects compare equal, then their hashCodes must have the same value too.

If you fail to follow these precautions, then any use of Maps on your object will give undefined values. You may know all the places that you use maps in your own code, but it's hard to be aware of when the run-time library is using a Map on some of your classes on your behalf. So the only safe course is to follow the rule, and make certain that if two objects compare equal, their hashCodes must have the same value too.

HashMap implements Map

The class java.util.HashMap implements the Map interface. It uses a hash table to minimize the searching on every lookup and it implements Map, hence, the name HashMap. You should now use this class where formerly you might have used JDK 1.0's Hashtable.

HashMap is a supremely useful class. Hash tables allow you store together any number of key/value pairs. Instead of storing items with index values 0, 1, 2, 3, as you would in an array, you provide the key to be associated with the object. Then in the future, you need provide only that key again, and voila, out pops the right object.

Here are the public members of HashMap, over and above what is promised by the Map interface that it implements:

```
public class java.util.HashMap <K, V>
      implements Map<K, V>, Cloneable, java.io.Serializable {

    public HashMap(int size, float load);
    public HashMap(int size);
    public HashMap();
    public HashMap(Map<? extends K,? extends V> m);

    public Object clone();
}
```

It has four constructors and a public clone() method. The size and load arguments to the constructors specify the initial size (number of elements) of the table, and the fraction of the table which can become full before it is reallocated to a bigger size. As a rule of thumb, a load factor of 0.75 seems to work quite well, and this is the default that the library uses. The last constructor does what you'd expect: constructs a new map with the same mappings as the given map.

HashMap has fail fast iterators, and is not synchronized. Here is some example code that uses a hash map to hold a company phone book containing names and corresponding extension numbers:

```
import java.util.*;
public class example2  {
    // the Map!
    Map<String, String> phonebook = new HashMap<String, String>();

    // constructor
    public example2(String n[], String nums[]) {
        for(int i=0; i< n.length; i++)
            phonebook.put ( n[i], nums[i] );
    }

    public static void main(String[] args) {
        // data
        String [] names = { "Lefty", "Guarav", "Wong", "Rupamay" };
        String [] extns = { "4873", "4810", "3769", "0" };

        // get an instance of this class
        example2 ex = new example2( names, extns );

        // dump out the map
        System.out.println("map:  " + ex.phonebook);

        // get the mappings
        Set<Map.Entry<String,String>> s = ex.phonebook.entrySet();

        // iterate over the mappings
        //    for (Iterator i = s.iterator(); i.hasNext(); ) {
        for (Map.Entry me : s) {
            Object ok = me.getKey();
            Object ov = me.getValue();
            System.out.print("key=" + ok );
            System.out.println(", value=" + ov );
        }
    }
}
```

Compiling and running the program results in this:

```
% javac -source 1.5 example2.java
% java example2
map:   {Wong=3769, Guarav=4810, Rupamay=0, Lefty=4873}
key=Wong, value=3769
key=Guarav, value=4810
key=Rupamay, value=0
key=Lefty, value=4873
```

You can see that the collection of key/value pairs has been stored into a HashMap and can be retrieved on demand.

TreeMap

The final Collections framework class to review here is java.util.TreeMap. TreeMap has the same relationship to HashMap that TreeSet has to HashSet. In other words, TreeMap implements the Map interface, and its underlying data structure is a red/black tree.

TreeMap takes some extra cycles to do its work of inserting and retrieving keys in the tree, but it will produce its keys in sorted order on demand. If you have no need to see the keys in sorted order, use HashMap instead. In the context of our phone directory example, we may well wish to have the keys in order, as this would be useful if we wanted to output the office phone directory in alphabetic order of names.

Here are the public members of TreeMap, over and above what is promised by the Map interface that it implements:

```
public class java.util.TreeMap <K, V>
    implements SortedMap<K,V>, Cloneable, java.io.Serializable {
    public TreeMap();  // constructors
    public TreeMap(Comparator<? super K> c);
    public TreeMap(Map<? extends K,? extends V> m);
    public TreeMap(SortedMap<K,? extends V> m);

    public Comparator<? super K> comparator();
    public K firstKey();
    public K lastKey();
    public Object clone();

    public SortedMap<K,V> headMap(K toKey);
    public SortedMap<K,V> tailMap(K fromKey);
    public SortedMap<K,V> subMap(K fromKey, K toKey);
}
```

The TreeMap class has four constructors which work in the obvious way. The first one creates an empty TreeMap. The second constructor creates an empty TreeMap that will use the Comparator passed as an argument. The third creates a TreeMap out of the elements in the given Map. The fourth constructor creates a TreeMap out of the elements in the given SortedMap.

A SortedMap is a subinterface of Map. TreeMap is the only current implementor of SortedMap. It is the interface that promises all the other methods of SortedMap that are over and above those promised by Map. The other methods will get you the comparator that is in use, or null if the TreeMap is using natural order. The firstKey() and lastKey() methods return the lowest and highest keys in the Map, respectively.

The method headMap() returns a view of this Map containing only elements that are strictly less than the argument object. The method tailMap() returns a view of elements that are greater than or equal to the argument object. The method subMap() returns a view into the Map that holds only objects starting at the from object inclusive, and going up to, but not including, the to object.

As an example use of TreeMap is the phone directory program, modified to use a TreeMap by changing one line.

```java
import java.util.*;
public class example3   {
    // the Map!
    Map<String, String> phonebook = new TreeMap<String, String>();

    // constructor
    public example3(String n[], String nums[]) {
        for(int i=0; i< n.length; i++)
            phonebook.put( n[i], nums[i] );
    }

    public static void main(String[] args) {
        // data
        String [] names = { "Lefty", "Guarav", "Wong", "Rupamay" };
        String [] extns = { "4873", "4810", "3769", "0" };

        // get an instance of this class
        example3 ex = new example3( names, extns );

        // dump out the map
        System.out.println("map:   " + ex.phonebook);

        // get the mappings
        Set<Map.Entry<String,String>> s = ex.phonebook.entrySet();

        // iterate over the mappings
        //    for (Iterator i = s.iterator(); i.hasNext(); ) {
        for (Map.Entry me : s) {
            Object ok = me.getKey();
            Object ov = me.getValue();
            System.out.print("key=" + ok );
            System.out.println(", value=" + ov );
        }
    }
}
```

The output of running this program is now in sorted order because we used TreeMap:

```
map:   {Guarav=4810, Lefty=4873, Rupamay=0, Wong=3769}
key=Guarav, value=4810
key=Lefty, value=4873
key=Rupamay, value=0
key=Wong, value=3769
```

Most of the time you won't be querying a Map for all its mappings. Most of the time you'll have a key and want to look up the corresponding value using this method:

```
public V get(Object key);
```

Or you'll be putting pairs into the table using this method:

```
public V put(K key, V value);
```

And that thought concludes this chapter.

Exercises

1. (Collections) Here is the outline of a class that provides access to its data structure through an iterator. Write the iterator.

```
class storage {

    private Object[] data = new Object[256];

    // don't allow access to anything not yet stored
    private int nextEmptySlot = 0;
    private int i=0;

    public Iterator iterator() {
        // returns a class that iterates over the data array
        return new Iterator() {
        // insert the body of the inner class here
        // 3 methods: remove(), hasNext(), next()
        };
    }
}
```

2. (Collections) Take the storage class from the previous question and add all the code necessary to make it implement the Collection interface. Make the type of the object stored a generic parameter. Limit the number of objects in the collection, and hence the size of the array to 128 elements. Throw an UnsupportedOperationException if someone tries to add element number 129.

3. (Collections) Take the storage class from the previous question and remove any limit on the number of data items held in the collection. If you try to add an element when there is no more room in the array, then allocate a new, larger array, and use System.arraycopy() to fill it with the contents of the old

array. Hint: Add the extra code in a subclass that overrides the methods of the parent class. That way, you simply inherit all the things that you do not need to change.

Some Light Relief—Early Names for Java

When Shakespeare wrote "A rose by any other name would smell as sweet" (Romeo and Juliet, Act II, Sc 1), he hadn't seen the effects of modern marketing, consumer branding, and product positioning. Names are incredibly important to the positioning of a product. First impressions count for way too much, and (you'll be horrified to learn) people do indeed judge books by their covers.

Names sometimes arise from the most fortuitous of circumstances. Linus Torvalds (himself named after two-time Nobel laureate Linus Pauling) planned to call Linux "Freax" because it was free and freaky. But his friend Ari Lemmke gave him an FTP directory called /pub/OS/Linux, and the name stuck. While still at college, Red Hat founder Marc Ewing was given his grandfather's Cornell lacrosse team cap (with red and white stripes). Marc lost track of it, and searched with increasing desperation. The manual for the original Red Hat Linux beta appealed to readers to return Marc's Red Hat if found. We're lucky that distribution isn't called Red-and-White-striped Lacrosse Cap Linux.

Would Java have been a runaway success if it was called "Oak"? It *was* called Oak for most of its early development years starting in 1991. James Gosling, the master programmer, Sun VP, and Sun Fellow behind the language, named it after the view from his office window. James's office was at 2180 Sand Hill Road, Palo Alto, California, on the fourth floor of the old Bank of America building. From the window he could see a large oak tree. When he needed a name for the language he was developing, what could be more handy than to look out of the window waiting for inspiration to strike?

The name Oak was short, natural, familiar, but it didn't have that edge, that buzz, that sizzle successful products need. But worse than that, years later, as Sun was planning to go public with Oak, the name failed a trademark search! There was a video card manufacturer called Oak Technology who held the rights. As a stop-gap, Oak was bogusly renamed to O.A.K. for Object Application Kernel. This was done so the source code didn't need to be changed, but a real name change was needed.

Oak was recognizably Java at this point. Patrick Naughton and Jonathan Payne had used it to create the Webrunner prototype web browser. The pair then got downloadable applets working in a weekend. By now it was January 1995, and the 1.0a2 semi-public alpha release was planned for March 1995. So a brainstorming session was called for all Oak team members, to come up with ideas for a new name. Table 16-1 is the shortlist taken into the meeting, and Java isn't even on it!

It was a impassioned meeting with a lot of suggestions and counter-suggestions hurled about. By now, the team had moved to new offices, the old DEC Western Research Lab at 100 Hamilton Avenue in Palo Alto. If you visit this building, you'll see it looks more like a water pipe factory than an office. Like the Pompidou Center in Paris, it makes a feature of exposing all the ducts and piping. At some point someone (no one recalls who) suggested Java, after the favorite brew from Peets Coffeehouse nearby. Some people liked it, some people didn't but it was added to the list. When the company lawyers reviewed all the names, they cleared three possibilities from a trademark standpoint: Java, DNA, and Silk.

A vote was then held. Every person ranked the three names in their order of preference. The vote revealed that the name DNA got the most "most liked" and the most "least liked" votes. So DNA was dropped. James Gosling seemed to favor Java over Silk, and Java now got the most votes. Kim Polese, as product manager, had the final say over the name. After four years as Oak, just a few weeks before release, the new name was Java. Sun started the trademark process, free access on the web soon ignited a firestorm of interest, and this rose could have no better name.

As a postscript, I should mention that there are some other stories about where the name came from. I'm almost afraid to write this down, in case it gives the stories more currency. One story claims Java was derived from the initials of individuals involved in the project. It's nonsense. We can form a backronym for anything! Another story has one team member saying they alone thought of the name. None of the other team members recollect it that way.

Table 16–1   Proposed names before Java was suggested

Candidate name	Comments from the Oak team
Calypso	Trademarked already?
Caravelle	Style of ship used for exploration (the Nina, Pinta and Santa Maria were caravelles).
C+-	
D	
OaK	CaPiTaLiZaTiOn?
Oak	Just leave well enough alone. How bad is the trademark situation really? Do we need a trademark?
Oak language	Does extending it make it trademarkable?
Sandal	Secure, Architecture-Neutral, Distributed Language. Has a friendly feeling to it.
Webjive	Sounds like fun, not a product...
Zygote	Just sounds cool.
Folio	Since I don't think we actually have the trademark for folio: Parquet – A mosaic made of wood Marquetry – A mosaic made of wood veneer
Silk	What webs are made out of.
Tycho, Turing, Descartes, Fermat, Azure, Crisp, Idyl, Intelliweb, Infolang, Netlang, Webscript, Webchat, DNA	

Simple Input Output

SCSI-wuzzy was a bus.
SCSI-wuzzy caused no fuss.
SCSI-wuzzy wasn't very SCSI, was he?

Designing input/output (henceforth "I/O") libraries is a lot harder than it might appear. There have been some spectacular blunders in the past. One language, Algol 60, gave up on I/O altogether, leaving it out of the language specification and making it an implementation-defined detail! Pascal has the deficiency that you can't test for end-of-file until you have read from the file, distorting all while loops that control input. The C library gets() call to read a string from a stream is probably the biggest single security hole in the history of computing.

It was responsible for the November 1988 Morris Worm that permeated all the then 50,000 (!) hosts on the Internet.[1] Classic Fortran I/O is so ugly because John Backus's team decided to reuse an existing IBM 704 assembler library instead of designing their own language support.

Getting to Know Java I/O

We'll start off by giving you an idea of what the problems are with Java I/O (we'll get all the gripes off our chest in one go). Then we'll look at the purpose of the java.io and mention the names of some of the many packages that make up the Java I/O library.

Java I/O problems

So what are the problems with Java I/O? It boils down to this: it is a very large library and it took six release with four different implementations to get it mostly right. Excessive use of the wrapper design pattern confuses rather than helps. It relies too much on the C I/O API.

Package java.io has about 75 classes and interfaces. Size alone doesn't make an API poor, but there are too many low-value classes (like SequenceInputStream) and it took until JDK 1.5 to get decent support for interactive I/O. Sun got I/O internationalization wrong the first time and had to add many more classes in JDK 1.1 to properly cope with Unicode. The Java I/O package is not intuitive to use, and there are a number of peculiar design choices often reflecting the use of the underlying standard C I/O library. That's the same mistake the Fortran team committed 40 years earlier. Finally, because this library makes heavy use of wrapper classes, you may need to use two or three classes to do simple I/O. Apart from all that, it's really a fine API.

Purpose of java.io package

Enough of the criticism. Obviously, the purpose of the java.io package is to conduct I/O on data and on objects. You will use the java.io package and others to write your data into disk files, into sockets, into URLs, and to the system console, and to read it back again. There is some support for formatting character data, and for processing zip and jar files. Several other packages are involved in this, and the key ones are listed in Table 17–1. The point of presenting this table is to indicate the vast range of Java I/O features.

1.   See The Cornell Commission on Morris and the worm; T. Eisenberg, D. Gries, J. Hartmanis, D. Holcomb, M. S. Lynn and T. Santoro; Commun. ACM vol. 32, 6 (June 1989), pp. 706–709).

What is a wrapper?

Wrapping an object means accessing its features through some other object, known as the "wrapper." The wrapper object will augment or improve the features available from the first object. You use the wrapper exclusively, and it in turn will invoke the wrapped object methods as it needs them. Wrapping is widely used in the Java I/O library. In the real world, you might "wrap" a sprinkler with a hosepipe so you get the functionality of water transmission through the hose, with the value-added feature at the end of distributing it in fine drops to irrigate your lawn.

As a programming example, say you had a class that takes ordinary text and prints it out as really nice reports, with page numbers and justified margins, etc. Suppose you also had a second class that translates French text into English text. You could design the translating class so that it "wrapped" the printing class.

The wrapper class would get a stream of French text and translate it into English, as before. Then it would automatically send the results directly on to the wrapped class, where they would be turned into a professional-quality printed document. The net effect would be a couple of classes that worked together to turn French text into nicely printed English documents. You would only need to learn the interface for the wrapper class, since you would invoke all your methods on the wrapper object.

There is even a code idiom for wrapper classes. They are written with a constructor whose argument is the object they will wrap. So, first you instantiate the object that will be wrapped:

```
NicePrinter iCanPrint = new NicePrinter();
```

then you instantiate a wrapper object, passing the to-be-wrapped object as an argument.

```
FrenchToEnglish wrapper = new FrenchToEnglish( iCanPrint );
```

Behind the scenes, the wrapper object will save a copy of the thing it's wrapping, and you only deal with the wrapper from that point on. When you call a wrapper method, it will do its work and then pass the results on for further processing as appropriate to the wrapped object it saved.

```
wrapper.setInput("LesMiserables.txt");
wrapper.translateAndPrint();
// automatically sends the translation into the wrapped object
// causing an English translation to get printed nicely.
```

Clearly, these fictitious FrenchToEnglish and NicePrinter classes have only a loose affinity. The wrapped/wrapper classes in Java I/O are much more tightly coupled. The java.io class that knows how to get data from a file is a "can be wrapped" object. The java.io class that knows how to interpret a data stream as binary values is a "can wrap" object. Put them together, and the wrapper can interpret a stream of binary data from a file. You can layer several wrappers on top of each other. You deal only with the outermost one, but each does its own special value-add and sends the bits on to the next one. Wrapping is a design pattern that is also known as the "Decorator" pattern.

Table 17–1   Java packages involved with I/O

Package name	Purpose
java.io	Contains the 75 or so classes and interfaces for I/O.
java.nio	New in JDK 1.4. An API for memory-mapped I/O, non-blocking I/O, and file locking.
java.text	For formatting text, dates, numbers, and messages according to national preferences and conventions. This task can now be achieved more easily by using java.util.Formatter in conjunction with PrintWriter.format or printf.
java.util.regex	New in JDK 1.4. For matching a string against a pattern or regular expression.
java.util.zip	Used to read and write zip files.
java.util.logging	New in JDK 1.4. A framework for recording and processing system or application messages to help with later problem diagnosis and resolution.
java.util.jar	Used to read and write jar files.
javax.xml.parsers	New in JDK 1.4. An API to read in and parse XML trees. Covered in Chapter 27.
javax.imageio	New in JDK 1.4. An API for image file I/O (JPEGs, GIFs, etc.) together with common operations for handling them, such as thumbnail processing, conversions between formats, and color model adjustment.
javax.print	New in JDK 1.4. The third attempt at providing a decent enterprise-ready printing service.
javax.comm	Support for accessing serial (RS-232) and parallel (IEEE-1284) port devices. Not part of the basic JDK.
javax.sound.midi	New in JDK 1.3. Provides interfaces and classes for I/O, sequencing, and synthesis of MIDI (Musical Instrument Digital Interface) data.
javax.speech	Speech recognition and output API under development. Third-party implementations are available now. This library will have the biggest impact in Java 2 Micro Edition on telephony applications.

In this chapter we will cover the I/O basics. Chapter 18 covers more advanced I/O topics. By the end of the two I/O chapters, you will be versed in the use of the first five packages listed in Table 17–1. *Further Reading* on page 423 points out resources for more information on some of the other packages.

Design Philosophy

The design philosophy for Java I/O is based on these principles:

- **Programs that do I/O should be portable**, even though I/O has some non-portable aspects. Platform differences in file names and line terminators must be handled in a way that ensures the code runs everywhere.

- **I/O is based on streams.** A stream has a physical "device" at one end, like a file or a location in memory. That physical device is managed by some class, and you wrap (layer) additional logical classes on top of that for specific kinds of I/O.

- **There are lots of small classes that do one thing**, instead of a few big classes that do many things. There is one class that interprets data in binary format, and another class that reads data from a file. If you want to read binary data from a file, you use both of these classes. The constructors make it convenient to use the classes together.

We'll see examples of these principles throughout the chapter. This is a long chapter, but a worthy one. To help you get the most out of it, Figure 17–1 represents the topics that will be covered, and how they are grouped together. As you can see, many of the I/O topics are freestanding and only relate to each other in a general way. If you feel lost at some point in this chapter, refer back to Figure 17–1.

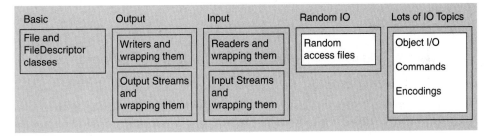

Figure 17–1   Topics in I/O

The first three boxes in Figure 17–1 are covered in this chapter, and the next two in Chapter 18, "Advanced Input Output." We'll start by looking at the File and FileDescriptor classes that provide a convenient way to represent a filename in Java. Then we'll cover Java support for interactive input (new in JDK 1.5). We'll round out the chapter by reviewing the most widely used input/output classes.

Portability of I/O

The basic portability approach of the Java run-time library is to have the same method do slightly different things appropriate to each platform. The standard end-of-line sequence on Windows is "carriage return, linefeed," while on Unix it is just "linefeed." Any library method that writes an end-of-line sequence, such as System.out.println(), will output a "carriage return, linefeed" pair on Windows, and a linefeed when running on Unix. In contrast, any string data where you wrote a literal '\n' (line feed) or '\r' (carriage return) in a string will be output on every platform exactly as you wrote it.

Table 17–2 shows some I/O-related platform differences. The column labelled *Java feature* shows the approach Java takes to minimize these differences.

Table 17–2   Platform differences in I/O

	MS Windows	Unix	Java feature
End-of-line characters	\r\n	\n	System.getProperty ("line.separator")
Filename separator	'\'	'/'	java.io.File.separator
Pathnames	*volume*:\b\c\d *or* *host**share*\c\d	/a/b/c/d	Pass pathname to program as an argument
Data byte order	Little-endian	Varies with hardware	Big-endian, see *Big-endian storage* on page 454

If you have some legacy code that requires the actual end-of-line sequence, you can obtain it with the following method call:

```
String actualEOL = java.lang.System.getProperty("line.separator");
```

That statement will put the EOL sequence used by this platform into the variable. The println() methods of PrintWriter and PrintStream also output the EOL sequence of the specific platform. The I/O API often allows a file to be identified in two parts: the directory it is in, and the filename. That allows you to split off the platform-sensitive directory pathname from the comparatively portable filename string.

There is a field in the class java.io.File that contains the filename separator, which is a backslash on Windows and a forward slash on Unix. Instead of writing a pathname as "/a/b/c.txt," you can write it using the separator character, ensuring that it will be correct on all platforms. If you insist on reducing portability by using literal strings for pathnames, remember that backslash is also the string escape character. Therefore, you have to write it twice (to escape itself) when writing literal file names for the PC. Here is an example:

```
String myFile = "\\a\\b\\c.txt";
```

You *can* actually use "/" to separate components in a Windows pathname in a program. The Windows file system calls all use it internally. The Windows interactive shell, COMMAND.COM, is the only part of the system that can't handle it. This is an interesting historical artifact, dating from the origins of MS-DOS as an unauthorized port (known as QDOS) of CP/M with a few trivial changes. That port was renamed to MS-DOS, licensed to IBM by Microsoft, only then bought by Microsoft so it could deliver on its licensing commitment, and the rest is history. Most programmers form a filename by declaring a variable with a briefer name to represent the separator character, like this:

```
final String s = java.io.File.separator;
String myFile = s + "a" + s + "b" + s + "c.txt";
```

This helps, but does not provide 100% data file portability because it doesn't mention the Windows drive. One approach to minimizing the differences is to tell the program its data filenames at run-time, either as command-line arguments or as system properties.

The Class java.io.File

The class java.io.File should really be called "Filename" since most of its methods are concerned with querying and adjusting filename, and pathname information, not the contents of a file. File can't actually do any I/O. Directory, filename and pathname information is often called "metadata," meaning "data about data." Methods of java.io.File allow you to access metadata to:

- Return a File object from a String containing a pathname

- Test whether a file exists, is readable/writable, or is a directory

- Say how many bytes are in the file and when it was last modified

- Delete the file, or create directory paths

- Get various forms of the file pathname.

Here are all the important public members of java.io.File. Method names are in bold for visibility.

Public members of java.io.File

```java
public class File implements Serializable, Comparable {
    public static final char separatorChar;
    public static final String separator;
    public static final char pathSeparatorChar;
    public static final String pathSeparator;

// constructors:
    public File(String path);
    public File(String directory,String file);
    public File(File directory,String file);

// about the file:
    public String getName();
    public String getParent();
    public File getParentFile();
    public String getPath();
    public String getAbsolutePath();
    public File getAbsoluteFile();
    public String getCanonicalPath() throws IOException;
    public File getCanonicalFile() throws IOException;

    public boolean canRead();
    public boolean canWrite();
    public boolean exists();
    public boolean isAbsolute();
    public boolean isDirectory();
    public boolean isFile();
    public boolean isHidden();
    public long lastModified();
    public long length();

// about the directory
    public String[] list();
    public String[] list(FilenameFilter);
    public File[] listFiles();
    public File[] listFiles(FilenameFilter);
    public File[] listFiles(FileFilter);
    public static File[] listRoots();
    public boolean mkdir();
    public boolean mkdirs();
// using temporary files
    public boolean createNewFile() throws IOException;
    public boolean delete();
    public void deleteOnExit();
    public static File createTempFile(String, String) throws IOException;
    public static File createTempFile(String, String, File) throws
IOException;

// miscellaneous:
    public boolean renameTo(File);
    public boolean setLastModified(long);
    public boolean setReadOnly();
    public int compareTo(File);
    public int compareTo(Object);
    public boolean equals(Object);
    public int hashCode();
    public String toString();
    public URL toURL() throws java.net.MalformedURLException;
}
```

You create a File object by giving strings for the directory and filename. The file doesn't actually have to exist when you instantiate the File object, and you can go on to create it using `createNewFile()`. You only bother to instantiate a File object if one of the operations listed previously is of interest to you. If you just want to do some I/O, then keep reading—that information is coming soon. Most of the method names in File give a clear indication of what they do. Here are the details on some of the less obvious ones.

```
public int compareTo(File);
```

This method compares the pathnames of two files for equality or otherwise. Filename comparisons are platform dependent, as Microsoft Windows does not distinguish letter case in filenames. A straight alphabetic comparison would give the wrong result on Windows, but the `compareTo()` method ensures the correct ordering for the platform.

```
public static File createTempFile(String prefix, String suffix) throws
IOException;
```

This routine creates a temporary file in the default temporary directory. A unique filename will be generated for you, and it will have the prefix and suffix that you provide. This lets you give all temporary files created by particular program names that start and end with specified letters. For instance, you could specify that all temporary files created by your mail program should use a name that starts with "mail-" and ends with ".tmp.", like mail-editchanges.tmp

There is another form of this method that takes a third parameter, a File object, to specify the directory.

```
public boolean createNewFile() throws IOException;
public void deleteOnExit();
```

These two routines could be used together to provide a simple file-locking protocol, giving exclusive access to some other file or resource. The `createNewFile()` method either atomically creates a new file, or returns "false" if the file already exists. "Atomically create" means that the check for the existence of the file, and the creation of the file if it does not exist, form a single operation. If there are several copies of your program running all making the same call at the same time, only one of them will succeed in creating the file. JDK 1.4 introduced the java.nio package, which provides more direct support for file locking.

```
public boolean mkdir();
public boolean mkdirs();
```

The first method creates just that directory. The second creates that directory plus any non-existent parent directories as needed.

```
public String[]  list();
public File[] listFiles();
```

The first method returns an array of strings representing the files and directories in the directory the method is invoked on. The second method returns the same information, but as File objects, not strings.

```
public static File[] listRoots();
```

This method lists all the available filesystems on this system. On Windows systems, the array will hold File objects for "A:\", "C:\", "D:\", and so on, allowing the programmer to learn what active drives there are. On Unix, the root drive is just "/" the root file system. On Windows, File objects for the root directories of the local and mapped network drives will be returned. Windows UNC pathnames (Universal Naming Convention pathnames that start with "//") indicate a non-local file and are not returned by this method.

FileDescriptor

The basic operating system object used to manipulate files is called a file descriptor, but you're not expected to create them or work with them much in Java.

Just to give you a brief overview, we will mention what descriptors are, and then move on to some tips on portable I/O. A file descriptor is a non-negative integer, such as0,1,2,3... etc.. It is used by the native I/O system calls to index a control structure containing data about each open file or socket. Each process has its own table of file descriptors, with each entry pointing to an entry in a system-wide file descriptor table. The size of the process descriptor table places a limit on the number of files or sockets that a process can have open simultaneously. A typical size is 256 or more file descriptors.

Java applications should not create their own file descriptors. The FileInputStream and FileOutputStream classes have methods that get the file descriptor for a file that you have open, and that open the file for a descriptor that you have. The class java.io.FileDescriptor is used when the operating system needs a file descriptor, perhaps for a JNI call, or as part of the run-time library.

Keyboard I/O

For the first nine years of its life, Java did not have any routines to do console input. The official spin from Sun was that you were supposed to use a GUI for interactive I/O. If you wanted to get input from the command line, you had to roll your own support using several classes. It was ugly, and it needlessly gave a bad impression of Java to generations of student programmers. Most teachers gave their students a class to do console I/O, and only taught the API support much later.

The JDK 1.5 release introduces a simple text scanner that can be used to read input. There is also a new method that provides a feature essentially the same as the `printf()` method used in C. We'll show examples of both of these over the next several pages.

System.in, out, and err

On all Unix operating systems and on Windows, three file descriptors are automatically opened by the shell and given to every process when it starts. File descriptor '0' is used for the standard input of the process. File descriptor '1' is used for the standard output of the process, and file descriptor '2' is used for the standard error of the process. The convention is so common because it is a part of the C language API.

These three standard connections are known as "standard in," "standard out," and "standard err" or error. Normally, the standard input gets input from the keyboard, while standard output and standard error write data to the terminal from which the process was started. Every Java program contains two predefined PrintStreams, known as "out" and "err." They are kept in Java.lang.System, and represent the command line output and error output, respectively. There is also an input stream called System.in that is the command line input. This is also referred to as console I/O or terminal I/O.

You can redirect the standard error, in, or out streams to a file or another stream (such as a socket) using these static methods:

```
System.setErr(PrintStream err);
System.setIn(InputStream in);
System.setOut(PrintStream out);
```

Stdin and stdout are used for interactive I/O. Stderr is intended for error messages only. That way, if the output of a program is redirected somewhere, the error messages still appear on the console.

Keyboard input

Before JDK 1.5, reading from System.in was a real problem. System.in had to be wrapped in a BufferedReader, and exceptions had to be handled by the programmer. To get numeric input, you needed a `readLine()` followed by a method call such as `Integer.parseInt()` to convert the String. The Scanner class simplifies this to the point where it is nearly sane.

We still don't have a single class that reads values from stdin. What we have is a more general mechanism. The new class, java.util.Scanner, can wrap certain classes that are sources of characters (in particular, any class that implements java.lang.Readable). You can then pull chunks of characters called *tokens* from the scanner, and get them interpreted as ints, longs, floats, Strings, etc.

The class java.util.Scanner

The word "scanner" is a term used by compiler-writers. Scanning means "splitting an input stream into groups-of-characters-that-belong-together (tokens)". By default, tokens are separated by whitespace (e.g. space, tab, newline). If you type at the keyboard "99 red balloons", scanning will split this into three tokens "99", "red" and "balloons". Here is how you wrap a scanner around stdin:

```
Scanner sc = new Scanner(System.in);
```

You get a scanner by calling one of the eight constructors of java.util.Scanner. The constructors of the scanner class are all private, and the static create() methods call them on your behalf. This leaves the door open for a future update that tries to *pool* or share instances of scanner (it's not done in the JDK 1.5 library).

If you know what type you are expecting to read from stdin (e.g. you just printed a message saying "Enter your age:"), you can get it like this:

```
int age = sc.nextInt();
```

This is not raw I/O that watches the input stream character-by-character. When reading from System.in, you have to type a carriage return before the input is given to your program. There is a next*Something*() method for each primitive type and for three object types, String, java.math.BigDecimal, and java.math.BigInteger.

Here are some of them:

```
public boolean nextBoolean();
public short nextShort();
public int nextInt();
public double nextDouble();
public String next();   // gets next string
public java.math.BigInteger nextBigInteger();
public java.math.BigDecimal nextBigDecimal(); /* and so on... */
```

All the next*Something*() methods skip over input that matches the delimiter pattern, and then attempt to return the next token as the stated type. All the next*Something*() methods will block if there is no input ready, which is exactly what you want with console I/O. There is no nextCharacter() because you can just read a character directly using InputStreamReader.read().

If the token cannot be interpreted as a type (e.g. you called sc.nextInt() and the next token is "red"), the method throws a java.util.InputMismatchException, which is a run-time exception. Recall that you do not have to provide a handler for run-time exceptions, but if there is no handler, your program will terminate when the exception occurs.

When a scanner throws an InputMismatchException, the token is not consumed. It remains in the scanner, ready to be retrieved or skipped over by some other method. As well as the next*Something*() methods, there is a hasNext*Something*() method for each primitive type and the three object types.

```
public boolean hasNext();   // has another token of any kind
public boolean hasNextBoolean();
public boolean hasNextShort();
public boolean hasNextInt();
public boolean hasNextDouble();
public boolean hasNextBigInteger();
public boolean hasNextBigDecimal();   /* and so on... */
```

This provides an easy way to check the input before reading it. Each hasNext*Something*() method returns true if the next token in this scanner's input can be interpreted as a value of the *Something* type. The scanner does not advance past the input that it checks.

Scanners can be wrapped around File objects, as well as around System.in. As an example, if you have a file of doubles separated by whitespace, you can read the whole file by:

```
Scanner sc2 = Scanner.create(new File("myNumbers.txt"));
while (sc2.hasNextDouble()) {
        double value = sc2.nextDouble();
}
```

Scanners have more features than described here. In particular, they can skip over or retrieve text that matches a regular expression pattern that you provide. They can scan strings in memory, as well as files and stdin. You can set the delimiters to a pattern other than whitespace (useful when reading a file of comma-separated values). The method takes an argument that is a String or Pattern object containing a regular expression (see Chapter 19) showing all the delimiters. The method is:

```
sc2.useDelimiter(String)
```

Scanners also have a notion of locale, so you can set the character that is used to separate groups of thousands in numbers. In the US, this separator is "," as in "1,000,000". Some other regions use a different character. There are other locale-specific characters used in java.util.Scanner. You can find them by reading the javadoc page for the class.

Keyboard output

Everyone is used to using the following to print information to the command line:

```
System.out.println("Your age is: " + age );
```

New!

JDK 1.5 adds a couple of `printf()` methods to the classes java.io.PrintStream and java.io.PrintWriter. The `printf()` method is very popular in C. Its first argument is a format string. The format string contains fixed text that you want to be output. It also contains *format specifiers* that specify how the remaining arguments should be inserted in the text. All format specifiers start with "%" and are followed by one or more other characters giving details of the desired formatting

As an example, you can use the format specifier "%d" to represent that the corresponding argument should be formatted as a decimal integer:

```
int age = 27;
System.out.printf("Your age is: %d \n", age );
```

When used to simply output a number as on the line above, there is no benefit to using printf. The power of `printf ()` is seen when you use the format specifiers to format and layout the other arguments that you want to print. You can specify the minimum width for an argument, and the number of decimal places:

```
System.out.printf("Pi is %7.3f \n", Math.PI);
```

That specifier "%7.3f" says to format the argument as a floating point number at least 7 characters wide, with 3 decimal places,. The argument, Math.PI here, is autoboxed and given to the method as an Object. The whole variable-arity feature described in chapter 5 was introduced into Java just so the `printf()` method would have a way to accept a variable number of arguments. Compiling and running the above code yields:

```
Pi is    3.142
```

Format specifiers—class java.util.Formatter

The format specifiers really compose a little programming language of their own. Their general format is:

```
% [ArgumentIndex$] [flags] [width] [.precision] ConversionSpecifier
```

The square brackets mean *that specifier is optional*. Not all combinations of specifiers are valid. We'll look at the required field, the conversion specifier, first. Table 17–3 shows some of the most popular conversion specifiers.

Table 17–3   Common conversion specifiers

Char	Meaning	Example	Argument	Output
s	Format as String. If Formattable, print arg.formatTo(), otherwise print arg.toString()	%s	"biff"	biff
d	Format as decimal integer	%d	myInt	57
f	Format as floating point number (by default, to six decimal places)	%f	Math.PI	3.141593
g	Format as floating point number, and using scientific notation for large exponents	%g	1000000000	1.000000e+09
x	Format as hexadecimal integer	%x	(int) 'A'	41
b	Format as boolean	%b	(i < 10)	true
c	Format as character	%c	'A'	A
h	For debugging. Print the hashcode(), which is usually the address of an object	%h	Math.PI	144d0ce3
n	New line. Use this instead of "\n" for cross-platform support of newlines.	%n	no argument	\n
tX	t indicates a Date conversion. The single character after t indicates what part of a date is needed, e.g. H means hour in the range 00 to 23. B means month name. See the javadoc on java.util.Formatter for full details.	%tB	Calendar.getInstance()	April

Each tX conversion for a date gets you one or more component of a date, like day, month, year, etc. To get a complete date string, you might need to pass in the Calendar argument more than once, like this:

```
Calendar c = Calendar.getInstance();
    System.out.printf("%tD, %tT \n", c, c );
05/06/04, 13:31:28
```

There are single character specifiers for some commonly used date formats.

```
    System.out.printf("%tc", c );
Thu May 06 13:31:28 PDT 2004
```

Other fields in a format specifier String

Recall that the general appearance of a format specifier string (used in printf) is:

```
% [ArgumentIndex$] [flags] [width] [.precision] ConversionSpecifier
```

The format specifiers are described at length in the javadoc for class java.util.Formatter. Table 17–3 described the *required* field, the conversion specifier. Now we give examples showing the *optional* fields:

- **ArgumentIndex** is a number/dollar pair like 1$, 2$, 3$. The number refers to the corresponding argument in the argument list starting at 1. You use this if you want to reorder the arguments, or format the same argument a couple of times in different ways. This is commonly seen with dates, where different conversions get the day, month, and year from the same Calendar object.

example using **ArgumentIndex**	output
```Calendar c = Calendar.getInstance();``` ```System.out.printf(``` ``` "%1$tB %1$te, %1$tY \n", c);```	May 9, 2004

- **Flags** adjust the output format. A flag of "^" converts it to upper case. A flag of "-" left justifies the field. Many flags can only be applied to numeric arguments: "+" always includes a sign, "(" puts negative numbers in parentheses.

example using **flag**	output
```System.out.printf("%(d \n", -23);```	(23)

- **Width** is the minimum number of characters to be written to the output. The asterisks in the example below are so you can see the padding space that has been inserted. Use the width flag to align fields in columns.

example using **width**	output
```System.out.printf("**%2d** \n", 0);```	** 0**

- **Precision** is the number of decimal places for floating point arguments. For non-numeric arguments, this is the maximum width of the field.

example using **precision**	output
```System.out.printf("%.4s \n", "lengthy");```	leng

- **Example using the full monty**: argument index, flag, width, precision and a conversion specifier:

example using **the full monty**	output
```System.out.printf(``` ``` "**%1$-7.2f** \n", -1.236);```	**-1.24 **

If that isn't ugly enough, there are format specifiers for everything you might want to print: dates, times, numbers, and so on. The format specifiers are similar to those in C, with some changes to accommodate the Java language and exploit some of its features. Like C's `sprintf()`, Strings may be formatted using the static method `String.format()`:

```
String printableDate = String.format("%1$tB %1$te, %1$tY \n",
                                       Calendar.getInstance());
```

Java formatting is more strict than that of C. Java will throw a java.util.IllegalFormatConversionException if a conversion is incompatible with a flag, where C silently ignores the flag. The format specifiers are meant to be readily recognizable to C programmers, but not necessarily 100% compatible with those in C.

Output

At last we're at the point where we'll talk about one of the major confusions in Java I/O, use of char (double byte) versus single byte I/O.

Readers versus OutputStreams

Originally, Java only had stream classes, and the streams only operated on bytes of data. However, characters in Java are two bytes wide, and byte-oriented I/O did not properly cope with internationalization.

So a wider type of stream was introduced in JDK 1.1 specifically for character-based I/O. **Reader** classes are able to get Unicode character input two bytes at a time. **Writer** classes are able to do Unicode character output two bytes at a time, as shown in Figure 17–2. Input and output **streams** operate on data one byte at a time.

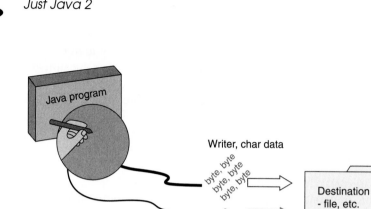

Writer, char data

Output Stream, binary data

Figure 17–2   Your program outputs data into a stream or writer

Java I/O is overly complicated to the newcomer because it relies on layering or wrapping classes. You need two or three classes to do anything. You determine exactly what classes to use by reviewing three attributes of your output:

- Whether you need 2-byte characters
- What you will be writing to (file, socket etc.)
- What format you want to write (binary or printable)

Here are the steps for choosing the classes in detail:

1. **Decide if your output includes any characters. If it does, do you want to output 16-bit characters or 8-bit characters?**

    If you are going to print a report in the USA or Europe, you'll probably use and choose 8-bit characters (apart from anything else, your printer probably can't print arbitrary 16-bit characters). If you have a database that uses Unicode, choose 16-bit. You want to make a choice that doesn't lose data.

    - 8-bit characters use an **OutputStream** class. Choose this by default.
    - 16-bit characters use a **Writer** class. Choose this if you want to write characters that have values outside the 8-bit byte ISO 8859-1 character set, such as Chinese or Hindi characters.

2. **Decide where you are going to write the data to.**

    Java programs access external data by instantiating a *stream* on the data. Most physical destinations (a place to where an output stream can flow) have a class dedicated to writing output there. There is only a limited number of destinations for data, shown in Table 17–4.

Table 17–4   Output destination and data width, determine the bottom layer class

Destination	8-bit OutputStream class or method	16-bit Writer class
A file	java.io.FileOutputStream	java.io.FileWriter
A socket	java.net.Socket.getOutputStream()	*Sockets never use 16-bit streams.*
A URL for GET/POST	java.net.URLConnection.getOutputStream()	*URLs are based on sockets, and so never use 16-bit streams.*
A pipe	java.io.PipedOutputStream	java.io.PipedWriter
A String in memory	*You can't create a String in memory from 8-bit operations.*	java.io.StringWriter
An array in memory	java.io.ByteArrayOutputStream	java.io.CharArrayWriter

You write to files, pipes, and in-memory data by instantiating a class that knows how to write to that destination. Sockets and URLs are treated differently because they can be read as well as written. Instead of instantiating a class, you call the getOutputStream() method on a socket or URLConnection object. Writing to a URL takes a little bit of URL-specific setup (you have to open a connection, create a connection object, configure the server to allow writing, etc.), but the other four destinations are very easy to use. Most of the time, you'll be writing to a file.

Let's call the class that you choose in this step the *bottom-layer class*.

3. **Decide what kind of output you will do, binary or printable.**

You can output binary values and 8-bit characters, of which the ASCII characters are just a subset. The full 8-bit character set is known as ISO 8859-1 Latin-1, but few have heard of that name and everyone has heard of ASCII, hence the title of Table 17–5. Both ASCII and 8859-1 are listed in Appendix B so you can review them.

As you probably know, there are different bit representations for same value held as different types. Take the number 29,012 as an example. It can be represented in a computer in (at least) three ways, as shown in Table 17–5.

Table 17–5   Differences among binary, ASCII, and String output determine the top layer class

Type	Format	Hexadecimal value	Class to use
Binary	4-byte binary integer	0000715B	java.io.DataOutputStream
ASCII bytes	Successive bytes	32 39 30 31 39	java.io.PrintOutputStream
String	Successive double-byte characters	0032 0039 0030 0031 0039	java.io.PrintWriter

These three different representations correspond to the three classes in java.io for writing output: DataOutputStream, PrintOutputStream, and PrintWriter. There's a fourth option too, namely to write out an entire object with all its fields. This is known as *serializing* an object, and we will look at it in a subsequent chapter.

Notice that it's not enough to say "I want to output the number 29012". You have to decide if you want to write it in binary or in a printable form. If a printable form, you will use a PrintWriter or PrintOutputStream to match your decision on 16-bit or 8-bit characters in step 1.

Let's call the class that you choose in this step the *top-layer class*.

Practical examples of output

Now that we know how to choose which classes to layer for output, let's look at three practical examples.

Example 1: You have an array of 1000 int values, and you want to put them in a file as binary data.

This output doesn't include any characters, so we know we're dealing with 8-bit output streams, not writers. The destination is a file, so consulting Table 17–4 the bottom-layer class will be java.io.FileOutputStream. Unless there is a special reason to make the output printable, we will save the data as binary ints. Table 17–5 tells us that the top-layer class is therefore java.io.DataOutputStream. When we wrap, the code will look like:

```
FileOutputStream fos = new FileOutputStream("ints.dat");
DataOutputStream dos = new DataOutputStream( fos );
```

This is almost always written in shortened form:

```
DataOutputStream dos = new DataOutputStream(
                    new FileOutputStream("ints.dat") );
```

We can now use methods of DataOutputStream to write data. These methods are listed in the next section, *java.io.DataOutputStream for binary output*.

Example 2: You want to write out the company book of spare parts, which is held in a Map of Integer, String pairs representing part number and part description. All the part descriptions can be accurately represented in ASCII characters.

The output does include characters, and the specification makes clear that 8-bit characters are adequate. Again the destination is a file, and Table 17–4 shows that the bottom layer class will be java.io.FileOutputStream. Since this is a phonebook, we surely want the output numbers to be printable ASCII bytes. Table 17–5 shows that the right top layer class is java.io.Print-Stream. The code will be:

```
PrintStream pos = new PrintStream(
                  new FileOutputStream("phonebk.txt") );
```

We will then use methods of PrintStream to write the ints and Strings.

Example 3: You have an array of all the names of employees in the Bangalore office. The names are in Hindi and other character sets. You want to write the names into a pipe to some other thread.

The specification makes clear that 16-bit characters are needed, combined with output to a pipe. Matching this in Table 17–4 shows that the bottom layer class will be java.io.PipedWriter. Table 17–5 shows that we will use java.io.PrintWriter as our top layer class. The code is:

```
PipedWriter piw = new PipedWriter();
PrintWriter pw = new PrintWriter( piw );
// we'll also need this to read from the other end of the pipe
PipedReader pir = new PipedReader(piw);
```

We will then use methods of PrintWriter to write the Strings.

Now that we have identified the three top-layer classes, the next three sections show the methods of the classes.

java.io.DataOutputStream for binary output

Here are the signatures of methods in the DataOutputStream class.

```
public class java.io.DataOutputStream
               extends java.io.FilterOutputStream
                 implements java.io.DataOutput {
   // constructor
   public DataOutputStream(java.io.OutputStream);
   public final void writeBoolean(boolean) throws java.io.IOException;
   public final void writeByte(int) throws java.io.IOException;
   public final void writeShort(int) throws java.io.IOException;
   public final void writeChar(int) throws java.io.IOException;
   public final void writeInt(int) throws java.io.IOException;
```

```
    public final void writeLong(long) throws java.io.IOException;
    public final void writeFloat(float) throws java.io.IOException;
    public final void writeDouble(double) throws java.io.IOException;
    public final void writeBytes(java.lang.String) throws java.io.IOException;
    public final void writeChars(java.lang.String) throws java.io.IOException;
    public final void writeUTF(java.lang.String) throws java.io.IOException;

    public void flush() throws java.io.IOException;
    public synchronized void write(int) throws java.io.IOException;
    public synchronized void write(byte[], int, int) throws java.io.IOException;
    public final int size();   // returns number-of-bytes written so far
}
```

Using DataOutputStream we can write the code to complete example 1, and output the int variables to a file. The whole thing will look like this:

```
                    // output binary data to a File
    DataOutputStream dos = new DataOutputStream(
                                new FileOutputStream("ints.dat") );
    // put next line in a for loop:
        dos.writeInt( myArray[i] );
    // when done writing, close the file:
        dos.close();
```

Whenever you do I/O, you usually need to wrap the statements in a handler for java.io.IOException.

java.io.PrintStream for printable ASCII output

Here are the signatures of methods in the PrintStream class.

```
public class java.io.PrintStream extends java.io.FilterOutputStream {
    public PrintStream(java.io.OutputStream);
    public PrintStream(String filename);          // new, improved
    public void print(boolean);
    public void print(char);
    public void print(int);
    public void print(long);
    public void print(float);
    public void print(double);
    public void print(char[]);
    public void print(java.lang.String);
    public void print(java.lang.Object);

    public PrintStream printf (String, Object...);   // ... means variable-arity

    public void println();
    public void println(boolean);
    // and so on for all the primitives ...

    public void flush();
    public void close();
    public boolean checkError();
```

```
    public void write(int);
    public void write(byte[], int, int);
}
```

Using PrintStream we can write the code to complete example 2, and output the parts to a file. The whole thing will look like this:

```
    // output <Integer, String> data from a Map to a File

    try {
        Map<Integer, String> partsBook = new HashMap<Integer, String>();
        partsBook.put(45678, "prop wash, 1 bucket"); // put some data

        PrintStream ps = new PrintStream(
                            new FileOutputStream("partsBk.txt") );

        // get the map set  and iterate over it
        Set<Map.Entry<Integer, String>> set = partsBook.entrySet();
        for (Map.Entry me : set)
            ps.printf( "%s %s \n", me.getKey(), me.getValue() );

    } catch (IOException iox) {
        System.err.println("Excpn: " + iox);
    }
```

The JDK 1.5 release introduced another constructor into class java.io.Printstream that lets you provide a filename argument directly:

```
    PrintStream ps = new PrintStream( "partsBook.txt" );
```

The library will then create the necessary bottom-layer OutputStream class automatically behind the scenes for you! PrintWriter has been similarly updated. You still need to know about layering, because this only works when the destination is a File, not for any of the other output sinks. Interestingly, you don't get this for a DataOutputStream. Java I/O is a riddle inside a puzzle wrapped up in used bubble gum.

Methods of java.io.PrintWriter for 16-bit character output

Here are the signatures of methods in the PrintWriter class.

```
public class java.io.PrintWriter extends java.io.Writer {
    public PrintWriter(java.io.Writer);
    public PrintWriter(java.io.Writer,boolean);
    public PrintWriter(java.io.OutputStream);
    public PrintWriter(String filename);            // new, improved
    public PrintWriter(java.io.OutputStream,boolean);
    public void flush();
    public void close();
    public boolean checkError();

    public void print(boolean);
```

```
    public void print(char);
    public void print(int);
    public void print(long);
    public void print(float);
    public void print(double);
    public void print(char[]);
    public void print(java.lang.String);
    public void print(java.lang.Object);

  public void println();
     // there are also println versions of all the above print methods,
e.g.
  public void println(boolean);    // and so on

  public PrintWriter printf(String, Object... );   // the new printf

  public void write(int);
  public void write(char[]);
  public void write(char[], int from, int to);
  public void write(java.lang.String);
  public void write(java.lang.String, int from, int to);
}
```

There is a print() method for most primitive types, and also a println() method that follows the output with the end of line sequence for that platform. There is a printf. There is no print(byte) because byte-oriented output is done with an OutputStream, not a Writer. The print() methods in PrintWriter don't throw IOException. The append() and printf() methods can throw IOException, and the javadoc is wrong to claim they can't (I filed the bug with the Java team). You can call the method checkError() to see if an I/O error occurred at some earlier point. Using PrintStream we can write the code to complete example 3, and output to a pipe between two threads. The whole thing will look like the following example.

```
    // output Strings through a pipe to another thread
try {
    PipedWriter piw = new PipedWriter();
    PrintWriter pw = new PrintWriter( piw );
    final PipedReader pir = new PipedReader(piw);

    Thread t = new Thread () {    // anon inner class
        public void run() {
            System.out.println("thread 2");
            Scanner sc = Scanner.create(pir);
            while (sc.hasNext()) System.out.println( sc.next() );
        }
    };
    System.out.println("thread 1");
    t.start();
    pw.print("data through the pipe");
    pw.close();
} catch (Exception e) { }
```

When compiled and run, the output will be:

```
thread 1
thread 2
data
through
the
pipe
```

The code in italics is a second thread that reads tokens from the pipe using a scanner. Those tokens are piped from one thread to another in a thread-safe way.

Flush after use?

Notice the `close()` method in java.io.PrintWriter. Even though there is no separate open for files, all I/O classes have a close method. Many of them have a `flush()` method, which forces bytes out from your process over to the OS. Java does not automatically flush and close streams just because you stop writing to them. Failing to close an output stream may leave it with some data not yet flushed to the underlying device. You should develop the habit of closing each stream as you are done with it.

Streams take up some OS resources, of which there is a limited quantity. By closing a stream when you are finished with it, you allow the JVM to give the file descriptor and buffers back to the OS. Also, closing pipes, sockets, and URLs allows the other end of the connection to see an end-of-file, and therefore is able to gracefully terminate instead of waiting for an event that may never happen.

We should conclude this description of PrintWriter by pointing out that, when writing to a file, the Java run-time system will convert 16-bit Character data into whatever the native encoding of the operating system is. If you have an 8-bit character set encoding as used in Western Europe and the US, then the high-order byte is dropped. For ISO 8859-1 characters, the dropped byte is 0 and makes no difference. You run into trouble if you are using characters where the high-order byte is used. Then your character data will be corrupted on output. This is why you shouldn't use a Stream when your data contains 16-bit characters.

Wrapping Additional Output Classes

As Figure 17–3 suggests, the java.io package has more classes that you can wrap around a Writer or OutputStream. The additional Writer wrapping classes can do things like filter the text as it goes by, or buffer it for performance. The additional OutputStream wrapping classes can bridge to a Writer class, filter, buffer, encrypt, and/or compress that data! When you wrap classes, only write from the outermost one. Otherwise, your I/O may get scrambled due to internal buffering.

All these additional wrappers go between what we have termed the top layer classes and the bottom layer classes. It makes sense—the bottom layer (like FileWriter) is the ultimate destination and nothing can come below that. The top-layer class has the methods that pour the bits into the stack, so nothing can come above that. Additional wrappers go between the two end points.

We'll present two examples here. First, we'll show an example of using a FilterWriter to modify text as it gets written. We'll also show how a BufferedWriter is used in this example. The second example will use OutputStream 8-bit wrappers to create a zip file archive. If you haven't seen this before, you may be surprised at the small amount of code that achieves these great results.

Additional writer wrappers

FilterWriter is an abstract class for you to extend and override. It provides the opportunity to look at and modify 16-bit characters as they are output. You could do the same thing by extending many of the other writer classes, but using this class makes your purpose explicit.

Here is an example program that post-processes the stream written into it and changes all "1"s to "2"s. A Filter can do other things like count lines, correct spelling mistakes, calculate checksums, or write an encrypted or compressed stream.

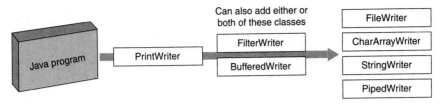

Figure 17–3   Wrapping more writer classes

A Filter to replace chars

In this example, the Filter overrides just two of the write() methods, but you may need to override any or all of the FilterWriter methods depending on which of them may be called by your code.

```
import java.io.*;
class MyFilter extends java.io.FilterWriter {
       public MyFilter(Writer w) { super(w); }

       public void write(String s, int off, int len) throws IOException {
              s = s.replace('1', '2');
              super.write(s, off, len);
       }

       public void write(char[] cbuf, int off, int len) throws IOException {
              String s= new String(cbuf);
              this.write(s, off, len);
       }
}
```

A class that uses a Filter

You can decorate a FileWriter (or other destination class from Table 17–4) with a BufferedWriter, if you want to improve performance. FileWriter by itself sends its output to the underlying stream as it receives it. Because of disk latency and system call context switch overhead, it's always much quicker to do one 512-character transfer than 512 individual one-character transfers.

```
import java.io.*;
public class Example2 {

       public static void main(String args[]) {
              FileWriter myFW = null;
              try {
                     myFW = new FileWriter( "dogs.txt" );
```

```
        } catch(IOException x) { System.err.println("IOExcpn: " + x); }

        PrintWriter myPW = new PrintWriter(
                                        new BufferedWriter(
                                          new MyFilter( myFW ) ) );
        myPW.println("101 Dalmatians");
        myPW.close();
    }
}
```

Wrapping a BufferedWriter around any Writer will achieve that efficiency by batching smaller writes until its internal buffer is full. The only place you don't want buffered I/O is with interactive I/O. Buffered I/O should have been the default behavior in the I/O package.

The API permits the BufferedWriter and the FilterWriter to be wrapped in either order. But to get the most performance benefit, you want as much of the pipeline as possible operating on buffers of data. So put the BufferedWriter as near to the start of the pipeline as possible (i.e., the BufferedWriter should be the outermost or next-outermost wrapper). This ensures that all wrapper objects downstream of the BufferedWriter are working with buffered data.

If you run the program and look at the output file dogs.txt, you will see the output has been filtered. It now contains "202 Dalmatians".

Output Stream wrappers

In the section above, we saw how a Writer could have a BufferedWriter and/or a subclass of FilterWriter interposed between the FileWriter (or other destination) and the PrintWriter. Output Streams can be wrapped in the same way to provide more functionality. You can wrap any or all of these output streams onto your original OutputStream:

- BufferedOutputStream
- Your subclass of FilterOutputStream
- OutputStreamWriter
- java.util.zip.ZipOutputStream
- java.util.zip.GZIPOutputStream
- java.util.jar.JarOutputStream
- javax.crypto.CipherOutputStream
- java.io.ObjectOutputStream
- Others in the release, and those which you write yourself.

The OutputStreamWriter class converts an OutputStream class to a Writer class, allowing you to layer any of the Writer classes on top of that. It provides a bridge from the 8-bit byte world to the 16-bit character world. The main motivation for doing so is that you can also specify the character set when you construct an OutputStreamWriter. Please review Chapter 18 for more information on character sets. Most of your programs won't need to change the character set, but Java has a solid way to do it when you need to.

The CipherOutputStream will encrypt the stream that it gets and write the encrypted bytes. You have to set it up with a Cipher object (and a key). There is (a little) more detail in the online API documentation.

The zip, gzip, and jar output streams will compress the bytes written into them using the zip, gzip, and jar algorithms, respectively. Jar format is identical to zip format, but with the addition of a manifest file listing the names of other files in the archive. (I use a command like "jar -xvf foo.jar" on Windows instead of fooling about with WinZip, but this won't work on encrypted files now that PKZip and WinZip have implemented incompatible encryption schemes). An example of writing an archive of several files in zip format is coming up soon.

The ObjectOutputStream class allows you to save an object and all the objects it references. You can wrap this class around any of the other output streams and send the object to a file, to a socket, down a pipe, etc. Chapter 18 shows an example of ObjectOutputStream in use.

Example of outputting a zip file

Zip is a multifile archive format popularized by the PC but available on almost all systems now. The zip format offers two principal benefits: it can bundle several files into one file, and it can compress the data as it writes it to the zip archive. It's more convenient to pass around one file than 20 separate files. Compressed files are faster and cheaper to download or e-mail than their uncompressed versions. Java Archives (.jar) files are in zip format. Support for zip and gzip files was introduced with JDK 1.1.

Gzip, an alternative to zip widely used on Unix, uses a different format for the data and can only hold one file (not a series of them). You are supposed to use the tar utility to aggregate all your files into one file, then use gzip to shrink it. Sometimes the Unix philosophy of "a different tool for everything" is not the most convenient approach.

Java has classes that will compress and expand files into either the gzip or the zip format. If you wrote a file out in zip format, you have to read it back in that way too. The same holds for gzip format. The formats are not interchangeable. If you have a choice, opt for zip over gzip because it does more and is much more widely used.

Files aren't the only possible destination for zip streams (or any output, compressed or otherwise). You can equally easily send streams through a socket to another computer across the Internet, put them in a String or byte array for later retrieval, or send them through a pipe to another thread.

The following is an example program showing how three files can be put into a
zip archive. You'll need three java source files to use as test data. Just make three
copies of this file and give them the names shown in the code. After running this
program, compare the size of the zip archive with the sum of the sizes of the three
files. Text strings compress well, binary data less so.

```java
import java.io.*;
import java.util.zip.*;
public class Example4 {

    // writing a zip archive
    static ZipOutputStream myZOS;

    public static void main(String args[]) throws IOException {
        myZOS = new ZipOutputStream (
                        new BufferedOutputStream (
                            new FileOutputStream("code.zip") )
);
        writeOneFile("Example1.java");
        writeOneFile("Example2.java");
        writeOneFile("Example3.java");
        myZOS.close();
    }

    static void writeOneFile(String name) throws IOException {
        ZipEntry myZE = new ZipEntry(name);
        myZOS.putNextEntry(myZE);

        BufferedInputStream myBIS = new BufferedInputStream(
                                        new FileInputStream(name)
);
        int c;
        while((c = myBIS.read()) != -1)       // read bytes until EOF
                myZOS.write(c);               // write the char we just
read
        myBIS.close();          }
}
```

Executing this program will create a zip archive called code.zip. Each file in a zip
archive is represented by an object called a ZipEntry. You can unpack it and
recover the original source files with class ZIPInputStream, or use any of the
standard zip tools like WinZip or Java's jar command.

That concludes output. Next, we'll look at Java's classes for input.

Input

The classes to do input are mostly the flip side of the output classes we have
already seen. Java programs access external data by instantiating a *stream* on the
data source. Each place from which an input stream can flow has a class

dedicated to getting that kind of input. Input is read from a stream of data representing the file, pipe, socket, memory array, or whatever. If you want to read 16-bit characters, you use a Reader class. If you want to read binary bytes or ASCII, you use an input stream.

Inputting double-byte characters

As usual, first decide between binary and character I/O, then choose your class based on where the data is coming from. For reading double-byte character data, you will use one of the Reader classes shown in Table 17–6. Note the symmetry with the Writer classes.

Table 17–6   **Choose the Reader class based on where the Input comes from**

Get input from	java.io class	Constructors

A **file**.	FileReader	`FileReader(java.lang.String) throws java.io.FileNotFoundException;`
		`FileReader(java.io.File) throws java.io.FileNotFoundException;`
		`FileReader(java.io.FileDescriptor);`

A **char array** in your program. You read from the array passed to the constructor.	CharArrayReader	`CharArrayReader(char[]);` `CharArrayReader(char[],int from,int to);`
A **String** in your program. You read from the String passed to the constructor.	StringReader	`StringReader( String s )`
A **pipe** that is written by a PipedWriter in another thread.	PipedReader	`PipedReader()` `PipedReader(PipedWriter source)`

There are only four places from which you can read chars with a Reader, and FileReader is by far the most common. That class opens a connection to a file. The constructors are shown in Table 17–6. The constructor takes an argument that is the String pathname to the file, or a File object or FileDescriptor object.

Basic Reader methods

All Readers give you at least these three somewhat basic input methods:

```
public int read()
public int read(char[] cbuf)
public int read(char[] cbuf, int from, int len)
```

These read into, respectively, a single character, an array of characters, and a range in an array of characters. The call will not return until some data is available to read, although it won't necessarily fill the array. The return value will be -1 if the Reader hits end of file (EOF). This is why the single char call returns a 32-bit int, even though it only reads a 16-bit character. The high-order 16 bits in the return value allow you to distinguish EOF from a character read. Those bits will be zero when a character is read, and 0xFFFF when EOF is reached. Test the return value for equality with -1 to see if you reached EOF.

An input problem rears its ugly head

At this point, from general symmetry, you are probably expecting to "wrap" another class on top of these Readers. That class will probably be called PrintReader, and it will have all the convenient methods for reading a String and returning a short, an int, a float, a boolean, etc. Bzzzt!

Sorry, the design falls apart here. There is no such class as PrintReader. Not only that, there is no class that *can* give you the desired feature of being able to read back in exactly the same number values as were output using PrintWriter. The problem is an algorithmic one. Numbers in printed format vary in length, so your code has no way of telling where one number ends and an immediately adjacent starts. For example, if you use PrintWriter to print two ints like this into a file (with no space between them):

```
myPW.print(293);
myPW.print(19);
```

The file will contain the string "29319", but if you try to read those numbers back in from that file, because of the variable length, there is no way of telling where one int ends and the next one starts. No program in any language can deduce whether the ints were originally 2 and 9319, or 29 and 319, or 293 and 19, or 2931 and 9. This problem does not arise with binary output, because all the binary types (short, int, float, etc.) have a fixed known size. This "where does a string of digits end?" problem is the reason that the XML language (see Chapter 27) always marks the end of a field with a closing tag.

Confused by number formats, by ASCII, Unicode, binary?
It *is* confusing until you understand the differences. You might find it helpful to review the different formats shown in Table 17–5 earlier in the chapter.

The best you can do when reading printed numbers is to read characters until you hit something that can't be part of a number (e.g., a space), then assemble a number out of the characters that preceded it. It's common to break up such files with end-of-line sequences, and it's convenient to be able to read a line at a time and tokenize (bundle together the groups of) the characters on that line.

This is exactly what the Scanner class does. Scanners make Java input a pleasure! See the following code example.

```
import java.io.*;
import java.util.Scanner;
import static java.lang.System.*;
public class Example5 {

        public static void main(String args[]) {
                FileReader myFR = null;
                try {
                  myFR = new FileReader( "Example5.java" );

                  Scanner sc = Scanner.create(new BufferedReader(myFR));
                  while(sc.hasNext())
                          out.println( sc.next() );
                } catch(IOException x) { err.println("Excp: " +x); }
        }
}
```

Another approach is to write all numeric strings into fixed length fields that are, say, 20 characters long. Then you can always read in fixed-length input. Another approach is to avoid reading/writing printable data; instead, do it all with binary byte streams. Another suggestion is to make your data totally portable and unambiguous by using XML. I'll be very glad when all word processors switch to saving in XML format. Have you ever had the experience of having a very old data file, but no longer have the application to read it? That data loss won't happen when all our data is in XML format.

Input is messier than output.

Reader Wrappers

There is the usual variety of wrapper classes that can wrap a Reader, shown in the Figure 17–4.

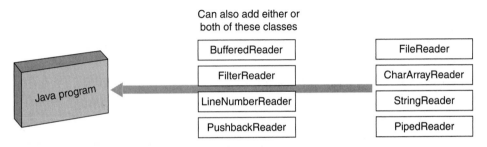

Figure 17–4   Wrapping the Reader classes

Classes that wrap readers

The classes that wrap a Reader are:

- **BufferedReader**. This class can provide a performance boost, and also has a readLine() method. The BufferedReader needs to wrap the class that actually accesses the data (e.g., the FileReader or whatever). Other classes may be layered on top of the BufferedReader, too.

- **FilterReader**. You subclass FilterReader, and your overriding methods allow you to see and modify individual characters as they come in—before the rest of your program sees them.

- **LineNumberReader**. This class keeps track of the line number count on this stream. You can find out the input line you are currently on by calling getLineNumber(). This class doesn't really offer enough value to justify its existence. It was written to support the first Java compiler and included in the API for no better reason than "Hey, we already had it written".

- **PushbackReader**. This class maintains an internal buffer that allows characters to be "pushed back" into the stream after they have been read, allowing the next read to get them again. The default buffer size is one character, but there is a constructor that lets you specify a larger size. You might use this if you were assembling successive characters into a number and you come to a character that can't be part of a number. You will push it back into the input stream so it can be ignored, but kept available for the next read attempt. This is less necessary now that we have the Scanner class.

Inputting ASCII Characters and Binary Values

You choose an input stream when you want to bring bytes into your program. As with Readers, you decide where you want to read from, and choose one of the InputStream classes accordingly (see Table 17–7).

Table 17–7   Choose the InputStream class based on the source of the input

Read binary input from	java.io Class	Constructors

A **file**	FileInputStream	`public FileInputStream(java.lang.String)`
		    `throws java.io.FileNotFoundException;`
		`public FileInputStream(java.io.File) throws`
		    `java.io.FileNotFoundException;`
		`public`
		    `FileInputStream(java.io.FileDescriptor);`

A **byte array** in your program	ByteArrayInputStream	`public ByteArrayInputStream(byte []);`
		`public ByteArrayInputStream(byte [], int`
		`from, int len);`

A **pipe** to be read by a PipedOutput-Stream in another thread	PipedInputStream	`public`
		`PipedInputStream(java.io.PipedOutputStream)`
		`throws java.io.IOException;`
		`public PipedInputStream();`

A StringBuffer object	StringBufferInputStream	*This class has been deprecated; don't use it.*

As before, you connect to socket and URL input streams using a method call, rather than a constructor. The method getInputStream() returns an input stream connected to the network resource, as shown in Table 17–8.

Table 17–8   Choose the getInputStream() method based on the source of the data

Read input from	Class	Method in that class to get an Input Stream
A **socket**	java.net.Socket	`public InputStream getInputStream() throws` `java.io.IOException;`
A **URL** connection	java.net.URLConnection	`public InputStream getInputStream() throws` `java.io.IOException;`

Using the constructors or method calls we can get an input stream that reads bytes from a file, a socket, a URL, a pipe, or a byte array. Once you have your input stream of whatever variety, it has certain basic methods available.

Basic InputStream methods

All InputStreams give you at least these three somewhat basic input methods:

```
public int read()
public int read(byte[] b)
public int read(byte[] b, int from, int len)
```

These read into, respectively, a single byte, an array of bytes, and a range in an array of bytes. The call will not return until some data is available to read, although it won't necessarily fill the array. The return value will be -1 if the InputStream hits end of file (EOF). This is why the single byte call returns a 32-bit int, even though it only reads a 8-bit byte. The high-order 24 bits in the return value allow you to distinguish EOF from a byte read. Those bits will be zero when a data byte is read and 0xFFFFFF when EOF is reached.

The ByteArrayInputStream allows you to take data from a byte array in your program using the read() methods rather than array indexing. There is a new package in JDK 1.4 called java.nio. This package supports methods that write out an array full of data to a stream with one statement. (See Chapter 18 for an example.)

All java.io classes with "InputStream" in their name have a few other methods, too, like close(), available(), and skip(). They are methods promised by the abstract class InputStream. Those three basic read() methods generally aren't enough, so you will wrap another class around your Input Stream. The most common wrapper is a DataInputStream class to read binary bytes. Anything written with a DataOutputStream can be read back in by a DataInputStream.

The DataInputStream class has these methods for binary input.

```
public class java.io.DataInputStream
        extends java.io.FilterInputStream implements java.io.DataInput {
    public DataInputStream(java.io.InputStream);
    public final int read(byte[]) throws java.io.IOException;
    public final int read(byte[], int, int) throws java.io.IOException;
    public final void readFully(byte[]) throws java.io.IOException;
    public final void readFully(byte[], int, int) throws java.io.IOException;
    public final int skipBytes(int) throws java.io.IOException;
    public final boolean readBoolean() throws java.io.IOException;
    public final byte readByte() throws java.io.IOException;
    public final int readUnsignedByte() throws java.io.IOException;
    public final short readShort() throws java.io.IOException;
    public final int readUnsignedShort() throws java.io.IOException;
    public final char readChar() throws java.io.IOException;
    public final int readInt() throws java.io.IOException;
    public final long readLong() throws java.io.IOException;
    public final float readFloat() throws java.io.IOException;
    public final double readDouble() throws java.io.IOException;
    public final String readLine() throws java.io.IOException;  // deprecated
    public final String readUTF() throws java.io.IOException;
    public static final String readUTF(java.io.DataInput) throws
                                                     java.io.IOException;
}
```

As you can see, there is a read method for all primitive types, e.g., readInt() to read an int. A line of 8-bit bytes can be read into a String using the readLine() method, but this has been deprecated because it lacks proper byte-to-double-byte conversion. You can also read a string that was written in the UTF-encoded format where characters are one to three bytes in length (readUTF() method). The UTF format string is preceded by a 16-bit length field, allowing your code to scoop up the right amount of data. Notice that, although there is a DataOutputStream.writeChars(), there is no DataInputStream.readChars(). You have to read chars one at a time, and you decide when you have read the entire string.

A word about IOExceptions

Let's say a few words on the subject of IOExceptions. If you look at the run-time source, you'll see that there are a dozen I/O-related exceptions. The most common I/O-related exceptions are:

FileNotFoundException   EOFException   InterruptedIOException   UTFDataFormatError

These are all subclasses of IOException. InterruptedIOException was supposed to be raised when you called the interrupt method of a thread that was blocked on I/O. It didn't work very well, and we'll look at the replacement (asynchronous I/O) in Chapter 18.

The name EOFException suggests that it is thrown whenever EOF (end of file) is encountered, and that therefore this exception might be used as the condition to break out of a loop. Unhappily, it can't always be used that way. EOFException is raised in only three classes: DataInputStream, ObjectInputStream, and RandomAccessFile (and their subclasses). The EOFException would be better named UnexpectedEOFException, as it is only raised when the programmer has asked for a fixed definite amount of input, and the end of file is reached before all the requested amount of data has been obtained.

EOFException is not a universal alert that the normal end of file has been reached. In FileInputStream or FileReader, you detect EOF by checking for the -1 return value from a read, not by trying to catch EOFException. So if you want to use an EOFException to terminate a loop, make sure that the methods you are using will throw you one. The compiler will warn you if you try to catch an exception that is not thrown.

FileNotFoundException is self-explanatory. UTFDataFormatException is thrown when the I/O library finds an inconsistency in reading some UTF data.

Dumping a file to hexadecimal example

Here is some sample code to read a file and dump its contents in hexadecimal.

Run the program with:

```
java Dump someFile
```

and it will create an output file based on the input filename, e.g. someFile.hex, that contains a hex dump of the input file.

```
import java.io.*;
import java.util.*;
import java.sql.Timestamp;
public class Dump {

    static FileInputStream myFIS = null;
    static FileOutputStream myFOS = null;
    static PrintStream myPOS = null;

    static public void main(String[] arg) {
        PrintStream e = System.err;
        try {
            myPOS = new PrintStream ( arg[0]+".hex" );
            long now = new Date().getTime();
            myPOS.printf("Hex dump of file %s %s %n", arg[0], new Timestamp(now));
            myFIS = new FileInputStream(arg[0]);

            while ( myFIS.available()>0 )
                    dump( (byte)myFIS.read() );
        } catch(IOException x) {
                e.println("Exception: " + x.getMessage() );
        }
    }

    static private long byteCount = 0;

    static private void dump(byte b) {
        if (byteCount % 16 == 0)
            myPOS.printf("%n%0^8x:", byteCount);
        // output a space every 4 bytes
        if (byteCount++ % 4 == 0)
            myPOS.print("  ");

        // dump the byte as 2 hex chars
        myPOS.printf("%0^2x", b);
    }
}
```

You can create a printable representation of a class file by running

```
java  Dump  Dump.class
```

You can use the Dump program to look at binary files that you create with DataOutputStream. Here is the beginning of the output you get from running this program on its own class file (it will vary with different compilers).

The output will be in file Dump.class.hex:

```
Hex dump of file Dump.class
00000000:  ca fe ba be    00 03 00 2d    00 8e 0a 00    2f 00 45 09
00000010:  00 46 00 47    07 00 48 0a    00 03 00 49    09 00 2e 00
00000020:  4a 07 00 4b    07 00 4c 0a    00 07 00 45    0a 00 07 00
00000030:  4d 08 00 4e    0a 00 07 00    4f 0a 00 06
```

The first int word of this class file is 0xCAFE 0xBABE. The first word of all Java class files is 0xCAFE 0xBABE. It is what is known as a "magic number"—a special value put at a special place in a file to confer the magical ability to distinguish this kind of file from any other. It allows Java tools like the JVM to check that they have been given a class file to execute against. If you are going to put a special value there, you might as well use one that is easy to recognize and remember!

We could wrap the FileInputStream in a BufferedInputStream as described in the next section. The program works without buffering, but may be slower for large input files.The default size of a buffer in BufferedInputStream is 8 KB. That's up from 0.5 KB in JDK 1.4 but still *much* too small. For large inputs, you should do some measurements and see what size gives you the performance you want.

Input Stream Wrappers

We have seen several times how a basic I/O class can be wrapped or "decorated" by another I/O class of the same parent class. So it should be no surprise that an InputStream can have a BufferedInputStream and/or a subclass of FilterInputStream interposed between the FileInputStream (or other data source) and the DataInputStream.

There is quite a variety of InputStreams that can decorate the basic access classes. Figure 17–5 shows some, but by no means all, of the most popular classes.

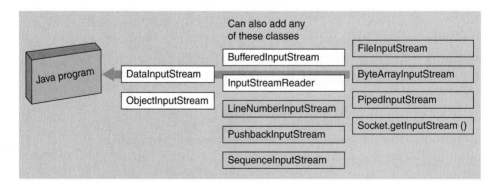

Figure 17–5   Classes that wrap InputStreams

You can wrap any or all of the following output streams onto your original InputStream:

- **BufferedInputStream**. This class must directly wrap the input source (e.g., the FileInputStream) to get the most performance benefit. You want the buffering to start as early as possible. Wrap any other classes around the buffered input stream.

- **Your subclass of FilterInputStream**. You will extend the class and override some or all of the read methods to filter the data on the way in.

- **LineNumberInputStream**. This class keeps track of the number of newlines it has seen in the input stream.

- **PushbackInputStream**. This class allows an arbitrary amount of data to be "pushed back" or returned to the input stream where it is available for re-reading. You might do this when you are trying to assemble a number out of digits in the input stream and you read past the end of the number.

- **SequenceInputStream**. This class provides the effect of gluing several input streams together, one after the other, so that as one stream is exhausted you seamlessly start reading from the next. You might use this when your data is spread across several data files with a similar format.

- **InputStreamReader**. This class converts an InputStream class to a Reader class, allowing you to layer any of the Reader classes on top of that. It provides a bridge from the 8-bit byte world to the 16-bit character world when you have an input stream and want a Reader. Remembering that the Reader methods are poor at processing anything with more structure than a character, the most common reason for going from an input stream to a Reader is to change the character set encoding—to convert from, for instance, ASCII to EBCDIC (an ancient IBM codeset).

- **java.util.zip.GZIPInputStream**. The zip, gzip, and jar output streams will uncompress the bytes read from them, using the zip, gzip, and jar algorithms, respectively. An example of reading and expanding a file in gzip format is shown in the next section.

- Various others in the release, and which you write yourself. For example, there is a CipherInputStream that will decrypt what is given to it. This is part of the javax.crypto extension library, which you have to set up with a Cipher object. There is more detail in the online API documentation.

At the very end of the chain of wrapped classes you generally have either a DataInputStream or an ObjectInputStream. The ObjectInputStream class allows you to read back in an object and all the objects it references. You can wrap this class around any of the other input streams, and read the object from a file, a socket, up from a pipe, etc. An example of object I/O is shown in Chapter 18.

gzip files and streams

The word *gzip* means GNU zip. The GNU organization (a loose organization of expert programmers founded at MIT by officially-recognized-as-a-genius Richard Stallman) has specified a simpler variant of a zip format that has become popular on Unix. It compresses its input by using the patent-free Lempel-Ziv coding. Here's the simplest example code to unpack a gzip file.

```java
//    Expand a .gz file into uncompressed form
//    Peter van der Linden

import java.io.*;
import java.util.zip.*;
public class expandgz {

    public static void main (String args[]) throws Exception {
            if (args.length == 0) {
                    System.out.println("usage:  java expandgz  filename.gz");
                    System.exit(0);
            }
            GZIPInputStream gzi = new GZIPInputStream(
                                        new FileInputStream( args[0] ));
            int to = args[0].lastIndexOf('.');
            if (to == -1) {
                    System.out.println("usage:  java expandgz  filename.gz");
                    System.exit(0);
            }
            String fout = args[0].substring(0, to);
            BufferedOutputStream bos = new BufferedOutputStream(
                                            new FileOutputStream(fout) );
            System.out.println("writing " + fout);

            int b;
             do {
                    b = gzi.read();
                    if (b==-1) break;
                    bos.write(b);
            } while (true);
            gzi.close();
            bos.close();
    }
}
```

Executing this program will expand the gzip file whose name (e.g., abc.gz) is given on the command line. There is a corresponding GZIPOutputStream class that you can use to write a file into compressed gzip form.

Further Reading

Table 17–9 shows some online resources for more information on other I/O packages.

Table 17–9   Online resources for other I/O packages

Package	Online resources
Image I/O	`java.sun.com/products/java-media/jai/whatis.html` API docs package javax.imageio
Speech	Programmer's guide at `java.sun.com/products/` `java-media/speech/forDevelopers/jsapi-guide/Preface.html`
Logging	Overview at `java.sun.com/j2se/1.5/docs/guide/util/logging/overview.html` API docs package java.util.logging
Communication ports (serial port)	See the home page at `java.sun.com/products/javacomm/` The home page has a pointer to a user guide.

Printing	What Java calls "printing" is actually "painting GUI objects onto paper". Be careful not to mistakenly read information on the older print APIs.
	`java.sun.com/printing/`
	API User Guide:
	`java.sun.com/j2se/1.5.0/docs/guide/jps/spec/JPSTOC.fm.html`
	API docs package javax.print. The API docs contain a small printing example.

Exercises

1. Measure the difference between buffered and non-buffered I/O operating with 10K 1-byte writes and one 10KB write, repeated 10,000 times in a loop. Draw a graph to illustrate your results. How do the results change with a buffer size of 128KB, 256KB, 512KB?

2. Modify the program that does a hex dump of a file so that it also outputs any printable bytes in a set of columns to the right of the hex dump on each line. Print the character if it has a printable form, and print a "." if it does not. This ensures that lines are the same length and columns line up.

3. Write a Java program whose output at run-time is an exact duplicate of the program's source code. Now that we have printf, the shortest Java program to do this is well under a page of code.

4. Write a program that prints a table of printable ISO 8859-1 characters and their bit patterns.

Just Java 2

5. Rewrite the hex dumper utility to use one or more Filter classes. The first filter can turn binary bytes into the equivalent printable hex characters. The second filter can insert the addresses and newlines at appropriate points.

6. Rewrite the deCSS utility (see *Some Light Relief—The Illegal Prime Number!*) in Java. For extra credit, look up the algorithms on the web to actually carry out the decryption of an encoded DVD stream, and write Java code to do that. Does it run quickly enough to decode and play in real time? Explain why or why not.

Some Light Relief—The Illegal Prime Number!

By now everyone is familiar with DVDs—originally an acronym for "Digital Video Disc," later changed to "Digital Versatile Disk" for pointless marketing reasons. DVDs are similar to CD-ROMs in many ways, with a crucial difference that commercial DVDs can hold about 8 GBytes, or more than ten times as much data as a CD. The tracks and the bits in the tracks are packed closer together on a DVD, which is why DVD players can read CDs but not vice-versa. If you use a suitable compression technology, you can actually squeeze up to 133 minutes of high-resolution video with several soundtracks and subtitles onto a DVD. The compression is essential, and the movie industry uses the MPEG-2 algorithm that was designed for this purpose, and which provides 40-1 compression. The more efficient MPEG-4 (DivX) compression, which provides another fivefold reduction, is also being introduced.

However, since the movie industry doesn't want to be Napstered (have their content ripped off and broadcast for free on the Internet), they encrypt the MPEG-2 files using an algorithm called the Content Scrambling System, or CSS. If you do a directory listing of a DVD, you'll see some large .VOB files. These are Video OBjects, a fancy name for content-scrambled .MPG2 files. Every maker of DVD players on the planet is supposed to license the decryption algorithm from the DVD Copy Control Association (DVD-CCA) for a fee, and they impose several restrictions on the player. DCC-CCA is believed to be a subsidiary of Matsushita, the company mainly responsible for the development of DVD and CSS. Some of its restrictions take away rights that consumers have long enjoyed under copyright law. They seem more geared towards controlling what consumers can do, rather than dealing with problems of rip-offs and piracy.

So what are the restrictions that licensed DVD players have to impose? CSS encryption allows the DVD industry to force region restrictions into all DVD players. There are six geographic regions (North America, Europe, etc.) and in 1999 they added a seventh for DVDs intended for airplanes. A player in region one will refuse to play disks labelled as belonging to any other region. Region restrictions allow the movie industry to sell the same DVD at different prices in different markets. It prevents any DVDs you buy on business trips outside your region from being played on your home system. The CSS encryption also prevents you from fast-forwarding past the copyright warning or advertisements or any other content the producer wants you to see. You can sell preview commercials for a much higher price if people cannot skip past them. Some people speculate that CSS is also paving the way for more restrictions such as DVDs with a limited lifetime or limited number of viewings. The movie industry blows a lot of smoke about CSS preventing large-scale piracy, but CSS does nothing whatever to prevent pirates from copying DVDs. Its only purpose is enforcing use limitations that take away the legal rights of consumers.

For a long time, there was no software to play DVDs available for Linux. If you had a shelf full of DVDs that you had bought, you could play them all on your TV or Windows box, but because of the CSS restrictions, not on your Linux or Solaris system. The CSS restrictions were the equivalent of a book publisher enforcing a restriction that you could read a book under incandescent lighting but not under fluorescent lighting or daylight. No one in the Linux community had the means to pay the "CSS tax" to the DVD-CCA. Then, in October 1999, anonymous German hackers reverse-engineered CSS. The source code to decrypt DVDs was published on the web by a 15-year-old boy from Norway. The program was called "deCSS" because it reverses CSS, turning the encrypted files into ordinary MPEG-2 files.

There then followed an extraordinary game of "whack-a-mole" as the DVD-CCA and the Motion Picture Association of America (MPAA) tried to chase the source code around the web and sue it out of existence. That game continues today. The 15-year-old boy was hauled off by the foolish Norwegian police who also seized his PC and his cell phone. The cell phone was a lucky guess on the part of the cops, because he did actually have a back-up copy of the source stored in it. Cell phones these days are effectively quite powerful computers, and a quarter of a billion cell phones (2004 figure) contain a JVM. After lengthy legal proceedings, the kid was eventually found not guilty.

The U.S. movie industry had the foresight (and the impudence) to get a law passed so that it is illegal to write, publish, possess, debug, talk about or run code like deCSS. The Digital Millennium Copyright Act (DMCA) made it illegal to circumvent a "technological protection measure" put in place by the copyright owner. That means the deCSS program is illegal. Write a program to play a DVD that you own, and you could go to jail! The DMCA is a poorly constructed law, written by the movie industry to advance its own interests at the expense of consumers. It will eventually be replaced by something more sensible but it all takes time. This is not theoretical. A software developer was arrested under the DMCA by FBI agents in Las Vegas in July 2001 one day after he publicly pointed out copyright protection weaknesses in Adobe software.

Hackers started to vie with each other for the most imaginative way to publish the deCSS code. America has very strong guarantees concerning freedom of speech, and there are long-standing precedents saying that printed text (even source code) counts as speech. Programmers embedded the code in JPEG files, put the algorithm in plain English, and one person even wrote the deCSS steps in the form of a *haiku* (Japanese poetry)! There is a whole gallery of these deCSS publications at `www.cs.cmu.edu/~dst/DeCSS/Gallery/` (assuming it hasn't been sued off the net yet).

My absolute favorite deCSS code exists in the form of a prime number. Computer scientist and number theory fan Phil Carmody found a prime number which expresses the deCSS code! Phil felt strongly that the Motion Picture Association was acting in bad faith, and to oppose this he wanted to make sure that the DeCSS code was archived somewhere beyond the reach of the law. Somewhere where the number would be allowed to be printed because it had some property that made it publishable, independent of whether it was "illegal" or not. Phil had done a lot of work with prime numbers and prime number proving. It can't be illegal to possess a prime number, can it? Or can it? Basic common sense says no, but the DCMA says yes!

Phil took the deCSS source file, which contains about 100 lines of C code, and gzipped it to make it smaller. That resulted in a binary file about 600 bytes long. Then Phil considered the file as, not a 4-byte integer or an 8-byte long integer, but a ~600-byte binary super-long integer, and he looked for a small number he could append so that the whole thing would be a prime number. In character terms, say the code gzipped to the string "100," Phil was looking for an odd number suffix like "9" that would make the whole string (in this case "1009") a prime number. That kind of search is quick and easy to program.

Number theory told Phil that his chances were about 1 in 1600 of finding a one or two byte suffix that would make the entire number prime. There wasn't a one byte suffix, so he went on to look for a two-byte suffix. Even though the chances were very slim, he found one! If he had not found one, he would have simply gone on to test longer suffixes and change variable names in the code until eventually a prime number was reached. The resulting prime number is shown Figure 17–6. It is 1,401 digits long.

```
48565078965739782930984189469428613770744208735135792401965207 36
86698513401047237446968797439926117510973777701027447528049058 83
13840375497099879096539552270117121570259746669932402268345966 19
60603485174249773584685188556745702571254749996482194184655710 08
41190862597169479707991520048667099759235960613207259737979936 18
86063169144735883002453369727818139147979555133999493948828998 46
91783610018259789010316019618350343448956870538452085380458424 15
65482488933380474758711283395989685223254460840897111977127694 12
07958624405471613210050064598201769617718094781136220027234482 72
24932325954723468800292777649790614812984042834572014634896854 71
69082354737835661972186224969431622716663939055430241564732924 85
52489912257394665486271404821171381243882177176029841255244647 44
50558346281448833563190272531959043928387376407391689125792405 50
15620889787163375999107887084908159097548019285768451988596305 32
38234905580920329996032344711407760198471635311617130785760848 62
23637028357010496125956818467859653331007701799161467447254927 28
33486916000647585917462781212690073518309241530106302893295665 84
36620008004767789679843820907976198594936463093805863367214696 95
97502796877120572499666698056145338207412031593377030994915274 69
18356593762102220068126798273445760938020304479122774980917955 93
83871210005887666892584487004707725524970604446521271304043211 82
61010359118647666296385849508744849737347686142088052 9443
```

Figure 17-6   The illegal prime number!

Following is a little Java program that takes a large number stored as a string (such as the one in Figure 17-6, hint, hint), turns that string into a super-long binary integer, and then writes that out as a gzip file.

You could then use standard tools like gunzip to turn it back into C source. Gunzip will balk at the wacky double-byte that Phil added at the end. Alternatively, you can easily use a Java program like the expandgz example shown earlier in this chapter to expand the gzip file into a C source code file. But remember, that would be the source code to deCSS and it is illegal to have or compile or run such a source code file under American law prevailing since 1998.

```
//   Convert a big number into binary and write it out
//   Peter van der Linden, June 2001

import java.io.*;
import java.math.*;
public class togz {

      static String illegalPrime =
"4856507896573978293098418946942861377074420873513579240196520736" +
"plug the rest of the number in here... " ;

      static BigInteger b = new BigInteger(illegalPrime);
      static final BigInteger two_five_six = new BigInteger("256");

      static byte[] result = new byte[illegalPrime.length()];

      public static void main (String args[]) throws Exception {
            BigInteger d_r [];

            if (b.isProbablePrime(3))
                       System.out.println("b is probably prime (good)");
            else System.out.println("b is probably not prime (bad!)");

            int i=0;
            do {
                    d_r = b.divideAndRemainder(two_five_six);
                    b = d_r[0];      // the multiple
                    result[i++] = (byte) d_r[1].intValue();  // the remainder
            } while ( b.compareTo( two_five_six ) >= 0);

            result[i] = (byte) b.intValue();

            System.out.println("writing bytes.gz");
            FileOutputStream fos = new FileOutputStream("bytes.gz");

            DataOutputStream dos = new DataOutputStream(fos);
            for (int j=i; j>0; j--) {
                    dos.writeByte( result[j] );
            }
            fos.close();
      }
}
```

What's wrong with this picture? The CSS descrambler that you get is just three or four utility routines, not a main program. To play DVDs on your Linux or Solaris box, you'll need to download the (allegedly illegal) software from one of several open source DVD players. I like the one at www.videolan.org.

Finally, you can try rewriting deCSS in Java for fun. Just don't blame me if the FBI knocks on your door with an MPAA warrant and seizes your debugger. Illegal code! The very idea! Next thing you know, they'll be declaring T-shirts illegal.

Advanced Input Output

I-O!
I-O!
It's off to work we go!
I-O, I/O, I/O.

This chapter follows on from the basic I/O chapter and provides information on more advanced I/O techniques in about a half-dozen sections, mostly independent. The section on the new I/O package (new in JDK 1.4 that is, with the name java.nio) is needed to understand the three other JDK 1.4 features of pattern matching, file locking, and character sets. You can read other sections in any order, or indeed skip the entire chapter now and return when you need information on any one of these topics.

Random Access File

Until now we have seen how input and output is done in a serial mode. However, sometimes we want to be able to move around inside a file and write to different locations, or read from different locations, without having to scan all the data. Traveling in a file stream in such a manner is called "random access".

Java has a random access file class that can do these operations. This is not an indexed sequential file or a direct access file of the kind supported by data processing languages. Those two techniques require the creation and maintenance of special indexes to address the file. The class java.io.RandomAccessFile does not use indices, but lets you access a file as though it were an array of bytes. There is an index or pointer that says where the next read or write will take place. You set the position of the file pointer with the method seek(), giving an argument that is the absolute offset into the file. When you set the file pointer, the next access will take place at the offset indicated. Because of the way operating systems store file contents, moving around in a file does not necessarily involve inefficient reading and rereading.

class java.io.RandomAccessFile

```
public class RandomAccessFile implements java.io.DataOutput, java.io.DataInput {
    public RandomAccessFile(java.lang.String,java.lang.String) throws
        java.io.FileNotFoundException;
    public RandomAccessFile(java.io.File,java.lang.String) throws
java.io.FileNotFoundException;
    public final java.nio.channels.FileChannel getChannel();  // used for locking
file
    public final java.io.FileDescriptor getFD() throws java.io.IOException;
    public native int read() throws java.io.IOException;
    public int read(byte[], int, int) throws java.io.IOException;
    public int read(byte[]) throws java.io.IOException;
    public final void readFully(byte[]) throws java.io.IOException;
    public final void readFully(byte[], int, int) throws java.io.IOException;
    public int skipBytes(int) throws java.io.IOException;
    public native void write(int) throws java.io.IOException;
    public void write(byte[]) throws java.io.IOException;
    public void write(byte[], int, int) throws java.io.IOException;

    public native long getFilePointer() throws java.io.IOException;
    public native void seek(long) throws java.io.IOException;
    public native long length() throws java.io.IOException;
    public native void setLength(long) throws java.io.IOException;
    public native void close() throws java.io.IOException;

    public final boolean readBoolean() throws java.io.IOException;
    public final byte readByte() throws java.io.IOException;
    public final int readUnsignedByte() throws java.io.IOException;
    public final short readShort() throws java.io.IOException;
    public final int readUnsignedShort() throws java.io.IOException;
    public final char readChar() throws java.io.IOException;
    public final int readInt() throws java.io.IOException;
    public final long readLong() throws java.io.IOException;
    public final float readFloat() throws java.io.IOException;
    public final double readDouble() throws java.io.IOException;
    public final java.lang.String readLine() throws java.io.IOException;
    public final java.lang.String readUTF() throws java.io.IOException;
    public final void writeBoolean(boolean) throws java.io.IOException;
    public final void writeByte(int) throws java.io.IOException;
    public final void writeShort(int) throws java.io.IOException;
    public final void writeChar(int) throws java.io.IOException;
    public final void writeInt(int) throws java.io.IOException;
    public final void writeLong(long) throws java.io.IOException;
    public final void writeFloat(float) throws java.io.IOException;
    public final void writeDouble(double) throws java.io.IOException;
    public final void writeBytes(java.lang.String) throws java.io.IOException;
    public final void writeChars(java.lang.String) throws java.io.IOException;
    public final void writeUTF(java.lang.String) throws java.io.IOException;
}
```

You instantiate a random access file with a mode string that says whether you plan to read the file or both read and write it. The mode string is "r" for reading, and "rw" for reading and writing. Throughout Java I/O, although there is a notion of closing files, there is no notion of opening a file. More precisely, when you instantiate of file object, that automatically opens the file for I/O. When you open for read/write access, if the file does not exist, it is created.

The following is an example of opening a random access file, seeking to the end, and then writing some more data. You should run this program and check that you get the expected output. When you run the program repeatedly, you will see it is appending to its output file.

```java
import java.io.*;
public class Raf {
    public static void main(String args[]) throws IOException {
        RandomAccessFile myRAF = new RandomAccessFile("myfile.dat", "rw");
        myRAF.seek( myRAF.length() ); // append to end of file
        myRAF.writeInt(5);
        myRAF.writeInt(0xBEEF);
        myRAF.writeBytes("at end.");
        myRAF.close();
        System.out.println("file myfile.dat written ok");
    }
}
```

You can use the program Dump.java from the previous chapter to look at the hex values written. You can run it and see something like this:

```
java Raf
file myfile.dat written ok
java Dump myfile.dat
type myfile.dat.hex
Hex dump of file myfile.dat 2004-04-29 15:02:11.093

00000000:  00000005  0000BEEF  61742065  6E642E
```

RandomAccessFile doesn't fit very well into the rest of the I/O framework, but nonetheless provides some useful features, including being able to read a line of data. It's in the Java API because it's in the underlying Unix API.

Running Commands and Getting Output From Them

This section explains how to execute a program from Java and read the output of that program back into your application. Just as a reminder, the use of OS commands in your code destroys portability.

If you can live with that limitation, there are four general steps to executing a program from your Java program.

1. Get the object representing the current run-time environment. A static method in class java.lang.Runtime does this.

2. Call the exec method in the run-time object, with your command as an argument string. Give the full path name to the executable, and make sure the executable really exists on the system. The call to exec() returns a Process object.

3. Connect the output of the Process (which will be coming to you as an input stream) to an input stream reader in your program.

4. You can either read individual characters from the input stream, or layer a BufferedReader on it and read a line at a time as in the code below.

Many books use the example of getting a list of files in a directory, even though there is already a Java method to do that in class File. The following code in class java.io.File will return an array of Strings, one string for each file name in the directory:

```
File f = new File(".");
String myFiles[] = f.list();
```

The file with the special name of "." is used on many operating systems to refer to the current working directory. We will use a different example here. We will execute a command in our Java program to make a file read-only. On Linux or other Unix, the command used would be "/bin/chmod a-w", on Windows we use the "attrib +R" command as shown in the following code.

Executing the attrib command from Java

```
import java.io.*;
public class ReadOnly {
    public static void main(String args[]) {
        try {
            Runtime rt = Runtime.getRuntime();   // step 1
            String cmd =
                // pathname changes in different versions of windows
                // "c:\\windows\\command\\attrib.exe  +R " + args[0]; // Win98
                    "c:\\windows\\system32\\attrib.exe  +R " + args[0];  // WinXP
            Process prcs = rt.exec(cmd);          // step 2
            InputStreamReader isr =                 // step 3
                new InputStreamReader( prcs.getInputStream() );
            BufferedReader in =
                new BufferedReader( isr );        // step 4.
            String line;
            System.out.printf("have set %s to read-only %n", args[0]);
            while (in.ready()) {
                System.out.println(in.readLine());
            }
            // Clean up
            prcs.waitFor();
            in.close();
        } catch(Exception e) { System.out.println(e); }
    }
}
```

This program uses the class java.lang.Runtime, which does several run-time-related things. The main use is to provide a way to execute other programs, but it can also load classes, request garbage collection, and do other memory-related things. It's a bit of a "grab-bag" for things that are done by the JVM.

The exec() method returns an object of class Process. That object allows you to get the in, out, and err streams from a process, and to wait for it to complete. You'll often see the lines of code reduced by directly wrapping the classes on each other, like this:

```
prcs = Runtime.getRuntime().exec(cmd);
in = new BufferedReader(
        new InputStreamReader( prcs.getInputStream()));
```

That replaces the lines commented as Steps 1, 2, 3, and 4 in the example. The attrib program that we have executed here doesn't produce any output, but we show how you can read lines from the InputStream for programs that do produce output. The waitFor() method lets the native program complete before the Java program continues on.

You can run the program and check the results with:

```
c:\ javac ReadOnly.java
c:\ java ReadOnly somefile
have set to read-only
c:\ dir /ar

 Volume in drive C has no label
 Volume Serial Number is 0D2B-14DC
 Directory of C:\JJ4\ch14io

SOMEFILE            6 08-24-01 7:56a somefile
       1 file(s)          6 bytes
       0 dir(s)    978.20 MB free
```

The "ar" option tells "dir" to only show files with the read-only attribute.

Note that there are half a dozen other versions of the Runtime.exec() method taking different arguments. These arguments can specify environment variables and the new working directory for the subprocess. Please refer to the API guide for the full list.

Limitations on running processes

An untrusted applet (Java program on a web page that is downloaded and run inside your browser when you visit that Web page) does not have permission to run executables. The Runtime.exec methods do not work well for special processes such as native windowing processes, daemon processes, Win16 or DOS processes on Win32, or shell scripts. In other words, many of the most useful things don't work! You can expect it to run a non-graphics program and that's about it. There are other problems, too:

- Most platforms provide limited buffer size for standard input and output streams. It might be as small as 1 or 2 Kbytes! If you do not promptly write to the input stream and read from the output stream of the subprocess, you may cause that subprocess to block and even deadlock. The same problem is often seen with Piped I/O, and it seems like everyone has to find out this limitation the hard way.

- The created subprocess is not started in an interactive shell, and so it does not have its own terminal or console. All its standard I/O (i.e., in, out, error) will take place to/from the parent process. The parent process uses the three streams (Process.getOutputStream(), Process.getInputStream(), Process.getErrorStream()) to feed input to and get output from the subprocess.

- Another implication of not running the program in an interactive shell is that the exec method does not have the ability to look for executables in the search path that your shell (or command interpreter) knows about. You should provide the complete path name for the command. This also means you cannot use commands that are built into a shell unless you explicitly call a shell as the program you wish to run (DIR and DEL are two Windows commands that are actually implemented by the shell). On Windows you can do a "find" for files with a ".exe" suffix to see which programs you can run.

- You will only be able to communicate with programs that use standard in, out, and err. Some programs like xterm open a new tty, or a GUI. These programs cannot be used as you would wish.

When you add all these restrictions together, plus the fact that a program that invokes an OS command or other program is usually not portable, the usefulness of the approach can be quite limited.

Formatted String Output

Support for formatted output was introduced with JDK 1.1, in package java.text. There is a class called java.text.DecimalFormat for formatting numbers, and a class DateFormat for formatting dates and times. Other classes provide support for collation (sorting order), and formatting program messages to users.

Most people now will prefer to use the standard formatting used in C and printf, available from JDK 1.5 in class java.util.Formatter. Please refer to the Chapter 17 for a description of these features.

Writing Objects to Disk

We've already seen how to write out strings, ints, doubles, etc., in both printable and binary forms. It may surprise you to learn that you can also write out, and later read back in, entire objects. When you serialize (write out) a single object to a data stream, it automatically saves the object, namely, all its instance data. If any of these non-static fields reference other objects, those objects are serialized too. That way, when you later deserialize (restore) the object, you get back the object and all its member fields pointing to all the things they pointed to before—everything needed to reconstitute the original object.

For example, if you serialize one element of a doubly linked list, everything it references, and everything the references reference, and so on, will be saved. For an element of a doubly linked list, that means the elements on each side of it, and the elements on each side of those (one of which is the original element—that doesn't get written out twice), and so on until the entire list has been written to disk.

The point of including everything that your object connects to, and all the things they connect to and so on, is to ensure that (when you read them back in) you can use those objects with the same state and contents that they had when you originally wrote them out. Doesn't this swell up the size of what you're writing until it's as big as your entire program? Objects contain references to their member fields, but members tend not to back reference the object of which they are a field. That means the links mostly go one way, and so serialized objects in practice remain a manageable size.

It's quite powerful to be able to do I/O on an entire graph of objects with one simple method call. If an object can be written to a stream, it can also be sent through a socket, compressed, encrypted, read out of a socket on another host, backed up onto a file, and later read back in again and reconstituted.

To make an object serializable, all you need do is make its class implement the Serializable interface. The interface java.io.Serializable doesn't have any methods or fields. It is an example of the Marker Interface design pattern. The purpose of requiring a class to implement an empty interface is to identify to other programmers and to the run-time library that it can be serialized. Here is a class that can be serialized:

```
package java.util;
public class Date implements java.io.Serializable { ...
```

Here is how you can serialize a Date object, and save it in a file:

```
// first create the file
ObjectOutputStream oos =new ObjectOutputStream (new
FileOutputStream("serial.bin") );
java.util.Date d = new java.util.Date();
oos.writeObject(d);
```

You can go on to write many more objects into the ObjectOutputStream. You need to be aware of the types that you are writing, so that you can cast them correctly back to their original type when you read them in again. Here is how you would read a serialized object back in again:

```
ObjectInputStream ois = new ObjectInputStream ( new FileInputStream("serial.bin")
);
java.util.Date restoredDate = (java.util.Date) ois.readObject();
```

It usually comes as a pleasant surprise to people to see that serialization is so easy! When you read an object back in, it has the type of Object. You need to cast it back to what it actually is. A ClassCastException will be thrown if you try to cast an object to a class it doesn't belong to. In the example, we really are reading in a Date, and so the cast takes place without a problem. If you put the above lines in a main program and add a couple of println's for the date before and after serialization, you will see output similar to this:

```
javac Serial.java
java Serial
date written out: Fri Apr 30 13:22:22
  date read back: Fri Apr 30 13:22:22
```

The important thing here is that the Date object survived its journey out into the filesystem, and came back in with the same value. Reading and writing objects is thankfully very simple.

Make sure you close an ObjectInputStream as soon as you have got the objects back that you need. ObjectInputStream hold references to all objects read from it, so their memory isn't eligible for garbage collection until the stream is closed or reset.

If a class is serializable, so are its subclasses (any interfaces of a parent are always inherited by the child). You can make a class serializable even if its parent isn't as long as the parent has a no-arg constructor and the child takes responsibility for restoring any parent context that wasn't serialized.

Serializing and security

Java object serialization was developed as an enabler for two other technologies: RMI and Java Beans. RMI (Remote Method Invocation) lets you make method calls across the network to processes running on other computers. Java Beans are a technique for modularizing code and manipulating them in a visual tool. Beans are enjoying some success in enterprise software, but have (surprisingly) been a total flop in desktop applications so far. Maybe the performance improvements of the 1.5 release will revive interest in desktop applications and hence in desktop beans.

When serialization was still in the design stage inside Sun, there was a great deal of debate about whether Java could allow serialization as the default setting. In other words, classes would have to opt out of allowing it, rather than opt in. After a lot of soul-searching, it was decided that programmers must take some explicit step to indicate that a class can be serializable (namely, we have to state that the class implements Serializable). The reason is that there are security implications to serializing a class.

If you serialize something like a file descriptor, someone could edit the file containing it and change some of the fields. When the file descriptor is read back in and deserialized, it will now be pointing at a different entry in the OS file descriptor table, or perhaps something outside the table altogether. Even though the exploit took place using native code, it would detract from the overall high level of security that Java enjoys.

So designers need to consider the security aspects when they make a class serializable. What happens if some field is given a different value while the object is in a file? Perhaps some kind of validation can be done after the object is read back in. Fields can be cross-checked for consistency with other data. You can also take complete control over the serialization process by doing it yourself. You take this approach by implementing the Externalizable interface and providing bodies for the two read and write methods therein.

Another step to improving the security of your serialized objects is to use the "transient" keyword. Any data field that is marked "transient" will not be written out when the class is serialized. You can often mark it "private" as well. A transient field is one that has a value that depends on some current state that will not be saved. For example, "current_speed" would be transient. You can also use the transient keyword to prevent the writing out of a field that is sensitive, such as "salary." If you do that, you will need to find some other way to restore the value after you have deserialized the object, perhaps by reading it from a secure database.

Some entire classes are not capable of being serialized. One such example is java.lang.Thread. Threads consist largely of Java code, but they also have a significant native code part. Each Java thread has two stacks: one for Java code and one for system code (usually C code). The native stack of a thread is not managed by Java, but by native code. The Java run-time doesn't know much about the native stack of a thread, and cannot save it. Thus, trying to serialize a thread will not be successful.

We already mentioned that only instance data is saved, not static data. You don't need to save the instructions in the methods of an object; that information is exactly what a class file is. So to successfully deserialize an object and use it, perhaps on another host, its class file must be accessible in the new environment.

XML support class

Just as I/O for ordinary types can be printable or binary, so too can objects be serialized into binary form or (incredibly) printable form. One of the main purposes of XML is to represent binary data in printable form. XML is described at length later in this book, and the one sentence summary is, "*XML is a portable way of storing data items in character form surrounded by tags that say what type each item is.*"

The Java 1.4 release introduced a class that let you serialize objects into XML form! The documentation says that this is intended solely for Java beans, including Swing GUI components. For your other classes (they say) you should continue using java.io.ObjectOuputStream. Those of us who like the advantages of XML will be the best judge of what to use where!

Here's an example of object persistence using XML:

```
import java.beans.*;
import java.io.*;
public class serial {
    public static void main(String args[]) throws Exception {
        java.util.Date d = new java.util.Date();
        FileOutputStream fos = new FileOutputStream("serial.xml");
        XMLEncoder xe = new XMLEncoder( fos );
        xe.writeObject(d);
        xe.close();
    }
}
```

After running the program, file serial.xml contains these lines:

```
<?xml version="1.0" encoding="UTF-8"?>
<java version="1.5.0" class="java.beans.XMLDecoder">
 <object class="java.util.Date">
  <long>1083282712203</long>
 </object>
</java>
```

XML makes a terrific serializable format for objects. I hope that Sun eventually blesses its use for all classes. The reason for their restriction is to maintain backwards compatibility with all the code that uses the earlier binary format. If you don't have any code that uses the earlier format, or you can convert it, then go ahead and serialize to XML.

Why would you serialize an object at all? The object may represent a customer record or a transaction that you wish to capture on backing store for archival, logging, or audit trail purposes. By writing it in XML, you are ensuring that it will be readable by any system at any time in the future, and can also be processed by a lot of automated tools that don't know about your specific data format.

New I/O Package

New!

JDK 1.4 introduced a package called java.nio. "Nio" stands for "new I/O" (so the JDK 1.5 I/O improvements must be "even newer than new I/O"). The java.nio package and subpackages support four important features not previously well-provisioned in Java:

- A non-blocking I/O facility for writing scalable servers
- A file interface that supports locks and memory mapping
- A pattern-matching facility based on Perl-style regular expressions
- Character-set encoders and decoders

Instead of building these on top of streams or file descriptors, these features are implemented using two new concepts: *buffers* and *channels*.

The right way to understand a buffer is to think of it as a big array in memory that holds data. Just like an array, a buffer can only hold things that are all the same type. So you can have a byte buffer, a char buffer, a short, double, float, and int buffer. If your file contains a mixture of floats and ints, you can pull them out of a Byte Buffer. Byte Buffer has methods to get and put all the primitive types except boolean.

The idea behind the Buffer class is to have a region of memory which can be accessed from both native code and Java at the same time, and that region has some special I/O characteristics in the native OS. Buffer is a kind of "native" array—native code can access it directly, and Java can use method calls to get its hands on the contents.

Because a buffer is essentially an area of memory, it can do things relating to memory, like clear its contents, support read/write or read-only operations, give you a range of elements, and tell you how many data elements it contains.

The second new concept in java.nio is the *channel*. A channel is a connection between a buffer and something that can give or receive data, such as a file or a socket. Because a channel connects to an underlying physical device, it can do things relating to an I/O device like support read/writes or provide file locks. There are channel classes specialized for files, for sockets, for pipes, and so on. You may think of a channel as an alternative to a stream. It has fewer fancy features (no elaborate wrapper classes), but it may have higher performance.

When to use channel I/O

Channel I/O is an alternative to basic stream I/O. Channels are similar to input or output streams, but also support the use of mapped I/O. Channel I/O also supports non-blocking I/O and can be faster than stream I/O.

You should use channel I/O for any high volume I/O (such as server applications). To improve performance, Sun reimplemented part of the Java classloader in JDK 1.5 using channels. When you need to do file locking or use a different character set from the default on your OS, channels provide an easy solution.

The following sections describe some features of java.nio and how to use them.

Multiplexed non-blocking server I/O

Channels have their own package at java.nio.channels. The package contains classes called DatagramChannel, SocketChannel, and ServerSocketChannel, among others. The single, critical feature that channels offer, and that classes DatagramSocket, Socket, ServerSocket do not, is the ability to do I/O without blocking the thread.

Non-blocking

The class java.nio.channels.SelectableChannel supports non-blocking I/O using what is called "selector-based multiplexing." Blocking I/O means that the I/O method does not return until the data transfer has taken place. If there is no input to read yet (because of network delays or because the user didn't type it yet), the entire thread will be blocked from continuing further. That's bad in terms of resource consumption. Simple non-blocking I/O, also known as "asynchronous I/O," means that you make the method call and it schedules the data transfer to take place at some future point, then returns almost immediately. No threads are blocked waiting.

Non-polling

Simple non-blocking I/O is helpful, but you can still burn up a lot of unproductive cpu time polling each descriptor to see if it is ready for more I/O yet. Selector-based multiplexing avoids this waste. It essentially says "monitor all these socket channels, and let me know when the next one of them is ready with data to transfer." The verb "to multiplex" means "to transmit several messages over the same medium all at the same time." Many different TV stations are multiplexed onto the cable of cable TV. The multiplexed part of selectors is that several data transfers may be underway at once, and the run-time system scans for pending data on the whole set of channels.

We won't review multiplexed I/O in depth, except to say that it provides the same kind of scalable I/O support as the select() system call available on all server operating systems. When select() is called, it blocks until one of a given set of socket descriptors is ready for reading or writing, or a timeout expires (whichever comes first).

Get a channel from a socket

To use multiplexed I/O in Java, first you get the channel from a socket. Then you register one or more channels with a Selector object, getting back a key. Finally, you do a select() on the Selector object. That waits until it can return a collection of keys that are ready for data transfer. Why is it OK for select() to block, but not other I/O methods? Because select() has a timeout feature. If no I/O becomes ready within so many milliseconds, the call returns. Also, you may be doing a select to get input from twenty sockets, but only one thread is blocked, not twenty.

Even if multiplexed I/O sounds involved, it is familiar to those who have used it in libraries for other languages. The additional objects of a key and a selector add a little more flexibility to the design. So now you can write non-blocking I/O in Java. When I/O is no longer a bottleneck in one thread, your web applications become scalable (when the load on the web server increases, you can speed it up by adding more processors).

Recovering from blocked server I/O

Channels support non-blocking I/O; they also make it easier to recover from blocked I/O. Server-based systems need to be reliable and scalable, but their threads can hang because of congestion, file mounting problems, or other remote access issues. Servers need the ability to get rid of threads that are "stuck" in network I/O. Scalability generally means that you assign a new thread to process each incoming request. That thread will be allocated to a socket, and that socket consumes a file descriptor. The system and each process have limited quantities of file descriptors. The idea is that the request comes in on a socket, where a thread serves it with any necessary I/O, database access, etc. The thread returns the answer to the client, then the thread and socket terminate and are reclaimed for further use.

All I/O in Java up to JDK 1.3 was synchronous or "blocking." When you execute a read or write instruction in Java, the method does not return until the data has been safely passed along. If there is a delay in the user response or the operating system or network, such that the data transfer cannot complete, then that thread hangs (waits indefinitely). When a thread becomes non-responsive for any reason, those file descriptors stay unavailable, eventually dragging down performance by reducing the number of sockets available to handle requests.

Some system designs rely on sockets *not* being consumed in this way. The designers of Java originally provided a method called interrupt() in class Thread. If some other thread called the interrupt() method of a Thread that was blocked, it was supposed to break out of the hang and get an InterruptedIOException while leaving the stream open for further attempts. Unfortunately, it turns out that the Windows API does not have any way to implement this that is both efficient and reliable. The interrupt method never worked well.

Workaround to blocking I/O

Instead, programmers used the workaround of closing the file descriptor or handle that was not responding to the I/O request. That unwedged the thread at the cost of leaving the I/O in an unknown state. The cost is generally acceptable. The most common reason to interrupt a thread is to ask it to shut down. If you plan to shut the thread down anyway, you might as well discard any socket in an unknown state and recover by opening a new connection.

Channels now officially provide the close-on-interrupt semantics that were in widespread unofficial use before. Any time you need to break threads out of blocking I/O operations, you should use a channel. You can either close the channel of a blocked thread, causing it to receive an AsynchronousCloseException, or you can call the interrupt() method of a thread that is blocked on channel I/O, thus closing the channel and delivering a ClosedByInterruptException to the blocked thread. File channels are always safe for use by multiple concurrent threads. Channels correctly support asynchronous interruption and closing.

Getting and using a file channel

There are several classes that support channels, but we'll only talk about FileChannels here. The network kinds of Channel (Datagrams and Sockets) are similar, but support slightly fewer operations because it doesn't make sense to lock sockets (they are inherently single-user). You get a FileChannel by calling the getChannel() method upon an instance of one of the classes FileInputStream, FileOutputStream, or RandomAccessFile in the java.io package.

```
RandomAccessFile raf = new RandomAccessFile("C:\\data.txt", "rw");
FileChannel myFileChannel = raf.getChannel();
```

The channel you get back is connected to the underlying physical file, and it will be open for read access in the case of FileInputStream, or for write access in the case of FileOutputStream. In the case of RandomAccessFile, the channel will be open for reading, or reading-and-writing, to match the mode that the random access file was instantiated with. In the code fragment above, you'll be able to read from and write into the channel to file c:\data.txt.

Once you have a file channel, there are several methods to read it into a buffer, or write it out from a buffer. The channel connects to the underlying file, while the buffer provides a place in memory to put the bytes. We'll finish up this summary of channels, then move on to buffers in the next section.

Channels also have methods to transfer data to and from another channel, to apply exclusive access locks to a file, and to map the file into memory. Mapping a file into memory is an advanced OS technique that uses the virtual memory subsystem to bring some or all of a file into the address space of a process. File mapping is an alternative to the read and write system calls used by streams. It is explained with an example a little later.

Here is the signature of a FileChannel method that reads from the channel (and hence from the file that the channel is connected to) into a byte buffer:

```
int read(ByteBuffer dst) throws IOException
```

You would use it like this:

```
ByteBuffer myBB = ByteBuffer.allocate(1024);
bytesRead = myFileChannel.read(myBB);
```

Channels, maps, and buffers maintain a notion of their "current position", just as file streams do. Bytes are read starting at this channel's current position, and then the position is updated with the number of bytes actually read. That number could be zero if nothing was read, or -1 to indicate that the channel has reached the end of stream. As with streams, you can "mark()" the current position to remember it, and then invoke `reset()` to return to that position later, and get the same input again (a fairly useless feature).

Here is the signature of a FileChannel method that writes from a byte buffer into the channel, and hence into the file that the channel is connected to:

```
int write(ByteBuffer src) throws IOException
```

It writes a sequence of bytes from the given buffer to the channel. It returns the number of bytes written, which may be zero. You would use it like this:

```
ByteBuffer myBB = ByteBuffer.allocate(1024);
// operations to put data into the byte buffer
myBB.put( ...    // we'll cover these soon
myBB.flip();    // changes over to writing the buffer
int bytesWritten = myFileChannel.write(myBB);
```

These lines of code write the bytes from the buffer through the channel into a file. Channels also support "scatter" reads into several buffers one after the other, and "gather" writes from several buffers into one channel. Scatter/gather I/O is convenient for certain protocol exchanges of fixed length messages. It also helps the kernel to use several small buffers instead of one big one.

What if you want to do filtering on the contents of a channel by wrapping additional classes, as we saw with the Reader/Writer and Streams classes? You cannot do that directly with a channel, but you can obtain a reader/writer/stream corresponding to a channel and then go on to wrap that in the usual way. The utility class java.nio.channels.Channels has half a dozen static methods that have the effect of converting each way between a channel and a Reader or a Writer or an InputStream or an OutputStream.

Buffers

You will create buffers either by an allocate method call, or by wrapping an existing array (or string for a character buffer) to form a buffer with the array contents, or by getting a buffer back from a channel map. You don't use a constructor to get a buffer: it's a hint that there is a lot more going on here than mere object allocation. Here's a sample line that obtains a 1 Kbyte buffer for you:

```
ByteBuffer bb1 = java.nio.ByteBuffer.allocate(1024);
```

Here's how you wrap an array to get a buffer that is filled with the contents of the array:

```
byte [] myByteArray = {0x11,0x22,0x33,0x44,0x55,0x66,0x77};
ByteBuffer bb2 = java.nio.ByteBuffer.wrap( myByteArray );
```

The wrapping is another example of the wrapper design pattern. A byte buffer can do pretty much all the things an array can do, and a few things of its own. As we saw above, you can write from a buffer into a channel, and thus into a file, pipe, or socket like this:

```
int count = fc.write(bb2);
```

This is very powerful. You can write an entire data array in two or three statements with no looping! Here's the entire program to read a file into a buffer:

Read a file using a Channel and a Buffer

```java
import java.io.*;
import java.nio.*;
import java.nio.channels.*;
public class MyBuffer {
    public static void main(String[] a) throws Exception {
        // Get a Channel for the file
        File f = new File("email.txt");
        FileInputStream fis = new FileInputStream(f);
        FileChannel fc = fis.getChannel();
        ByteBuffer bb1 = java.nio.ByteBuffer.allocate((int)f.length());

        // Once you have a buffer, you can read a file into it like this:
        int count = fc.read(bb1);
        System.out.println("read "+ count + " bytes from email.txt");
        fc.close();
    }
}
```

Other Buffer methods

Once your buffer is loaded with data from a channel, how do you access that in your program, and can you change the buffer? There are several kinds of operations upon buffers. They are as follows:

- After reading into a buffer, you need to rewind() it, to reset the position mark to the beginning. If you are about to start writing or getting from the buffer after a series of reads or puts, you need to call the flip() method.

- The get() and put() methods that read and write the next single data item, e.g.:

```java
byte b = bb1.get(); // gets the next byte
Double d = bb1.getDouble(); // gets the next 8 bytes into a double
ByteBuffer result = bb1.putChar('X'); // puts a char into the buffer
```

Gets and puts are done at the current index position in the buffer, and move the position immediately past what was just transferred. All the putSomething() methods are optional. They will only be supported if the underlying operating system supports this operation on a buffer.

There are get() and put() operations for these types: byte, char, double, float, int, long, and short. Notice that you read bytes into a buffer, but are able to get() and put() larger pieces of data. As always, you have to know the types of data that are stored in your files. A program cannot figure that out from looking at the bits.

* Absolute get() and put() methods that read and write a datum at a given offset, e.g.,

```
bb1.put(319, (byte) 0xF); // puts this byte at offset 319 in the buffer
bb1.putLong(256, 1234567890L); // puts this long at offset 256 in the buffer
```

* Bulk get() methods that transfer a sequence of bytes from this buffer into a byte array, e.g.,

```
byte[] destination = new byte[2048];
bb1.rewind();
bb1.get( destination ); // fills the array from the buffer
```

You should avoid unnecessary copying of data for performance reasons. Work directly with the buffer where possible.

* Bulk put() methods that transfer contiguous sequences of bytes from an array into this buffer, e.g.,

```
byte[] b2 = { 1,2,3,4,5,6,7,8,9,0xA };
bb1.put(b2);
```

You can also "wrap" an array around a buffer. That causes the buffer to be filled with the contents of the array. Unlike put(), it also causes further changes to either of the buffer or the array to be reflected in the other. One way to implement this is to relocate the buffer to occupy the same storage as the array.

```
byte[] b3 = { 1,2,3,4,5,6,7,8,9,0xA };
bb1.wrap(b3);
```

The buffer's capacity changes to match that of the wrapping array.

* Methods for allocating, compacting, duplicating, and extracting a subrange of ("slicing") a buffer.

View Buffers

Channels can only read from or write into a byte buffer. Even if the underlying file contains ints or longs, a channel cannot write into an int buffer. However, after you have read in the bytes, you can open a *view buffer* that is a differently typed interpretation of the underlying byte buffer. A view buffer is simply another buffer whose content is backed by the byte buffer. Changes to the byte buffer's content will be visible in the view buffer, and vice versa; the two buffers' current position and sizes are independent.

Here is how you get a view buffer that interprets its data as floats:

```
bb1.rewind();  // need to move buffer index back to beginning
FloatBuffer myFB = bb1.asFloatBuffer();
```

There are corresponding as*Something*Buffer() methods for the types char, short, int, long, and double. View buffers have a couple of advantages compared with the type-specific get and put methods described above. A view buffer is indexed in terms of the size of its values, not individual bytes. If you execute myFB.put(8, 3.14159F), it will make the 8th float in the buffer (bytes 56 to 63), not the 8th to 11th bytes, have the value of pi. A view buffer also provides bulk get and put methods for its type, as shown in the following complete program.

A bulk transfer from a buffer to an int array

```
import java.io.*;
import java.nio.*;
import java.nio.channels.*;
public class Buffer2 {
    public static void main(String[] a) throws Exception {
        // Get a Channel for the file
        FileInputStream fis =
                        new FileInputStream("numbers.bin");
        FileChannel fc = fis.getChannel();
        ByteBuffer bb = java.nio.ByteBuffer.allocate(400);
        // fill the buffer from the file
        int count = fc.read(bb);

        bb.rewind(); // need to move buffer index back to start
        IntBuffer ib = bb.asIntBuffer();
        // bulk get into an int array
        int[] myIntArray = new int[50];
        ib.get( myIntArray );
        for (int i=0; i<5; i++) {
            System.out.println( "arr["+i+"]="+ myIntArray[i] );
        }
        fc.close();
    }
}
```

If you compile and run this program, you will see printed the first few values in the file numbers.bin. Create the file first and put any junk in there. The contents are brought into the program with a channel that is read into a byte buffer. The byte buffer is rewound and then overlayed with an int view buffer. An int array is then filled with data from the int view buffer in a single get operation. Finally, the first five ints in the array are printed. You should compare them with the values you get by reading numbers.bin with a data input stream. Depending on what is in the file originally, you will see output like this:

```
arr[0]=2003461731
arr[1]=1751280235
arr[2]=1986164595
arr[3]=1986947691
arr[4]=1646294541
```

View buffers and characters

There is one further note about buffers. You may have noticed that the first example, MyBuffer.java in the buffer section, used a file called "email.txt" that obviously contained characters. When we read it in, these characters ended up in Java 8-bit bytes, not in Java 16-bit characters. What if we wanted to move each single ASCII byte in the file into a Java double-byte char? It turns out that this is now simple to do automatically.

Once you have the data from your file in a byte buffer, you can specify a new encoding and decode it from one buffer into another. The last section of this chapter is a lengthy description of character set encodings and the order in which bytes may appear. Here is the code that reads ASCII characters from a file, and ensures that they end up in Java Unicode double-byte chars:

```java
// Get a Channel for the source file
FileInputStream fis = new FileInputStream("email.txt");
FileChannel fc = fis.getChannel();

// Get a Buffer from the source file
MappedByteBuffer bb =
    fc.map(FileChannel.MapMode.READ_ONLY, 0, (int)fc.size());

Charset cs = Charset.forName("8859_1");
CharsetDecoder cd = cs.newDecoder();
CharBuffer cb = cd.decode(bb);
```

These lines are part of a complete example presented later.

Memory Mapped I/O

Let's return to the topic of memory-mapped I/O. We stated that file channels/buffers are an alternative to reads/writes on streams. Memory-mapped I/O is an alternative to both, implemented as a refinement to channels/buffers. The whole point of mapped I/O is faster I/O. When transferring large amounts of data, mapped I/O can be faster because it uses virtual memory to make the file contents appear in your address space. It takes some initial setup and puts more work on the virtual memory subsystem, but mapped I/O avoids the extra copying from buffers in kernel memory into buffers in your process.

When you read with a stream, the OS reads from the disk into a buffer owned by the device driver and then moves the contents from kernel space to your buffer in user space. Memory mapping only needs a couple of bits twiddled in the VM system to say "that disk page is now part of this process address space." So why doesn't everyone use mapped I/O all the time? Kernel whackers do, and the rest of the world is still hearing about the feature. Also, it's not part of the ANSI C API, which is one of the most widely used I/O APIs.

It came from Multics

Mapped memory is also known as shared memory. As well as offering performance improvements for larger files, it can be used for bulk data transfer between cooperating processes that all map in the same file. These processes don't even have to be on the same system, as long as the same file is visible to each. Mapped files were first used in Multics, the 1960s operating system that was wildly over budget and schedule, but which was the stepfather of Unix (and thus the ancestor of Linux, MaxOS X, and Solaris, too).

When you do a map operation on a FileChannel to map a file into memory, your return value is a mapped byte buffer that is connected to the file. The run-time system is expected to use the operating system features for memory mapping. The result is that when you write in the buffer, that data appears in the file. If you read from the buffer, you get the data that is in the file. Everyone is familiar with the way an operating system can read an executable file and make the instructions appear in the address space of a process. Mapped I/O does essentially the same thing for data files. The signature of FileChannel's map method is:

```
MappedByteBuffer map(int mode, long position, int size)
     throws IOException;
```

The position argument is the offset in the file where you want the mapping to start. This will usually be offset zero, to start at the beginning. The size is the number of bytes that you want from the file. This will usually be `myFile.length()` to get the whole thing.

The mode argument is one of FileChannel.MapMode.READ_ONLY, FileChannel.MapMode.READ_WRITE, or FileChannel.MapMode.PRIVATE, for read-only, read-and-write, or copy-on-write mapping. Copy-on-write is a variation of read-and-write mapping that says "if any process changes the content of this map it gets its own private copy with its change; everyone else can carry on sharing the unchanged version." It's mostly used in systems programming to share data pages of executables, and there was little reason to hide the semantics from Java, even though it's not something used much by applications.

Here's an example of mapping a FileChannel and, hence, the underlying File into memory:

```
File f = new File("data.txt");
FileInputStream fis = new FileInputStream(f);
FileChannel fc = fis.getChannel();

MappedByteBuffer mbb = fc.map(FileChannel.MapMode.READ_ONLY, 0, (int)
f.length() );
```

Note that file lengths are given in a long, but that you can only map an int's worth of memory (2 GByte) in any one map, so you must make sure the map size argument is typed as an int. We do that here by using the cast "(int)". If the physical memory available to your JVM cannot hold all the file, the virtual memory subsystem will bring in pieces of it as needed without you doing anything, or even being aware of it.

Direct buffers

A MappedByteBuffer is also termed a "direct" buffer. A direct byte buffer may also be created by invoking the allocateDirect factory method of this class. The buffers returned by this method typically have somewhat higher allocation and deallocation costs than non-direct buffers. So direct buffers should only be used for large, long-lived buffers that are subject to the underlying system's native I/O operations. The code that follows shows a file being written using a channel and buffer. Then the same file is read back in using mapped I/O. The data is compared with what was written, and it had better match.

Mapped I/O example

```
import java.io.*;
import java.nio.*;
import java.nio.channels.*;
public class MyMap {
    public static void main(String args[]) throws Exception {
        FileOutputStream fos = new FileOutputStream("ints.bin");
        FileChannel c = fos.getChannel();
        ///////////// write using channel and buffer //////////
        ByteBuffer bb = ByteBuffer.allocate(40);
        IntBuffer ib = bb.asIntBuffer();    // this is a view
        // fill the buffer
        for (int i=0; i<10; i++)  ib.put(i);
        // write the buffer full of ints to the channel and thus file
        c.write(bb);
        c.force(true);    // commit to disk
        c.close();

        ////////////////////// read back using mapped I/O //////////
        // read back loads of ints into a channel
        FileInputStream fis = new FileInputStream("ints.bin");
        c = fis.getChannel();
        MappedByteBuffer mbb = c.map(FileChannel.MapMode.READ_ONLY, 0, 40);
        // int num = c.read(mbb);    // you don't read a mapped buffer!
        System.out.println("byte buff capacity: " + mbb.capacity() );
        System.out.println("byte buff position: " + mbb.position() );
        System.out.println("byte buff    limit: " + mbb.limit() );
        for (int i=0; i<10; i++)   {
            int j = mbb.getInt();
            if (j != i) System.out.println("data mismatch: "+i+","+j);
        }
        System.out.println("Read the ints back from file ok");
    }
}
```

Many details of memory-mapped file behavior are inherently dependent upon the underlying operating system, and so they are not specified in Java.

File Locking

As we saw in the threads chapter, sometimes you have two things going on at once in a program, and to keep them straight you may need to stop them from doing the same thing together. This situation can occur in file handling. An example would be a data file that several programs want to update at the same time. Let's say the last record in the file contains the total of all the other records in the file. When a program updates the file, it first writes the new data value, then it reads the current total, adjusts it for the new value, and writes it back. If another program should happen to come along at just the wrong time, both programs may read the old total, then they will both update it, but one update of the total will overwrite the other. Result: two data changes, but only one change to the total, so the file is now inaccurate.

One way to avoid this situation is to use threads and synchronize them on some suitable object. That only works when all the threads trying to update the file are running in one JVM. Many applications cannot accept that limitation, which is where file locking comes in. Using the new FileLock class introduced in JDK 1.4 as part of package java.nio, the programmer can lock part or all of a file for exclusive access.

As a reminder, a method called getChannel() has been added to each of the FileInputStream, FileOutputStream, and RandomAccessFile classes. Invoking the getChannel() method upon an instance of one of those classes will return a file channel connected to the underlying file.

Once you have the FileChannel object for an output file, you call its lock() or tryLock() method. Lock is a blocking call—it won't return until it has the lock, or the channel is closed, or the thread interrupted. The method tryLock() is not a blocking call. It returns at once, whether it got the lock or not. The return value from both these calls is a FileLock object or null. Both of these methods have variants that let you provide arguments to specify that a region of the file (rather than the whole thing) is locked. That allows finer control over how much different processes stay out of each others way, with consequently better performance.

Here is an example program that repeatedly tries to acquire a lock. When it gets the lock, it prints a message saying so, and sleeps for two seconds to simulate doing some work with the file. It then releases the lock. It sleeps a further third of a second and does the whole thing over again.

```
import java.io.*;
import java.nio.channels.*;
public class Lock {
    public static void main(String[] a) throws Exception {
        // Get a Channel for the file
        FileOutputStream fos = new FileOutputStream("data.txt");
        FileChannel fc = fos.getChannel();
        while (true) {
            // Try to get a lock
            FileLock lock = fc.tryLock();
            if (lock !=null) {
                System.out.println("got lock");
                Thread.sleep(2000);    // simulate some work
                lock.release();
            }
            Thread.sleep(333);
        }
    }
}
```

If you compile this lock program and run several different copies of it at the same time, you will see messages indicating that the locks have been acquired and released.

The file-locking API maps directly onto the native locking facility of the underlying operating system. Thus, the locks held on a file are visible to all programs that have access to the file, regardless of the language in which those programs are written.

Whether or not a lock actually physically prevents another program from accessing the content of the locked region is system-dependent and therefore unspecified. The native file-locking facilities of some systems are advisory, meaning that programs must cooperate to observe a known locking protocol in order to guarantee data integrity. On other systems native file locks are mandatory, meaning that if one program locks a region of a file, then all other programs are prevented from accessing that region in a way that would violate the lock. To ensure consistent and correct behavior across platforms, all programmers should treat the locks provided by this API as if they were advisory locks. Everyone should use the java.nio features to do file locking going forward.

Charsets and Endian-ness

A character set, also known as an "encoding," is the set of bit patterns used to represent a set of characters. ASCII is one popular encoding. EBCDIC is a family of character sets with regional variations used on IBM mainframes. Unicode is a third encoding. Before describing the character sets available to Java, we need to explain "big-endian" and "little-endian" storage conventions.

Big-endian storage

Endian-ness refers to the order in memory in which bytes are stored for a multi-byte quantity. The term is a whimsical reference to the fable *Gulliver's Travels*, in which Jonathan Swift described a war between the Big-Endians and the Little-Endians, whose only difference was in where to crack open a hard-boiled egg. It was popularized in the famous paper, *"On Holy Wars and a Plea for Peace"* by Danny Cohen, USC/ISI IEN 137, dated April 1, 1980. It's a cool paper, well worth reading, and you can easily find it on the web if you search.

All modern computer architectures are byte-addressable, meaning every byte of main memory has a unique address. If you store a multibyte datum in several successive addresses, should the most significant byte of the datum go at the highest address or the lowest address? Big-endian means that the most significant byte of an integer is stored at the lowest address, and the least significant byte at the highest address (the big end comes first).

In other words, if you have an int value of 0x11223344, the four bytes:

```
0x11, 0x22, 0x33, 0x44
```

will be laid out in memory as follows on a big-endian system:

```
base address +0:    0x11
base address +1:    0x22
base address +2:    0x33
base address +3:    0x44
```

The SPARC, Motorola 68K, and the IBM 390 series are all big-endian architectures. Big-endian has the advantage of telling if a number is positive or negative by just looking at the first byte. It's also the way we read and write numbers in Western cultures in both word and digit form.

Little-endian storage

Little-endian contrasts with this by storing the *least* significant byte of an integer at the lowest address, and the highest byte at the highest address (the little end comes first). The number is "the other way up." On a little-endian system the same four bytes will be arranged in memory as follows:

```
base address +0:    0x44
base address +1:    0x33
base address +2:    0x22
base address +3:    0x11
```

The Intel x86 is a little-endian architecture, as was the DEC VAX. Little-endian has the advantage of telling if a number is odd or even by just looking at the first byte (not all that frequent a need).

Java uses big-endian ordering when it processes data, regardless of the platform it is on. Big-endian is also known as "network byte order" because the fundamental Internet TCP/IP standard is defined to use big-endian. The only time endianness is an issue is when you are trying to read data that was written by a non-Java program on a PC. Then you have to remember to swap multibyte values on the way in, or wrap a buffer around an array, as explained shortly.

Supported encodings

Table 18–1 shows some popular encodings. Every implementation of the Java platform from JDK 1.4 on is required to support these standard charsets. For character sets that include multibyte characters, endianness is an issue.

Table 18–1   Required encodings

Name	Size	Description
US-ASCII	7 bits	The American Standard Code for Information Interchange
ISO-8859-1	8 bits	The problem with ASCII is that it is the *American* Standard Code, and has no provision for accented characters. ISO-8859-1 contains the 7-bit ASCII character set, and the eighth bit is used to represent a variety of European accented and national characters. ISO 8859-1 is shown in an appendix at the end of this text.
UTF-8	8-24 bits	A UCS Transformation Format is an interim code that allows systems to operate with both ASCII and Unicode. "UCS" means Universal Character Set. In UTF-8, a character is either 1, 2, or 3 bytes long. The first few bits of a UTF character identify how long it is. • ASCII values (less than 0x7F) are written as one byte. • Unicode values less than 0x7FF are written as two bytes. The first byte starts with 110. • Other Unicode values are written as three bytes. The first byte starts with 1110. The second or third bytes of a multibyte sequence start with the bits set to 10. UTF is a hack best avoided if possible. It complicates code quite a bit when you can no longer rely on all characters being the same size. However, UTF offers the benefit of backward compatibility with existing ASCII-based data, and forward compatibility with Unicode data. There are several variations of UTF to accommodate byte order.
UTF-16BE	16 bits	Sixteen-bit UCS Transformation Format, big-endian byte order.
UTF-16LE	16 bits	Sixteen-bit UCS Transformation Format, little-endian byte order.
UTF-16	16 bits	Sixteen-bit UCS Transformation Format, byte order identified by an optional byte-order mark. When writing out data, it uses big-endian byte order and writes a big-endian byte-order mark at the beginning.

You gain the use of one of these encodings by passing a string containing the desired encoding as an argument to the constructor of OutputStreamWriter (for output) or InputStreamReader (for input). Recall from the previous chapter that these two classes provide a bridge between the world of 8-bit characters and the world of 16-bit characters.

What actually happens is that the bit patterns you have in your program are potentially changed in length and content, according to the encoding you specify. If you are reading in ISO 8859 single-byte characters, and mention that as the encoding, each one will be expanded to two bytes as it is read into Java Unicode characters.

Here's an example program that writes character values using an explicit encoding.

Using a specific character set

```
//   Write chars using UTF-Big Endian encoding
import java.io.*;
import java.util.*;
public class Codeset {
  public static void main (String args[]) throws Exception {
    FileOutputStream fos = new FileOutputStream("results.txt");
    OutputStreamWriter osw = new OutputStreamWriter(fos, "utf-16be");
    char data[] = { 0x11, 0x22, 0x33, 0x44, 0x55, 0x66, 0x77,
                        0x88, 0x99, 0xAA, 0xBB, 0xCC, 0xDD, 0xEE };
    osw.write( data );
    osw.close();
  }
}
```

If you run this program and try "utf-16be" and other character sets, you will see results as shown in Table 18–2. Appendix C shows the 8859-1, ASCII, and EBCDIC character sets.

Table 18–2   Character set results

Charset name	Output	Notes
Data written	11,22,33,44,55,66,77,8 8,99,AA,BB,CC,DD,EE	This is the data that is written using the various encodings.
"US-ASCII"	n/a	It's illegal to try to write 16-bit characters when you have specified a 7-bit encoding. The results are unspecified.
"ISO-8859-1"	n/a	It's illegal to try to write 16-bit characters when you have specified an 8-bit encoding. The results are unspecified.
"UTF-8"	11,22,33,44,55,66,77, C2,88,C2,99,C2,AA,C2,B B,C3,8C,C3,9D,C3,AE	The first few bits of a UTF character identify how long it is.
"UTF-16BE"	00,11,00,22,00,33,00,4 4,00,55,00,66,00,77, 00,88,00,99,00,AA,00,B B,00,CC,00,DD,00,EE	Sixteen-bit UCS Transformation Format, big-endian byte order. Big-endian is network byte order.
"UTF-16LE"	11,00,22,00,33,00,44,0 0,55,00,66,00,77,00 88,00,99,00,AA,00,BB,0 0,CC,00,DD,00,EE,00	Sixteen-bit UCS Transformation Format, little-endian byte order
"UTF-16"	FE,FF,00,11,00,22,00,3 3,00,44,00,55,00,66,00 ,77 00,88,00,99,00,AA,00,B B,00,CC,00,DD,00,EE	Sixteen-bit UCS Transformation Format. The initial FE, FF is the byte-order mark signifying big-endian.

Consult the release documentation for your implementation to see if any other charsets are supported.

Table 18–3 lists some popular encodings that may be supported on your system. There are literally dozens and dozens of other encodings.

Table 18–3   Other popular encodings

Name	Size	Description	Code for letter 'A'
windows-1252	8 bits	The default file.encoding property for most of Windows is "cp1252." Microsoft diverged from the standard ISO 8859-1 Latin-1 character set (which is shown in an appendix at the end of this book) by changing 27 characters in the range 0x80 to 0x9f, and called the result Code Page 1252. Complicating the situation, under Windows the shell uses a different encoding set to the rest of the system. It uses an older encoding for compatibility with MS-DOS. The shell uses either code page cp850 or cp437. To find out what code page is being used by the command shell, execute the DOS command "chcp" and see what it returns.	0x41
Unicode	16 bits	The problem with 8859_1 is that it can represent only 256 distinct characters. That's barely enough for all the accented and diacritical characters used in western Europe, let alone the many alphabets used around the rest of the world. Unicode is a 16-bit character set developed to solve this problem by allowing for 65,536 different characters. Strings in Java are made up of Unicode characters.	hex 0041
EBCDIC	8 bits	The Extended Binary Coded Decimal Interchange Code is an 8-bit code used on IBM mainframes instead of ASCII. It was originally intended to simplify conversion from 12 bit punch card codes to 8-bit internal codes. As a result, it has some horrible properties, like the letters not being contiguous in the character set. EBCDIC is really a family of related character sets with country-specific variations. An EBCDIC chart is shown in Appendix C.	0xC1
ISO/IEC 10646	32 bits	This is the Universal Character Set. There are two forms: UCS-2 and UCS-4. UCS-2 is a 2-byte encoding, and UCS-4 uses a 4-byte per-character encoding. This enormous encoding space is divided into 64K "planes" of 64K characters each. The ISO people want everyone to think of Unicode as just a shorthand way of referring to Plane Zero of the complete 4-byte ISO/IEC 10646 encoding space. Unicode, in other words, is UCS-2, which is a subset of the full UCS-4. They call this the "Basic Multilingual Plane" or BMP.	0x0000 0041

Byte-swapping binary data

The character sets only affect character I/O. You cannot apply an encoding to do automatic endian-swapping of binary data. But if you are using Java to read little-endian binary data, i.e., binary data that was written by a native program on a PC, you need to do this byte-swapping. We use the buffer class introduced in JDK 1.4. In Java 1.4, you can fill a buffer directly from a file, then pull values out of it with your choice of endian-order. To byte-swap a buffer, use code like this:

```
FileInputStream fis = new FileInputStream("ints.bin");
FileChannel c = fis.getChannel();
ByteBuffer bb = ByteBuffer.allocate(40);
int num = c.read(bb);

bb.rewind();
bb.order(ByteOrder.LITTLE_ENDIAN);

Float f1 = bb.getFloat();
```

Summary of charsets

- Most native file systems are based on 8-bit characters.
- Streams automatically handle the translation to Unicode strings used internally in Java.
- You get the right thing by default.
- If you want something different, you can ask for it.

Exercises

1. (Random Access Files) Create a data file that contains ten ints and a long. The long value holds the total of the ints. Write a program that repeatedly checks the total is correct, chooses one of the ten ints at random, changes it to a random value, and updates the total.

2. (Serialization) Write a program that creates a java.util.Vector object and adds various arrays to it. Serialize the Vector to a file. Read the Vector back in, and write the code to check that it contains the same contents that it had when written out. Modify the serialized file to give one of the arrays different content. (Hint: strings are easy to update in a file.) Check that your program detects the change.

3. (Channels, Buffers) Write a program that has two threads. One thread should engage in I/O using a channel. It should contain a handler for ClosedByInterruptException and AsynchronousCloseException. The other thread should call the interrupt method of the first thread. The first thread should catch the exception, re-open another channel and carry on with I/O. Put the whole thing in a loop and run it overnight. Is it reliable enough that it is still running in the morning? Is your operating system reliable enough to cope with this?

4. (Channels, Buffers) Write a program to measure the difference in performance between I/O through a direct (mapped) buffer and a non-direct buffer. Your program should output a 512 KByte array of ints 1,000 times in a loop to the same random access file. Is the performance of input any different? Account for any differences.

5. (Channels, Buffers) Take the example program that shows memory-mapped I/O for an input file and modify it so that the output is done by mapped I/O too.

6. (Locking) Take the program written for the random access file exercise (question 1 above). Run two copies of the program and demonstrate that the total quickly goes awry.

7. (Locking) Update the program in the previous exercise to protect the file by locking it. Run several copies of the program overnight to show that it works correctly.

8. (Locking) Update the program in the previous exercise so that it locks only the regions of the file that it is going to update: the random int and the total field. Measure the performance of this code and compare it with the code from the previous exercise. Is it faster or slower? Account for any performance differences.

9. (Encodings) Write a program that prints a neat table of EBCDIC and ASCII characters and their associated bit patterns.

10. (Encodings) Write a codeset program to write out data in all the standard encodings and confirm how the bytes are swapped with the different character sets.

Some Light Relief—The Illegal T-shirt!

The story so far: The light relief in the previous chapter described how the Motion Picture Association of America, combined with a shadowy Japanese-controlled organization known as the DVD-CCA, were furiously trying to stuff the toothpaste of DVD decryption back into the tube of secrecy. Their efforts were aided by a bad U.S. law known as the 1998 Digital Millennium Copyright Act.

The DMCA is not the first piece of bad law affecting the Internet. The Communications Decency Act lasted less than a year before the U.S. Supreme Court struck it down as unconstitutional in 1997. The DMCA is a bad law because it tilts the balance between consumers and copyright holders too heavily toward copyright holders. Many kinds of ordinary legal uses of DVDs, such as playing them with your DVD player of choice on the computer of your choice, have become effectively illegal under the DMCA.

Every once in a while, common sense collides with the law. It's not quite the irresistible force meeting the immovable object because the law must always yield to common sense in the long run. But it can be pretty entertaining in the short run. Take a look at the picture of this T-shirt (Figure 18-1).

Figure 18–1   Wear a T-shirt; go to jail!

The T-shirt contains a few lines of C code on the back, and the DVD Copy Control Association (DVD-CCA) is suing the vendor to try to drive this T-shirt off the market!

The dispute centers around those few lines of C code on the back of the shirt. They are just regular lines of C code, looking like this:

```
void CSSdecrypttitlekey(
            unsigned char *tkey,
            unsigned char *dkey) {
      int i;
      unsigned char im1[6];
      unsigned char im2[6]={0x51,0x67,0x67,0xc5,0xe0,0x00};

      for(i=0;i<6;i++)
            im1[i]=dkey[i];

      CSStitlekey1(im1,im2);
      CSStitlekey2(tkey,im1);
}
```

So why all the fuss? The answer lies in a vicious struggle over money, trade secrets, and a new U.S. copyright law affecting DVDs. DVDs (i.e., video films stored on high capacity CDs) hold ordinary MPEG-2 files that have been encrypted. The encryption is called the Content Scrambling System, or CSS. The DVD industry makes a lot of noise implying that CSS helps with protection against pirates. But, shiver me timbers mateys, the CSS encryption has no effect at all on piracy. Pirates just copy the entire disk bit-for-bit and resell them. DVD players don't have any magical way to tell if the same bits are coming from a genuine DVD or a pirate copy.

The CSS encryption is really there to give the DVD industry control over how *you* play back the titles you bought. If the bits are encrypted, they can only be played on a DVD player that is approved by the DVD industry. The industry can then enforce all kinds of restrictions, from not being able to fast forward past the trailers and adverts at the beginning, to not being able to play DVDs from other countries, to refusing to play content that has gone out of copyright and should therefore be freely available.

The movie and publishing industry has quite a history of rewriting copyright laws to favor itself. The period of copyright protection was originally up to 28 years from date of creation. By the 1920s the law afforded a maximum of 56 years of copyright protection. This period was expanded to 75 years in 1976, after strenuous lobbying from the Walt Disney corporation concerned about losing exclusive rights to the material created by the grandfathers of current employees. Even with the 1976 extension, the copyright on Mickey Mouse would expire on January 1 2004, so in the late 1990s Disney went back for another helping. Congress obligingly rolled over again and retroactively extended copyright another 20 years through the Sonny Bono Copyright Term Extension Act of 1998. Some time in the 2010s, the industry will surely want to reduce consumer rights even further and try to write itself an infinite lifetime on copyright. Even patents, flawed as they are, have a much more limited lifetime.

There are rights other than those of content producers at stake here. America has very strong guarantees concerning freedom of speech, and there are long-standing precedents saying that printed text (even source code) counts as speech. When the deCSS code was printed on a T-shirt, nobody seriously thought they'd be sued over it. Of course, the suit is really aimed at discouraging programmers from spreading knowledge about deCSS, and from playing their DVDs with software that hasn't been approved by the DVD-CCA.

The DVD industry won't achieve those goals. You can't legislate knowledge out of existence. This is the same nonsense that the U.S. government tried a few years ago, classifying some forms of encryption software as "munitions" and thereby regulating their export under the same rules as machine guns, tanks, and artillery pieces. That software ban lasted right up until the time it collided with the need to put encryption in browsers as an enabler for e-commerce. One possible outcome is that the DMCA will be found unconstitutional (i.e. contrary to the most fundamental principles of U.S. law). But until that happens, you can wear your illegal T-shirt with pride—you're striking a blow for freedom of speech, for consumer rights, and for writing and running whatever damn code you like on your own computers.

See also the book *Free Culture: How Big Media Uses Technology and the Law to Lock Down Culture and Control Creativity* by Lawrence Lessig. This important book can be freely downloaded from `http://www.free-culture.cc/freecontent/`. Lessig is a Professor of Law at Stanford Law School and founder of the school's Center for Internet and Society. Prior to joining the Stanford faculty, he was the Berkman Professor of Law at Harvard Law School. He is a great advocate for net values, open source code, and the rights of individuals on the internet.

4

Client Java

Chapter 19

Regular Expressions

This chapter provides an introduction to some classes in the java.util and related packages that have utilities for your code to use. We start with the regular expression support that allows you to do pattern matching of Strings. After that, we look at the Date and Calendar-related classes, which have confused and frustrated many people.

The chapter finishes with a brief look at some data structure classes that predate Collections, but are still useful. The rest of this book is devoted to explaining more Java libraries and showing examples of their use. Let's get going with regular expressions and pattern matching.

Regular Expressions And Pattern Matching

This section uses the I/O features described in the previous chapters and describes the regular expression pattern matching feature that was introduced with JDK 1.4.

If you have typed "dir *.java" to see all the Java files in a directory, you have used a regular expression for pattern matching. A regular expression is a String that can contain some special characters to help you match patterns in text. In this case, the asterisk is shorthand for "any characters at all". The name "regular expression" was coined by American mathematician Stephen Kleene who

467

developed the expressions as a notation for describing what he called "the algebra of regular sets". The asterisk is also called a "Kleene star".

JDK 1.4 introduced a package called java.util.regex that supports the use of regular expressions. Using the classes in that package lets you answer questions like "Does this kind of pattern occur anywhere in that String?", and you can split Strings apart and create new Strings with changed contents. These sorts of operations are very useful in the following contexts:

- Web searches (you can use regular expressions in many search engines).
- Email filtering (discard email where the "From:" line matches well-known spammers)
- Text-manipulation tasks. Source code editors usually have a way to search using regular expressions. If you don't know how to do pattern matching in the editor you use to edit programs, you aren't yet reaching your full potential as a programmer. Plus, it's a great way to beguile other programmers who look over your shoulder.

There's lots of good news about regular expressions in Java. First, the language of regular expressions (the way you form regular expressions, the special symbols and their meaning) is very similar to that used by Perl. There are a few obscure things supported by Java that Perl 5 doesn't support, and vice versa. Java is less forgiving about badly formed expressions. But if you already know Perl, there's less to learn about Java pattern matching. If you don't use Perl, your Java regex knowledge will get you jump-started.

Best of all, Java regular expressions are simple. There are only three classes in the package, and one of those is an exception! Well, you can't really judge the complexity of a library by the number of classes it has, but regular expressions are straightforward. Pattern matching is important, and we'll cover it in some detail.

Let's say you have a String somewhere, and you want to look for a pattern in it. A pattern will be something like "at least one letter or digit (and maybe many) followed by a colon followed by a space, followed by at least one letter or digit (and maybe many)". The steps to look for a pattern in a String, s, include:

1. You specify the pattern with a String, p, holding a regular expression representing the pattern.
2. You then turn String p into a pattern object by invoking the static method `java.util.regex.Pattern.compile(p)`. The `compile()` hands you back a pattern object.
3. Using the pattern object from Step 2, you invoke the `matcher()` method, giving it the input String s that you want to look through. Matcher(s) will give you back a `java.util.regex.Matcher` object. That matcher object has the methods for matching, splitting, and replacing parts of input Strings.

Therefore, two of your classes are pattern and matcher. The third class is the exception PatternSyntaxException. That exception is thrown if you provide a faulty regular expression to `Pattern.compile()`.

Under the covers, the `Pattern.compile()` method builds a tree to represent the regular expression. Each node in the tree represents one component of the regular expression. Each node contains the code that does a comparison on an input String and gives an answer about whether it matches that part of the pattern. It is similar to the work an ordinary compiler does to turn source code into executable code, so "compile()" is a reasonable name for the method. The programmers could have made a constructor available. The use of a static method called `compile()` to return an instance is a hint that there is a lot more work going on here than memory allocation and initialization. It also leaves the door open to a future release which tries to share pattern matchers or provide several alternative implementations that can be swapped in at run-time.

Two cautions

There are two cautions to observe.

First, patterns very quickly become very hard to read. Take every step to keep them as simple as possible.

Second, the regular expression language used in the Windows command shell is *different* to the regular expression language used everywhere else in computer science. If you have three files on a Windows system (containing, oh, I don't know, chapter 19 of a Java book):

```
ch19.fm.may06
ch19.fm.apr25
ch19.fm
```

Say you wish to delete the two files with the date in the name, and keep the third. Typing

```
del ch19.fm.???
```

is correct for Java/Perl patterns but a big mistake on Windows. Windows will delete all three files. Words fail me on this one.

Matching a pattern

Just as you don't directly instantiate a pattern object, you don't directly instantiate a matcher. You get an instance of the Matcher class by calling the `matcher()` method of your pattern object. Then you send it input from anything that implements the CharSequence interface. String, StringBuffer, and CharBuffer implement CharSequence, so they are easy to pattern match. If you want to match patterns in a text file, this is also easy to do using the new Channel I/O feature. You get the Channel for the file, then you get a Buffer from the Channel. Character Buffers implement the CharSequence interface. If you need to pattern match from some other source, you can implement the CharSequence interface yourself (it's small and easy).

After you have a matcher object, it supports three kinds of match operations:

- The **find()** method scans the input sequence looking for the next sequence that matches the pattern.

- The **matches()** method tries to match all the input sequence against the pattern.

- The **lookingAt()** method tries to match some or all of the input sequence, starting at the beginning, against the pattern.

Forming patterns

A regular expression, or pattern, is a String that describes the kind of thing you want to match. Most letters represent themselves. If you compile a literal pattern of "To: pvdl@aaa.com", it will match exactly those letters in that order. If you have a file containing old email, you could use this pattern to find all the email addressed that way.

After you have compiled a pattern and have a matcher object, you can invoke its find() method to look for the next occurrence of the pattern in the input. You can then call its group() method to get back the input sequence that was matched by the previous match operation. The code is similar to the following:

```
Pattern p = Pattern.compile("To: ted@sun.com");
Matcher m = p.matcher( someBuffer );
while (m.find())
    System.out.println("Found text: "+m.group());
```

The find() method returns a Boolean result indicating if the next occurrence of the pattern was found in the input. The group() method returns a String containing the most recent part of the input to match. If you provide a main program and run the code on a file containing my email, it prints the matches with output similar to the following:

```
Found text: To: ted@sun.com
Found text: To: ted@sun.com
```

The following sections use this example data file of email. It contains five email messages, each of which starts with "From:" and continues until the next "From:".

Sample email data file

```
From: aaa@sun.com
To: bbb@sun.com
Subject: weather
The weather is fine today.
From: aaa@sun.com
To: ccc@sun.com
 Hello
From: aaa@sun.com
To: ddd@xyz.com,eee@home.com
Subject: no change!
--[booo!]
Weather still fine!
    He said he was a British Subject: born in London
From: aaa@sun.com
To: bbb@sun.com
Subject: Help - no rain.
We are in a drought,
    Bill.
From: aaa@sun.com
To: BBB@SUN.COM
Subject: SHIFT KEY
HELP! SHIFT KEY IS STUCK _ BILL
```

The following sections use this program as a framework for trying different patterns. The pattern line is marked in bold. If you want to experiment with the different patterns shown, this is the line to update. This program and the data file are on the web site afu.com/jj6.

Sample pattern-matching program

```
import java.util.regex.*;
import java.io.*;
import java.nio.*;
import java.nio.charset.*;
import java.nio.channels.*;
public class Extract {
    public static void main(String[] args) throws Exception {
        // Create a pattern to match comments
        Pattern p = Pattern.compile("To: bbb@sun.com");

        // Get a Channel for the source file
        FileInputStream fis = new FileInputStream("email.txt");
        FileChannel fc = fis.getChannel();

        // Map a Buffer in from the data file, and decode the bytes
        MappedByteBuffer bb =
            fc.map(FileChannel.MapMode.READ_ONLY, 0, (int)fc.size());
        Charset cs = Charset.forName("8859_1");
        CharsetDecoder cd = cs.newDecoder();
        CharBuffer cb = cd.decode(bb);

        // Run some matches
        Matcher m = p.matcher(cb);
        while (m.find())
            System.out.println("Found text: "+m.group());
    }
}
```

Running the program creates the following output:

```
java Extract
Found text: To: bbb@sun.com
Found text: To: bbb@sun.com
```

The following three lines of code may be unfamiliar:

```
Charset cs = Charset.forName("8859_1");
CharsetDecoder cd = cs.newDecoder();
CharBuffer cb = cd.decode(bb);
```

The three lines of code specify how the bytes in the file are translated into characters as they are brought into the buffer. The earlier examples of mapped I/O just took bytes from the file and put them into bytes in the buffer. In this case, we get an object that represents the ISO 8859 Latin-1 character set (shown in Appendix B). Using that object we get a decoder object. The decoder object has the ability to "decode" or translate bytes into double-byte characters. The 8859 example is a single byte character set and the translation turns each byte in the file into two bytes in the buffer; zero is the most significant byte. For more details about character sets and encodings, see the second I/O chapter.

Range

The pattern "To: bbb@sun.com" won't find *all* email to bbb. Email should be delivered whether the domain part of the address is in upper or lowercase. This pattern matches only lowercase. As frequently happens with regular expressions, there are several different ways of writing a pattern. We can make the pattern ignore letter case by passing a flag when we compile the pattern, as shown in the following example:

```
Pattern p = Pattern.compile("To: bbb@sun.com",
                         Pattern.CASE_INSENSITIVE);
```

Another way to achieve the same effect is to use a range. When the pattern object sees square brackets, it tries to match one of the characters inside the brackets. If we want to match "sun" without regard to case of the first letter, we could use this pattern:

```
"[Ss]un"
```

The pattern in one pair of square brackets matches one character. You can use a hyphen to indicate a range of characters (hence the name for this feature). Both of the following patterns will match any single digit:

```
"[0123456789]"
"[0-9]"
```

To exactly match two digits "00" to "99" we could use "[0-9][0-9]".

A powerful feature of the range function is the ability to match "anything but" the list of characters in the range. If the first character in a range is "^" (caret), it means "match any character *except* the ones that follow". In order to extract the "To:" lines for all names except those that start with "j" we could use this pattern:

```
"To: [^j]"
```

Similarly, "[^]" matches any character other than a space, and "[^0-9]" matches any one character that is not a digit. If you need to match against one of the special characters like square bracket or caret, you can "escape" them in the String. You escape a special character (treat it literally) by putting two backslashes before it in the String. Rather than use one backslash, use two because the rules of Java Strings take precedence over the rules of regular expression patterns. To get one backslash in a Java String, you must escape it with its own backslash.

This is really and truly lame

The backslash character `\` is used in Java Strings to escape certain characters, i.e., give them some different meaning. For example, "n" in a String means the lowercase letter n. But "\n" tells the compiler that the linefeed character, ASCII 0x0A, should be substituted. Similarly, "\r" means that you get a carriage return, ASCII 0x0D. Since backslash has this special meaning, to get a backslash in a String, you must escape the backslash itself. (JLS 3.10.6)

As a result, every time you want one backslash in a Java String, you have to write two. We have already seen how this means rewriting all path names for Windows:

```
String myFileName = "\\a\b\\c.txt";
```

This requirement means that you must rewrite many pattern matching Strings when you place them in Java Strings, so these no longer look the same as Perl regular expressions. The metacharacter to match a digit is \d, or in a String:

```
String matchDigit = "\\d";
```

If you want to look for a String that's a path name, your pattern may end up like this:

```
String myFilePattern = "\\\\a\\\\b\\\\c.txt";
```

Obviously, this is *really* lame. One way to avoid it would have been to have a new class that is like String but which doesn't do character escaping.

You might blame Dennis Ritchie, who popularized this "backslash means escape in a String" protocol in C, except C was laid down in 1970. You could blame Seattle Computer Products, who created the product sold under the name MS-DOS and made backslash the path name separator, apparently in ignorance of C and Unix. You can blame Larry Wall, who invented Perl, or James Gosling, who reused C's String escape convention in Java. Or you could just live with it.

Ranges can be used to match literal Strings. But we are often in a situation where we want to match a String that conforms to some pattern. The email subject line, for example, starts with "Subject: ", then has some kind of text, and ends with an end-of-line character. To match a pattern that includes some arbitrary text, use metacharacters.

Single-character metacharacters

Let's say we want to match the Subject line of email. We want a pattern to match "Subject: *anything*" on one line. We will use the *metacharacter* "." (dot) that matches any single character. There are other metacharacters besides dot that match a single character. These metacharacters are shown in Pattern metacharacters.

Table 19–1   Pattern metacharacters

Metacharacter	Written in Java String	Single character matched	Express with a range
.	"."	Any character	n/a
\d	"\\d"	A digit	[0-9]
\D	"\\D"	A non-digit	[^0-9]
\s	"\\s"	A whitespace character	[\t\n\x0B\f\r]
\S	"\\S"	A non-whitespace character	[^\s]
\w	"\\w"	A character that can be part of a word	[a-zA-Z_0-9]
\W	"\\W"	A character that isn't part of a word	[^\w]

We use "." to match any character. We also need to apply a *quantifier* that says how many times to do this. The quantifier "*" means "any number of times." It applies to whatever immediately precedes it. Putting together the "match any character" dot with the "any number of times" quantifier, our pattern to match the subject line of email is the following:

```
"Subject: .*"
```

This matches up to the end of a line because, by default, the dot does not match line terminator characters. If you put that pattern into a suitable program and run it, you get output similar to the following:

```
Found text: Subject: weather
Found text: Subject: no change!
Found text: Subject: Born in London
Found text: Subject: Help - no rain.
Found text: Subject: SHIFT KEY
```

If you look back at the email.txt file, you'll see that the "Born in London" text is not actually a subject line. We will fix that in a later section.

Quantifiers

There are other quantifiers that can express different amounts of repetition. Table 19–2 on page 476 shows some quantifiers that specify the number of times a particular character or pattern should match. In this table, "X" represents any pattern.

Table 19–2   Quantifiers

Pattern	Meaning
X?	X, zero or one time
X*	X, zero or more times
X+	X, one or more times
X{n}	X, exactly n times
X{n, }	X, at least n times
X{n,m}	X, between n and m times

You can group patterns in parentheses to indicate exactly what is being repeated. So "(\\w*: \\w*)*" will match any number of sequences that consist of wordcharacters-colon-space-wordcharacters. This is a pattern for email headers. Don't be fooled by the name "wordcharacter". It only matches a single character, not an entire word. If you want it to match a word, you have to use a quantifier to repeat it, as shown in the email example.

All quantifier operators (+, *, ?, {m,n}) are greedy by default, meaning that they match as many elements of the String as possible without causing the overall match to fail. In contrast, a reluctant closure will match as few elements of the String as possible when finding matches. You can make a quantifier reluctant by appending a '?' to the quantifier. An example of a reluctant quantifier is shown later.

Capturing groups and back references

Another use for parentheses is to represent matching subpatterns within the overall pattern. These subpatterns are called *capturing groups*, and you can retrieve them independently from the matcher you use in your code. You can also refer to one of these capturing groups later in the expression itself with a backslash-escaped number. A backslash followed by a number is always interpreted as a back reference. The first back reference in a regular expression is denoted by \1, the second by \2, and so on. Therefore, the expression: "([0-9]+)==\1" would match input like "2==2" or "17==17." Remember to double those backslashes when you want to put them in a Java String!

Back references let you match against patterns that contain *Reader's Digest* style junk mail. If you've never received a *Reader's Digest* letter, it is personalized by repeating your name and other details they have on file about you. A typical phony letter would be similar to the following:

Dear Peter,
Excuse the intrusion, Peter, but we just wanted to ask you who would
look after your family at 123 Main Street, if anything should happen to you,
Peter?
Life insurance is not that expensive, Peter, and surely the family is worth it.
Please contact us for more details, Peter.

The following pattern would match against this:

```
Pattern p = Pattern.compile(
          "^Dear (\\w+),$"      // matches "Dear name,"
          + "(^"                //   any number of lines
          +    ".* \\1.*"
//    each line has the name we captured in group 1.

          + "$)*"               //   end line
        , Pattern.MULTILINE );
```

As you can see, patterns quickly become difficult to read. This pattern matches
the greeting and then up to the first line not containing the name. The important
things in the *Reader's Digest* example are the expression in parentheses on the first
line (the parentheses make it a capturing group), and the "\\1" on the third line
of the pattern, which is a back reference to capturing group 1. The back references
are numbered according to the order in which their opening parenthesis appears.
Capturing groups can nest inside each other.

Whenever you use parentheses, the bracketed part of the pattern becomes a
capturing group (there is a way to turn that off). The method Matcher.group(int i)
returns the input sequence captured by group i during the most recent match. To
extract the actual name and print it, we would add the following code:

```
Matcher m = p.matcher( someBuffer );
if (m.find()) {
   System.out.println("Letter personalized for: " + m.group(1));
   System.out.println("line from letter: " + m.group(2));
}
```

Group 1 is the name. The call to group(2) will return the String "Please contact us
for more details, Peter," since that is the most recent match of all the lines that the
group captured.

Anchors

Returning to our email example, the pattern "Subject: .*" will also find non-
subject lines, where text similar to the following exists:

```
How to be a British Subject: marry into the Royal Family.
```

That's not an email subject line, but it contains characters that match our pattern. If we really only want Subject lines, we need to be able to specify that the pattern only matches something at the beginning of a line. To do this we use a set of metacharacters called "anchors", which attach the pattern to a particular place. Anchor characters shows some anchor characters and how they affect matching. In this email example, anchoring the pattern to the beginning of a line is still not enough. The pattern could occur in the body of an email message at the beginning of a line. To get this exactly right, you will need to match on the whole message, and distinguish headers from the body. An exercise at the end of the chapter allows you to do that.

Table 19–3   Anchor characters

Anchor	Effect
^	The beginning of a line (also needs the multiline flag)
$	The end of a line (also needs the multiline flag)
<	The beginning of a word
>	The end of a word
\b	A word boundary
\B	A non-word boundary
\A	The beginning of the input
\Z	The end of the input but for the final terminator, if any
\z	The end of the input

Notice that the anchor for the beginning of a line is a caret. Don't get confused by the fact that caret is also used in ranges with a different meaning. There are so many metacharacters needed that it's inevitable that a few would be reused. We can anchor our email subject search to the beginning of a line with a pattern similar to the following:

```
"^Subject: .*"
```

By default, the expressions for beginning and end of line don't do that! They only match the beginning and end of the input. You must set a pattern flag for multiple lines, as we did previously for letter case. The multiline flag will cause pattern matching to extend across line boundaries in the input. The following example shows you how to set the pattern and a couple of flags in one statement:

```
Pattern p = Pattern.compile("^Subject: .*$",
                Pattern.MULTILINE | Pattern.CASE_INSENSITIVE );
```

The flags are actually integer constants, and you "or" them together to combine their effect, as shown in the previous line of code.

Alternation

Let's make this example more realistic by writing a pattern to extract a series of entire email messages. A mail message is defined as everything between one "From:" at the start of a line, and the next one. There is a method in pattern that splits an input sequence into pieces that are separated by the pattern. This is similar to what a Scanner does with a delimiter. It returns an array of Strings, and is perfect for this purpose. The code to use it looks similar to the following example:

```
Pattern p = Pattern.compile("^From:", Pattern.MULTILINE);
String[] messages = p.split( someBuffer );
```

This code will split our file into Strings, each of which contains one e-mail. The delimiter pattern is not copied into the resulting messages array.

Now let's look at a couple of other topics relating to pattern matching. The first one is alternation, which uses the " | " (vertical bar) meta character. The second topic is how to say "anything except this word"?

When you place a " | " in a pattern, it means "or". The pattern will match if either the left side of the " | " or the right side matches the input. That's all there is to alternation! You can use parentheses to group the alternate things more explicitly if needed. There is no corresponding "and" feature, because you get that effect by writing two subpatterns one after the other. So "XY" means "match an X followed by a Y," while "X | Y" means "match if you see either an X or a Y."

Word negation

The next topic we will cover in this section is how to match the negation of a word. Ranges provide an easy way to match the negation of a single character. There is no built-in support for negation ("everything but") of an entire word. Most people's first guess at a pattern to exclude all lines that start with "From" is "^[^F][^r][^o][^m]".

This doesn't do what you want! It matches everything where the first character is not an "F", *and* the second character is not an "r", *and* the third character is not an "o", and so on. Because these "not equal to" conditions are "anded" together, if you have a word for which *any* of these letters-and-positions is a F... or .r.. or ..o. or ...m; for example, "Frob" or "grin" or "shot" or "glum" you will find that the pattern rejects that line overall as a match. Regular expressions really ought to have an operator that matches the negation of a word.

You have to create the idiom of "exclude this word" from other primitive operations that are available. To extract complete email messages, we want to start with a "From:" at the beginning of a line, and go up to but not including the next "From:" at the beginning of a line.

One way to express this is with a pattern in three parts: a "^From:" matched literally, then an "everything except a '^From'", then a "^From:" or an end-of-input (using alternation). Following is the code example:

```
Pattern p = Pattern.compile(
"^From:.*$"          // first "From:"
+ "(^.*$)*?"          // anything, over several lines
+ "^(?=From:|\\z)"    // second "From:" or end of input
, Pattern.MULTILINE);
```

The "?" in pattern "*?" is the "reluctant quantifier" that we mentioned earlier. It matches zero or more times reluctantly. For example, if there is another way to interpret this match, that other part of the pattern is preferred. Similarly, the "?=From" is a special construct that provides a match with lookahead. The matching characters are not regarded as part of the captured group but remain in the buffer for the next find() attempt. Finally, the "|\\z" causes a match on either the "From" or the end of input.

One place where regular expressions can be used is in the accept method of the class javax.swing.filechooser.FileFilter. The class java.io.File has a method: File[] listFiles(FileFilter filter). You can write a class implementing FileFilter and supply the only method there, which is accept(File). You can put your file selection logic in there, and base it on desired filename patterns.

Metawords

There are also metawords that match entire categories, as shown in POSIX character classes.

Table 19–4   POSIX character classes

(US-ASCII only)	Meaning
\p{Lower}	A lower-case alphabetic character: [a-z]
\p{Upper}	An upper-case alphabetic character:[A-Z]
\p{Alpha}	An alphabetic character:[{lower}{upper}]
\p{Digit}	A decimal digit: [0-9]
\p{Alnum}	An alphanumeric character: [{alpha}{digit}]
\p{Punct}	Punctuation: one of !"#$%&'()*+,-./:;<=>?@[\]^_`{|}~
\p{Graph}	A visible character: [\p{Alnum}\p{Punct}]
\p{Print}	A printable character: [\p{Graph}]
\p{Blank}	A space or a tab: [\t]
\p{Cntrl}	A control character: [\x00-\x1F\x7F]
\p{Xdigit}	A hexadecimal digit: [0-9a-fA-F]
\p{Space}	A white space character: [\t\n\x0B\f\r]

All of the state involved in performing a match is in the matcher, so many matchers can share the same pattern. But matcher objects are not thread safe, and one matcher should not be invoked from different threads at the same time.

Finally, the JDK comes with an example program that searches for regular expressions in files. This program is also a Unix utility known as "grep," which stands for "globally search for regular expression and print." A much simplified version of the program follows. Please review it carefully, as it provides a non-trivial practical example of the use of regular expressions.

Java grep program

```java
// Search a list of files for lines that match a given regular-expression
// pattern.  Demonstrates NIO mapped byte buffers, charsets, and regular
// expressions.
import java.io.*;
import java.nio.*;
import java.nio.channels.*;
import java.nio.charset.*;
import java.util.regex.*;
public class Grep {
    public static void main(String[] args) {
        if (args.length < 2) {
            System.err.println("Usage: java Grep pattern file...");
            return;
        }
        doCompile(args[0]);
        for (int i = 1; i < args.length; i++) {
            File f = new File(args[i]);
            try {                    CharBuffer cb = mapInFile(f);
                grep(f, cb);
            } catch (IOException x) {
                System.err.println(f + ": " + x);
            }
        }
    }
    // Charset and decoder for ISO-8859-15
    private static Charset charset = Charset.forName("ISO-8859-15");
    private static CharsetDecoder decoder = charset.newDecoder();
    // Pattern used to separate files into lines
    private static Pattern linePattern = Pattern.compile(".*\r?\n");
    // The input pattern that we're looking for
    private static Pattern pattern;
    // Compile the pattern from the command line
    //
    private static void doCompile(String pat) {
      try {
          pattern = Pattern.compile(pat);
      } catch (PatternSyntaxException x) {
          System.err.println(x.getMessage());
          System.exit(1);
      }
    }
    // Use the linePattern to break the given CharBuffer into lines,
    // applying
```

```
    // the input pattern to each line to see if we have a match
    private static void grep(File f, CharBuffer cb) {
        Matcher lm = linePattern.matcher(cb); // Line matcher
        Matcher pm = null;   // Pattern matcher
        int lines = 0;
        while (lm.find()) {
            lines++;
            CharSequence cs = lm.group();  // The current line
            if (pm == null)
                pm = pattern.matcher(cs);
            else
                pm.reset(cs);
            if (pm.find())
                System.out.print(f + ":" + lines + ":" + cs);
            if (lm.end() == cb.limit())
                break;
        }
    }
    // Search for occurrences of the input pattern in the given file
    private static CharBuffer mapInFile(File f) throws IOException {
        // Open the file and then get a channel from the stream
        FileInputStream fis = new FileInputStream(f);
        FileChannel fc = fis.getChannel();
        int size = (int)fc.size();
        MappedByteBuffer mbb = fc.map(FileChannel.MapMode.READ_ONLY, 0,
                                                                  size);

        // Decode the file into a char buffer
        CharBuffer cb = decoder.decode(mbb);
        return cb;
    }
}
```

That concludes the discussion of regular expressions. Now let's describe some more classes from package java.util.

Calendar Utilities

The JDK 1.0 support for dates was poorly designed. With the benefit of hindsight, it would have been better to throw it out and start over again, but backward compatibility was seen as the more important goal. In JDK 1.1 most of the constructors and methods of java.util.Date class were deprecated, and other classes were provided to offer better support for time zones and internationalization.

The following classes specifically relate to date and time:

- The class Date represents a specific instant in time with millisecond precision. It's really a timestamp, not a date.

- The class Calendar is an abstract class for converting between a Date object and a set of integer fields such as year, month, day, and hour.

- The class GregorianCalendar is the only concrete subclass of Calendar in the jdk. It does the date-to-fields conversions for the calendar system in common use.

- The class DateFormat is an abstract class that lets you convert a Date to a printable String with fields in the way you want (for example, dd/mm/yy or dd.MMM.yyyy).

- The class SimpleDateFormat is the only concrete subclass of DateFormat in the jdk. It takes a format String and either parses a String to produce a date or takes a date and produces a String.

- The class TimeZone is an abstract class that represents a time zone offset and also calculates daylight savings time adjustments.

- The class SimpleTimeZone is the only concrete subclass of TimeZone in the JDK. The class defines an ordinary time zone with a simple daylight savings and daylight savings time period.

Not only was date and time support poorly designed, it was poorly implemented and full of bugs. The good news is that many of the bugs were corrected in 1.1.4 and 1.1.6. In JDK 1.2, the most common problems were corrected. This part of the JDK has been maintained by IBM.

You can instantiate Date with no arguments to represent the current moment.

```
Date now = new Date();
```

In the past, you could provide arguments (year, month, day, hour, and so on) to "build me a Date that represents this date/time." That use is now deprecated and you should use the class GregorianCalendar instead.

Java uses a 64-bit long to represent an instant in time. The value is interpreted as "milliseconds since Jan 1 00:00:00, 1970." The scheme is sufficient to represent dates from 292,269,053 B.C. to A.D. 292,272,993 (64 bits covers minus 9,223,372,036,854,775,808 to plus 9,223,372,036,854,775,807 milliseconds), which seems like a lot, but is really only about 12% of the age of the planet, or 6% if you only count the portion in the past. Note that prior to JDK 1.2, a GregorianCalendar did not accept values earlier than 4716 B.C. In addition to all its other sins, the class Date was misnamed; it should be thought of as "Instant" or "Timestamp."

Calendar and Gregorian calendar

The class Calendar translates between an instant in time and individual fields like year, month, day, hour, and so on. Date used to do this, but it did it in a way that didn't properly internationalize, so those methods have been deprecated.

Deprecated interfaces

Compatibility between releases is a major goal of JavaSoft. In most cases this works very well, but there are a small number of cases where an API has had to be changed. When an API is replaced by a different one, JavaSoft assures software compatibility by leaving the old API in place and marking it as "deprecated." To deprecate something means to disapprove of it. Deprecated features will eventually be removed from the API. When you compile a program that uses a deprecated API, the compiler issues a single line error message similar to the following:

```
% javac foo.java
Note: foo.java uses a deprecated API.  Recompile with "-
deprecation" for details.
1 warning
```

The purpose of this warning is to tell you that you are using an old feature that has been replaced. The warning will not cause compilation to fail, but it reminds you that the class will eventually be removed from the JDK and you need to bring your code up to date. Only one deprecation warning is issued for a compilation, even if you use dozens of outmoded classes or methods. To view the full list of deprecated features that you used, use the following example to compile:

```
% javac -deprecation foo.java
foo.java:4: Note: The constructor java.util.Date(int,int,int)
has been deprecated.
Date d1 = new Date(97,12,2);
               ^
Note: foo.java uses a deprecated API.
Please consult the documentation for a better alternative.
3 warnings
```

This example shows you the deprecated feature; in this case it is one of the constructors in java.util.Date. You then look at the source code to see the suggested replacement. In this case, that piece of code refers you to java.util.Calendar. The Calendar class is the replacement for some methods in the Date class.

Calendar also knows about time zones, and therefore, about things like summertime. The time zone information has a class of its own: TimeZone. DateFormat class provides elementary Date formatting.

Calendar is an abstract base class, which is meant to be overridden by a subclass that implements a specific calendar system. It's a dumb approach; it makes the common case of simple date processing not obvious. Most of the world uses the Gregorian calendar (named after the Pope who established it in 1582). Excessive generality in a design is as bad or worse than excessive rigidity.

The class java.util.GregorianCalendar extends Calendar and provides more methods. Since Calendar is an abstract class, and the parent of

GregorianCalendar, I recommend that you simply use GregorianCalendar all the time. The following example shows how you would get a date of a particular value:

```
GregorianCalendar g = new GregorianCalendar(61,7,13);
```

That represents the day the Berlin wall was constructed (August 13, 1961) in the European central time (ECT) zone. A better way to construct that date is to first set the correct time zone, and then set the date.

```
TimeZone z_ect = TimeZone.getTimeZone("ECT");
GregorianCalendar g = new GregorianCalendar(z_ect);
g.set(61,7,13);
```

Note that (incredibly stupidly) months are in the range 0 to 11, and years are represented by the four-digit year less 1900. If you don't specify a time zone, GregorianCalendar defaults to the time zone in place on the OS where the program is running. For example, for a program running in Japan, the OS default is probably Japanese standard time (JST). A list of all time zones can be found by looking in the source for java.util.TimeZone.java.

You can retrieve the individual values out of a date by following this example:

```
int year = g.get(Calendar.YEAR);
int month = g.get(Calendar.MONTH);
int date = g.get(Calendar.DATE);
int day = g.get(Calendar.DAY_OF_WEEK);
```

You can also check if one date is before or after another date. There is no simple way to get the amount of time between two dates. There are two "helper" classes: TimeZone and SimpleTimeZone. Again, SimpleTimeZone is a concrete subclass of TimeZone, and can be used exclusively. You can create a time zone object for any time zone you want, and then pass it to GregorianCalendar so it will work with values in that time zone.

```
TimeZone z_ect = TimeZone.getTimeZone("ECT");
GregorianCalendar g2 = new GregorianCalendar(z_ect);
g2.set(89, 10, 9, 19, 0); // Berlin Wall Down  Nov 9 1989 7pm
g2.set(89, Calendar.NOVEMBER, 9, 19, 0); // better
```

You can do simple date and time formatting with static methods from the class java.text.DateFormat, as shown in the following example:

```
public static void main( String[] args ) {
    Date d = new Date();
    String s1 = DateFormat.getDateInstance().format( d );
    String s2 = DateFormat.getTimeInstance().format( d );
    String s3 = DateFormat.getDateTimeInstance().format( d );

    System.out.println("Date is " + s1 );
    System.out.println("Time is " + s2 );
    System.out.println("DateTime is " + s3 );
}
```

The program fragment runs to produce the following result:

```
Date is Nov 10, 2003
Time is 7:55:23 PM
DateTime is Nov 10, 2003 7:55:23 PM
```

You can also parse or convert a String into a DateFormat using that class. With methods from java.text.SimpleDateFormat, more flexible parsing and formatting is available. You provide a format String argument to the constructor in which different letters represent different fields of a date (day, hour, year, A.M., P.M., and so on) and the style in which you want to see them. Then you call the format() method with your date as the argument, and it passes it back as a String of the requested form.

```
import java.text.*;
import java.util.*;
public class df {

    public static void main( String[] args ) {
        SimpleDateFormat df1 =
         new SimpleDateFormat ("yyyy-MM-dd hh:mm:ss.S");
        SimpleDateFormat df2 = new SimpleDateFormat ("dd-MMM-yy");
        String startdatetime = "2003-11-10 19:23:27.0";
        try {
            Date d = df1.parse(startdatetime);
            String s = df2.format( d );
            System.out.println("Date is " + s );
        } catch (ParseException pe) {
            System.out.println("ParseException " + pe );
        }
    }
}
```

When you run that code, a String is parsed to get a Date, and then the Date is parsed to get a String in a different format. Following is the output:

```
Date is 10-Nov-03
```

The number of times a pattern letter is repeated determines whether the short or long form of a text field is used. If at least four pattern letters are used (for example, "EEEE"), the long form of "Tuesday" is used. Otherwise, the short form (if there is one) will be used. For a number field (for example, "SSSSS"), the field will be zero-padded to that amount. Year is handled specially; a field of "yy" indicates that the year should be truncated to two digits.

The class SimpleDateFormat is in the java.text package, rather than java.util because it is primarily concerned with internationalized and localized ways of formatting the date.

The database crowd fixed Date a little in java.sql.Date by overriding java.util.Date, and making it deal only with dates and not times. That's another possibility for you to use.

Table 19–5   SimpleDateFormat

Symbol	Meaning	Presentation	Example
G	Era designator	(Text)	AD
y	Year	(Number)	1996
M	Month in year	(Text & Number)	July & 07
d	Day in month	(Number)	10
h	Hour in A.M./P.M. (1-12)	(Number)	12
H	Hour in day (0-23)	(Number)	0
m	Minute in hour	(Number)	30
s	Second in minute	(Number)	55
S	Millisecond	(Number)	978
E	Day in week	(Text)	Tuesday
D	Day in year	(Number)	189
F	Day of week in month	(Number)	2 (2nd Wed in July)
w	Week in year	(Number)	27
W	Week in month	(Number)	2
a	A.M./P.M. marker	(Text)	PM
k	Hour in day (1-24)	(Number)	24
K	Hour in A.M./P.M. (0-11)	(Number)	0
z	Time zone	(Text)	Pacific Standard Time
'	Escape for text	(Delimiter)	
''	Single quote	(Literal)	'

Other Utility Classes

BitSet

This class maintains a set of bits that are identified by the value of an integer, like an array index. You can have over two billion individual bits in a set (if you have enough virtual memory), each of which can be queried, set, cleared, and so on. The bit set will increase dynamically as needed to accommodate extra bits you add.

```
public BitSet();  // constructor
public BitSet(int N);  // constructor for set of size N bits

public void or (BitSet s); // OR's one bit set against another.

public void set (int i); // sets bit number i.

public int size(); // returns the number of bits in the set.
```

Stack

The Stack class maintains a Last-In-First-Out stack of Objects. You can push (store) objects to arbitrary depth. The methods include:

```
public Object push(Object item);   // add to top of stack.

public Object pop();   // get top of stack.
```

In addition, there are three other methods not usually provided for stacks:

```
public boolean empty(); // nothing on the stack?

public Object peek();   // returns top Object without popping it.

public int search (Object o); // returns how far down the stack
// this object is (1 is at the top), or -1 if not found.
```

The original author of this class made an interesting mistake. He made Stack a subclass of Vector, so that he would get the vector behavior of allowing unbounded input. He failed to notice that it meant all the methods of Vector would be available in Stack—including inappropriate methods like removeElementAt() to pull something out of the middle of a vector. Therefore, Stack does not guarantee Last-In-First-Out behavior. Hans Rohnert from Germany pointed this out in email. As Hans put it, it is not true that Stack "is a" Vector, rather it should "have a" Vector in which to store.

The usual way to "hide" unwanted methods from a base class is to override them with private versions, empty versions, or versions that throw a run-time exception. In this case, Vector.removeElementAt(int) is final, and final methods

Just Java 2

can't be overriden. Never call `removeElementAt()` on your stack, and you'll stay out of trouble.

Some of these early 1.0 utility packages were written very quickly by skilled programmers who were more interested in getting the code working than achieving a perfect design. It's easier to find flaws in code than it is to write faultless software. Pointing out the occasional blemish is done in the spirit of learning, not as a criticism of the work of others.

The java.math API

Don't confuse the java.math package with the class java.lang.Math. Class java.lang.Math has trig operations on doubles. The java.math package described here contains three classes that support arithmetic with more decimal places than the hardware type *double* can provide. It also has an enum that describes rounding modes. The java.math package is slow (because it is implemented in software) but gives results of arbitrary accuracy.

The java.math package was added to JDK 1.1 for three reasons:

- To be used in the java.security Digital Signature Algorithm interfaces.

- To complete the support for all SQL types used in database programming and to allow arithmetic on types larger than long and double. If you do database programming, you'll be comfortable with the two java.math.BigDecimal and java.math.BigInteger classes, which can represent the SQL types DECIMAL and NUMERIC.

- To do arithmetic on numbers of arbitrary size, even if you don't use cryptography or database programming.

As the names suggest, BigInteger deals with integers of unbounded size and BigDecimal deals with unbounded numbers with fractional parts. BigDecimal is essentially BigInteger with some extra code to keep track of the scale (where the decimal point is). If you want to manipulate a number that takes a megabyte to store all its decimal places, you can. BigInteger provides versions of all of Java's primitive integer operators and all relevant static methods from java.lang.Math. Additionally, BigInteger provides operations for modular arithmetic, greatest common divisor calculation, primality testing, prime generation, single-bit manipulation, and a few other odds and ends.

The following is an example of BigInteger used to perform a calculation that is listed in the 1989 *Guinness Book of World Records* under "Human Computer":

```
BigInteger bi1 = new BigInteger("7686369774870");
BigInteger bi2 = new BigInteger("2465099745779");
bi1 = bi1.multiply(bi2);
System.out.println( "The value is "+ bi1 );
```

When compiled and run, the correct answer appears:

```
The value is 18947668177995426462773730
```

BigInteger naturally does it faster than the human record holder who took 28 seconds. The following is an example of BigDecimal used to round a number to four decimal places of precision:

```
BigDecimal bd1 = new BigDecimal( java.lang.Math.PI );
System.out.println( "The value is "+ bd1 );

int digsrightofradix = 4;
bd1 = bd1.setScale(digsrightofradix, BigDecimal.ROUND_HALF_UP);
System.out.println( "The value to 4 places is "+ bd1 );
```

When compiled and run, the following output appears:

```
The value is 3.141592653589793115997963468544185161590576171875
The value to 4 places is 3.1416
```

The true value is 3.1415926535 8979323846 2643383279 5028841971 693993751, so you can see that our value of pi is wrong in the 16th decimal place.

This is because we got the value from a double, and that's the limit on accuracy for doubles (refer back to Chapter 7 if you don't remember this). If we calculate pi from a formula using BigDecimal, we can get arbitrary precision.

Class BigDecimal also contains many other options for rounding numbers.

Random

This is a class to provide pseudo-random numbers. We call them pseudo-random rather than random because the source of bits is an algorithm. To the casual observer it looks like a random stream of bits, and for most applications we can pretend that they are. The numbers aren't really random, though, and sequences tend to get stuck in repetitive cycles after a large number of iterations.

If you just quickly want a random number between 0.0 and (just less than) 1.0, then the Math package has a random method, which is just a wrapper for instantiating Random one time and then supplying values. Use the following example to call the Random method:

```
double d = Math.random();   // returns value in range 0.0 .. 1.0
```

How to look at the API of a class
You can run javap on a fully qualified classname to list the methods in the class. The class java.util.Random was listed this way:
```
% javap java.util.Random
```
That gives you a very quick way to remind yourself of the API at the command line.

The Random class contains the following items:

```
public class java.util.Random implements java.io.Serializable {
    public java.util.Random();
    public java.util.Random(long);

    public boolean nextBoolean();
    public void nextBytes(byte[]);
    public int nextInt();
    public int nextInt(int);
    public long nextLong();

    public float nextFloat();
    public double nextDouble();

    // a Gaussian distribution has mean 0.0, standard deviation 1.0.
    public synchronized double nextGaussian();
    public synchronized void setSeed(long);
}
```

The nextGaussian() provides numbers symmetrically distributed around zero, and successively more unlikely to be picked the further away from zero you get. If we collected a group of these numbers and plotted them, they would form the shape of a bell curve. The algorithm used here for taking random values from a Gaussian distribution is from *The Art of Computer Programming* by Donald Knuth (Addison-Wesley, 1994: Section 3.4.1, Algorithm C).

You can instantiate Random with or without a seed. The following example uses a seed:

```
java.util.Random r = new java.util.Random(344L);
```

If you don't give Random a seed, it uses the current reading from the day and time clock (the millisecond part of this is going to be pretty close to random). If you choose to supply the seed, you will get the same series of random numbers every time you supply that same seed. This is useful in testing and debugging code.

To get a random int value in a certain range (for example, 0 to 5) to simulate the cast of a die, you would use the following:

```
int myturn = r.nextInt(6);
```

The method nextDouble returns a value between 0.0 and 1.0. To get a random double value in a certain range (for example, 0.0 to 100.0) to simulate a percentage, you would scale it up with multiplication:

```
double mypercent = r.nextDouble() * 100.0;
```

How to time your code
Follow this example to time your Java code:

```
long start = System.currentTimeMillis();
    :    // do the work here
    :
long stop = System.currentTimeMillis();
System.out.println("time: " + (stop-start) + "millisecs");
```

Properties

Java has a platform-independent way to communicate extra information at run-time to a program. Known as *properties*, these work like environment variables. Environment variables were shunned for being too platform-specific. A programmer can read the value of a property by calling getProperty() and passing an argument String for the property of interest:

```
String dir = System.getProperty("user.dir");
```

A long list of predefined properties appears in the file java/lang/System.java and in Table 19–6 on page 494. You can also define a new property on the command line when you invoke the program:

```
java -Drate=10.0  myprogram
```

That value "10.0" will be returned as a String when querying the property "rate."

```
String r = System.getProperty("rate");
```

It can be converted to a floating-point number and used as a value in the program. In this case, it's an alternative to a command line argument, but with the advantage that its' value is visible everywhere, not just in main.

Predefined properties lists the predefined properties guaranteed to have a value on every Java client. Others also exist.

Table 19–6   Predefined properties

Property Name	Explanation
java.version	Version number of the Java system
java.vendor	Vendor-specific String
java.vendor.url	Vendor URL
java.home	Java installation directory
java.class.version	Java class version number
java.class.path	Java classpath
os.name	Operating System Name
os.arch	Operating System Architecture
os.version	Operating System Version
file.separator	File separator ("/" on Unix)
path.separator	Path separator (":" on Unix)
line.separator	Line separator ("\n" on Unix)
user.name	User account name
user.home	User home directory
user.dir	User's current working directory

Most programs don't need to access these properties at all. But if they do, it's nice to be able to do it in a platform-independent way.

The java.util.Properties class

You will be happy to hear that there is a java.util class to help you read in and process properties. The java.util.Properties class is just a subclass of java.util.Hashtable with a few extra methods added. The concept of properties also exists in other languages, such as Lisp and Forth. The Java system comes with a whole set of predefined properties holding information about the implementation.

This utility class has two purposes: it allows a property table to be read in and written out via streams and it allows programmers to search more than one property table with a single command. If you don't need either of these benefits, you could use a HashMap instead of a Properties table.

Typical methods include the following:

```
public String getProperty(String key);

public synchronized void load(InputStream in)
    throws IOException;
// reads key/value pairs in from a stream, stores them in this

public synchronized void save(OutputStream out, String header);
// writes the key/value pairs out as text
// the header is just a comment String you provide to label
// the property table. The current date is also appended.
```

To put entries in a Properties object, use the put(Object key, Object element) method inherited from HashTable. So that you don't feel obliged to start adding to the predefined system property table, there's a feature that allows you to provide an existing properties table to a constructor. This creates an empty properties list that you can populate. Whenever you do a getProperty, it will search your table. If nothing is found, it will go on to search the table provided to the constructor. Here is an example:

```
Properties sp = System.getProperties();
Properties mytable = new Properties(sp);
mytable.list(System.out);
```

The first line gets the standard predefined properties table. The second line piggybacks it onto a second Properties table that we create and can fill with a call, such as mytable.put (propertyname, propertyvalue). When we do a lookup in mytable, it will look first in mytable and then in the system properties table. The third line prints mytable (intended for debugging, but it's not clear why you can't just use the save() method). The method public String getProperty(String key, String default) will return the default String if there is no entry for this key in the table.

Note on the Java native interface

The Java Native Interface is an API that allows you to make calls into C and C++ programs from Java. You can also make calls into any other programming language that follows the C calling and linking conventions. Non-Java code is referred to as native code; therefore, it is a native interface.

If you use the JNI, you tie your code to a single platform and operating system, losing a major benefit of Java. The JNI should be used only as a last resort. Most programs don't need it and won't use it.

Readers who want to put JNI into practice can browse the JavaSoft web page for an introduction to JNI. Use the search facility on the home page at java.sun.com, and look for "JNI." Avoid the use of native methods if you can.

Further Reading

The book *Java Regular Expressions: Taming the java.util.regex Engine* by Mehran Habibi (published by APress, 2004) is generally regarded as a good study on the topic. If you are interested enough to want to play around with Perl, you can visit the www.perl.com/ website to find tutorials and download a free copy of the software. O'Reilly sponsors the Perl website, and they also support a corresponding "Java in the Enterprise" website at www.onjava.com/. They have some good Java articles and other resources.

See developer.java.sun.com/developer/technicalArticles/releases/1.4regex/ for more information on Java regular expressions.

Exercises

1.   (Patterns, easy) Do a web search to find all the pieces that comprise a URL in its full generality. State what these pieces are. Write a pattern-matching program that checks URLs for validity (such as no embedded spaces). Show the output of your program when run on both good and bad URLs.

2.   (Patterns, medium) An email message consists of an arbitrary number of headers, then a blank line, then the body of the text. The headers all have a label followed by a colon, a space, and some optional text all on one line. The "From:" and "To:" headers are required, and come first in that order. The pattern would begin something like this:

```
Pattern email = Pattern.compile(
            "^From: .*$"      // "From" line
       + "^To: .*$"      // "To" line
```

Write the rest of a pattern to match an email message, and use capturing groups to separate the individual parts. Don't forget to make this a multiline pattern.

3.   (Patterns, harder) Write a pattern that matches the Java regular expressions presented in this text. This is several days of work. Run your meta-pattern matcher on all the Java regular expression Strings shown in this chapter. Account for any that it does not accept.

4.   (Math, medium) Convince yourself that the nextGaussian() numbers form a bell curve by writing a program to actually do it. *Hint:* You'll find it easier to plot a graph using ASCII text if you generate the values first, save them, and sort them into order before plotting the values. Which of the collection classes is a good choice to help with storing and sorting?

Some Light Relief—Exchanging Apples And Crays

There's an old story that "The people at Cray design their supercomputers with Apple systems, and the Apple designers use Crays!" Apart from this being a terrific example of recurring rotational serendipity (what goes around, comes around) is there any truth to it?

Like many urban legends, this one contains a nugget of truth. The 1991 Annual Report of Cray Research, Inc., contained a short article describing how Apple used a Cray for designing Macintosh cases. The Cray is used to simulate the injection molding of the plastic enclosure cases. The Mac II case was the first Apple system to benefit from the modeling, and the trial was successful. The simulation identified warping problems that were solved by prototyping, thus saving money in tooling and production. Apple also uses its Cray for simulating air flow inside the enclosure to check for hot spots. The Cray magazine also reported that the Apple PowerBook continues to use supercomputer simulations. (Cray Channels, Spring 1996, pp.10-12 "Apple Computer PowerBook computer molding simulation").

The inverse story holds that Seymour Cray himself used a Macintosh to design Crays. The story seems to have originated with an off-the-cuff remark from Seymour Cray, who had a Macintosh at home and used it to store some of his work for the Cray 3. Common sense suggests that the simulation of discrete circuitry (Verilog runs, logic analysis, and so on), which is part of all modern integrated circuit design, is done far more cost-effectively on a large server farm than on a microprocessor. Cray probably has a lot of supercomputer hardware ready for testing as it comes off the production line.

It's conceivable that a Macintosh could be used to draft the layout of blinking lights for the front of a Cray, or choose some nice color combinations, or some other non-CPU intensive work. A Macintosh is a very good system for writing design notes, sending email, and drawing diagrams, all of which are equally essential parts of designing a computer system.

The good folks at Cray Research have confirmed in a Cray Users' Group newsletter that they have a few Macs on the premises.While it's unlikely that they run logic simulations on their Macs, we can indeed chalk it up as only-slightly-varnished truth that "the people at Cray design their supercomputers with Apple systems, and the Apple designers use Crays".

All the action in supercomputers is in clusters these days, not in super-powerful monolithic mainframes. Also bear in mind that Moore's Law means that the desk-side G5 Mac in 2004 (236 MFLOP) is more powerful than the Cray 1 (160 MFLOP) super computer reigning nearly 30 years earlier in 1976.

Chapter 20

GUI Basics and Event Handling

▼   ALL ABOUT EVENT HANDLING

▼   TIPS FOR SLIMMING DOWN HANDLER CODE

▼   SUMMARY OF EVENT HANDLING

▼   EXERCISES

▼   SOME LIGHT RELIEF—THE MOUSE THAT ROARED

All GUI libraries have four basic areas of functionality:

- Creation of user interface "controls" or components, such as scroll bars, buttons, and labels.

- Support for giving behavior to the controls by connecting GUI events (for example, clicking a button) to code that you write.

- Support for grouping and arranging the controls on the screen.

- Support for accessing window manager facilities, such as specifying which window has the input focus, reading JPEG and other image files, and printing.

Related graphics libraries also provide support for graphics operations, such as drawing an arc, filling a polygon, and clipping a rectangle. There may even be a complete 2-D and 3-D drawing library, similar to the ones in Java.

For the first couple of major releases, Java supported GUI operations with a package called java.awt. The "AWT" stands for "Abstract Window Toolkit." The AWT supported the portability goals of Java. The toolkit gave user programs a common binary window interface on systems with different native window systems. That's a very unusual feature, like having your favorite Macintosh program run on a Windows PC and still do GUI operations. You might wonder how it is done.

You can call methods in the AWT run-time to pop up a native menu, resize a window, get the location of a mouse click, and so on. Java then calls through to the native GUI library. Events coming back from the GUI go into the Java run-time, and are passed on to your code as appropriate. The *Java bytecode* is the same on each platform, but the *native library* behind the Java run-time library is specific to each platform. The AWT code uses the underlying native (or "peer") window system to manipulate GUI objects.

The AWT is a series of abstract interfaces along with Java code to map them into the actual native code on each system. This is why it is an *abstract* window toolkit: it is not tailored for a specific computer, but it offers the same API on all. Too much different native behavior leaked through and, eventually IBM persuaded Sun to move to an all-Java GUI known as Swing. Swing is almost wholly implemented in Java. It uses native canvases on which to display widgets controlled and drawn by Java.

We mentioned the list of services that any GUI library must support. This chapter focuses on one of these services: an event-handling system that notices when the user adjusts one of the components and interrupts the program to tell it what happened.

You must know how to handle the events that controls can generate before you can make sense of the controls themselves. Event handling is a dull but necessary prerequisite, like eating your vegetables before you can have dessert. We will deal with controls in the next chapter. The basic idea with Java GUI programs is that you do the following actions:

1. Declare controls. These controls include buttons, menus, and choices. You can extend these classes to add your own ideas/needs to the behavior, but this is often unnecessary.

2. Implement event handlers to respond to clicking, menu selection, button presses, window re-sizing and other activity. Your implementing class will often be an anonymous class. Using an anonymous class reduces the amount of code and puts the class declaration close to where it is used.

3. Add the controls to a container. You may choose to extend the container class, but this is frequently unnecessary. Containers display on the screen. Containers can hold several related controls that you want to appear next to each other onscreen. For example, a frame can hold two buttons and a scrolling panel.

It's a challenge to explain all this. The first three topics—declaring controls, handling their events, and putting them in containers—fit together so closely that you have to understand a bit of each before you can fully understand any of them. The topics are so big that each requires a whole chapter, and we will take them serially.

All About Event Handling

First, a few necessary words of explanation about the programming model for window systems. Unlike procedural programs in which things happen sequentially, windowing programs are *asynchronous*, because actions occur at unpredictable times. You never know which of the onscreen buttons, menus, frames, or other elements the user will touch next. Accordingly, a model known as *event-driven programming* is used.

In event-driven programming, the logic of your code is inverted. Instead of one flow of control from beginning to end, the run-time system sits in a "window main loop" simply waiting for user input. When the user clicks the mouse, the operating system passes it to the window manager which turns it into an *event* and passes it on to a handler you supplied earlier. This is known as a *callback*. Your handler is a *callback routine*, because the window system calls back to it when the event happens. Your event handler deals with the graphics event and any work associated with it.

If a button says "press here to read the file," your code must arrange for the file to be read when called. Handling a button event means noticing that it occurred and doing the associated action, but other events may involve some drawing on the screen. For example, dragging something with the mouse is just repeatedly drawing it under the mouse coordinates as it moves.

Java event model

The *event model* is the name for the framework that turns a GUI interaction (mouse click, menu selection, button press, etc.) into a call for your code to process it. The event model can also be used for something unrelated to the GUI, like a timer going off. In other words, the event model is the design for connecting your code to any kind of asynchronous actions, called *events*, for handling.

The window manager can't directly call your event-handling routines because the run-time library doesn't even see your code until it is asked to run it. Therefore, at run-time the event model has to be told which of your routines handle events.

Java originally used inheritance to tie together your code and the event model. JDK 1.1 introduced a better approach called the *delegation-based* model. Some of the Java documentation still refers to "1.1-style events," which is the current model. To get any events, your code has to begin by telling the window system, "send those events of yours to these methods of mine". You connect the controls that generate events by registering a callback with your event-handling classes, as Figure 20–1 shows.

Threads, the event dispatcher, and your code

You will notice that once you put a GUI component onscreen, your program does not end when it reaches the end of the `main()` method. This is not a new rule—it's the same old rule about a program not ending while it still has one or more threads running.

When you make a GUI component visible, a thread is started inside the Java run-time library to receive events that may be generated by that component. The underlying OS window system library is told to pass all events to this Java run-time library thread, and this thread is responsible for forwarding the events on to your code. The fact that this event thread is live prevents your program from exiting when it falls off the end of `main()`. So the GUI stays on the screen, and the program now runs in response to user input on the GUI.

This Java library thread is called the "event dispatching thread." It runs in your address space, in parallel with all your code, but spends most of its time blocked waiting for a GUI event. When a GUI event occurs, the event dispatching thread either consumes the event itself, or calls back to the event-handler code that you wrote and registered.

Therefore, your event handlers are executed by one of the Java run-time library threads, not by one of *your* threads! One implication of this is that your event handlers will block the delivery of other GUI events, and so must be brief and quick to execute. You *never* want to undertake a time-consuming operation like reading a file in an event handler. Instead, spawn it off into a thread of its own. You can do this with an inner (or not) class in your event handler, and get it to run like this:

```
new Thread() {     // run it in a different thread to event handler
    public void run() {
        // put your lengthy non-GUI statements here
    }
}.start();
```

Conversely, there is a static method in the SwingUtilities class that will take a Runnable object and execute it later *in* the event handler thread. Any and all GUI adjustments you want to make after the GUI first becomes visible, must be done in the event handler thread. We show an example of this in the next chapter.

GUI events are automatically added to a queue in the run-time library as they happen. The event dispatching thread empties this queue by dispatching the events to your handler code.

Since all event dispatching is handled by one library thread alone, another implication is that the library can do less synchronization than would be required if many threads were running. Less synchronization equals better overall performance, as long as the synchronization is still correct.

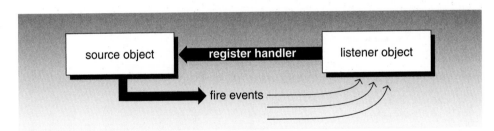

Figure 20–1   How events are passed in JDK **1.1**

You register your handler code once at the beginning with the GUI object that will be generating events. After that, those events are fired (or sent) to you when they occur. In particular, your handler code is called and passed the event object as an argument.

If you do not completely understand callbacks, go back and read that section in Chapter 11. It is essential that you understand callbacks because they form the basis of the new event-handling model.

The events that are fired from the source to the listener are simply objects passed as arguments to a method call. An event object has several data fields holding information, such as where the event took place on the screen, a description of the event, the number of mouse clicks, the state of a checkbox, and so on. There is a general java.util.EventObject type and all AWT events are children of that, as Figure 20–2 shows.

The JFrame example

A JFrame, a subclass of the AWT class Frame, has a title string and a menu bar on which you can add several menus. Following is the code to put a JFrame on the screen from an application:

```
import javax.swing.*;
public class FrameDemo {
    public static void main(String[] args) {
        JFrame jframe = new JFrame("Example");
        jframe.setSize(400,100);
        jframe.setVisible(true);
    }
}
```

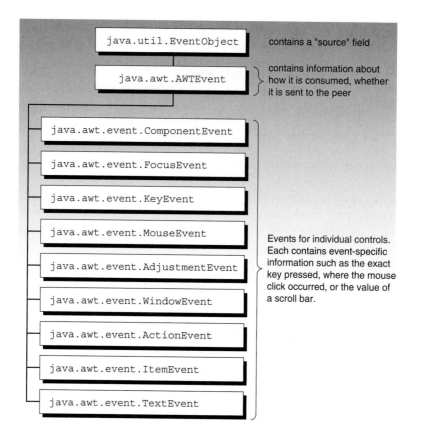

Figure 20–2   The hierarchy of event objects in JDK 1.1

Compiling and executing this program results in a frame similar to Figure 20–3 to appear on the screen. Here, we just gave it the name on the title bar of "Example."

Figure 20–3   The JFrame is a subclass of Frame, which is a subclass of Window

Since it is a Window, JFrame is capable of receiving events generated by Windows. Clicking a Window to close it generates an event. If you try this with the program we described, you'll notice that the JFrame goes away but your program stays active. You must press Control-C to exit the program because you need to write code to handle the "window closing" event. The code should quit the program when it is invoked.

Let's add an event handler to our JFrame that notices when the WindowClosing event takes place. That event will be delivered when you click to close a Window.

First, tell our JFrame that Window events are handled by an object that I call "mwh" here—a nice short name which is an abbreviation of "my window handler." The code appears exactly as before, and we add the following line to the main() routine:

```
jframe.addWindowListener(mwh);
```

The callback for a Window event is registered by calling the AWT method addWindowListener. This is a method in the Window superclass of JFrame that takes as a parameter an interface called WindowListener. Your applet must declare an instance of a class that implements the WindowListener interface and that will be the event handler for this button. You still have to write that class, but assuming it has the name shown below, you can instantiate an object according to the following example:

```
myCodeToHandleWinClose mwh = new myCodeToHandleWinClose();
```

The last step is to write the myCodeToHandleWinClose class that implements the java.awt.event.WindowListener interface and provides the promised methods. The class can be in a separate file or contained in the same one.

```
class myCodeToHandleWinClose implements WindowListener {
    public void windowClosing(WindowEvent e) {System.exit(0);}
    public void windowClosed(WindowEvent e) { }
    public void windowOpened(WindowEvent e) { }
    public void windowIconified(WindowEvent e) { }
    public void windowDeiconified(WindowEvent e) { }
    public void windowActivated(WindowEvent e) { }
    public void windowDeactivated(WindowEvent e) { }
}
```

The windowClosing() method of the myCodeToHandleWinClose class is called whenever the Window "close" choice is made. Notice that it was necessary to provide declarations for all the routines in the interface. Since we are interested only in WindowClosing, there are empty bodies for the other methods. We'll show a way of simplifying this later in the chapter.

The WindowListener interface (like many of the SomethingListener interfaces) is declared in the java.awt.event package. There are other event and Listeners declared in the javax.swing.event package. The WindowListener interface promises that there will be half a dozen methods with specific names. The methods will be called for different Window events now that we have delegated the task to the object "mwh" that contains the methods.

One advantage of the Java event framework is that the GUI-related code is easily separated from the application logic code. This flows from good use of OOP: put everything in a class of its own and declare instances of the class as needed. In this way, encapsulation works for you. If you want to change what happens on window close, you just update the class that deals specifically with it. In a non-OOP implementation, it's too easy to mix everything together, making program maintenance and testing ten times harder than it should be. The same event framework is used for JavaBeans (component software), as well as the AWT.

Putting the whole thing together and into our JFrame example, the following code handles the window closing event:

```
import javax.swing.*;
import java.awt.event.*;
public class CloseDemo {
    public static void main(String[] args) {
        JFrame jframe = new JFrame("Example");
        jframe.setSize(400,100);
        jframe.setVisible(true);
        myCodeToHandleWinClose m = new myCodeToHandleWinClose();
        jframe.addWindowListener(m);
    }
}


class myCodeToHandleWinClose implements WindowListener {

    public void windowClosing(WindowEvent e) {System.exit(0);}
    public void windowClosed(WindowEvent e) { }
    public void windowOpened(WindowEvent e) { }
    public void windowIconified(WindowEvent e) { }
    public void windowDeiconified(WindowEvent e) { }
    public void windowActivated(WindowEvent e) { }
    public void windowDeactivated(WindowEvent e) { }
}
```

Notice that the code inside the WindowClosing method calls System.exit() to quit the program. When you run this, you'll see the same frame as before, but when you click on the window to close it, the program will now exit gracefully. Well done! You have finished your first example of an event handler.

You may wonder what events exist, what interfaces deal with them, and what methods the Listener interfaces use. Table 20–1 summarizes the answers to all three questions. You should also review the javadoc pages for classes and interfaces in package java.awt.event. The source code for the interfaces and their methods can also be reviewed in the directory $JAVAHOME/src/java/awt/event.

The same framework is used by all the event handlers:

1. Write a class that implements a `SomethingListener` interface.

2. Declare an object (for example, `myHandler`) of your class.

3. On your component, call the `addSomethingListener(myHandler)` method.

You can reduce the amount of code with inner classes. See *Tips for Slimming Down Handler Code* on page 508.

Table 20–1   Categories, events, and interfaces

General category	Events that it generates	Interface that the event-handle implements
Mouse	Dragging or moving mouse causes a MouseEvent.	MouseMotionListener
	Clicking, selecting, releasing causes a MouseEvent.	MouseListener
Mouse wheel	Mouse wheel events (new in 1.4).	MouseWheelListener
Keyboard	Key press or key release causes a KeyEvent.	KeyListener
Selecting (an item from a list, checkbox, etc.)	When item is selected causes an ItemEvent.	ItemListener
Text input controls	When newline is entered causes a TextEvent.	TextListener
Scrolling controls	When a scroll bar slider is moved causes an AdjustmentEvent.	AdjustmentListener
Other controls (button, menu, etc.)	When pressed causes an ActionEvent.	ActionListener
Window changes	Open, close, iconify, etc., causes a WindowEvent.	WindowListener
Keyboard focus changes	Tabbing to next field or requesting focus causes a FocusEvent. A component must have the focus to generate key events.	FocusListener
Component change	Resizing, hiding, revealing, or moving a component causes a ComponentEvent.	ComponentListener
Container change	Adding or removing a component to a container causes a ContainerEvent.	ContainerListener

Tips for Slimming Down Handler Code

Inner classes are intended for event handlers. The inner classes allow you to put the event-handling class and method right next to where you declare the control or register the callback listener. Anonymous classes are a refinement of inner classes, allowing you to combine the definition of the class with the instance allocation. The following example shows the code rewritten using an anonymous class:

```java
import javax.swing.*;
import java.awt.event.*;
public class CloseDemo2 {

    public static void main(String[] args) {
        JFrame jframe = new JFrame("Example");
        jframe.setSize(400,100);
        jframe.setVisible(true);

        jframe.addWindowListener( new WindowListener() { // anon. class
            public void windowClosing(WindowEvent e) {System.exit(0);}
            public void windowClosed(WindowEvent e) { }
            public void windowOpened(WindowEvent e) { }
            public void windowIconified(WindowEvent e) { }
            public void windowDeiconified(WindowEvent e) { }
            public void windowActivated(WindowEvent e) { }
            public void windowDeactivated(WindowEvent e) { }
        } ); // end of anonymous class.
    }
}
```

Try to compile and run this code example. Your CloseDemo2.java file generates class files called CloseDemo2.class and CloseDemo2$1.class. The second item represents the anonymous WindowListener inner class.

You should use inner classes and anonymous classes only where the event handler is just a few lines long. If the event handler is more than a screenful of text, it should be in a named top-level class. We have to admit, however, that the notational convenience for smaller cases is considerable—just don't get carried away.

There are two further refinements: make your top-level class implement the appropriate listener interface and use an adapter class. These techniques further reduce the amount of "housekeeping code" you need to write. You'll see them in other programmers' code. I'll present them here so you can recognize the pattern.

Making a top-level class into a listener

You don't *have* to declare a separate class to implement the listener interface. You can make any of your existing classes do the work by adding the handler methods and the "implements somethingListener" clause.

The following code demonstrates this idea:

```java
import javax.swing.*;
import java.awt.event.*;
public class CloseDemo3 implements WindowListener {

    public static void main(String[] args) {
        JFrame jframe = new JFrame("Example");
        jframe.setSize(400,100);
        jframe.setVisible(true);

        jframe.addWindowListener( new CloseDemo3() );
    }

    public void windowClosing(WindowEvent e) {System.exit(0);}

    public void windowClosed(WindowEvent e) { }
    public void windowOpened(WindowEvent e) { }
    public void windowIconified(WindowEvent e) { }
    public void windowDeiconified(WindowEvent e) { }
    public void windowActivated(WindowEvent e) { }
    public void windowDeactivated(WindowEvent e) { }
}
```

In this example, you make the demo class itself implement WindowListener. The body of the class provides all the methods that WindowListener demands. When you want to add the WindowListener, you just instantiate an object of the demo class and the work is done in the main method (which is static). If you were making that call in an instance method, the line would be even simpler:

```java
jframe.addWindowListener( this );
```

It's a handy technique, but you're not done yet. You can make the code even shorter, as the next section explains.

Using a listener adapter class

Even though you were interested only in the windowClosing event, you had to supply null bodies for all the methods in the WindowListener interface. To make things a little more convenient, a concept called *adapter classes* can be used. An adapter is one specific example of a design pattern. An adapter is the design pattern that converts the API of some class into a different, more convenient API.

In Java AWT event handling, you might want to implement only one or two functions to handle the one or two events of interest for some of the Listener interfaces (such as WindowListener). The SomethingListener interface may specify half a dozen methods. The language rules are such that you must implement all the functions in an interface even if you just give them empty bodies, as shown earlier in the WindowListener. The package java.awt.event provides adapters that help by allowing you to override as few methods as you like. The adapters include the following:

- ComponentAdapter
- MouseMotionAdapter
- WindowAdapter
- ContainerAdapter
- MouseAdapter
- FocusAdapter
- KeyAdapter

These adapters are classes that provide empty bodies for all the methods in the corresponding SomethingListener interface. Following is an example of the WindowAdapter.java adapter:

```
public abstract class WindowAdapter implements WindowListener {
    public void windowOpened(WindowEvent e) { }
    public void windowClosing(WindowEvent e) { }
    public void windowClosed(WindowEvent e) { }
    public void windowIconified(WindowEvent e) { }
    public void windowDeiconified(WindowEvent e) { }
    public void windowActivated(WindowEvent e) { }
    public void windowDeactivated(WindowEvent e) {}
}
```

If you can declare your event handler as a subclass of one of these adapters, you can provide only the one or two methods you want, instead of implementing all the methods in the interface. This way, you let inheritance do the work. Another way to do this is to have one Adapter class implement all the Listener classes with null methods for all of them. This way you don't have to remember all the individual adapter names. That's the way I would have done it, which is probably why I'm not on the Swing design team.

Since Java classes have only one parent, you can't use this technique if you already inherit from some other class (although you can always create a new class just to make it a subclass of some adapter).

The following code is an example of how the WindowAdapter class is used when you are interested only in the windowClosing event:

```
import javax.swing.*;
import java.awt.event.*;
public class CloseDemo4 extends WindowAdapter {

    public static void main(String[] args) {
        JFrame jframe = new JFrame("Example");
        jframe.setSize(400,100);
        jframe.setVisible(true);

        jframe.addWindowListener( new CloseDemo4() );
    }

    public void windowClosing(WindowEvent e) {System.exit(0);}
}
```

The code is much shorter and easier to understand. What could be simpler than an adapter? Well, it turns out that there is a major pitfall with adapter classes, and it's one of those awful problems that leaves you swearing at the keyboard the first time you encounter it. You'll know to check for it after that, but the first time is a little frustrating.

We'll use KeyAdapter to show the problem, rather than WindowListener. The KeyListener is an interface used to send keyboard events. A keyboard event is generated when a key is pressed, released, and typed (pressed and released). There are KeyListener methods for all three of these. For this example, let's say you are going to use an adapter because you're interested only in the event that comes to keyPressed() and none of the other key-related events. Let's create an anonymous class for the KeyAdapter.

When you create an inner class for an adapter class, you simply supply the one or two methods that you wish to override. This concept is shown in the following code:

```
new KeyAdapter() {
    public void keyPressed(java.awt.event.KeyEvent e)
    { System.out.println("got "+e.getKeyChar()); }
} // end anon class
```

You may, however, make a small spelling or letter case error in supplying your method. This error is shown in the following code:

```
new KeyAdapter() {
    public void KeyPressed(java.awt.event.KeyEvent e)
    // Notice capital "K" in "KeyPressed" WRONG!
    { System.out.println("got "+e.getKeyChar()); }
} // end anon class
```

A spelling mistake like this means that your method will not override the intended method in the adapter class. Instead, you have added a new method that never gets invoked! The empty body of the correctly spelled method in the adapter class will be invoked instead, and it will do nothing. If your event handler seems to do nothing and you used an adapter, you should first check that the method name and signature exactly match something in the adapter class.

As I mentioned at the start of the chapter, learning how to handle events is like clearing your plate of vegetables before being allowed to have dessert. You've now eaten enough vegetables, so I'll wrap up this chapter with a summary.

Summary of Event Handling

We have seen a specific example of handling the event generated by closing a Window. It can be written more compactly if you write it as an inner class or even as an anonymous class. You can junk even more unneeded code if you use an adapter class.

There are several kinds of events for the different controls: a button generates one kind of event, a text field another, and so on. To impose order and to divide them up according to what they do, there are approximately 12 individual Listener interfaces shown in Table 20–1 on page 507. They all work the same way: you write a handler class that implements the interface, and register it with the control. When the control fires an event, the method in the handler object that you registered is called.

The key points about GUI handling include the following:

- Each SomethingListener interface has one or more methods showing the signature of a method that is called when the corresponding SomethingEvent occurs.

- Your handler code implements the SomethingListener interface and therefore has methods with signatures that fulfill those promised in the interface.

- Each control has a method called addSomethingListener(). The addSomethinglistener() method takes a single argument, an object that implements the SomethingListener interface.

- Swing requires that all code that might affect GUI components be executed from the event-dispatching thread. A section in Chapter 21 explains this concept.

- You call addSomethingListener(), using an instance of your handler class as the parameter. This registers your object as the handler for that kind of event for that control.

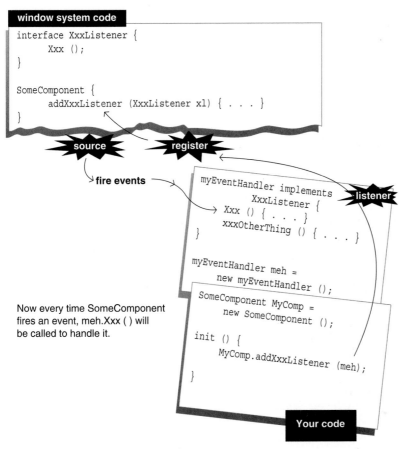

Figure 20–4   Design pattern of JDK 1.1 event handling

The SomethingEvent class is a subclass of class AWTEvent and stores all the information about what just happened, where, and when. An object of the SomethingEvent class is passed to the method in the SomethingListener interface. It sounds more complicated than it is. Figure 20–4 shows the design pattern.

You can register several handlers to receive the same single event. You can dynamically (at run-time) remove or add an event handler from a control. You add an event handler with a call shown to the following example:

```
myComponent.addWindowListener( myEventHandler );
```

You won't be too surprised to learn that the method to remove one is shown in the following example:

```
myComponent.removeWindowListener( myEventHandler );
```

We won't show all of the *Something*Event classes and *Something*Listener interfaces here. You should review them by typing the following:

```
javap java.awt.event.MouseEvent
```

Compiled from MouseEvent.java:

```
public synchronized class java.awt.event.MouseEvent
        extends java.awt.event.InputEvent
{
    public static final int MOUSE_FIRST;
    public static final int MOUSE_LAST;
    public static final int MOUSE_CLICKED;
    public static final int MOUSE_PRESSED;
    public static final int MOUSE_RELEASED;
    public static final int MOUSE_MOVED;
    public static final int MOUSE_ENTERED;
    public static final int MOUSE_EXITED;
    public static final int MOUSE_DRAGGED;
    int x;
    int y;
    int clickCount;
    boolean popupTrigger;
    public int getX();
    public int getY();
    public java.awt.Point getPoint();
    public synchronized void translatePoint(int, int);
    public int getClickCount();
    public boolean isPopupTrigger();
    public java.lang.String paramString();
    // constructor
    public java.awt.event.MouseEvent(java.awt.Component,
        int,long,int,int,int,int,boolean);
}
```

Similarly, you can check on the interface that is implemented by your handler by typing the following:

```
javap java.awt.event.MouseListener
```

Compiled from MouseListener.java:

```
public interface java.awt.event.MouseListener extends
        java.lang.Object implements java.util.EventListener {
    public void mouseClicked(java.awt.event.MouseEvent);
    public void mousePressed(java.awt.event.MouseEvent);
    public void mouseReleased(java.awt.event.MouseEvent);
    public void mouseEntered(java.awt.event.MouseEvent);
    public void mouseExited(java.awt.event.MouseEvent);
}
```

We don't need to show the java.awt.event.MouseAdapter class because it has all the same methods, only with empty bodies. You should use the online browser documentation to look at the public fields and methods of all the other Events and Listeners. A full list of the events and listeners is provided in Chapter 21.

There are a lot of new ideas presented by event handling, so don't worry if it doesn't all make sense now. Sleep on it, reread it, try the sample programs, and it will all come together. Understand the event handling before moving on.

Exercises

1. Review the javadoc pages for classes and interfaces in package java.awt.event. How many classes and interfaces exist?

2. Write a program that displays a JFrame. Install a key listener and the three kinds of mouse listener on the frame. Print out each event that is received. Are you surprised at the number of mouse motion events?

3. The source code for the event interfaces and their methods can also be reviewed in the directory $JAVAHOME/src/java/awt/event. ($JAVAHOME is the location where you installed the release. On my system it is C:\jdk1.4.)

    Take a look at MouseWheelEvent.java, which shows how support for the new mouse wheels was added in JDK 1.4. What information can a mouse wheel event convey?

4. After doing the previous exercise, design and describe the event that represents a Zap. Zaps are delivered from the new "Wendy Wand" hardware that can be pointed at any component and invoked with a wink and a shake. Zaps have a location on the screen, a Zap-strength field (wimpy, medium, stun, or to-frog), and a Zap-Color.

5. Write a program that displays a JFrame and handles Zap events. Simulate Zap events by instantiating them and posting them to the event queue. Class java.awt.EventQueue has a method postEvent() that will do this for you. Perhaps you could make a mouse click generate a Zap event in its handler.

Some Light Relief—The Mouse That Roared

Just about everything computer-related must have been designed for the first time or done for the first time by somebody. At some point there must have been the first editor, the first debugger, the first core dump, the first disk drive.

Sometimes these events are surprisingly recent. Sometimes they are old. The term "core dump", which is a copy of the contents of a process's memory, is pretty old. It dates back to the early 1950s when computer memories really were composed of cores. Main memory was built out of tiny ferrite rings or "cores" threaded on fine wires which could induce or reverse a magnetic polarity in the cores. Memory was literally made up of cores that each held one bit, and the contents of memory was a "core dump". Switching time was slow, but it didn't matter because processors were slow too, with cycle times in the milliseconds.

One of the computer "firsts" was the first mouse pointing device. We even know where this was launched: at the Fall Joint Computer Conference in San Francisco in October 1968. It took another 16 years before memory and graphics software got cheap enough to bring the mouse into everyday use with the 1984 Apple Macintosh.

The pioneering inventor of the mouse was computer scientist Doug Englebart (pictured in Figure 20-5 in 2001), who worked at the Stanford Research Institute in Menlo Park, CA. Doug was interested in graphical displays and ways of improving the human-computer interface. He had the idea for a hand-operated pointing device in 1964, and it took four years to complete it.

Figure 20–5   Mouse inventor Englebart

At that time, there were no computers for personal use. Time-sharing was just beginning, and the only people with graphical displays were radar operators. Doug had to persuade managers at SRI to buy an $80,000 graphics console to support his research project. He could foresee a time when screens would replace teletypes, and computers would be cheap enough to have several at home.

The world's first computer mouse still exists, as Figure 20–6 shows. Doug brings it along to seminars and shows it off. It's about the size of a house brick, and it is carved out of a block of pine wood. Pieces have been chipped off it over the years. The mouse size was determined by the internal mechanism. It uses two large potentiometers to track movements. The pots are essentially wheels that have an electrical resistance that changes as the wheel rotates. Doug wanted a sideways mouse movement of 6 inches to correspond to a complete move across the screen; 2.pi.r equals 6, so you need pots about two inches in diameter, and a case the size of a house brick to hold everything.

Figure 20–6   The first mouse

Figure 20–7 shows the underside of the prototype mouse, clearly showing the workings.

Figure 20–7   The belly of the mouse

The pot wheels are mounted at right angles to each other. As you push the mouse, the wheels rotate in proportion to the amount it moves up and along. The resistance of the pots varies, and an analog-to-digital converter turns the measurements into numbers that are sent down the cable to the computer. The computer displays those changing numbers in the form of a moving cursor. The wheels are chamfered so they turn even when pushed diagonally.

The world's first mouse had a single red button at the top right. Notice that the tail comes out of the front of the mouse, not the rear. Clearly, the first priority was to prove the concept, then improve the ergonomics. The device was named early in its development, and nobody remembers who named it. With its original size, it could easily have been labeled a "cat" instead of a mouse.

Later studies at Xerox PARC showed that the mouse was near optimal in terms of access time and accuracy. It is twice as good as some other kinds of pointing devices: eye tracking systems, light pens, and graphics tablets. The mouse will be with us for some time to come.

The new area in input devices is speech. You can buy several voice recognition products today, but they are nowhere near as good as the speaking computer on the Starship Enterprise. Speech is generally a poor way of communicating with a computer. It's tiring and tiresome. You probably won't use it much where a keyboard is available, but it will be a boon to control your cell phone or pocket organizer.

The software has to improve substantially before real-time spoken I/O becomes common. That is partly a matter of boosting CPU power, which is driven by Moore's Law. In mid 2004, the fastest Intel chip you can buy runs at 3.4 GHz. By 2010, it is likely to be eight times faster at 27 GHz.

A Java Speech API was developed under the Java Community Process as specification JSR-113. You can read more about it at `java.sun.com/products/javamedia/speech/`. There are several implementations available today to let you put speech technology into your user interfaces in a future-proof way. When better implementations using more processor power are released, you can plug them in underneath your Java code without changing a single line. That's not guaranteed to happen if you program directly to the third-party APIs. I'm still thinking about those 27 GHz CPUs. That's a lot of processor power to soak up. We'd better get busy! Bridge to computer: The helm is yours.

JFC and the Swing Package

In Chapter 20, we saw that the basic idea behind Java GUI programs is that you perform the following actions:

- Declare controls. You can subclass them to add to the behavior, but this is often unnecessary.

- Implement an interface to get the event handler that responds to control activity.

- Add the controls to a container. Again, subclassing is possible but frequently unnecessary.

Chapter 20 explained how to handle the events that controls generate. This chapter dives into the details of the controls themselves: what they look like, how you use them, and what they do. Chapter 22 wraps up by describing containers and how you use them to lay out controls neatly on the screen.

Java Foundation Classes

Supporting a Java interface to the underlying native window libraries achieves the goal of making Java GUI programs highly portable, but it comes at the cost of inefficiency. Peer events must be translated into Java events before they can be handled by Java code. Worse, native libraries aren't identical on each platform, and sometimes the differences leak into the Java layer.

Example of how native library behavior leaked into the AWT

Sun never did get file name filtering to work for the AWT "file selection dialog" on Windows systems. This was bug 4031440 on the Java Developer Connection at `java.sun.com/jdc`.

To support FilenameFilter, the AWT FileDialog needs to issue a callback for each file to display, and you supply a FilenameFilter that can accept or reject the file. But on Win32, the FileDialog control works in a completely different way. It doesn't issue callbacks. Instead, it accepts simple wildcard patterns to match against file names. That's a reasonable alternative to FilenameFilters, but that model isn't supported by the current Java API. As a result, AWT filename filtering never worked on Win32. This is an example of the difficulties of trying to make a common window library above several different native libraries. Swing solved these difficulties, since there is minimal reliance on native library support. The javax.swing.JFileChooser class lets the user select a file without dependence on the native components.

The Java Foundation Classes (JFC) are a set of GUI-related classes created to solve the AWT problem of platform idiosyncrasies. JFC also supports the following items:

- A pluggable look-and-feel, so that when you run the program, you can choose whether you want it to look like a Windows GUI, a Macintosh GUI, or some other style.

- An accessibility API for features like larger text for the visually impaired.

- The Java 2-D drawing API.

- A drag-and-drop library and an "undo last command" library.

- The Swing component set.

The Swing components (scroll bar, button, textfield, label, etc.) replace the AWT versions of these components. The AWT is still used for the other areas of GUI functionality, such as layout control and printing. We're describing and working with Swing/JFC from here on.

JFC was bundled with JDK 1.2 as a standard part of Java and was also available unbundled for JDK 1.1. Although it's a core library now, the "x" in the package name in JDK 1.2, javax.swing, reflects the fact that the package first became available as an optional extension library. There was quite a bit of churn over the correct package name for Swing, and the unbundled version for JDK 1.1 was released as package com.sun.java.swing. You should use Swing, rather than AWT components, in new programs you write. All browsers now support Swing through the use of the plug-in.

The Java Foundation Classes are aimed squarely at programmers who want to build enterprise-ready software at least as good as (often better than) software built with native GUI libraries. The JFC has the additional advantage of being a lot simpler than competing window systems and producing code that runs on all systems. It is also future-proof. Your programs won't stop working on your next OS change.

Some terminology

In Win32, the term *control* means the group of all the GUI things that users can press, scroll, choose between, type into, draw on, and so forth. In the Unix XWindows world, a control is called a *widget*.

Control and widget are not Java terms. Instead, we use the term *component*, or, when talking specifically about Swing, the *JComponent* subclass of Component. Each Swing control is a subclass of javax.swing.JComponent, so each control inherits all the methods and data fields of JComponent. JComponents are serializable, meaning the object can be written out to disk, can be read in again later, and can become an object again. They follow the rules for JavaBeans, so they can be coupled together in visual builder tools.

This chapter is about explaining the Swing components and how you use them. You will build up your GUI programs using these components. The first thing to note is that the Swing components are no longer peer-based, but are written in Java and are thus consistent on all platforms. Under the AWT, a button ended up being a Win32 button on Windows, a Macintosh button on the Macintosh, and a Motif button on Unix. With Swing, the button is rendered on a little bit of screen area that belongs to some ancestor Java component, and Swing puts all the button semantics on top of that. Swing draws the button so it looks armed (ready to push), pushed, or disabled. Because the code is written in Java, the button has identical behavior no matter where it runs.

JFC is quite a big topic. There are more than three hundred classes in the Swing library alone. We'll present nine or 10 individual Swing JComponents here, and provide pointers on the rest. This amounts to several pages, so I recommend you read one or two in depth, then just look at the figures to get an idea of what each does. Return to the appropriate section in the chapter as you need actual code examples.

Heavyweight versus lightweight components

In AWT, all components are based on peer components. A Java AWT button really is a Win32 button on Windows. This is termed a *heavyweight component.*
A *lightweight component,* like all the Swing JComponents, is one that doesn't use a peer or native component. Instead, it is drawn by Java code on a piece of the screen that already belongs to Java. It is drawn onto its container. The most important differences include the following:

- Lightweight components can have transparent areas in them, so they don't have to look rectangular in shape.
- Mouse events on a lightweight component are delivered to its container. If you want a JButton to get mouse events for some reason (a button press causes an ActionEvent), add the listener to the container.
- When they overlap, lightweight components are never drawn on top of heavyweight components. This is because you can't draw half of a lightweight component on one component and the other half on another. Lightweight components exist wholly within their parent heavyweight component.

JavaSoft recommends that you not mix Swing JComponents with AWT components because of the poor behavior when overlapping.

Overview of JComponent

Object-oriented programming fits well with window systems. The concept of making new controls by subclassing existing ones and overriding part of their behavior saves time and effort. Another similarity is the way that controls have to handle events just as objects handle messages. (Method calls are equivalent to sending a message to an object, and some OOP languages refer to making a method call as "sending a message").

There is an abstract class called JComponent, which is the parent class for most things that can appear on screen. The basic ingredients of a GUI are all subclasses of the class called JComponent. JComponent is the superclass that holds the common information about an onscreen control and provides higher-level features common to each control, as shown in the following list:

- Size (preferred, minimum, and maximum).
- Double buffering (a technique to make frequently changing components look smoother with less flickering).
- Support for accessibility and internationalization.
- Tooltips (pop-up help when you linger on a JComponent).
- Support for operating the control with the keyboard instead of the mouse.

523

- Some help for debugging by slowing component rendering so you can see what's happening.
- The thickness of lines or insets around the edge of the control.

Components correspond to "things that interact with the user" and containers are "backdrops to put them on". The superclass of javax.swing.JComponent is java.awt.Container. The parent of container is the java.awt component.

The behavior and appearance of each specific control is one level down in the subclasses of JComponent. The Swing lightweight controls can be divided as shown in Table 21–1. We will look at just one or two components from each of these categories.

Each control has methods appropriate to what it does. The JFileChooser control has methods to get and set the current directory, get the selected filename(s), apply a file name filter, and so on. We'll examine these individual JComponents later in the chapter.

Table 21–1   Swing lightweight controls

GUI category	Control	Swing class name
Basic controls	Button	JButton, JCheckBox, JRadioButton
	Combo box	JComboBox
	List	JList
	Menu	JMenu, JMenuBar, JMenuItem
	Slider	JSlider
	Toolbar	JToolbar
	Text fields	JTextField, JPasswordField, JTextArea, JFormattedTextField
Uneditable displays	Label	JLabel
	Tooltip	JToolTip
	Progress bar	JProgressBar
Editable displays	Table	JTable
	Text	JTextPane, JTextArea, JEditorPane
	Tree	JTree
	Color chooser	JColorChooser
	File chooser	JFileChooser
	Value chooser	JSpinner

Table 21–1   Swing lightweight controls *(cont.)*

GUI category	Control	Swing class name
Space-Saving Containers	Scroll pane	JScrollPane, JScrollBar
	Split pane	JSplitPane
	Tabbed pane	JTabbedPane
Top-Level Containers	Frame	JFrame
	Applet	JApplet
	Dialog	JDialog, JOptionPane
Other Containers	Panel	JPanel
	Internal frame	JInternalFrame
	Layered pane	JLayeredPane
	Root pane	JRootPane

All About Controls (JComponents)

We now have enough knowledge to start looking at individual controls in detail and to describe the kinds of events they can generate. Most of window programming is learning about the different controls that you can put on the screen and how to drive them. This section describes some individual controls. The controls shown in Figure 21–1 are all subclasses of the general class JComponent that we have already seen.

These classes are the controls or building blocks from which you create your GUI. You can perform the following actions with these components:

1. Add them to a container (often `JFrame` or `JApplet`) with a call such as the following example:

    ```
    MyJContainer.add( myJComponent );
    ```

    Up until JDK 1.5 you could not add a component directly to a container. You had to add it to an object called the *content pane* of the container, as shown in the following example:

    ```
    MyJContainer.getContentPane().add( myJComponent );
    ```

    The content pane is a layer within a container whose purpose is to have controls added to it. It was always a terrible idea. Sun actually added a special check for this at run-time. If you add to a container instead of a

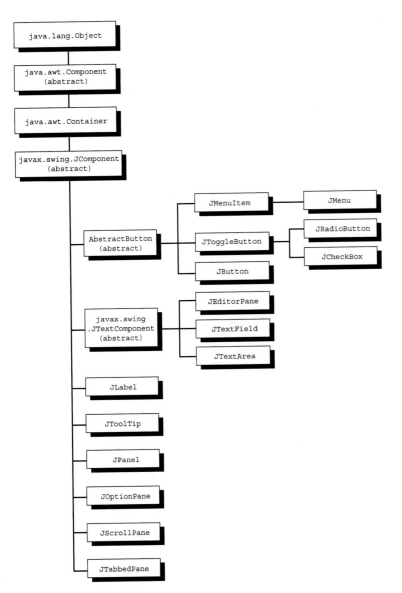

Figure 21–1 Some JComponent controls (visible GUI objects) of Java

container's content pane, it throws an exception and the message reminds you of the "right" way to do it! Sun finally fixed it. We'll use both approaches here, to get you accustomed to seeing both.

2. Register your event handler using the addSomeListener() method of the control. This tells the window system which routine of yours should be called when the user presses buttons or otherwise makes selections to process the event.

Fortunately, both of these activities are quite straightforward, and we'll cover them here in source code, words, and pictures. The add method can be applied to a JFrame in an application similar to the following example:

```
JFrame jf = new JFrame();
                    . . .
jf.add( something );
// or    jf.getContentPane().add( something );
```

It can also be applied to the JApplet's panel, as shown in the following example:

```
public static void init () {
    this.getContentPane().add( something );
```

In the Applet/JApplet life cycle, there is an init() method which your applet code should override. It is called when the applet is loaded, and it is a good place to place the code that creates these GUI objects. We will use init() for that purpose. If you are writing an applet with Swing components, you must use JApplet (not Applet) as your parent class to ensure that all drawing and updates take place correctly.

Whenever a user operates a JComponent (presses a button or clicks a choice), an event is generated. The source code for the event class can be seen in the $JAVAHOME/src/java/awt/event directory. It contains information about the coordinates of the event, the time it occurred, and the kind of event that it was. If the event was a key press, it has the value of the key. If the event was a selection from a list, it has the string chosen.

As we saw in Chapter 20, the run-time library creates one of these event objects for each occurrence of an event and queues them up on the event queue. The event dispatching thread takes event objects off the queue and calls your appropriate event handlers with the event object as an argument.

How to display components

Containers are the objects that are displayed directly on the screen. Controls must be added to a container if you want to see them. The container in this example driver program is called *JFrame*. JFrame will be the main window for most of your Swing applications.

Let's create a JFrame, set its size, set it visible, tell it how to arrange JComponents that are added, and add some event-handler code to exit the program when it detects that you have clicked on the JFrame to close it. That's quite a list of tasks, so we'll split them off into a separate method. Make everything static. In this way, we can use it from the main() method, and we get the following:

```
import java.awt.*;
import java.awt.event.*;
import javax.swing.*;
public class Demo {
    static JFrame jframe = new JFrame("Example");

    public static void setupJFrame() {
        jframe.setSize(400,100);
        jframe.setVisible(true);
        jframe.setLayout( new FlowLayout() );

        WindowListener l = new WindowAdapter() {
            public void windowClosing(WindowEvent e) {
                System.exit(0);}
        };
        jframe.addWindowListener(l);
    }

    public static void main(String[] args) {
        setupJFrame();
        JButton jb = new JButton("pressure");
        jframe.getContentPane().add( jb );
        jframe.setVisible(true);
    }
}
```

The JButton Component that we are demonstrating is printed in bold type. The line that follows adds the JComponent to the JFrame's content pane. To cut down on the extraneous code in the pages ahead, I'll show only the statements that directly deal with the JComponent. That means I'll show only the two bold statements in the example above. You should supply all the missing code when you compile and run the examples. Next, a thread caution, and then on to the first example!

Swing Threads—A Caution!

The GUI components are maintained on the screen by a thread of their own, separate to any threads that you have running in your code. This GUI thread is called the *event-dispatching thread*, and it takes care of rendering the GUI components and processing any GUI events that take place. An example of a GUI event would be a mouse click, a selection from a menu, or a keystroke on a text field.

The need for thread safety occurs in the system libraries just as much as it does in your code. To work properly, *Swing requires that all code that might affect GUI components be executed from the event-dispatching thread!* The reason is performance: the GUI library does not have to do synchronization that would be required if multiple threads were potentially adjusting data.

As you know, events are handled by a callback from the window system to an event-handler object you supply. That means that your event-handler code automatically executes in the event-dispatching thread, as it should. But should you try to create new GUI components in another of your threads, your thread will not be synchronized with run-time library data structures. Therefore, the only place where you should create, modify, set visible, set size, or otherwise adjust GUI components is in your event-handler code. Otherwise, you will bring yourself synchronization problems that are difficult to debug.

The following example is erroneous natural-looking code:

```java
public static void main (String[] args) {
    createSomeFrame(); // created in the main thread
    showThatFrame();   // shown by main thread,
    // now that first component is displayed, no more
    // code that affects components may be run from
    // any thread other than the event-dispatching thread
    createSomeOtherGUIComponent(); // WRONG!!!
}
```

There is one exception to the rule of doing GUI work only in the event-dispatching thread, which fortunately allows us to write our programs in the most natural way. You are allowed to construct a GUI in the application's main method or the JApplet's init method, providing there are no GUI components already on the screen from your program and that you do not further adjust it from this thread after the GUI becomes visible. Most people obey these rules by accident, but you should know about them. For practical purposes, this means if you want to create a new GUI component in response to a GUI event, you *must* do the instantiation in the code that handles the GUI event.

If you have to do more GUI work from one of your own threads, you can easily put it into the correct thread by using the Runnable interface. One of the Swing utilities takes a Runnable as an argument and runs it in the event dispatching thread. The code is as follows:

```java
Runnable toDoInEvHandlerThread = new Runnable() {
    public void run() {
        // things to do in the event-dispatching thread
        doTheWork();
    }
};

javax.swing.SwingUtilities.invokeLater(toDoInEvHandlerThread);
```

You should follow this protocol in Swing programs. If you ignore this warning, sooner or later, one of your Swing programs will hit a data race bug, and it will be nearly impossible to reproduce, let alone debug it. When maintaining Swing programs check that invokeLater() has been used where needed.

Now let's look at some Swing components.

Swing Components

JLabel

What it is: JLabel is the simplest JComponent. It is a string, image, or both that appears onscreen. The contents can be left-, right-, or center-aligned according to an argument to the constructor. The default is left-aligned. JLabel is a cheap, fast way to get a picture or text on the screen.

How it appears onscreen:

Figure 21–2   How JLabel appears onscreen

The code to create it:

```
//   remember, we are only showing relevant statements from main()
     ImageIcon icon = new ImageIcon("star.gif");
     JLabel jl = new JLabel("You are a star", icon, JLabel.CENTER);

     frame.add( jl );
     frame.pack(); // size the JFrame to fit its contents
```

Note the way we can bring in an image from a GIF or JPEG file by constructing an ImageIcon with a pathname to a file. Labels do not generate any events in and of themselves. It is possible, however, to get and set the text of a label. You might do that in response to an event from a different component. The constructors for JLabel include the following:

```
public javax.swing.JLabel(java.lang.String);
public javax.swing.JLabel(java.lang.String,int);
public javax.swing.JLabel(java.lang.String,javax.swing.Icon,int);
public javax.swing.JLabel(javax.swing.Icon);
public javax.swing.JLabel(javax.swing.Icon,int);
```

The int parameter is a constant from the JLabel class specifying left-, right- or center-alignment in the area where the label is displayed.

JLabels are typically used to augment other controls with descriptions or instructions. Most JComponents that display some text (such as JButton, JLabel, JOptionPane etc.) are happy to display HTML. Start the text with <html> and end with </html>. You can easily display multi-line buttons, and mix fonts and colors. Here is a JButton with two lines of text:

```
JButton jb = new JButton("<html>Multi<br>line</html>");
```

JButton

What it is: This is a GUI button. You supply code for the action that is to take place when the button is pressed.

How it appears onscreen:

Figure 21–3   How JButton appears onscreen

The code to create it:

```
JButton jb = new JButton("pressure");
jframe.add( jb );
```

The code to handle events from it:

```
jb.addActionListener( new ActionListener() {
    int i = 1;
    public void actionPerformed(ActionEvent e)
        { System.out.println("pressed "+ i++); }
    } );
```

When you press this button, the event handler prints out the number of times it has been pressed. You can easily create buttons with images as well, similar to this example:

```
Icon spIcon = new ImageIcon("spam.jpg");
JButton jb = new JButton("press here for Spam", spIcon);
```

Figure 21–4   How code looks onscreen

You can add a keyboard accelerator to a button, and you can give it a symbolic name for the text string that it displays. This helps with internationalizing code.

Program an "Alice in Wonderland" JFrame with two buttons, one of which makes the frame grow larger, the other smaller. The Component method setSize(int, int) will resize a component. (Easy; approximately 20 lines of code.)

JToolTip

What it is: This is a text string that acts as a hint or further explanation. You can set it for any JComponent. It appears automatically when the mouse lingers on that component and it disappears when you roll the mouse away.

Tooltips don't generate any events so there is nothing to handle.

How it appears onscreen: We'll add a tooltip to the JLabel that we showed on the previous page.

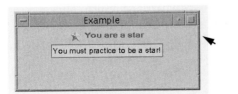

Figure 21–5   How JToolTip appears onscreen

The code to create it:

```
JLabel jl = ...
jl.setToolTipText("You must practice to be a star!");
```

Notice that you don't directly create a JToolTip object. That is done for you behind the scenes. You invoke the setToolTipText() method of JComponent.

It's quick and easy to create tooltips; use them generously.

JTextField

What it is: This is an area of the screen where you can enter a line of text. There are two subclasses: JTextArea (several lines in size) and JPasswordField (which doesn't echo what you type). You can display some initial text. The text is selectable (you can highlight it with the cursor) and can be set to be editable or not editable.

How it appears onscreen:

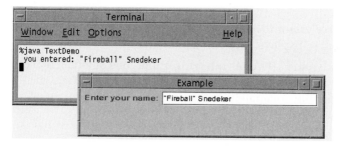

Figure 21–6   How JTextField appears onscreen

The code to create it:

```
JLabel jl = new JLabel("Enter your name:");
JTextField jtf = new JTextField(25); // field is 25 chars wide
```

The code to retrieve user input from it: Text fields generate key events on each keystroke and an ActionEvent when the user presses a carriage return. This makes it convenient to validate individual keystrokes as they are typed (as in ensuring that a field is wholly numeric) and to retrieve all the text when the user has finished typing. The following code gets the text:

```
jtf.addActionListener( new ActionListener() {
    public void actionPerformed(ActionEvent e)
    {  System.out.println(
        " you entered: " + e.getActionCommand() ); }
    } );

Container c = jframe.getContentPane();
c.add( jl );
c.add( jtf );
```

In this example, running the program, typing a name, and hitting carriage return will cause the name to be echoed on system.out. You should write some code to try to implement a listener for each keystroke.

JCheckBox

What it is: A checkbox screen object that represents a boolean choice: pressed, not pressed, on, or off. Usually some text explains the choice. For example, a "Press for fries" JLabel would have a JCheckBox "button" allowing yes or no. You can also add an icon to the JCheckBox, just the way you can with JButton.

How it appears onscreen:

Figure 21–7   How JCheckBox appears onscreen

The code to create it:

```
JCheckBox jck1 = new JCheckBox("Pepperoni");
JCheckBox jck2 = new JCheckBox("Mushroom");
JCheckBox jck3 = new JCheckBox("Black olives");
JCheckBox jck4 = new JCheckBox("Tomato");
Container c = jframe.getContentPane();
c.add( jck1 ); c.add( jck2 ); // etc...
```

The code to retrieve user input from it: Checkbox generates both ActionEvent and ItemEvent every time you change it. This seems to be for backward compatibility with AWT. We already saw the code to handle ActionEvents with Button. The following code registers an ItemListener:

```
jck2.addItemListener( new ItemListener()
{ // anonymous class
    public void itemStateChanged(ItemEvent e) {
        if (e.getStateChange()==e.SELECTED)
            System.out.print("selected ");
        else System.out.print("de-selected ");
        System.out.print("Mushroom\n");
    }
} );
```

In this example, running the program and clicking the "Mushroom" checkbox will cause the output of selected Mushroom in the system console.

Handlers in real programs will do more useful actions as necessary like assigning values and creating objects. The ItemEvent contains fields and methods that specify which object generated the event and whether it was selected or deselected.

JPanel

What it is: There is an AWT component known as Canvas. It is a screen area that you can use for drawing graphics or receiving user input. When you need to draw arbitrary shapes and text in arbitrary places (e.g. a graph or a drawing program) you extend Canvas and override its paint() method to add the behavior you need. A Canvas has few methods. All its functionality is either inherited from Component (setting font, color, size) or from functionality you add when you extend the class.

There is no JCanvas component in Swing. The AWT component Canvas was just like the AWT component Panel, except Panel was also a container. The Swing version of Panel, JPanel, does double duty. It replaces both Canvas and Panel.

To draw on a JPanel, you supply your own version of the method paintComponent(Graphics g). To do that, you need to extend the class and override the paintComponent() method[1] for this Container. That gives you a Graphics context—the argument to paintComponent()—which is used in all drawing operations. The many methods of java.awt.Graphics let you render (the fancy graphics word for "draw") lines, shapes, text, etc., on the screen.

A simpler alternative for simpler drawings is to use JLabel to create the picture and add it to JPanel as shown in the following code.

The code to create it: Figure 21–8 is the result from running the following code:

```
class MyJPanel extends JPanel {
    JLabel jl = new JLabel(new ImageIcon( "bmw.jpg"));
    { add(jl); // instance initializer just for fun

        addKeyListener( new KeyAdapter() {
            public void keyPressed(KeyEvent e) {
                char c = e.getKeyChar();
                System.out.println("got char "+c);
            }
        } );
    }
}

. . .

    public static void main(String[] args) {
        setupFrame();
        MyJPanel mjp = new MyJPanel();
        jframe.getContentPane().add(mjp);
        jframe.setVisible(true);
        mjp.requestFocus();
    }
```

---

1. A more descriptive name for the paintComponent() method would be how_to_draw_me().

I like this picture because it looks the same in black and white as it does in color.

Figure 21–8   JPanel replaces panel and canvas

I have also added a KeyListener for the JPanel here. That allows you to make keystrokes on top of the JPanel and have the callback take place for each one individually. All you do is echo the characters to prove you got them. With the picture backdrop and the capture of individual keystrokes, you have the basics of a computer game right there.

You have to request the focus for a component before key events will be sent to it, and the component has to be visible at the time you do that.

JRadioButton and ButtonGroup

What it is: JRadioButtons are used when you have a group of checkboxes and you want a maximum of one of them to be selected. This was done with a CheckboxGroup in the AWT, but the design has been cleaned up and simplified in Swing. JRadioButton, JCheckBox, and JButton are now subclasses of AbstractButton and have common consistent behavior, can be given images, can be embedded in menus, and so on.

The term "radio buttons" arises from the old manual station selection buttons in car radios. When you pressed in one of the buttons, all the others would pop out and be deselected. ButtonGroups work the same way.

How it appears onscreen:

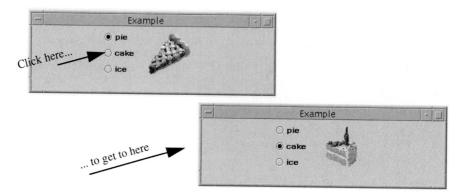

Figure 21–9 **How JRadioButton appears onscreen**

On Windows, mutually exclusive checkboxes are round, while multiple selection checkboxes are square. This is one of those "look and feel" differences between window systems.

The code to create it: This example shows some more sophisticated things you can do in your event handler. In this example, we have a JLabel with a picture of the choice. In the event handler, we set the label to correspond to the RadioButton choice.

The ButtonGroup class automatically takes care of arming the previous radio button when you press another. Review the following code example:

```
// JRadioButton code
    final JLabel piclabel
        = new JLabel(new ImageIcon( pieString + ".gif"));

    /** Listens to the radio buttons. */
    class RadioListener implements ActionListener {
        public void actionPerformed(ActionEvent e) {
        // getting the event causes update on Jlabel icon
        piclabel.setIcon(
            new ImageIcon( e.getActionCommand()+".gif"));
        }
    }

    JRadioButton pieButton = new JRadioButton(pieString);
    pieButton.setMnemonic('b');
    pieButton.setActionCommand(pieString);
    pieButton.setSelected(true);

    JRadioButton cakeButton = new JRadioButton(cakeString);
    JRadioButton iceButton = new JRadioButton(iceString);

    // Group the radio buttons.
    ButtonGroup group = new ButtonGroup();
    group.add(pieButton);
    group.add(cakeButton);
    group.add(iceButton);

    // Register a listener for the radio buttons.
    RadioListener myListener = new RadioListener();
    pieButton.addActionListener(myListener);
    cakeButton.addActionListener(myListener);
    iceButton.addActionListener(myListener);

    // Put the radio buttons in a column in a panel to line up
    JPanel radioPanel = new JPanel();
    radioPanel.setLayout(new GridLayout(0, 1));
    radioPanel.add(pieButton);
    radioPanel.add(cakeButton);
    radioPanel.add(iceButton);

    jframe.getContentPane().add(radioPanel);
    jframe.getContentPane().add(piclabel);
    jframe.setVisible(true);
```

JOptionPane

What it is: This is a utility pane that can pop up some common warning and error messages. It's as easy to use as JToolTip, and it works the same way. You don't instantiate it directly, but you call a method to make it happen.

How it appears onscreen:

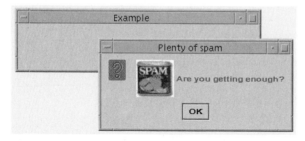

Figure 21–10   How JOptionPane appears onscreen

The code to create it: JOptionPane is similar to a VB msgbox or dialog. There are several different types of JOptionPane, some of which just display a message (click OK to dismiss it). Others ask the user to input a String or click a radio button. You get the input by calling a method such as getValue(). See the javadoc for more details.

```
Icon s = new ImageIcon("spam.jpg");
JLabel jl = new JLabel("Are you getting enough?", s,JLabel.CENTER);

JOptionPane.showMessageDialog( null, // parent frame
                   jl,   // Object to display
                   "Plenty of spam", // title bar message
                   JOptionPane.QUESTION_MESSAGE );
```

The code to retrieve user input from it: No input comes back from this component. When the user clicks on the button, the pane is dismissed automatically. There are many choices and methods that fine-tune this JComponent to let you convey exactly the information you want.

JScrollPane

What it is: Of all the JComponents, this one is probably my favorite. It works so hard for you with so little effort on your part.

A JScrollPane provides a scrollable view of any lightweight component. You instantiate a JScrollPane with the thing you want to scroll as an argument to the constructor. Then you set the ScrollPane's preferred size with a method call, add it to your container, and you're done! This is so much easier than messing around with individual and highly buggy scrollbars that we had in JDK 1.0.

By default, a scroll pane attempts to size itself so that its client displays at its preferred size. Many components have a simple preferred size that's big enough to display the entire component. You can customize a scroll pane with many refinements on how much to scroll, which of the scroll bars to show, custom decorations around the sides, and so on. The visible area in the pane is called the "viewport."

How it appears onscreen:

Figure 21–11   How JScrollPane appears onscreen

The code to create it: In this code, we put the JPanel subclass that we created earlier into a JScrollPane:

```
MyJPanel mjp = new MyJPanel();
JScrollPane jsp = new JScrollPane( mjp );
jsp.setPreferredSize( new Dimension(150, 150));
jframe.getContentPane().add(jsp);
```

The code to retrieve user input from it: You won't need to interact with your scroll pane very frequently, as it does so much of the right thing by default. However, you can implement the Scrollable interface if your enthusiasm extends to wanting to get callbacks for individual clicks on the scroll bars.

JTabbedPane

What it is: A Tabbed Pane is a component that lets you economize on-screen real estate. It simulates a folder with tabbed page dividers. You have a series of "tabs" (labels) along the top, associated with components on a larger rectangular area beneath. By clicking a tab label, you bring its associated component to the front. We'll show an example using the JEditorPane and the JPanel.

How it appears onscreen:

Clicking here…

…brings that pane

to the front.

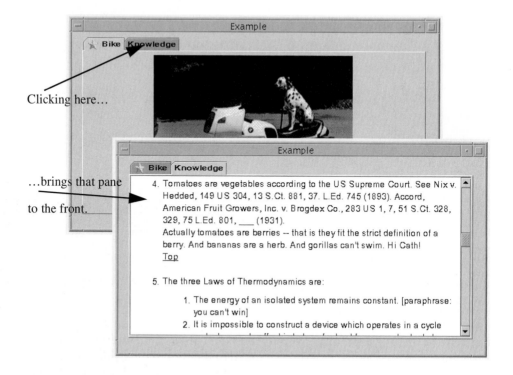

Figure 21–12   How JTabbedPane appears onscreen

You can make the tabs appear on any of the four sides of the TabbedPane. You can even have more than one row of tabs, but the human factors of that are so appalling that Sun added new behavior in JDK 1.4. Usually, when you have multiple rows in a tabbed pane, any tab that's clicked jumps to the bottom row of tabs (so its pane appears in front). As a result, clicking on some tabs causes all of them to change places. To prevent this, you can pass an argument to the constructor saying that you want tabs to scroll, not to wrap, when you have more tabs than will fit on one line.

The code to create it:

```
// set up the editor pane, as before
    JEditorPane jep =null;
    try {
        jep = new JEditorPane( "file:///tmp/know.html" );
    } catch (Exception e) {System.out.println("error: "+e); }

    jep.setEditable(false); // turns off the ability to edit
    JScrollPane jsp = new JScrollPane( jep );
    jsp.setPreferredSize( new Dimension(550, 250));

// set up the JPanel, as before
    MyJPanel mjp = new MyJPanel();
    jframe.getContentPane().add(mjp);

// create a tabbed pane and add them to it.
    JTabbedPane jtp = new JTabbedPane();
    ImageIcon ic = new ImageIcon("star.gif");
    jtp.addTab("Bike", ic, mjp,
               "1989 BWM RS100/1996 Dalmatian Annie");
    jtp.addTab("Knowledge", null, jsp, "who knew?");

    jframe.getContentPane().add(jtp);
    jframe.setVisible(true);
}
```

The method to add a tab and the component together takes the following four arguments:

```
public void addTab(String title,
                   Icon icon,
                   Component component,
                   String tip)
```

The title is the phrase to put on the tab. The icon is a little picture with which you can decorate the phrase. For example, on the "Bike" pane I use a star, and on the "Knowledge" pane I use null to signify no picture. The third parameter is the component that you want associated with that tab. The final parameter is a String representing tooltip text that you get for free with this component.

JEditorPane

What it is: This is a very powerful JComponent! JEditorPane allows you to display and edit documents that contain HTML, Rich Text Format, or straight Unicode characters. It formats the text and displays it.

How it appears onscreen:

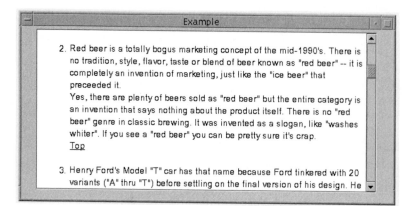

Figure 21–13   How JEditorPane appears onscreen

You can load the component from a URL or a String containing a URL as shown here, or from the contents of a String itself. In the following example, the JEditor pane is placed in a ScrollPane so it displays and scrolls well.

The code to create it:

```
JEditorPane jep =null;
try {
    jep = new JEditorPane( "file:///tmp/know.html" );
} catch (Exception e) {System.out.println("error: "+e); }

jep.setEditable(false); // turns off the ability to edit
JScrollPane jsp = new JScrollPane( jep );
jsp.setPreferredSize( new Dimension(550, 250));

jframe.getContentPane().add(jsp);
```

Notice how trivial it is to display an HTML file and to wrap a JScrollPane around it. JEditorPane is a subclass of the less specialized JTextComponent.

Let's quickly review the match between components and events shown in Components and events.

Table 21–2   Components and events

Component	Event handler interface	Method(s) the interface promises
JButton JMenu JMenuItem JRadioButton JCheckBox	ActionListener	`public void actionPerformed(ActionEvent e);`

Component	ComponentListener	`public void componentResized(ComponentEvent);`
		`public void componentMoved(ComponentEvent);`
		`public void componentShown(ComponentEvent);`
		`public void componentHidden(ComponentEvent);`

Container	ContainerListener	`public void componentAdded(ContainerEvent);` `public void componentRemoved(ContainerEvent);`
Component	FocusListener	`public void focusGained(FocusEvent e);` `public void focusLost(FocusEvent e);`
JButton JMenu JMenuItem JRadioButton JCheckBox	ItemListener	`public void itemStateChanged(ItemEvent e);`

Component	KeyListener	`public void keyTyped(KeyEvent e);`
		`public void keyPressed(KeyEvent e);`
		`public void keyReleased(KeyEvent e);`

Component	MouseListener	`public void mouseClicked(MouseEvent e);`
		`public void mousePressed(MouseEvent e);`
		`public void mouseReleased(MouseEvent e);`
		`public void mouseEntered(MouseEvent e);`
		`public void mouseExited(MouseEvent e);`

Table 21–2   **Components and events** *(cont.)*

Component	Event handler interface	Method(s) the interface promises
Component	MouseMotionListener	`public void mouseDragged(MouseEvent e);`
		`public void mouseMoved(MouseEvent e);`
JTextField	ActionListener	`public void actionPerformed(ActionEvent e);`
Dialog	WindowListener	`public void windowOpened(WindowEvent e);`
JDialog		`public void windowClosing(WindowEvent e);`
Frame		`public void windowClosed(WindowEvent e);`
JFrame		`public void windowIconified(WindowEvent e);`
Window		`public void windowDeiconified(WindowEvent e):`
JWindow		`public void windowActivated(WindowEvent e);`
		`public void WindowDeactivated (WindowEvent e);`

More About Swing Components

Components and events named all the significant JComponents, and there were about forty in all (including all the subclasses of subclasses). We've briefly presented some of the more important ones here. That's certainly enough to get you started writing GUI programs. To keep the book to a manageable size, however, and still fit in all the other information, we don't show all of them.

Here are some pointers on how to find out more about the other components when you're ready to. The first resource is the good (if somewhat fluid) online tutorial on Java in general, and Swing in particular, that Sun Microsystems maintains at `java.sun.com/docs/books/tutorial/ui/swing/`.

The second resource is a book that examines JFC, including the Swing components in depth. These books are frequently intimidating in size. One such book that I like is *The JFC Swing Tutorial: A Guide to Constructing GUIs*, Second Edition by Walrath, Campione, Huml, and Zakhour (Addison-Wesley, 2004, ISBN 0201914670). It weighs in at 800 pages, so be prepared to put in a few evenings and weekends.

Debugging lightweight components

JComponent supports a method to help the implementation team debug the Swing library, but you can use it, too. You can call the following code:

```
RepaintManager.currentManager(yourContainer.getRootPane()).
            setDoubleBufferingEnabled(false);
anyJComponent.setDebugGraphicsOptions( options );
```

The first statement turns off double buffering for the container your component is in. The "options" parameter on the second statement is an int which is 0 to switch debugging off, or contains any of these flags OR'd together:

• DebugGraphics.FLASH_OPTION // flash the component as it is accessed

• DebugGraphics.BUFFER_OPTION // show the offscreen graphics work

• DebugGraphics.LOG_OPTION // print a text summary of graphics work

The flash option is pretty spectacular and allows you to see lightweight components being drawn.

Finally, I have the same advice that Obi-Wan gave Luke Skywalker on his quest to defeat the forces of evil: *Use the Source*. The Java platform is almost unique among commercial products in that the complete source code for the run-time library is distributed with the system.

Having the source is a triple blessing. You can read the code to find out how something works and what features it offers (the code is heavily commented). You can recompile the code with more of your own debugging information, and use that instead of the standard run-time library (not everyone will want to tackle this, but in fact, it is trivial to use the "update" option to jar to replace a single class file in rt.jar. Make a backup copy of rt.jar before you change anything, and don't tell anyone you heard this idea from me). You will also be exposed to the ideas, style, and designs that are used by the best Java programmers in the world. The best programmers in the world learn from each other by reading each other's code. Now you have this opportunity, too. Seize it.

I really like Swing. It passes the golden rule of software: it's simple to do simple things. Just be aware that all the components have many more features than are presented here and you can get sophisticated effects when you start combining them and using them to full advantage.

Further Reading

The first Java website that you visit should be Sun's at `java.sun.com`. But the Java website that you visit most frequently should be the Java Lobby at `www.javalobby.org`.

The Java Lobby is an independent group representing Java developers. Led by software entrepreneur Rick Ross, the Lobby has tens of thousands of members. It is a great place for thoughtful discussion and late-breaking news on Java. You can even get advice on coding. The Java Lobby is a great resource and membership is free.

Exercises

1. Review the javadoc-generated description of the javax.swing.SwingUtilities class. Write a program that demonstrates the use of two of the utilities in that class.

2. Add the JEditorPane that can render HTML to some code that can make a socket inquiry in the HTTP protocol (chapter 25 shows the code for this). Create a basic web browser in less than 150 lines of code. You can do this in one evening, and spend the rest of the year adding refinements to it.

3. Review the class java.awt.Robot. It is intended to generate native system input events for test programs. Instead, use it to develop an automatic player for Minesweeper or other favorite game.

Some Light Relief—The Bible Code

The concept of "Bible codes" was something that became popular in 1997, helped by a mass marketed book on the subject. It's a completely bogus idea that there are hidden strings in the first five books of the Bible, and these hidden strings foretell the future.

The hidden strings, or *Bible codes,* are allegedly found by looking at individual characters of the Bible, starting at some offset, and taking every Nth letter thereafter to form a phrase. It works much better with a Bible in Hebrew because the classic written form of that language does not have any vowels. Hence, you can construct many possible phrases depending on which vowels you choose to put in and where you choose to end a word. "BLLGTS" can be interpreted as "Boil leg & toes" or "Be a li'l gutsy" or even "Bill Gates."

When you find a Bible "code" you frequently find other related phrases around it. Of course, you can often find clouds in the sky that have shapes that look like animals, and the reason is exactly the same: people tend to see what they want to see. There's a huge amount of sky and clouds to look at, and you can always find something if you look at enough random stuff.

I thought it would be fun to write some Bible code software in Java, so I put it on the book website at afu.com/jj6. There's a program there that you can run to search for arbitrary patterns in the Bible (a copy of the King James Version is also there). See Figure 21–14 for the results when I set it to search for the string "Java", which is a place and language unknown in biblical times.

As you can see, it has found the word along with other astonishing and highly meaningful phrases ("knowledge of Java, a great blessing, bit, net"). You can run the program for yourself and find other phrases of your choice.

```
                          bible code

         look for pattern:    java          go!

  treeof(knowledge)ofgoodandevilan d ariverwentouto(redentowaterthe
  ochwasborniradandiradbegatmehu|j|aelandmehujae(be(gatmethusaela
  henthefloodofwaterswasuponthee|a|rthandnoahwan(i)andhissonsand
  sthetokenofthecovenantwhichiha|v|eestablishedbetyeenmeandallfl
  eeandmakethyname(great)ndthoush|a|1tbe(blessing)ndiwillblessthe
  ndblessedbethemosthighgodwhich h athdeliveredthineenemiesintot



  starts at offset:  9864     gap between chars:   5765
```

Figure 21–14   Bible code says "Java a great blessing!"

One of the promoters of the Bible code concept challenged his critics to find hidden messages in non-Bible texts like *Moby Dick*. He thought there weren't any. He was dead wrong!

You will find that *Moby Dick* contains predictions for the deaths of Indira Gandhi, President Rene Moawad of Lebanon, Martin Luther King, Chancellor Engelbert Dollfuss of Austria, Leon Trotsky, Sirhan Sirhan, John F. Kennedy, Robert Kennedy, and Princess Diana, among others! Figure 21–15 shows the Diana prediction from *Moby Dick*.

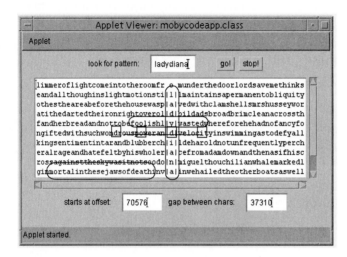

Figure 21–15   Bible code links Lady Di and Dodi

"Lady Diana, Dodi, foolishly wasted, mortal in these jaws of death!" There are two likely conclusions. Either Herman Melville was the Supreme Creator of the Universe and he encoded Bible code style predictions in *Moby Dick* as well as in the Bible. Or, another possibility is that the notion of hidden messages encoded in revered works is a bunch of nonsense put about by some people who should know better. I don't know about you, but I'm going with the simpler of the two explanations. The meaninglessness of the codes doesn't impugn the origin of the Bible. It just says that people can be wrong when they try to project their own interpretations onto any text.

There's a copy of *Moby Dick* on the website, along with the Bible code software to search it. I'd like to find out what hidden messages there are in the Sherlock Holmes books. This is what programmers do when they have too much time on their hands.

Chapter **22**

Containers, Layouts, and AWT Loose Ends

▼ PLUGGABLE LOOK AND FEEL

▼ ALL ABOUT CONTAINERS

▼ LAYOUT IN A CONTAINER

▼ TYING UP THE LOOSE ENDS

▼ EXERCISES

▼ SOME LIGHT RELIEF—SKY VIEW CAFE: A HIGH QUALITY APPLET

We're now two-thirds of the way through our tour of JFC and Swing. This chapter completes the topic by presenting some containers and an explanation of how you use them to lay out your components neatly on the screen. We also give some information on a couple of topics that are related to the window system in general.

Pluggable Look and Feel

Let's start off the chapter with something that, while not unique to Java, is certainly not widely available. I'm referring to the *Pluggable Look and Feel* or *PLAF* as it is usually abbreviated. By default, a Swing program has the *Metal* look and feel, which is a look and feel designed especially for Java. You can easily change that so a program has the look and feel of Windows, the Macintosh, or of Motif. PLAF means that you, the programmer, can add a few extra lines of code to allow users to select which look and feel they want anytime they run your program, regardless of which operating system is running underneath.

The Pluggable Look and Feel is a win for software portability. Not only do your Java programs run everywhere, but they can even look the same everywhere.

549

This is a great boon for users who have become comfortable with a program on one particular platform. Now that same knowledge and familiarity can be retained regardless of the execution environment.

As a programmer, you might share my opinion that the look and feel of a window system is not the most important topic in software today. All window systems do roughly the same set of things, and it's no big deal. The fact remains that, for some users, it *is* a most important topic. Those users buy the software that pays the wages that keep us employed.

Figure 22–1 is an example of the kind of differences you see on different window systems. The three panels show the same controls in three different "look and feel" ways. The top panel is the Metal look and feel. If you choose to have your GUIs display in Metal, your programs will have a consistent look regardless of the operating system or window libraries. The second panel has the Motif look and feel. The lines are so delicate and thin that some of them don't reproduce completely on this screen capture. The bottom panel is the basic Windows look and feel. Pay no attention to the relative sizes of fonts and buttons. That can all be resized to suit the program. The difference is in how much shading appears around a button, how thick the dot is in a selected radio button, whether components are given a 3-D look, and so on.

Here's the really cool thing: there is only one program here! And they are all running on a Windows PC. When you select one of those JRadioButtons, it transforms the program to display in that style. I started up three copies of the program, chose a different look and feel in each, put them next to each other, and took a screen shot. This is less than 150 lines long, and the key area is a couple of lines. It declares the JComponents and a listener for the radio buttons.

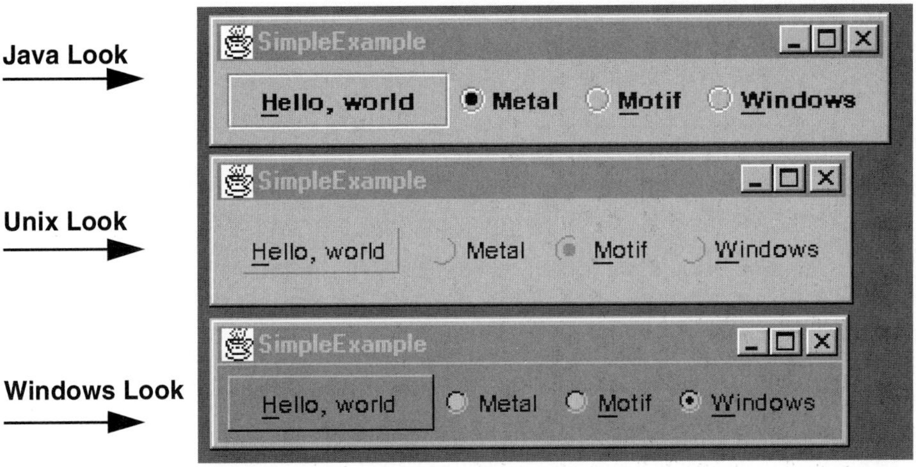

Java Look ⟶

Unix Look ⟶

Windows Look ⟶

Figure 22–1   A Pluggable Look and Feel (PLAF)

The listener has the code (shown here) that does the magic:

```
String metalPLAFName = "javax.swing.plaf.metal.MetalLookAndFeel";
String motifPLAFName = "com.sun.java.swing.plaf.motif.MotifLookAndFeel";
String winPLAFName = "com.sun.java.swing.plaf.windows.WindowsLookAndFeel";
String lnfName = e.getActionCommand();
try {
    UIManager.setLookAndFeel(lnfName);
    SwingUtilities.updateComponentTreeUI(frame);
    frame.pack();
} catch (Exception exc) { ...
```

There are a couple of methods in the library to let you force the look and feel to match the system on which you are running. The following code does that:

```
UIManager.setLookAndFeel(UIManager.getSystemLookAndFeelClassName());
```

The following code forces a program to use the common Metal look:

```
UIManager.setLookAndFeel(UIManager.getCrossPlatformLookAndFeelClassName());
```

Since the look and feel is rendered by Java code, not by use of native libraries, it is feasible to have any look and feel on any platform. Microsoft and Apple, however, have chosen not to grant permission for their look and feel to be used on other platforms.

Model/View/Controller architecture

You may hear people talk about the *Model/View/Controller,* or *MVC,* architecture of Swing. MVC is a design pattern or framework originally developed by Professor Trygve Reenskaug at Xerox PARC in 1978. The purpose of MVC was to provide convenient GUI support in Smalltalk.

Model/View/Controller is used extensively in Swing. For the basic components, you don't notice it. For more complicated components like JTree and JTable, you need to know a little about it. A one-line summary of MVC would be: rather than having one big class for each JComponent, different GUI responsibilities have been split out into different classes. MVC makes the Platform Look and Feel possible, or at least a lot simpler.

Basically, the *model* contains your data, the *view* is the graphical representation, and the *controller* is responsible for the interaction between the other two. As an example, think of a program that keeps time and displays it as part of a user interface desktop, such as the example program we developed in chapter 2. The Model will be the part of the program that reads the real-time clock, turns it into hours and minutes, and adjusts for time zone. There is only one model, but there can be multiple views of it. One view would be a display in the form of a clock with hands. Another view would be a digital display of hours, minutes, and seconds. A third view would be a clockface with Roman numerals. The controller is any "glue" code connecting the model and its views.

In practice, the controller and the view are often put in the same class. Swing initially kept them separate, but realized it was easier to let the model and views talk to each other directly. Model and views are separate, though.

All About Containers

We come now to the third of the three ideas common to all Java GUI programs: grouping together controls and arranging them neatly by adding them to a container.

We've seen this when we added the JComponents to the content pane of a JFrame, and the JFrame showed up on the screen. The piece that is new is that a container can have different *layout policies* for where components go on the screen when you add them. A layout policy might be, "Add components from left to right across the container. When you reach the right-hand margin, start a new line of them." Another layout policy might be, "Components can go to the north, south, east, west, or in the center of the component. You have to tell me where you add one." There are a number of classes, called *Layout Managers*, that implement layout policies like these. We are going to describe them at length in this chapter. Before we do, we'll look at containers a bit more closely.

Controls, containers, component...where will it all end?

Here's the way to tell these three similar-sounding names apart!

Control This is not a Java term. This is the PC term for what is called a widget in the Unix world. A control is a software element on the screen, such as a button or a scroll bar.

Container These are screen windows that physically contain groups of controls or other containers. You can move, hide, or show a container and all its contents in one operation. Top-level containers can be displayed on the screen. Non top-level containers have to be in a top-level container to be displayed.

Component This is a collective name for controls and containers. Since they have some common operations, component is their common parent class. Swing's JComponents are a subclass of component.

The Container class hierarchy

The previous chapter described many controls of JDK 1.2. Now let's take a look at the containers that hold them. Figure 22–2 shows the class hierarchy for containers. Notice that most of the Swing containers are not JComponents, but are specializations of existing AWT containers.

On the following pages, we will outline these containers, suggest typical uses, and show code examples. Container is the class that groups together a number of controls and provides a framework for how they are positioned on the screen.

Container has fields and methods to deal with the following items:

- The layout manager used to automatically position controls.
- Forcing the layout to be done.
- The thickness of any lines or insets (Borders) around its edges.
- Adding a ContainerListener for ContainerEvents.
- Adding, removing, and retrieving a list of any of the controls.
- Size (current, preferred, minimum, and maximum).
- Requesting the keyboard focus.
- A paint() routine that renders it on the screen.

The AWT class called Container is the superclass for components whose purpose is to hold several controls. A Container is essentially a rectangular portion of the screen that allows you to treat several individual controls as a group. You don't display a control directly; you add it to a Container, and it is the container that is displayed.

Container also has methods to get and set many attributes and to add and remove Components from itself. Containers must have either their pack() method called or have their initial size set before they will show up on the screen. Set their size by using the following code:

```
public void setSize(int width, int height)
```

The units are pixels (dots on the screen). Since a Container is a subclass of Component, it also has all the Component fields. You should review the Container methods by running javap java.awt.Container.

When you have finished adding or changing the components in a Container, you typically call the first three of these methods on the container.

```
myContainer.invalidate();  // tell AWT it needs laying out
myContainer.validate();    // ask AWT to lay it out
myContainer.show();        // make it visible

myContainer.pack();        // squeeze it down smaller
```

What's in a Swing container?

In this section, we look at what a Swing container has that an AWT container doesn't, and why you must use a Swing container to contain Swing components. Most of it comes down to the difference between lightweight and heavyweight components and making lightweight components work properly.

You add a component to an AWT container with a statement similar to the following:

```
myAWTContainer.add(myAWTComponent)
```

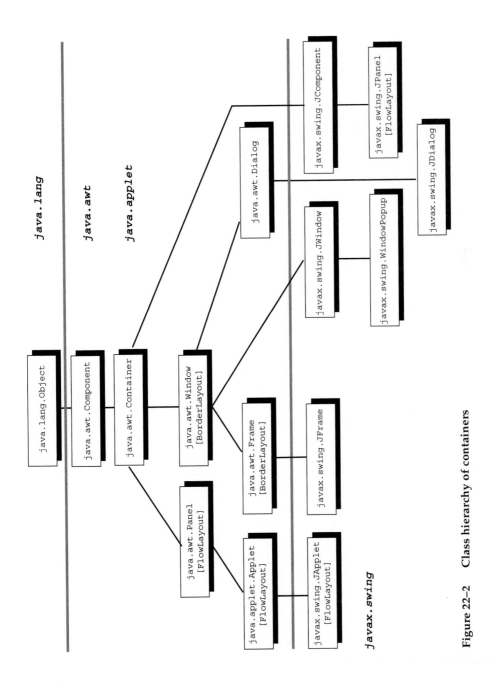

Figure 22–2   Class hierarchy of containers

Swing containers are different. They have several layers, as Figure 22–3 shows. The different layers are used for different effects.

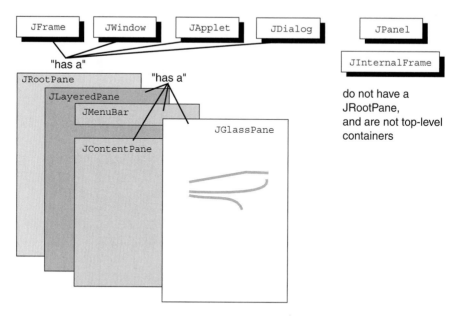

Figure 22–3   Layers of Swing containers

The JRootPane is the data structure that holds all the various other panes that Swing containers have. The JLayeredPane manages the JMenuBar and the content pane. It also maintains a notion of z-order (which components are on top of other components within the container). It has several default depth ranges, including one for floating toolbars, one for modal dialogs, one for things being dragged, and so on. The JLayeredPane does the right thing by default, but also allows you to "get under the hood" and set things explicitly where you want them.

The JContentPane is the object within a Swing container to which you add your JComponents and set layout policies. The default layout policy is border layout. Border layout components are added around the four edges and in the center of the container. The JMenuBar is an object that keeps track of any menus associated with the container. In many cases there won't be any.

The JGlassPane is a transparent pane that lays over everything and allows you to intercept mouse events or draw over the whole container without getting distracted by the components within it.

A JPanel is a lightweight container whose purpose is to be drawn on, and to group controls together. The Swing containers have methods to get and adjust these individual pane layers. We saw many times in the previous chapter how you add components to a Swing container. You add them to the container's content pane with the following code:

```
mySwingContainer.getContentPane().add(child);
```

Now we'll look at some individual Swing containers.

JFrame

A JFrame is a window that also has a title bar, a menubar, a border (known as the inset), and that can be closed to an icon. JFrame is the Swing version of frame. You should avoid mixing Swing and AWT controls and containers.

We've seen the code to create, resize, and show a JFrame throughout the previous chapter. That was done as an application, but frames can also be displayed from an applet. When you create a JFrame, it is not displayed physically inside the applet or other container but is a separate free-floating window on the monitor.

A JFrame is a specialization of frame in the Swing package. It has more refined default behavior on closing the frame, and it adds a number of methods for getting the different "layers" of a Swing container. Following is how you associate a file containing an icon with a frame so that when you close the frame, it collapses to the icon.

```
// load the image from a file Toolkit
Toolkit t = MyFrame.getToolkit();
Image FrameIcon = t.getImage(filename);
MyFrame.setIconImage(FrameIcon);
```

The file name should point to a GIF or JPEG file that is the icon you want to use. Typically, this image will be thumbnail-sized, 32 x 32 pixels or so.

Other ways to bring in an image

We saw in the previous chapter that it is convenient to use ImageIcon to import an image file into a Java program. Following are the constructors for ImageIcon:

```
// constructors of ImageIcon
public javax.swing.ImageIcon();
public javax.swing.ImageIcon(java.awt.Image);
public javax.swing.ImageIcon(java.awt.Image,java.lang.String);
public javax.swing.ImageIcon(java.lang.String); // a filename
public javax.swing.ImageIcon(java.lang.String,java.lang.String);
public javax.swing.ImageIcon(java.net.URL);
public javax.swing.ImageIcon(java.net.URL,java.lang.String);
public javax.swing.ImageIcon(byte[]);
public javax.swing.ImageIcon(byte[],java.lang.String);
```

Once you have an ImageIcon, you can retrieve the image from it with the following:

```
Image myImage = myImageIcon.getImage();
```

JPanel

A JPanel is a generic container that is always in some other container. It does not float loose on the desktop, as JWindow and JFrame do. A JPanel is used when you want to group several controls inside your GUI. For example, you might have several buttons that go together. Adding them to a panel can treat them as one unit, display them together, and lay them out on the screen under the same set of rules (more about this later).

Note that the Swing JPanel isn't descended from the AWT panel. They still fulfill the same kind of role: to be a generic non-top-level container. By being a JComponent, JPanel can also provide other support not present in AWT. It can provide automatic double buffering and the accessibility help. Double buffering is a technique that uses more memory to obtain flicker-free updates to components that are being updated frequently on the screen.

Applet and JApplet

Applet is a subclass of Panel. This means that applets come ready-made with some GUI features. JApplet is the Swing subclass of Applet. Figure 22–4 shows an applet.

```
Applet Viewer: plum.class
Applet

    I am in the Applet



Applet started.
```

Figure 22–4   Another applet

Following is the code that created that applet:

```java
// <applet code=plum.class height=100 width=200> </applet>

import java.awt.*;
import javax.swing.*;

public class plum extends JApplet {

    public void init() {
        setBackground(Color.green);
        resize(250,100);
    }

    public void paint(Graphics g) {
        g.drawString("I am in the Applet", 35,15);
    }
}
```

As with Panel and JPanel, JApplet adds some Swing conveniences and is required when your applet consists of Swing components. Since JApplet is a subclass of Applet, it has all the Applet methods described in *Popular Applet methods*.

One advantage of an applet over an application for a GUI program is that you can start adding and displaying components without creating an underlying backdrop. With an applet, one already exists.

Popular Applet methods

Here are some popular methods of Applet:

```
public URL getDocumentBase() //the URL of the HTML page
                             // containing the applet
public URL getCodeBase() //the URL of the applet code

public String getParameter(String name)
public void resize(int width, int height)

public void showStatus(String msg)
public Image getImage(URL url) //bring in an image
public Image getImage(URL url, String name)

public static AudioClip newAudioClip(URL url) // NEW in 1.2
public AudioClip getAudioClip(URL url) //bring in a sound file
public void play(URL url)
```

The following four methods are used for the stages in the applet life cycle:

```
public void init()
public void start()
public void stop()
public void destroy()
```

As you can see, Applet has several methods that deal with sounds and pictures. For both of these, it uses a URL to pinpoint the file containing the goodies. You can now obtain an audio clip from a URL with a static method. That means you can do it in an application, not just in an applet. You do not have to do anything special to make an applet retrieve media from its server over the Internet—it is a built-in method. A URL can locate something that is local to your system or anywhere on Internet.

The DocumentBase referred to in the first method is simply the directory containing the HTML page that you are currently visiting. Similarly, the CodeBase is the directory that contains the applet you are currently executing. For security purposes, the machine with the codebase is regarded as the server. Often, these two directories will be the same, but since the codebase is a URL, it can be anywhere on the Internet.

Window and JWindow

This container is a totally blank window. It doesn't even have a border. You can display messages by putting Labels on it. Typically, you don't use Window directly but instead use its more useful subclasses, Frame and Dialog. The Swing class JWindow is really only there to help with pop-up menus.

Windows can be modal, which means they prevent all other windows from responding until they are dealt with (e.g., dismissed with a checkbox). Window has a few methods for bringing it to the front or back, packing (resizing to preferred size), or showing (making it visible). Now that we've met containers, we are ready to move on to the next section and tackle layouts!

Another debugging tip

If you ever want to see what components are in a Java GUI, you can press Control + Shift + F1.

These three keys will dump out on system.error the text representation of the components that are on the screen. You will see results similar to the following:

```
java.awt.Frame[frame0,0,0,500x275,layout=java.awt.FlowLayout,
resizable,title=bible code]
   java.awt.Label[label0,130,32,98x24,align=left,text=look for pattern:]
   java.awt.TextField[textfield0,233,29,76x31,text=,editable,selection=0-0]
   java.awt.Label[label1,314,32,20x24,align=left,text=  ]
   java.awt.Button[button0,339,32,31x24,label=go!]
   java.awt.TextArea[text0,20,65,459x175,text=,editable,selection=0-
         0,rows=10,columns=62, scrollbarVisibility=both]
   java.awt.Label[label2,67,248,91x24,align=left,text=starts at offset:]
   java.awt.TextField[textfield1,163,245,69x31,text=,editable,selection=0-0]
   java.awt.Label[label3,237,248,121x24,align=left,text=gap between chars:]
   java.awt.TextField[textfield2,363,245,69x31,text=,editable,selection=0-0]
```

It's a bit of a "brute force" technique, but it's nice to know.

Layout in a Container

Figure 22–5 shows a frame to which we have added several controls. They are positioned automatically as we add them.

Figure 22–5   Arranging controls on the screen

The code for this is on the CD in the directory containing all the other AWT programming material. The problem is the end result doesn't look very professional because nothing is neatly aligned. Solution: layout managers!

Layout Managers are classes that specify how components should be placed in a container. You choose a layout manager for a container with a call similar to the following invoked on the content pane:

```
setLayout ( new FlowLayout() );
```

We'll look at six layout managers: the five that are part of AWT and a sixth one that comes with Swing. The first and most basic layout manager is FlowLayout.

FlowLayout

Figure 22–6 uses the same code as previously, but the FlowLayout was used and the JFrame was pulled out wide to the right.

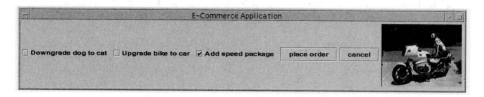

Figure 22–6   **In this window, buttons are positioned left to right and centered**

A flow layout means that components are added left to right, keeping them centered in the container and starting a new line whenever necessary. When you resize the window, components might move to a new line. There are possible "left" and "right" arguments to the constructor to make the components be left- or right-justified instead of centered, as shown in the following example:

```
setLayout (new FlowLayout (FlowLayout.RIGHT));
```

Most of the layouts allow you to specify the gap in pixels between adjacent components by specifying the values to the constructor. One FlowLayout constructor uses the following code:

```
public FlowLayout(int align, int hgap, int vgap);
```

Our first example on the previous page was actually a FlowLayout, too. As we made the JFrame less wide, it folded the flowing line of components with the result seen there.

The following code sets a flow layout on a JFrame:

```
myJframe.getContentPane().setLayout ( new FlowLayout() );
```

Some layout managers adjust their components to fit the container, and some layout managers just lay out components unchanged. FlowLayout doesn't change the sizes of contained components at all. The BorderLayout tells its enclosing container the size to allow for each control by invoking the preferredSize() methods of each control. Other layout managers (GridBagLayout and

GridLayout) force the components to adjust their size according to the actual dimensions of the container.

Every component has methods to getMinimumSize(), getPreferredSize(), and getMaximumSize(). These methods inform layout managers how much they can adjust the size of a component to fit the layout. You can extend a component and override one or more of these methods to change the behavior. You can also use the setter versions of the methods, shown in Figure 22–10 with an example.

Next you'll see the code used to generate Figure 22–6 and the following two examples (commenting and uncommenting code as needed):

```java
import java.awt.*;
import java.awt.event.*;
import javax.swing.*;
public class BorderDemo {
    static JFrame jframe = new JFrame("E-Commerce Application");

    public static void setupjframe() {
        jframe.setSize(400,400);
        jframe.setVisible(true);
// jframe.getContentPane().setLayout( new FlowLayout() );
        jframe.getContentPane().setLayout( new BorderLayout(10,7) );
// jframe.getContentPane().setLayout( new GridLayout(3,2, 10, 7));
        WindowListener l = new WindowAdapter() {
        public void windowClosing(WindowEvent e){System.exit(0);}
        };
        jframe.addWindowListener(l);
    }

    public static void main(String[] args) {
        setupjframe();
        // JCheckBox jck1 = new JCheckBox("Downgrade dog to cat");
        JCheckBox jck2 = new JCheckBox("Upgrade bike to car");
        JCheckBox jck3 = new JCheckBox("Add speed package");
        // p.add( jck1, "North" ); //max. 5 components
        Container p = jframe.getContentPane();
        p.add( jck2, "East" );
        p.add( jck3, "South" );

        JButton jb1 = new JButton("place order");
        p.add( jb1, "North" );
        JButton jb2 = new JButton("cancel");
        p.add( jb2, "West" );

        JLabel jl = new JLabel(new ImageIcon( "bmw.jpg"));
        p.add(jl, "Center");
        jframe.pack();
    }
}
```

GridLayout

Figure 22–7 shows the same code with a one-line change to give it a grid (m-by-n) layout.

Figure 22–7   A grid layout puts things in equal-sized boxes starting from the top left

In the constructor, you specify the number of rows and columns, as shown in the following code:

```
int rows=7, cols=3;
setLayout( new GridLayout(rows, cols) );
```

This code creates seven lines on a grid that is three boxes wide.

Grid layouts are simple and somewhat rigid. One thing that always surprises and annoys programmers is the way the components change in size to match the grid size. Compare the size and shape of the buttons here with those in the previous layout. To avoid this, add a component to a panel, and add the panel to the container with the grid layout.

The following code sets a grid layout on a JFrame:

```
jframe.getContentPane().setLayout( new GridLayout(3,2, 10, 7) );
```

The "3, 2" are the 3 rows and 2 columns. The "10, 7" are the horizontal gap and the vertical gap in pixels to leave between components.

BorderLayout

The third popular type of layout is BorderLayout. As the name suggests, you can put four components around the four edges of the Frame, with a fifth component taking any remaining space in the middle. The default layout for a Window and its subclasses Frame and JFrame is BorderLayout. You can set a border layout in a ContentPane with a line similar to the following:

565

```
setLayout( new BorderLayout() );
```

You then add up to five widgets, specifying whether they go at the north (top), east (right), and so on. Figure 22–8 shows the same application with a one-line change to use BorderLayout. Note the size of the buttons.

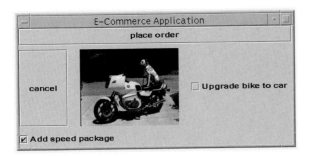

Figure 22–8   Frame using BorderLayout

It's obviously inconvenient to have a maximum of five widgets, and that brings us to the real way layouts are used. There probably isn't a single layout manager that will do exactly what you want. Instead, group related components onto panels, and then add the panels to a Frame, using another layout manager. We'll explain how this works using BoxLayout, introduced with Swing. The following code sets a border layout on a JFrame:

```
jframe.getContentPane().setLayout( new BorderLayout(10, 7) );
```

Again, the "10, 7" are the horizontal and vertical gaps. The following code is for a component to container with a Border Layout:

```
myFrame.getContentPane().add( myComponent, "East" );
```

The directions can be "North", "South", "East", "West", and "Center."

There are two important points to note with BorderLayout. First, you have to set BorderLayout before adding components. Otherwise, you mysteriously see nothing (this isn't true, however, for the other two layout managers). Second, letter case is significant when setting the position. For example, you can't use "north" instead of "North."

BoxLayout

A fourth kind of layout manager is BoxLayout, named because of its ability to align a group of components horizontally or vertically, as Figure 22–9 shows.

Figure 22–9   A screen shot using BoxLayout

The code to apply a BoxLayout to a container looks like this:

```
Container c = jframe.getContentPane();
c.setLayout( new BoxLayout(c, BoxLayout.Y_AXIS));
```

Note that unlike the other layout managers, this one takes the content pane as an argument as well as being invoked on the content pane. The second argument says whether to stack vertically (as here) or horizontally, BoxLayout.X_AXIS.

You add components exactly the same way as in the previous layout managers, as shown in the following example:

```
JButton jb1 = new JButton("place order");
p.add( jb1 );
```

For example, box layout gives us the ability to stack all the radio buttons on one panel, the Jbuttons on another panel, and add them to a Frame in three columns with grid layout or border layout. Let's try that.

Combining layouts

Figure 22–10 shows the results of putting the three radio buttons on their own panel, putting the two buttons on their own panel, then adding the two panels and the Jlabel to the Frame with a border layout. This is already starting to look more normal. The size, shape, and positioning of the components won't fly all over the place when you resize the frame.

The following the important part of the code to produce these results:

```
JPanel p1 = new JPanel();
p1.setLayout( new BoxLayout(p1, BoxLayout.Y_AXIS));
JCheckBox jck1 = new JCheckBox("Downgrade dog to cat");
JCheckBox jck2 = new JCheckBox("Upgrade bike to car");
JCheckBox jck3 = new JCheckBox("Add speed package");
p1.add( jck1 );
p1.add( jck2 );
p1.add( jck3 );

JPanel p2 = new JPanel();
p2.setLayout( new BoxLayout(p2, BoxLayout.Y_AXIS));
JButton jb1 = new JButton("place order");    p2.add( jb1 );
JButton jb2 = new JButton("cancel");    p2.add( jb2 );

JLabel j1 = new JLabel(new ImageIcon( "bmw.jpg"));

Container c2 = jframe.getContentPane();
c2.add(j1, "Center");
c2.add(p1, "West");
c2.add(p2, "East");
jframe.pack();
```

That layout can still be improved. You can do the following actions:

- Move the radio buttons in from the edge of the panel. Do this by adding a *border* to the panel. The following code adds a ten-pixel border all around the component:

  ```
  JPanel p1 = new JPanel();
  p1.setBorder(BorderFactory.createEmptyBorder(10, 10, 10, 10));
  ```

- Ensure the two buttons are the same length by setting the maximum size of the shorter button to the preferred (or regular) size of the longer button, as shown in the following example:

  ```
  JButton jb2 = new JButton("cancel");
  jb2.setMaximumSize( jb1.getPreferredSize() );
  ```

- Add a bit of spacing between the buttons by adding a blank area, as shown in the following example:

  ```
  p2.add(Box.createRigidArea(new Dimension(0, 15)));
  ```

  Box is a helper class for BoxLayout. It has various methods to create space-fillers.

- Finally, we can add a border around the panel on which the buttons are located, as shown in the following example:

  ```
  JPanel p2 = new JPanel();
  p2.setBorder(BorderFactory.createEmptyBorder(14, 14, 14, 14));
  ```

Put it all together and you have a pleasing and professional looking GUI, as Figure 22–10 shows.

Figure 22–10   Adding multiple elements to a layout

The only new this is the `BorderFactory.createEmptyBorder(14, 14, 14, 14)` call. A *factory* is a class that can create other classes and return them to you. Here, it will send you some instance of a border class, possibly shared if you're using the same kind of border in two places. I've only scratched the surface of the many ways you can improve alignment and appearance in Swing. Although there are many more features available to the expert, the features we have reviewed will serve your basic needs.

Other layout managers

AWT has a CardLayout manager. It does exactly the same thing as a tabbed pane, but without the finesse. There's no reason to use CardLayout now that we have tabbed panes.

The final kind of AWT layout manager is GridBagLayout, which is a variation of GridLayout. Rather than force you to fit components one per grid position, it allows you to let a component take up the space of several adjacent grid positions. It uses a series of constraints and weights to determine what goes where.

GridBagLayout is excessively complicated for what it does, and I recommend helping it fall into disuse by not bothering with it. If you really want to spend time on GridBagLayout, there is a tutorial about it online at `java.sun.com/docs/books/tutorial/uiswing/layout/using.html`.

JDK 1.4 introduced the SpringLayout class. It provides layouts that are similar to absolute positioning of Components, but also supports the helpful feature of resizing appropriately to changes in container size or component fonts (which absolute positioning does not support). SpringLayout is intended to be used by tool-builders who implement IDEs. It gives them a way to let programmers drag-and-drop components where they want them to show the preferred layout appearance by example. SpringLayout (like GridBagLayout) does its work using

Constraints objects that specify preferred, maximum, minimum, and current values for where it is relative to its neighbors. You probably won't code SpringLayout explicitly in your programs.

Most of the use of GridBagLayout and SpringLayout comes from programmers who use IDEs. The layout code is generated automatically, and programmers don't have to wrangle it by hand (unless they later try to fix it up without the visual tool). It's just drag-and-drop-and-hope.

Layouts are useful and provide automatic component resizing when you resize the container. You probably won't find any one layout that does exactly what you want. The solution is to divide your Panels and Frames into subpanels, use an appropriate layout manager for each panel, and then display the different panels together in a single frame. You may then use borders and boxes to hone the results. Skilled programmers can write their own layout managers. AWT contains enough power for you to do that. You might consider it if you're trying to match the look and feel of some existing custom application. In Java, you can write your own look and feel, not just layout, if you care to go down that path.

Finally, you always have the option of setting a null layout manager and positioning controls at absolute coordinates using `public void setLocation (int x, int y)`. It is almost always better to use a layout manager than to use absolute positions. It's less work for you, and the GUI will look better when run on different platforms. An absolute layout that looks good on one platform frequently looks terrible on another platform.

Tying up the Loose Ends

At this point, we have dealt with events, components, and containers both in summary and in depth. There are just a few other topics to cover to conclude the chapter.

JDK 1.4 image I/O

Java at last has an API for image I/O, allowing you to read and write files in several popular formats both locally and across the net. It's nicely-designed and extensible so that as new formats appear they can quickly be supported by Java.

Image I/O (introduced in JDK1.4) supports reading GIF, JPEG, and PNG formats. GIF is not supported for writing because it uses LZW compression, the algorithm for which is encumbered by a patent held by Unisys. One patent expired in June 2003, but Unisys has indicated that it thinks it holds some other patents that continue its ownership of GIF.

PNG is "Portable Network Graphics," a newer standard intended to replace GIF, and not encumbered by patents. You can read about the formats (any format, in fact) at *www.wotsit.org*.

There are five packages in Java Image I/O, but most of them are concerned with the implementation and plugability of new support. You will probably find that the class javax.imageio.ImageIO contains static methods to do all the simple things you need. You can read a JPEG file into an Image with the following two lines:

```
import javax.imageio.*;


File f = new File("c:\images\myimage.jpg");
BufferedImage bi = ImageIO.read(f);
```

It is equally easy to write out an image in PNG or JPEG format. If you refer back to the previous chapter, we showed code to do screen capture into an object of type java.awt.Image. When you have one of these, check if it is the BufferedImage subclass. You can write BufferedImages to a file with the following lines:

```
BufferedImage bi = (BufferedImage) myImage;
File f = new File("c:\images\myimage.jpg");
ImageIO.write(bi, "jpg", f);
```

When you have something as an image, you can easily get its graphics context and draw on it, as shown in the following code:

```
Graphics2D big = bi.createGraphics();
big.setPaint(Color.red);
big.drawString ("Date: Oct 2004", 20, 20);
```

Those lines of code let you put a date or other caption in the top left of your digital photos.

The javax.imageio package contains the basic classes and interfaces for reading and writing thumbnails and for controlling the image reading process (ImageReader, ImageReadParam, and ImageTypeSpecifier) and the image writing process (ImageWriter and ImageWriteParam). It also supports conversion between formats (ImageTranscoder).

More information about Java 1.4 Image I/O is online at
java.sun.com/j2se/1.4/docs/guide/imageio/spec/apps.fm1.html

Games programmers will love the "full screen exclusive mode" of JDK 1.4. It lets the programmer suspend the windowing system and write directly into video memory, and onto the screen. Because you are writing directly to memory rather than through many layers of GUI software, it is very fast, although it lacks the features of a window system.

A similar mode is available using Microsoft's DirectX library, which is widely used by games programmers. Now games programmers can get the performance they need, and the future-proofing/portability of Java code too. Full-screen exclusive mode is handled through a java.awt.GraphicsDevice object . For a list of all available screen graphics devices (in single or multi-monitor systems), you can call the method `getScreenDevices` on the local `java.awt.GraphicsEnvironment()`.

The toolkit

A Component method called `getToolkit()` returns a reference to the toolkit. The name *toolkit* just means "a collection of generally useful window-related things" and is the "T" in AWT. Once you have a `Toolkit`, you can call any of its methods, which can do the following:

- Set things up for printing the screen.

- Get information about the screen size and resolution.

- Beep the keyboard.

- Get information about the color model in use.

- Get information about font size.

- Transfer data to and from the system clipboard.

- Set the icon image of the Frame.

For example, `java.awt.Toolkit.getDefaultToolkit().getScreenSize()` returns a `java.awt.Dimension` object, which has ints representing height and width. As usual, you can view all the methods by typing `javap java.awt.Toolkit`.

JFC introduced the ability to transfer data to and from the system clipboard and to drag-and-drop components. The topics are a bit outside the scope of this book, but you can find the source files in $JAVAHOME/src/java/awt/datatransfer and dnd, (dnd is drag'n'drop). There's a tutorial online at
`java.sun.com/docs/books/tutorial/uiswing/misc/dnd.html`

Printing the screen

Java's world view of printing is a little strange. It regards the purpose of printing as being to transfer GUI content onto paper. Most people think that printing is about transferring the content of files onto paper with neat margins and fonts. Once you understand that Java printing means rendering frames and panels onto paper instead of the screen, some of the features become clearer. If you really want to print files, bring them up in a GUI or use the OS-specific commands.

Java support for printing has evolved over the years, and JDK 1.4 introduced the third variation on a printing API. JDK 1.0 had no support for printing. JDK 1.1 offered some basic low-resolution printing to a printer based on the class PrintJob. JDK 1.2 introduced the java.awt.print package, and the ability to print anything that can be rendered on the screen. It uses callbacks; the application provides information on the components that it wants printed. The printing system will call back to the paintComponent() method when it is read to print. Instead of passing it a Graphics context that relates to the screen, it passes one that will eventually get sent to the printer. There's a certain convenience for everyone in this approach. It makes it easy for the printing subsystem to print pages repeatedly or in a different order. Just as the window system can call on any component to repaint itself at any time, the printing system has the same ability, and callbacks provide it.

JDK 1.3 added two new classes giving finer control over properties of a print job (like destination or number of copies) and attributes of a printed page (like paper size, orientation, and quality).

JDK 1.4 implements JSR006, the unified printing API. It is unified in the sense that it allows printing on all platforms, including the Java 2 Micro Edition. It builds on the JDK 1.2 print API, and has a new package, javax.print. That package lets you discover and select print servers. You also get improved formatting options, and there is an interface for plug-ins, so third parties can provide their own plug-in printing services.

Changing cursor appearance

In JDK 1.0.2, the cursor could be set only for a Frame. In jdk 1.1, this restriction was lifted, and the cursor can now be set for each individual Component. The cursor is the little icon that moves about the screen tracking the mouse movements. There are fourteen different cursor icons listed in Table 22–1.

Table 22–1   Fourteen cursor icons

Appearance	Name
Eight different directions for resizing	Cursor.SW_RESIZE_CURSOR, etc.
One default cursor	Cursor.DEFAULT_CURSOR
One crosshair cursor	Cursor.CROSSHAIR_CURSOR
One text cursor	Cursor.TEXT_CURSOR
One busy waiting cursor	Cursor.WAIT_CURSOR
One hand cursor	Cursor.HAND_CURSOR
One move cursor	Cursor.MOVE_CURSOR

Figure 22–11 shows some of these icons.

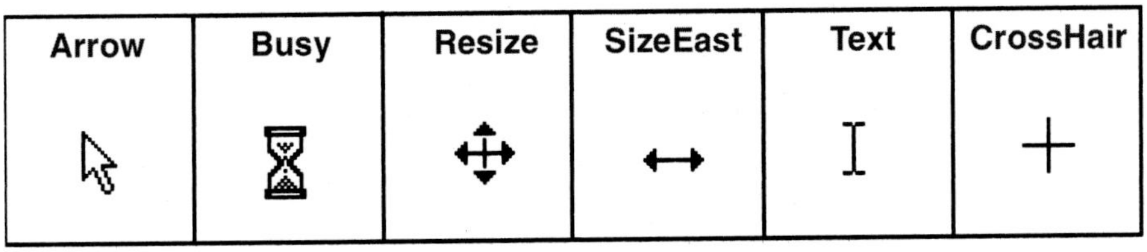

Arrow	Busy	Resize	SizeEast	Text	CrossHair
↖	⌛	✥	↔	I	+

Figure 22–11   Some of the cursor icons

The cursor appearance can be set for any component with the following method:

```
public synchronized void setCursor(Cursor cursor)
```

For example, to set the hand cursor, use the following:

```
this.setCursor(new Cursor(Cursor.HAND_CURSOR) );
```

There is a getCursor() method, too. There is no way in JDK 1.1 to supply your own bitmap for a custom cursor, though obviously this is a reasonable thing to do. Custom cursors arrived in JDK 1.2 with the following toolkit method:

```
Cursor createCustomCursor(Image cursor, Point hotSpot, String id)
        throws IndexOutOfBoundsException
```

You must override that method, and then call setCursor().

Exercises

1. Take the MyFrame program that demonstrates the thread bug and update it to reproduce the race condition more easily. Change the arithmetic that updates variable i into two statements, and put a `sleep()` or a `yield()` statement between them. Observe the failure.

2. Update the MyFrame program to remove the race condition by making the reading and writing of the variables mutually exclude each other. Test your code by running it on a version of the program that quickly reproduces the race condition failure.

3. Write a small Java program to capture the screen, display it in a scroll panel inside a frame, and allow the user to trim its size. Write the cropped region to a file on request. Allow the user to choose any output file format that the Image I/O library on that platform supports.

4. Write a program that uses Image I/O to display a thumbnail display of all the GIFs, JPEGs, and PNG files in a directory. Let the user select one, and display that full size in a new window. Allow the user to change the size of it, crop a region, and save it in a new format. That is the beginning of a general-purpose Java image editing application. You can take it as far as your interests run.

5. The following code will grab a screen image.

```
Robot ro = new Robot();
Toolkit t = Toolkit.getDefaultToolkit();
final Dimension d = t.getScreenSize();
Rectangle re = new Rectangle(d.width, d.height);
final Image image = ro.createScreenCapture( re );
```

Write code to display it half size, and allow the user to crop the image. Use the class javax.imageio.ImageIO to write the image out as a JPEG file. Refer to the javadoc to see the `write()` methods.

Some Light Relief—Sky View Cafe: A High Quality Applet

For the end of this chapter, I want to introduce you to the Sky View Cafe program and its author, Kerry Shetline. Sky View Cafe is an astronomy applet, but even if you have no interest in astronomy, it's a terrific showcase for the very professional graphics effects that a careful programmer can achieve.

In case you are interested in astronomy, I'll mention that Sky View Cafe displays many types of astronomical information, and is particularly easy to use. It shows star charts, rise and set times for the Sun, Moon, and planets, Moon phases,

orbital paths of the planets in 3-D (I love animating that one!), a perpetual
calendar with astronomical events, lunar and solar eclipses, the moons of Jupiter
and Saturn, and more. See Figure 22–12 for the main screen.

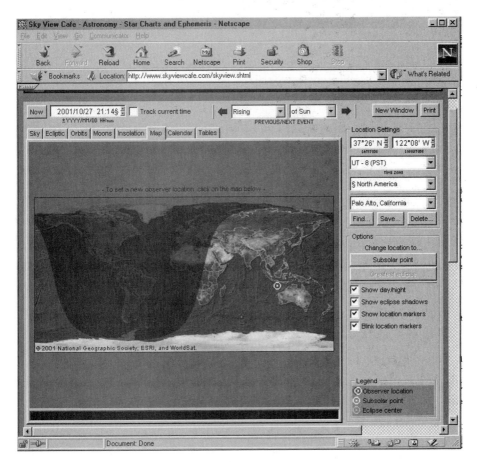

Figure 22–12   The Sky View Cafe astronomy applet

That screen shows the half of the world that is in darkness and the half that's in
daylight at that moment. It's a funny shape because the world is round and
flattened out into an unrolled cylinder on the screen. You can see that the
Antarctic is enjoying 24 hours of daylight at the moment.

The first thing to do is to click on the map to tell the program where you are on
the planet. That makes the night sky maps accurate for your position. Instead of
clicking, you can look up your city name by clicking the Find button on the right
hand side. Since ordinary applets can't write locally, it will tell the server to set a
client side cookie, saving your location for future runs. Now you can select one of
the other tabs on the tabbed pane. Printing is done in a very clever way: it causes

a showDocument (), which brings up a new browser containing the thing you want printed. Then you use the browser's print command! Clever—and it avoids much tricky code.

We won't run through all the features of Sky View Cafe here. Part of the fun is exploring it for yourself. Kerry has a strong background in writing "what if" software that makes it easy to try things and easy to back out of them. He started professional programming writing programs for that excellent magazine, *Creative Computing* (long since defunct). Later, Kerry worked in C++ for seven years. He has used Java for the last six years, and points out that he can get more done faster in Java because his programs run on all computers and operating systems.

Following is a code snippet from the class that represents our solar system:

```
package org.shetline.astronomy;

import java.util.*;
import java.io.*;
import org.shetline.util.*;
import org.shetline.math.*;

public class SolarSystem extends MathUser implements AstroConstants
{
    protected HeliocentricPlanets     planets = null;
    protected EclipticBody            moon = null;
    protected Pluto                   pluto = null;
    protected String[]                planetNames;

    // Result in days per revolution.
    //
    public double getMeanOrbitalPeriod(int planet)
    {
        if (planet < MERCURY || planet > PLUTO)
            return 0.0;

        // Convert degrees per Julian century into days per revolution.
        return 100.0 * 365.25 * 360.0 / elems[planet - MERCURY][0][1];
    }
```

This code implements, in part, one of the Sky View Cafe features that I really like, which is the animated model of the solar system known as an Orrery. It's the third tabbed pane, "Orbits." Clicking it brings up a display showing the paths of the nine planets, including Earth, that orbit our star. You can adjust the angle from which you're viewing the solar system by dragging on it (Figure 22–13 illustrates this).

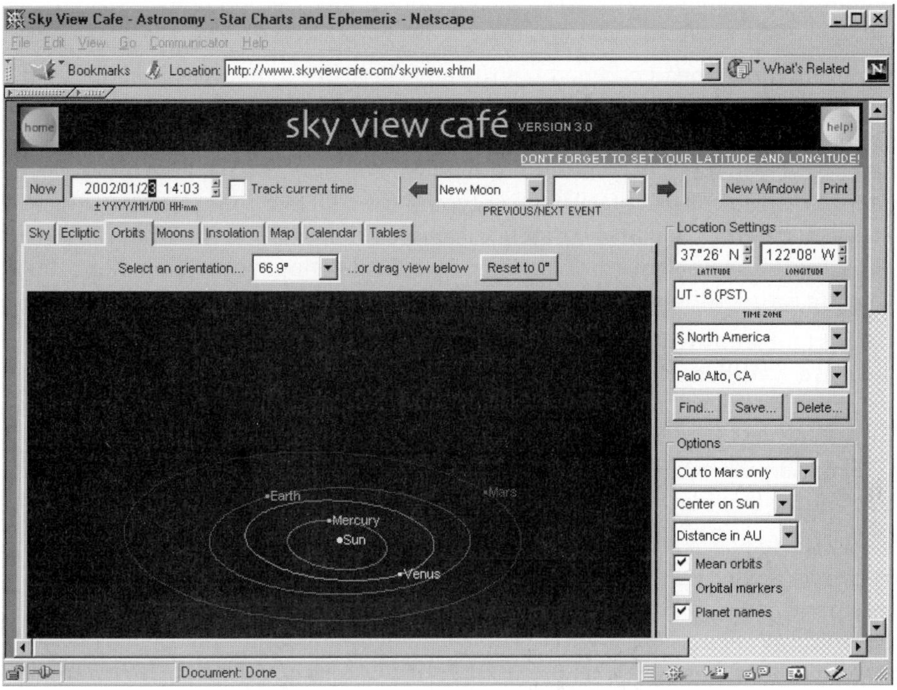

Figure 22–13   Moving model of the solar system

If you highlight a single digit in the "Date" field at the top left and then press the spinner (one of a pair of small arrows to the right) to adjust the date, you can advance the model by that amount (minute, hour, day, month, year, decade, etc.). When you do this, the planets move in their orbits correspondingly. If you keep the spinner pressed, it keeps incrementing time, and keeps moving the planets around. Beautiful!

The name "Orrery" (for a moving model of the solar system) comes from the Earl of Orrery (a small place in Ireland) who paid a clock maker to build him one in 1712. The device was created by George Graham, so it really should be a "Graham."

Kerry explained how he designed and coded Sky View Cafe. You have to have a strong interest in the subject area that you're programming. It helps to look for other programs that do related things. Other programs might have some good ideas you can re implement, or have some bad ideas that you can avoid.

Newsgroups can provide helpful information, and Sun hosts some Java-specific newsgroups at the Java Developer Connection at developer.java.sun.com. Kerry also urges programmers to read the javadoc-generated API documentation for each library class they want to use. There's lots of information in there, but it won't do you any good unless you read it.

You need to think ahead when you write any class. Try to imagine how it might be reused somewhere later, and write it accordingly. Don't build in knowledge about the current context, but pass it in as parameters. Perhaps the class can be generalized by making it abstract, and then subclassing it to provide more detail. Kerry is a firm supporter of early prototyping for GUI code. Get a basic framework running reliably so that you can see how your ideas work in practice. Add to this framework in gradual steps. Avoid a development style where you are coding for months without having enough to test or run.

An important feature of Sky View Cafe is the amount of effort that went into making it a well-behaved applet. Although it's big at approximately 375 Kbytes (one minute to download on a phone line), it has been crafted to run in just about any browser, and to avoid many known browser bugs. The code is all in JDK 1.1 for this reason. Kerry develops on a Macintosh using the CodeWarrior IDE, and tests on almost all platform/browser revision combinations.

Sky View Cafe was a labor of love, and it took Kerry about 18 months of hobby project time (evenings and weekends) to bring it to this state. Too many open source projects reach version 0.8, and the programmer loses interest. Sky View Cafe is now at version 3.0.4 with 4.0 under development, and it is open source shareware. Kerry has generously published the source so others can learn from his work, and he invites people to register if they find the program useful. The current version of Sky View Cafe is online at the website www.shetline.com.

5

Enterprise Java

Relational Databases and SQL

In the first half of this chapter we'll look at the most widely used kind of database, the relational database. We'll examine the model for using it, and we'll introduce some of the special terms that database experts use. We will work through a couple of small examples to show the techniques that apply equally well to much larger databases. The second half of the chapter is a primer on SQL, the specialized programming language used to talk to a database and update information in it. We'll look at the way you create database tables and populate them with data. Then we'll describe the SQL statements to extract, update, and remove information from a database. SQL has its own data types and operators, presented here.

All this will prepare us to use JDBC, the Java library that supports access to databases, in Chapter 24, "JDBC." If you are already well versed in databases and SQL, you can safely go straight on to that chapter now.

The JDBC library is one of the most important Java libraries, right up there with the XML library and the servlet library. JDBC solves a problem that has previously been a drawback to all other database programming approaches, namely, platform lock-in. When you write your database access code in Java using JDBC, your database can easily be moved to another database vendor and another OS environment. If you outgrow the capacities of either of these, it's straightforward to trade up to a more capable platform with minimal or no changes to your software. If you want to change database vendors for any reason, your software is easily portable to the new environment.

Database programming is a central part of modern enterprise software systems. All professional programmers should understand the basics. This chapter gives you a solid grounding in programming database queries in SQL. JDBC uses SQL to do its work. We focus on SQL here and defer the Java part to Chapter 24.

Finally, we'll use a really terrific open source database known as the Mckoi database as our example. This is a free, open source database, written in 100% Java, and available for easy download. The Mckoi database comes with a small GUI program that lets you run SQL queries against the example database. It is an excellent tool for learning and experimenting with SQL without wasting a lot of time.

Introduction to Relational Databases

A database is a structured collection of data. It may be anything from a simple list of members of a sports club, to the inventory of a store, or the huge amounts of information in a corporate network. To retrieve and update data stored in a computer database, you need database management software. There are several approaches to database software architecture: relational, hierarchical, and Codasyl network. Here, we'll focus on relational databases, which is the most widely used approach by far.

The relational database concept

Like so many of the best ideas in computer science (e.g., TCP/IP, HTTP, XML, ethernet, sockets, or the JVM), relational databases are based on a simple fundamental concept. The idea behind relational databases is that you can organize your data into tables. Other approaches to databases have tried to keep everything in one big repository. Having individual tables that keep the related pieces of data together simplifies the design and programming. It also adds speed and flexibility to the implementation.

What is a table?

What specifically do we mean by a "table"? We mean the data can be represented in tabular form with columns that all contain values of one type, and where a row holds the related data on one thing (one customer, one account, one order, one product, etc.). The table format is a logical, not a physical, organization. Under the covers, the database management software will typically store the data in indexed files and cache it in memory in tree structures when the program is running. But it will always present the appearance of tables to your programs.

Table 23–1 shows some (fictional) people, their age, favorite bands, and where they live.

Table 23–1   The "People and Music" table

Name	Age	Lives in	Listens to
Robert Bellamy	24	England	Beatles
Robert Bellamy	24	England	Abba
Robert Bellamy	24	England	Oasis
Judith Brown	34	Africa	Muddy Ibe
Judith Brown	34	Africa	Abba
Butch Fad	53	USA	Metallica
Timothy French	24	Africa	Oasis
Timothy French	24	Africa	Nirvana
Grayham Downer	59	Africa	Beatles

Tricky terminology

There are some special database terms that go with tables. A single row of data is known as a *tuple,* or more commonly a *record* or *row.* It's effectively a set of data that belong together in some way. In our first table, the record (Robert Bellamy, 24, England, Beatles) is saying that the age, place, and music preferences are those of Robert Bellamy. The second record stores another music preference for Robert: he also listens to Abba.

The name of the data in a column is called an *attribute.* Age is an attribute here. An attribute is the term for an individual field of a record. If math scares you, forget the rest of this paragraph, but it's how database maestros talk to each other at conferences. A *domain* is the set of allowable values for an attribute. An example domain for the age attribute could be "integers between 0 and 125." The domain is a constraint on the values of the attribute. A *relation* is (informally) a table with columns and rows. The number of attributes in a relation (i.e., how many fields a record has) is called its *degree.* The number of tuples in a relation (i.e., the number of data records you have in it) is called its *cardinality.* We'll prefer the more widely used terms of record, column, etc. from this point.

Mathematics makes databases work perfectly

We have special terms for all these things because they are mathematical concepts. Relational databases are based on the mathematical concepts known as set theory and predicate logic. People often think that the "relational" part of the name comes because we store related things together. Actually, it is because the architecture uses *mathematical relations* that say how one group of data is associated with another. There is a formal underpinning to our data manipulation, and it can be proved that certain operations will yield the correct result, are equivalent to some longer operation, and so on. To make certain that our databases remain true to the mathematics, these qualities are required to be true at all times:

- Each table has a different name from all the others in the database.

- Each column has a different name from all the others in the database.

- Each row has a different value from all the others in the table. There is never a duplicate row in a table.

- Each "cell" (attribute) in a table contains exactly one value.

- The order in which the rows and columns appear has no significance. If you want order to be significant, you create a new column to store that value.

- Values of a column are all from the same domain, i.e., if a column starts off representing age, it doesn't suddenly change into salary halfway through a table.

Database design

Referring to Table 23–1, say we want to find all the people who live in Africa and listen to Abba. We simply look at each record and compare the "Lives in" and "Listens to" attributes, printing out the ones that match "Africa" and "Abba," respectively. It works well for this query, but there are some big disadvantages to storing the data all in one table. If someone moves out of the country, we have to find every record in which their name appears and update it. As we are going through the database trying to update records, we have to lock out other read attempts to stop them seeing inconsistent data. Because so much data is duplicated, our storage needs will be bigger, and all programs which run against the database will take longer. The amount of data here is very small, but keep in mind that all the sizes scale up. A company could easily have a database containing hundreds of tables, some of which have millions of rows.

The recommended approach to designing databases is to try to minimize the amount of data duplication. You try to have one relation for each kind of entity (customer, employee, order, cd catalog, shipment, etc.) and store in there only the attributes directly associated with that kind of entity, not every possible attribute it has. In this case, we will probably create a couple of tables, such as Table 23–2.

Table 23–2   The "Person" table

Name	Age	Lives in
Robert Bellamy	24	England
Grayham Downer	59	Africa
Timothy French	24	Africa
Butch Fad	53	USA
Judith Brown	34	Africa

In Table 23–3, we store attributes called "Name" and "Music Group Name." There, each record represents a person and a group that they listen to regularly.

Table 23–3   The "ListensTo" table

Name	Music Group Name
Robert Bellamy	Beatles
Robert Bellamy	Abba
Robert Bellamy	Oasis
Butch Fad	Metallica
Judith Brown	Muddy Ibe
Judith Brown	Abba
Timothy French	Oasis
Timothy French	Nirvana
Grayham Downer	Beatles

Do you see what we have done? We have "factored out" the common data of name, age, and lives in into one table, leaving name and music group name in Table 23–3. Now when Robert Bellamy moves to the USA, that information only needs to be updated in exactly one record. The data in "Listens To" is related to the data in "Person" by matching the name attribute. If Robert stops listening to Abba, we can delete that row without also dropping Robert, his age, and his country from the database.

We will be using these tables with this data for the rest of the chapter, so you may want to put a post-it note on this page so you can easily refer back to this section. Now we dive into some low-level details for a few paragraphs. You need these terms to understand how to use SQL, so don't go on until you have understood it.

Primary and Foreign Keys

It's one thing to put data into a database. You also need to be able to retrieve it on demand. The way we get data out of the database is to present it with the right unique identifier, known as a *key*. For example, in a database of vehicle license records, the VIN or Vehicle Identification Number will be the key to the table of vehicles.

Primary keys

Every table must and will have an attribute (or group of attributes together) that uniquely identifies every record. This attribute or group of attributes is called the *primary key* to the table. By "uniquely identify every record," we mean that each record has a different value for that attribute or group of attributes. The primary key to our Person table is the "Name" attribute. We can never allow two different people to have the same name in this small database, although that is an unrealistic restriction in real life. That's why banks and other agencies identify you by social security number or an account number, which is guaranteed to be unique.

In our "Listens To" table, we need both attributes (person name and group name) to uniquely identify a row of data. People who like two bands are in there once for each band, so person name is not unique. And since several people can listen to the same band, music group names are duplicated too. But the combination of person name plus music group name is unique. So the primary key to our "Listens To" table is both these attributes.

Foreign keys

As well as primary keys, many tables contain *foreign keys*. These are attributes in one table that are a primary key in some other table. The "Listens To" table has a foreign key of Name, which is the primary key for Person. The Person table does not contain any foreign keys. Although it has the Name attribute, that is only part of the key for the "Listens To" table, not the whole key. It's called a "foreign" key because it is not a key in this table, but for a table in some other distant place.

When you have a value of a foreign key, for instance, "Judith Brown" in the "Listens To" table, that value *must* also occur in the table for which it is the primary key. In other words, there must be a "Judith Brown" entry in the Person table. In fact, the purpose of keys is to be able to get to related data in other tables. Keys are how we navigate through the database. When the foreign key existence requirement is met, then the database is said to have *referential integrity*.

Referential integrity

You keep referential integrity in a database by being careful about the data you remove. If you drop a customer account because of lack of activity, you must also drop all references to that customer in all tables in your database. The onus is on the programmer to keep referential integrity; the database cannot do it for you. If your database lacks referential integrity, you'll get funny results when you try to extract data from more than one table together.

Entity and transaction integrity

There are two other forms of integrity that databases need: entity integrity and database integrity. If you don't have a value for some attribute, perhaps because you are still acquiring data for that table, there is a special value called "null" that can be assigned. Null doesn't mean zero. It means "no value has yet been assigned." An expression involving null evaluates to null. We could use null in the age column, when someone does not wish to give us their age. We must never use null in any column that is part of a primary or foreign key. This is referred to as *entity integrity*. The entity integrity rule ensures that all our keys are always valid keys.

To understand *transaction integrity*, think of an update to a database that moves money from one account to another. There will probably be a row of data for the source account and the destination account. You need to write a statement that deducts the money from the first account, and a second statement that adds that sum to the second account. You want to be absolutely sure that either both statements are executed or neither of them are. You never want to be in a situation where the money was deducted but not paid in to the second account. If you have a way to group statements and ensure that all parts of the transfer occurs or none of it occurs, you can maintain transaction integrity.

Relationships

Let's say more about the relationship between a foreign key and the table where it is a primary key. That relationship can be *one-to-one*, *one-to-many*, or *many-to-many*.

One-to-one relationships

A one-to-one relationship says that the two things are matched exactly. The relationship between ship and captain is one-to-one. Each ship has one captain, and each captain has one ship (ignoring real world details like mutinous ships, captains waiting for a command, etc.).

One-to-many relationships

As you might guess, a one-to-many relationship means that one thing in this table corresponds to potentially many things in that table. Each individual ship has multiple sailors, so the ship/crew member relationship is one-to-many. All the sailors on a given ship will have the same value for the "belongs to the crew of" attribute. The "one" side of a one-to-many relationship will be a primary key, as shown in Figure 23–1. The ship's name would be a primary key in the table of a shipping line's fleet.

Many-to-many relationships

Many-to-many relationships occur when multiple records in one table are somehow related to multiple records in another table. We can see what this means if we introduce a "MusicGroup" table that is a list of bands. We could store any band-specific information in it too, such as the land of origin for each music group. Take, for example, Table 23–4.

Table 23–4   The "MusicGroup" table

Music Group Name	Land of Origin
Beatles	England
Abba	Sweden
Oasis	England
Metallica	USA
Muddy Ibe	Africa
Nirvana	USA

Now our database has tables that hold a many-to-many relationship. Some people listen to several bands, and some bands are listened to by several people. That's a many-to-many relationship between the Person and MusicGroup tables.

Solving the key problem of many-to-many

Many-to-many relationships can't be processed directly in relational databases (though it's clearly possible to create the table). The reason is that a primary key can only link tables on a one-to-many basis. Unless you take other steps, the restriction on many-to-many means we cannot make direct queries based on band name (e.g., "who listens to a given band?"). That may be acceptable if you never want to make that kind of query, but you want to build flexibility into your designs, do not rule it out.

Stating the many-to-many limitation in terms of Java code, you can think of a primary key as being like the index variable in a Java "for" loop. It lets you process the whole table without missing any rows out, or considering any primary keys twice. Many-to-many would be like resetting the index variable several times in the looping. Luckily, there is an easy way to get over the restriction that many-to-many relationships can't be processed directly. You resolve many-to-many relationships by adding a new table that can express the relationship in terms of two one-to-many tables.

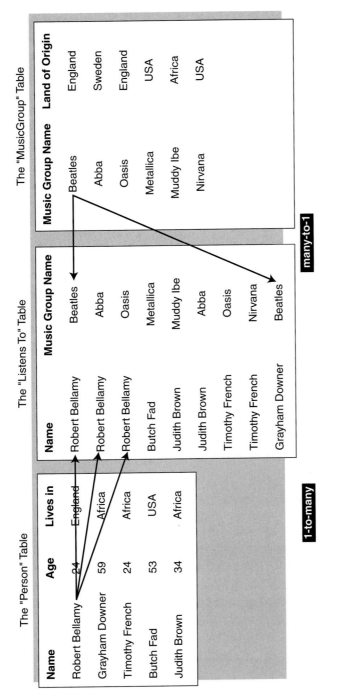

Figure 23–1 Breaking up a many-to-many relationship: "Many people listen to many bands"

Adding a table

We simply need a new table that, for each band, has a record for each person who listens to it. That new table is on the "many" end of a one-to-many relationship with the MusicGroup table. The new table must also have for each person, a record for each band they listen to. So the new table will also be on the "many" end of a one-to-many relationship with the Person table. And that's an exact description of our existing ListensTo table! (Of course, the design was chosen with this in mind.) Each name there is related to several music group names, and each music group is related to several names. You can see that Robert is associated with the Beatles, Abba, and Oasis, while Oasis is associated with Timothy and Robert.

Using the ListensTo table we represent the many-to-many relationship between MusicGroup and Person. We can now do the SQL equivalent of "for each MusicGroupName in MusicGroup table, find the matching MusicGroupName in the ListensTo table, and print out the person name." This new table allows us to do queries by band.

To summarize, we resolve many-to-many relationships in a relational database by decomposing them into two one-to-many relationships, adding a new table as needed.

Normal Forms

Tables need to follow a set of numbered rules known as "normal form." (It's "normal" in the sense of "normalized" or conforming to a standard). First normal form says that all attributes must be atomic. That means there can be no lists of items in an attribute. You can't have an attribute that is "contents of a shopping cart," because that could contain several items. Atomic means "only one, and it cannot be subdivided any further."

Second normal norm

Second normal form says that it is in first normal form (atomic) and every non-key attribute depends fully on the key. The Person table has non-key attributes of "age" and "lives in" and both of these are completely dependent on the person we are identifying by the "name" attribute. However, if we added a column to the table to hold, say, the land of origin of the band, we would be breaking second normal form. A band's land does not depend on the primary key (the person name).

Third normal norm

A table is in third normal form if it is in second normal form and all non-key columns are mutually independent. In the Person table, the non-key columns are "age" and "lives in." These are mutually independent because they can change without affecting the other. If we were to add a column to store "is a minor" data in Person, the table would no longer be in third normal form. Whether or not someone is a minor depends on their age, which is another attribute in the Person relation.

Add tables to taste

If you find your table designs break a normal form rule, you can always fix it by adding an extra table as we did above to resolve a many-to-many relationship. You may need to move columns from one table to another or to add an identification number to a couple of tables to relate records between them. Raw data can always be put into third normal form. There are additional normal forms beyond this, but third normal form is enough for most purposes. If you make sure all your tables are in third normal form, you will be able to use relational database operations on them and get the right results. A database that has been designed to be in third normal form is said to be "normalized." There's a great memory aid for the form in which you want your tables: the data in a table has to *depend on the key, the whole key, and nothing but the key.*

Relational Database Glossary

Table 23–5 is a glossary of terms that you can review and refer to as necessary. There are a few terms in here that appear later in the chapter.

Table 23–5   Relational database glossary

Name	Description
attribute	A column in a table, e.g., the "Name" attribute.
cardinality	The number of rows in a relation.
database integrity	You maintain database integrity by grouping statements in a "transaction" that is either executed as a whole, or has no part of it executed.
degree	The number of columns in a table.
domain	The set of permissible values for an attribute.
entity integrity	The requirement that key attributes never contain a null.
first normal form	A table in which no attributes have lists of data items.
foreign key	The attribute or group of attributes in one table that form a primary key for some other table.
join	An operation that combines the data in two or more tables by using foreign keys in the first table to access related data in a subsequent table. This is an "inner join" or "equijoin".
prepared statement	An SQL statement which is cached in native code form to allow faster processing.
primary key	The attribute or group of attributes that together uniquely identify a record in a table.
referential integrity	The requirement that all foreign keys are present in the table where they are a primary key.

Table 23–5   **Relational database glossary**

Name	Description
relation	A table in a relational database. It corresponds to a file of records.
relational database	A collection of relations in third normal form.
second normal form	A table is in second normal from when it is in first normal form and also every non-key attribute depends on the primary key.
stored procedure	A group of related SQL statements, which are kept in precompiled form inside the database, and can be invoked just like a method call.
third normal form	A table is in third normal form when it is in second normal form and also all non-key attributes are independent of each other.
trigger	A trigger is an SQL statement that is stored in the database, and that executes automatically when a specified event occurs in the database, such as a column update. It will usually be some kind of automatic delete, insert, or update of some other attribute.
tuple	A tuple is a row of related data in a table. It is essentially a record of related data.

Once we have our tables, SQL is the language we use to access and process them. The JDBC library is a way of connecting to a database, shipping it SQL statements, and getting back the results in a form that Java can process. We will shortly present a primer on SQL, showing the highlights of the language for those who have never seen it before. First we need to download the open source Mckoi database, which includes a GUI tool for submitting SQL queries.

Download and Install Mckoi

At this point you should download and install the Mckoi database software, so you can try running the SQL queries, and get the results visually.

To get started, go to the Mckoi website at

```
www.mckoi.com/database
```

Click on the "latest version" link under "Download the software." Download the zip file to your C:\ top level directory. It is about 2MB in size, so it downloads quite quickly. After the mckoi zip file is on your disk, unpack its contents using a command like this:

```
cd c:\
jar -xvf mckoi1.0.2.zip
```

That creates a directory called mckoi1.0.2 containing the database binaries and Java source, some documentation, and sample programs.

Set up the Mckoi jar files

Next, make the Mckoi libraries visible to your Java compiler and JVM. There are three jar files in the directory where you just extracted the release. These jar files are:

file name	contents
mckoidb.jar	The database management software
gnu-regexp-1.1.4.jar	GNU regular expression package
mkjdbc.jar	The JDBC driver software

There are several alternative ways of making the Mckoi libraries visible to the compiler and JVM. The simplest is to move the jar files to the ...\lib\ext directory of your Java run-time installation. Jar files in here are automatically regarded as part of the standard run-time library.

Be careful to move them to the right directory! The directory or directories that the system actually uses for compiling and for execution can be seen by using the "-verbose" option when you run the compiler or JVM. Look for the pathnames of where the system libraries are picked up. On WinXP, with default installations, the files can be copied as follows:

```
copy \mckoi1.0.2\*.jar  "c:\program files\java\j2sdk1.5.0\jre\lib\ext\"

copy \mckoi1.0.2\*.jar  "c:\program files\java\j2re1.5.0\lib\ext\"
```

The first copy makes the Mckoi libraries visible to the compiler; the second makes them visible to the JVM. (It seems like a gigantic bug waiting to happen that Sun has set things up so the compiler and JVM use different pathnames to (what we hope are the same) libraries).

Running the Mckoi example code

The next step is to run one of the example database programs that accompany the release. Go to the demo directory with this command:

```
cd c:\mckoi1.0.2\demo\simple
```

Then run the sample database application that comes with the release. Use this command (assuming you have put the Mckoi jar files in the ...\lib\ext directories):

```
java  SimpleApplicationDemo
```

If all is well, you will see some output similar to the following, assuring you that the database libraries have been properly installed.

```
Rows in 'Person' table: 12
Average age of people:  30.0833333333
All people that live in Africa:
  Grayham Downer
  Judith Brown
  Timothy French
  ...
```

If you do not see output like this, you will need to resolve the installation problem based on the output you do see.

Running the Mckoi SQL query tool

This step is the one we have been leading up to. Mckoi comes with visual SQL query tool, as shown in Figure 23–2.

This is a Swing application that allows you to type in SQL queries in the upper window, press the "run" button, and see the results interactively. You can run it on the demo database that comes with mckoi, or on a database that you create. It provides a very good way to learn SQL interactively.

Person.name	Person.age	Person.lives_in
Robert Bellamy	24	England
Grayham Downer	59	Africa
Timothy French	24	Africa
Butch Fad	53	USA
Judith Brown	34	Africa
Elizabeth Kramer	24	USA
Yamnik Wordsworth	14	Australia
Domonic Smith	25	England
Ivan Wilson	23	England
Lisa Williams	24	England
Xenia, Warrior Princess	32	Rome
David Powell	25	New Zealand

Query Time: 0.33 seconds.   Row Count: 12

Figure 23–2   Mckoi SQL query tool

Start the query tool running with these commands:

```
cd \mckoi1.0.2\demo\simple
```

```
java com.mckoi.tools.JDBCQueryTool -url "jdbc:mckoi:local://ExampleDB.conf"
                                    -u user -p "pass1212"
```

There are two commands there, shown on three lines to fit on this page. You should use this tool to type in the examples in the pages ahead.

Basic SQL Primer

At first, every database vendor had its own special database query language. Users eventually got fed up enough to create an industry standard around IBM's SQL. There was the SQL'89 standard, followed by the SQL'92 standard, both created under the umbrella of ANSI (American National Standards Institute). SQL version 3 was published in 1999, and is known as "SQL:1999" or SQL-3. SQL is also a FIPS standard, FIPS PUB 127-2. FIPS is a Federal Information Processing Standard issued with the full weight and authority of the U.S. Government, after approval by the Secretary of Commerce. In practice, SQL is fragmented with many slightly incompatible dialects from database vendors. We keep to the current ANSI standard and do not present any vendor-specific code. You should follow the same practice in your programs, too.

SQL is an abbreviation for "Structured Query Language" and is a programming language in its own right. It's usually pronounced like the word "sequel" or spelled out as individual letters s-q-l. SQL is specialized for its application area, and is not used for general purpose programming. But all of the operations that you are likely to want to do to a database are built-in functions in SQL.

One attractive feature of SQL is that you express what you want to do in English-like text such as this.

```
SELECT name FROM Person
    WHERE lives_in = 'Africa'
    ORDER BY name;
```

By convention, the SQL keywords are written in uppercase. In SQL, you describe the results you want, not the steps to carry out to get them. This style of programming is known as "functional programming" and it contrasts with the "procedural programming" of more familiar languages like Java. Because you don't give the steps to get what you want, database implementors are free to find the most efficient way to get it. The big database companies put a lot of effort into their query optimizers, and this is one of the big advantages of SQL over earlier query languages.

The designers of SQL could have chosen to make programmers express the operations in terms of mathematical formulas or algebra, instead of words. That would make programs harder to read for many people and raise an unnecessary barrier to learning and teaching. Thank heavens they shunned that temptation. Executing the above SQL statement on our Person table yields a result set of:

Grayham Downer

Judith Brown

Timothy French

Try typing the SQL statement into the visual query tool and confirm you get these results.

So far we have outlined the way a relational database stores data and extracts it from a single table. The power of the technology comes from the flexible way you can extract and combine data from several tables to create new tables. It's a little contrived to show this in a small example, so keep in mind that this works equally well on the huge datasets common in industry, and the benefits are proportionately larger.

There are four categories of SQL statement:

- CREATE and INSERT to create tables and put records into them
- SELECT to query the database and get back data that matches your criteria
- UPDATE to change the values in existing records
- DELETE and DROP to remove records and tables from the database

There is a surprisingly rich variety of options that can be added to these statements, allowing a large amount of work to be done with a few simple English phrases. JDBC issues SQL commands by putting them in a String, and passing that String to various methods in the JDBC library. So to program in JDBC we need to know what the SQL phrases look like. Or to put it another way, you don't have to learn another database language if you know SQL. So why bother with JDBC and Java at all? Because you want to do something with the data you pull out of the database: send it to a client, wrap an email around it, mark it up with XML, and so on. Java is frequently the best way to do that something.

These SQL statements are powerful, but they seem to have been designed in a way that makes it very hard to present them in an easy-to-read format! So they are shown here in terms of a template, which is annotated on the right-hand side with some additional remarks. If you try to show the formal grammar for SQL, it explodes in size and gets in the way of clarity. Even so, it's a bit of work to show the four different kinds of statement. You may want to make one quick pass through the remainder of this section, and then come back to it when you need specific information.

Creating and Populating Tables

The CREATE statement is used to create a new table, and the INSERT statement is used to add a new record to a table.

The CREATE statement has this general format:

Format of SQL CREATE statement	Additional information
| ```
CREATE TABLE tablename(
    colName   dataType
optionalConstraint
);
``` | <— *can repeat this line, separated by commas* |

Here is an example of the use of the CREATE statement:

Example of SQL CREATE statement	Additional information
| ```
CREATE TABLE Person (
    name      VARCHAR(100) PRIMARY KEY,
    age       INTEGER,
    lives_in  VARCHAR(100)
);
``` | *"PRIMARY KEY" is a constraint* |

This statement will create the Person table that we saw earlier in the chapter. It will have three columns called "name," "age," and "lives in." The "optionalConstraint" shown in the first example means that you can add or omit a constraint to a column, giving more information about what kind of values are legal there. We have added a constraint to the "name" column, saying that this is the primary key of the table. That has the effect of making sure that records always have a non-null unique value there when the records are inserted into the table. "Not null" and "unique" are also constraints that can be applied individually.

Try typing the SQL statement into the visual query tool and confirm you get these results. There is already a table called Person in this database, so you will get an error message to that effect. Enter the query again, changing the table name to Person2. You need to completely overwrite the old query with the new one, when using the Mckoi GUI tool.

Some datatypes that SQL understands and the corresponding Java types are shown in Table 23–6. The SQL keywords and datatypes can use any letter case. The convention is to write them all in uppercase.

Table 23–6   Some SQL datatypes

SQL datatype	Corresponding Java type
CHAR(n)	String, exactly n chars
VARCHAR(n)	String, up to n chars
INTEGER *or* INT	int
DOUBLE	double
DATE	java.sql.Date
TIMESTAMP	java.sql.Timestamp
BLOB	java.sql.Blob
ARRAY	java.sql.Array
DECIMAL, NUMERIC	java.math.BigDecimal

The BLOB datatype means "Binary Large Object." There are also CLOBs, "Character Large Objects." SQL arrays are sequences of data. Think back to earlier in the chapter where we said that first normal form means that there are no lists of items in an attribute. There's a question of where you draw the line though. If you are recording student marks over 12 weeks of homework assignments, it's overkill to store each mark in a new record. Instead, we'll have a student/course marks record, and the course marks will be held as a fixed length array that gets updated with a new mark each week. BLOBs, CLOBs, and arrays are represented by classes in the java.sql package, and they have methods to get their values.

The CREATE statement just creates an empty table. As yet it has no records in it. We will put records in using the INSERT statement, which has this general appearance:

Format of SQL INSERT statement	Additional information

`INSERT INTO tablename`
    `(colName1  ,colName2  ,colName3 ...)`
    `VALUES`
	<— can provide a value for all attributes or just some

`    (value1    ,value2    ,value3 ...)` `;`	*<— can repeat this line, separated by commas these values are inserted into the attributes listed*

Here is an example of the use of the INSERT statement:

Examples of SQL INSERT statement   **Additional information**

```
INSERT INTO Person ( name, age, lives_in )
    VALUES ('Robert Bellamy', 24, 'England' ),
        ( 'Grayham Downer', null, 'Africa' ),
        ( 'Judith Brown', 34, 'Africa' );
```

Note the use of single quotes to surround a String

Downer doesn't want to give his age

This statement will start to populate (fill in with data) the Person table that we saw earlier in the chapter. The values are inserted into the record in the order in which the attributes are named. The number of values given in each of the value lists should match the number of attributes in the list before the "values" keyword. SQL is very picky about the requirement that character strings be enclosed in single quotes.

Note that some database vendors have not implemented support for inserting multiple rows with one statement. So to retain maximum portability you would want to restrict yourself to adding one record per insert statement.

Try typing the INSERT statement into the visual query tool and confirm you get these results. Put the data into the table named Person2. You should try each subsequent SQL statement in the visual tool from here on.

Querying and Retrieving Data

The SELECT statement is used to query a database and get back the data that matches your query.

The SELECT statement has this general format:

Format of SQL SELECT statement   **Additional information**

```
SELECT
    Name1  ,Name2  ,Name3 ...
FROM
    tablename1, tableName2, ...
WHERE
        conditions
ORDER BY  colNames
;
```

<— can mention one or more columns, or "" for all columns*

<— can mention one or more tables

<— the "WHERE" clause is optional and can be omitted

<— the "ORDER BY" clause is optional and can be omitted
It returns the data sorted by this field

We have already seen an example of a basic select from a single table. The power of the statement arises when you select from two or more tables at once. So to find all the people in Africa in our database who listen to the Beatles or the band Fela Kuti, we could use the SQL command shown below. Numbers have been added on the left to help with commenting on the code; these will not appear in actual SQL code.

```
1    SELECT Person.name, Person.lives_in, ListensTo.music_group_name
2    FROM Person, ListensTo
3    WHERE ListensTo.music_group_name IN ( 'Fela Kuti', 'Beatles' )
4    AND Person.name = ListensTo.person_name
5    AND Person.lives_in = 'Africa' ;
```

Going through the statement line by line, we can make the following observations:

Line 1 gives the columns that we want to get back in our answer. Notice that the table name can be used to qualify the column so that there is no ambiguity.

Line 2 gives the names of the tables that we will be running the query on.

Line 3 starts our "where" clause. It says which data values or rows will be returned as the answer, based on matching the criteria that follow. The first criterion is that the music_group_name must be one of those in the list given. Notice the way you can compare against a list of items in parentheses.

Line 4 adds another condition. It says that whenever we have found one of those two bands, we look for the same name in the Person table.

Line 5 is the final part of the condition. It says that the "lives in" field for that person should hold the value "Africa." Voila, we are done. Running the query produces the output:

<figure>
Mckoi JDBC Query Tool

File Options

```
SELECT Person.name, Person.lives_in, ListensTo.music_group_name
    FROM Person, ListensTo
    WHERE ListensTo.music_group_name IN ( 'Fela Kuti', 'Beatles' )
    AND Person.name = ListensTo.person_name
    AND Person.lives_in = 'Africa' ;
```

[Run Query] [Stop Query]

name	lives_in	music_group_name
Grayham Downer	Africa	Fela Kuti
Grayham Downer	Africa	Beatles
Judith Brown	Africa	Fela Kuti

Query Time: 0.0 seconds. Row Count: 3
</figure>

Figure 23–3   Running the query

Grayham Downer appears in the list twice because he matches the criteria twice. He listens to both the target bands. If you were sending out promotional mail based on this query, you would want to ensure that you did not send two mails to him. Database inquiries frequently have results that may seem surprising if you are not familiar with set theory. The keyword "DISTINCT" after "SELECT" will eliminate duplicate records from being returned to you. If you sent the SQL command:

```
SELECT DISTINCT Person.name
    FROM Person, ListensTo
    WHERE ListensTo.music_group_name IN ( 'Fela Kuti', 'Beatles' )
    AND Person.name = ListensTo.person_name
    AND Person.lives_in = 'Africa' ;
```

The result set will be:

```
Grayham Downer
Judith Brown
```

The significance of primary key and foreign key should now be clearer. You always use a foreign key to relate one table to another. The operation is called "join" because you are merging or joining the data in two or more tables where the data match your conditions. In this case we used person_name which is a foreign key in the ListensTo table and the primary key for the Person table. Because it is a key, that allows us to retrieve the data from Person that corresponds to the name we found in ListensTo. This kind of join is an "inner join" or "equijoin." In set theory terms, it is data that falls in the intersection of the two tables. There are also "outer joins," which get you the data that is in one table, but not the other. These are outside the scope of this basic primer.

Let's elaborate on the conditional selections. You can use all the operators shown in Table 23–7 to compare attributes.

Table 23–7   SQL comparison operators

Meaning	SQL operator	Example
equals	=	WHERE lives_in = 'Africa'
greater than	>	WHERE age > 39
less than	<	WHERE age < 21
greater than or equal	>=	WHERE name >= 'Brown'
less than or equal	<=	WHERE age <= 65
not equal to	<>	WHERE name <> 'Brown'
pattern match	LIKE	WHERE name LIKE '%own'
matches any of several choices	IN	WHERE age IN (18, 19, 20)

When you compare a string for being greater than some other string, it does a lexical comparison of the characters. So the name "Crown" is greater than

"Brown." The "like" operator is for pattern-matching, and uses a "%" as a wild card. The example shown in table 23-7 "`name LIKE '%own'`" will match any names that end with "own." There are other operators in SQL. The name we select from a table can be a mathematical function of some column in the table. That's expressed like this:

```
SELECT COUNT(*) FROM Person;
```

That statement gives you the number of rows in the Person table. There are other functions too. Table 23–8 shows some of them. These come after the SELECT keyword, and the entire statement may also have a WHERE clause that restricts the records that are input to the function.

Table 23–8   Some SQL functions

Meaning	SQL function	Example
Gives the number of rows satisfying the WHERE condition if present.	COUNT(*)	SELECT COUNT(*) FROM Person;
Gives the total of the named column, for all rows that meet the condition. This example adds the ages of people over 21 in our database.	SUM(*col*)	SELECT SUM(age) FROM Person WHERE age > 21;
Calculates the average of the named column. This example gives the average age of the minors.	AVG(*col*)	SELECT AVG(age) FROM Person WHERE age < 21;
Returns the largest value in that column.	MAX(*col*)	SELECT MAX(age) FROM Person;
Returns the smallest value in that column.	MIN(*col*)	SELECT MIN(age) FROM Person;

Subquery Selections

Quite frequently you want to submit a further select on the result of a select. There are several ways to do that, one way being to nest a select statement inside another. A nested select statement is called a subquery.

Here is an example of a subquery:

```
SELECT Person.name FROM Person
WHERE
    Person.lives_in IN ('England', 'USA')
AND
    Person.name NOT IN
      ( SELECT ListensTo.person_name FROM ListensTo
        WHERE
            ListensTo.music_group_name = 'Beatles' );
```

The simplest way to understand subqueries is to look at them piece by piece, starting from the innermost nested one. In this case, the nested select statement is:

```
( SELECT ListensTo.name FROM ListensTo
  WHERE
      ListensTo.music_group_name = 'Beatles' );
```

A moment's reading should convince you that this provides a result set of names of people who listen to the Beatles. So substitute that into the entire statement, and we get:

```
SELECT Person.name FROM Person
WHERE
    Person.lives_in IN ('England', 'USA')
AND
    Person.name NOT IN ( names-of-people-who-listen-to-Beatles ) ;
```

That can quickly be seen as all the people who live in England or the USA, and who do not listen to the Beatles. Be careful. Excessive use of subqueries results in SQL code that is hard to understand and hard to debug. As an alternative to subqueries you can often create, insert into, select from, and then drop temporary tables. Another alternative is to generate the queries dynamically. That is, to use one query to get the list of names, hold that in a variable, and use that variable in the second query. This will become clearer after reading the next chapter.

SELECT and all the SQL statements have even more features than are shown here, but this is enough to start writing real applications.

Result Set of a SELECT Query

We've seen informally in previous examples how the results of a SELECT statement are returned to you. The results of a query come back as rows-in-a-table, held in an object called a *result set*.

Contents of a result set

The result set contains zero or more rows which are retrieved and examined individually using something called a *cursor*. Just as a GUI cursor marks your position on the screen, a database cursor indicates the row of the result set that you are currently looking at. A cursor is usually implemented as an unsigned integer that holds the offset into the file containing your result set. It has enough knowledge to move forward row by row through the result set.

The cursor

Database management systems typically provide a cursor to the SQL programmer automatically. The programmer can use it to iterate through the result set. JDBC 2 upgrades the features of a cursor available to Java. Now you can move the cursor backward as well as forward, providing the underlying database supports that. You can also move the cursor to an absolute position (e.g., the fifth row in the result set) or to a position relative to where it is now (e.g., go to the immediate previous record).

Getting a sorted result set

We can ask for our result set to come to us sorted by some column or columns. We achieve this by using the "ORDER BY" clause in the query. When you do that, it makes sense to use the cursor to ask for the record before the one we are currently looking at. For example, if you order by "billing price" you can go backward until you reach orders under $10. That way, you can process your most valuable orders first, and stop invoicing when the amount is smaller than the cost of processing.

SELECT pitfalls

Here are some common pitfalls encountered when using the SELECT statement. When you hit an error in your programs in the next chapter, check if it is one of these!

- Not surrounding a literal string in single quotes.

- Spelling the table name or the column name wrongly.

- Only mentioning the tables that you are extracting from in the "from" clause. You need to mention all the tables that you will be looking at in the "where" clause.

- Failing to specify "distinct" and thus getting duplicate values in certain columns.

- Failing to leave a space between keywords when creating a Java String on several lines containing SQL.

Updating Values

The UPDATE statement is used to change the values in an existing record.

The UPDATE statement has this general format:

Format of SQL UPDATE statement	Additional information

`UPDATE tablename`
   `SET`
      `colName1=value1  ,colName2=value2 ...`
   `WHERE`
      `colNamei  someOperator  valuei   ...`
`;`
	←— can provide a value for all attributes or just some
	
	←— can repeat this line, separated by AND or OR

Here is an example of the use of the UPDATE statement:

Example of SQL UPDATE statement	Additional information

`UPDATE Person`
   `SET  age = 25, lives_in = 'USA'`
   `WHERE name='Robert Bellamy' ;`
	Robert celebrated his birthday by moving to the USA.

This statement will start to populate (fill in with data) the Person table that we saw earlier in the chapter. The values are inserted into the record in the order in which the attributes are named.

Deleting Records and Tables

The DELETE statement is used to remove records from a table, and the DROP statement is used to completely remove all trace of a table from the database.

The DELETE statement has this general format:

Format of SQL DELETE statement	Additional information

`DELETE FROM tablename`
   `WHERE`
      `colName  someOperator  value   ...`
`;`
	←— can repeat this line, separated by AND/OR to further refine which records get deleted

If you forget the "where" clause, all records in the table are deleted! A table with no records still exists in the database, and can be queried, updated, etc. To get rid of all traces of a table (not a common operation in most databases), use the DROP statement.

The DROP statement has this general format.

Format of SQL DROP statement	Additional information
`DROP TABLE tablename ;`	

There is frequently more than one way to write an SQL query. Some of the ways will do less work than other ways. Nowadays it is the database's responsibility to reorder queries for the best performance.

SQL Prepared Statements and Stored Procedures

Prepared statements and *stored procedures* are two different ways of organizing your SQL code and getting it to run faster. When you send an SQL statement to your database, there is an SQL interpreter that reads the statement, figures out what it means and which database files are involved, and then issues the lower-level native instructions to carry it out. Depending on what the statement is exactly, it may be quite a lot of work to analyze and interpret it.

Prepared statement

If you find that you are issuing a statement over and over again, the database will be doing a lot of work that can be avoided. The way to do this is with a prepared statement. As the name implies, the prepared statement is constructed and sent to the SQL interpreter. The output of the interpreter (the native code instructions) is then saved. The prepared statement can later be reissued, perhaps with different parameters, and it will run much more quickly because the interpretation step has already been done. Does this remind you of anything? This is exactly how Just-In-Time (JIT) Java compilers speed up execution—by compiling to native code and caching the results.

Stored procedure

A stored procedure is a similar idea to prepared statements but taken one step further. Instead of caching an individual statement, you can save a whole series of statements as a procedure. A stored procedure will typically implement one entire operation on a database, like adding an employee to all the relevant tables (payroll, department, benefits, social club, etc.). It is typical to provide parameters to a stored procedure; for example, giving the details of the employee who is being added to the company.

The vast majority of database systems support stored procedures, but a major sticking point has been the variation in the exact syntax used. JDBC 2 solves this issue by allowing you to write stored procedures in Java. That means your library of stored procedures is now portable to all databases, which is a major step forward!

This concludes our tour of the concepts of SQL and databases, and we now proceed to Chapter 24 to look at how you put it all together in Java.

Exercises

1. Define and give examples of the following database terms: *tuple*, *attribute*, *relation*.

2. What does it mean to normalize a database design? Describe first, second, and third normal forms.

3. Reinforce your knowledge by reviewing the basic SQL course at www.sqlcourse.com. It allows you to formulate and run SQL queries online.

4. Write an SQL statement to display the name and age of everyone in the Person table who is older than 39.

5. Write an SQL statement to display the name of everyone in the Person table who lives in a NATO country and listens to the Beatles. There are 19 member nations of the North Atlantic Treaty Organization, including the USA, UK, Canada, France, Germany, Greece, and Poland. New members join from time to time, so top students will keep the list in a table, rather than a set of literals.

6. What is an SQL subquery, and when would you use one?

7. Write an SQL statement to display the name of everyone in the Person table who lives in a NATO country and *does not* listen to the Beatles. Be careful to exclude people who listen to the Beatles, and also listen to other bands as well. The simplest way to do this is to use a subquery.

8. Explain, using examples, the difference between a primary key and a foreign key.

Some Light Relief—Reading the Docs

How do you tell if a user has read the software documentation? If users are anything like us programmers, it's a pretty safe assumption that they have *not* read the documentation. Time is short, and reading manuals is tedious and time-consuming.

I once knew someone who worked on the support desk for a large internal software application. He cut his workload by 85% using one simple technique. Whenever someone reported a problem with the software, he asked them which page of the manual it violated before he would investigate it. Most users preferred to live with any bug rather than spend hours tunneling through the manual, and Perkins' technique saved him a lot of bother right up until the time he got fired.

Another way of encouraging people to read the manual is to have the program ask "Did you read the manual, answer y/n:" The program won't proceed until it gets the right answer. And neither "yes" nor "no" is the right answer. Somewhere in the manual, buried deep in an obscure paragraph, is the information that, to continue, this question expects the answer "Teletubbies." But you'll only know that if you read the manual thoroughly.

Are you a student reading this chapter for an "Advanced Java" class? OK, then! Please demonstrate that you have read this chapter by writing your favorite color at the top right of the front sheet of your homework for this chapter. If blue is your favorite color, write "blue." Write "black" if you like black best, etc. Professors: see how many of your students really do the assigned reading. But be careful—last time I did this, one of the students wrote a little note buried in his next homework setting me a similar challenge, to test if I really read each page of all the homework that was submitted!

Chapter 24

JDBC

In this chapter we'll build on the relational database and SQL knowledge from Chapter 23. We'll show how to use one of the several excellent open source Java-friendly relational databases available. This will let you run a database management system on your own computer and try the features in practice. The bulk of the chapter to describes JDBC, the Java library that supports access to databases. We'll walk through its classes and the way they are used. We will reuse the data from the previous chapter, involving a database holding the music preferences for a group of people. Finally, we'll show code to create and update a database, and give you the information needed to write more Java-database code yourself.

Introduction to JDBC

JDBC is made up of about two dozen Java classes in the package `java.sql`. The classes provide access to relational data stored in a database or other table-oriented form. JDBC works in a similar way to Microsoft's database access library (known as ODBC), but redesigned, simplified, and based on Java, not C. ODBC imposed a single library that let your Windows code interface to any database. If you are familiar with ODBC, JDBC will be a snap to learn. And even if you are not, it's still pretty straightforward. JDBC works with the largest database servers such as Oracle, DB2 and mySQL, and with the smallest desktop database systems, such as xBase files, FoxPro, and MS Access. JDBC can even access text files and Excel spreadsheets using the ODBC bridge.

Building database systems in Java

An exciting development (new in 2004) is Sun's product Java Studio Creator. It is a development environment that has all the forms, GUIs, and visual tools to make it very easy to put together a Java client/server/database system. You can get more details on Java Studio Creator at

`http://developers.sun.com/prodtech/javatools/jscreator/index.jsp`

There are white papers and tutorials, as well as a free download of the tool itself.

JDBC classes allow the programmer to use modern database features like simultaneous connections to several databases, transaction management, pre-compiled statements with bind variables, calls to stored procedures, and access to metadata in the database dictionary. JDBC supports both static and dynamic SQL (a query or update constructed at run-time). JDBC and SQL greatly simplify deployment issues, because you can now rely on the presence of a set of vendor-independent standard Java interfaces for queries and updates to your relational database.

Installing the Mckoi Database Software

A major goal of this chapter is to give readers the means to actually try some hands-on relational database programming. That's an ambitious goal, because relational databases are industrial-strength and industrial-sized pieces of software. Up until a few years ago, the only choice in a database management system was which of the commercial vendors would you buy from. More recently, the explosion of interest in open source software has led to a much larger number of choices, some of which require no financial outlay. Table 24–1 and

Table 24–2 show some popular commercial and non-commercial products and their characteristics.

There are some truly excellent databases available for free download over the Internet. Some of them even come with the source code, which provides additional learning opportunities. The last three in Table 24–2 are all implemented completely in Java and run on any up-to-date JVM. The first three products are only available on certain platforms.

The Mckoi database software is used as the example here because it comes with example programs, has good documentation, and is very easy to get running. Mckoi is largely the work of talented English programmer Toby Downer, backed by his employer Diehl and Associates, who support the goals of the open source movement. This chapter was tested using the 1.0.2 release of Mckoi. To get started, go to the Mckoi website at

`www.mckoi.com/database`

Download and install the Mckoi database as described in Chapter 23. If you already installed it for Chapter 23, delete the \mckoi directory and reinstall the software. This is to ensure that the example database is restored to its initial configuration, so that the examples given in this chapter will work.

Table 24–1   Some commercial databases

Company	Product	Product attributes	Website	Java support
Oracle	Oracle 9i family	Supports even very large datasets, and also effective for small businesses. Available for Solaris and Windows.	www.oracle.com	Full support
IBM/ Informix	DB2, Informix	Large capacity, multi-platform database.	www.ibm.com	Full support
Sybase	Adaptive Server IQ	Large capacity, multi-platform database.	www.sybase.com	Full support
Microsoft	SQL server	Runs only on the NT line, limited by the capacity of the underlying PC.	www.microsoft.com	No vendor support
IBM/ Informix	Cloudscape	A commercially supported pure Java database that is included with Java 2 Enterprise Edition. It is the reference implementation of an embedded Java database.	www.informix.com/ cloudscape	Full support

Table 24–2   **Some non-commercial databases**

Organization	Software	Product attributes	Website	Java support
PostgreSQL	PostgreSQL 7.1	Written in C, open source, commercial support available, excellent SQL support. Supports medium- to lower-end large databases.	`www.postgresql.org`	Full support
MySQL AB	MySQL 3.23	Written in C, open source, commercial support available. Supports small- to medium-size databases.	`www.mysql.com`	Full support
Hughes Technologies	mSQL	Lightweight relational database, free for non-commercial use.	`www.Hughes.com.au/ products/`	Full support
Diehl & Assoc.	Mckoi SQL database	Written in Java, open source, very easy to start using. Supports small- to medium-size databases.	`www.mckoi.com/ database`	Full support
Lutris Technologies	InstantDB	Written in Java, free, no source, has GUI tools. Supports small- to medium-size databases.	`instantdb.enhydra. org`	Full support
FFE Software	FirstSQL/J	Written in Java, commercial support available. Supports small- to medium-size databases.	`www.firstsql.com`	Full support

Running the Mckoi database

The Mckoi JDBC driver has two modes of execution—embedded and client/server mode.

- **In embedded mode**, your program is linked with the database. So this is quick and convenient for test programs where everything runs on one system. Embedded mode is designed for standalone applications that need database functionality. The database does not run as a separate process and does not have to be started separately. To use embedded mode, simply make the jar files visible in your class path as described in Chapter 23.
- **In client/server mode**, the JDBC driver uses TCP/IP to communicate with a Mckoi database server running on a remote machine. To use client/server mode, start the database server with this command:

  ```
  java -jar mckoidb.jar
  ```

  Then use this kind of URL for the JDBC connection:
  `"jdbc:mckoi://host[:port]/"` where host is a DNS hostname, and port is a non-default port that you have configured Mckoi to use.

For the purposes of this chapter, you can execute the database and sample programs in embedded mode. Embedded mode is simpler to get running because it only involves one computer and one process. If you use the software in a production system, use client/server mode because that supports the use of the JDBCQueryTool or other application using the database while your program is running.

Running the Example Code

The next step is to try running one of the example database programs that accompany the release. Go to the demo directory with this command:

```
cd c:\mckoi1.0.2\demo\simple
```

Then run the sample database application that comes with the release. Use this command (assuming you have put the mckoi jar file in the jre\lib\ext directory):

```
java  SimpleApplicationDemo
```

If all is well, you will see some sample output similar to this, assuring you that the database libraries have been properly installed.

```
Rows in 'Person' table: 12
Average age of people:  30.0833333333
All people that live in Africa:
  Grayham Downer
  Judith Brown
  Timothy French
  . . .
```

If you do not see output like this, you will need to debug the problem based on the output you do see. After you have the database example running, go to *Connecting to the Database* on page 615,to see how your Java application code establishes a connection with a database prior to sending across various SQL commands. We will finish up this section by saying a few words about the evolution of the JDBC.

JDBC was originally an acronym for "Java Data Base Connectivity," and is now held by Sun marketing not to be an acronym at all. JDBC was developed independently of the JDK, and first bundled with it in JDK 1.1. The package name is java.sql. Your database code may also use the java.math package that supports arbitrary-precision arithmetic. JDBC development continued to add more advanced features, creating JDBC version 2.0. Part of the JDBC 2.0 library was bundled with Java 2 (the release that is also known as JDK 1.2), and part of it was not. Table 24–3 summarizes the situation.

Table 24–3   JDBC versions

JDBC version	Bundled with	Package name	Contents
JDBC 1.0 (previously called 1.2)	JDK 1.1	java.sql	Basic Java client to database connectivity.
JDBC 2.0 core API	JDK 1.2 and later	java.sql	Added features such as scrollable results sets, batch updates, new datatypes for SQL-3, and programmatic updates using the result set.
JDBC 2.0 optional API	J2EE 1.2 and later	javax.sql	Can be downloaded from java.sun.com/products/jdbc/. Contains database server-side functionality. Prepares the ground for the use of database-aware Java beans.
JDBC 2.1 optional API	Not bundled	javax.sql	Incremental improvement and additions over the 2.0 API.
JDBC 3.0 core API	JDK 1.4 and later	java.sql	Adds support for connection pooling, statement pooling, and a migration path to the Connector Architecture.

The Mckoi database manager implements the JDBC 2.0 core API.

Connecting to the Database

A database works in the classic client/server way. There is one database and many clients talk to it. (Larger enterprises may have multiple databases, but these can be considered independently for our purposes.) The clients are typically remote systems communicating over TCP/IP networks. They may talk directly to the database (called a "2-tier" system) or to a business logic server that talks to the database (known as a "3-tier" system).

How does a client or business logic program open a dialog with a database manager? JDBC uses a piece of software called a *database driver*. The database driver is specific to each vendor, and it is a library-level example of the Adaptor design pattern. It knows how to connect to its database, send requests over TCP/IP, and how to listen for replies from the database and pass them on to your code. Just as an operating system device driver hides the peculiarities of an I/O device from the kernel and presents a standard interface for system calls, each JDBC driver hides the vagaries of its particular database and presents a standard interface to Java programs that use JDBC.

Putting it another way, the purpose of a JDBC database driver is to know the low-level protocol for talking with its database at one end, and with JDBC classes and methods at the other end. It acts like a human language interpreter, moving information from one end and putting it in a standard form that is comprehensible to the other end (see Figure 24–1). You typically get a JDBC database driver from the database vendor. There are several different kinds of database drivers, depending on whether it is written in Java or native code, or whether it talks directly to the database or through another data access protocol such as Microsoft's ODBC. None of that matters much to the applications programmer. As long as you have a working JDBC driver, you don't care how it works. Essentially, all commercial and non-commercial databases now have excellent support for access from Java programs. There are good third-party libraries that can be used to access the Microsoft database products.

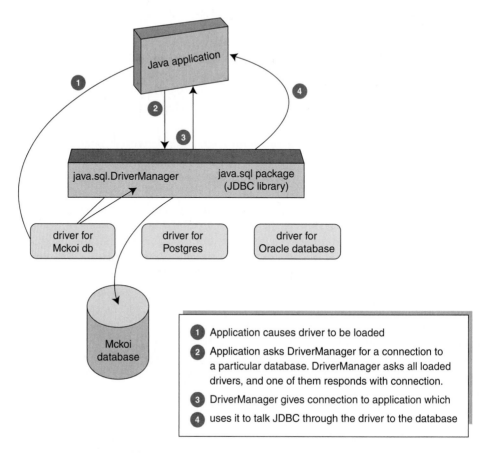

1 Application causes driver to be loaded

2 Application asks DriverManager for a connection to a particular database. DriverManager asks all loaded drivers, and one of them responds with connection.

3 DriverManager gives connection to application which

4 uses it to talk JDBC through the driver to the database

Figure 24–1   How JDBC establishes a connection between your code and a database

Load a JDBC driver

First, you do a class.forName on the JDBC driver name. That causes its class to be loaded into the JVM that's executing your program.

```
Class.forName("com.mckoi.JDBCDriver");
```

You don't need to create an instance of the driver class. Simply getting the class loaded is enough. Here's how it works. Each JDBC driver has a static initializer that is run when the class is loaded, and in that code the driver registers itself with the JDBC. You can also load a JDBC driver into the DriverManager by adding an entry to the sql.drivers property of the JVM. For example:

```
java -Dsql.drivers=com.mckoi.JDBCDriver   ...
```

If you do this, you don't need the previous call to Class.forName. Whichever approach you take, JDBC now knows about this driver, and can make calls to it. The JDBC driver does 90% of the work that is done in JDBC. Since Mckoi is an open source product, you can inspect the code to confirm how this works for yourself.

Get a database connection using a URL-like string

Next, your Java application program asks for a connection to the database, using a string that looks like a URL as an argument. The JDBC library has a class called java.sql.Connection that knows how to use that string to guide it in its search for the right database.

The exact format of the pseudo-URL string will vary with each database, but it typically starts with "jdbc:" to indicate the protocol you will be using, just as "http:" indicates to a web server that you will be using the hypertext transport protocol. The string will then go on to give some indication of the database host name, the port number, and a database-specific subprotocol to use. The Mckoi database uses a pseudo-URL like this:

```
String url = "jdbc:mckoi:local://ExampleDB.conf?create=true";
```

That URL names a file called "ExampleDB.conf" on the local host in the current working directory that holds configuration information on the database. The parameter in the URL "create=true" says that we intend to create the database in our program. Sun seems to want database implementors to cope with database creation commands based on SQL, not attributes passed in the URL. Sun's preferred approach adds complexity because it requires a database to be able to parse SQL commands before it exists.

The "create=true" parameter to create a database is vendor-specific, but it's also how Cloudscape (see Table 24–1) works for embedded databases. The exact form of the pseudo-URL will vary from vendor to vendor. You need to read the documentation that comes with the database. Then your code will call a static method of the overall JDBC driver manager to get you a connection based on that string, and strings representing a username and password.

```
connection = java.sql.DriverManager.getConnection(url, user, passwd);
```

Behind the scenes, the DriverManager calls every JDBC driver that has registered, and asks it if that is a URL it can use to guide it to its database. If we have prepared the ground correctly, the URL will be recognized by at least one of the drivers. The first driver to connect to its database with this URL, username, and password, will be used as the channel of communication. The application program gets back a "Connection" object. (Strictly speaking, it gets an object that implements the Connection interface.) The session has been established, and the connection is now used for communication between your program and the database. Why doesn't the application simply talk directly to the driver? It could

---

Interface versus class that implements the interface

Some of the key JDBC things, like Connection, Statement, and ResultSet, are actually interfaces, not classes. Here and throughout, we don't make an unnecessary distinction between an interface and a class that implements that interface. When we say "you get a Connection," you actually get an instance of some class that implements the Connection interface. You can store references to it in variables of type Connection, and you can use it to call all the methods defined in the Connection interface.

If you're ever curious about what class is behind some interface, you can easily find out its name. For any non-null reference x,

```
x.getClass().getName()
```

returns the fully qualified name of the class of the object referenced by x. If you are even more curious, you can then use reflection to dump out the names of its fields and methods.

As Patricia Shanahan (an expert programmer who sometimes answers questions on Usenet's Java groups) put it: "Never depend on this information in your programming. A method whose contract requires it to return a Connection may return instances of different classes in different implementations. It may even return instances of different classes in the same implementation under subtly different circumstances. The fact that it returns a Connection is part of its contract. The actual class of the returned object is implementation. Part of the art of object-oriented programming is firmly ignoring implementation details of one class when working on another class. Focus instead on the contracts between the classes, and the implementation details of the class you are working on."

---

do that, but then you don't have a single standard library anymore—you have a collection of 50 different protocols and conventions for talking to 50 different databases. The point of the JDBC is to avoid that.

Connecting to a database is an expensive (time-consuming) operation. You would never design a servlet system that opened a new connection for every doPost() request. Most databases have a way to share connections among several different processes. This arrangement is known as "connection pooling." JDBC 2.0 introduced a new and preferred approach to getting a connection. Instead of using a Driver directly, you use a DataSource object which you configure and register with a naming service (e.g., LDAP, YP, NIS+) that uses the Java Naming and Directory Interface (JNDI). That is intended for enterprise-level software and takes a lot more setting up, so we'll stick to simple drivers in this chapter.

In summary, your application program knows which database it wants to talk to, and hence which database driver it needs to load. The JDBC driver manager knows how to establish the JDBC end of a database connection, and the driver knows how to establish the database end. They do it. The driver manager gives you back a connection into which you can pour standard SQL queries and get results.

Executing SQL Statements

Now we are at the point where we can start issuing SQL commands to our database and getting back results. We do this through a Statement object that we get from the connection object described in the previous section. Table 24–4 shows several methods in Connection.

Table 24–4   Some methods of `java.sql.Connection`

Method	Purpose
`Statement createStatement()`	Returns a statement object that is used to send SQL to the database.
`PreparedStatement prepareStatement(String sql)`	Returns an object that can be used for sending parameterized SQL statements.
`CallableStatement prepareCall(String sql)`	Returns an object that can be used for calling stored procedures.
`DataBaseMetaData getMetaData()`	Gets an object that supplies database configuration information.
`boolean isClosed()`	Reports whether the database is currently open or not.
`void setReadonly(boolean yn)`	Restores/removes read-only mode, allowing certain database optimizations.
`void commit()`	Makes all changes permanent since the previous commit/rollback.
`void rollback()`	Undoes and discards all changes done since the previous commit/rollback.
`void setAutoCommit(boolean yn)`	Restores/removes auto-commit mode, which does an automatic commit after each statement.
`void close()`	Closes the connection and releases the JDBC resources for it.

You will invoke these methods on the `java.sql.Connection` object that you get back from the JDBC driver manager, as shown in an upcoming example. You use a connection to create a Statement object. The statement object has methods that let you send SQL to the database. Thankfully, statements are blissfully simple. You send SQL queries as Strings. In other words, the JDBC designers did not try to force-fit object-oriented programming onto SQL, perhaps by creating a Select class. Here's how you send a select query to the database:

```
Statement myStmt = connection.createStatement();
ResultSet myResult;
myResult= myStmt.executeQuery( "SELECT * FROM Person;" );
```

The executeQuery() method takes a string as an argument. The string contains the SQL statement that you want to execute. In the code fragment show previously, the SQL asks for all data to be returned from the Person table. There is an object that holds your result set. Here, we've called it myResult and it belongs to the ResultSet class. We'll talk more about ResultSet in a minute. Once you have a Statement object, you call one of its methods, shown in Table 24–5, to send SQL to the database. Statement has more methods than these, but these are the ones you'll use most.

Standard SQL has an optional ";" at the end of each SQL statement. You can leave it off. It is omitted in all the tutorials at Javasoft.

Table 24–5   java.sql.statement methods to execute SQL

SQL statement	JDBC statement to use	Type of its return value	Comment
SELECT	executeQuery(String sql)	ResultSet	The return value will hold the data extracted from the database.
INSERT, UPDATE, DELETE, CREATE, DROP	executeUpdate(String sql)	int	The return value will give the count of the number of rows changed (for insert, update, or delete statements), or zero otherwise.
Stored procedure with multiple results	execute(String sql)	boolean	The return value is true if the first result is a ResultSet, false otherwise. You get the actual results by calling another method of the statement class.

The different SQL statements have different return values. Some of them have no return value, some of them return the number of rows they affected, and the select statement returns all the data it pulled out of the database. To cope with these different possible results, you need to call a different method depending on what kind of SQL statement you are executing. The most interesting case is the select statement that gets back an entire result set of data. The next section, *Result Sets*, describes how this data is conveyed to your Java program.

Almost every JDBC interaction with a database can throw an exception, and you need to handle it appropriately in your code. JDBC defines four exceptions at present: SQLException (the most common), SQLWarning, BatchUpdateException, and DataTruncation. It is very important to write each handler so it outputs

meaningful error messages for every exception it gets. If you don't pay attention
to this, you will find it much harder to debug database problems and error
situations.

Threads and database programming

Older databases sometimes have support for asynchronous SQL operations,
meaning that you can start another SQL statement before you get the results back
from the past one. Java doesn't need to use this kind of SQL because you can get
the same effect by issuing the statements in separate Java threads. Your JDBC
programs will be more portable if you use Java threads (supported everywhere)
and not asynchronous SQL (may or may not be supported).

When you write multithreaded Java code that uses JDBC, you must synchronize
all your accesses to all shared data. Shared data means any data that is accessed in
more than one thread and also written by at least one of the threads. If you do not
properly synchronize data access, the data can be updated or read inconsistently
(with a value partly from one thread and partly from another). That leaves your
code with hard-to-debug data races and data corruption problems.

Result Sets

As we saw in the previous chapter, the SELECT statement extracts data from a
database. Here's an example which should be prefaced with the warning that
columns are numbered starting with 1, not zero. That is an SQL convention that
really had to be respected by Java. If we run this Java code fragment,

```
ResultSet result;
result = statement.executeQuery( " SELECT Person.name, Person.age "
                              + "FROM Person "
                              + "WHERE Person.age = 24 " );
while (result.next()) {
    String p = result.getString(1);
    int a = result.getInt(2);

        System.out.println( p + " is " + a + " years");

}
```

we'll get output like this:

```
Robert Bellamy is 24 years
Timothy French is 24 years
Elizabeth Kramer is 24 years
```

Relating that output to the code fragment shows how the ResultSet object can
hold multiple values. I like to think of ResultSet as being similar to a 2D array.
Instead of incrementing the most significant index variable, you call the result
method next(). Each time you call next(), you are moved on to the next record in

the result set. You need to call next() before you can see the first result record, and it returns false when there are no more result records, so it is convenient for controlling a while loop. That does make it different from an Iterator, however, so be alert to that difference. As a reminder, the Iterator next() method returns the next *object*, not a true/false value. A true/false value can be returned for a result set next() because there is another group of methods for actually getting the data. Read on to find out what!

You get individual values from a column within a record by calling one of the many methods whose signature looks like this:

```
SomeType  getSomeType( colNumberOrName );
```

The argument can be the name of the attribute, or the column number (which starts at 1, remember). Thus, the class ResultSet has methods getBlob(), getBigDecimal(), getDate(), getBytes(), getInt(), getLong(), getString(), getObject(), and so on, for all the Java types that represent SQL types and for a column name and column number argument. The getObject() is interesting. If the database supports it, you can put a Java object into the database! You can then retrieve it later, and invoke methods on it. So your database may be able to store and catalog serialized Java objects as well as data.

Column numbers should be used for columns that are not explicitly named in the query, such as when you do a "select '*'". Column names can be unreliable in this case, but otherwise they document the intent of your program better. Another advantage of using column names versus column index for the ResultSet 'get' methods is that your code doesn't break when your query changes to include more columns. Access by name might run into limitations of JDBC drivers, though. Some drivers allow access to the result set columns only in the order of the index. If you use by name and try to access columns out of order, you will get an exception. You can see all of the get-methods if you review the javadoc HTML pages for java.sql.ResultSet.

Good programming practice says that you should close Statement objects explicitly when they are no longer needed, with a statement like this:

```
myStmt.close();
```

Closing a statement when you are finished with it is important because it frees up resources (like locks and caches) on both the server and the client.

Pitfall: Reusing statements

Notice that a result set is assigned by the return value of a method of `Statement`. Normally, we would expect to be able to invoke a second `execute()` method on the same statement, assign the return value to a different result set, and proceed on our merry way. There is, however, a hidden pitfall to this!

Only one result set at a time can be open for a given statement. When you re-use a statement object, it closes whatever the previous result set was for that statement object. That means if you are going through a result set and executing more statements based on what you find, you must use an additional statement object. Otherwise, the second statement makes you lose the results of the first statement, which you are still processing. Here's some invalid code that shows what can go wrong:

```
ResultSet result1, result2
result1 = myStmt.executeQuery( someSQLString );
while (result1.next()) {
     /* more code */
     result2 = myStmt.executeQuery( someSQLString2 ); // NO!  blows
                                                       //away result1

}
```

The problem is that the while loop uses `result1`, but `result1` is destroyed when a second query is issued from the same `myStmt` object. Reusing the `myStmt` object will close the `result1` result set. Instead, do this:

```
/* code... */
Statement myOtherStmt = connection.createStatement();
while (result1.next()) {
     /* more code... */
     result2 = myOtherStmt.executeQuery( someSQLString ); // OK.
}
```

Of course, if you never have two statements active simultaneously, you only need one statement and result set object, which you can reuse for all your queries.

Cursor support

A default ResultSet object is not updatable and has a cursor that moves forward only. With this type of Result Set you can only go through the result records once, and only from the first row to the last row in order. That's not very convenient, so JDBC 2.0 brought in some new methods that let you specify (when you create a statement) that you want something better than the default. In this code example,

```
Statement stmt = conn.createStatement(
                  ResultSet.TYPE_SCROLL_INSENSITIVE,
                  ResultSet.CONCUR_UPDATABLE  );
```

all result sets created by that statement will:

- Be scrollable. You can move backwards and forwards among the records of the result set. A cursor indicates the current position in the result set.

- Not sense updates by others that occur after your result set was constructed. That is, despite possible updates to the database from elsewhere, your result set will not change. This may or may not be what you want.

- Be updatable. If a result set is updatable, it means you can call a method to change its value, and then another method to put that same change back in the database too. This is very handy when the query results are being reviewed by a person online. They can type a new value for some field, and your program can move that to the result set and get it to update the database without formulating a whole new SQL query.

If a database cannot support the result set configuration you have requested, it will carry on processing and return a result set that it can complete. It will also add a warning to your connection object. So it is a good idea to check for warnings before and after creating a customized result set. The method getWarnings() of the Connection class will do this check. If you try to do something that is not supported on your result set, it will raise an SQLException. See the fields of the ResultSet class for other options.

Batching SQL Statements and Transactions

Performance has always been one of the top concerns of database vendors, and they often go to some lengths to find ways to speed up queries. One of the bottlenecks is the time taken to package up a query, ship it over TCP/IP, and get it into the database where the SQL interpreter can start working on it. In other words, the network latency has a cost.

To reduce the overhead of network latency, many vendors support a way to batch several SQL statements together and send them to the database as a group. You can batch together any statements that have an int return type, which basically means "any SQL statements except for select." You can see why. You are sending over a group of SQL statements to be executed together, but there is no mechanism defined for getting back the result set for each select. It is not that hard to invent such a mechanism (e.g., executing a batch returns an array of ResultSet), but this has not been done.

To bundle a group of SQL statements in a batch, you create a Statement object as usual:

```
Statement myStmt = conn.createStatement();
```

Then, instead of issuing an execute call for the statement, you instead do a series of addBatch(), like this:

```
myStmt.addBatch( myNonSelectSQL0 );
myStmt.addBatch( myNonSelectSQL1 );
myStmt.addBatch( myNonSelectSQL2 );
```

Finally, when you are ready to send the whole batch to the database, invoke the executeBatch() method:

```
int [] res = myStmt.executeBatch();
```

Batching SQL statements is so easy, there's no reason to avoid it. That will cause all the statements to be sent to the database, and executed as a batch one after the other. The results come back in the form of an array of int, where the ith element holds the row count result of the ith statement in the batch (or zero if it did not return a row count). Support for batches of statements came in with JDBC 2.0.

Transactions

In Chapter 23 we referred to "transaction integrity" and explained how a fairly common situation required either all of a group of statements to be executed or else none of them. The way you do this is to group the statements in a "transaction." You execute the transaction in a temporary working area internal to the database. Then, based on other information from your environment, you either "commit" or "rollback" the transaction. Committing the transaction means you let all the data from the working area be copied to the database so your statements have taken effect. A rollback of the transaction means you delete the working area without copying it to the main database so none of your statements affect the database.

Transaction commitment is done through the Connection object. When a JDBC driver starts up, the Connection is in auto-commit mode. That means the Connection automatically commits changes after executing each individual statement. You can turn that off and control when commits or rollbacks are done by invoking this method on your Connection object:

```
boolean savedCommitValue = conn.getAutoCommit();  // save the current value
conn.setAutoCommit(false);      // turn off stmt-by-stmt commits
```

Then execute as many SQL statements as makes sense for your transaction; these will frequently be grouped in a batch. Look to see if they all completed successfully, and commit the transaction. You can also restore the old setting of autocommit:

```
int [] res = myStmt.executeBatch();
conn.commit();     // commit the changes
conn.setAutoCommit(savedCommitValue);  // restore previous value.
```

If, however, an SQLException was raised, part of the recovery from that might be to issue a rollback:

```
conn.rollback();  // drop the partially completed changes.
```

The statements within a transaction are all the statements that you issued on a given connection since the previous commit() or rollback() Another way of looking at this is to note that Connection and transaction are almost synonymous—you can only have one open transaction per connection. So if you want to update a database concurrently and transactionally, the most practical way can be to use one connection per transaction per thread.

Prepared Statements and Stored Procedures

Another way to boost performance is to precompile the SQL statement using what is termed a "prepared statement." That technique and the related one of "stored procedures" are described in this section.

Prepared statements

A SQL statement is precompiled and stored in a PreparedStatement object. This object can then be used to efficiently execute this statement repeatedly, often changing some of the argument values at run-time. You get a PreparedStatement using a method of your Connection object. It's easiest to see with a code example:

```
PreparedStatement pstmt = conn.prepareStatement(
    "UPDATE EMPLOYEES SET SALARY = ? WHERE ID = ?");

pstmt.setBigDecimal(1, 150000.00);
pstmt.setInt(2, linden4303);
pstmt.executeUpdate();
 // other code goes here
pstmt.setBigDecimal(1, 85000.00);
pstmt.setInt(2, jenkins2705);
pstmt.executeUpdate();
```

That code will set employee linden4303's salary to $150,000, and employee jenkins2705's salary to $85,000. The question marks in the SQL query represent data values that will be filled in before the statement is executed. It works like arguments to a procedure, with one difference: any of the question mark fields that you don't change will retain whatever value you have previously set them to, so you only need to set fields that change.

PreparedStatement has its own versions of the methods executeQuery(), executeUpdate(), and execute(). In particular, PreparedStatement objects do not take an SQL string as a parameter because they already contain the precompiled SQL statement you previously created.

Stored procedures

Let's move on to take a look at stored procedures. These are a group of SQL statements bundled together as one unit that can be called from your program. That's where the "procedure" part of the name comes from. The "stored" part of the name is because the procedure can be pre-compiled by the SQL interpreter and actually stored within the database. Stored procedures improve database performance by reducing the amount of information that is sent over a network. A stored procedure is used when you have a group of SQL statements that, taken together, carry out some task like adding a new account and initializing it.

Up until now, stored procedures could not be moved outside the database, and could not be linked to software components or external libraries. These disadvantages disappear when you write stored procedures in Java. You have two choices for creating stored procedures.

- You can create them using SQL commands to install and manage stored procedures, and submit these commands using `executeUpdate()` in the normal way.

- You can write the stored procedure following the SQLJ conventions. SQLJ is an industry standard covering how to embed SQL statements into Java methods and how to use Java methods for stored procedures. There is more information on SQLJ at `www.sqlj.org`.

Using SQLJ means writing a stand-alone Java program to contain your stored procedure. This is exciting and interesting because it means that even your stored procedures are now portable between different databases. Write a public static void method in a Java class. That method will have the usual code to get a Connection, create a Statement, and execute it. You compile it and put it in a jar file. Then you use the SQLJ library to install the jar file in the database management system. There is a special SQL syntax (which varies between databases) that lets you invoke your stored procedure. We won't cover the specialized technique here, except to say that there are examples in *Further Reading* on page 631.

Complete Example

This section shows the complete program to create, update, and select from a database using JDBC. A longer version of this code comes with the Mckoi database and can be found in directory `c:\mckoi\demo\simple`. The code has been split into two programs there for convenience, one to create the tables, and one to query them.

```java
/**
 * Demonstrates how to use JDBC.
 */

import java.sql.*;

public class Example {

  public static void main(String[] args) {

    // Register the Mckoi JDBC Driver
    try {
      Class.forName("com.mckoi.JDBCDriver");
    }
    catch (Exception e) {
      System.out.println("Can't load JDBC Driver. " +
                        "Make sure classpath is correct");
      return;
    }

    // This URL specifies we are creating a local database. The
    // config file for the database is found at './ExampleDB.conf'
    // The 'create=true' argument means we want to create the database.
    // If the database already exists, it can not be created.
    // So delete .\data\*  when you want to run this again.
    String url = "jdbc:mckoi:local://ExampleDB.conf?create=true";

    //  Use a real username/password in a real application
    String username = "user";
    String password = "pass1212";

    // Make a connection with the database.
    Connection connection;
    try {
      connection = DriverManager.getConnection(url, username, password);
    }
    catch (SQLException e) {
      System.out.println("Connect problem: " + e.getMessage());
      return;
    }

    // --- Set up the database ---
    try {
      // Create a Statement object to execute the queries on,
      Statement statement = connection.createStatement();
      ResultSet result;

      System.out.println("-- Creating Tables --");

      // Create a Person table,
      statement.executeUpdate(
"     CREATE TABLE Person ( " +
"       name        VARCHAR(100) PRIMARY KEY, " +
"       age         INTEGER, " +
```

```
"        lives_in  VARCHAR(100) ) " );

    System.out.println("-- Inserting Data --");

    statement.executeUpdate(
"    INSERT INTO Person ( name, age, lives_in ) VALUES "
+ "        ( 'Robert Bellamy', 24, 'England' ), "
+ "        ( 'Grayham Downer', null, 'Africa' ), "
+ "        ( 'Timothy French', 24, 'Africa' ), "
+ "        ( 'Butch Fad', 53, 'USA' ), "
+ "        ( 'Judith Brown', 34, 'Africa' ) ");

    System.out.println("-- SQL queries --");
    // get average age of the people
    result = statement.executeQuery("SELECT AVG(age) FROM Person");
    if (result.next()) {
       System.out.println("Av. age:  " + result.getDouble(1));
    }
    System.out.println();
    // List the names of all the people that live in Africa
    result = statement.executeQuery(
       "SELECT name FROM Person WHERE lives_in = 'Africa' ");

    System.out.println("All people that live in Africa:");
    while (result.next()) {
       System.out.println("   " + result.getString(1));
    }

    // Close the statement and the connection.
    statement.close();
    connection.close();

  }
  catch (SQLException e) {
    System.out.println(
    "An SQLException occurred: " + e.getMessage());
  }
  catch (Exception e) {
    e.printStackTrace(System.err);
  }
 }
}
```

Make sure the three Mckoi jar files are in your classpath, then you can compile and run this code with these commands:

```
mkdir \mckoi1.0.2\demo\basic
cd \mckoi1.0.2\demo\basic
(now create the source file Example.java in this directory)

javac Example.java
java Example
```

The output will look like this:

```
-- Creating Tables --
-- Inserting Data --
-- SQL queries --
Av. age:  27.0

All people that live in Africa:
  Grayham Downer
  Timothy French
  Judith Brown
```

Database and Result Set Metadata

"Meta-*anything*" is a higher or second-order version of the *anything*. Metadata is data about data. The classic example of metadata is file and directory information on your disk drive. You don't directly put it there, but you need it to keep track of your real data, and it is maintained by the system on your behalf. Databases have a large amount of metadata describing their particular capabilities and configuration.

The database metadata is going to be different for each database, and JDBC lets you get hold of it through the `java.sql.DatabaseMetaData` interface. You get an instance of the Metadata class by invoking a method of Connection. There you will find 100 or so fields and methods that you can use to find out specific details on the database. For example, it can tell you if the database supports transactions, and if so, to what level.

You use the database metadata when you know your code is going to run against several different databases. By looking at the metadata, your code can discover the individual features of a database, and perhaps take advantage of performance-related options. Often, but not always, there is a slower more standard way to achieve an effect, and you may prefer to write your database application code that uses that, instead of querying the database about its advanced features. Using database metadata is an advanced technique, beyond the scope of this book. The javadoc documentation is extensive if you want to pursue this topic further.

Result sets also have metadata. An object of type `java.sql.ResultSetMetaData` can get information about the columns in a ResultSet object. Here is an example. The following code fragment creates a ResultSet and gets the corresponding ResultSetMetaData object from it. The code then uses that object to find out two pieces of information about the result set. It calls two methods, one to find out how many columns the result has, and one to learn whether the first column in the result set can be used in a WHERE clause (i.e., it is a "searchable" column).

```
ResultSet result = statement.executeQuery(
    "SELECT c1, c2 FROM myTable; "

ResultSetMetaData rsmd = result.getMetaData();
int numberCols = rsmd.getColumnCount();
boolean b = rsmd.isSearchable(1);
```

Further Reading

There are some excellent book-length treatments of relational databases and JDBC in particular. One book I like is the *JDBC API Tutorial and Reference* (Addison Wesley, Reading: MA, 1999), in successive editions by Graham Hamilton and Rick Cattell, and then by Maydene Fisher, and then by Seth White and Mark Hapner, and finally by Maydene and Seth again. If you buy this book, be sure to get the most up-to-date edition!

In addition, Sun has an online tutorial on JDBC that contains some of the same material in the JDBC API Tutorial book.

`java.sun.com/docs/books/tutorial/jdbc/index.html.`

Exercises

1. Run the javadoc tool to create the javadoc files for the packages of the Mckoi database, and browse the API. The database comes with the Java source code that implements it. The file is called src.zip. Unzip it, cd to the src directory that it creates, work out what the package names are (they mirror the directory names), and run javadoc on them. Look at some of the source code with an editor, and browse the javadoc-generated API documentation for the same files. How useful is javadoc to you? Why? How far does the code follow the Sun recommended code conventions at `java.sun.com/docs/codeconv/html/CodeConvTOC.doc.html` ?

2. Write a JDBC program to display the name and age of everyone in the Person table who is older than 39. This question builds on a similar one in Chapter 23 that asked you to write the SQL statement. Now the exercise asks that you put it into a JDBC program and actually run it.

3. Write a JDBC program to display the name of everyone in the Person table who lives in a NATO country and doesn't listen to the Beatles. You can google to find out which nations belong to NATO. Be careful to exclude people who listen to other bands as well as the Beatles. You will need a subquery for this.This question builds on a similar one in the previous chapter that asked you to write the SQL statement. Now the exercise asks that you put it into a JDBC program and actually run it.

4. Modify your program from the previous question to submit an invalid SQL query. How do the database and your program respond?

5. Write the JDBC code to create and populate a table for the CD inventory of an online store. Each CD is either domestic or imported. These details are stored for all CDs: artist, title, price, and quantity in stock. Imported CDs also have these fields: country of origin, genre, non-discount status, language, and lead time for reorder. Write some instance data describing your five favorite CDs (include a couple of imported CDs, too), and populate your database.

6. Update your code from the previous exercise question to allow it to work interactively with the user. The user should be able to type in the title of a CD, and the database should return all the data it holds on that CD.

Heavy Light Relief—In Which "I" Spam Myself

It's official: my email is out of control. Actually, everybody's email is out of control. I have 50 MB in my inbox alone, some of this unanswered email dating back three or more years. There's another few hundred MB in other folders. This is why Google Mail or something like it will be successful. I need a halfway decent tool to search my email and other files of concentrated knowledge and keep them secure, searchable, encrypted and archived. Find and grep just aren't good enough.

Managing files is worth paying for

I don't want Google's (or anyone else's) scripts reading my email, so I am prepared to pay for this service, but no one offers it yet. In the USA, the Stored Communications Act (part of the decades-old wiretap legislation package known as the Electronic Communications Privacy Act) says that any electronic data stored with a third party for more than 180 days can be subpoenaed by law enforcement without notifying the owner of that data. So to discourage government fishing expeditions, the data needs to be stored encrypted on the server and only be decryptable by the client. Some companies, like Hushmail.com offer some of these services. *[Note to venture capitalists: I can fix this for $10M, business plan on request. Just don't make your request by email.]*

Spam, spam, spam, lovely spam

Spam isn't clogging up my mailbox. That's a separate problem. I get a *lot* of spam, currently more than 2,500 spam messages each and every day just like everyone else who posted to usenet in the 1990s and still uses the same account. With an average spam size around 10KB, that's more than 2 MB a day flowing in, and being automatically filtered out and junked. The signal-to-noise ratio is 0.004 and dropping by the month. Yet nobody seems able to fix the spam onslaught.

I remember the very first spam email I got. I was slightly surprised to get email from someone I didn't know, who seemed to be suggesting a product for me to buy. Why would they do that, and why would they choose *me*, out of all the thousands of people on the Internet? This was a couple of years before April 1994 when two deadbeat lawyers from Arizona, Canter and Siegel, spammed all 6000 Usenet newsgroups with their unwanted adverts. They offered to help people enter the Green Card immigration lottery for $145, suppressing the information that people could enter by themselves for free.

After my first email spam, several weeks went by, and then a different one arrived. I kept that too, for its novelty value. I stopped saving them pretty quickly. Currently spam flows in at 100,000 bytes/hour in ever-increasing torrents. So I have three email problems: answering it, searching it, and fending off spam.

The dead-level limit came in April 2004, when I hit all three problems in one email. Specifically, I got three spam emails that were apparently sent *by* me. I was spamming myself! OK, I wasn't really spamming myself. Spammers are up to all kinds of tricks to get you to read the pitch and/or click on the viral attachment. They forge sender names at random. Friends had complained in the past of getting spam that was forged to look like it came from me, and finally I got three of them myself within a week.

The email header showed all three of these spams came from the same ISP:

```
Received: from unknown (HELO pvdl.com) ([212.20.141.190])(<pvdl@afu.com>)
```

Spam-merchants can (and do) forge all the other headers, but they cannot forge the last hop before it reaches your site. They lie about the domain and user name, but must put their true IP address in there, otherwise your ISP's mail program cannot talk to them and accept mail for delivery.

Blacklisting a clueless ISP

A reverse DNS search (try dnsstuff.com or samspade.org) on that IP address showed that it belonged to a company called Global Access Telecommunications, Inc. of Frankfurt in Germany. One of their customers was the spammer, but G.A.T. were responsible for not enforcing their terms of service, and allowing the spammer to get away with it. G.A.T. was quickly put on a worldwide blacklist of organizations from whom email is rejected, for being clueless ISPs. These blacklists are maintained by volunteers like spamhaus.org and cbl.abuseat.org, but they have the same limitation as virus scanners—they are reactive and only come into effect after a large number of people have already suffered the ill effects.

[6]34 *Just Java 2*

The payload in all three of these spams was a Trojan Horse executable attachment. When installed, that would turn my PC into a zombie spam-bot under the control of the spammers. This is an open proxy server, that will accept connections from anywhere, and act as a blind intermediary to any other network addresses/services. The spammers would then use my PC to continue their spamming.

It's got to stop

This has got to stop. The whole thing: the spamming, the viruses, the trojan horses, the worms, the phishing for credit data, the remote control of thousands of other peoples' PCs, the distributed denial of service attacks, the 419 frauds, the Windows operating system that provides such a nutritious environment for these; all of it has to stop. If Windows was a car that failed this badly, the Federal government would have forced the manufacturer to recall it and fix it years ago.

The email problem is actually the same kind of problem that plagues Windows itself. It is hard to build a secure, trustworthy application on top of an insecure foundation. In the case of email and Windows, the design in use today did not have security as a goal. The insecurity of Windows actively contributes to the degradation of the Internet.

Other operating systems like Linux, MacOS X, and Solaris, don't have the constant, recurring security problems of Windows. It's not just because Windows is the default big target. It's because security is still not seen as an important goal in the design of Windows, and it was and is a goal in the other operating systems.

Non-technical people often don't realize the magnitude of the problem, and propose naive solutions to solve the piece of it that they understand. This happens so frequently that the Net has developed a checklist for pointing out the flaws. It outlines many of the issues:

```
Your idea proposes a
(x) technical ( ) legislative (x) market-based ( ) vigilante
approach to fighting spam. Your idea will not work. Here is why it won't
work. (One or more of the following may apply to your particular idea, and
it may have other flaws which used to vary from state to  state before a
bad federal law was passed.)

( ) Spammers can easily use it to harvest email addresses
(x) Mailing lists and other legitimate email uses would be affected
(x) No one will be able to find the guy or collect the money
( ) It is defenseless against brute force attacks
(x) It will stop spam for two weeks and then we'll be stuck with it
(x) Users of email will not put up with it
( ) Microsoft will not put up with it
( ) The police will not put up with it
(x) Requires too much cooperation from spammers
(x) Requires immediate total cooperation from everybody at once
(x) Many email users cannot afford to lose business or alienate potential
    employers
```

```
( ) Spammers don't care about invalid addresses in their lists
( ) Anyone could anonymously destroy anyone else's career or business

Specifically, your plan fails to account for

( ) Laws expressly prohibiting it
(x) Lack of centrally controlling authority for email
( ) Open relays in foreign countries
( ) Ease of searching tiny alphanumeric address space of all email addresses
( ) Asshats
( ) Jurisdictional problems
(x) Unpopularity of weird new taxes
(x) Public reluctance to accept weird new forms of money
(x) Huge existing software investment in SMTP
(x) Susceptibility of protocols other than SMTP to attack
( ) Willingness of users to install OS patches received by email
( ) Armies of worm-riddled broadband-connected Windows boxes
(x) Eternal arms race involved in all filtering approaches
( ) Extreme profitability of spam
( ) Joe jobs and/or identity theft
( ) Technically illiterate politicians
(x) Extreme stupidity on the part of people who do business with spammers
(x) Extreme stupidity on the part of people who do business with Microsoft
(x) Extreme stupidity on the part of people who do business with Yahoo
(x) Dishonesty on the part of spammers themselves
(x) Bandwidth costs that are unaffected by client filtering
( ) Outlook

and the following philosophical objections may also apply:
(x) Ideas like yours are easy to come up with, yet none have ever been
shown practical
(x) Any scheme based on opt-out is unacceptable
( ) SMTP headers should not be the subject of legislation
( ) Blacklists suck
( ) Whitelists suck
( ) We should be able to talk about Viagra without being censored
( ) Countermeasures should not involve wire fraud or credit card fraud
( ) Countermeasures should not involve sabotage of public networks
(x) Countermeasures must work if phased in gradually
(x) Sending email should be free
(x) Why should we have to trust you and your servers?
( ) Incompatibility with open source or open source licenses
( ) Feel-good measures do nothing to solve the problem
( ) Temporary/one-time email addresses are cumbersome
( ) I don't want the government reading my email
( ) Killing them that way is not slow and painful enough

Furthermore, this is what I think about you:
( ) Sorry dude, but I don't think it would work.
(x) This is a stupid idea, and you're a stupid person for suggesting it.
```

What this is saying is that, short of a major technological miracle, the only way we'll get relief is to build the Internet version 2.

Email is a tough problem because I want to get email from people who have never emailed me in the past (old school friends, book readers, students) but I don't want to a deluge of spam. The way to solve it is to remove anonymity from email transactions. If abuse occurs, you go back up the chain, your ISP, the spammer's ISP, to the spammer, and you have an identifiable perpetrator to hold accountable. If they are in a region where your laws don't apply, and their ISP lets it happen repeatedly, their ISP gets blacklisted. Other ISPs in law-abiding nations refuse to make connections or route packets from them, so they quickly isolate themselves from the net. It may be that bulk mail is no longer an economically feasible service for ISPs to offer without bond guarantees—great!

There are a couple of proposals for reducing spam. The Sender Policy Framework (SPF) is an effort to stop forged mail headers. At each mail hop, the IP addresses are validated against the domain names the mail says it has. Mis-matches are very likely forgeries, and can be discarded. SPF won't help much with spam sent by zombie spambots, Windows PCs that have been taken over, and remotely controlled to channel spam. Domain Keys is a similar proposal for validating message headers. These proposals are helpful as far as they go, but we need authentication and privacy in many protocols not just the Simple Mail Transfer Protocol. We need a solution not just for mail, but for blogs, for web services, for secure e-commerce, for browsers, for everything online that needs privacy, authentication, and security. Why reinvent it for each protocol?

TIP: Trusted Internet Protocol

The right way to do all this is to implement TIP—trusted Internet Protocol—IPv6 with cryptographically based identity checking implemented in hardware. That is what Intel should be working on, instead of dabbling with the symptoms (like the NX—No eXecute—hardware change supported in Windows XP SP2 to prevent stack cracking).

TIP will require people to log on (authenticate) before can they reach out and use other people's resources on the network. Your home PC will do this for you automatically, just like your home phone. PCs in libraries or internet cafes will either be untrusted, and thus restricted to read-only remote operations. Or users can authenticate manually to be allowed to send email, run ssh, etc.

This won't stop spam. Nothing can stop spam, short of stopping email. Email is a protocol that allows other people to write content onto your server. There is no 100% perfect algorithm to automatically distinguish content you like, from content you don't like. Identity authentication will diminish the volume and provide accountability.

It's not like this kind of need has never arisen before in the history of the planet. How bad did things get before we had building codes? Before we got traffic laws? Before we realized that unbridled power of sovereigns or presidents was a terrible idea? Before we registered shipping? Before we put customs and immigration officers at the borders? Before we had copyrights for written works? Before we licensed the radio spectrum? Before we stopped free MP3 music piracy online? OK, strike that last one.

How much worse do things have to get on the Internet before people are desperate to get automated trust assurance for our fundamental tool for information sharing? For me, the answer came in the week of April 19 2004, when "I" sent myself 3 spam messages that were designed to take control of my PC.

Networking in Java

"If a packet hits a pocket on a socket on a port,
and the bus is interrupted and the interrupt's not caught,
then the socket packet pocket has an error to report."

— *Programmer's traditional nursery rhyme*

The biggest barrier to understanding Java networking features is getting familiar with network terms and techniques. If you speak French, it doesn't mean that you can understand an article from a French medical journal.

Similarly, when you learn Java, you also need to have an understanding of the network services and terminology before you can write Internet code. So this chapter starts with the basics of TCP/IP networking, *Everything You Need To Know about TCP/IP but Failed to Learn in Kindergarten*, followed by a description of Java support, starting with *A Client Socket in Java*.

There is a lot of knowledge in this chapter. After the TCP/IP basics, we'll develop some socket examples. We'll see how a client gets services from a remote server using sockets. Then we will look at server sockets to see how incoming connections are accepted. Our first example will merely print HTTP headers. We will add to it little by little until it is a complete HTTP web server.

Everything You Need To Know about TCP/IP but Failed to Learn in Kindergarten

Networking at heart is about shifting bits from point A to point B. We bundle the data bits into a packet, and add some more bits to say where they are to go. That, in a nutshell, is the Internet Protocol or IP. If we want to send more bits than will fit into a single packet, we can divide the bits into groups and send them in several successive packets. The units that we send are called *user datagrams* or *packets*. Packet is the more common term these days.

User datagrams can be sent across the Internet using the User Datagram Protocol (UDP), which relies on the Internet Protocol for addressing and routing. UDP is like going to the post office, sticking on a stamp, and dropping off the packet. IP is what the Postal Service does to sort, route and deliver the packet. Two common applications that use the UDP are: SNMP, the Simple Network Management Protocol, and TFTP, the Trivial File Transfer Protocol. See Figure 25–1.

When we send several pieces of postal mail to the same address, the packages might arrive in any order. Some of them might even be delayed, or even on occasion lost altogether. This is true for UDP too; you wave goodbye to the bits as they leave your workstation, and you have no idea when they will arrive where you sent them, or even if they did.

Uncertain delivery is equally undesirable for postal mail and for network bit streams. We deal with the problem in the postal mail world (when the importance warrants the cost) by paying an extra fee to register the mail and have the mail carrier collect and bring back a signature acknowledging delivery. A similar protocol is used in the network work to guarantee reliable delivery in the order in which the packets were sent. This protocol is known as Transmission Control Protocol or TCP. Some applications that run on top of (i.e. use) TCP are: FTP, the File Transfer Protocol, SMTP (sending email), POP3 (downloading email from server), IMAP (manipulation of email on the server), HTTP (requests from a browser and fulfillment by a web server), and Telnet.

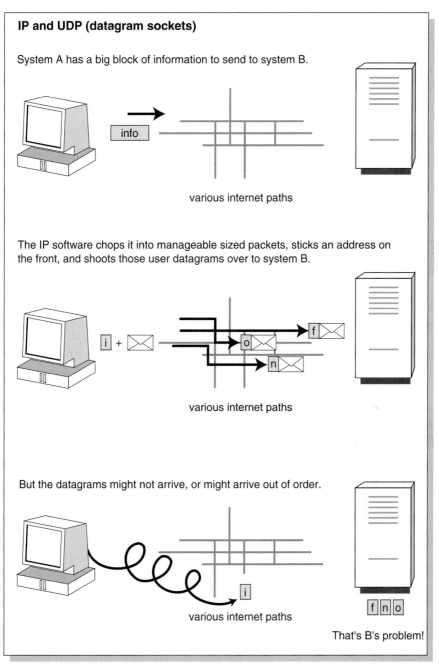

Figure 25–1   IP and UDP (datagram sockets)

What is your IP address?

On Unix workstations including MacOS and Linux, you can run the "ifconfig" (interface configuration) program to find out your IP address.

On Windows 2K and XP, you can run "ipconfig" to get some of the information. Type this in a command tool:

```
c:\> ipconfig/all
```

On 9x, the command is "winipcfg". It will pop up a window that lists the host name, IP address, subnet mask, gateway, and even the MAC address of your network card. The MAC (Media Access Control) address is the address burned into ROM on your network interface card. It is not used in TCP/IP because, unlike IP addresses, it does not have a hierarchy of Internet/WAN/LAN/switch/host. To route packets using MAC addresses, each router would need a list of every MAC address in the world. The very last hop of a packet (from a switch to a computer) *is* addressed to the computer's MAC address.

An IPv4 address looks like:	207.142.131.236 - 32 bits in 4 bytes separated by periods
An IPv6 address looks like:	1080:0:0:0:0:800:0:417A - 128 bits in eight groups of 4 hex digits
A MAC address looks like:	E0:0A:42:F3:56:25 - 48 bits, in six pairs of hex digits

TCP uses IP as its underlying protocol (just as UDP does) for routing and delivering the bits to the correct address. The "correct address" means the IP address; every computer on the Internet has an IP address. However, TCP is more like a phone call than a registered mail delivery in that it supports an end-to-end connection for the duration of the transmission session. It takes a while to set up this stream connection, and it costs more to assure reliable sequenced delivery, but the cost is usually justified. See Figure 25–2.

The access device at each endpoint of a phone conversation is a telephone. The access object at each endpoint of a TCP/IP session is a socket. Sockets were developed in Berkeley, Calif in the late 1970's for Berkeley Unix. Today, every operating system has adopted IP and Berkeley Unix sockets. Sockets are connection endpoints between processes on (usually) different machines connected by a TCP/IP network.

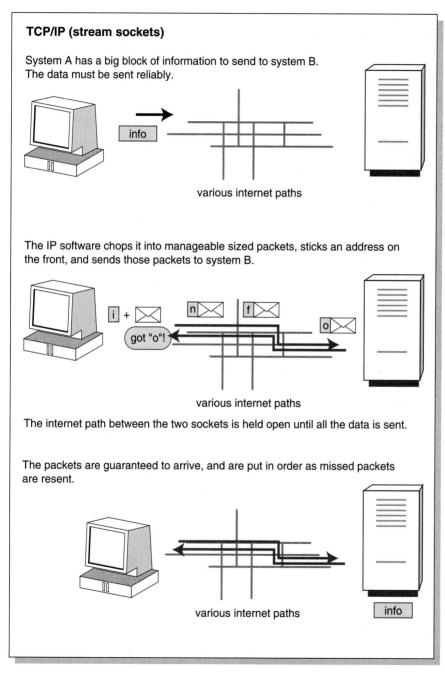

TCP/IP (stream sockets)

System A has a big block of information to send to system B.
The data must be sent reliably.

various internet paths

The IP software chops it into manageable sized packets, sticks an address on the front, and sends those packets to system B.

various internet paths

The internet path between the two sockets is held open until all the data is sent.

The packets are guaranteed to arrive, and are put in order as missed packets are resent.

various internet paths

Figure 25–2   TCP/IP (stream sockets)

Please do not teach students poor acronyms

There is an architectural model of networking, known as the ISO seven-layer model. It doesn't exactly match any real network, but it's a good tool for understanding networking. The seven-layer model says that there are seven layers in a network connection. Each layer only talks to the layer immediately above or below it, but its communications are directed to the *same* layer on the remote computer. Together they form what the marketing droids call an "IP stack" though it's really a FIFO-queue of course. The layers are shown in Table 25–1. Read it from the bottom up.

Table 25–1   The ISO seven-layer model for networks

Layer	Layer name	Description
7	**Application**	This layer defines protocols for programs to communicate. HTTP is an application layer protocol
6	**Presentation**	This layer does any necessary character set conversion (such as Unicode to ASCII) so two systems can talk.
5	**Session**	This is the layer that sets up, maintains, then tears down the active connection between two users. The connection stays in place even if not continuously sending data. Each endpoint of a session is a socket.
4	**Transport**	It sets up a logical connection with the remote host, and sends data over it. It manages the flow of data so neither end is overrun.
3	**Network**	The most complex layer. It maintains a connection between two endpoints. This layer handles IP addresses and packets, and does addressing and routing.
2	**Datalink**	This layer splits a transmission into frames with a MAC address. It provides device independence and the appearance of error-free transmission to the layers above.
1	**Physical**	An example of a physical layer is the 100 base T ethernet wiring standard.

People use the acronym *All People Seem To Need Data Processing* to remember the seven layers, but I think it makes more sense to consider the stack from the bottom up, so *Please Do Not Teach Students Poor Acronyms*.

The TCP/IP four-layer reality

TCP/IP is actually built from four layers:

4 The application layer (the networking protocols like HTTP, POP3 and IMAP).

3 The transport layer (TCP and UDP),

2 The network layer (packets and IP addresses),

1 The datalink or link layer (frames and MAC addresses),

Protocols built on IP

There are three big protocols built on top of IP. Both ends of the protocol have an OS data structure called a socket. A socket does the same job for an IP connection that a telephone handset does for a phone conversation: it is an object that makes it convenient to send and receive. In the case of a phone handset we send and receive noises. In the case of an IP connection, we send and receive bytes.

IP supports the following protocols, using socket connections:

• Slower, reliable delivery using TCP (this is termed a *stream socket*).

• Faster but unguaranteed delivery using UDP (this is a *datagram socket*).

• Fast raw bits using ICMP (Internet Control Message Protocol) datagrams. They are not delivered to the application layer at all. Their purpose is to ask one of the lower layers at the remote end to do something or respond in some way.

ICMP is a low-level protocol for message control and error reporting. It uses IP packets, but its messages are directed at the IP software itself and don't come through to the application layer. Java doesn't support ICMP and we won't say anything more about it.

Client versus server sockets

A client socket is different from a server socket. The client socket is good at asking for something, while the server socket is good at listening for requests. In the phone world, a server socket is the equivalent of a call center that only takes calls and never initiates outgoing calls. A client socket is the equivalent of someone who dials into the call center for support. The phone world is a great analogy for understanding many things about networked communication (because the phone world *is* networked communication, but of a type where everyone is familiar with the end point features).

Note that the number of socket writes is not at all synchronized with the number or timing of socket reads. A packet may be broken into smaller packets as it is sent across the network, so your code should *never* assume that a read will get the same number of bytes that were just written into the socket.

IPv4 versus IPv6

The most widely used version of IP today is Internet Protocol Version 4 (IPv4). However, IP Version 6 (IPv6 or IPng) is also beginning to enter the market. IPv6 uses 128 bit addresses, not 32 bit, and so allows many more Internet users. IPv6 is fully backward compatible with (can process packets sent using) IPv4, but it will take a long time before IPv4 is displaced by v6. IPv4 is supported with hardware-based routing at wire speed on 2.5Gb links. IPv6 currently uses software routing.

An IPv4 feature called "Network Address Translation" (NAT) has greatly reduced the pressure to move to v6. A few years ago, it looked like we were going to run out of IP addresses. Today NAT lets your big site have just one assigned address, which you use for the computer with the internet connection. You use any IP address you like for the computers on your side of the firewall. You may be duplicating numbers that someone else uses behind their firewall, but the two systems don't interfere with each other. When you access the internet, NAT updates your packets dynamically. It rewrites your internal IP address in packets changing it into the externally visible one, and rewrites IP addresses in incoming packets so they'll go to your host. A NAT server keeps track of who's doing what, so it knows who should get which packets from the outside. From the outside, it looks like all your traffic is coming from your server computer that runs the NAT service.

Common network hardware

Here are some common pieces of hardware in the network world. When we talk about "layer 3" etc. in the following definitions, it is with reference to the OSI 7-layer model.

Router. A router is a computer with at least two interfaces, connecting it to two different networks. It looks at IP addresses and moves packets from one of these networks to the other (that is the definition of *routing*) when necessary. Since it looks at IP addresses, by definition it is a layer 3 device. Routers look at the IP headers and consult their forwarding tables to determine the best path for forwarding the packets. They use protocols such as ICMP to communicate with each other and guess the best router to pass a packet, to send it from source to destination. As we saw in the previous traceroute example, a packet might be forwarded between 20 routers, with each hop bringing it closer to its destination.

Companies also sell products called "layer 3 switches", or *routing switches*. They are actually routers rather than switches. They mean that the router also does some layer 2 switching functions.

Switch. A switch is like a telephone exchange. In fact, *switch* is the modern name for both a telephone exchange and the computer inside it. Instead of phone numbers, a network switch uses MAC addresses. Years ago, we connected a computer to the ethernet by physically attaching the computer to a piece of ether

Looking at a packet traveling over the Net

Packets are moved along by routers, which are special-purpose computers that connect networks. Every IP packet that leaves your computer goes to a nearby router which will move the packet to another router closer to the destination. This transfer continues until finally the packet is brought to a router that is directly connected to the subnet serving the destination computer.

Routers maintain large configuration tables of what addresses are served by what routers, what the priorities are, and what rules they should use for security and load balancing. These tables can be updated dynamically as the network runs.

Windows has a program that lets you trace a packet's movement between routers. Here's the output from a sample run, tracing the route between my PC and java.sun.com. Unix has a similar program, called "traceroute."

```
c:\> tracert java.sun.com
Tracing route to java.sun.com [192.18.97.71]over a maximum of 30 hops:
...
7    15 ms    16 ms    15 ms    28.ge13-0.mpr2.pao1.us.above.net [64.125.12.61]

8    15 ms    17 ms    16 ms    so-6-1-0.mpr4.sjc2.us.above.net [64.125.29.126]

9    16 ms    17 ms    16 ms    so-0-0-0.cr2.sjc3.us.above.net [64.125.29.138]

10   16 ms    16 ms    16 ms    pos1-0.er2a.sjc3.us.above.net [64.125.28.198]

11   17 ms    17 ms    16 ms    64.124.81.56.sun.com [64.124.81.56] Trace
complete.
```

traceroute can be problematical if one is behind a firewall. You may have to use the "-I" option, "traceroute -I java.sun.com". Traceroute is good for troubleshooting network connectivity. Here it tells us that overall packets travel from me to Java-World HQ (ten miles) in under a fiftieth of a second.

---

cable that also ran to 20 other computers. Today, each computer has a dedicated line to a switch, and runs at the full speed, e.g. Gb ether, on every line. The switch filters and forwards packets either to the final destination, or to a router to move it nearer the final destination. When a frame comes in, the switch looks at its MAC address, and sends that frame to the one port that is connected to that MAC address. A switch is the modern incarnation of a bridge.

Hub. A hub is a frame repeater. It doesn't read addresses. It just copies each incoming frame to every connection it has. Computers discard packets that are not addressed to them, so you can use a hub to share a network connection between several computers. The drawback is that everyone is delayed by everyone else's traffic. A hub is a layer 1 device, and is also known as a *multi-port repeater*.

These days, switches have become so cheap that the default is to buy a switch instead of a hub; switches lead to less congestion on a LAN since each host only sees its own traffic.

DNS server. There will be a local server known as the Domain Name Server (usually one per subnet, per campus, or per company) that resolves the symbolic name into an IP address. That allows people to deal with names. Programs will make calls to the DNS server to convert IP addresses to names and vice versa. The premier DNS software is the Berkeley Internet Name Daemon (BIND).

Firewall. A firewall can be hardware or software or a combination. Its purpose is to discard unauthorized packets, and stop them coming from the Internet into your private network. There are several different techniques for this. Packet filtering looks at each individual packet and accepts or rejects it based on configurable rules such as "deny all ftp requests except to host foo".

Proxy server. A proxy server sits between a client application, such as a Web browser, and a real server. It intercepts all requests to the real server, and may be able to fulfill the requests itself, e.g. it may be able to retrieve a web page from a from a local cache. If not, it makes the request to the real server. A proxy server can be used to deny clients access to a set of websites or network services. Finally and most importantly a proxy server hides the details of your internal network from the outside world. Proxy servers are often part of a firewall server.

If you use a proxy server you will need to tell Java the details in order to access hosts outside the firewall. You do this by defining properties, perhaps when starting the code:

```
java -DproxySet=true -DproxyHost=SOMEHOST -DproxyPort=SOMENUM code.java
```

Without this, you'll get an UnknownHostException. At work, your systems administrator will know the values. At home, you won't be using a proxy server unless you set it up yourself.

There! Now you know everything you need to use the Java networking features.

What's in the networking library?

If you browse the network library API, you'll find the following classes. There are a few other classes, but these are the key ones.

- Socket   This is the client Socket class. It lets you open a connection to another machine, anywhere on the Internet (anywhere that the remote end permits, that is).

- ServerSocket   This is the server Socket class. ServerSocket lets an application accept TCP connections from other systems and exchange I/O with them.

- URL

The class represents a Uniform Resource Locator—a reference to an object on the web. You can create a URL reference with this class.

- URLConnection

You can open a URL and retrieve the contents, or write to it, using this class.

- HttpURLConnection

The class extends URLConnection and supports functions specific to HTTP, like GET, POST, PUT, HEAD, TRACE, and OPTIONS.

- URLEncoder/URLDecoder

These two classes have static methods to allow you to convert a String to and from MIME x-www-form-urlencoded form. This is convenient for posting data to servlets or CGI scripts.

The class DatagramSocket supports the use of UDP packets. We don't deal with UDP here because it is less widely used than TCP. Most people want the reliability feature that TCP offers. Ironically, the widespread use of subnets using directly connected switches (instead of shared ethernet segments) has made UDP much more reliable, to the point where people are using it on LANs instead of TCP, and getting performance *and* reliability.

Let me try that last sentence again. When we started extensive networking in the late 1970s, ethernet was the medium of choice. You strung a single ethernet cable down a corridor and workstations physically attached to the net by tapping into the cable. That meant that all the network traffic was visible to all the workstations that used that cable. It was electronically noisy and slow. Today, nearly everyone uses 10baseT or 100baseT wiring. The number is the speed in Megabits, and the "T" part means "Twisted pair." There is a twisted pair wire from your workstation directly to the switch that controls your subnet. No other workstation shares your twisted pair wiring. Result: faster performance, less electronic noise, and more reliable subnets, leading to greater confidence using UDP.

TCP/IP client/server model

Before we look at actual Java code, a diagram is in order showing how a client and server typically communicate over a TCP/IP network connection. Figure 25–3 shows the way processes contact each other by using IP address and a port number. The IP address identifies a unique computer on the Internet. The port number is a simple data structure that the OS maintains to direct an incoming network connection to a specific process.

An IP address is like a telephone number, and a port number is like an extension at that number. Together they specify a computer and a service request. The combination of an IP address plus a port number is the definition of a socket. To talk to each other, the client and server must open a dialog using the same port number.

For simplicity, in Java network socket connections are made to look like I/O streams. You simply read and write data using the usual stream methods (all socket communication is in 8-bit bytes), and it automagically appears at the other end. Unlike a stream, a socket supports two-way communication. There is a method to get the input stream of a socket, and another method to get the output stream. This allows the client and server to talk back and forth.

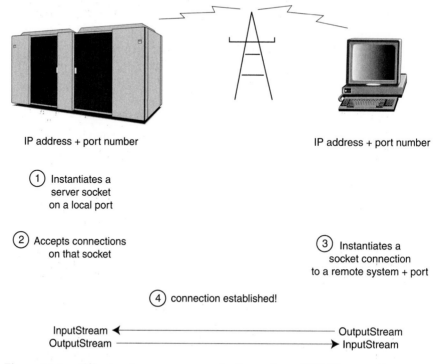

Figure 25–3   Client and server communication using a TCP/IP connection

Almost all Internet programs work as client/server pairs. The server is on a host system somewhere in cyberspace, and the client is a program running on your local system. When the client wants an Internet service (such as retrieving a web page from an HTTP server), it issues a request, usually to a symbolic address such as www.sun.com rather than to an IP address (though that works just fine, too).

The bits forming the request are assembled into a *packet* and routed to the server. The server reads the incoming packet, notes what the request is, where it came from, and then tries to respond to it. It does so by providing either the service (web page, shell account, file contents, etc.) or a sensible error message. The response is sent back across the Internet to the client.

All the standard Internet utilities (telnet, rdist, FTP, ping, rcp, NFS, and so on) operate in client/server mode connected by a TCP or UDP socket. Programs that send mail don't *really* know how to send mail—they just know how to take it to the Post Office port. In this case, mail has a socket connection and talks to a demon at the other end with a fairly simple protocol. The standard mail demon knows how to accept text and addresses from clients and transmit it for delivery. If you can talk to the mail demon, you can send mail. There is little else to it.

Many of the Internet services are actually quite simple. But often considerable frustration comes in doing the socket programming in C and in learning the correct protocol. The socket programming API presented to C is quite low level and all too easy to screw up. Errors are poorly handled and diagnosed. As a result, many programmers naturally conclude that sockets are brittle and hard to use. Sockets aren't hard to use. The C socket API is hard to use.

Port = service;   socket = IP address + port

An IP address says which computer you are trying to reach. You still need to tell that computer what you want from it. That is done with a port number.

A port number is an integer under 65,536 (16 bits). A large number of Internet services are at predefined port numbers. If you want to ask for this kind of service from a specific computer, you would send a request to this port number at its IP address:

port number	service
20	ftp data
21	ftp control
22	secure shell remote login protocol
23	telnet
25	Simple Mail Transfer Protocol
37	time service
80	http connection
110	Post Office Protocol 3
135	The dcom rpc server port that Microsoft left open on Windows, allowing the Blaster worm to penetrate millions of PCs from August 2003.
194	Internet Relay Chat
445	The "Local Security Authority Subsystem Service" that Microsoft left open on Windows, allowing the Sasser worm to penetrate hundred of thousands of PCs in May 2004
458	Apple QuickTime
1080	Alternative port for http
5190	Alternative port for SMTP

A firewall works in part by looking at the port number in incoming packets and throwing away ones that ask for a service you don't want to offer. Port numbers under 1024 on Unix can only be accessed by the superuser. So http and some other services are sometimes bumped up, e.g. to port 1080. A socket is defined as *an IP address plus a port on that computer.*

Don't believe me? Take a look. The C code to establish a socket connection is:

```
int set_up_socket(u_short port) {
    char    myname[MAXHOSTNAME+1];          Horrid C / C++ Sockets
    int     s;
    struct sockaddr_in sa;
    struct hostent *he;

    bzero(&sa,sizeof(struct sockaddr_in));  /* clear the address */
    gethostname(myname,MAXHOSTNAME);        /* establish identity */
    he= gethostbyname(myname);              /* get our address   */
    if (he == NULL)                         /* if addr not found... */
        return(-1);
    sa.sin_family= he->h_addrtype;          /* host address */
    sa.sin_port= htons(port);               /* port number */

if ((s= socket(AF_INET,SOCK_STREAM,0)) <0) /* finally, create socket */
        return(-1);
    if (bind(s, &sa, sizeof(sa), 0) < 0) {
        close(s);
        return(-1);                         /* bind address to socket */
    }

    listen(s, 3);                           /* max queued connections */
    return(s);
}
```

By way of contrast, the equivalent Java code is:

```
ServerSocket servsock = new ServerSocket(port, 3);
```

That's it! Just one line of Java code to do all the things the C code does.

Java handles all that socket complexity "under the covers" for you. It doesn't expose the full range of socket possibilities, so Java avoids the novice socketeer choosing contradictory options. On the other hand, a few obscure sockety things cannot be done in Java. You cannot create a raw socket in Java, and hence cannot write a ping program that relies on raw sockets (you can do something just as good, though). The benefit is overwhelming: You can open sockets and start writing to another system just as easily as you open a file and start writing to hard disk.

A "ping program," in case you're wondering, is a program that sends ICMP control packets over to another machine anywhere on the Internet. This action is called "pinging" the remote system, rather like the sonar in a ship "pings" for submarines or schools of fish. The control packets aren't passed up to the application layer, but tell the TCP/IP library at the remote end to send back a reply. The reply lets the pinger calculate how quickly data can pass between the two systems.

The story about ping
If you want to know how quickly your packets can reach a system, use ping.

```
c:\> ping java.sun.com
Pinging java.sun.com [64.124.81.57] with 32 bytes of data:
Reply from 64.124.81.57: bytes=32 time=17ms TTL=245
Reply from 64.124.81.57: bytes=32 time=17ms TTL=245
Ping statistics for 64.124.81.57:
Packets: Sent = 4, Received = 4, Lost = 0 (0% loss),

Approximate round trip times in milli-seconds:
Minimum = 17ms, Maximum = 22ms, Average = 18ms
```

This confirms that the time for a packet to hustle over from Mountain View to Santa Clara is about 0.16 seconds on this particular day and time. "TTL" is "Time To Live." To prevent infinite loops, each router hop decrements this field in a packet, and if it reaches zero, the packet just expires where it is.

I can't resist mentioning that a book review at Amazon.com for *The Story About Ping* is refreshing—especially the review by John E. Fracisco. Check it out.

The most-used methods in the API for the client end of a socket are:

```java
public class Socket extends Object {
    public Socket();
    public Socket(String,int) throws UnknownHostException,
                                      java.io.IOException;
    public Socket(InetAddress,int) throws java.io.IOException;

    public java.nio.channels.SocketChannel getChannel();
    public InputStream getInputStream() throws IOException;
    public OutputStream getOutputStream()
                                   throws IOException;

     public synchronized void setSoTimeout(int) throws SocketException;
     public synchronized void close() throws IOException;

    public boolean isConnected();
    public boolean isBound();
    public boolean isClosed();
    public boolean isInputShutdown();
    public boolean isOutputShutdown();

     public boolean shutdownOutput() throws IOException;
     public boolean shutdownInput() throws IOException;
     public static void setSocketImplFactory(
                                       SocketImplFactory fac);
}
```

The constructor with no arguments creates an unconnected socket which you can later bind() to a host and port you specify. After binding, you will connect() it. It's easier just to do all this by specifying these arguments in the constructor, if you know them at that point.

The setSoTimeout(int ms) will set a timeout on the socket of ms milliseconds. When this is a non-zero amount, a read call on the input stream will block for only this amount of time. Then it will break out of it by throwing a java.net.SocketTimeoutException, but leaving the socket still valid for further use.

The setSocketImplFactory() method is a hook for those sites that want to provide their own implementation of sockets, usually to deal with firewall or proxy issues. If this is done, it will be done on a site-wide basis, and individual programmers won't have to worry about it.

The socket API has one or two dozen other get/set methods for TCP socket options. Most of the time you don't need these and can ignore them.

A Client Socket in Java

This section shows a simple example of using a socket to communicate with another computer. You should type this code in and try it. If you haven't done much network programming, you'll find it a gleeful experience as you network with systems around the planet, and even in space. The space shuttle has a TCP/IP network connection to Mission Control, but the spoilsports at NASA keep its address secret, so we'll use a different host.

There is an Internet protocol known as Network Time Protocol or NTP. NTP is used to synchronize the clocks of some computers. Without periodic sync'ing, computer clocks tend to drift out of alignment, causing problems for times they need to agree on, like email and file timestamps. NTP is pretty fancy these days, but a simple part of the protocol involves making a socket connection to a NTP server to get the time.

Our example program will open a socket connection to an NTP server and print out the time it gets back. The way a client asks for the time is simply to make a socket connection to port 13 on an NTP server. Port 13 is the Internet standard on all computers for the time of day port. You don't have to identify yourself or write some data indicating what you want. Just making the socket connection is enough to get the server to give you an answer. Java does all the work of assembling the bytes into packets, sending them, and giving you an input stream with the bytes coming back from the server.

Here is a Java program that connects to an NTP server and asks the time:

```java
import java.io.*;
import java.net.*;
public class AskTime {

    public static void main(String a[]) throws Exception {
        if (a.length!=1) {
            System.out.println("usage:  java AskTime <systemname> ");
            System.exit(0);
        }

        String machine = a[0];
        final int daytimeport = 13;
        Socket so = new Socket(machine, daytimeport);
        BufferedReader br =
                new BufferedReader( new InputStreamReader(
                        so.getInputStream() ) );
        String time = br.readLine();
        System.out.printf("%s says it is %s %n", machine, time);
    }
}
```

The program expects the name of an NTP server to be passed to it on the command line. There are about 200,000 NTP servers on the Internet. Several national standards organizations allow reading the time via NTP. Table 25–2 gives a couple of addresses for the service.

Table 25–2   Some global timeservers

Organization	NTP server	IP address
Physikalisch-Technischen Bundesanstalt, Germany	ptbtime1.ptb.de	192.53.103.103
US Naval Observatory, Washington, DC	tock.usno.navy.mil	192.5.41.41

These servers come and go. Do a web search on "NTP server" for a current list. When you run the program, giving a hostname as argument, you see this:

```
% java AskTime ptbtime1.ptb.de
ptbtime1.ptb.de says it is 02 MAY 2004 01:43:56 METDST
```

TCP/IP on Windows

Your Java network programs are going to work only if you are using a computer that has an IP address and a connection to a TCP/IP network.

On a Unix workstation, TCP/IP support is a standard part of the operating system. If you're still using that quaint old antique, Windows 95, you'll need to have the TCP/IP protocol stack (library) installed.

Networking in Windows 9x can be fussy, as well as buggy and insecure. You'll find that you need to have an active network connection to your ISP to get any part of it to work. WinXP has acceptable networking support, apart from not having a good firewall (no support for seeing what outbound connections are doing). Get the free Zone Alarm from download.com to plug this gap.

You can provide the IP address instead of the server name, and the AskTime program will work equally well.

This program demonstrates how easy it is to open a socket connection to a port on another computer using the Java networking library. It's just flat-out impressive to write a dozen lines of code that can ask a computer anywhere on the planet to tell you the time. Maybe there's something to this Internet thing, after all.

Sockets are used in client or in server mode. The program shown previously is an example of the client use of socket. The client side initiates the contact. It is like knocking on a door or calling a phone number and starting a conversation with whoever answers.

The server side is just sitting there, waiting on a socket until someone shows up to ask for something. We will show how to write a server socket a little later in the chapter, in *A Server Socket in Java* on page 660. The next topic, *Sending Email by Java*, is another example of how a client can obtain a service by opening a socket connection and writing to it. The example here is sending email by writing to the mailserver port which (as another Internet standard) lives on port 25.

Sending Email by Java

As our next example, let's write a Java program to send some email. Email is sent by socketed communication with port 25 on a computer system. All we are going to do is open a socket connected to port 25 on some system that is running a mail server and speak "mail protocol" to the sendmail demon at the other end. If we speak the mail protocol correctly, it will listen to what we say, and send the email for us.

The following requires an Internet standard mail (SMTP) program running on the server. If your server has some non-standard proprietary mail program on it, you're out of luck. If your ISP uses a different port for mail (mine uses port 5190) use that instead. You can check which program you have by telnetting to port 25 on the server, and seeing if you get a mail server to talk to you.

Here's how you use telnet to say helo to the SMTP program on port 25 (the bold lines are what you type, the other lines are responses to you):

```
telnet yourisp.com 25
220 yourisp.com SMTP
HELO
250 yourISP.com
QUIT
221 yourisp.com
```

You could feed email to the server by hand, if you memorized the protocol and had the patience. There are two wrinkles to connecting to SMTP servers. First, it became common for spammers to steal time on other people's mailservers to relay their spam. As a result, most mail servers are now selective about who they accept a connection from. You won't be able to get mailers around the world to talk to you, just your ISP mail server. Second, Java now has a mail API with a somewhat higher-level interface, so you don't need to understand individual mail commands. But the point here is to show some give and take over a socket connection. Again, this example shows the client end of the socket connection.

The code to send email is:

```
import java.io.*;
import java.net.*;
public class email {

    public static void main(String args[]) throws IOException {
        Socket sock;
        BufferedReader bis;
        PrintStream ps;

        sock = new Socket("localhost", 25);
        bis = new BufferedReader(
                    new InputStreamReader(sock.getInputStream()));
        ps = new PrintStream(sock.getOutputStream());

        ps.println("mail from: trelford");
        //System.out.println( dis.readLine() );
        // Exercise for student:
        // check all responses from the SMTP server
        // They should all start with "2nn" or "3nn"
        // Any different reply code means a failure to send mail.
        System.out.println(bis.readLine());

        String Addressee= "linden";
        ps.println("rcpt to: " + Addressee);
        //System.out.println( dis.readLine() );
        System.out.println(bis.readLine());

        ps.println("data");
        //System.out.println( dis.readLine() );
        System.out.println(bis.readLine());

        ps.println("This is the message\n that Java sent");
        ps.println(".");
        System.out.println(bis.readLine());

        ps.flush();
        sock.close();
    }
}
```

Running this program will send email to the addressee. Many of the Internet services are like this one. You set up a socket connection and talk a simple text request-and-response protocol to tell the server at the other end what you want.

Note that the main() routine has been declared as throwing an Exception. This is a shortcut, permissible in development, to save the necessity of handling any exceptions that might be raised. It only works because exceptions are not considered part of the signature of a method. In production code, it is important to catch and handle any exceptions.

You can find all the Internet Protocols described in documents in *Request For Comments* (RFCs), the format in which they were originally issued, available online. Do a web search to find a mirror near you. The mail RFC is RFC821.txt. A careful study of some of these documents will often answer any protocol questions you have.

You can find more information on the Java mail API at java.sun.com/products/javamail/.

If you write a simple Swing GUI around this mail-sending code, you've written a mailer program! It's not that hard to get the RFCs for the POP3 and IMAP[1] protocols and write the code to read and display incoming mail, too.

A Server Socket in Java

This section shows a simple example of creating a *server* socket to listen for incoming requests. We could write the server side of a simple NTP server, but let's try something a little more ambitious. It should be fairly clear at this point that HTTP is just another of the many protocols that use sockets to run over the Internet.

A web *browser* is a client program that sends requests through a socket to the HTTP port on a server and displays the data that the server sends back. A basic web browser can be written in a couple of hundred lines of code if you have a GUI component that renders HTML, which Java does.

---

1. POP3 is "Post Office Protocol 3," and IMAP is "Internet Mail Access Protocol," different standards for the client end of mail systems. POP3 downloads mail and keeps it on the client. IMAP keeps the mail on the server, which is more convenient if you read it from several different computers.

A web *server* is a server program that waits for incoming requests on the HTTP port and acts on those to send the contents of local files back to the requestor. It can be implemented in just a few dozen lines of code.

Security of network programs—a cautionary tale!

Be very careful when you start developing networked programs on your computer. Before you try it at work, check if there is a company policy about network use. You can get fired for doing the wrong thing!

The problem is that any server sockets you create may be visible more widely than you intended. If you are running this at home, and you are not using a firewall, your server socket will be visible to the entire net. That's like leaving the front door of your home wide open.

When I was developing the HTTP server in Java for this chapter, I left it running on my PC to test it. Someone's automated port scanner script soon noticed my server, made an unauthorized connection to it, and issued this HTTP command:

```
GET /scripts/..%%35c../winnt/system32/cmd.exe?/c+dir HTTP/1.0
```

This is an attempt to break out of the scripts directory, run a shell, and do a "dir" to see what's on my system. This is the NIMDA worm that pushes its way into the straw house that is Microsoft's IIS. Once in, crackers will try to add their own back door on your computer where you'll never find it. Then they can use your system whenever it's on the net (they love cable modems) for such things as distributed denial of service attacks.

My server was logging client requests, but not fulfilling them, so the nimda-nimrod was out of luck. Be careful out there; people are actively looking for systems to break into 24x7.

The example here is part of the code for a web server. This is the code that opens a server socket on the http port, port 80, and listens for requests from web browsers. We echo the requests, but don't act on them.

The code is split into two classes to better show what's happening. The first class is the main program. It instantiates a server socket on port 80 (use port 1080 if you're writing the test code on a system without root access). The code then does an accept() on the server socket, waiting for client connections to come in. When one does come in, the program creates a new object to deal with that one connection and invokes its getRequest() method.

```
public class HTTPServer {
    public static void main(String a[]) throws Exception {
        final int httpd = 80;
        ServerSocket ssock = new ServerSocket(httpd);
        System.out.println("have opened port 80 locally");

        Socket sock = ssock.accept();
        System.out.println("client has made socket connection");

        OneConnection client = new OneConnection(sock);
        String s = client.getRequest();
    }
}
```

There are only two new lines of code in this server program. This line:

```
ServerSocket ssock = new ServerSocket(httpd);
```

and this line:

```
Socket sock = ssock.accept(); // on the server
```

The first line instantiates a server socket on the given port (httpd is an int with the value 80). The second line does an `accept()` on this server socket. It will block or wait here until some client somewhere on the net opens a connection to the same port, like this:

```
clientSock = new Socket("somehost", 80); // on the client
```

At that point, the `accept()` method is able to complete, and it returns a new instance of a socket to the server. The rest of this conversation will be conducted over the new socket, thus freeing up the original socket to do another `accept()` and wait for another client. At the client end, the socket doesn't appear to change.

In a real server, the code will loop around and accept another connection. We'll get to that. Here is the second half of the code: the OneConnection class that the main program uses to do the work for a single client request.

```
import java.io.*;
import java.net.*;
class OneConnection {
    Socket sock;
    BufferedReader in = null;
    DataOutputStream out = null;

    OneConnection(Socket sock) throws Exception{
        this.sock = sock;
        in  = new BufferedReader(
        new InputStreamReader( sock.getInputStream() ) );
        out = new DataOutputStream(sock.getOutputStream());
    }

    String getRequest() throws Exception {
        String s=null;
        while ( (s=in.readLine())!=null) {
            System.out.println("got: "+s);
        }
        return s;
    }
}
}
```

The constructor keeps a copy of the socket that leads back to the client and opens the input and output streams. Sockets always do I/O on bytes, not Unicode chars. HTTP is a line-oriented protocol. We push a BufferedReader onto the input stream so we can use the convenient readLine() method. We could equally use java.util.Scanner.create() to wrap the input stream, and then call nextLine() on the scanner object that create() returns.

If you're using a binary protocol, do everything with streams, not readers/writers. We wrap a DataOutputStream on the output side of the socket. We don't write anything in this version of the program, but we will soon develop it and start writing.

Socket protocols

The getRequest() method reads successive lines from the socket and echoes them on the server. How does it know when to stop reading lines? This is one of the tricky things with sockets—they cannot tell the difference between "end of input" and "there is more input, but it is delayed coming through the network."

To cope with this inability to know when it's done, socket protocols use one of three approaches:

• Have the client precede each message by a number giving the length of the following message. Or use some other indication to end transmission, such as sending a blank line or the word BYE as in SMTP.

- Have the client close its output stream, using `sock.shutDownOutput()`. That causes the next read at the server end to return -1.

- Set a timeout on the socket, using `sock.setSoTimeout(int ms)`. With this set to a non-zero amount, a read call on the input stream will block for only this amount of time. Then it will break out of it by throwing a java.net.SocketTimeoutException, but leaving the socket still valid for further use.

The third approach, using timeouts, is the least reliable because timeouts are always too long (wasting time) or too short (missing input). HTTP uses a mixture of approaches one and two.

Running the HTTP server program

Compile the code and then run the program. Make sure you run it on a computer that is not already running a web server; otherwise it will find that it cannot claim port 80. If all is well, the program will print out:

```
java HTTPServer
have opened port 80 locally
```

then it will block, waiting for an incoming request on the port. This is exactly what a web server does: opens port 80 and waits for incoming socket connections from clients.

Loopback address

Every computer system on the Internet has a unique IP address consisting of four groups of digits separated by periods like this: 204.156.141.229

They are currently revising and increasing the IP address specification so that there will be enough new IP addresses to give one to every conceivable embedded processor on earth, and a few nearby friendly planets. These IP version 6 addresses look like: 1080:0:0:0:8:800:200C:417A

One special IPv4 address is: 127.0.0.1. This is the "loopback" address used in testing and debugging. If a computer sends a packet to this address, it is routed to itself, without actually leaving the system. This special address is used to run Internet software even if you are not connected to the Internet. Set your system up so that the Internet services it will be requesting are all at the loopback address. Make sure your system is actually running the demons corresponding to the services you want to use.

The hostname for the loopback address is "localhost," if you are requesting services by name rather than IP address. On any system, you should be able to enter the command "ping localhost" and have it echo a reply from the loopback IP address. If you can't do this, it indicates that your TCP/IP stack is not set up properly.

Here's the interesting part. You can make that connection using any web browser! Just start up your browser and direct it to the computer where you are running the Java program. You can run your browser on a different system altogether, and give it the name of the computer running the Java program. Or, if you are running everything on one computer, the name will be "localhost," and the URL will be something like:

```
http://localhost/a/b/c/d.html
```

The rest of the URL doesn't matter since our server program doesn't (yet) do anything with the incoming request. You will see the Java server print out the message that a socket connection has been made ("got a socket"), and then print the HTTP text it receives on the socket from the browser!

```
got a socket
got: GET /a/b/c/d.html HTTP/1.1
got: Accept: image/gif, image/x-xbitmap, image/jpeg, image/pjpeg, */*
got: Accept-Language: en-us
got: Accept-Encoding: gzip, deflate
got: User-Agent: Mozilla/4.0 (compatible; MSIE 5.5; Windows NT 4.0)
got: Host: localhost
got: Connection: Keep-Alive
got:
```

These strings are HTTP headers. They are created by the browser to tell the server what file it has asked for, and they provide information about what kinds of formats the browser can accept back.

A couple more points to note here. First, almost all servers uses threads. That way, they can serve the client and at the same time accept further requests. We will shortly show the code to do this. Second, these dozen or so lines of server code are at the heart of every webserver. If you add a couple of routines to read whatever file the browser asks for and write it into the socket, you have written a webserver. Let's do it.

The ServerSocket API is:

```
public class ServerSocket {
    public ServerSocket() throws IOException;
    public ServerSocket(int) throws IOException;
    public ServerSocket(int,int) throws IOException;
    public ServerSocket(int,int,InetAddress) throws IOException;

    public Socket accept() throws java.io.IOException;
    public void close() throws java.io.IOException;
    public java.nio.channels.ServerSocketChannel getChannel();

    public void bind(SocketAddress) throws IOException;
    public void bind(SocketAddress, int) throws IOException;
    public boolean isBound();
    public InetAddress getInetAddress();
    public int getLocalPort();

    public boolean isClosed();
    public synchronized void setSoTimeout(int) throws SocketException;
    public synchronized int getSoTimeout() throws java.io.IOException;
    public static synchronized void setSocketFactory(SocketImplFactory)
            throws IOException;
    public synchronized void setReceiveBufferSize(int) throws
SocketException;
    public synchronized int getReceiveBufferSize() throws SocketException;
}
```

The accept() method listens for a client trying to make a connection and accepts it. It creates a fresh socket for the server end of the connection, leaving the server socket free to do more accepts.

The bind() method is used to connect an existing socket to a particular IP address and port. (This use of bind is unrelated to the DNS bind program). You use this when you want to use channels instead of streams for socket I/O.

The other methods should be clear from their names. There are other methods in the API, but these are the main ones you will use.

Debugging sockets

The little HTTPServer program we just saw can be used to help debug some server socket problems. You can see exactly what headers the browser sends you for different HTML requests. It works for other protocols too. If you make the code listen on another port, you can look at the incoming stream there.

Standing on the corner, watching all the packets go by

The server program, shown on the previous pages, will echo all the input that is sent to one socket. This is similar to the way that the FBI's controversial Carnivore program works.

Carnivore was created so that the FBI could do the online equivalent of phone tapping. It works at the more fundamental level of individual packets rather than sockets, but the principle is the same.

Carnivore is basically a packet sniffer that can be installed at an ISP and directed to copy packets that meet certain criteria (to or from a given IP address, for example). In this way, Carnivore can give the FBI a copy of all the email, all the website visits, all the telnet sessions for a particular target over the course of a month or more. A court order is needed to authorize each use of Carnivore.

The FBI made a PR error by giving the program such an aggressive name. Law enforcement needs access to these tools to track down online fraud, network disruption, and other crimes. But they would have done themselves a favor by calling the software something calmer like "Old Packet Collector."

Another debugging technique uses the telnet program to look at incoming text to a client socket. Telnet's actual purpose is to open a command shell on a remote computer. The lines you type are sent over the socket connection, and the responses sent back the same way. However, you can tell telnet to use any port. The stream that it receives on that port will be displayed in the telnet window (or command tool—Microsoft discontinued using a GUI telnet), and the things you type will be sent through the socket back to the server. The characters you type will be sent to the other end, but not echoed, however.

TELNET is just a quick and dirty debugging technique to help you see what's going on. Figure 25–4 uses telnet to see what an NTP server is sending back. Most servers will close a socket as soon as they have given you the requested information, hence the "connection lost" pop-up window. There is also a "keep-alive" option to a socket that requests the connection be retained for expected use in the very near future. This is useful for HTTP.

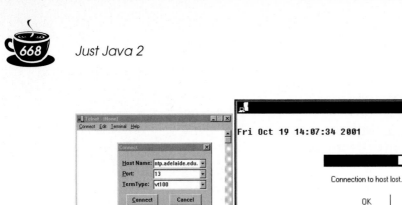

Figure 25–4   Debugging with telnet

These days you should avoid the use of telnet and FTP for their main purpose, as
they send passwords "in the clear" to the remote socket. They are thus vulnerable
to packet-sniffing by crackers at routers. Use SSH, the secure shell, instead. SSH
can be started with options that let it do an FTP transfer.

Using netstat

Another useful tool for seeing what is going on with your network connection is
netstat. It is available on Windows and Unix. Run netstat like this:

```
c:\> netstat
Active Connections
    Proto  Local Address    Foreign Address            State
    TCP    h:1891           images-vdc.amazon.com:80   ESTABLISHED
    TCP    h:1902           images-vdc.amazon.com:80   ESTABLISHED
    TCP    h:1426           afu.com:143                ESTABLISHED
    TCP    h:1025           localhost:1028             ESTABLISHED
    TCP    h:1028           localhost:1025             ESTABLISHED
```

This shows all the current IP connections, the local socket, the remote socket, and the
state. Netstat lets you see if you can at least make a connection to a remote system.
The "-?" option to netstat will give you a message about other options.

Finally, there's a helpful website at rikers.org. You can use one of their web
pages (specifically, http://rikers.org/cgi-bin/test.cgi) to see what is
happening with your HTML pages. If you specify that web page as the "Action"
value for an HTML form, when you press the "submit" button, the script will
echo back to you everything that your form sent across. If this site goes off the net,
try doing a web search for "CGI test forms". Using an echo script makes it easy to
see what is going on, and hence what you need to correct.

Getting the HTTP command

Let's add a few lines of code (in bold) to our server to extract the HTTP GET command that says what file the browser is looking for. We will develop this example by extending the OneConnection class. That way, we will add just the new code in the child class, and use the existing methods from the parent. The code in the new child class is:

```
class OneConnection_A extends OneConnection {

    OneConnection_A(Socket sock) throws Exception {
        super(sock);
    }

    String getRequest() throws Exception {
        String s=null;
        while ( (s=in.readLine())!=null) {
            System.out.println("got: "+s);
            if (s.indexOf("GET") > -1) {
                out.writeBytes("HTTP-1.0 200 OK\r\n");
                s = s.substring(4);
                int i = s.indexOf(" ");
                    System.out.println("file: "+ s.substring(0, i));
                return s.substring(0, i);
            }
        }
        return null;
    }
}
```

The getRequest() method now looks at incoming HTTP headers to find the one containing a GET command. When it finds it, it writes an acknowledgement back to the browser (the "200 OK" line), and extracts the filename from the GET header. The filename is the return value of the method.

The main program will need to construct the OneConnection_A object and then call its getRequest() method. From here it is a small step to actually get that file and write it into the socket.

Here's a new class that is a child of OneConnection_A; it adds a method to get the file of the given name and write it into the socket. Since it knows how big the file is, it might as well generate the HTTP header that gives that information.

```
class OneConnection_B extends OneConnection_A {

    OneConnection_B(Socket sock) throws Exception {
        super(sock);
    }

    void sendFile(String fname) throws Exception {
        String where = "/tmp/" + fname;   // create dir if necessary
        if (where.indexOf("..") > -1)
            throw new SecurityException("No access to parent dirs");
        System.out.println("looking for " + where);
        File f = new File(where);
        DataInputStream din = new DataInputStream(
                                    new FileInputStream(f) );
        int len = (int) f.length();
        byte[] buf = new byte[len];
        din.readFully(buf);
        out.writeBytes("Content-Length: " + len + "\r\n");
        out.writeBytes("Content-Type: text/html\r\n\r\n");
        out.write(buf);
        out.flush();
        out.close();
    }
}
```

Never use println() with sockets!

The `println()` method is defined to output the platform specific line separator. This will be "\n" on Unix, "\r" on Macs before MacOS X, and "\r\n" on Windows. However, lots of TCP/IP protocols are line based, and the line is defined to end with carriage return line feed "\r\n", or just line feed "\n". So if you're an archaeologist-coder who runs Mac OS9, the println method won't output something that a socket server recognizes as a complete end of line sequence.

The Mac client will do a println, which sends a "\r", and then wait for a response from the server. The server will get the "\r" and wait for a "\n" to complete the end of line sequence. Result: deadlock! Each end is waiting for something from the other. See Apple Tech Note 1157 for more on this:

`developer.apple.com/technotes/tn/tn1157.html`

The solution is to *never use println with remote protocols* on any platform. Always use explicit "\n" characters when writing to a socket.

The main program will need to construct the OneConnection_B object and then add a call to its sendfile method. Sendfile will serve files out of /tmp, so create that directory if you are using a Windows computer. Now that our server has the ability to return files we need to build in some security. The first few lines of the method prepend the string "/tmp/" onto the filename. The code also checks that the filename does not contain the string ".." to enter a parent directory. These two limitations together ensure that the server will only return files from your /tmp directory.

The "Content-Length" and "Content-Type" are two standard HTTP headers that help the browser deal with what you send it. The blank line tells the browser that is the end of the headers and the text that follows should be displayed.

At this point you should try compiling the code, placing a test html file in the \tmp directory, and then starting the server. Browse the URL localhost/tmp/example.html and check that the browser displays the output correctly.

We have completed a basic web server. That's quite an accomplishment! The next section looks at client-side sockets again, in particular how to use a socket to pull information from a web page. It then shows the same task done by a URLConnection. We then describe the class that represents IP addresses and finish the chapter by making the web server multithreaded.

HTTP and Web Browsing: Retrieving HTTP Pages

Here is an example of interacting with an HTTP server to retrieve a web page from a system on the network. This shows how easy it is to post information to HTML forms. Forms are covered in more depth in Chapter 26, and you can peek ahead if you want.

HTML forms allow you to type some information in your browser, which is sent back to the server for processing. The information may be encoded as part of the URL, or sent separately in name/value pairs.

The Yahoo site is a wide-ranging access portal. They offer online stock quotes that you can read in your browser. I happen to know (by looking at the URL field of my browser) that a request for a stock quote for ABCD is translated to a socket connection of:

```
http://finance.yahoo.com/q?s=abcd
```

That's equivalent to opening a socket on port 80 of finance.yahoo.com and sending a "get /q?s=abcd." You can make that same request yourself, in either of two ways. You can open a socket connection to port 80, the HTTP port. Or you can open a URL connection, which offers a simpler, higher-level interface. We'll show both of these here.

Here's the stock finder done with sockets:

```java
import java.io.*;
import java.net.*;
public class Stock {

    public static void main(String a[]) throws Exception {
        if (a.length!=1) {
            System.out.println("usage:  java Stock <symbol> ");
            System.exit(0);
        }

        String yahoo = "finance.yahoo.com";
        final int httpd = 80;
        Socket sock = new Socket(yahoo, httpd);

        PrintStream out =
                new PrintStream( sock.getOutputStream() );

        String cmd = "GET /q?" +"s=" +a[0] +"\n";
        out.print(cmd);
        out.flush();

        BufferedReader in =new BufferedReader(
          new InputStreamReader( sock.getInputStream() ) );
        String s=null;
        int i, j;
    // pick out the stock price from the pile of HTML
    // it's in big bold, get the number following "<big><b>"
        while ( (s=in.readLine()) != null)   {
            if ((i=s.indexOf("<big><b>")) < 0) continue;
            j = s.indexOf("</b>");
            s=s.substring(i+8,j);
            System.out.println(a[0] +" is at "+s);
            break;
        }
    }
}
```

The Yahoo page that returns stock quotes contains thousands of characters of hrefs to ads and formatting information. Luckily it's fairly easy to pull out the stock price. From inspecting the output, it's on a line bracketed by <big><b> ... </b>, which is HTML formatting to print the number in bold face. This type of program is called a "screenscraper" and it has been replaced by XML markup, as we'll see in Chapter 27, "XML and Java.". Screenscrapers are horribly unreliable and break as soon as the web page appearance changes. Check the book website for the latest.

Given all that, running the program provides this output:

```
java Stock ibm
ibm is at 88.19
```

It was a whole lot more fun running this program in the ancient Bubbylonian era (spring 2000), than it is today. Here is the same program, rewritten to use the classes URL and URLConnection. Obviously, URL represents a URL, and URLConnection represents a socket connection to that URL. The code to do the same work as before, but using URLConnection is:

```java
import java.io.*;
import java.net.*;
public class Stock2 {

    public static void main(String a[]) throws Exception {
        if (a.length!=1) {
            System.out.println("usage:  java Stock2 <symbol> ");
            System.exit(0);
        }

        String yahoo = "http://finance.yahoo.com/q?s=" + a[0];

        URL url = new URL(yahoo);
        URLConnection conn = url.openConnection();

        BufferedReader in = new BufferedReader( new InputStreamReader(
                                          conn.getInputStream())));
        String s=null;
        int i=0,j=0;
        while ( (s=in.readLine()) != null)   {
            if ((i=s.indexOf("<big><b>")) < 0) continue;
            j = s.indexOf("</b>");
            s=s.substring(i+8,j);
            System.out.println(a[0] +" is at "+s);
            break;
        }
    }
}
```

The main difference here is that we form a URL for the site and file (script) that we want to reference. We finish up as before, reading what the socket writes back and extracting the characters of interest.

Clearly, both programs will stop working when Yahoo changes the format of the page, but it demonstrates how we can use a URL and URLConnection for a slightly higher-level interface than a socket connection. We could even go one step further and use the class HttpURLConnection which is a subclass of URLConnection. Please look at the HTML documentation for information on these classes.

How to find the IP address given to a machine name

The class java.net.InetAddress represents IP addresses and about one dozen common operations on them. The class should have been called IP or IPAddress, but was not (presumably because such a name does not match the coding conventions for classnames). Common operations on IP addresses are things like: turning an IP address into the characters that represent the corresponding domain name, turning a host name into an IP address, determining if a given address belongs to the system you are currently executing on, and so on.

InetAddress has two subclasses:

- `Inet4Address`   The class that represents classic, version 4, 32-bit IP addresses

- `Inet6Address`   The class that represents version 6 128-bit IP addresses

Your programs will not use these classes directly very much, as you can create sockets using domain and host names. Further, in most of the places where a hostname is expected (such as in a URL), a String that contains an IP address will work equally well. However, if native code passes you an IP address, these classes give you a way to work on it.

The InetAddress class does not have any public constructors. Applications should use the methods `getLocalHost()`, `getByName()`, or `getAllByName()` to create a new InetAddress instance. The program that follows show examples of each of these.

This code will be able to find the IP address of all computers it knows about. That may mean all systems that have an entry in the local hosts table, or (if it is served by a name server) the domain of the name server, which could be as extensive as a large subnet or the entire organization.

```java
import java.io.*;
import java.net.*;
public class addr {

    public static void main(String a[]) throws Exception {

        InetAddress me = InetAddress.getByName("localhost");
        PrintStream o = System.out;
        o.println("localhost by name =" + me );

        InetAddress me2 = InetAddress.getLocalHost();
        o.println("localhost by getLocalHost =" + me2 );

        InetAddress[] many = InetAddress.getAllByName("microsoft.com");
        for (int i=0; i<many.length; i++)
                o.println( many[i] );
    }
}
```

Run it with:

```
java addr

localhost by name =localhost/127.0.0.1
localhost by getLocalHost =zap/10.0.10.175
Microsoft: microsoft.com/207.46.230.218
Microsoft: microsoft.com/207.46.230.219
Microsoft: microsoft.com/207.46.197.100
Microsoft: microsoft.com/207.46.197.101
Microsoft: microsoft.com/207.46.197.102
```

The getAllByName() method reports all the IP addresses associated with a domain name. You can see from the output above that Microsoft.com, like most big sites, is served by multiple IP addresses, on two different subnets (probably for fault tolerance). Each of those five IP addresses probably represents load balancer hardware fanning out to dozens of server nodes.

A Multithreaded HTTP Server

There's one improvement that is customary in servers, and we will make it here. For all but the smallest of servers, it is usual to spawn a new thread to handle each request. This has three big advantages:

1. Foremost, it makes the server scalable. The server can accept new requests independent of its speed in handling them. (Of course, you need to run a server that has the mippage to keep up with requests.)

2. By handling each request in a new thread, clients do not have to wait for every request ahead of them to be served.

3. The program source can be better organized, as the server processing is written in a different class.

The following code demonstrates how we would modify our HTTP web server to a new thread for each client request. The first step is to make another child in the OneConnection hierarchy to implement the Runnable interface. Give it a run method that will actually do all the work: get the request, then send the file.

```
import java.io.*;
import java.net.*;
class OneConnection_C extends OneConnection_B
                        implements Runnable {

    OneConnection_C(Socket sock) throws Exception {
        super(sock);
    }

    public void run() {
      try {
        String filename = getRequest();
        sendFile(filename);
      } catch (Exception e) {
        System.out.println("Excpn: " + e);}
    }

}
```

The main program will have the server socket and it will put the accept in a loop,
so that we can handle many requests, not just the first one. It will instantiate our
connection class as before, turn it into a thread, and invoke its start method. The
code follows:

```
public class HTTPServer4 {
    public static void main(String a[]) throws Exception {

        final int httpd = 80;
        ServerSocket ssock = new ServerSocket(httpd);
        while (true) {
            Socket sock = ssock.accept();
            System.out.println("client has made socket connection");
            OneConnection_C client = new OneConnection_C(sock);
            new Thread(client).start();
        }
    }
}
```

The code seems so brief because we have draped the functionality across several
classes in an inheritance hierarchy. That was done so that the example code
would be smaller and easier to present. You should try putting the code back into
one or two classes. It's still only 50 or 60 lines long. This has got to be the world
record for the smallest HTTP server.

A Mapped I/O HTTP Server

The final section of this chapter presents the code to use the new mapped I/O facility in a socket server. As a refresher, here is a program that uses channel I/O to duplicate a file:

```java
import java.io.*;
import java.nio.*;
import java.nio.channels.*;
import java.net.*;
class DupFile {

    void copyThruChannel(String fname) throws Exception {
        File f = new File(fname);
        FileInputStream fin = new FileInputStream(f);
        int len = (int) f.length();

        FileChannel fc = fin.getChannel();
        System.out.println("allocating buff");
        ByteBuffer myBB = ByteBuffer.allocate(len);
        int bytesRead = fc.read(myBB);
        myBB.flip();

        System.out.println("getting fout channel");
        FileOutputStream fos = new FileOutputStream(fname+".copy");
        FileChannel fco = fos.getChannel();
        int bytesWritten = fco.write(myBB);
        fco.close();
    }

    public static void main(String a[]) throws Exception {

        DupFile client = new DupFile();
        client.copyThruChannel(a[0]);
    }
}
```

In a similar way, the code to update our HTTP server, so that it uses channel I/O, looks like this:

```
import java.io.*;
import java.nio.*;
import java.nio.channels.*;
import java.net.*;
class OneConnection_D extends OneConnection_C  {

    OneConnection_D(Socket sock) throws Exception {
        super(sock);
    }

    void sendThruChannel(String fname) throws Exception {
        File f = new File(fname);
        FileInputStream fin = new FileInputStream(f);
        int len = (int) f.length();

        FileChannel fc = fin.getChannel();
        System.out.println("allocating buff");
        ByteBuffer myBB = ByteBuffer.allocate(len);
        int bytesRead = fc.read(myBB);
        myBB.flip();

        System.out.println("getting sock channel");
        SocketChannel sc = sock.getChannel();
        int bytesWritten = sc.write(myBB);
        sc.close();
    }
}

public class HTTPServer4 {
    public static void main(String a[]) throws Exception {

        final int httpd = 80;
        ServerSocketChannel ssc = ServerSocketChannel.open();
        InetSocketAddress isa
               = new InetSocketAddress(InetAddress.getLocalHost(), httpd);
        ssc.socket().bind(isa);
        System.out.println("have opened port 80 locally!");

        System.out.println("waiting for accept");
        Socket sock = ssc.accept();
        System.out.println("client has made socket connection");

        OneConnection_D client = new OneConnection_D(sock);
        String filename = client.getRequest();
        client.sendThruChannel(filename);
    }
}
```

This server is single-threaded to keep the code focused on I/O. The main routine shows how you open a server socket channel, then bind it to the port of interest. From here it is easy to use mapped I/O, as shown in method sendThruChannel().

Further Reading

TCP/IP Network Administration, by Craig Hunt (O'Reilly & Associates, Sebastopol CA, 2002), ISBN 0596002971.

> The modest title hides the fact that this book will be useful to a wider audience than just network administrators. It is a very good practical guide to TCP/IP written as a tutorial introduction.

Internet Core Protocols: The Definitive Guide by Eric A. Hall (O'Reilly, 2000)

> It's a cover-to-cover read. The book's only defect is the reliance on a now-unavailable commercial tool. (The tool can be recreated for free using Ethereal, instead).

Unix Network Programming, by W. Richard Stevens (Prentice Hall, NJ, 1990)

> The canonical guide to network programming.

Exercises

1. Extend the previous example mail program so that it prompts for user input and generally provides a friendly front end to sending mail.

2. Write a socket server program that simply returns the time on the current system. Write a client that calls the server and sends you mail to report on how far apart the time on the local system is versus the time on the current system.

3. In the previous exercise, the server can only state what time it is at the instant the request reaches it, but that answer will take a certain amount of time to travel back to the client. Devise a strategy to minimize or correct for errors due to transmission time. (Hard—use a heuristic to make a good guess.)

4. Read the API for java.net.URLEncoder and URLDecoder and write a program that encodes a string into the MIME format called x-www-form-urlencoded.

5. Update the multithreaded webserver so that it can also serve JPG and GIF files and correctly identify their type to the browser. You can just use the file extension as an indicator of the contents.

Some Light Relief—500 Mile Limit on Email

This chapter's light relief is a true story about networks and system administration.

Trey Harris is a senior systems engineer, and a vice president of SAGE, the System Administrators Guild (www.sage.org). Trust me, if you have a mission-critical server, you want a guy like Trey to keep it running.

A few years ago, Trey was responsible for email at a university in the Research Triangle area of North Carolina. One day, a peculiar problem report came in from the Dean of the Statistics Department. The dean reported that there was a 500-mile limit on their email. Email to places closer than about 500 miles was usually delivered just fine. But as the Dean said, "500 miles, or a little bit more, is our current email limit."

College deans are creatures with god-like powers on campus. Even when they report something blatantly ridiculous they have to be treated with care. Trey cautiously pointed out that email didn't really work that way. The dean replied that, no, he had all the data that proved it did. When they had first noticed the problem a few days ago, the dean assigned one of the geostatisticians to gather data. After all, this was a Statistics department and that's what they do.

The geostatistician had experimented with a great many email addresses, and had drawn up a map correlating geography and email results. The map showed that the Statistics department could send email to most sites closer than 500 miles, but there was a hard cutoff much beyond that. There were some places within that radius that they couldn't reach or could only reach sporadically, but they could never send email farther than that distance.

Trey knew that whatever this problem was, it was probably caused by someone changing the system configuration. Sure enough, the dean acknowledged that the problem started after a consultant patched the Statistics department server and rebooted it. However, the consultant was certain that he hadn't touched the mail system.

Trey logged into the department's mails server and sent a few test mails. Email to his own local test account went fine. The same thing for email to Raleigh, Atlanta, and Washington. Then he emailed a user in Memphis (600 miles away). It failed. Boston failed. So did Detroit. Trey was seeing exactly the ridiculous problem that the dean reported! At this point, Trey pulled out his address book and an atlas and tried to narrow it down. New York (420 miles) worked, but Providence (580 miles) failed.

One of the first things to check on a mail delivery problem when the system has been patched and rebooted, is the sendmail.cf configuration file. It was fine. Thinking about what to try next, Trey telnetted to the SMTP port to issue a few mail commands by hand. Ah! The first clue! The system responded with the old "Sendmail 5" response that was standard with Solaris at that time, even though Trey had installed the more up-to-date Sendmail 8 throughout the campus.

The pieces quickly came together after that. The consultant had upgraded the version of Solaris, which had wiped out the mail upgrade. The version of Sendmail 5 that Sun shipped as standard could deal with most of the Sendmail 8 sendmail.cf. But the new configuration options that Trey had written with more meaningful names were all ignored and therefore defaulted to zero. One of the settings that became zero was the timeout value to allow while connecting to a remote SMTP server. Some experimentation established that on the Stats department mail server, a zero timeout would abort a connect call in slightly over three milliseconds.

Now, an odd feature of the campus network at the time was that it was 100% switched. An outgoing packet wouldn't incur any processing delay until it reached a router on the far side. So the time to connect to a lightly loaded remote host on a nearby network would actually largely be governed by the speed of light distance to the destination rather than by incidental router delays.

As Trey says, "Feeling slightly giddy, I fired up the units command." Units is a Unix command that converts between different measurement units. You tell it what units you have (like centimeters) and what units you want (like fathoms), and it tells you the conversion factor. Trey typed in the critical numbers to find out how many miles the speed-of-a-signal-in-a-wire (the physics constant "c") goes in 3 milliseconds:

```
$ units
500 units, 54 prefixes
You have: c
You want: miles  /  3 millisecond
        * 558.84719
```

There you go! "500 miles, or a little bit more."

Chapter 26

Servlets and JSP

This chapter describes two key Java technologies that are used in server-side Java: servlets and JSP.

Overview of Servlets and JSP

The first of these technologies, servlets, provides a way for a browser to cause a program to run on the server. The server calculates something, possibly accesses a database, and sends HTML output back to the browser on the client. In a nutshell, that is the architecture of all web-based B2C (business-to-consumer) e-commerce systems, from Amazon.com to the Zdnet.com online store. These are applications where the end-user interface is provided by a web browser, and the back-end logic runs on a server.

Servlets for creating web pages with the latest data

An ordinary page of HTML is static. Each time the server sends it out, it sends the exact same bytes. The only way it changes is if someone updates the HTML file with an editor. But many kinds of information change dynamically: stock prices, the weather, seats available on a flight, amount of inventory on hand, account balance, contents of an online shopping cart, and so on. Servlets and JSP are a great way to get this dynamic information into a web page. The pages that the user sees are calculated by general-purpose programs that can reference and update databases as part of serving the request.

Servlets are the most popular way for a browser to get a dynamic web page from a program on the server. The old way used an interface called CGI, and your scripts would be written in Perl or Visual Basic or some other language. With servlets, your code is written in Java. There is a size/complexity tradeoff here: small scripts (less than a couple of pages) can be written at the drop of a hat and are well suited to Perl or PHP.

What web servers and web browsers do

- **A web browser** is just a program that sends requests to the HTTP port (port 80 by default) on a server, and displays the data that the server sends back. A basic web browser can be written in a couple of hundred lines of code (if you have a GUI component that renders HTML, which Java does). It's only when people start adding support for newsreaders, mail, instant messaging, HTML editing, SETI analysis, and so on, that a browser balloons up in size.

- **A web server** is just a program that waits for incoming requests on the HTTP port, and responds by sending the contents of local HTML and image files back to the requestor.

- **A servlet container** (such as Apache's Tomcat) is an add-on to a web server. It will run a servlet program in response to a request on port 8080 by default. The output (usually HTML) of the servlet program will be sent back to the requestor.

The larger and more complicated your code, the more you will benefit from using a Java servlet. If you need to access a database, you can use Java's JDBC library. If you need threading or network libraries, Java has them. If your code needs to run with permissions-based access control, Java supports this. Instead of a mixture of different tools and libraries, you can write the whole thing in one consistent language. Perhaps the biggest advantage is that servlets free you from being tied to one kind of hardware or one software vendor. Because of Java's portability, you can easily move to more capable hardware as your processing needs increase. Your servlet code can be run by any servlet server. It's easy to add new capacity and leave the software unchanged.

JavaServer Pages for embedding dynamic web page content

The second technology we will visit in this chapter is called "Java Server Pages," modelled after the ColdFusion technology invented by the Allaire company of Boston, Massachusetts. Allaire now makes a Java servlet and JSP execution environment known as JRun that can be plugged into any web server.

Allaire's ColdFusion product was copied by Microsoft and given the name ASP— "Active Server Pages." ColdFusion, ASP, and JSP are all ways of mixing ("embedding") programming statements, scripts, and components in web pages on the server side. When the server gets a request for the page, it executes the embedded programming statements, and sends to the browser the ordinary HTML plus the HTML dynamically generated by executing the embedded code. If you are familiar with ASP, you can pick up JSP in a few minutes. To put it another way, JSP looks a lot like fragments of Java code, but embedded in an HTML page.

For small programs, JSP is simpler than a servlet. Servlets require the programmer to write Java code to output all the HTML (the fixed part and the dynamically varying part) along with all the headers that a web server adds automatically. JSP allows a programmer to write down the fixed HTML content. Then you write Java code fragments in the same web page. When a browser browses the page, the server executes the Java fragments to create the dynamically varying HTML. Then the server sends all the HTML over to the browser. The whole page looks like static content to the browser. This approach allows the server to send the full HTTP headers, including one that tells the browser the page length.

JSP is (in theory) a good way to separate the dynamic and static parts of your web page. In practice, it takes considerable discipline to prevent your JSP programs from becoming hard to maintain. So people have invented additional frameworks to help with this; the most popular is Struts from the Apache group at http://jakarta.apache.org/struts. It's an open source framework with a free download.

JSP doesn't have any extra capabilities compared with servlets, and indeed JSP is usually implemented in terms of servlets. Both servlets and JSP are big topics, covered at book length elsewhere. In this chapter we map out the territory and show working examples of each. The goals are to show you how to write basic servlets, and to cover the key points of server-side Java. This chapter can be

Just Java 2

worked through in an afternoon, and gives you enough information to know

Portability and common sense

Web-based software decouples the server from the clients and lets them run
you can keep your options open for the future. If your development team doesn't
pay attention to this, you might start a new project with Active Server Pages, and
condemn the software to only ever run on a single platform, a single operating

Mike Keating, a systems analyst in Storrs, Connecticut, explained, "IIS, ASP, VB, COM,
MTS were convenient to use because they were preinstalled on our systems, or easily
integrated, so I used them when I started building web applications a few years
ago." When the organization became interested in the Linux server operating system
for its stability, performance and low cost, the price of Window's convenience
became evident: none of the existing web applications could run on the Linux

"Having our web applications isolated on the NT platform is a big headache," Mike
commented. "We're trying to get off Microsoft-only solutions as quickly as we can.
By using Java, if we change our server OS again in the future, we can still run our
applications on any platform that supports Java—which is pretty much everything."
"If anyone is evaluating Java-based technology against Microsoft-only software,
don't think 'it can't happen to me'—you may very well find yourself some day in the
near future wishing you paid more attention to platform independence. We're
writing new projects in Java and rescuing our stranded applications as resources
permit." Even if your company will only ever be a Microsoft shop, you can avoid the
trauma of periodic Microsoft upgrades by using Java. People who tried to keep
applications running while changing from MS-DOS to Win 3.1 to Win 95 to NT 4 know

Why Use Servlets?

Server-side web programming is well established on the web. It lets you build
systems with a client part that can run in a browser on any computer, with any

Clients and servers

The HTTP protocol provides a framework for communicating with a server, where
all the real work is done. The server-side code may do load-balancing to move
incoming requests to the system best equipped to handle them. The server code
can access/update your database and process any data using the most up-to-date

The client cannot call server routines directly. It can only send over HTTP requests saying what it wants. Opportunities to subvert the server are more restricted than when everything runs on one physical system. You still need to code defensively because people may try to access your page in a way that could make the server spend all its time trying to service their request.

Client/server programming was popular even before the web went mainstream, and bringing the two together was a natural marriage. CGI—the "Common Gateway Interface"—was the first attempt to get dynamic content into web pages. CGI got the job done, but it had big problems with security and performance. CGI implementations often start up an entire new process to run a script. It doesn't have to be done that way, but in practice it usually was. Servlets are loaded into memory once, and stay around ready to handle all future requests. So there can be a big performance advantage to using servlets. It also means that servlets can choose to hold system resources (such as a database connection) between requests. Since opening and closing a database connection is a lengthy operation, this is another win for servlets.

Servlets make it easier to separate the business logic used to generate results from the HTML that displays those results. JSP takes that one step further. Separation of logic from presentation has benefits. It's an enabler for the use of component software such as Java Beans. Component software lets a system designer deploy the same code to handle a transaction whatever the origin is: web-based, online transaction, or batch processing. We're getting into enterprise-level software issues here, but servlets deliver consistency and code reuse.

What servlets replace

Servlet technology replaces the family of server plugins such as the Netscape API, CGI, or the Microsoft ISAPI, none of which are standardized or multiplatform like the servlet API. Servlets today are the most popular choice for building portable interactive web applications. Add-on software to run servlets is available for Apache Web Server, iPlanet Web Server, Microsoft IIS, and others. Servlet containers can also be integrated with web-enabled application servers such as BEA WebLogic Application Server, IBM WebSphere, iPlanet Application Server, and others.

Servlets as web services

Servlets are highly effective in implementing web services. Chapter 28 reviews two public implementations of web services. For now, think web services = "a way for a program here to run a program on a remote server and get the output back here in easily processed form".

"Apps on tap"—provisioning

People are currently driving the technology even further with a technique called "ASP" or Application Service Provision. Don't confuse Application Service

Provision with "Active Server Pages." Provisioning is all about extending the benefits of client/server systems to all kinds of application software. The idea is that instead of *buying* software and installing it locally on your PC, you *rent* access to the software at the ASP site. Instead of running a spreadsheet locally, the program executes on a server at the ASP site and sends you the equivalent data for display on your screen. Instead of running a mail program on your system, you pay Google to filter, store and serve your email to a browser client. You pay Google "in kind" by accepting the ads they insert into your messages, then Google brokers the ads for real money. Google has done pretty well with the ASP model; its 2004 revenue was about $1 Bn.

Ideally, you don't see a feature difference between using an ASP and running your programs locally, but the total cost of ownership is lower. The ASP takes care of all the system administration tasks, data backup, etc., and your PC is just used as a communications device to reach the ASP. You don't even need an expensive heavyweight PC. You can use any number of cheap or portable or wireless devices to connect to the ASP. Servlets are ideal for use in an ASP, providing a simple way to connect clients to server processing.

The ASP model has some compelling advantages and is winning acceptance. If you think this sounds like a rerun of X-Windows or Citrix technology, you are right, but the web aspect adds a significant new dimension: the ability to run from any computer, any OS, anywhere. Nobody yet knows when Application Service Providers can deliver on the early promise, but there are a number of smart people working hard to make it happen.

Releases and Versions

By agreement with Sun Microsystems, the reference implementation for servlets and JSP is maintained by the Apache Software Foundation. The Apache web server is an open source project, and by far the most widely used web server in the world. You can look up more information about the Apache Software Foundation at www.apache.org. Apache uses the project name "Jakarta" for their Java-specific work.

The servlet library is part of the Enterprise Edition of Java, so must be downloaded separately if you are using the Standard Edition. The servlet design underwent some rapid evolution at first with a number of versions and releases, but it has settled down now. Table 26–1 and Table 26–2 spell out the details, so you can relate everything to other versions you may have heard about. At the time of this writing (2004), the most up-to-date version of the servlet API is version 2.4, and that is used in this chapter. Check the Apache website listed in Table 26–2 for any later version and download and use that in preference. This technology is mature enough that there shouldn't be any drastic changes in future revisions.

The main product of Apache's Java-based Jakarta project is a servlet-and-JSP container known as Tomcat. Tomcat can run standalone as a servlet server, or it can be added on to most other web servers to process any Java requests. Tomcat was based on an earlier program known as "JServ" (in case you hear that term used somewhere). A "servlet container" is the new name for what older books refer to as a "servlet engine." It simply means the software framework within which servlets execute. We will use Tomcat as the container throughout this chapter. Tomcat is used because it is the reference implementation for servlets, because it is available for free download, and because it is compatible with the most widely deployed web server in the world, Apache. Tomcat is written in Java, so you can get it running on any computer with an up-to-date JVM.

Table 26–1   Server/servlet versions

Date shipped	Servlet container version	Compatible with servlet version	Compatible with Java Server Pages version
2003	Tomcat 5	Servlet 2.4	JSP 2.0

The servlet and JSP specifications have changed and improved as people got practical experience with the technology. JSP 1.0 allowed the use of Java beans. JSP 1.1 added support for custom JSP tags. The Servlet specification 2.3 introduced filters that allow you to do preprocessing on an HTTP request before the servlet gets it. Servlets 2.4 had a host of small improvements and a couple of features deprecated or clarified. There are additional products that combine Java and web servers at the Apache website, and it is worth visiting jakarta.apache.org to review these for yourself.

Table 26-3 lists a glossary covering all the new terms, so you can refresh your memory or refer back to it as needed.

Table 26–2   Glossary

Term	Definition
Apache	The Apache Software Foundation is a volunteer organization which has produced the most popular web server in the world, and made it available for free download. Their website is www.apache.org
Ant	A utility that accompanies Tomcat, used when Tomcat has to compile some servlet code automatically. Ant is a Java-based build utility that works out the correct dependency order in which to compile each file. It works cross-platform, unlike non-Java based tools. Ant is a replacement for "make" when used with Java.
Catalina	The servlet container (engine) part of Tomcat version 5.
CGI	The Common Gateway Interface was the first server-side scripting technology. It specifies how the server should execute a script when a particular web page is referenced. CGI scripts can be written in different languages, and Perl is a popular choice.

Table 26–2   **Glossary** *(cont.)*

Term	Definition
cookie	A cookie is a few bytes of information that the server asks the browser to store on the client, and return on demand. This token can be used to keep track of what pages the client has already seen, whether they have already given a password, and other information about the current session with the server.
HTTP	Hyper-Text Transfer Protocol. The vocabulary and standard way in which a browser and a server take turns to exchange information with each other.
Jakarta	The part of the Apache Software Foundation that focuses on Java server technology, and maintains the Java part of the Apache website. It has the Tomcat software as its centerpiece.
Jasper	The JSP server part of Tomcat.
JServ	An early implementation of the Java Servlet API from the Apache Software Foundation. It has been replaced by the Tomcat project.
JSP	Java Server Pages is a technology that allows programmers to mix together programming statements and HTML in web pages. The statements are executed and replaced with their output when the page is referenced. This server-side scripting approach was pioneered by Allaire's ColdFusion product on Windows.
Servlet	A servlet is any Java class that implements the javax.servlet.Servlet interface. It is executable by any compliant servlet container. The most common form of servlet is an HTTP servlet that responds to browser requests.
Tomcat	An open source servlet-and-JSP engine, written in Java, from the Jakarta project of Apache. Tomcat also includes a rudimentary web server, making it easy to use for development (you don't need to set up a separate web server).
POST	A request made by a browser that will upload user-entered data to the server and get back a new page. The contents of the new page will be calculated on the fly by the server. The client parameters (e.g. form data) are sent as a separate message.
GET	Similar to POST, except the browser or server may return a cached version of the page rather than calculating it anew. The client parameters (i.e. the form data) are appended onto the end of the URL.

Installing the Tomcat Software

This section describes how to download and install the Tomcat servlet web server software. Note that there is a FAQ at `http://jakarta.apache.org/tomcat/faq`. To get started on your first servlet, follow these steps.

1. Go to `http://jakarta.apache.org`, follow the links to the download page, and download the binary of the most recent version of Tomcat 5. Get the right version for your system. For Windows this is an exe file. It's a 10MB download.

2. Unpack the file you downloaded (if a zip or gz file). Run the file if it is an exe file. You'll need to provide the admin password on Windows. Accepting all the defaults works fine, although it is a Very Good Idea to install into a directory called "\tc5" instead of the default. The default pathname is way too long and contains embedded spaces, so you have to quote it every place you use it.

3. The last step in the installation asks you if you want to start Tomcat. You do. You can also stop and start Tomcat manually on WinXP through Control Panel/Performance and Maintenance/Administrative Tools/Services/ Apache Tomcat.

4. After you have started Tomcat, browse `http://localhost:8080` If everything went smoothly, you will see a page served back to you by Tomcat that looks like this:

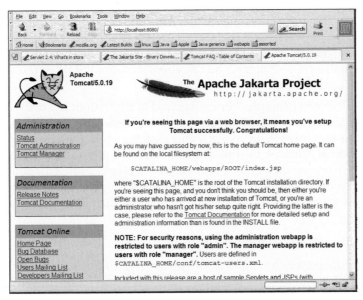

Figure 26–1   Home page of Tomcat on your system

Running the Example Servlets

Tomcat will run as a stand-alone web server, which is very convenient for development. It can also be configured to run as an adjunct to most other web servers to handle only the servlet/JSP requests. That's useful for deployment in real IT environments, and we won't get into it here.

The next step is to try running Tomcat on one of the example servlets that accompany it. First, shut down any other web servers that you have running on your system, so they don't interfere with this example. Then start Tomcat by following the steps in the following box.

Starting and stopping Tomcat

Tomcat is installed as a system service on WinXP. Start Tomcat on WinXP using the Control Panel -> (category view) -> Performance and Maintenance -> Administrative Tools -> Services -> Apache Tomcat.
On Unix, you can use the startup and shutdown scripts in the bin directory.

```
% cd $TOMCAT_HOME
% bin\startup
```

For security reasons, you should not leave a web server running on your system where outsiders may see it. There is a corresponding shutdown script in "bin/shutdown."

Tomcat serves web pages to requests that come through port 8080, so start a browser and give it the URL `http://localhost:8080`. You can use the name "localhost" or the special IP address "127.0.0.1" that means "this system." Or if your computer has a DNS name, you can also use that in the URL. You should see the page in Figure 26–1 again.

Click on the "Servlet Examples" link displayed at the bottom left of the page, and you will bring up a new page that has the top half-a-dozen examples of servlet-related things you want to do, along with a skeleton of the source code that implements them. Click on the link marked "Hello World execute". You will see the browser change to a dynamic page reading "Hello World". This demonstrates that you can successfully run the example servlets on your system. After you have read the basic example here, you can return to this URL and find sample code for the following:

- Getting the HTTP headers of this request
- Reading the parameters passed with an HTTP GET request
- Setting and retrieving a cookie
- Creating and examining session information

We cover the first two of these in this chapter. Cookies and sessions should be studied with the online Tomcat examples.

We'll now cover the material that you need to understand how servlets work. All this information might look somewhat involved, but writing servlets and JSP is easily done. One of the links reachable from the Tomcat home page is the *Servlet API documentation* at `http://127.0.0.1:8080/tomcat-docs/servletapi/index.html`

It's a good idea to keep a browser tab open on that page, and review each class as it is mentioned in the rest of this chapter.

Ports and Protocols

As we saw in Chapter 25, you use input and output streams on sockets just as though you were reading/writing a file. The class `java.net.ServerSocket` lets your server program accept incoming data by spawning off a thread with a socket that you can read client requests from. The class `java.net.Socket` lets you send data to a server socket on another computer, or read response data that is coming back into the local host.

Servlets are a higher-level alternative to reading/writing sockets. Servlets can be used to service *any* request that is made via a socket (such as FTP), not just web page requests via HTTP. A servlet that talks something other than HTTP is called a "generic servlet" and it will extend the class `javax.servlet.GenericServlet`. The vast majority of servlets are used to serve HTTP requests. These are known as "HTTP servlets," and they extend the class `javax.servlet.http.HttpServlet`.

The computer science term "protocol" means "an agreement on how to talk to each other." Browsers and servers talk to each other using HTTP, HyperText Transfer Protocol. The browser starts the conversation, and then each end takes its turn to say something. It goes back and forth over the net like a game of tennis. Each HTTP request from a browser is replied to with a response from the server.

A commercial web server is multithreaded and typically deals with many clients (browsers) at any moment, but is either reading a request or sending the response to each. The key concept of servlets is that when you browse a page on the client, it causes the servlet to run on the server.

The servlet does whatever processing was coded, and then (usually) writes some HTML to represent the answer The web server sends that newly generated HTML back to the browser for display. Just as with a regular HTML page, a servlet can be invoked many times. A servlet can cope with several concurrent requests, and it may call another servlet or forward the original request to it for processing.

The HTML to Invoke a Servlet

This section describes the HTML that will be displayed on the client and cause a servlet to run on the server. The most common way for a browser to invoke a servlet is via an HTML button that causes the entire form, with all the data the user typed in, to be sent over to the server.

There are about ten different GUI input types, but the most often used are *text, radio, checkbox,* and *submit.* For a complete list of all the input types and other attributes, do a web search on "HTML, form, guide." To make it all line up nicely on the screen, everything inside a form is often put in an HTML table.

Figure 26–2 shows an example of an HTML form, some INPUT tags, and the web page they generate. You should create a web page with the HTML shown here, and confirm that you can browse it, enter data, and click the submit button.

How form data is sent to a URL

Now we come to the question of how and where the browser sends the data from the form. The form tag will always have two attributes (omitted in Figure 26–2, for simplicity) that specify how and where the form data goes. These attributes are called *"action"* and *"method."* There are also additional possible attributes, to give the whole form a name, and to say how the data should be encoded before it is sent to the server. The default values are fine for these. An example of a complete form tag would be

```
<form  action="/servlet/petform"   method="post">
```

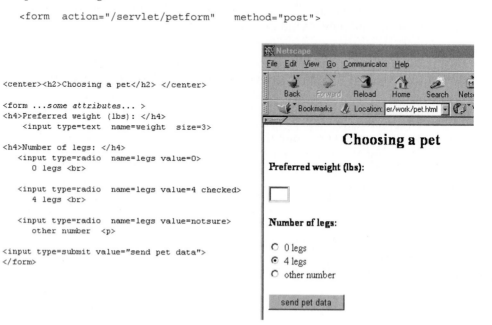

```
<center><h2>Choosing a pet</h2> </center>

<form ...some attributes... >
<h4>Preferred weight (lbs): </h4>
    <input type=text  name=weight  size=3>

<h4>Number of legs: </h4>
    <input type=radio  name=legs value=0>
       0 legs <br>

    <input type=radio  name=legs value=4 checked>
       4 legs <br>

    <input type=radio  name=legs value=notsure>
       other number  <p>

<input type=submit value="send pet data">
</form>
```

Figure 26–2   HTML example form

- The *action* attribute in a <FORM> gives the URL for the script or servlet that will process the data. It doesn't need to be a URL on the same server that served the form. It doesn't need to be a full URL. It can be a partial URL that is based on the URL of the page already being served.

- The *method* attribute specifies the HTTP approach that the browser should use when sending over the data. The two possibilities are GET and POST.

In HTML, attributes *may* be enclosed in quotation marks. In XML (which we'll meet in Chapter 27) attributes *must* be enclosed in quotation marks. So you may as well get into the habit now.

Differences between POST and GET

Reams of pages have been written about using POST versus GET in an HTML form. Originally, GET was used to ask for a file from the server, and POST was used to send data to the server. Today, either can be used to transmit form data to a server-side application. The differences boil down to this:

- POST passes the form data to the server as a series of fields in the body of the HTTP request. GET sends the data appended to the URL as a query string, like this

  ```
  http://www.yahoo.com/stocks.htm?somename=somevalue
  ```

  Since the GET data is actually added onto the end of the URL string, the user can bookmark it, and submit the same data later by going to the bookmark. This is why search engines often use GET. As it is part of the URL, the user can also see it and play around with it, which you may not want.

- GET is limited to a small amount of text data that can be appended to the address (less than 255 characters). POST handles an arbitrary amount of text and binary data and it does not show up as part of the address URL. Many web servers log URLs. If you don't want your logs to contain sensitive user data (like account names and passwords), you *must* POST it.

- GET responses can be cached anywhere along the way—by your browser, by your company's proxy server, or by the web server. With POST, the page request is required to go through all the caching layers to the server and extract the data again. So POST should be used when the servlet is counting accesses, or making a charge to see the page, or controlling who can see the page.

You will typically post form data to a servlet. The browser will send the data to the server according to the HTTP protocol. The HTTP protocol defines the contents of HTTP *requests* and *responses*. The user does not see all the text that makes up an HTTP request sent to the browser. All they see is the URL in the location field at the top of the browser. But the browser also assembles several other text strings, specifying extra administrative details that will help the server answer. These are known as "header fields." All of this together forms the "HTTP request," as shown in Figure 26–3.

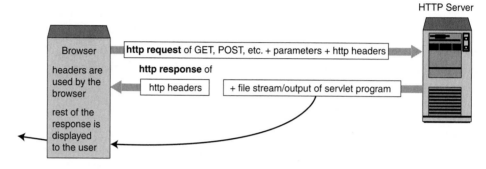

Figure 26–3   An HTTP request and response

The browser sends requests, and the server sends back responses.

The HTTP response

The header information, together with the HTML body forms the "HTTP response." The browser consumes the headers, and displays the rest of the response on the screen for the user to read. Some of the HTTP headers defined in RFC2616 are shown in Table 26–3.

Table 26–3   HTTP headers

Header	Purpose
Content-Encoding	This header tells the browser that the content has been encoded for transmission, so the browser knows it has to change it back before displaying it. The content might be zip compressed, for example.
Content-Language	This header specifies the language in which the content is written. The value is one of the language codes laid down by RFC 1766, e.g., "en" (English), "en-us" (North American dialect), etc.
Expires	This header specifies the time when the content is considered out of date, and hence should no longer be cached.
Connection	This header can have a value of "keep-alive" when persistent connections are being used, or "close" when they are not.

When you fill out and submit a form, your browser automatically adds on any necessary headers for the HTTP request. If you want to get more details on headers that can appear in an HTTP request or response, the best resource is RFC 2616 (the

Internet standard for HTTP) available at www.rfc-editor.org. You will need this information if you craft an HTTP request or response by hand in a program.

A Servlet and Its Request/Response

In this section we will present the skeleton of a servlet, and also look at the objects that it uses to learn about a request and send a response. A servlet is just like any other Java program, but one that runs inside a web server engine, termed the "container."

There are some configurations or conventions that tell the servlet container where your servlet is and what URL should invoke it. The servlet container will call your overriding methods when that URL is requested, and pass in parameters that convey all the information in the form sent from the client browser.

You create your servlet by extending one of the javax.servlet classes, and overriding one or more of the methods in it with your own code. The skeleton of an HTTP servlet looks like this:

```
public class MyServlet extends javax.servlet.http.HttpServlet {

    public void init() { /* code */ }
    public void doGet() { /* code */ }
    public void doPost() { /* code */ }
    public void destroy() { /* code */ }
}
```

This code is simplified slightly by leaving off the method parameters and the exceptions they can throw. They are shown a couple of paragraphs later. The init() method is called only once when the class is first loaded. You would use this for one-time initialization, such as opening a connection to a database. The destroy() method is also called only once when the servlet is unloaded. This method is used to free any remaining resources or do final housekeeping on shutting down. If you don't have any special startup or shutdown code, you don't need to override these methods.

The doGet() or doPost() methods are the ones that do the work of the servlet. Obviously, doGet() is called when the HTML form used a get method, while doPost() is invoked by a form with a post method.

There are other less important doSomething() methods, too, corresponding to the other things that an HTML form may do. For example, there is a doDelete() method that can be overridden for the less-common HTTP request DELETE. This request is rarely implemented because you generally don't want to empower users with the ability to delete files on the server. You might allow it on a server on your intranet. You can review other methods in the API docs that are part of the servlet kit.

All the "do" methods, like doGet() and doPost(), take the same parameters and have a void return value. E.g.

```
protected void doGet(HttpServletRequest req, HttpServletResponse resp)
                throws javax.servlet.ServletException, java.io.IOException;
```

You call methods on the HttpServletRequest argument to find out what the browser is asking for exactly. There's a method you call to get a PrintWriter from the HttpServletResponse, and you write your resulting plain text, HTML, image file, audio file, or Javascript using it. What you write gets sent back to the browser. It's as simple as that.

Note that the two routines are labelled as "protected," meaning that they can only be called by routines in the same package or in a subclass. That makes sense. It is probably not meaningful for your servlet to be called other than to process an HTTP request. If it *is* meaningful to invoke your doPost() routine otherwise, then your system design probably needs some refactoring, perhaps to split out a chunk of the common code into a Java bean.

Servlet Request

The first part of a request will be the HTTP headers, followed by the parameters. Headers are the bookkeeping information supplied automatically by the browser or server, stating things like the locale, and the version of HTTP in use. Parameters are provided by the user and passed in the query string or in the form data. A parameter name is whatever name the HTML form designer gave the parameter in an attribute. It is legal for parameter or headers to have a comma-separated list of values, so you need to be alert to this possibility in your code.

Let's take a look at the classes that implement request and response objects to see what information comes and goes. We'll start with the Java class that represents an HTTP request. Tomcat will create an object that implements this interface to hold all the data in the incoming request. Tomcat will then invoke your servlet, and pass the request object to it as an argument.

These methods are just the highlights of an HTTP servlet request object. There are about 20 get*Something*() methods in HttpServletRequest, and another 20 in its parent, ServletRequest, allowing all information in the request to be retrieved. You will invoke these methods (shown in Table 26–5) on the javax.servlet.http.HttpServletRequest parameter, as shown in the example coming up.

Notice that some of these methods, such as getHeaders(), return Enumeration objects, rather than the newer Iterator object that was intended to replace Enumeration and was part of JDK 1.2. This is for backwards compatibility with existing servlet code.

Table 26–4   Key methods of `javax.servlet.http.HttpServletRequest`

Method	Purpose
`getHeader(String s)`	Returns the first value of the header whose name you provide, or null if there isn't one of that name.
`getHeaderNames()`	Returns an Enumeration of all the header names in this request.
`getHeaders (String s)`	Returns an Enumeration of all the values of the header whose name you provide, or an empty Enumeration if there isn't one of that name. Some headers, such as Accept-Language, can be sent by clients as several headers each with a different value rather than sending the header as a comma-separated list.
`getIntHeader (String s)`	Used when you want to pull an integer out of the headers. String s is the name of the header. It will return the int value of the header, or throw a NumberFormatException, or return -1 if there is no header with this name.
`getParameter (String s)`	Returns the value of the parameter whose name you provide, or null if there isn't one.
`getParameterValues (String s)`	Works like `getParameter()`, but is used when the parameter can have several values, e.g., it may be a set of checkboxes or a multiselection list. It returns an array of String containing all the values.
`getParameterNames()`	Returns a java.util.Enumeration object containing all the parameter names in this request.
`getServerName()`	Returns the hostname of the server that received the request.
`getCookies()`	Returns an array of the cookies that came with this request. A cookie is a few bytes of data that the server sends to the browser and gets back in later requests, allowing the server to keep track of the client.

Response to a Servlet Request

Tomcat will also pass your servlet one of these response objects as an argument. The object has lots of methods that let you give values to its fields. You send back the actual data by writing to a print writer that you get from the response object.

Just Java 2

Table 26–5 shows the most frequently called methods of your response object, the HTTP servlet response.

Table 26–5   Key Methods of `javax.servlet.http.HttpServletResponse`

Method	Purpose
`getWriter()`	Returns a PrintWriter that will get written with the data part of the servlet response.
`setHeader(String n, String v)`	Adds a response header with the given name and value.
`setDateHeader(String s, long d)`	Adds a response header with the given name and time value.
`setIntHeader(String s, int v)`	Adds a response header with the given name and int value.
`addCookie(Cookie c)`	Adds the specified cookie to the response.
`setStatus(int sc)`	Set the status code for this response.
`setContentType (String s)`	Sets the response's MIME content type.
`setContentLength (int size)`	Sets the Content-Length header of the response.

You will invoke these methods on the `javax.servlet.http.HttpServletResponse` parameter, as shown in the example coming up. There are about 20 methods in HttpServletResponse and its parent class, ServletResponse, allowing just about any field to be set and returned to the browser. There are about 20 static final variables giving names to each of the status codes. You should review the javadoc descriptions of these classes.

There are about a dozen HTTP headers, but you can ignore them unless you need the special effects that they cause. The content type is the only one you need to set. You can also look a few pages further on in this chapter, in *Java Server Pages* on page 710, where we write a JSP program to echo the headers received from the browser. That shows you some typical headers.

Writing Your Own Servlet

Here is the code for a servlet that can process the HTML form that we created in the section *How form data is sent to a URL* on page 694. We're going to send a reply that suggests a suitable pet based on the weight and leg count the user submitted.

Compiling your servlet

Make sure that your CLASSPATH has the servlet jar files in it, as shown in the following command, applicable to Windows:

```
javac -Djava.ext.dirs="\program files\apache software foundation\Tomcat
5.0\common\lib" PetServlet.java
```

Note: The example command is just one line, but is too wide to print that way in a book. The "-D*property*=*value*" option defines a property with that value to the compiler system. The "java.ext.dirs" property is the pathname to a directory of jar files (in this case the Tomcat jar files) that you want to be available to the compiler or run-time. The servlet library is not part of the JDK standard edition. It is part of the Enterprise Edition. It is also bundled with Tomcat.

```java
import javax.servlet.*;
import javax.servlet.http.*;
import java.io.*;
import java.text.*;
import java.util.*;

public class PetServlet extends HttpServlet {

    private String recommendedPet(int weight, int legs) {
        if (legs ==0) return "a goldfish";
        if (legs ==4) {
            if (weight<20) return "a cat";
            if (weight<100) return "a dog";
        }
        return "a house plant";
    }

    public void doPost(HttpServletRequest req,
                       HttpServletResponse resp )
        throws ServletException, IOException {

        // get the input field values
        int petWeight = 0, petLegs = 0;
        try {
          petWeight = Integer.parseInt(req.getParameter("weight"));
          petLegs = Integer.parseInt(req.getParameter("legs"));
        } catch (NumberFormatException nfe) {
          petWeight=petLegs=-1; // indicates that we got an invalid number
        }

        resp.setContentType("text/html");

        PrintWriter out = resp.getWriter();

        out.println(" <html> <body> <h1>Recommended Pet</h1> <p>");
        out.println("You want a " + petLegs + "-legged pet weighing "
                    + petWeight + "lbs.");

        String pet = recommendedPet(petWeight, petLegs);
        out.println("<P> We recommend getting <b>" + pet );
        out.println("</b> <hr> </body> </html> ");

        out.close();
    }
}
```

Note the line that says "resp.setContentType("text/html")." It is putting some standard information in the HTML headers that are sent back to the browser. We have to provide the minimal set of headers for the HTTP response. If you are going to set any headers, make sure you do it before you start writing the content of the response. A common content type is "text/plain" for ordinary character files, and "text/html" for HTML files. It refers to the MIME encoding of the strings that follow.

MIME—Multipurpose Internet Mail Exchange

MIME encoding is a way of turning arbitrary binary files into ASCII and labelling what the data represents. MIME was developed so that binary files like JPEG images could be mailed around more easily, and it is equally useful for HTTP transactions. MIME is an abbreviation for "Multipurpose Internet Mail Exchange," and is laid down in RFCs 1521 and 1522 if you want to look it up. In this example you don't need to set any other headers.

HTTP versions 1.0 and 1.1

There are two versions of HTTP: 1.0 and 1.1. If you use any contemporary browser you get support for 1.1, which is good, but a few people out there are not using modern browsers. Among other improvements, HTTP 1.1 allows clients to send more requests to the server on the same socket that it just used. That saves time if you're getting some more content on the same web page, e.g., if you are displaying some HTML with image files. Normally, the client knows when it has got all the content because the server ends by breaking the socket connection. But if the server tells the client how many bytes are in the current response body, the client can count them as they arrive and will know when the server has sent everything and is ready for another request on this socket.

So it's good practice to set a header giving the length of the content part of each response when you know it. You can do that by assembling all the content in a ByteArrayOutputStream before sending it. ByteArrayOutputStream grows automatically as needed. Write everything to a ByteArrayOutputStream. After you have written all the data, call the size() methodof the ByteArrayOutputStream to find out how much you wrote, and do a setContentLength(). Finish up by doing a response.getOutputStream() and passing that as an argument to the ByteArrayOutputStream's writeTo() method. You don't have to copy anything anywhere. The code fragment that follows illustrates this approach. Needless to say, you must have completely finished writing any headers before you start writing the content of the response.

Keeping track of content length

```
ByteArrayOutputStream ba = null;
    private void writeBytes(String s) throws IOException {
        byte buf[] = s.getBytes();
        ba.write(buf);
    }
    public void service(HttpServletRequest req,
                        HttpServletResponse resp )
        throws ServletException, IOException {
        resp.setContentType("text/html");
        // How to calculate content length
        ba = new ByteArrayOutputStream();
        writeBytes("<P> some text <HR> ");
        resp.setContentLength(ba.size());
        OutputStream out = resp.getOutputStream();
        ba.writeTo(out);
        out.close();
    }
}
```

Three servlet tips

First, always close the output stream when you are not going to write any more to it.

Second, examine your exception handling, and try to express any problem in terms of an appropriate HTML status code if there is one. The HTML status codes are static int constants that can be found in javax.servlet.http.HttpServletResponse. For example, 404 is the dreaded "requested resource is not available".

Third, each servlet container has some way to log unexpected situations. Find out what that way is for your web server, and write log records as part of running each servlet.

Configuring Tomcat to find your servlet

Now compile and run this servlet. You can put this first example source file anywhere, but for simplicity and convenience I recommend that you put the source file and its class file in the same directory along with the examples that come with Tomcat. If you do this, no other configuration of Tomcat is needed. Tomcat configuration is still not quite as easy as it should be.

Apache and Tomcat are great web-serving engines: free, open source, widely used. Their weakness is that the information needed to configure them is not very accessible. Every web server is going to have its own configuration rules, and some are easier than others. Make sure you have set the environment variables listed at the beginning of this chapter. Then complete the example by compiling the source file in the directory specified in the following examples, setting up the HTML, starting the Tomcat server, and finally browsing the URL for this servlet.

Set up all the pathnames according to Table 26–6. This re-uses the existing Tomcat examples directory, and you can get away with minimal extra configuration

The petform.html file will contain these lines:

```
<html> <body>
<b>Choose a Pet</B>
<P>
<form  action=servlet/PetServlet method=post>

   <h4> preferred weight: </h4>
       <input type=text  name=weight  size=3>

   <h4> number of legs: </h4>
       <input type=radio  name=legs  value=0>
       0 legs <br>

       <input type=radio  name=legs  value=4  checked>
       4 legs <br>

       <input type=radio  name=legs  value=notsure  checked>
       other number <p>
    <input type=submit value="send pet data" >
</form>
```

You do need to add eight lines to the file `$TOMCAT_HOME\webapps\servlets-examples\WEB-INF\web.xml` . That file describes the URL-to-Java program mapping in XML form. Just use your favorite text editor, and find the helloworld phrase:

```
<servlet>
    <servlet-name>HelloWorldExample</servlet-name>
    <servlet-class>HelloWorldExample</servlet-class>
</servlet>
```

Copy those lines, and change it to our servlet name, PetServlet:

```
<servlet>
    <servlet-name>PetServlet</servlet-name>
    <servlet-class>PetServlet</servlet-class>
</servlet>
```

Do a similar thing a little later in the file, inserting these (different) lines:

```
<servlet-mapping>
    <servlet-name>PetServlet</servlet-name>
    <url-pattern>/servlet/PetServlet</url-pattern>
</servlet-mapping>
```

Table 26–6   Pathnames to execute your servlet

Purpose	Value
%TOMCAT_HOME% environment variable	`c:\program files\apache software foundation\tomcat 5.0`
Servlet source file	`%TOMCAT_HOME%\webapps\servlets-examples\WEB-INF\classes\PetServlet.java`

When compiling, your CLASSPATH must include (the path may differ on non-Windows platforms)	`%TOMCAT_HOME%\common\lib\*.jar`
	
	`(use the "-Djava.ext.dirs=" flag shown below)`

Command to compile the servlet	`javac -Djava.ext.dirs=%TOMCAT_HOME%\common\lib` `                PetServlet.java`
Form HTML file	`%TOMCAT_HOME%\webapps\servlets-examples\petform.html`
HTML tag that invokes the servlet	`<form  action=servlet/PetServlet  method=post>`
Browse this URL to run	`http://127.0.0.1:8080/servlets-examples/petform.html`

Be very, very careful to use the correct pathnames. If you get even one character in one of the names wrong, the example won't work, and Tomcat will give you a not very helpful 404 error.

Browser results from running the servlet

The petservlet produces a result in the browser as shown in Figure 26–4.

Figure 26–4   Result of the petservlet

Servlet deployment

To help deploy all the files to your application server, in a real system you'll create a Web Archive (WAR) of your JSPs. In this sample pet system, we'll leverage the existing file and directories for the bundled demos.

A war file is just like a jar file of your compiled servlet code, along with a WEB-INF directory and a web.xml file that describes the application to Tomcat. You can use the jar tool that comes with the JDK to create it. The file format is the same, but a different extension name was chosen to highlight the different uses of a .jar and a .war file. You write the configuration XML, and move the war file into the webapps directory. It is deployed when the servlet container restarts.

- **A .jar file** contains a set of classfiles that can be placed in a classpath. It might also be double-clickable, containing everything including a GUI needed to run an application.

- **A .war file** contains servlet and JSP class files that can only be run in the context of a web server. It will also hold a web.xml file that maps servlet pathnames used in the browser to Java servlet programs in the server filesystem.

The Tomcat configuration files use XML, which is a human-readable form that looks a bit like lots of new HTML markup tags. Chapter 27 has more information on XML. You will find that you need to stop and start Tomcat again so that it can pick up changes in your servlets. It is possible to change the configuration file so that it always looks for a newer version classfile before running a servlet. This is called making the servlet *reloadable*, but there is a large performance cost to this feature, so if you enable it, you want to turn it off again once development is complete.

Servlet development and debugging tips

Debugging a servlet presents some new challenges because the servlet container may not provide a lot of support. Tomcat allows you to set a variable in its configuration file for each servlet that represents the "debugging level" from 1 to 10. The higher the number, the more events that are logged.

Another possibility is to use `print()` statements, but since the container probably doesn't have a console window, you need to use `System.setOut()` to redirect the output to a file. This affects the whole JVM. Turn it off before production use. Another choice is to learn and use the debugger that comes with your IDE, and do your preliminary testing in that environment rather than in a real web server.

If a servlet hits an unhandled exception, the container will typically pass the Java run-time error message back to the client. That's meaningful while you are debugging a system, but should be avoided in deployed systems. You can find out the call chain at the point where an exception is handled by putting this in your code:

```
try { ...
} catch (Throwable ex) {
      ex.printStackTrace();
}
```

That stack trace will go to System.err—you probably want to redirect it somewhere useful (depending on the container.) Alternatively, you can specify a PrintWriter to send the trace to.

Finally, servlet expert Jon Skeet suggests thinking about servlets from the browser's point of view. Jon offers the following advice. A browser doesn't know there's a servlet behind the scenes; it's just talking to a web server. This simplifies program creation and debugging, because you can apply all your HTML knowledge when designing servlets.

You can design the user interface, putting in dummy static data where necessary, and then write your servlet so that it outputs the HTML you've written, along with any images needed. Each request only gets one response, so to get a page with two pictures on it, there are three requests. First, the browser requests the HTML for the page, e.g., index.html. Second, when it gets the HTML, it notices that there are two img tags, so it requests each of the images. As far as the servlet programmer is concerned, these are all independent requests. With HTTP/1.1, they may come on the same connection, but that doesn't affect you. The servlet should just write each image or page as it's requested.

HTML Frames are similar to images—there's one request for the frameset, then one request per frame. Stick to the idea that each HTML page you've written corresponds to one request, and everything will work like a charm.

Servlet Operating Cycle and Threading

Servlets typically have the operating cycle, as shown in Figure 26–5.

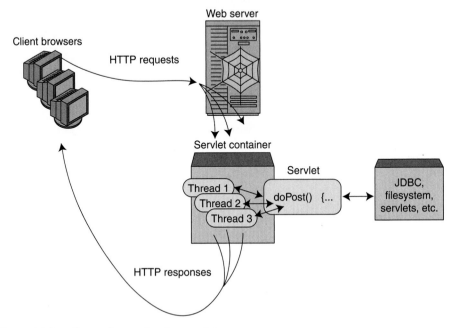

Figure 26–5   Operating cycle of a servlet

Servlet life cycle

The sequence of events in a servlet's lifetime is:

1. The servlet container starts up, and at some point constructs an instance of the servlet and calls its init() method. The init() method is only called once. Not once per request, not once per session, but once at the beginning of the servlet's lifetime. The init() method is a good place to put code to open a database connection.

2. Unlike, say, a GUI, there is no background thread always running code in the servlet. The servlet instance object just stays ready in memory, waiting for a request. This makes servlets very efficient. Eventually, a request comes to the web server, and the web server passes the request to the servlet container.

3. The servlet container instantiates a new thread to process the request. Note that the container does not instantiate a new servlet object. The newly created thread representing the request calls the doPost() method (or whatever is appropriate for this request) of the existing instance of your

servlet. The servlet can access a database, the filesystem, other servlets, etc. It creates the HTTP response, which the container returns to the client. Thread-per-request makes servlets scalable and high performance.

4. Repeat steps 2 and 3 for each request. Eventually the web server will be requested to shut down. At that point, the servlet's destroy() method is called. Then it is a candidate for garbage collection and finalization. A servlet instance will also be destroyed if you have set things up so that newer versions of a servlet are loaded automatically.

Servlets and threads

Servlets typically run on multithreaded servers and instantiate a new thread for each incoming request. This is the usual way that servers process incoming requests on a socket—create a new thread for each request for service. The use of threads means that two requests might be executing in your servlet code at the same time. Your code will need to synchronize access to any resources that are shared. This will include resources like instance variables, database connections, and static data. If you don't properly synchronize access to instance data, you will run into trouble with data race bugs.

Consider a servlet that accesses a database and puts data in an instance variable of the servlet. The servlet specification stipulates that you get a new *thread* for each invocation of a servlet, but not a new *instance* of the servlet object.

If two requests come in together and you are unlucky with scheduling, it could happen that request A gets its data out of the database, but it is overwritten in the instance variable with B's data from the database before A can use it. Then the servlet returns B's data to both A and B, confusing everyone. Chapter 14, "Advanced Thread Topics," explains synchronization in more detail.

Performance tip

Synchronization is costly in terms of time, and drags down performance. The fastest approach is to avoid class and instance variables, and thus the need for synchronization in your servlets (and other code too). Instead nest all your variables inside any method (i.e., make them local variables), and pass them as parameters as needed.
Variables local to a method can't be seen outside the method (unless you take some special action to export them). So local variables don't need to be synchronized. Similarly, objects instantiated inside a method do not need to be synchronized *as long as you don't do anything to cause them to be shared*. But you must always synchronize access to data that is visible in more than one thread.

There used to be an alternative to making your servlet thread safe. You were able to declare that your servlet implemented javax.servlet.SingleThreadModel. This has now been deprecated and should no longer be used.

Additional servlet information

There is really not much more to servlets than we have now seen. The topics outside the scope of this chapter are cookies, setting a session, security, filtering, and redirecting the request to another servlet.

A cookie is a morsel of tasty data that a server sends back to the client and can retrieve on demand. It allows the server to retain some state information for each of its clients. The information is typically something like, "what pages has the user seen?" or "has this user given the password yet?" Unless configured otherwise, the client send its cookie tokens back to the web server that they originally came from, with every web page request to that server.

A session is a way for the server to keep track of a user across a series of page requests. You would use a session to conduct an entire e-commerce transaction, with all the different pages for choosing goods, submitting credit card numbers, and so on. Cookies are often used to maintain session information. Readers who want to know more about these two matters can look at the examples in the sample code that comes with Tomcat. Start Tomcat running and then browse the URL `//127.0.0.1:8080` to see these pages.

All of these topics, including filtering and redirecting, are covered at length in the Servlet version 2.4 Specification, which can be downloaded from the Sun website. Although they call it a specification, and it's more than 200 pages long, it's easy to read and worth taking a look at. You can find it at `java.sun.com/products/servlet/index.html`.

Java Server Pages

We will conclude this tour of server-side Java with a description of Java Server Pages (JSP), and an example JSP program. One way of understanding JSP is to say that JSP is ASP, without the restriction to Windows only. Another way of understanding it is to say that JSP programs are a variant on ordinary servlets, where some of the simple tasks are automated for you. In fact, the container implements JSPs by automatically translating them into the equivalent servlet which is then run in the usual way.

A JSP is a slick way of writing a servlet

An ordinary unchanging web page contains HTML (plus Javascript perhaps). A servlet is a compiled Java program. A JSP program is a hybrid of these two. It lets you mix individual Java statements in with your HTML code. The Java code will be executed on the server when the page is browsed, and it will provide some dynamic content to the page. You might do some calculations, or put something in a loop.

Your JSP Java code fragments automatically have the missing boilerplate code added, to make a complete servlet. This servlet is automatically compiled for you by the JSP container when the page is browsed. As with servlets, JSP code is compiled once and loaded into memory on first use. A developer will typically browse all the JSP pages when deploying a system, so that users don't see the "first time through" compilation time penalty.

JSP syntax

A large part of a servlet is "boilerplate," meaning text that is the same in all servlets. The class declaration, the method signatures, and so on, are needed to make sure your code compiles, but they are the same in every servlet. JSP eliminates all that standard context. It is provided for you automatically. This can dramatically shorten the amount of code you need to write, and also makes it simple enough for non-programmers to produce JSP.

JSP uses special tags to separate the Java from the HTML. The JSP opening tag is "<%" and the closing tag is "%>". The opening tag "<%" might be followed by another character such as "!" or "@" or "="to further specialize its meaning. A very brief example here will show you best. These lines in a JSP file:

```
<b> current time is:
    <%=  new java.util.Date() %>
</b>
```

will produce a line of output like this when you browse the JSP:

current time is: Mon Feb 19 18:37:23 PST 2001

When you try this, it may take 30 seconds or so to appear because the container has to compile your JSP file the first time you browse it. If the automatic JSP compilation results in compiler error messages, these will be sent back to the client for display in the browser. When you browse the same HTML file a minute later without changing anything, the resulting page will show a different time, demonstrating that the JSP provides dynamic page content.

The piece that is new is the second line in the JSP file. It starts with the tag `<%=` which means "evaluate the Java expression that follows, convert it to String, and write it to the HTML output." Other JSP tags have their own meaning, as shown in Table 26–7.

Table 26–7   JSP tags and meanings

Start of JSP tag	Meaning of JSP tag
<%	Everything up to the closing tag "%>" is Java code (blocks, statements, declarations, etc.).
<%=	Evaluates the Java expression that follows, converts it to String, and writes it to the HTML output. Ends with "%>".
<%!	This is a Java declaration that is inserted into the body of the servlet, where it is available to all methods in the servlet.
<%@	This tag can be followed by one of several different strings, such as "method," "import," "implements," "extends." These are followed by a string that specifies the name for a Java method, package, interface, etc. This tag affects the generated Java, rather than the HTML it will output.
<jsp: useBean .../>	Has a list of attributes that specify a Java bean to invoke, and parameters to pass to it. Note that it ends with "/>". This tag uses the XML conventions.

As a further example, the following JSP code echoes back all the headers that the page received. Note that there are some variables predefined within JSP for the coder's convenience. The response PrintWriter is "out," the HttpServletRequest is "req," and the HttpServletResponse is "resp."

```
<html>
<body bgcolor="white">
<h1>The Echo JSP</h1>
<%    java.util.Enumeration eh = request.getHeaderNames();
      while (eh.hasMoreElements()) {
          String h = (String) eh.nextElement();
          out.print("<br> header: " + h );
          out.println(" value: " + request.getHeader(h));
      }
%>
</body>
</html>
```

Type this in to a file called echo.jsp and try running it using the pathnames shown in Table 26–8. Make sure Tomcat is running when you try this program, otherwise there is nothing to handle the request!

Table 26–8   Executing your JSP

Purpose	Value
Copy compiler library to Tomcat library. **Then stop and restart Tomcat.**	`copy "c:\program files\java\j2sdk1.5.0\lib\tools.jar" %TOMCAT_HOME%\common\lib`
JSP source file	`%TOMCAT_HOME%\webapps\jsp-examples\echo.jsp`
JSP class file	Generated automatically for you
Browse this URL to run	`http://127.0.0.1:8080/jsp-examples/echo.jsp`

Since we aren't sending across any parameters, we don't need to invoke the JSP with a form, and we can just directly browse the JSP file itself. If you have connected up everything correctly, there will be a small pause while Tomcat automatically generates a servlet for the JSP and compiles it. Then you should see something like Figure 26–6 appear in your browser.

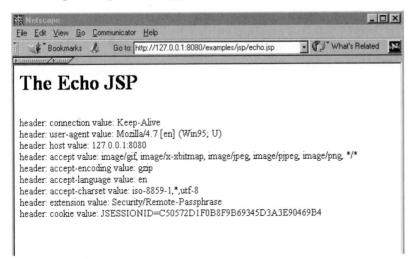

Figure 26–6   Results of browsing your JSP file

A browser doesn't know if there's a servlet, JSP, or static web page at the other end of the URL. These are the kind of headers that the client sends with any request. The headers will vary slightly on different systems and browsers. It is possible to shorten this JSP example by using the JSP tag that automatically does the output, as shown in this next JSP example.

Second example of JSP

Here's another example of JSP.

```
<html>
<body bgcolor="white">
<h1>The Echo 2 JSP</h1>
<%    java.util.Enumeration eh = request.getHeaderNames();
      while (eh.hasMoreElements()) {
          String h = (String) eh.nextElement();
%>
          <br> header: <%=  h  %>
                value: <%=  request.getHeader(h) %>
<%
      }
%>
</body>
</html>
```

Put this code in a file called echo2.jsp in directory called
%TOMCAT_HOME%\webapps\jsp-examples.
Browse URL http://127.0.0.1:8080/jsp-examples/echo2.jsp to run it. You'll see
something like Figure 26–7.

The Echo 2 JSP

header: host value: 127.0.0.1:8080
header: user-agent value: Mozilla/5.0 (Windows; U; Windows NT 5.1; en-US; rv:1.6) Gecko/20040113
header: accept value:
text/xml,application/xml,application/xhtml+xml,text/html;q=0.9,text/plain;q=0.8,image/png,image/jpeg,image/gif;q=0..
header: accept-language value: en-us,en;q=0.5
header: accept-encoding value: gzip,deflate
header: accept-charset value: ISO-8859-1,utf-8;q=0.7,*;q=0.7
header: keep-alive value: 300
header: connection value: keep-alive
header: cookie value: JSESSIONID=9A64F08FD1ED6A85EA045B4759D50B81

Figure 26–7   echo2.jsp

Use Struts to avoid JSP tangles

JSP code can become messy if you are not careful, as this example shows. Tangled
messes seem much more common than nicely separated code. People have put
effort into additional servlet-based technologies such as WebMacro
(sourceforge.net/projects/webmacro/), Enhydra (xmlc.enhydra.org), Velocity

(`jakarta.apache.org/velocity`) and Jakarta Struts, to try to enforce the separation more cleanly.

Struts in particular is gaining great acceptance. Struts is a presentation framework for building servlet and JSP applications. It encourages application architecture that uses the Model-View-Controller separation. To look into Struts, start at `http://jakarta.apache.org/struts`.

Java Beans in Servlets and JSP

This chapter wouldn't be complete without pointing out the role of Java beans on the server side. Java beans are software components, namely well-specified "modules" that do a specific job and can easily be reused in many applications. Microsoft makes extensive use of software components under the product name ActiveX, often for some visual or GUI feature.

For example, a programmer might write a piece of code that can display a set of numbers as a pie chart. That routine is very suitable for turning into a software component, making it available to any program on the system.

The point of JSP is to use lots of Java beans that cover your business processes. You might have one bean that encompasses everything you can do with a customer record, another for an order, and a third that represents a payment transaction. JSP lets you easily integrate these beans in a web-based display framework. JSP has a special tag that lets web pages on the server easily interact with beans with hardly any "glue" code needed. People call this a "tag library."

Here's an example of the tags that connect a JSP page to a Java bean that manages database access.

```
<%@ page language="java" import="java.sql.*" %>

<jsp:useBean id="db" scope="request"
  class="com.afu.database.DbBean" />

<jsp:setProperty name="db" property="*" />
```

You use the same beans (the same logic) for your non-web-based processing so you have the advantages of consistency, familiarity, and software reuse. The combination of Java beans and JSP is a major use of JSP.

Last Words on JSP, Beans, and Tag Libraries

The main reason for using JSP is that it allows web developers to quickly build web pages that interface to enterprise systems. The JSP tags let HTML designers tie web information into corporate business logic contained in Java objects without having to learn all about Java object-oriented programming.

A separate, smaller programming team can create libraries of software components. Then web designers can use those libraries by writing markup tags that they are familiar with. Use of tag libraries is one of the cornerstones of JSP. JSP thus provides a rapid prototyping framework for building two tiers (the client and the front-end server) of an N-tier distributed system.

Servlets can act as a middleware gateway to existing legacy systems, providing an easy way to web-enable your current systems. Furthermore, since all the code is on the server (not the client), when you want to update your application you just roll the code out to a few servers and your entire user base gets the newest code at once.

Further Reading

If you are interested in a more detailed study of servlets, download and read the Java Servlet 2.4 Specification from the java.sun.com website. Although its title is "Specification," it actually contains some good explanations of the details of servlets.

After you master the basics here, you can go on to get deeper knowledge from either Hall and Brown's *Core Servlets and JavaServer Pages*, 2d ed, 2003, Prentice Hall PTR, (make sure you get the latest edition) or *Servlets and JSP: The J2EE Web Tier* by Jayson Falkner, Kevin R. Jones, Addison-Wesley, 2003.

If you want to know what kind of web server a site is running, or you want to see the market share of different web servers, look at www.netcraft.com. Finally, the website www.servlets.com is a great resource for programmers writing servlets and JSP code.

Exercises

1. Modify the petform servlet so that it includes the content length in its response.

2. Write a servlet that sends back to the client (for display) all the parameters and HTTP request headers that it received. Have the servlet get enumerations of all the headers and all the parameters, and echo them back to the client.

3. Write a JSP that handles our pet selection form.

4. Earlier in this chapter, we showed an HTML form that invoked a servlet. It's actually possible to write a servlet or JSP that delivers that form as well as responding to it. When the servlet is invoked by a URL, it should respond with the HTML representing the form for pet selection. When the servlet is invoked by submitting the form, it should make the pet selection. That keeps everything relating to pet selection in one file, possibly easing maintenance. You can tell if a form was submitted by doing a requestParameter() on any of the argument names, like this: `String formSent = request.getParameter("legs")`. If the string comes back null, there wasn't a form submitted (or at least that argument was not filled in), so the servlet must have been invoked with a URL reference. The service routine should then generate the form. Otherwise, the servlet should send back the HTML with the pet selection. Write a JSP file so that it delivers the pet selection form in this way, and responds to it too.

Some Light Relief—Using Java to Stuff an Online Poll

The email to me was brief. It just read:

```
From billg@Central Mon May  4 11:57:41 PDT
Subject: Hank the Angry Dwarf
To: jokes@Sun.COM

Hey everyone.  If you've got five seconds to spare, go to the following
url:
      http://www.pathfinder.com/people/50most/1998/vote/index.html

and vote for:
      Hank the Angry, Drunken Dwarf

This is a huge joke.  We want to try to get Hank way up there on the People
Magazine 50 most beautiful people of the year list.  As of 2:00AM, he's
already up to number 5!
```

Well, I can recognize a high priority when I see one. I put down the critical bug fix I was working on, went right to the website, and checked what this was all about.

What this was all about

Every year the celebrity gossip magazine *People* prints a list of "the 50 most beautiful people in the world," and this year they were soliciting votes on their website. *People* had started the ball rolling with nominations for actors like Kate Winslet and Leonardo DiCaprio, who were in the public eye because of their roles in the Titanic movie.

People magazine gave web surfers the opportunity to write in names of people for whom they wanted to vote. A fan of the Howard Stern radio show nominated "Hank the angry, drunken dwarf" for *People*'s list. When Stern heard about Hank's nomination as one of the most beautiful people in the world, he started plugging the candidacy on the radio. A similar phenomenon took place on the Internet, and many people received email like I did. Another write-in stealth candidate widely favored by netizens was flamboyant, blond-haired, veteran pro-wrestler Ric Flair.

Hank is an occasional guest on Stern's syndicated radio program. Hank is a very short 36-year old dude who lives in Boston with his mother and enjoyed his 15 minutes of fame as a belligerent, if diminutive, devotee of beer, tequila, and Pamela Anderson.

The *People* website soon crashed under the strain of incoming votes for Hank. When the *People* poll closed, the results were as follows:

230,169 votes	Hank the dwarf	Angry, drunken dwarf and Stern radio guest
17,145 votes	Ric Flair	25-year pro-wrestling performer
14,471 votes	Leonardo DiCaprio	High school dropout
7,057 votes	Gillian Anderson	Actress
5,941 votes	Kate Winslet	High school dropout

Hank Nassif, the angry, drunken dwarf, was officially the most beautiful person in the world, by a margin of more than 10-to-1 over the runner-up! Unhappily, *People* magazine showed their true colors at this point, ignored the clear mandate from the website, and went ahead with a cover story naming the guy who came in third as the official "most beautiful person in the world" for 1998. What a rip-off.

The Java votebot

There were dark allegations here of automated voting programs, or votebots. I was shocked. But not too shocked to show you how to write a votebot using your new-found Java servlet skills.

First, find any online poll. Lots of sites run them because they are a lot cheaper than having actual meaningful content. Let's pick on, I don't know, say,

CNN.com. The goofballs in the media are always running some kind of "scientific" poll in an attempt to seem "with it" and "hip" to the latest trends and "cool slang." In October 2001, they were running a poll asking, "Is al Qaeda sending coded messages to followers via video statements?" You could answer "yes" or "no." There wasn't a box for people to respond "This kind of inane question only trivializes serious matters, and distracts attention from the real issues".

Do a "view source" on a poll web page in your browser to see how they are submitting the results. The part of the HTML page that deals with the poll will probably be a form looking something like this:

```
<FORM METHOD=POST ACTION="http://poll.cnn.com/poll?1682781"
TARGET="popuppoll">
<INPUT TYPE=HIDDEN NAME="Poll" VALUE="168278">
<!-- Question 1 --><INPUT TYPE=HIDDEN NAME="Question" VALUE="1">
<SPAN class="BoxStory">
Is al Qaeda sending coded messages to followers via video statements?
<BR><BR></SPAN>
</TD> </TR>

<!-- Answer 1 -->
<TR> <TD>
<SPAN class="BoxStory"> Yes </SPAN>
</TD>
<TD align=center><INPUT TYPE=RADIO NAME="Answer168279" VALUE=1>
</TD> </TR> <!-- /end Answer 1 -->

<!-- Answer 2 -->
<TR> <TD>
<SPAN class="BoxStory"> No </SPAN>
</TD>
<TD align=center><INPUT TYPE=RADIO NAME="Answer168279" VALUE=2>
</TD> </TR>
```

So that tells us this is a simple form which is posted to URL "http://poll.cnn.com/," the script is called "poll," its argument is called "1682781," and the name/value posted is "Answer168279=1" for yes, and "Answer168279=2" for no. There is a hidden attribute giving the question number, too.

It doesn't matter which way you stuff this or any poll; the point is that a news organization needs to decide if it is in the news business or the entertainment business.

Here's the program to do it.

```
// implements a votebot to stuff Internet polls
import java.io.*;
import java.net.*;
public class votebot {
    public static void main (String args[]) {
        try {
            for (int i=0; i<1000; i++) {
                URL u = new URL ("http://poll.cnn.com");
                URLConnection uc = u.openConnection();
                uc.setDoOutput (true);
                OutputStream os = uc.getOutputStream();
                PrintStream ps = new PrintStream (os);
                ps.print ("GET /poll?1682781p\r\n");
                ps.print ("Question=1&Answer168279=2\r\n");
                System.out.print (".");
            }
        } catch (Exception ex) {
            System.out.println ("Excpn: "+ex.getMessage());
        }
    }
}
```

If this doesn't work for you, the likeliest reason is the polling site employing electronic countermeasures, such as discarding multiple inputs from one IP address. Or the "poll" may in fact be completely fake and discard all input from anyone at all times. If they are caching IP addresses to prevent multiple votes, then you need to forge your outgoing IP address. There is no way to do that from Java. But if you have a better idea, please send me email!

Chapter 27

XML and Java

This chapter is in three parts. The first part describes XML, what it's for, and how you use it. It's straightforward and is described in a couple of sections in the chapter. The largest part of this chapter describes Java support for XML, covering how you access and update XML documents. The XML world defines two different algorithms for accessing XML documents ("everything at once" versus "piece by piece"), and Java supports them both. We put together a Java program that uses each of these algorithms. The third part of the chapter explains how to use the Java library for XML so you can trying running the code for yourself.

XML Versus HTML

You'll probably be relieved to hear that the basics of XML can be learned in a few minutes, though it takes a while longer to master the accompanying tools and standards. XML is a set of rules, guidelines, and conventions for describing structured data in a plain text editable file. The abbreviation XML stands for "eXtensible Mark-up Language."

XML is related to the HTML used to write web pages, and has a similar appearance of text with mark-up tags sprinkled through it.

- HTML mark-up tags are things like `<br>` (break to a new line), `<table>` (start a table), and `<li>` (make an entry in a list). In HTML the set of mark-up tags are fixed in advance, and the only purpose for most of them is to guide the way something looks on the screen.

- With XML, you define your own tags and attributes (and thus it is "extensible") and you give them meaning, and that meaning goes way beyond minor points like the font size to use when printing something out.

XML advantages over HTML

Don't make the mistake of thinking that XML is merely "HTML on steroids." Although we approach it from HTML to make it easy to explain, XML does much more than HTML does. XML offers the following advantages:

- It is an archival representation of data. Because its format is in plain text and carried around with the data, it can never be lost. That contrasts with binary representations of a file which all too easily become outdated. If this was all it did, it would be enough to justify its existence.

- It provides a way to web-publish files that can be directly processed by computer, rather than merely human-readable text and pictures.

- It is plain text, so it can be read by people without special tools.

- It can easily be transformed into HTML, or PDF, or data structures internal to a program, or any other format yet to be dreamed up, so it is "future-proof."

- It's portable, open, and a standard, which makes it a great fit with Java.

We will see these benefits as we go through this chapter. XML holds the promise of taking web-based systems to the next level by supporting data interchange everywhere. The web made everyone into a publisher of human-readable HTML files. XML lets everyone become a publisher or consumer of computer-readable data files.

Keep that concept in mind as we go through this example.

HTML—a good display format and not much else

We'll start with HTML because it's a good way to get into XML. Let's say you have an online business selling CDs of popular music. You'll probably have a catalog of your inventory online, so that customers know what's in stock. Amazon.com works exactly like this. One possibility for storing your inventory is to put it in an HTML table. Each row will hold information on a particular CD title, and each column will be the details you keep about a CD—the title, artist, price, number in stock, and so on. The HTML for some of your online inventory might look like this:

```
<table>
<tr> <th>title</th>   <th>artist</th>   <th>price</th>   <th>stock</th>   </tr>

<tr> <td>The Tubes</td>   <td>The Tubes</td>   <td>22</td>  <td>3</td>   </tr>

<tr> <td>Some Girls</td>   <td>Rolling Stones</td>   <td>25</td>  <td>5</td>   </tr>

<tr> <td>Tubthumper</td>   <td>Chumbawamba</td>   <td>17</td>  <td>6</td>   </tr>
</table>
```

We are using tags like `<tr>` to define table rows. When you display it in a web page, it looks like Figure 27–1.

```
 Bookmarks   Location: file://c:/jj4/table1.html
 Instant Message   Internet   Lookup   New&Cool   R

  title       artist      price stock
The Tubes   The Tubes      22    3
Some Girls  Rolling Stones 25    5
Tubthumper  Chumbawamba    17    6
```

Figure 27–1   HTML table displayed in a browser

The HTML table is a reasonable format for displaying data, but it's no help for all the other things you might want to do with your data, like search it, update it, or share it with others.

Say we want to find all CDs by some particular artist. We can look for that string in the HTML file, but HTML doesn't have any way to restrict the search to the "artist" column. When we find the string, we can't easily tell if it's in the title column or the artist column or somewhere else again. HTML tables aren't very useful for holding data with a variable number of elements. Say imported CDs have additional fields relating to country, genre, non-discount status, and so on. With HTML, we have to add those fields to all CDs, or put imported CDs in a special table of their own, or find some other hack.

XML does things that HTML cannot

This is where XML comes in. The basic idea is that you represent your data in character form, and each field (or "element," as it is properly called) has tags that say what it is. It looks that straightforward! Just as with HTML, XML tags consist of an opening angle bracket followed by a string and a closing angle bracket. The XML version of your online CD catalog might look like this:

```
<cd> <title>The Tubes</title>    <artist>The Tubes</artist>
     <price>22</price>           <qty>3</qty>   </cd>

<cd> <title>Some Girls</title>   <artist>Rolling Stones</artist>
     <price>25</price>   <qty>5</qty>   </cd>

<cd> <title>Tubthumper</title>   <artist>Chumbawamba</artist>
     <price>17</price>   <qty>6</qty>   </cd>
```

It looks trivial, but the simple act of storing everything as character data and wrapping it with a pair of labels saying what it is opens up some powerful possibilities that we will get into shortly. XML is intended for some entirely different uses than displaying in a browser. In fact, most browsers ignore tags that they don't recognize, so if you browse an XML file you'll just get the embedded text without tags (unless the browser recognizes XML, as recent versions of Microsoft's Internet Explorer do).

Don't double-wrap data; transform it

Should we also wrap HTML around the XML so it can be displayed in a browser? You could do that, but it is not the usual approach. XML is usually consumed by data-processing programs, not by a browser. The purpose of XML is to make it easy for enterprise programs to pass around data together with their structure.

It's much more common to keep the data as records in a database, extract and convert it into XML on demand, pass the XML around, then have a servlet or JSP program read the XML and transform it into HTML on the fly as it sends the data to a browser. The Java XSLT library, in package javax.xml.transform, does exactly that. Let us go on to make a few perhaps obvious remarks about the rules of XML.

Summary of the XML/HTML key differences
- HTML was created to *display data* and focus on *how the data looks*
- XML was created to *describe data* and focus on *what the data is*
- HTML is used to make text presentable and readable by people
- XML is a format to store and exchange data. It can be read by computers and people
- XML is a portable way to describe data for a program
- Java is a portable way to process data in a program

Some Rules of XML

XML follows the same kind of hierarchical data structuring rules that apply throughout most programming languages, and therefore XML can represent the same kind of data that we are used to dealing with in our programs. As we'll see later in the chapter, you can always build a tree data structure out of a well-formed XML file and you can always write out a tree into an XML file. When you want to send XML data to someone, the XML file form is handy. When you want to process the data, the in-memory tree-form is handy. The purpose of the Java XML API is to provide classes that make it easy to go from one form to the other, and to grab data on the way.

The XML element

Notice that all XML tags come in matched pairs of a begin tag and an end tag that surround the data they are describing, like this:

```
<someTagName>    some data appears here    </someTagName>
```

The whole thing—start tag, data, and end tag—is called an *element*.

You can nest elements inside elements, and the end tag for a nested element must come before the end tag of the thing that contains it. Here is an example of some XML that is not valid:

```
<cd>    <title>White Christmas  </cd>  </title>
```

It's not valid because the title field (or "element" to use the proper term) is nested inside the cd element, but there is no end tag for it before we reach the cd end tag. This proper nesting requirement makes it really easy to check if a file has properly nested XML. You can just push start tags onto a stack as they come in. When you reach an end tag, it should match the tag on the top of the stack. If it does, pop the opening tag from the stack. If the tag doesn't match, the file has badly nested XML.

XML attributes

Just as some HTML tags can have several extra arguments or "attributes," so can XML tags. The HTML `<img>` tag is an example of an HTML tag with several attributes. The `<img>` tag has attributes that specify the name of an image file, the kind of alignment on the page, and even the width and height in pixels of the image. It might look like this:

```
<img  src="cover.jpg"  height="150"  width="100"  align="right">
```

In HTML, we can leave off the quotes around attribute values unless the values contain spaces. In XML, attribute values are *always* placed in quotation marks, and you must not put commas in between attributes. We could equally describe our CD inventory using attributes like this:

```
<cd  title="The Tubes"  artist="The Tubes"  price="22"  qty="3"> </cd>
```

As frequently happens in programming, a software designer can express an idea in several different ways. Some experts recommend avoiding the use of attributes in XML where possible, for technical reasons having to do with expressiveness.

XML comments

Comments have the same appearance as in HTML, and can be put in a file using this tag (everything between the two pairs of dashes is a comment):

```
<!-- comments  -->
```

Well-formed XML documents

XML tags are case-sensitive.

XML is generally much stricter about what constitutes a good document than is HTML. This strictness makes it easier for a program to read in an XML file and understand its structure. It doesn't have to check for 50 different ways of doing something. An XML document that keeps all the rules about always having a matching closing tag, all tags being properly nested, and so on is called a "*well-formed*" document. There is a complete list of all the rules in the XML FAQ at www.ucc.ie/xml/.

The Document Type Definition (DTD)

There is another level of data validation in addition to a document being "well-formed." You also want to be able to check that the document contains only elements that you expect, all the elements that you expect, and that they only appear where expected. For example, we know this is not a valid CD inventory entry:

```
<cd>  <price>22</price>  <qty>3</qty>  </cd>
```

It's not valid because it doesn't have a title or artist field. Although we have three in stock, we can't say what it is three of.

What a DTD does

XML files therefore usually have a Document Type Definition or "DTD" that specifies how the elements can appear. The DTD expresses which tags can appear, in what order, and how they can be nested. The DTD can be part of the same file, or stored separately in another place. A well-formed document that also has a DTD and that conforms to its DTD is called *valid*.

DTD syntax

The DTD is itself written using something close to XML tags, and there is a proposal underway to align the DTD language more closely to XML. You don't need to be able to read or write a DTD to understand this chapter, but we'll go over the basics anyway. There is a way to specify that some fields are optional and thus might not be present. In other words, it's the usual type of "a *foo* is any number of *bars* followed by at least one *frotz*" grammar that we see throughout programming, with its own set of rules for how you express it. Here's a DTD that specifies our CD inventory XML file.

```
<!ELEMENT inventory (cd)* >
    <!ELEMENT cd (title, artist, price, qty)>
        <!ELEMENT title (#PCDATA)>
        <!ELEMENT artist (#PCDATA)>
        <!ELEMENT price (#PCDATA)>
        <!ELEMENT qty (#PCDATA)>
```

White space is not significant in an XML file, so we can indent elements to suggest to the human reader how they are nested. The first line says that the outermost tag, the top-level of our document, will be named "inventory," and this is followed by zero or more "cd" elements (that's what the asterisk indicates). Each cd element has four parts: title, artist, price, and qty, in that order. Definitions of those follow in the DTD. "#PCDATA" means that the element contains only "parsed character data," and not tags or other XML information.

XML documents are trees

When you get down to the bottom level, every element is either "CDATA"—character data that is not examined by the parser—or "PCDATA"—parsed character data meaning the string of an element. The nesting rule automatically forces a certain simplicity on every XML document which takes on the structure known in computer science circles as a tree.

XML documents begin with a tag that says which version of XML they contain, like this:

```
<?xml version="1.0"?>
```

This line is known as the "declaration" and it may also contain additional information, in the form of more attributes, about the character set and so on. By convention, the next tag gives the name of the root element of the document. It also has the DTD nested within it, or it gives the filename if the DTD is in another file. Here's what the tag looks like when it says "the DTD is in a file called "invfile.dtd":

```
<!DOCTYPE inventory  SYSTEM "inv-file.dtd" >
```

The version and DTD information is called the "prolog," which comes at the start of an XML document. The marked-up data part of the XML file is called the "document instance." It's an instance of the data described by the DTD.

Sections of an XML document

Figure 27–2 shows the different sections of an XML document and the names given to them. This example shows how the DTD looks when it is part of the XML file, rather than a separate file.

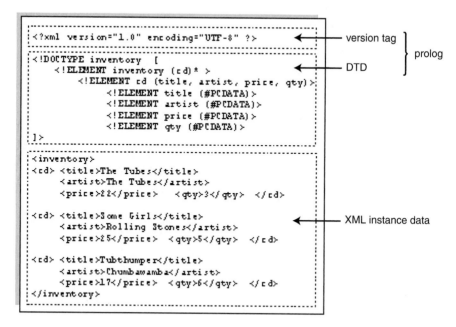

Figure 27–2   The parts of an XML file

XML and namespaces

An important recent feature of XML is "namespaces." A "namespace" is a computer science term for a place where a bunch of names (identifiers) can exist without interfering with any other bunches of names that you might have laying around. For instance, an individual Java method forms a namespace. You can give variables in a method any names you like, and they won't collide with the names you have in any other method. A Java package forms a namespace.

When you refer to something by its full name, including the package name and class name, you unambiguously say what it is, and it cannot get mixed up with any other name that has identical parts. If we refer to "List" in our Java code, it may not be clear what we mean. If we write java.util.List or java.awt.List, we are saying which List we mean unambiguously by stating the namespace (the package) it belongs to. The reference cannot be confused with any other.

XML supports namespaces, so the markup tags that you define won't collide with any similarly named tags from someone else. When you give the name of a tag at the start of an element, you can also supply an attribute for that tag, saying which namespace it comes from. The attribute name is "xmlns" meaning "XML NameSpace," and it looks like this:

```
<artist xmlns="http://www.example.com/inventory" >
Rolling Stones
</artist>
```

This says that the artist element, and any elements contained within it, are the ones that belong to the namespace defined at www.example.com/inventory. You define a namespace within a DTD by adding a "xmlns=something" attribute to the element's tag. By mentioning a namespace in the XML as in the example above, the CD inventory "artist" element will not be confused with any other element that uses the name "artist." Namespaces are useful when you are building up big DTDs describing data from several domains. However, note that the Java XML parsers do not support namespaces in the current release.

DTD for Shakespeare's plays

Here's a longer example of a DTD giving the XML format of Shakespearean plays! This shows the power of XML—you can use it to describe just about any structured data. This example is taken from the documentation accompanying Sun's JAXP library. It was written by Jon Bosak, the chief architect of XML. You'll notice a few more DTD conventions. A "?" means that element is optional. A "+" means there must be at least one of those things, and possibly more. You can group elements together inside parentheses.

DTD for Shakespeare's plays

```
<!-- DTD for Shakespeare    J. Bosak    1994.03.01, 1997.01.02 -->
<!-- Revised for case sensitivity 1997.09.10 -->
<!-- Revised for XML 1.0 conformity 1998.01.27 (thanks to Eve Maler) -->

<!-- <!ENTITY amp "&#38;#38;"> -->
<!ELEMENT PLAY      (TITLE, FM, PERSONAE, SCNDESCR, PLAYSUBT, INDUCT?,
                                          PROLOGUE?, ACT+, EPILOGUE?) >
<!ELEMENT TITLE    (#PCDATA) >
<!ELEMENT FM       (P+) >
<!ELEMENT P        (#PCDATA) >
<!ELEMENT PERSONAE (TITLE, (PERSONA | PGROUP)+) >
<!ELEMENT PGROUP   (PERSONA+, GRPDESCR) >
<!ELEMENT PERSONA  (#PCDATA) >
<!ELEMENT GRPDESCR (#PCDATA) >
<!ELEMENT SCNDESCR (#PCDATA) >
<!ELEMENT PLAYSUBT (#PCDATA) >
<!ELEMENT INDUCT   (TITLE, SUBTITLE*, (SCENE+|(SPEECH|STAGEDIR|SUBHEAD)+)) >
<!ELEMENT ACT      (TITLE, SUBTITLE*, PROLOGUE?, SCENE+, EPILOGUE?) >
<!ELEMENT SCENE    (TITLE, SUBTITLE*, (SPEECH | STAGEDIR | SUBHEAD)+) >
<!ELEMENT PROLOGUE (TITLE, SUBTITLE*, (STAGEDIR | SPEECH)+) >
<!ELEMENT EPILOGUE (TITLE, SUBTITLE*, (STAGEDIR | SPEECH)+) >
<!ELEMENT SPEECH   (SPEAKER+, (LINE | STAGEDIR | SUBHEAD)+) >
<!ELEMENT SPEAKER  (#PCDATA) >
<!ELEMENT LINE     (#PCDATA | STAGEDIR)*>
<!ELEMENT STAGEDIR (#PCDATA) >
<!ELEMENT SUBTITLE (#PCDATA) >
<!ELEMENT SUBHEAD  (#PCDATA) >
```

The DTD says that a Shakespearean play consists of the title, followed by the FM ("Front Matter"—a publishing term), personae, a scene description, a play subtext, a possible induction, a possible prologue, at least one (and maybe many) act, then finally, an optional epilogue. I asked Jon Bosak why he didn't use white space to better format this DTD. He explained that it's hard to do for non-trivial DTDs, although people are doing it more now with schemas (data descriptions) that are truly based on XML.

One programmer recently wrote a DTD describing the format of strip cartoons and published it on the `slashdot.com` website. It's a very flexible data description language! You don't need to be able to read and write DTDs as part of your work, but it doesn't hurt. There are automated tools called DTD editors that let you specify data relationships in a user-friendly way and automatically generate the corresponding DTD. There are a few additional DTD entries and conventions, but this summary provides a strong enough foundation of XML to present the Java features in the rest of the chapter.

What Is XML Used For?

There seems to be agreement from all sides that XML has a bright future. Microsoft chief executive Steve Ballmer said that he thinks use of XML will be a critically important trend in the industry. Why is this? What motivated XML's design?

The origins of XML

XML was developed in the mid 1990s under the leadership of Sun Microsystems employee Jon Bosak. Jon was looking for ways to use the Internet for more than just information delivery and presentation. He wanted to create a framework that would allow information to be self-describing. That way applications could guarantee that they could access just about any data. That in turn would clear the path to intelligent data-sharing between different organizations. And *that* in turn would allow more and much better applications to be written and increase the demand for servers to run them on. Well, that last part isn't a goal, but it's certainly a great side effect for anyone in the computer hardware industry.

XML solves data incompatibility

Information access might not sound like a problem in these days of web publishing, but it used to be a significant barrier. The web is still not a good medium for arbitrary binary data or data that is not text, pictures, or audio. A few years ago, every hardware manufacturer had a different implementation of floating-point hardware, and the formats were incompatible between different computers. If you had a tape of floating-point data from an application run on a DEC minicomputer, you had to go through unreasonable effort to process it on another manufacturer's mainframe. IBM promoted its EBCDIC (Extended Binary Coded Decimal Interchange Code) convention over the ASCII (American Standard Code for Information Interchange) codeset standardized in the rest of the Western world. People who wanted to see their printouts in Japanese resorted to a variety of non-standard approaches.

By storing everything in character strings, XML avoids problems of incompatible byte order (big-endian/little-endian) that continue to plague people sharing data in binary formats. By stipulating Unicode or UTF encoding for the strings, XML opens up access to all the locales in the world, just as Java does.

XML makes your data independent of any vendor or implementation or application software. In the 1960s, IBM launched a transaction processing environment called CICS. CICS was an acronym for "Customer Information Control System." When a site used CICS, after a while it usually became completely dependent on it, and had to buy large and continuing amounts of hardware and support from IBM in order to keep functioning. People used to joke that it was the customer that was being controlled, not the information. But it was no joke if you were in that position. Modern software applications cause the same kind of single-vendor lock-in today. XML goes a long way to freeing your data from this hidden burden. But note this key point: just because something is published in XML does not make it openly available. The DTD and semantic meaning of the tags must also be published before anyone can make sense of non-trivial documents.

XML means we can all just get along

So XML makes it possible for otherwise incompatible computer systems to share data in a way that all can read and write. XML markup can also be read by people because it is just ordinary text. So what new things can be done with XML? XML opens up the prospect of data comparisons and data sharing at every level on the web. If you want to buy a digital camera online today, you might spend a few hours visiting several retailer websites and jotting down your comparison shopping notes. With XML, you take a copy of the merchants' product datasheets and run an automated comparison sorted in order of the product characteristics that matter most to you. Even more important, if you're a business that needs to buy 1,000 digital cameras for resale, XML lets you put this business-to-business transaction up for bid in an automated way.

Requirements for B2B XML processes

Two things have to happen for business-to-business (B2B) automated XML bids and comparisons to occur.

• First, suppliers have to use a common DTD for describing their wares online.

• Second, someone has to write the comparison software, probably as a web service (see Chapter 28).

Neither of these is outlandish. Various industry groups have already started to cooperate on common data descriptions. The best known are RosettaNet for electronics, and Acord for insurance. The development community is also working on XML-based protocols to let software components and applications communicate using over HTTP. One contender here is SOAP—Simple Object Access Protocol—from IBM, HP, Microsoft, and others.

XML gives content providers a data format that does not tie them to particular script languages, authoring tools, and delivery engines. XML supports a standardized, vendor-independent, level playing field upon which different authoring and delivery tools may freely compete.

XML Versions and Glossary

Table 27–1 contains the latest version numbers relating to XML. This chapter describes the most up-to-date version of everything available at the time of this writing (Summer 2004).

Table 27–1   XML-related version numbers

API	Version number	Description
JAXP	Ver. 1.2	Java API for XML processing. Includes an XSLT framework based on TrAX (Transformation API for XML) plus updates to the parsing API to support DOM Level 2 and SAX version 2.0. The remainder of this chapter has more information on JAXP.
XSLT	Ver. 1	XSLT is a conversion language standardized by W3C that can be used to put XML data in some other form such as HTML, PDF, or a different XML format. For example, you can use XSLT to convert an XML document in a format used by one company to the format used by another company. See www.zvon.org for a tutorial on "eXtensible Stylesheet Language Transformations" (XSLT).
SAXP	Ver. 2.0	Simple API for XML Parsing. This is covered later in this chapter.
DOM	Level 2	Document Object Model, which is another API for XML parsing. This is covered later in this chapter.
JAXM	Ver. 1.1.2	Java Architecture for XML Messaging. A new specification that describes a Java library for XML-based messaging protocols. Objects and arguments (messages) will be turned into XML and sent to other processes and processors as streams of characters.
JAXB	Ver. 1.0	Java Architecture for XML Binding. A convenient new Java library for XML parsing under development by Sun.

Table 27–2 contains a glossary of terms that you can review and refer back to as necessary.

As should be clear from the alphabet soup of different libraries and versions, XML is an emerging technology, and Java support for XML is evolving rapidly—on Internet time in fact.

Table 27–2   XML-related glossary

Name	Example	Description
start tag	`<artist>`	Marks the beginning of an element.
end tag	`</artist>`	Marks the end of an element.
element	`<price>17</price>`	A unit of XML data, complete with start and end tags.
DTD	See *The Document Type Definition (DTD)* on page 726	Document Type Definition, specifying which tags are valid, and what are the acceptable ways of nesting them in the document.
entity	`&LT;`	An entity is essentially a shorthand way of referring to something. Here, the four characters "<" form an entity representing a left chevron, which has special meaning if it appears literally. An entity is a distinct individual item that is included in an XML document by referencing its name. This item might be as small as an individual character, or a text string, or a complete other XML file, or it may be a reference to something defined earlier in this XML file. All entities have to be declared in the DTD before they can be used.
attribute	`<foo someName="someValue" ...`	The **someName="someValue"** string pair holds additional information or detail about an element.
JAXP	See chapter text	The Java API for XML processing. A package of classes that support a Java interface to XML. The package name is javax.xml, introduced in JDK 1.4
JAXB	N/A	The Java Architecture for XML Binding— a follow-up library to JAXP, which handles all the details of XML parsing and formatting. It can be more efficient than using a SAX (Simple API for XML) parser or an implementation of the DOM (Document Object Model) API. An early draft was released in July 2001.
XML	See chapter text	eXtensible Mark-up Language.
XSLT	See chapter text	eXtensible Stylesheet Language Transformations, a standard for transforming XML into text or other XML documents. An XSLT implementation was introduced with JDK 1.4.
URI	`ftp://ftp.best.com`	Uniform Resource Identifier. The generic term for all types of names and addresses that refer to objects on the World Wide Web. A URL is one kind of URI.
URL	`http://www.afu.com`	Uniform Resource Locator. The address of a website or web page. The first part of the address specifies the protocol to use (e.g., FTP, HTTP). The second part of the address gives the IP address or domain name where the resource is located.

JAXP Library Contents

This is a good point to review the packages that make up the Java XML library, their purpose, and their classes. The different package names reflect the different origins of the code. The Java interfaces came from Sun Microsystems, the DOM implementation came from the W3C, and the SAX parser implementation came from yet a third organization.

Package: `javax.xml.parsers`

- Purpose: Is the Java interface to the XML standard for parsing.

- Contains these classes/interfaces: DocumentBuilderFactory, DocumentBuilder, SAXParserFactory, SAXParser. These get instances of a Parser and undertake a parse on an XML file.

Package: `javax.xml.transform`

- Purpose: is the Java interface to the XML standard for tree transformation

- Contains: classes to convert an XML tree into an HTML file or XML with a different DTD. Tree transformation is beyond the scope of this text, but you can read more about it by searching for "transform" at java.sun.com.

Package: `org.w3c.dom`

- Purpose: has the classes that make up a DOM tree in memory

- Contains these classes/interfaces: Node plus its subtypes: Document, DocumentType, Element, Entity, Attr, Text, etc.

Package: `org.xml.sax`

- Purpose: has the classes that can be used to navigate the data returned in a SAX parse

- Contains: two packages org.xml.sax.ext (extensions) and org.xml.sax.helpers plus these classes/interfaces: Attributes, ContentHandler, EntityResolver, DTDHandler, XMLReader. The helpers package contains the DefaultHandler class which is typically extended by one of your classes to handle a SAX parse, as explained below.

All the listed packages are kept in a file called jaxp.jar. The JAXP distribution also includes two other jar files: crimson.jar and xalan.jar. Crimson.jar holds the DOM and SAX parser implementations. Xalan.jar contains the implementation of the xml transformation interface. Make sure that the right jar files are in your path for the features you are using.

Because of the seemingly unrelated package names, XML parsing may appear a little unorganized. Just remember it this way: You always need the java.xml.parsers package. And you need the package with "dom" in its name to do a DOM parse, or "sax" in its name to do a SAX parse. The SAX packages also have the error-handling classes for both kinds of parse.

Reading XML With DOM Parsers

XML documents are just text files, so you could read and write them using ordinary file I/O. But you'd miss the benefits of XML if you did that. Valid XML documents have a lot of structure to them, and we want to read them in a way that lets us check their validity, and also preserve the information about what fields they have and how they are laid out.

What we need is a program that reads a flat XML file and generates a tree data structure in memory containing all the information from the file. Ideally, this program should be general enough to build that structure for all possible valid XML files. Processing an XML file is called "parsing" it. Parsing is the computer science term (borrowed from compiler terminology) for reading something that has a fixed grammar, and checking that it corresponds to its grammar. The program is known as an "XML parser." The parser provides a service to application programs. Application programs hand the parser a stream of XML from a document file or URL, the parser does its work and then hands back a tree of Java objects that represents or "models" the document.

An XML parser that works this way is said to be a "Document Object Model" or "DOM" parser. The key aspect is that once the DOM parser starts, it carries on until the end and then hands back a complete tree representing the XML file. The DOM parser is very general and doesn't know anything about your customized XML tags. So how does it give you a tree that represents your XML? Well, the DOM API has some interfaces that allow any kind of data to be held in a tree. The parser has some classes that implement those interfaces, and it instantiates objects of those classes.

It's all kept pretty flexible, and allows different parsers to be plugged in and out without affecting your application code. Similarly, you get information out of the tree by calling routines specified in the DOM API. The Node interface is the primary datatype for the Document Object Model. It represents a single node in the document tree, and provides methods for navigating to child Node. Most of the other interfaces, like Document, Element, Entity, and Attr, extend Node. In the next section we will review the code for a simple program that uses a DOM parser. DOM parsers can be and are written in any language, but we are only concerned with Java implementations here.

A Program That Uses a DOM Parser

This section walks through a code example that instantiates and uses a DOM parser. The DOM parser is just a utility that takes incoming XML data and creates a data structure for your application program (servlet, or whatever) to do the real work. See Figure 27–3 for the diagram form of this situation.

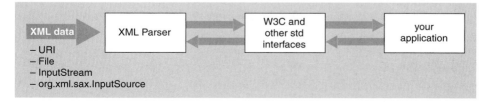

Figure 27–3   The flow of data from XML to your code

The code we show in this section is the code that is "your application" in Figure 27–3. The JAXP library has code for the other two boxes. The interface is a little more involved than simply having our class call the parser methods. This unexpected slight complication happens because the Java library implementors wanted to make absolutely sure that the installations never got locked into one particular XML parser. It's always possible to swap the parser that comes with the library for another. To retain that flexibility, we instantiate the parser object in a funny way (the Factory design pattern), which we will explain later.

The program is going to read an XML file, get it parsed, and get back the output which is a tree of Java objects that mirror and represent the XML text file. Then the program will walk the tree, printing out what it finds. We hope it will be identical with what was read. In a real application, the code would do a lot more than merely echo the data; it would process it in some fashion, extracting, comparing, summarizing. However, adding a heavyweight application would complicate the example without any benefit. So our application simply echoes what it gets. The program we are presenting here is a simplified version of an example program called DOMEcho.java that comes with the JAXP library. The general skeleton of the code is as follows.

```
// import statements

public class DOMEcho {

    main(String[] args) {
      // get a Parser from the Factory
      // Parse the file, and get back a Document

      // do our application code
      // walk the Document, printing out nodes
      echo( myDoc );
    }

    echo( Node n ) {
      // print the data in this node

        for each child of this node,
            echo(child);
    }

}
```

The first part of the program, the import statements, looks like this:

```
import javax.xml.parsers.*;
import org.xml.sax.*;
import org.xml.sax.helpers.*;
import org.w3c.dom.*;
import java.io.*;
```

That shows the JAXP and I/O packages our program will use. The next part of the program is the fancy footwork that we warned you about to obtain an instance of a parser—without mentioning the actual class name of the concrete parser we are going to use.

This is known as the Factory design pattern, and the description is coming up soon. For now, take it for granted that steps 1 and 2 give us a DOM parser instance.

```
public class DOMEcho {
    public static void main(String[] args) throws Exception {

        // Step 1: create a DocumentBuilderFactory
          DocumentBuilderFactory dbf =
             DocumentBuilderFactory.newInstance();
        // We can set various configuration choices on dbf now
        // (to ignore comments, do validation, etc)

        // Step 2: create a DocumentBuilder
          DocumentBuilder db = null;
          try {
              db = dbf.newDocumentBuilder();
          } catch (ParserConfigurationException pce) {
              System.err.println(pce);
              System.exit(1);
          }
          // Step 3: parse the input file
          Document doc = null;
          try {
              doc = db.parse(new File(args[0]));
          } catch (SAXException se) {
              System.err.println(se.getMessage());
              System.exit(1);
          } catch (IOException ioe) {
              System.err.println(ioe);
              System.exit(1);
          }

        // Step 4: echo the document
         echo( doc );

        }
```

That shows the key pieces of the main program. We will look at the code that echoes the document shortly, as it is an example of the data structure that the DOM parse hands back to your application.

When you check the javadoc HTML files for the JAXP library, you will see that the parse gives you back an object that fulfills the Document interface. Document in turn is a subclass of the more general Node interface shown in Table 27–3.

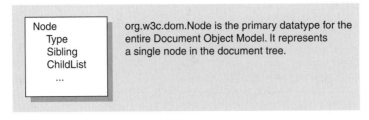

Figure 27–4   A Node represents an element, a comment, a CDATA section, an entity, and so on

Your tree is a tree of Nodes as shown in Figure 27–5. Each element, entity, PCData, Attribute, etc., in your XML file will have a corresponding Node that represents it in the data structure handed back by the DOM parse. Node is an interface promising a dozen or so common operations: get siblings, get children, get type, get name, and so on.

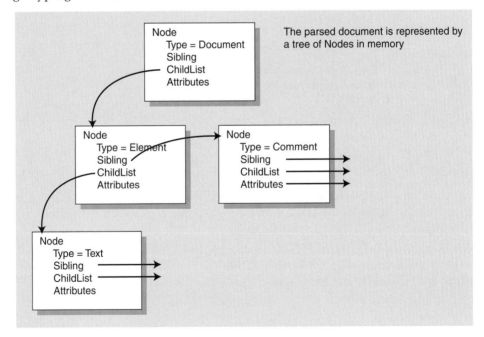

Figure 27–5   A DOM parse builds up a tree of Nodes

Each Node has a list of child Nodes that are the elements contained within it. There is also a field that points to a collection of attributes, if the node has attributes. When you examine the class org.w3c.dom.Node using javadoc, you will see that it has10 or 20 fields and methods allowing you to get and set data associated with the Node, as shown in Table 27–3.

Table 27–3   **Methods of `org.w3c.dom.Node`**

Method	Purpose
getChildNodes()	Returns a NodeList that contains all children of this node.
hasChildNodes()	Returns a boolean signifying if the node has children or not.
getNextSibling()	Returns the node immediately following this node, i.e., its next sibling.
getNodeType()	Returns an int code representing the type of the node, e.g., attribute, cdata section, comment, document, element, entity, etc.
getNodeName()	Returns a String representing the name of the node. For an element, this is its tag name.
getNodeValue()	Returns a String that means different things depending on what type of Node this is. An Element that just has PCData will have a child Node of type "text" and the node value that is the element's PCData.
getParentNode()	Returns the parent of this node.

You invoke these Node methods on the document value returned from the parse, as shown in the following example. Here is the remainder of the code. It does a depth-first traversal of a DOM tree and prints out what it finds. Once again, real application programs will do much more than just echo the data. We have omitted any processing of the XML data for simplicity here.

All we do here is echo the XML to prove that we have a tree that accurately reflects it.

```java
/**
 * Recursive routine to print out DOM tree nodes
 */
private void echo(Node n) {
    int type = n.getNodeType();
    switch (type) {
    case Node.DOCUMENT_NODE:
        out.print("DOC:");
        break;
    case Node.DOCUMENT_TYPE_NODE:
        out.print("DOC_TYPE:");
        break;
    case Node.ELEMENT_NODE:
        out.print("ELEM:");
        break;
    case Node.TEXT_NODE:
        out.print("TEXT:");
        break;
    default:
        out.print("OTHER NODE: " + type);
        break;
    }

    out.print(" nodeName=\"" + n.getNodeName() + "\"");

    String val = n.getNodeValue();
    if (val != null) {
        if ( !(val.trim().equals(""))) {
            out.print(" nodeValue \""
                + n.getNodeValue() + "\"");
        }
    }
    out.println();

// Print children if any
    for (Node child = n.getFirstChild(); child != null;
            child = child.getNextSibling()) {
        echo(child);
    }
}
```

Use instanceof, not switch( )

The code shown previously (taken from a Sun example) switches on the NodeType int field to deal with different types of Node. A better, more object-oriented way to do this is to use the instanceof operator:

```
private void echo(Node n) {
    if (n instanceof Document)
        out.print("DOC:");
    else if (n instanceof DocumentType)
        out.print("DOC_TYPE:");
    else if (n instanceof Element)
        out.print("ELEM:");
```

The Node interface is further specialized by child interfaces that extend it. The interfaces that extend the Node interface are Attr, CDATASection, CharacterData, Comment, Document, DocumentFragment, DocumentType, Element, Entity, EntityReference, Notation, ProcessingInstruction, and Text. These sub-interfaces can do all the things that a Node can do, and have additional operations peculiar to their type that allow the getting and setting of data specific to that subtype.

As an example, the org.w3c.dom.CharacterData subinterface of Node adds a few methods to allow the inserting, deleting, and replacing of Strings. Table 27–4 lists the key methods of CharacterData. You should review Node and all its child interfaces using javadoc when you start to use XML parsers.

Table 27–4   Methods of org.w3c.dom.CharacterData

Method	Purpose
getData()	Returns the CharacterData of this Node.
appendData(String s)	Appends this string onto the end of the existing character data.
insertData(int offset, String s)	Inserts this string at the specified offset in the character data.
replaceData(int offset, int count, String s)	Replaces 'count' characters starting at the specified offset with the string s.
setData(String s)	Replaces the entire CharacterData of this node with this string.

You will invoke these methods on any Node to modify its character data.

The Document subinterface of Node is particularly useful, having a number of methods that allow you to retrieve information about the document as a whole, e.g.,get all the elements with a specified tagname. Some of the most important methods of Document are outlined in Table 27–5.

Table 27–5   Methods of `org.w3c.dom.Document`

Method	Purpose
getElementsByTagName(String t)	Returns a NodeList of all the Elements with a given tag name in the order in which they are encountered in a preorder traversal of the Document tree.
createElement(String e)	Creates an Element of the type specified.
getDoctype()	Returns the DTD for this document. The type of the return value is DocumentType.

You will invoke these methods on the document value returned from the parse.

Once you have parsed an XML file, it is really easy to query it, extract from it, update it, and so on. The XML is for storing data, moving data around, sharing data with applications that haven't yet been thought of, and sharing data with others outside your own organization (e.g., an industry group or an auction site). The purpose of the parser is to rapidly convert a flat XML file into the equivalent tree data structure that your code can easily access and process.

Reading an XML File—SAX Parsers

DOM level 1 was recommended as a standard by the World Wide Web consortium, W3C, in October 1998. In the years since then, a weakness in the DOM approach has become evident. It works fine for small and medium-sized amounts of data, up to, say, hundreds of megabytes. But DOM parsing doesn't work well for very large amounts of data, in the range of gigabytes, which cannot necessarily fit in memory at once. In addition, it can waste a lot of time to process an entire document when you know that all you need is one small element a little way into the file.

To resolve these problems, a second algorithm for XML parsing was invented. It became known as the "Simple API for XML" or "SAX," and its distinguishing characteristic is that it passes back XML elements to the calling program as it finds them. In other words, a SAX parser starts reading an XML stream, and whenever it notices a tag that starts an element, it tells the calling program. It does the same thing for closing tags too. The way a SAX parser communicates with the invoking program is via callbacks, just like event handlers for GUI programs.

The application program registers itself with the SAX parser, saying in effect "when you see one of these tags start, call this routine of mine." It is up to the application program what it does with the information. It may need to build a data structure, or add up values, or process all elements with one particular value, or whatever. For example, to search for all CDs by The Jam, you would look for all the artist elements where the PCDATA is "The Jam."

SAX parsing is very efficient with machine resources, but it also has a couple of drawbacks. The programmer has to write more code to interface to a SAX parser than to a DOM parser. Also, the programmer has to manually keep track of where he is in the parse in case the application needs this information (and that's a pretty big disadvantage). Finally, you can't "back up" to an earlier part of the document, or rearrange it, anymore than you can back up a serial data stream. You get the data as it flies by, and that's it.

The error handling for JAXP SAX and DOM applications are identical in that they share the same exceptions. The specifications require that validation errors are ignored by default. If you want to throw an exception in the event of a validation error, then you need to write a brief class that implements the `org.xml.sax.ErrorHandler` interface, and register it with your parser by calling the `setErrorHandler()` method of either `javax.xml.parsers.DocumentBuilder` or `org.xml.sax.XMLReader`. Error handling is the reason why DOM programs import classes from the `org.xml.sax` and `org.xml.sax.helpers` packages.

JAXP includes both SAX and DOM parsers. So which should you use in a given program? You will want to choose the parser with an eye on the following characteristics:

- SAX parsers are generally faster and use fewer resources, so they are a good choice for servlets and other transaction oriented requirements.

- SAX parsers require more programming effort to set them up and interact with them.

- SAX parsers are well suited to XML that contains structured data (e.g., serialized objects).

- DOM parsers are simpler to use.

- DOM parsers require more memory and processor work.

- DOM parsers are well suited to XML that contains actual documents (e.g., Microsoft Word or Excel documents in XML form, assuming Microsoft publishes the DTDs).

If it's still not clear, use a DOM parser, as it needs less coding on your part.

A Program That Uses a SAX Parser

This section walks through a code example of a SAX parser. Because we have already covered much of the background, it will seem shorter than the DOM example. Don't be fooled. The general skeleton of the code is as follows.

```
// import statements: see below

public class MySAXEcho extends DefaultSAXHandler {

    main(String[] args) {
      // get a Parser
      // register my callbacks, and parse the file
    }

    // my routines that get called back
    public void startDocument() { /*code...*/}
    public void startElement( /*code...*/
    public void characters ( /*code...*/
    public void endElement(
  /*code...*/
}
```

The first part of the program, the import statements, looks like this:

```
import java.io.*;
import org.xml.sax.*;
import org.xml.sax.helpers.DefaultHandler;
import javax.xml.parsers.SAXParserFactory;
import javax.xml.parsers.ParserConfigurationException;
import javax.xml.parsers.SAXParser;
```

That shows the JAXP and I/O packages our program will use. The next part of the program is the fancy footwork to obtain an instance of a parser without mentioning the actual class name of the concrete parser we are going to use. As a reminder, it will be explained before the end of the chapter. For now, take it for granted that we end up with a SAX parser instance.

The next part of the program is critical. It shows how we register our routines for the callbacks. Rather than register each individual routine, the way we do with basic event handling in Swing, we make our class extend the class `org.xml.sax.helpers.DefaultHandler`.

That class has 20 or so methods and is the default base class for SAX2 event handlers. When we extend that class, we can provide new implementations for any of the methods. Where we provide a new implementation, our version will be called when the corresponding SAX event occurs.

For those familiar with Swing, this is exactly the way the various Adapter classes, e.g., MouseAdapter, work.

```
public class MySAXEcho extends org.xml.sax.helpers.DefaultHandler {

    public static void main(String argv[]) {
        // Get a SAX Factory
        SAXParserFactory factory = SAXParserFactory.newInstance();

        // Use an instance of ourselves as the SAX event handler
        DefaultHandler me = new MySAXEcho();

        try {
            SAXParser sp  = factory.newSAXParser();

            // Parse the input
            sp.parse( new File(argv[0]), me);

        } catch (Throwable t) {
            t.printStackTrace();
        }
    }

    static private PrintStream  o = System.out;
```

The two lines in bold show where we create an instance of our class and then pass it as an argument to the parse routine, along with the XML file. At that point, our routines will start to be invoked by the SAX parser.

The routines we have provided in this case are shown in the following example.

```
//=============================================================
    // SAX DocumentHandler methods
    //=============================================================

    public void startDocument()
    throws SAXException
    {
        o.println("In startDocument");
    }

    public void startElement(String namespaceURI,
                            String sName, // simple name (localName)
                            String qName, // qualified name
                            Attributes attrs)
    throws SAXException
    {
        o.print( "got elem <"+sName);
        if (attrs != null) {
            for (int i = 0; i < attrs.getLength(); i++) {

o.println(attrs.getLocalName(i)+"=\""+attrs.getValue(i)+"\"");
            }
        }
        o.println("");
    }

    public void characters (char buf[], int offset, int len)
            throws SAXException {
        String s = new String(buf, offset, len);
        o.print(s);
    }

    public void endElement(String namespaceURI,
                            String sName, // simple name
                            String qName  // qualified name
                            )
    throws SAXException
    {
        o.println("</"+sName+"");
    }

}
```

And that's our complete SAX parser. In this case, we have provided the routines to get callbacks for the start of the document and each element, for the character data inside each element, and for the end of each element. A review of the DefaultHandler class will show all the possibilities. You should download, compile and run the program.

A sample data file of a CD, complete with DTD, looks like this:

```
<?xml version="1.0"?>
<!DOCTYPE inventory  [
<!ELEMENT inventory (cd)* >
    <!ELEMENT cd (title, artist, price, qty)>
        <!ELEMENT title (#PCDATA)>
        <!ELEMENT artist (#PCDATA)>
        <!ELEMENT price (#PCDATA)>
        <!ELEMENT qty (#PCDATA)>
]>

<inventory>
  <cd> <title>Some Girls</title>    <artist>Rolling Stones</artist>
        <price>25</price>   <qty>5</qty>   </cd>
</inventory>
```

Compile and execute the program, giving the name of the data file on the command line:

```
javac SAXEcho.java
java SAXEcho   cd.xml
```

You will see output from the echo part of the code like this:

```
In startDocument
Some Girls</>
got elt <
>
Rolling Stones</>
got elt <
>
25</>
```

One of the exercises at the end of the chapter is to update the program to provide more readable output about the elements it finds.

The Factory Design Pattern

You can safely skip this section on first reading, as it simply describes how and why you use a design pattern with the JAXP library.

If you implement an XML parser in the most straightforward way, code that uses the parser will need implementation-specific knowledge of the parser (such as its classname). That's very undesirable. The whole XML initiative is intended to free your data from single platform lock-ins, so having your code tied to a particular parser undermines the objective. The Java API for XML Processing (JAXP) takes special steps to insulate the API from the specifics of any individual parser.

This makes the parser "pluggable," meaning you can replace the parsers that come with the library with any other compliant SAX or DOM parser. This is achieved by making sure that you never get a reference to the implementation class directly; you only ever work using an object of the interface type in the JAXP library. It's known as the "Factory" design pattern.

Factories have a simple function: churn out objects. Obviously, a Factory is not needed to make an object. A simple call to a constructor will do it for you. However, the use of Factory allows the library-writer to define an interface for creating an object, but let the Factory decide which exact class to instantiate. The Factory method allows your application classes use a general interface or abstract class, rather than a specific implementation. The interface or abstract class defines the methods that do the work. The implementation fulfills that interface, and is used by the application, but never directly seen by the application.

Figure 27–6 shows an abstract class called "Worker." Worker has exactly two methods: a() and b(). An interface can equally be used, but let's stick with an abstract class for the example. You also have some concrete classes that extend the abstract class (WorkByJane, WorkByPete, etc.). These are the different implementations that are available to you. They might differ in anything: one is fast but uses a lot of memory, another is slow but uses encryption to secure the data, a third might be able to reach remote resources.

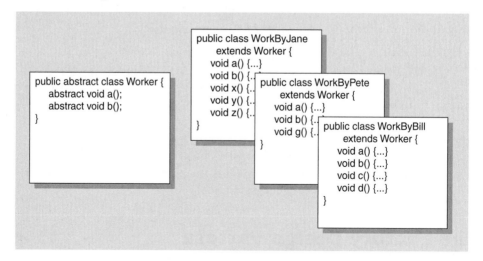

Figure 27–6   Worker abstract class, and subclasses with different methods

The idea behind the Factory pattern is that you don't want your application code to know about these implementation classes. You don't want it to be able to invoke the extra methods in the implementation, for example. You want a way to declare and use an instance of one of the implementation classes but have it be typed as the abstract worker class. You further want to do that with your application code seeing as little as possible of the implementation and ideally none.

Figure 27–7 shows the Factory pattern that achieves this:

```
public class MyFactory {

    static Worker getWorker( params... ) {
        //based on params,
        //choose Pete, Bill, or Jane
        ...
        return new WorkByPete();
    }
    ...
}
```

Figure 27–7   The Factory pattern

The factory has a method (usually static, though it doesn't have to be) that will return something that is the type of our abstract class, Worker. Here we have called this routine getWorker. It will actually send back a subtype of Worker, but as you know, if Dog is a subtype of Mammal, wherever a parameter or assignment calls for a Mammal you can give it a Dog. This is not true the other way around, of course, as you cannot supply a general class when a more specific one is called for. The Factory method getWorker will look at the parameters it was sent and decide which kind of Worker implementation is the best one to use: a fast one, a secure one, a small memory one, or whatever. Then it will instantiate one of these subclasses, and return it. Notice that *the return type is that of our abstract class, not one of the concrete subtypes.*

Our code that calls into the Factory will resemble Figure 27–8.

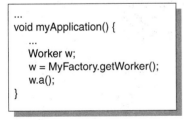
```
...
void myApplication() {
    ...
    Worker w;
    w = MyFactory.getWorker();
    w.a();
}
```

Figure 27–8   Getting an object from a Factory

It gets back a Worker, and the only thing that can be done with a worker is to call a() or b(). There is no opportunity to call any of Pete or Jane's extra methods, shown in Figure 27–6.

You cannot instantiate a Worker object, because it's an abstract class. But by using the Factory pattern, you now hold a concrete object that is of type Worker. Describing how this works with XML parsers will bring some clarity to the Factory pattern.

When using an interface, you don't want to access the underlying implementation classes. If you break this rule, you might as well not be using an interface at all; you have locked yourself into one implementation. In the case of a DOM parser, you want to do everything through the interface, and not directly use the actual DOM parser that implements the interface. The interface is:

```
package org.w3c.dom;
public interface Document ... { ...
```

And the concrete class that implements the DOM parser currently looks something like this:

```
public class PetesPrettyGoodParser implements org.w3c.dom.Document { ...
```

But we don't want our code to be tied to any one implementation. That means you *don't* want your code to say:

```
class MyXMLApp { ...
    Document myDoc = new PetesPrettyGoodParser();    // Avoid this!
         ... = myDoc.petesSpecialMethod();       // Avoid this!
```

If you did that, you are building knowledge of Pete's Parser into your code and you can accidentally start calling additional methods of Pete's, which violates the intended API. Instead, we want a way to instantiate and access something that is a "PetesPrettyGoodParser," but without actually naming it. We want to create it and use it totally using interface methods. This is where the Factory Design Pattern comes in. The library code will have a ParserFactory class. The ParserFactory will have a static field or method that will give you a reference to the thing you are trying to keep out of your code. This field or method will typically be called something like getInstance or newInstance. (If the library writer gave it a name of newInstance, don't confuse it with the method of the same name that has a similar purpose in class java.lang.Class.) The Factory method will look like this:

```
package javax.xml.parsers;
class DocumentBuilderFactory { ...
      static DocumentBuilderFactory newInstance() {

            . . .
```

Design Pattern Summary

In summary, a classic Factory design pattern looks like this:

1. You have an interface or abstract class, Worker.

2. You have some implementations of that, WorkerBill, WorkerJane, WorkerFred.

3. You have a Factory that has a method, often static, often called `getSomething` or `newSomething`." It returns something of type Worker. That method chooses which of the implementors to use. It does a new WorkerBill (let's say) and returns it as the supertype.

The application code now has a concrete class, but typed as the abstract superclass or interface. It cannot use more methods than are in the interface. Voila.

Other Java XML Notes

The Document building code is not guaranteed to be well behaved in threads. You may very well have many XML files to parse, and you may want to use a thread for each. An implementation of the DocumentBuilderFactory class is not guaranteed to be thread safe. To avoid problems, the application can get a new instance of the DocumentBuilderFactory per thread, and they can be configured differently in terms of how much validation they do, whether they ignore comments and so on.

Here's how we use the Factory instance to get back a Parser that has the type of the abstract class `javax.xml.parsers.DocumentBuilder`:

```
... myDb = myDbf.newDocumentBuilder();
```

Now that we have a DocumentBuilder (which is actually a Pete'sPrettyGoodParser, or equivalent), we can use it in a type-safe, future-proof way to parse an XML file and build the corresponding document, like this:

```
org.w3c.dom.Document doc = myDb.parse( new File("myData.xml"));
```

We did not simply move the dependency from your code into the run-time library. The JAXP run-time library has put the hooks in place to make it possible to switch parser implementations. The full details are the in the Specification document which you will download. However, to summarize, the run-time looks for a property file that contains the class name of any different parser you want to use. If the property is not found, it uses the default. So it all works as desired. Everything is hands-off. You're manipulating the tree by remote control, which admittedly makes this harder to follow.

Factory pattern confusion in Java XML

The folks at Javasoft designed this with a double example of the factory pattern. First, you get a Factory, from that you get a ParserFactory, then you get a parser, then you parse. Even worse, they made the code more confusing by using the same class (DocumentBuilderFactory) for both Factories! The code looks like this:

```
// Step 1: instantiate a DocumentBuilderFactory
    DocumentBuilderFactory dbf =
        DocumentBuilderFactory.newInstance();
// Step 2:   Use the factory pattern again to get db
    DocumentBuilder db = dbf.newDocumentBuilder();
// Step 3: now actually use db as a parser
    Document doc = db.parse( "cd.xml" );
```

They wrote code to get a Factory using the Factory pattern! The algorithm used is "first get a factory instance, then use that to get a parser instance," but it would work just as well and be a lot clearer if DocumentBuilderFactory had a static factory method to return a DocumentBuilder directly.

I asked around in Javasoft to see why this was done, and the answer was it was a holdover from the early days of the API. The intent was to keep all the methods that configure the parser in one factory. Then once a parser had been configured and set up to be instantiated, you could use the builder class to get hold of the parser that had been configured and also use the convenience methods in there. For example, say you had just one factory and you started parsing and building a document. Then what would it mean if you changed one of the configurations in the middle? Does it affect the current parser or does it instantiate a new parser and take effect from then on? To avoid all this, once a parser has been configured, you can't change the configuration unless you get a new instance of the parser.

A much better way to solve the problem is to do what SAX 2.0 does if you try to reconfigure the parser during a parse, which is to throw an exception. This has the advantage of eliminating an extra class in the API and makes it easier to use. It's water under the bridge at this point, and we have to live with the unnecessary complexity. Moral: Keep your code obvious, and it will be easier to maintain.

Further Reading

There is a centralized portal for people developing with XML languages at www.xml.org. The website was formed in 1999 by OASIS, the non-profit Organization for the Advancement of Structured Information Systems, to provide public access to XML information and XML Schemas. You can find everything there from tutorials to case studies.

The website www.w3schools.com/dtd/default.asp has a good DTD Tutorial under the title "Welcome to DTD School." It also has links to many other tutorials of interest to XML developers.

If you're interested in getting more information on XML and the Java XML API, be aware there are a few items we haven't covered. First, there is an additional XML mark-up tag, known as a "processing instruction." This is a piece of XML inherited from SGML, but not really a good fit. (SGML is the mother of all mark-up languages, too large and too complicated to ever get much use in the real world. XML and HTML are simplifications of SGML.) A processing instruction is used to link style sheets (regular HTML CSS style sheets) into documents. Second, the topics of both elements and attributes are deeper than we have room for here. We have not covered the third library in JAXP: the transformation library in javax.xml.transform.

There is an independently developed open source library called JDOM. This is a Java API that does the same job as W3C's DOM. It was created as a more object-oriented and easier to use alternative to DOM, and there is a good possibility it will be adopted into JAXP (or even replace it). It has been adopted as Java Specification Request number 102, if you want to check on its progress. Please see the JDOM website at www.jdom.org for the most up-to-date information.

IBM offers a series of free tutorials on their website. There are tutorials covering parsers, DOM, SAX, and the transformation library. Go to www.ibm.com/developerworks and click or search on XML. You have to register at the site, but it is free and quick.

Exercises

1. Describe the Factory design pattern and state its use.
2. Write a DTD that describes a CD inventory file. Each CD is either domestic or imported. These details are stored for all CDs: artist, title, price, quantity in stock. Imported CDs also have these fields: country of origin, genre, non-discount status, language, and lead time for reorder. Write some XML instance data describing your five favorite CDs (include a couple of imported CDs, too).
3. Validate your XML file from the previous question by running it against the DOMEcho program that comes with the Java XML library. In the output you get, explain what the text nodes with a value of "[WS]" are. Hint: Try varying the number of spaces and blank lines in your instance data, and seeing how that changes the output.
4. Rewrite the DTD describing Shakespearean plays making better use of names, comments, and indenting.
5. It is possible to implement a DOM parser using a SAX parser, and vice versa, although not particularly efficiently. Write a couple of paragraphs of explanation suggesting how both of these cases might be done.

6. Write a servlet that reads an XML file of a CD inventory and sends HTML to the browser, putting the data into a table.

7. Improve the output of the SAXEcho program to make it more presentable and understandable.

8. Write an application that uses a DOM parser to get CD information and outputs the total number of all kinds of CDs that you have in stock, and the total number by each artist. Remember that some artists may have several titles in print at once.

Some Light Relief—View Source on Kevin's Life

The 5K Contest first ran in the year 2000. It's a new annual challenge for web developers and HTML gurus to create the most interesting web page in less than 5120 bytes. That's right, all HTML, scripts, image, style sheets, and any other associated files must collectively total less than 5 kilobytes in size and be entirely self-contained (no server-side processing).

The 5k competition was originally conceived in the fall of 1999 after an argument about the acceptable file size of a template for a project at work. The creator says, "It took a long time to actually get it organized because, back in those days, we all worked hard at our soul-destroying dot.com jobs and didn't have time for fun personal projects."

The 5K size limit is pretty much the only rule, and some of the entries are a bit too Zen for a meat-and-potatoes guy like me, but everyone seems to be having a good time. There is the usual crop of games written in Javascript. You've got your Space Invaders, your Maze solvers, your Game of Life. It's the International Obfuscated C Code Competition (see my text *Expert C Programming*), updated for the new medium and the new millennium. 3D Tetris, post modernism, poetry, art, angst—it's all there, with clever use of Javascript, style sheets, and DHTML. You can even enter an applet if you want.

One nice entry in 2001 is the Timepiece (shown in Figure 27–9). This is an animated clock showing seconds, minutes, hours, date, day-of-week, month, phase of moon, and year. You can choose the time zone.

Timepiece is incredibly busy to look at, but somehow the complexity adds to its appeal. All umpteen axes grind past each other as seconds tick away, a fusion of traffic, tectonics, and time. (Sorry, that Zen poetry style is catching. In less than 5K of Javascript code.) You can see all the 5K winners at www.the5k.org/.

One of the unexpected winners this year was, amazingly and appropriately, an XML entry. Think about it: XML is a "storing" thing, not a "doing" thing! So how can it compete with flashy graphic entries like the 3D Tetris or the Virtual Reality

757

Dolphin? It competed with imagination. People are always looking for something fresh, something original, something that hasn't been done to death before.

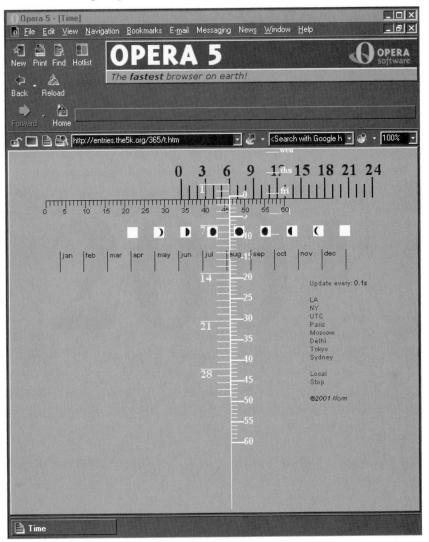

Figure 27–9   The Timepiece in under 5K bytes.

Winner Kevin Conboy described his entry as "a subtle comment on the pervasive nature of the Internet." He tried to imagine doing a "view source" on his life to see what an actual day would look like. Here is an extract from Kevin's essay entry—an XML diary. Kevin starts by getting up, washing, and dressing.

```
<!DOCTYPE KCML PUBLIC "-//KVC//DTD KCML 1.0 EXPERIMENTAL//EN"
"http://www.alternate.org/TR/REC-html40/loose.dtd"><br>
<day length='24' start='730' end='1046' name='kevinconboy'>
<wake>

<home temp='70' ac='true' tv='true' computer='false'>
<shower length='12' soap='ivory' shave='true'> </shower>
<style shirt='bananaRepublic' shorts='#000000'
shoes='bananaRepublic('sandals');'
  hat='false' boxers='true'> </style>
<kiss wife='true' son='true'></kiss>
<elevator down='true' up='false' occupied='true' conversation='no'>
</elevator>
</home>
```

Kevin lunches at a Mexican restaurant with three friends, and spends the afternoon working on graphics production for a client.

```
<lunch type='external' length='1' transport='walk' location='wahoos'>
<meal type='mexican' companions='('vijayPatel','jeffVoreis','triciaChaya')'
src='chickenQuesadillas' beverage='mountainDew' refill='true'></meal>
</lunch>

<afternoon>
<task type='graphicsProduction' client='pearlIzumi'></task>
```

Finally, he drives home, has an evening meal, bathes his son, and soothes him, and tucks him in bed before watching a little TV and turning in himself.

```
<son activity='bath' cry='false'>
<bath length='15' clean='true' curSanity='('prevSanity+20');'> </bath>
<toSleep length='15' cry='true' blanket='false' pacifier='true'
bottle='false' curSanity='('prevSanity+30');'> </toSleep>
</son>

<television>
<program src='HBO' type='dennisMiller' entertain='true'>
</television>

</wake>
</day>
```

That very human sentiment of soothing his family strikes a chord. You (the reader) and I are both now near the end of the day, at the last sentence in this chapter, and maybe we both feel the same way too: curSanity++; good night, dear programmer, sleep tight, and don't let the Tera byte.

Chapter 28

Web Services at Google and Amazon

Web services have had a lot of publicity proclaiming them the new "new thing", but they haven't yet achieved the universal use that would justify that publicity. There are several reasons behind that. One factor was the end of the Y2K upgrade spending, followed a few months later by the collapse of dot-communism. Together these led to a multi-year world-wide recession in the computer industry. Companies have been deferring new IT investments where they can.

In other words, the fact that web services aren't yet ubiquitous may have more to do with the economic climate than with the technology. But another factor is that web services often aren't secure. There is no trivial universally accepted security solution. You can prevent people snooping on the bits by encrypting them using SSL (Secure Sockets Layer, as used in https: protocols everywhere). But we also need a way to ensure that only authorized clients call the server. There are several alternatives for this (such as authentication tokens), but industry has yet to converge on one.

Regardless, organizations are now increasing their use of web services. Two of the premier websites on the internet, Google and Amazon, have launched web services Beta programs. These two initiatives are not related to each other, and they have taken slightly different technical approaches.

The goals of the two Beta programs are the same though. Amazon and Google are both predicting that web services are going to grow greatly in significance.

Amazon and Google are planting a flag in the ground, saying that they intend to be part of that growth, and help shape the future of web services. For you as a programmer, the benefit is getting early exposure to a technology that's got a great future.

In this chapter we'll give you a clear picture of what web services are, and the problems they can solve for an organization. We will show how client programs send XML requests to web services. The work that a web service server does to fulfill a request is beyond our scope here. We will look at some XML that is sent back in response, but not how it is generated or transformed. In the second section, we'll look at the Google web services beta, and walk through an example that uses it. The Google package is quite reasonable, and most programmers could figure it out for themselves. It saves your time, if I put the steps together in a list, and point out the pitfalls. We'll end up with a way to do google searches from inside one of your programs.

The third section describes the beta program for Amazon web services. There are some enormously talented people working hard at Amazon to bring the program to you free of charge. But, ironically for a company working in the books-and-information-online business, Amazon's documentation isn't good enough and there are errors in the beta release that prevent it from working out of the box. Overall Amazon has done a good job though.

The current form of this chapter will have a limited lifetime, starting in June 2004. Beta programs come to an end. My belief is that Amazon and Google and many other companies will soon establish permanent web services interfaces. At that point I'll update the chapter, and may put it on my website at afu.com/jj6. Let's get started by describing what web services in general do for you.

Web Services Introduction

Chapter 27 described XML. That mark-up language lets you label pieces of data with a description of what they are. If you give an XML file to another program (including a program outside your organization) it can easily find within the file the pieces in which it is interested. Web services consist of XML files, plus a way of sending them to a server that will execute a program (probably a servlet) based on the request in the XML, and send back the results.

What are web services?

There are a lot of different perspectives on web services, but in principle, the technology is straightforward. Here is the programmer's perspective.

A web service says "*Here's my URL you can post XML files to (exactly like posting an HTML form). I'll read the XML to find out what you are asking me to do, then I'll do it, and send the answer back as a web page of more XML*". Instead of a browser at one end, there's a program at both ends.

Web services provide a service-oriented architecture that lets IT groups develop and deploy centrally, while supporting any platform anywhere that is connected to the 'net. Web services are likely to supplant past systems that have tried to do this (CORBA, DCOM, IIOP, RPC and, yes, Java's RMI), but which have all had interoperability limitations in talking to each other. For example, RMI only works when there is a Java system at both ends.

The problem that web services solve

If you've never worked in IT you may doubt this, but if you have worked in IT, you'll immediately recognize it as true. A significant IT expense for large organizations is the cost of moving data from one system to another. You store data for system A in a database, then requirements change and some of the data needs to be shared with System B in real time. But systems A and B are hosted on different computers, and use databases from different vendors. Just getting them to agree on the format of a calendar date is a problem. Actually moving the bulk data reliably and repeatedly is an expensive and fragile undertaking.

Some companies try to avoid the costs of data migration by moving everything into a gigantic data repository known as a data warehouse. That has some advantages and some drawbacks of its own. Other companies, like Vitria Inc., have built a substantial business out of providing software channels that reliably feed data from one system to another.

Today's browser-based web architecture has two potential improvements for business data use:

- Get rid of manual steps. At present, people read web pages. In a business environment, you want to eliminate manual steps. They are error-prone and can cause delays. If web pages are being used for data retrieval (e.g. inventory levels), it is desirable to turn the person-to-computer process into a computer-to-computer process.

- Integrate "islands of data". When data comes from several websites (e.g. comparing the cost and timing of a trip by rail versus airplane) a person has to take notes, summarize and re-package the data. It can introduce clerical errors, and does not scale well when the number of alternatives or trips increases.

People have written "screen-scraper" programs that address these issues, but each one of those is a custom job. Screen-scrapers work in intranets, but may need modification when they poll external websites that change. Now that the world is connected by the internet, there has to be a better way to publish and move data.

Anything that automates the flow of data can directly reduce IT costs. For example, a company can permit trusted suppliers view its internal inventory levels, so suppliers can replenish stocks automatically under a just-in-time delivery system. Web services provide the basic messaging and service-description functions for this kind of electronic relationship.

Web services infrastructure

Bill Gates recently described the infrastructure needed for web services. He identified four necessary pieces:

1. The hardware and software for communication. The internet provides this.

2. A standard way for services to describe what they do, and to find each other on the internet. Web Services Description Language (WSDL) supplies the first, and UDDI, the Universal Description Discovery and Integration standard, the second.

3. A common format for data. XML provides this.

4. A protocol for servers and clients to exchange XML messages with each other. There are two or three contenders here: REST (fast, simple, but basic), SOAP (slower, more complex, but more capable), and XML-RPC (somewhere in the middle between REST and SOAP). Like the email protocols or the FTP protocol, a web services protocol says *"If you talk to me on this port, and say these kinds of sentences, then I'll understand what you need and give it to you."*

This is the promise of web services: it moves the web beyond being a gigantic reading room, and lets it become an API for client/server or peer-to-peer programs. By using XML over HTTP connections, the client and server are completely decoupled. They don't have to match in hardware, architecture, or operating system.

When Bill Gates outlined these components for web services, the client/server independence was a major *dis*advantage for him. All his past software frameworks (like COM, DCOM, and .Net) have been Windows-only. Microsoft supports web services, even though they do not reinforce the Microsoft monopoly, because they give Bill something else he really wants. Web services encourage the move from "software as product" to "software as service", where apps-on-tap software can be accessed remotely and rented per-use or per-time-period.

Deutsche Telekom uses Web Services today to connect about 100 content providers with 5 million mobile phone service subscribers. By 2015, when Moore's Law will make it economically feasible, tiny computers may run the light switches, pet doors, and fridges in our homes. They may all have IP addresses, and they may all use web services to talk to other authorized systems.

Information architects have great hopes that web services will one day make it easy to create aggregate systems by combining smaller web services. People always have these kind of hopes for every new software technology. Web services are strong enough to stand on their own regardless of whether this particular ambition is realized.

Web services and your code

This chapter will show you how to write a client program that makes calls to a web service. Let's list the steps to be done by such a program. The service could be as simple as doing a Google search. The point here is that, as a web service, the search results come back in a format which is meant to be easy for a program to use. If a person is doing a web search interactively, use a browser, not a web service.

1. Identify the server that offers the resource that you want. This may be done by querying using UDDI, the Universal Description Discovery and Integration standard.

2. Obtain the XML file (written in Web Services Description Language) that describes how to make a request to the server. The description will include the URL, and what kind of fields are needed in the XML file that will be sent over and in the answer that will be sent back.

3. Run the WSDL file through a tool that converts it into a library of Java calls. The premier tool for doing this translation is Axis—the Apache Extensible Interaction System. Axis is open source, and can do a lot of other things as well.

4. Write your code to call into the library produced by Axis. Your code will provide a number of parameters. The library will assemble these into an XML file, put a SOAP (Simple Object Access Protocol) envelope around it, and send it via an HTTP GET or POST to the web service URL.

5. The web service will process the SOAP request, create an XML file with the results, and send it back to your system. In the case of Google, this will be a search request. In the case of Amazon, this will be information about a book, or the confirmation of a step in completing a book purchase.

6. The web services client library on your system will handle the incoming XML, and pass it on to your code as a return value. You may get raw XML, which you can further process using XSLT—Extensible Stylesheet Language Transformations. XSLT is a way of converting XML into HTML or plain text

or XML that uses another vocabulary. Or the library may do all the work of converting the XML response into something your program finds easier to deal with.

This is the theory, and in practice some of these steps may not be necessary. If you already know that you intend to search Google or Amazon, you don't need a UDDI enquiry. If you want to find several alternative providers, e.g. to convert some foreign currency, a UDDI enquiry will tell you who offers the service.

The profusion of evolving standards, and the consequent alphabetti spaghetti, present a formidable barrier to a programmer trying to master this technology. Realizing this, both Amazon and Google provide some client software that does some or most of the hard parts. That's quite likely to become a standard feature of web services in future. With this theoretical background in mind, let's go on to look at the Google web service.

Google Web Services

The first step is to download the beta kit (or the actual web services package if this has turned into a product by the time you're reading this). Go to `http://www.google.com/apis/` read the license and click to download the zip file.

The license makes clear this is for personal use; you're not allowed to build this into commercial products. You're also restricted to fewer than 1000 queries a day, and not more frequently than one a second. Google may well offer a different license in future. You've got to respect their trademarks and agree this is beta software which might not work. The download is less than one MB, so only takes a few seconds.

Before you can go any further, you need to create a Google account. This is really just a free registration of your email address and a password. Google will send you an email, and when you click on the link in it, you're able to proceed. Your Google account can also be used to post to Usenet through the Google servers, to access Google mail, and a couple of other things.

Google will then send you a license key, also called a *client key*, by email. This is a 32-character (not -bit) string of mixed case alphabetics and punctuation. This isn't a valid key, but a key will look something like this:
`hNpM%kKY6+k;j1hxkO3KnwQmso+/UH2g`

You have to include your individual client key in all program interactions with the Google web service. That lets Google keep track of who is doing what, and selectively disable the service if necessary.

Contents of the Google Beta Kit

After you have downloaded the beta kit, unzip it. It's well behaved, and will unpack into a directory called "googleapi" that contains:

- A brief program written in Java that demonstrates how to call the web service.

- An HTML document that explains in detail the semantics of the function calls you can make using the Google Web APIs service. If you didn't already know how to filter a Google search by date-published, or only get details from one site, this will give you the inside information.

- A jar file that you link against. This jar file does *all* the heavy lifting of XML formulation, SOAP communication, and result parsing of the return value. Seriously, this is so easy to use, that you might get the wrong impression that all web services are that easy.

- The WSDL file that describes the Google web services in XML.

- Javadoc for the Google library contained in the jar file.

- A readme file describing the above, and telling you how to run the demo immediately.

Let's look at some of these individual pieces.

The googleapi.jar library

The jar file googleapi.jar contains the items shown in Table 28–1.

Table 28–1   Contents of file googleapi.jar

File	Description
The jar file for package com.google.soap.search	Google's Java wrapper for the API SOAP calls.
activation.jar	Jar file for the JavaBeans Activation Framework. The Framework is a library for determining the MIME type of files— is it a GIF, a JPEG, an audio file, etc.
mailapi.jar	The Javamail library. This is used for its character encoding features. UFT-8 is used everywhere, not Latin-1. ASCII is not affected, but clients will get accented characters as two bytes not one, and must handle that.
apache-soap-22.jar	The Apache SOAP 2.2 library.
crimson.jar	The Apache Crimson 1.1.3 library. This is an XML parser.

The library has google's SOAP endpoint address
`http://api.google.com/search/beta2` built in to it. You don't actually need to know any of these libraries, except the first one. You don't need to understand SOAP or UDDI or WSDL or even XML to use the Google web services API!

When you compile and when you run your own search programs, you need to make sure that library googleapi.jar is on your classpath for both the compiler and the JVM.

The Google WSDL file

The WSDL file provides a standard description of Google's search services. The file is included with the beta kit, and is also at http://api.google.com/GoogleSearch.wsdl. This XML file is about 200 lines long, and the first few lines look like the following example.

```xml
<?xml version="1.0"?>
<!-- WSDL description of the Google Web APIs.
     The Google Web APIs are in beta release. All interfaces are subject to
     change as we refine and extend our APIs. Please see the terms of use
     for more information. -->

<!-- Revision 2002-08-16 -->

<definitions name="GoogleSearch"
             targetNamespace="urn:GoogleSearch"
             xmlns:typens="urn:GoogleSearch"
             xmlns:xsd="http://www.w3.org/2001/XMLSchema"
             xmlns:soap="http://schemas.xmlsoap.org/wsdl/soap/"
             xmlns:soapenc="http://schemas.xmlsoap.org/soap/encoding/"
             xmlns:wsdl="http://schemas.xmlsoap.org/wsdl/"
             xmlns="http://schemas.xmlsoap.org/wsdl/">

  <!-- Types for search - result elements, directory categories -->

  <types>
     <xsd:schema xmlns="http://www.w3.org/2001/XMLSchema"
                 targetNamespace="urn:GoogleSearch">

        <xsd:complexType name="GoogleSearchResult">
          <xsd:all>
            <xsd:element name="documentFiltering"          type="xsd:boolean"/>
            <xsd:element name="searchComments"             type="xsd:string"/>
            <xsd:element name="estimatedTotalResultsCount" type="xsd:int"/>
            <xsd:element name="estimateIsExact"            type="xsd:boolean"/>
            <xsd:element name="resultElements"
                              type="typens:ResultElementArray"/>
            <xsd:element name="searchQuery"                type="xsd:string"/>
            <xsd:element name="startIndex"                 type="xsd:int"/>
            <xsd:element name="endIndex"                   type="xsd:int"/>
            <xsd:element name="searchTips"                 type="xsd:string"/>
            <xsd:element name="directoryCategories"
                              type="typens:DirectoryCategoryArray"/>
            <xsd:element name="searchTime"                 type="xsd:double"/>
          </xsd:all>
        </xsd:complexType>

        <xsd:complexType name="ResultElement">
          <xsd:all>
            <xsd:element name="summary" type="xsd:string"/>
            <xsd:element name="URL" type="xsd:string"/>
            <xsd:element name="snippet" type="xsd:string"/>
            <xsd:element name="title" type="xsd:string"/>
            <xsd:element name="cachedSize" type="xsd:string"/>
            <xsd:element name="relatedInformationPresent" type="xsd:boolean"/>
            <xsd:element name="hostName" type="xsd:string"/>
            <xsd:element name="directoryCategory" type="typens:DirectoryCategory"/>
            <xsd:element name="directoryTitle" type="xsd:string"/>
          </xsd:all>
        </xsd:complexType>
```

It describes the web services in a form that software can understand. You don't need to use it when you use the Google web services. You would need to use other people's Web Services Description Language files if you want your programs to connect to arbitrary web services dynamically.

Running the example program

The very first thing to try is running the example program that Google provides. You can do that by typing this command line, using your actual client key and any search term you want. If you have several search terms, enclose them in double quotes.

```
java -cp googleapi.jar com.google.soap.search.GoogleAPIDemo <key> search  honey
```

Here, "honey" is the search term we give Google, and <key> represents your client key. You'll either need to cd to the directory with the googleapi.jar file, or give its full pathname in the above command. When you do that successfully, the demo program will echo the parameters you have given it:

```
Parameters:
Client key = <your key>
Directive  = search
Args       = honey
```

There will be a pause of a second or two while the request is formulated in XML, wrapped in a SOAP bar, put on the wire, serviced by Google, and the XML response sent back to your system.

Then you'll see an answer starting like this:

```
Google Search Results:
======================
{
TM = 0.129773
Q  = "honey"
CT = ""
TT = ""
CATs =
   {
   {SE="",
FVN="Top/Business/Industries/Food_and_Related_Products/Sweeteners/Honey"},
   {SE="", FVN="Top/Shopping/Food/Sweeteners/Honey"}
   }
Start Index = 1
End   Index = 10
Estimated Total Results Number = 3760000
Document Filtering = true
Estimate Correct = false
Rs =
   {

   [
   URL  = "http://www.honey-movie.com/"
   Title = "<b>Honey</b> DVD :: Hip Hop Dance Movie Stars Jessica Alba, Missy Elliot
<b>...</b>"
   Snippet = ""
   Directory Category = {SE="", FVN="Top/Arts/Movies/Titles/H/Honey_-_2003"}
   Directory Title = "<b>Honey</b>"
   Summary = "Official site from Universal Pictures. Contains synopsis, trailer,
photographs, cast and crew"
   Cached Size = "8k"
   Related information present = true
   Host Name = ""
   ],

   [
   URL  = "http://www.honey.com/"
   Title = "<b>Honey</b>.com - The <b>Honey</b> Expert"
   Snippet = "<b>Honey</b>.com is your source for <b>honey</b> information<br> and
recipes. <b>Honey</b>.com -- the <b>honey</b> expert. <b>...</b>  "
   Directory Category = {SE="", FVN=""}
   Directory Title = ""
   Summary = ""
   Cached Size = "18k"
   Related information present = true
   Host Name = ""
   ],
```

You get up to ten results returned in this beta system. The Google web service
gives you the results back in the form of an object, not in the form of XML. You
call methods of that object to drill down on individual finds. The results returned

will be the same as the first ten results you would get from an interactive query made in a browser at the same time.

Coding your own Google search

You can review the javadoc description of Google's web api in the directory created when you unzipped the download. It's in googleapi/javadoc/index.html.

You'll see that you can make three kinds of requests:

- Search for web pages containing a term you provide.

- Ask for spelling correction on a word you provide (did you know Google could do that?).

- Ask for web pages from Google's cache that contain a term you provide. This is for looking at web pages that are not currently on the web, either because that web server is swamped, or because the owner has removed them.

You construct a request, and set the two mandatory attributes like this:

```
GoogleSearch s = new GoogleSearch();
s.setKey("your key goes here");
s.setQueryString("honey");
```

You initiate the web service request like this:

```
GoogleSearchResult r = s.doSearch();
```

It needs to be inside a try statement that catches the GoogleSearchFault exception. Those four lines above are enough to search, but you can also set dozens of other attributes on the query (such as restricting results to the English language and so on).

A short complete program looks like this:

```
import com.google.soap.search.*;
public class search {
  public static void main(String[] args) {

    GoogleSearch s = new GoogleSearch();
    s.setKey("your key goes here");
    s.setQueryString("honey");
    try {
        GoogleSearchResult r = s.doSearch();

        System.out.println(r.toString());
    } catch (GoogleSearchFault f) {
        System.out.print("The call to the Google Web APIs failed: ");
        System.out.println(f.toString());
    }
  }
}
```

When you compile and run the search program, you have to be careful to provide all the classpaths you need. The compiler needs to see the googleapi.jar class libraries:

```
javac -cp googleapi.jar  search.java
```

The JVM needs to see the library, and your search.class class file, so you probably want to include a "." to represent current directory in the class path:

```
java -cp googleapi.jar;.  search
```

(On Unix, use a ":" not a ";" as the path separator, of course.) As you will see, you can just do a print() on the search results object returned to you. It has a pretty comprehensive toString() method that turns it into human readable output. Inside a program you'll want to call methods on the GoogleSearchResult object to get to the individual elements, and to get the fields out of the elements.

Google searches can return millions of web pages. Some limits have been set on the Beta implementation to keep it real. A search string cannot be more than 2KB, or have more than 10 words in the query. Each query will return you no more than 10 results. The javadoc html and the googleapi/APIs_Reference.html pages have more details on this. The Google API is not constrained to a particular version of the JDK.

What a delightful surprise the Google web service API turned out to be. It's surprisingly hard to make software easy to use. The Google folks obviously put some real thought into hiding the underlying complexities, and they did an excellent job. Let's go on and look at the Amazon web services.

Amazon Web Services

Many of the steps in using the Amazon web services mirror those of the Google web services. There is a beta kit that you download, you have to register in order to get a key, a Java library is provided along with a sample application, and so on.

The Amazon people have not gone to quite so much trouble to hide the underlying complexities, so the process of getting code running is a bit more involved than with Google. On the other hand, you get a more realistic experience of engaging with web services. There were some bugs which prevented compilation in the beta version of the Amazon kit at the time I downloaded it. However it is possible to resolve all these and get code running.

Start by visiting http://www.amazon.com/gp/browse.html/?node=3434641 which is the download page. If this 404's, then search Google for "Amazon Web Services". When you get to the right Amazon page, notice the links on the left of that page for a FAQ, the license details, and obtaining the client key, which Amazon calls a *token*. Obtain your token by clicking on the link and filling in your email address and a password. Your browser will load a new page, which shows your 14-character token. This will also be emailed to the address you gave.

Web services and security

Amazon and Google are both using a featherweight security mechanism for their beta services. Sending a client key in clear text over HTTP is bad enough, but if the transport uses an HTTP GET, the key is appended to the URL. Since URLs are tracked and cached, this is like broadcasting your secret information.

When these services go fully commercial, Google and Amazon will certainly choose a more secure alternative, like SSL, Kerberos tickets, or X.509 certificates.

Although it is still in Beta, the license agreement for Amazon web services is a bit longer than Google's, because Amazon is encouraging people to deploy applications around this. Indeed, they even sell one such application, written by an early adopter in the Beta program. That developer could have been you, if you'd tackled this a few months ago!

Contents of the Amazon Beta Kit

After downloading the file kit.zip, unzip it to create a directory called "kit" that contains a directory AmazonWebServices with these contents:

- A readmefirst file describing the following information, giving advice, and telling you how to run the demo.

- A directory containing some information on writing programs to use the services. Click on index.html to enter at the correct place.

- A directory containing the Java code for the demo

- A directory containing SOAP **request** Java code examples.

- A directory containing SOAP **response** Java code examples.

- A directory of XML response examples.

- A directory of XSLT style sheet examples, showing how to use the Extensible Stylesheet Language Transformations library to morph the XML into more convenient forms.

When you put all this together, what you get is programmatic access to all the features of the Amazon website. This would allow you to build your own interface to Amazon.com, specialized to your own business. Amazon still runs an affiliate program paying a small kickback to websites that bring purchasers too them. Another possibility is to search Amazon and suggest books to people who are using some other application of yours. Say you run a travel agent business. As the last step in booking a vacation package for someone, you could automatically offer them a choice of guidebooks for that area.

Running the example program

Amazon supports two alternative entry points to their web services, one simple, the other complicated:

- A REST entry point. REST is an acronym for Representational State Transfer, and it is the simple approach. It means you send web service requests in the form of requests to URLs. If there are any parameters, they are tacked onto the end of the URL, or posted like an HTML form in XML. The result comes back as text or an XML file, and may include more URLs where additional details are available. The server is essentially guiding the client through a state machine in which each URL in a response represents a new state that can be transferred to (hence Representational State Transfer). The REST protocol lets developers start building Web services right away, without needing any toolkits beyond what they normally use for network application development.

- A SOAP (Simple Object Access Protocol) entry point. This is the complicated approach. It requires specific knowledge of the SOAP XML specification, and a SOAP toolkit to form requests and parse the results.

Here's what you need to do to run Amazon's SOAP example. I don't recommend you do this, except to convince yourself of the practical drawbacks of SOAP. It's more complicated than it needs to be.

1. Download and install the Apache Axis package. There are eight jar files that you have to make visible to Java. Put them in any directory, and then put the pathname of the directory on the commandline like this:

    ```
    java -Djava.ext.dirs=/your/path/to/axisjars  rest-of-line
    ```

2. The Axis code will read a WSDL file, and generate a Java library of classes and methods to access the promised services. The site is
    `http://ws.apache.org/axis/`

3. Download the Amazon WSDL file, and run it through Axis. The file is at
    `http://soap.amazon.com/schemas3/AmazonWebServices.wsdl`

4. Compile all the Java code created in step 2. These files can be found at
    `kit\AmazonWebServices\JavaCodeSample\com\amazon\soap\axis\*.java`

    You must compile under JDK 1.4. JDK 1.5 will issue compiler warnings about the use of the word enum.

5. Now compile the example application code in directory
    `\AmazonWebServices\JavaCodeSample`

You will need to fix compilation errors in seven files. These are caused by incorrect use of letter case in several variable names. E.g., a method is declared as setWishlist_id() but it is invoked in another file as setWishlist_Id(). Change the files where it is invoked, not the files where it is declared.

6. Run the program, by typing java run. That will bring up a Swing window looking like Figure 28–1.

Figure 28–1   Window displayed when you type java run

7. On the "XML" tab in the window, select "ASIN/UPC code".

8. Paste your Amazon token in the field marked "Developer Token".

9. Paste "0131774298 " in the field labelled "AsinSearch".

10. Press "send".

More quickly than a browser reference (because it does not have to render images or HTML), the text details for book with ISBN 0-13-1774-298, the Ugly Fish C Book, will show up in the lower panel, under the JTree icon that is labelled "result". If you click on that icon you can open up successive levels of detail on the book.

A more RESTful way to access Amazon web services

Amazon's chief web services designer Jeff Barr has been quoted as saying 85% of Amazon's web service use is REST, and only 15% use SOAP. The REST approach is much, much simpler and quicker to get working. SOAP is more flexible if you need to do something unusual like secure http communication between three or more parties.

A SOAP envelope in XML will look something like this:

```
<soap:Envelope xmlns:soap="http://schemas.xmlsoap.org/soap/envelope/">
<soap:Body>
<gs:doAmazonSearch xmlns:gs="urn:AmazonSearch">
<token>myToken</token>
<asin>0-13-1774-298</asin>
</gs:doAmazonSearch>
</soap:Body>

</soap:Envelope>
```

The word "ASIN" is "Amazon Standard ID Number" which, for a book, is the ISBN. You can see how the SOAP includes the name of the method to call, and the names/values of the parameters.

What WSDL and UDDI give you

Even if you don't know what "doAmazonSearch" does, by reading the WSDL you know how to call it, what parameters it expects, and what kind of results it will return (not shown in previous example, to keep it readable).

It is just about feasible to write a program that can read a WSDL file and automatically marshall the data, make the call, and parse the results. Using a WSDL description a programmer can interface two applications in hours, not weeks.

The next problem is finding other people's web services, and having them find yours. The UDDI—Universal Description, Discovery, and Integration—standard addresses this. UDDI provides a searchable index of WSDL service descriptions. And its searching and update functions are themselves web services so they can be accessed from a program.

REST (REpresentational State Transfer) is an architectural style, not a complicated over-the-wire protocol like SOAP. REST says that the web already has set of remote commands that can be applied to any URL on any server—the HTTP commands GET, POST, PUT, DELETE. These commands tell a web server which HTML page or image file to send. REST says that they can be used equally well to interact with programs. If the program needs data, HTTP/POST already allows the client to upload a stream of text. If there's only a small amount of data (a customer ID and an ISBN, say), tack it onto the end of the URL in the established practice of HTTP/GET.

Here's an example. Amazon supports REST queries. You can retrieve the same information by constructing the following URL. For ease of reading, I have broken it up onto several lines. To see it work without any programming at all, type the following text into a browser URL field. Use your actual client key, and do not type spaces or line feeds:

```
http://xml.amazon.com/onca/xml3?
   t=webservices-20
 & devt=<your client key>
 & AsinSearch=0131774298
 & type=lite

 & f=xml
```

The Amazon web service will respond with XML, the first few lines of which look like this:

```
<Request>
     <Args></Args>
</Request>
     <Details
url="http://www.amazon.com/exec/obidos/ASIN/0131774298/webservices-20?dev-
t=your key%26camp=2025%26link_code=xm2">
<Asin>0131774298</Asin>
<ProductName>Expert C Programming</ProductName>
<Catalog>Book</Catalog>
     <Authors>
        <Author>Peter van der Linden</Author>
     </Authors>
     <ReleaseDate>14 June, 1994</ReleaseDate>
     <Manufacturer>Prentice Hall PTR</Manufacturer>

     <ImageUrlSmall>
      http://images.amazon.com/images/P/0131774298.01.THUMBZZZ.jpg
     </ImageUrlSmall>
```

This is the same information sent to the demo SOAP program, which parsed it and displayed the results graphically. For learning purposes, it would probably be better if Amazon's SOAP program GUI just displayed the raw XML.

If you can assemble that URL, type it in manually and get results, it's trivial to see how a Java program can do the same thing. Chapter 27 shows code to do that, so I won't repeat it here.

As soon as your program reads the XML returned by the web service, it will parse it and extract the data of interest. The program may also use an XSLT (Extensible Stylesheet Language Transformation) library to transform the XML output into other markup languages, such as HTML or plain text. An XSLT stylesheet is a template governing the transformation, and is not related to the similarly named Cascading Style Sheet (CSS).

Conclusions

The computer industry has been doing electronic data interchange for years. Web services is a way of standardizing and turning it into Remote Procedure Calls, using ubiquitous web servers and XML. REST is a way of simplifying *that*, reusing existing HTTP protocols instead of inventing new ones.

The two giants of the Web, Amazon and Google, both concluded that UDDI and SOAP were not suitable for exposure in their Beta web services initiatives. Google layered a completely new, and much simpler custom library on top. Amazon provided thousands of lines of sample code in 35 Java files. But they also supported the REST approach which the overwhelming majority of their Beta users prefer.

Web services have always been led from in front by the evolving technology, not driven from behind by a pressing need. One result has been the profusion of industry groups rolling the frontiers forward, anticipating problems in advance of users encountering them. There are grand visions of automatically locating global services and connecting to them in real-time to consume billable services. But down on the ground, there are IT managers who just want the data from the customer repair system to flow to authorized service dealers so the dealers can order parts, and get reimbursement for warranty repairs. For these people UDDI, SOAP, and maybe WSDL is an unnecessary expense.

Web services support in MacOS X

There's only one desktop operating system in 2004 with built-in support for web services: MacOS X (pronounced "MacOS ten") from Apple.

MacOS X is BSD Unix with a first-class window system on top, and it is full of hidden treasures. It comes with DVD authoring software. It has speech recognition and speech synthesis as a standard feature (turn it on with apple/system preferences/speech). MacOS ships with Java preinstalled, and native support for Java is part of the OS. MacOS comes with the world's best http server, Apache, built right into the OS and easy to run.

You can run Apple's Sherlock program to see web services in use. It accesses commercial web services, and can do things like tell you movie showtimes in your local area. Sherlock offers a custom view into many web services like airline flights, stock prices, online auctions, language translation and more. You can easily write your own code to work with web services on MacOS X. See the apple page at
`www.apple.com/webobjects/web_services.html`

It would be trivial to reimplement the Google web service so that it used a REST approach, and there would no longer be any complexity that would need to be hidden. The Google developers are generally regarded as clueful, so one wonders if the web services team deliberately chose SOAP for a reason like "exploring a new technology".

That question was posed on the Google developer newsgroup, and an official answer came back: "We chose to deliver Google Web APIs via SOAP because we believe that the SOAP developer tools make Google Web APIs accessible to the broadest developer community." So they're claiming that they think the Java and .NET libraries that interface to SOAP outweigh simplicity. But then they wrapped the SOAP library with their own special easy-to-use library, which pretty clearly proclaims "we think SOAP is not ready for prime time exposure." Time will tell if this was a well-considered decision. In the meantime, there are signs that Google will make a Beta3 release that supports REST.

SOAP itself has evolved over the years. Even the name has been retrospectively deemed no longer an acronym. While SOAP, UDDI and WSDL are solid, some standardization efforts in other areas of web services look premature.

It's debatable whether any advantages of SOAP are worth the increased effort and performance cost. Why use an elaborate SOAP message to communicate the remote method name and the parameters, when you can encode this in a URL? If you already know the service you want to use and its format, why use WSDL to repeat that information? In the face of changing technology, sticking to simple tried and tested mechanisms, like REST, is about as prudent as you can get.

Some Light Relief—Googlewhacking

This is a great place to mention "googlewhacking", the game invented by Gary Stock (or someone else, there are several who claim to have coined the term). Googlewhacking is for people who have not just too much time on their hands, but entire clocksful of too much time on their hands. The idea is to discover a set of two words in a Google search that out of the bazillions of pages on the web, return exactly one match. Recent googlewhacks:

- ambidextrous scallywags
- squirreling dervishes
- panfish interrogation
- disenthralled nimrod
- insolvent pachyderms
- hellkite flamingo

There are only three rules:

1.   Do not put your words in quotes. Quoting a string tells Google to find the words in that order next to each other, and that's just too easy.

2.   Both words must be listed in the online dictionary at `dictionary.reference.com`

3.   Online lists of words (dictionaries, glossaries, etc.) don't count as web page results.

Few of these terms stay googlewhacks for long. People put them in blogs, then the Google webcrawlers index those pages, and poof!

You can tell the world of your tremendous accomplishments by posting true googlewhacks to the website at `www.googlewhack.com`. There's a FAQ there, written in a delightfully sarcastic and insouciant tone, offering this justification for why three-letter abbreviations are not accepted as googlewhack terms:

The web and the 'net are not qat zek, nor pij sdo... and not all men

can say pyx unp, but, yes... you may. But not now, and not for our use.

On the grounds that you can't have too much of a good thing, software developer Kevin Marks introduced the Marks scoring system for googlewhacks. When you find a whack, you search for the two terms individually and multiply the two page counts together. The product is the score for that googlewhack. The current record-breaker is the 292,698,000,000 of RCassidy's "linux checkerspot".

The whole Googlewhack phenomenon says something about the speed with which a meme propagates around the web. Googlewhacks just seem so 2002 now, as passé as bell-bottoms, beehive hair, and blogging. But, hey, whatever shorts your ports.

Stay well, write good code, and never pass an unexpectedly long string argument to a C routine that pushes an unbounded length parameter on the stack, particularly not when the string argument overwrites the return address with a pointer back into the part of the stack where another piece of your string argument contains carefully crafted machine instructions that will turn your computer into yet another zombie spambot. The world would be a better place if we'd all stick to Just Java.

Appendix **A**

Downloading Java

Here are the steps to download and install the latest free Java compiler.

1. Go to the website java.sun.com

    Click on the link to "downloads".

    You want the most up-to-date version of the Java development kit. From time to time, Sun Marketing re-badges the JDK, using ever more silly and awkward names. Most recently, it has been called Java 2 Platform, Standard Edition (J2SE) Software Development Kit (SDK). In summer 2004, the most up-to-date version was 1.5 (yes, "Java 2" is at version 1.5).

2. You want the SDK (the compiler, tools, and run-time library). The JRE is just the part of the SDK needed to run Java programs, but not the development tools (the JRE is a smaller download intended for users). Click through the license (it says you can use the tools for free, but you're not to use them to build any nuclear reactors).

3. You reach a page where you choose which platform on which you will be running the compiler. Wherever you choose to compile, your executable programs will run on all platforms.

    Sun distributes compilers for Solaris, Linux, and Windows. Solaris has been a 64-bit operating system since we re-architected the kernel for Solaris 7 in 1998. Almost everyone else is still running 32-bit versions of Linux and Windows so choose one of those, unless you installed 64-bit Linux or Windows.

    If you are running something other than Solaris, Linux, or Windows, go to the home page of the manufacturer and search for their Java download. MacOS X comes with the JDK preinstalled, but new releases of Java may come out after you buy your Apple, so check the Apple website for the latest.

4. For Windows, Sun offers an "offline" installation and an "online" one. The "offline" installation gives you the entire 50MB release in one download. (It's so big because it also installs the NetBeans IDE, the Java browser plug-in, and Java webstart). Use the offline download if you have a reliable broadband service. The result is a file that you execute to do the installation.

781

The "online" download is a small (under 1MB) download of a program. When you run it, it does the real download and installation. It's restartable, if the connection is lost. There's a FAQ of common issues/answers at the download web page.

5.   When the installation wizard runs, accept all defaults and optional features (demos, source code, etc.). If you choose a different installation directory, write down where! You need that pathname (plus "\bin" added to the end) in step 7. For Windows, the default install is in:

```
"c:\Program Files\Java\j2sdk1.5.0"
```

With jdk142 and later, installing Java on Windows also installs an auto update feature. It's a background program that checks for a newer release at 10pm each night. You can configure this with control panel -> (classic) -> Java -> update.

6.   *Read the installation notes* (this is currently a link near the top of the download page on Sun's website). Do not omit this step. The notes have information about hardware requirements, limitations, late-breaking news, workarounds, etc. Sun: this should really be popped up as the last step in the install wizard.

7.   Set the path variable on your operating system, so that you don't have to type the full pathname to the java compiler tools. The pathname will be the one you made note of in step 5, with "\bin" added to the end.

In older versions of Windows, you might add the pathname to the start of the existing PATH in file \autoexec.bat.

In XP, you will navigate the following panels: start, control panel, (possibly switch to category view), performance and maintenance, system, click "advanced" tab, click "environment variables" down at the bottom of the advanced panel. Then choose "path" on the "System variables" part of the panel. Add the pathname

"c:\Program Files\Java\j2sdk1.5.0\bin"

to the start of the path. Note the "\bin" needed on the end of the pathname. Different pathnames in the Path system variable are separated by ";" so add that too.

8.   Start a new command window, and type "path" to check what you did in step 8. You should see the entire list of directories that are checked for each command you enter, and the pathname to the java bin directory should be on that list.

9.   Type this command, to invoke the java compiler:

```
javac -verbose
```

You should get back a dozen lines of output, starting like this:

```
javac: no source files
Usage: javac <options> <source files>
where possible options include:
  -g                        Generate all debugging info
  -g:none                   Generate no debugging info
  -g:{lines,vars,source}    Generate only some debugging info
  -nowarn                   Generate no warnings
  -verbose                  Output messages about the compiler
```

Using no source file is even easier than the "hello world" program, and demonstrates just as well that the compiler is installed.

Now it's Hello World

Java programs are made up of code organized into classes. If you are not using an IDE, the classes go into java source files. Important classes should go in a file of the same name as the class. For example, a class called "hello" should go in a file called "hello.java". Here is the source you can put in such a file:

```
public class hello {
    public static void main(String[] args) {
        System.out.println("hello sailor");
    }
}
```

You compile that with the command:

```
javac hello.java
```

That compilation will create a file called hello.class. It contains the executable program binary. You can run it with the command:

```
java hello
```

Note you use the name of the class, not the name of the file. Try it now. Then, on to the big picture of Java!

Appendix **B**

Powers of Two Table

Refer to Table B–1 for powers of two.

With n bits in integer two's complement format, you can count:

- Unsigned from 0 to (one less than 2^n)
- Signed from -2^{n-1} to (one less than 2^{n-1})

Table B–1 Powers-of-Two from 2^1 to 2^{64}

2^1	2	2^{17}	131,072	2^{33}	8,589,934,592	2^{49}	562,949,953,421,312
2^2	4	2^{18}	262,144	2^{34}	17,179,869,184	2^{50}	1,125,899,906,842,624
2^3	8	2^{19}	524,288	2^{35}	34,359,738,368	2^{51}	2,251,799,813,685,248
2^4	16	2^{20} megabyte	1,048,576	2^{36}	68,719,476,736	2^{52}	4,503,599,627,370,496
2^5	32	2^{21}	2,097,152	2^{37}	137,438,953,472	2^{53}	9,007,199,254,740,992
2^6	64	2^{22}	4,194,304	238	274,877,906,944	2^{54}	18,014,398,509,481,984
2^7	128	2^{23}	8,388,608	2^{39}	549,755,813,888	2^{55}	36,028,797,018,963,968
2^8	256	2^{24}	16,777,216	2^{40} terabyte	1,099,511,627,776	2^{56}	72,057,594,037,927,936
2^9	512	2^{25}	33,554,432	2^{41}	2,199,023,255,552	2^{57}	144,115,188,075,855,872
2^{10} kilobyte	1,024	2^{26}	67,108,864	2^{42}	4,398,046,511,104	2^{58}	288,230,376,151,711,744
2^{11}	2,048	2^{27}	134,217,728	2^{43}	8,796,093,022,208	2^{59}	576,460,752,303,423,488
2^{12}	4,096	2^{28}	268,435,456	2^{44}	17,592,186,044,416	2^{60}	1,152,921,504,606,846,976
2^{13}	8,192	2^{29}	536,870,912	2^{45}	35,184,372,088,832	2^{61}	2,305,843,009,213,693,952
2^{14}	16,384	2^{30} gigabyte	1,073,741,824	2^{46}	70,368,744,177,664	2^{62}	4,611,686,018,427,387,904
2^{15}	32,768	2^{31}	2,147,483,648	2^{47}	140,737,488,355,328	2^{63}	9,223,372,036,854,775,808
2^{16}	65,536	2^{32}	4,294,967,296	2^{48}	281,474,976,710,656	2^{64} bubbabyte	18,446,744,073,709,551,616

Appendix C

Codesets

Table C-1 shows 256 decimal and hexadecimal codes that represent characters and control characters in different codesets. The codesets shown are:

- ISO 8859 Latin-1 codeset. ISO 8859-1 is identical to the first 256 Unicode characters.

- ANSI_X3.4-1968 ASCII. The ASCII characters are a subset of the 8859-1 code, and codes within the ASCII range are indicated by shading in the leftmost column in the table below.

- IBM's nearly obsolete EBCDIC codeset.

Table C–1 ISO 8859-1, ASCII and EBCDIC codes

ISO 8859-1 and ASCII		Dec	Hex	EBCDIC	
NUL	Null	0	00	Null	NUL
SOH	Start of Heading (CC)	1	01	Start of Heading	SOH
STX	Start of Text (CC)	2	02	Start of Text	STX
ETX	End of Text (CC)	3	03	End of Text	ETX
EOT	End of Transmission (CC)	4	04	Punch Off	PF
ENQ	Enquiry (CC)	5	05	Horizontal Tab	HT
ACK	Acknowledge (CC)	6	06	Lower Case	LC
BEL	Bell	7	07	Delete	DEL
BS	Backspace (FE)	8	08		
HT	Horizontal Tabulation (FE)	9	09		
LF	Line Feed (FE)	10	0A	Start of Manual Message	SMM
VT	Vertical Tabulation (FE)	11	0B	Vertical Tab	VT
FF	Form Feed (FE)	12	0C	Form Feed	FF
CR	Carriage Return (FE)	13	0D	Carriage Return	CR
SO	Shift Out	14	0E	Shift Out	SO
SI	Shift In	15	0F	Shift In	SI
DLE	Data Link Escape (CC)	16	10	Data Link Escape	DLE
DC1	Device Control 1	17	11	Device Control 1	DC1
DC2	Device Control 2	18	12	Device Control 2	DC2
DC3	Device Control 3	19	13	Tape Mark	TM
DC4	Device Control 4	20	14	Restore	RES
NAK	Negative Acknowledge (CC)	21	15	New Line	NL

787

Table C–1   ISO 8859-1, ASCII and EBCDIC codes *(cont.)*

	ISO 8859-1 and ASCII	Dec	Hex	EBCDIC	
SYN	Synchronous Idle (CC)	22	16	Backspace	BS
ETB	End of Transmission Block (CC)	23	17	Idle	IL
CAN	Cancel	24	18	Cancel	CAN
EM	End of Medium	25	19	End of Medium	EM
SUB	Substitute	26	1A	Cursor Control	CC
ESC	Escape	27	1B	Customer Use 1	CU1
FS	File Separator (IS)	28	1C	Interchange File Separator	IFS
GS	Group Separator (IS)	29	1D	Interchange Group Separator	IGS
RS	Record Separator (IS)	30	1E	Interchange Record Separator	IRS
US	Unit Separator (IS)	31	1F	Interchange Unit Separator	IUS
SP	Space	32	20	Digit Select	DS
!	Exclamation Point	33	21	Start of Significance	SOS
"	Quotation Mark	34	22	Field Separator	FS
#	Number Sign, Octothorp, "pound"	35	23		
$	Dollar Sign	36	24	Bypass	BYP
%	Percent	37	25	Line Feed	LF
&	Ampersand	38	26	End of Transmission Block	ETB
'	Apostrophe, Prime	39	27	Escape	ESC
(	Left Parenthesis	40	28		
)	Right Parenthesis	41	29		
*	Asterisk, "star"	42	2A	Set Mode	SM
+	Plus Sign	43	2B	Customer Use 2	CU2
,	Comma	44	2C		
-	Hyphen, Minus Sign	45	2D	Enquiry	ENQ
.	Period, Decimal Point, "dot"	46	2E	Acknowledge	ACK
/	Slash, Virgule	47	2F	Bell	BEL
0	0	48	30		
1	1	49	31		
2	2	50	32	Synchronous Idle	SYN
3	3	51	33		
4	4	52	34	Punch On	PN
5	5	53	35	Reader Stop	RS
6	6	54	36	Upper Case	UC
7	7	55	37	End of Transmission	EOT
8	8	56	38		
9	9	57	39		
:	Colon	58	3A		
;	Semicolon	59	3B	Customer Use 3	CU3
<	Less-than Sign	60	3C	Device Control 4	DC4
=	Equal Sign	61	3D	Negative Acknowledge	NAK
>	Greater-than Sign	62	3E		

Table C–1   ISO 8859-1, ASCII and EBCDIC codes *(cont.)*

ISO 8859-1 and ASCII		Dec	Hex	EBCDIC	
?	Question Mark	63	3F	Substitute	SUB
@	At Sign	64	40	Space	SP
A	A	65	41		
B	B	66	42		
C	C	67	43		
D	D	68	44		
E	E	69	45		
F	F	70	46		
G	G	71	47		
H	H	72	48		
I	I	73	49		
J	J	74	4A	Cent Sign	¢
K	K	75	4B	Period, Decimal Point, "dot"	.
L	L	76	4C	Less-than Sign	<
M	M	77	4D	Left Parenthesis	(
N	N	78	4E	Plus Sign	+
O	O	79	4F	Logical OR	|
P	P	80	50	Ampersand	&
Q	Q	81	51		
R	R	82	52		
S	S	83	53		
T	T	84	54		
U	U	85	55		
V	V	86	56		
W	W	87	57		
X	X	88	58		
Y	Y	89	59		
Z	Z	90	5A	Exclamation Point	!
[	Opening Bracket	91	5B	Dollar Sign	$
\	Reverse Slant	92	5C	Asterisk, "star"	*
]	Closing Bracket	93	5D	Right Parenthesis	)
^	Circumflex, Caret	94	5E	Semicolon	;
_	Underline, Underscore	95	5F	Logical NOT	¬
`	Grave Accent	96	60	Hyphen, Minus Sign	-
a	a	97	61	Slash, Virgule	/
b	b	98	62		
c	c	99	63		
d	d	100	64		
e	e	101	65		
f	f	102	66		
g	g	103	67		
h	h	104	68		
i	i	105	69		
j	j	106	6A		
k	k	107	6B	Comma	,

Table C–1 ISO 8859-1, ASCII and EBCDIC codes *(cont.)*

ISO 8859-1 and ASCII		Dec	Hex	EBCDIC	
l	l	108	6C	Percent	%
m	m	109	6D	Underline, Underscore	_
n	n	110	6E	Greater-than Sign	>
o	o	111	6F	Question Mark	?
p	p	112	70		
q	q	113	71		
r	r	114	72		
s	s	115	73		
t	t	116	74		
u	u	117	75		
v	v	118	76		
w	w	119	77		
x	x	120	78		
y	y	121	79		
z	z	122	7A	Colon	:
{	Opening Brace	123	7B	Number Sign, Octothorp, "pound"	#
|	Vertical Line	124	7C	At Sign	@
}	Closing Brace	125	7D	Apostrophe, Prime	'
~	Tilde	126	7E	Equal Sign	=
DEL	Delete	127	7F	Quotation Mark	"
	Reserved	128	80		
	Reserved	129	81	a	a
	Reserved	130	82	b	b
	Reserved	131	83	c	c
IND	Index (FE)	132	84	d	d
NEL	Next Line (FE)	133	85	e	e
SSA	Start of Selected Area	134	86		f
ESA	End of Selected Area	135	87	g	g
HTS	Horizontal Tabulation Set (FE)	136	88	h	h
HTJ	Horizontal Tabulation with Justification (FE)	137	89	i	i
VTS	Vertical Tabulation Set (FE)	138	8A		
PLD	Partial Line Down (FE)	139	8B		
PLU	Partial Line Up (FE)	140	8C		
RI	Reverse Index (FE)	141	8D		
SS2	Single Shift Two (1)	142	8E		
SS3	Single Shift Three (1)	143	8F		
DCS	Device Control String (2)	144	90		
PU1	Private Use One	145	91	j	j
PU2	Private Use Two	146	92	k	k
STS	Set Transmit State	147	93	l	l
CCH	Cancel Character	148	94	m	m
MW	Message Waiting	149	95	n	n
SPA	Start of Protected Area	150	96	o	o

Table C–1 ISO 8859-1, ASCII and EBCDIC codes *(cont.)*

	ISO 8859-1 and ASCII	Dec	Hex	EBCDIC	
EPA	End of Protected Area	151	97	p	p
	Reserved	152	98	q	q
	Reserved	153	99	r	r
	Reserved	154	9A		
CSI	Control Sequence Introducer (1)	155	9B		
ST	String Terminator (2)	156	9C		
OSC	Operating System Command (2)	157	9D		
PM	Privacy Message (2)	158	9E		
APC	Application Program Command (2)	159	9F		
		160	A0		
¡	inverted exclamation mark	161	A1		
¢	cent sign	162	A2	s	s
£	pound sterling sign	163	A3	t	t
¤	general currency sign	164	A4	u	u
¥	yen sign	165	A5	v	v
¦	broken vertical bar	166	A6	w	w
§	section sign	167	A7	x	x
¨	spacing dieresis or umlaut	168	A8	y	y
©	copyright sign	169	A9	z	z
ª	feminine ordinal sign	170	AA		
«	left double angle quote or guillemet	171	AB		
¬	logical not sign	172	AC		
	soft hyphen	173	AD		
®	registered trademark sign	174	AE		
¯	spacing macron long accent	175	AF		
°	degree sign	176	B0		
±	plus-or-minus sign	177	B1		
²	superscript 2	178	B2		
³	superscript 3	179	B3		
´	spacing accute accent	180	B4		
µ	micro sign, mu	181	B5		
¶	paragraph sign, pilcrow sign	182	B6		
·	middle dot, centered dot	183	B7		
¸	spacing cedilla	184	B8		
¹	superscript 1	185	B9	Grave Accent	`
º	masculine ordinal indicator	186	BA		
»	right double angle quote or guillemet	187	BB		
¼	fraction 1/4	188	BC		
½	fraction 1/2	189	BD		
¾	fraction 3/4	190	BE		
¿	inverted question mark	191	BF		

Table C–1   ISO 8859-1, ASCII and EBCDIC codes *(cont.)*

ISO 8859-1 and ASCII		Dec	Hex	EBCDIC	
À	capital A grave	192	C0		
Á	capital A acute	193	C1	A	A
Â	capital A circumflex	194	C2	B	B
Ã	capital A tilde	195	C3	C	C
Ä	capital A dieresis or umlaut	196	C4	D	D
Å	capital A ring	197	C5	E	E
Æ	capital AE ligature	198	C6	F	F
Ç	capital C cedilla	199	C7	G	G
È	capital E grave	200	C8	H	H
É	capital E acute	201	C9	I	I
Ê	capital E circumflex	202	CA		
Ë	capital E dieresis or umlaut	203	CB		
Ì	capital I grave	204	CC		
Í	capital I acute	205	CD		
Î	capital I circumflex	206	CE		
Ï	capital I dieresis or umlaut	207	CF		
Ð	capital ETH	208	D0		
Ñ	capital N tilde	209	D1	J	J
Ò	capital O grave	210	D2	K	K
Ó	capital O acute	211	D3	L	L
Ô	capital O circumflex	212	D4	M	M
Õ	capital O tilde	213	D5	N	N
Ö	capital O dieresis or umlaut	214	D6	O	O
×	multiplication sign	215	D7	P	P
Ø	capital O slash	216	D8	Q	Q
Ù	capital U grave	217	D9	R	R
Ú	capital U acute	218	DA		
Û	capital U circumflex	219	DB		
Ü	capital U dieresis or umlaut	220	DC		
Ý	capital Y acute	221	DD		
Þ	capital THORN	222	DE		
ß	small sharp s, sz ligature	223	DF		
à	small a grave	224	E0		
á	small a acute	225	E1		
â	small a circumflex	226	E2	S	S
ã	small a tilde	227	E3	T	T
ä	small a dieresis or umlaut	228	E4	U	U
å	small a ring	229	E5	V	V
æ	small ae ligature	230	E6	W	W
ç	small c cedilla	231	E7	X	X
è	small e grave	232	E8	Y	Y
é	small e acute	233	E9	Z	Z
ê	small e circumflex	234	EA		
ë	small edieresis or umlaut	235	EB		
ì	small i grave	236	EC		

Table C–1 ISO 8859-1, ASCII and EBCDIC codes *(cont.)*

ISO 8859-1 and ASCII		Dec	Hex	EBCDIC	
í	small iacute	237	ED		
î	small i circumflex	238	EE		
ï	small idieresis or umlaut	239	EF		
ð	small ETH	240	F0	0	0
ñ	small n tilde	241	F1	1	1
ò	small o grave	242	F2	2	2
ó	small o acute	243	F3	3	3
ô	small o circumflex	244	F4	4	4
õ	small o tilde	245	F5	5	5
ö	small o dieresis or umlaut	246	F6	6	6
÷	division sign	247	F7	7	7
ø	small o slash	248	F8	8	8
ù	small U grave	249	F9	9	9
ú	small U acute	250	FA		
û	small U circumflex	251	FB		
ü	small U dieresis or umlaut	252	FC		
ý	small Y acute	253	FD		
þ	small thorn	254	FE		
ÿ	small y dieresis or umlaut	255	FF		

Index

Wouldn't it be great

if the world's leading technical publishers joined forces to deliver their best tech books in a common digital reference platform?

They have. Introducing
InformIT Online Books
powered by Safari.

■ **Specific answers to specific questions.**
InformIT Online Books' powerful search engine gives you relevance-ranked results in a matter of seconds.

■ **Immediate results.**
With InformIT Online Books, you can select the book you want and view the chapter or section you need immediately.

■ **Cut, paste and annotate.**
Paste code to save time and eliminate typographical errors. Make notes on the material you find useful and choose whether or not to share them with your work group.

■ **Customized for your enterprise.**
Customize a library for you, your department or your entire organization. You only pay for what you need.

Get your first 14 days **FREE!**
For a limited time, InformIT Online Books is offering its members a 10 book subscription risk-free for 14 days. Visit **http://www.informit.com/online-books** for details.

POWERED BY Safari

inform IT
Online Books

informit.com/onlinebooks

inform IT

www.informit.com

YOUR GUIDE TO IT REFERENCE

Articles

Keep your edge with thousands of free articles, in-depth features, interviews, and IT reference recommendations – all written by experts you know and trust.

Online Books

Answers in an instant from **InformIT Online Book's** 600+ fully searchable on line books. For a limited time, you can get your first 14 days **free**.

Catalog

Review online sample chapters, author biographies and customer rankings and choose exactly the right book from a selection of over 5,000 titles.

Prentice Hall PTR   InformIT   InformIT Online Books   Financial Times Prentice Hall   ft.com   PTG Interactive   Reuters

TOMORROW'S SOLUTIONS FOR TODAY'S PROFESSIONALS

Prentice Hall **Professional Technical Reference**

| Browse | Book Series | What's New | User Groups | Alliances | Special Sales | Contact Us |

Search | Help | **Home**

Quick Search

PTR Favorites

Find a Bookstore

Book Series

Special Interests

Newsletters

Press Room

International

Best Sellers

Solutions Beyond the Book

 Shopping Bag

Keep Up to Date with

PH PTR Online

We strive to stay on the cutting edge of what's happening in professional computer science and engineering. Here's a bit of what you'll find when you stop by **www.phptr.com**:

What's new at PHPTR? We don't just publish books for the professional community, we're a part of it. Check out our convention schedule, keep up with your favorite authors, and get the latest reviews and press releases on topics of interest to you.

Special interest areas offering our latest books, book series, features of the month, related links, and other useful information to help you get the job done.

User Groups Prentice Hall Professional Technical Reference's User Group Program helps volunteer, not-for-profit user groups provide their members with training and information about cutting-edge technology.

Companion Websites Our Companion Websites provide valuable solutions beyond the book. Here you can download the source code, get updates and corrections, chat with other users and the author about the book, or discover links to other websites on this topic.

Need to find a bookstore? Chances are, there's a bookseller near you that carries a broad selection of PTR titles. Locate a Magnet bookstore near you at www.phptr.com.

Subscribe today! Join PHPTR's monthly email newsletter! Want to be kept up-to-date on your area of interest? Choose a targeted category on our website, and we'll keep you informed of the latest PHPTR products, author events, reviews and conferences in your interest area.

Visit our mailroom to subscribe today! **http://www.phptr.com/mail_lists**